# Psychology and Education
## of the Gifted

*SECOND EDITION*

# Psychology and Education
# of the
# GIFTED

---

*second edition*

*Edited by WALTER B. BARBE*

*and JOSEPH S. RENZULLI*

*IRVINGTON PUBLISHERS, Inc., New York*

**HALSTED PRESS Division of**
**JOHN WILEY & SONS**

*NEW YORK   LONDON   SYDNEY   TORONTO*

Distributed by Halsted Press Division of
John Wiley & Sons, New York.

Library of Congress Cataloging in Publication Data

Barbe, Walter Burke, 1926–    ed.
    Psychology and education of the gifted. Second Edition

    Includes bibliographies and indexes.
    1. Gifted children—Education—Addresses, essays,
lectures.    I. Renzulli, Joseph S.    II. Title.
[DNLM:    1. Education, special child, gifted—Educa-
tion.    LC3993 P974]
LC3993.B36    1975         371.9′5         75–14330
ISBN 0–470–04775–5

Printed in the United States of America

*To our wives*
*Marilyn W. Barbe*
*Mary Jo Renzulli*

# Contents

Preface                                                                     xi

**Part I**
**INTRODUCTION TO THE**
**STUDY OF THE GIFTED**

Section A
Historical Development

1. The Discovery and Encouragement of Exceptional
   Talent—*Lewis M. Terman*                                                  6

2. A Backward and Forward Glance at the Gifted
   —*Abraham J. Tannenbaum*                                                 21

3. A New Approach to the Study of Genius—*Lewis M. Terman*                  32

4. The Education of the Gifted and Creative in the U. S. A.
   —*Paul A. Witty*                                                         39

Section B
Concepts and Concerns about Giftedness

1. Emerging Concepts of Giftedness—*E. Paul Torrance*                       48

2. The Meaning of 'Giftedness'—An Examination of an
   Expanding Concept—*J. W. Getzels and P. W. Jackson*                      56

3. Basic Concepts—*Virgil S. Ward*                                         61

**Part II**
**CHARACTERISTICS OF THE**
**GIFTED AND CREATIVE**

Section C
Facets or Traits of Mental Giftedness

1. Three Facets of Intellect—*J. P. Guilford*                              75

2. Primary Mental Abilities of Children—*Thelma G. Thurstone*              91

3. The Study of Giftedness: A Multidimensional
   Approach—*J. W. Getzels and P. W. Jackson*                              99

Section D
Characteristics of the Gifted

1. A Study of the Family Background of the Gifted
   —*Walter B. Barbe*                                                 111

2. A Psychologist Examines 64 Eminent Scientists—*Anne Roe*         119

3. Research Summary of Characteristics of the Gifted
   —*James J. Gallagher*                                            127

Section E
Characteristics of the Highly Creative

1. The Nature and Nurture of Creative Talent
   —*Donald W. MacKinnon*                                           151

2. Originality in Relation to Personality and Intellect
   —*Frank Barron*                                                  168

3. Identification of Creativity—The Individual—*Marie Dellas
   and Eugene L. Gaier*                                             179

Section F
Social and Emotional Characteristics

1. Adjustment Problems of the Gifted—*Edith H. Grotberg*           208

2. Problems of Highly Creative Children—*E. Paul Torrance*         214

3. Friendship and the Intellectually Gifted Child
   —*Harriet E. O'Shea*                                            220

**Part III
IDENTIFICATION AND
MEASUREMENT OF
GIFTEDNESS**

Section G
Problems and Issues in Identification

1. Problems in the Identification of Intellectually Gifted
   Pupils—*Ruth A. Martinson and Leon M. Lessinger*                232

2. Problems in the Assessment of Creative Thinking—*Donald J.
   Treffinger, Joseph S. Renzulli, and John F. Feldhusen*          240

3. Locating Gifted Children in Junior High School
   —*Carl W. Pegnano and Jack W. Birch*                            248

4. Identification of the Socially Gifted—*Roy K. Jarecky*          256

*VIII*

Section H
Identification Procedures

1. Scale for Rating the Behavioral Characteristics of Superior
   Students—*Joseph S. Renzulli, Robert K. Hartman, and
   Carolyn M. Callahan*                                         264

2. "What Kind of Person Are You?" A Brief Screening Device
   for Identifying Creatively Gifted Adolescents and Adults
   —*E. Paul Torrance and Joe Khatena*                          274

3. Identification: Responsibility of Both Principal and
   Teachers—*John C. Gowan*                                     280

4. The Measurement of Individual Differences in Originality
   —*R. C. Wilson, J. P. Guilford, and P. R. Christensen*       282

**Part IV**
**DEVELOPING AND**
**ENCOURAGING GIFTEDNESS**

Section I
Planning for the Gifted

1. Program Organization and Implementation—*Virgil S. Ward*    295

2. Early School Admission for Mentally Advanced
   Children—*Jack W. Birch*                                     303

3. Homogenous Grouping for Gifted Children
   —*Walter B. Barbe*                                           308

4. Designing and Implementing a Program for the Gifted and
   Talented—*Leonard G. Lanza and William G. Vassar*           316

5. Identifying Key Features in Programs for the Gifted
   —*Joseph S. Renzulli*                                        324

Section J
Instructional Approaches

1. Schedules, Bells, Groups, and Independent Study
   —*William M. Griffin*                                        330

2. A Model for the Analysis of Inquiry—*Richard Suchman*       336

3. Learning by Discovery: Psychological and Educational
   Rationale—*Hilda Taba*                                       346

4. Learning and the Learning Center—*Mildred L. Krohn*         355

IX

Section K
The Highly Creative

1. The Enhancement of Creativity—*Harold K. Hughes*  361

2. Methods and Educational Programs for Stimulating
   Creativity—*Donald J. Treffinger and John Curtis Gowan*  371

3. Developing Imagination Through SCAMPER
   —*Robert F. Eberle*  387

4. Methods for Encouraging Creativity in the Classroom
   —*Robert A. Goodale*  391

Section L
Issues in Motivating Underdeveloped Talent

1. The Gifted and the Disadvantaged—*A. Harry Passow*  402

2. Talent Potential in Minority Group Students
   —*Joseph S. Renzulli*  411

3. Cultivating New Talents: A Way to Reach the Educationally
   Deprived—*Calvin W. Taylor*  424

4. The Highly Intelligent Dropout—*Joseph L. French*  431

Part V
TEACHING THE GIFTED

Section M
Teaching the Gifted and Creative

1. Teaching the Gifted—A New Frame of Reference
   —*Walter B. Barbe and Edward C. Frierson*  435

2. The Role of the Teacher of Gifted and Creative
   Children—*Joan B. Nelson and Donald L. Cleland*  439

3. Characteristics of Teachers Judged Successful by
   Intellectually Gifted, High Achieving High School
   Students—*William E. Bishop*  449

4. Creative Teaching Makes a Difference—*E. Paul Torrance*  460

Index  475

# Preface

*T*he growing interest in the psychology and education of gifted and talented persons has resulted in a substantial increase in the number and variety of contributions to the literature in this area of study. In selecting readings for this book we have attempted to include a representative sample of recent research and commentary on various aspects of giftedness. At the same time, an effort has been made to preserve the important contributions of the past by including several selections that are clearly a part of the foundation upon which this special area of psychology and education was built.

With so much excellent material to draw upon, the task of determining which articles to include was indeed a difficult one. We have attempted to include material that deals with philosophical and theoretical issues, significant research findings, and practical suggestions for identifying and providing programs for the gifted and talented. Significant and sometimes contradictory points of view are presented, as are the results of research studies which are not always in complete agreement. A conscientious effort has been made to include what the editors believe to be those materials that will be of most value to theorists, researchers, and practitioners in both the fields of psychology and education.

The intended purposes of the book are varied. As a collection of much of the outstanding literature in this area, it can serve as a text in a course on the gifted or as a supplementary set of resource materials for such a course. We also hope that bringing together this many articles dealing with the theoretical and practical aspects of a particular problem area will make the book a useful resource for both serious scholars and program developers.

The book is divided into five major sections and thirteen subsections. Included are materials on the historical development of the psychology and education of the gifted, characteristics of the gifted and creative, and issues related to identifying and providing programs for highly able students. Special attention is given to the topic of underdeveloped talent and teaching the gifted. We have attempted to include selections that deal with both the elementary and high school levels.

Appreciation is expressed to the authors and publishers of the articles for permission to reprint their material in this book. The cause of the gifted is furthered today by the increased awareness and understanding of the problems of the gifted which is due in no small measure to the writings of those whose materials are reprinted here. The Author Index contains the name of virtually every person who has worked in the area of the gifted.

The editors express their sincere appreciation to those persons who aided us in the preparation of this manuscript. LeAnn Gordon and Robert A. Carson provided invaluable assistance by locating articles and obtaining permissions from authors and publishers. Ann Mignon and Gary Zaremski made an important contribution in the preparation of materials as did Robin D. Froman in the important task of indexing the entire volume. We would like to thank a number of graduate students who were kind enough to complete a questionnaire dealing with the types of materials that they would find most useful in a book of this type. Finally, special gratitude is expressed to Linda Harris Smith for her conscientious efforts in supervising the production of the entire manuscript.

W.B.B.
J.S.R.

# Psychology and Education
## of the Gifted

### SECOND EDITION

# Part I
## Introduction to the Study of the Gifted

The psychology of gifted children has been too long neglected. Now that the social climate has changed so radically in attitudes toward gifted children, there is hope that more research on the psychology of the intellectually superior will aid teachers and administrators in assisting the gifted to realize their potential.

More and more is being learned about the physical characteristics, interests, attitudes, and mental abilities of all children—the retarded, average and gifted—but far less research has been done on the psychology of gifted children. If psychology is to be defined as the study of man in relation to his environment, there is definitely a need to devote more attention to the psychological problems involved both in the study and education of the gifted individual. The study of the gifted is well underway; an understanding of the gifted will come about only from using what is known in an attempt to aid him in his adjustments.

The misconceptions concerning gifted individuals, widely believed before Terman disproved them, and to some extent still believed by many people today, probably come from the writings in the late nineteenth century of such men as Lombroso and Nisbet. In *The Man of Genius* (1), published in 1895 in London and New York, and widely read throughout the world, Lombroso attempted to show that insanity was closely related to genius. In *The Insanity of Genius* (2), Nisbet purports to prove this same theory.

While no intelligent person today believes that "genius and insanity go hand in hand," there is evidence that those individuals scoring in the highest ranges of the intelligence test (over 180) are characterized by different adjustment problems from those of the average child. Leta Hollingworth recognizes this in *Gifted Children* in which she states, "Another generalization that can be made about these children (over 180 I.Q.) is that nearly all have been school problems (3)."

Perhaps the very existence of abilities so far superior to those of the average makes for this poorer adjustment. It must be remembered, however, that gifted children in general are better adjusted than the average. This does not mean that they have fewer adjustments to make, but rather that even though they may face more adjustments than do the average, they generally make such adjustments successfully.

Probably no change in the attitude of the American public has been so great as that toward gifted children. At one time the gifted child was thought to be a physical weakling and a social misfit, so parents' determination to have only an average child was to be expected. But long after the bespectacled introvert concept had been completely disproved, parents held on to the popular notion that "average" was really good enough. What they really meant, of course, was that they wanted a child potentially capable of achieving at a higher level than they did, but one who would have none of the negative traits that were supposed to go along with mental superiority. Being very unrealistic about the fact that "average" was not good enough to achieve near the level to which they aspired for their children, parents nevertheless felt that they must maintain the "average" label for their child. Fortunately, this universal worship of the average has changed. Today, for the first time in nearly a century, parents are saying that they hope they have a gifted child. The freedom that allows parents to make this statement is perhaps the greatest change since Terman's original studies which disproved the previously held notions about the eccentricity of giftedness. There is indeed hope for the gifted that was not present even a few years ago.

The beginning of the change in attitudes toward the gifted can be marked at the time Lewis Terman began to study gifted children in California. This was climaxed by the presentation in 1947 of Volume IV of *Genetic Studies of Genius,* entitled *The Gifted Child Grows Up* (4). To Lewis Terman must go the credit for having started us on the path toward a new era, one in which all children will be accepted for what they are and will be allowed to develop those innate abilities they possess without fear of ridicule from a society characterized by mediocrity.

The establishment of the American Association for Gifted Children in 1947 is another landmark in the increasing attention to children who are exceptional in a different way. The appearance, in 1951, of *The Gifted Child* (5), edited by Paul Witty, gave new impetus to the movement. The Educational Policies Commission booklet, *Education for the Gifted* (6), in 1950, drew still more attention to the gifted.

In 1953 the National Association for Gifted Children (7) was formed, with the purpose of providing an organization for both teachers and parents concerned with the problem of the gifted child. *The Gifted Child Quarterly* is a publication of this organization which provides valuable information to teachers and parents, bibliographies, and reviews of recent books on the gifted. The Association for the Gifted (8), a division of the Council for Exceptional Children, is another organization which has in recent years provided influential leadership in furthering the cause of education for the

4

gifted. This organization has been especially active in sponsoring federal legislation that led to a nationwide study of educational provisions for the gifted and the areas of gifted education that are still in need of further development. The study also led to the establishment of the Office of the Gifted and Talented in the United States Office of Education and to the first National/State Leadership Training Institute for the Gifted and Talented.

The articles in Part I of this book represent an attempt to provide the reader with a chronicle of historically significant contributions to the study of giftedness. Some of the articles have helped to dispel the misconceptions about giftedness described above and other selections have been influential in calling both professional and public attention to the importance of providing a better education for what has often been described as "our nation's most valuable natural resource." The articles range from a summary of Terman's classic study about the characteristics of intellectually gifted youngsters to more recent concerns about the broad range of talents that can and should be developed by our educational system.

## References

1. Lombroso, C., *The Man of Genius*. New York: Charles Scribner's Sons, 1895.

2. Nisbet, J. F., *The Insanity of Genius*. London: DeLaNore Press, 1895.

3. Hollingworth, Leta, *Gifted Children*. New York: The Macmillan Company, 1926, p. 265.

4. Terman and Oden, *The Gifted Child Grows Up*, op. cit.

5. Witty, Paul (editor), *The Gifted Child*. Boston: D. C. Heath & Company, 1951.

6. Educational Policies Commission, *Education of the Gifted*. Washington, D. C.: National Education Association, 1950.

7. National Association for Gifted Children (8080 Springvalley Drive, Cincinnati, Ohio).

8. The Association for the Gifted, Council for Exceptional Children (1920 Association Drive, Reston, Virginia 22091).

*Lewis M. Terman*

# The Discovery and Encouragement of Exceptional Talent

*I* am deeply sensible of the honor of being invited by the American Psychological Association, through its special committee, to give the initial lecture in the Walter V. Bingham Lecturship series.

I am especially happy that Chancellor Kerr and the psychology department of the University of California graciously acceded to my request that the address be given here, where I have many friends and where so much notable research has been done on the mental, physical and personality development of children; where such famous experiments have been made on the purposive behavior of rats, both gifted and dull; where authoritarian minds have been so exhaustively probed; and where the recently established Institute of Personality Assessment is engaged in such promising investigations.

Before beginning my lecture I should like to pay tribute to the life work of the late Walter Van Dyke Bingham, at whose request this lectureship was established by Mrs. Bingham. Born in Iowa in 1880, young Walter early demonstrated his exceptional gifts by skipping both the third and fourth grades and by graduating from high school at the age of 16. As a freshman in college he was the youngest in his class and the only one to make a straight A record. After graduating from Beloit College he taught in high schools for four years, then entered the graduate school of the University of Chicago and in 1908 won his doctorate in psychology with honors. From 1908 to 1910 he was instructor at Teachers College and assistant to Edward L. Thorndike. In 1910 he was appointed assistant professor at Dartmouth to

Reprinted from *American Psychologist,* Vol. 9, No. 6 (June, 1954), pp. 221-230. By permission of the American Psychological Association.

teach all their classes in psychology, but when he left there five years later the staff included an instructor and two full professors, all selected by Dr. Bingham. His rare ability to recognize exceptional talent is indicated by the fact that both of these professors became college presidents.

From 1915 to 1924 Dr. Bingham was professor of psychology and the head of the division of applied psychology at the Carnegie Institute of Technology, and it was here that he found the opportunity he had long wanted to promote large-scale investigations in applied psychology. The faculty he assembled for that purpose was one of the most distinguished ever brought together anywhere in this country. Among them were J.B. Miner, L.L. Thurstone, Walter Dill Scott, Kate Gordon, and E.K. Strong. Three others appointed as consultants were F.L. Wells, G.M. Whipple, and Raymond Dodge. It was this faculty that, under the wise leadership of Dr. Bingham, laid the solid foundation for vocational and industrial psychology in America.

When our country entered the war in 1917, nearly all of the Carnegie group were soon engaged in psychological work either for the Surgeon General or for the War Department or for both. Dr. Bingham was a member of Yerkes' committee of seven that devised the army mental tests, in 1917-1918 was a member of the Committee on Classification of Personnel (the committee charged with devising and administering vocational tests in all the army camps), and in 1918-1919 was Lt. Colonel in the Personnel Branch of the Army General Staff.

During World War II even greater service was rendered by Dr. Bingham as chief psychologist for the Office of Adjutant General from 1940 to 1946. In this capacity he and his committee were responsible not only for the Army General Classification Test that was administered tt the many millions of inductees, but also for advising on the entire program of psychological services in the armed forces. In this capacity too he was in position to influence the selection of men best qualified to head the various branches of military psychology. I have no doubt that the extraordinary success of the work accomplished by psychologists during the war was largely due to his leadership and to his judgment of men.

If time permitted, I should like to tell you about his more than 200 publications, about the great variety of problems they dealt with, and the contributions they made in several fields of psychology, but I am sure that if Dr. Bingham were here he would want me to get on with our scheduled program.

I have often been asked how I happened to become interested in mental tests and gifted children. My first introduction to the scientific problems posed by intellectual differences occurred well over a half-century ago when I was a senior in psychology at Indiana University and was asked to prepare two reports for a seminar, one on mental deficiency and one on genius. Up to that time, despite the fact that I had graduated from a normal college as a Bachelor of Pedagogy and had taught school for five years, I had never so much as heard of a mental test. The reading for those two reports opened up

**7**

a new world to me, the world of Galton, Binet and their contemporaries. The following year my MA thesis on leadership among children (10) was based in part on tests used by Binet in his studies of suggestibility.

Then I entered Clark University, where I spent considerable time during the first year in reading on mental tests and precocious children. Child prodigies, I soon learned, were in that time in bad repute because of the prevailing belief that they were usually psychotic or otherwise abnormal and almost sure to burn themselves out quickly or to develop postadolescent stupidity. "Early ripe, early rot" was a slogan frequently encountered. By the time I reached my last graduate year, I decided to find out for myself how precocious children differ from the mentally backward, and accordingly chose as my doctoral dissertation an experimental study of the intellectual processes of fourteen boys, seven of them picked as the brightest and seven as the dullest in a large city school (11). These subjects I put through a great variety of intelligence tests, some of them borrowed from Binet, and others, many of them new. The tests were given individually and required a total of 40 or 50 hours for each subject. The experiment contributed little or nothing to science, but it contributed a lot to my future thinking. Besides "selling" me completely on the value of mental tests as a research method, it offered an ideal escape from the kinds of laboratory work which I disliked and in which I was more than ordinarily inept. (Edward Thorndike confessed to me once that *his* lack of mechanical skill was party responsible for turning *him* to mental tests and to the kinds of experiments on learning that required no apparatus.)

However, it was not until I got to Stanford in 1910 that I was able to pick up with mental tests where I had left off at Clark University. By that time Binet's 1905 and 1908 scales had been published, and the first thing I undertook at Stanford was a tentative revision of the 1908 scale. This, after further revisions, was published in 1916. The standardization of the scale was based on tests of a thousand children whose IQ's ranged from 60 to 145. The contrast in intellectual performance between the dullest and the brightest of a given age so intensified my earlier interest in the gifted that I decided to launch an ambitious study of such children at the earliest opportunity.

My dream was realized in the spring of 1921 when I obtained a generous grant from the Commonwealth Fund of New York City for the purpose of locating a thousand subjects of IQ 140 or higher. More than that number were selected by Stanford-Binet tests from the kindergarten through the eighth grade, and a group mental test given in 95 high schools provided nearly 400 additional subjects. The latter, plus those I had located before 1921, brought the number close to 1,500. The average IQ was approximately 150, and 80 were 170 or higher (13).

The twofold purpose of the project was, first of all, to find what traits characterize children of high IQ, and secondly, to follow them for as many years as possible to see what kinds of adults they might become. This meant that it was necessary to select a group representative of high-testing children in general. With the help of four field assistants, we canvassed a school population of nearly a quartermillion in the urban and semi-urban areas of California. Two careful checks on the methods used showed that not more than 10 or 12 per cent of the children who could have qualified for the group in the schools canvassed were missed. A sample of close to 90 per cent insured that whatever traits were typical of these children would be typical of high-testing children in any comparable school population.

Time does not permit me to describe the physical measurements, medical examinations, achievement tests, character and interest tests, or the trait ratings and other supplementary information obtained from parents and teachers. Nor can I here describe the comparative data we obtained for control groups of unselected children. The more important results, however, can be stated briefly: children of IQ of 140 or higher are, in general, appreciably superior to unselected children in physique, health, and social adjustment; markedly superior in moral attitudes as measured either by character tests or by trait ratings; and vastly superior in their mastery of school subjects as shown by a three-hour battery of achievement tests. In fact, the typical child of the group had mastered the school subjects to a point about two grades beyond the one in which he was enrolled, some of them three or four gardes beyond. Moreover, his ability as evidenced by achievement in the different school subjects is so general as to refute completely the traditional belief that gifted children are usually one-sided. I take some pride in the fact that not one of the major conclusions we drew in the early 1920's regarding the traits that are typical of gifted children has been overthrown in the three decades since then.

Results of thirty years' follow-up of these subjects by field studies in 1927-1928, 1939-1940, and 1951-1952, and by mail follow-up at other dates, show that the incidence of mortality, ill health, insanity, and alcoholism is in each case below that for the generality of corresponding age, that the great majority are still well adjusted socially, and that the delinquency rate is but a fraction of what it is in the general population. Two forms of our difficult Concept Mastery Test, devised especially to reach into the stratosphere of adult intelligence, have been administered to all members of the group who could be visited by the field assistants, including some 950 tested in 1939-1940 and more than 1,000 in 1951-1952. On both tests they scored on the average about as far above the generality of adults as they had scored above the generality of children when we selected them. Moreover, as Dr. Bayley and Mrs. Oden have shown, in the twelve-year interval between the two tests, 90 per cent increased their intellectual stature as measured by this test. "Early ripe, early rot" simply does not hold for these subjects. So far, no one has developed postadolescent stupidity!

As for schooling, close to 90 per cent entered college and 70 per cent graduated. Of those graduating, 30 per cent were awarded honors and about two-thirds remained for graduate work. The educational record would have been still better but for the fact that a majority reached college age during the great depression. In their undergraduate years 40 per cent of the men and 20 per cent of the women earned half or more of their college expenses, and the total of undergraduate and graduate expenses earned amounted to $670,000, not counting stipends from scholarships and fellowships, which amounted to $350,000.

The cooperation of the subjects is indicated by the fact that we have been able to keep track of more than 98 per cent of the original group, thanks to the rapport fostered by the incomparable field and office assistants I have had from the beginning of the study to the present. I dislike to think how differently things could have gone with helpers even a little less competent.

The achievement of the group to midlife is best illustrated by the case histories of the 800 men, since only a minority of the women have gone out for professional careers (15). By 1950, when the men had an average age of 40 years, they had published 67 books (including 46 in the fields of science, arts and the humanities, and 21 books of fiction). They had published more than 1,400 scientific, technical, and professional articles; over 200 short stories, novelettes, and plays; and 236 miscellaneous articles on a great variety of subjects. They had also authorized more than 150 patents. The figures on publications do not include the hundreds of publications by journalists that classify as news stories, editorials, or newspaper columns; nor do they include the hundred, if not thousands of radio and TV scripts.

The 800 men include 78 who have taken a PhD degree or its equivalent, 48 with a medical degree, 85 with a law degree, 74 who are teaching or have taught in a four-year college or university, 51 who have done basic research in the physical sciences or engineering, and 104 who are engineers but have done only applied research or none. Of the scientists, 47 are listed in the 1949 edition of *American Men of Science*. Nearly all of these numbers are from 10 to 20 or 30 times as large as would be found for 800 men of corresponding age picked at random in the general population, and are sufficient answer to those who belittle the significance of IQ differences.

The follow-up of these gifted subjects has proved beyond question that tests of "general intelligence," given as early as six, eight, or ten years, tells a great deal about the ability to achieve either presently or 30 years hence. Such tests do not, however, enable us to predict what direction the achievement will take, and least of all do they tell us what personality factors or what accidents of fortune will affect the fruition of exceptional ability. Granting that both interest patterns and special aptitudes play important roles in the making of a gifted scientist, mathematician, mechanic, artist, poet, or musical composer, I am convinced that to achieve greatly in almost any field, the special talents have to be backed up by a lot of Spearman's g, by which is meant the kind of general intelligence that requires ability to form many sharply defined concepts, to manipulate them, and to perceive subtle relationships between them; in other words, the ability to engage in abstract thinking.

The study by Catherine Cox of the childhood traits of historical geniuses gives additional evidence regarding the role of general intelligence in exceptional achievement. That study was part of our original plan to investigate superior ability by two methods of approach: (a) by identifying and following living gifted subjects from childhood onward; and (b) by preceeding in the opposite direction and tracing the mature genius back to his childhood promise. With a second grant from the Commonwealth Fund, the latter approach got under way only a year later than the former and resulted in the magnum opus by Cox entitled *The Early Mental Traits of Three Hundred Geniuses* (1). Her subjects represented an unbiased selection from the top 510 in Cattell's objectively compiled list of the 1,000 most eminent men of history. Cox and two able assistants then scanned some 3,000 biographies in search of information that would throw light on the early mental development of these subjects. The information thus obtained filled more than 6,000 typed pages. Next, three psychologists familiar with mental age norms read the documentary evidence on all the subjects and estimated for each the IQ that presumably would be necessary to account for the intellectual behavior recorded for given chronological ages. Average of the three IQ estimates was used as the index of intelligence. In fact two IQ's were estimated for each subject, one based on the evidence to age 17, and the other on evidence to the mid-twenties. The recorded evidence on development to age 17 varied from very little to an amount that yielded about as valid an IQ as a good intelligence test would give. Examples of the latter are Goethe, John Stuart Mill, and Francis Galton. It was the documentary information on Galton, which I summarized and published in 1917 (12), that decided me to prepare plans for the kind of study that was carried out by Cox. The average of estimated IQ's for her 300 geniuses was 155, with many going as high as 175 and several as high as 200. Estimates below 120 occurred only when there was little biographical evidence about the early years.

It is easy to scoff at these post-mortem IQ's, but as one of the three psychologists who examined the evidence and made the IQ ratings, I think the author's main conclusion is fully warranted; namely, that "the genius who achieves highest eminence is one whom intelligence tests would have identified as gifted in childhood."

Special attention was given the geniuses who had sometime or other been labeled as backward in childhood, and in every one of these cases the facts clearly contradicted the legend. One of them was Oliver Goldsmith, of whom his childhood teacher is said to have said "Never was so dull a boy." The fact is that little Oliver was writing clever verse at 7 years and at 8 was reading Ovid and Horace. Another was Sir Walter Scott, who at 7 not only read widely in poetry but was using correctly in his written prose such words as "melancholy" and "exotic." Other alleged childhood dullards included a number who disliked the usual diet of Latin and Greek but had a natural talent for science. Among these were the celebrated German chemist Justus von Liebig, the great English anatomist John Hunter, and the naturalist Alexander von Humboldt, whose name is scattered so widely over the maps of the world.

In the cases just cited one notes a tendency for the direction of later achievement to be foreshadowed by the interests and preoccupations of childhood. I have tried to determine how frequently this was true of the 100 subjects in Cox's group whose childhood was best documented. Very marked foreshadowing was noted in the case of more than half of the group, none at all in less than a fourth. Macaulay, for example, began his career as historian at the age of 6 with what he called a "Compendium of Universal History " filling a quire of paper before he lost interest in the project. Ben Franklin before the age of 17 had displayed nearly all the traits that characterized him in middle life: scientific curiosity, religious heterodoxy, wit and buffoonery, political and business shrewdness, and ability to write. At 11 Pascal was so interested in mathematics that his father thought it best to deprive him of books on this subject until he had first mastered Latin and Greek. Pascal secretly proceeded to construct a geometry of his own and covered the ground as far as the 32nd proposition of Euclid. His father then relented. At 14 Leibnitz was writing on logic and philosophy and composing what he called "An Alphabet of Human Thought." He relates that at this age he took a walk one afternoon to consider whether he should accept the "doctrine of substantial forms."

Similar foreshadowing is disclosed by the case histories of my gifted subjects. A recent study of the scientists and nonscientists among our 800 gifted men (15) showed many highly significant differences between the early interests and social attitudes of those who became physical scientists and those who majored in the social sciences, law, or the humanities. Those in medical or biological sciences usually rated on such varaibles somewhere between the physical scientists and the nonscientists.

What I especially want to emphasize, however, is that both the evidence on early mental development of historical geniuses and that obtained by follow-up of gifted subjects selected in childhood by mental tests point to the conclusion that capacity to achieve far beyond the average can be detected early in life by a well-constructed ability test that is heavily weighted with the g factor. It remains to be seen how much the prediction of future achievement can be made more specific as to field by getting, in addition, measures of ability factors that are largely independent of g. It would seem that a 20-year follow-up of the thousands of school children who have been given Thurstone's test of seven "primary mental abilities" would help to provide the answer. At present the factor analysts don't agree on how many "primary" mental abilities there are, nor exactly on what they are. The experts in this field are divided into two schools. The British school, represented by Thomson, Vernon, and Burt, usually stop with the identification of at most three or four group factors in addition to g, while some representing the American school feel the scores of 40 or 50 kinds of tests into a hopper and manage to extract from them what they believe to be a dozen or fifteen separate factors. Members of the British school are as a rule very skeptical about the realities underlying the minor group factors. There are also American psychologists, highly skilled in psychometrics, who share this skepticism. It is to be hoped that further research will give us more information that we now have about the predictive value of the group factors. Until such information is available, the scores on group factors can contribute little to vocational guidance beyond what a good test of general intelligence will provide.

I have always stressed the importance of *early* discovery of exceptional abilities. Its importance is now highlighted by the facts Harvey Lehman has disclosed in his monumental studies of the relation between age and creative achievement (8). The striking thing about his age curves is how early in life the period of maximum creativity is reached. In nearly all fields of science, the best work is done between ages 25 and 35, and rarely later than 40. The peak productivity for works of lesser merit is usually reached 5 to 10 years later; this is true in some twenty fields of science, in philosophy, in most kinds of musical composition, in art, and in literature of many varieties. The lesson for us us from Lehman's statistics is that the youth of high achievement potential should be well trained for his life work before too many of his creative years have been passed.

This raises the issue of educational acceleration for the gifted. It seems that the schools are more opposed to acceleration now than they were thirty years ago. The lockstep seems to have become more and more the fashion, notwithstanding the fact that practically everyone who has investigated the subject is against it. Of my gifted group, 29 per cent managed to graduate from high school before the age of 16 ½ years (62 of these before 15 ½), but I doubt if so many would be allowed to do so now. The other 71 per cent graduated between 16 ½ and 18 ½. We have compared the accelerated with the nonaccelerated on numerous case history variables. The two groups differed very little in childhood IQ, their health records are equally good, and as adults they are equally well adjusted socially. More of the accelerates graduated from college, and on the avergae nearly a year and a half earlier than the nonaccelerates; they averaged high in college grades and more often remained for graduate work. Moreover, the accelerates on the average married .7 of a year earlier, have a trifle lower divorce rate, and test just a little higher on a test of marital happiness (14). So far as college records of accelerates and nonaccelerates are concerned, our data closely parallel those obtained by the late Noel Keys (3) at the University of California and those by Pressey (9) and his associates at Ohio State University.

The Ford Fund for the advancement of Education has awarded annually since 1951 some 400 college scholarships to gifted students who are not over 16 ½ years old, are a year or even two years short of high school graduation, but show good evidence of ability to do college work. Three quarters of them are between 15 ½ and 16 ½ at the time of college entrance. A dozen colleges and universities accept these students and are keeping close track of their success. A summary of their records for the first year shows that they not only get higher grades than their classmates, who average about two years older, but that they are also equally well adjusted socially and participate in as many extracurricular activities (17). The main problem the boys have is in finding girls to date who are not too old for them! Some of them have started a campagn to remedy the situation by urging that more of these scholarships be awarded to girls.

The facts I have given do not mean that all gifted children should be rushed through school just as rapidly as possible. If that were done, a majority with IQ of 140 could graduate from high school before the age of 15. I do believe, however, that such children should be promoted rapidly enough to permit college entrance by the age of 17 at least, and that a majority would be better off to enter at 16. The exceptionally bright student who is kept with his age group finds little to challenge his intelligence and all too often develops habits of laziness that later wreck his college career. I could give you some choice examples of this in my gifted group. In the case of a college student who is preparing for a profession in science, medicine, law, or any field of advanced scholarship, graduation at 20 instead of the usual 22 means two years added to his professional career; or the two years saved could be used for additional training beyond the doctorate, if that were deemed preferable.

Learned and Wood (7) have shown by objective achievement tests in some 40 Pennsylvania colleges how little correlation there is between the student's knowledge and the number of months or years of his college attendance. They found some beginning sophomores who had acquired more knowledge than some seniors near their graduation. They found similarly low correlations between the number of course units a student had in a given field and the amount he knew in that field. Some with only one year of Latin had learned more than others with three years. And, believe it or not, they even found boys just graduating from high school who had more knowledge of science and were about to begin teaching science in high schools! The sensible thing to do, it seems, would be to quit crediting the individual high school or the individual college and begin crediting the individual student. That, essentially, is what the Ford Fund scholarships are intended to encourage.

Instruments that permit the identification of gifted subjects are available in great variety and at nearly all levels from the primary grades to the graduate schools in universities. My rough guess is that at the present time tests of achievement in the school subjects are being given in this country to children below high school at a rate of perhaps ten or twelve million a year, and to high school students another million or two. In addition, perhaps two million tests of intelligence are given annually in the elementary and high schools. The testing of college students began in a small way only 30 years ago; now almost every college in the country requires applicants for admission to take some kind of aptitude test. This is usally a test of general aptitude, but subject-matter tests and tests of special aptitudes are sometimes given to supplement the tests of general aptitude.

The testing movement has also spread rapidly in other countries, especialy in Britain and the Commonwealth countries. Godfrey Thomson devised what is now called the Moray House test of intelligence in 1921 to aid in selecting the more gifted 11-year olds in the primary schools for the privilege of free secondary education. This test has been revised and is given annually to about a half million scholarship candidates. The Moray House tests now include tests of English, arithmetic, and history. In 1932 the Scottish Council for Research in Education (18) arranged to give the Moray House test of intelligence (a group test) to all the 90,000 children in Scotland who were born in 1921, and actually tested some 87,000 of them. The Stanford-Binet tests have been translated and adapted for use in nearly all the countries of Europe and in several countries of Asia and Latin America. Behind the Iron Curtain, however, mental tests are now banned.

I have discussed only tests of intelligence and of school achievement. There is time to mention only a few of the many kinds of personality tests that have been developed during the last thirty-five years: personality inventories, projective techniques by the dozen, attitude scales by the hundred, interest tests, tests of psychotic and predelinquent tendencies, tests of leadership, marital aptitude, masculinity-femininity, et cetera. The current output of research on personality tests probably equals or exceeds that on intelligence and achievement tests, and is even more exciting.

Along with the increasing use of tests, and perhaps largely a result of it, there is a growing interest, both here and abroad, in improving educational methods for the gifted. Acceleration of a year or two or three, however desirable, is but a fraction of what is needed to keep the gifted child or youth working at his intellectual best. The method most often advocated is curriculum achievement for the gifted without segregating them from the ordinary class. Under ideal conditions enrichment can accomplish much, but in these days of crowded schools, when so many teachers are overworked, underpaid, and inadequately trained, curriculum enrichment for a few gifted in a large mixed class cannot begin to solve the problem. The best survey of thought and action in this field of education is the book entitled *The Gifted Child*, written by many authors and published in 1951 (16). In planning for and sponsoring this book, The American Association for Gifted Children has rendered a great service to education.

But however efficient our tests may be in discovering exceptional talents, and whatever the school may do to foster those discovered, it is the prevailing *Zeitgeist* that will decide, by the rewards it gives or withholds, what talents will come to flower. In Western Europe of the Middle Ages, the favored talents were those that served the Church by providing its priests, the architects of its cathedrals, and the painters of religious themes. A few centuries later the same countries had a renaissance that included science and literature as well as the arts. Although presumably there are as many potential composers of great music as there ever were, and as many potentially great artists as in the days of Leonardo da Vinci and Michaelangelo, I am reliably informed that in this country today it is almost impossible for a composer of *serious* music to earn a living except by teaching, and that the situation is much the same, though somewhat less critical, with respect to artists.

The talents most favored by the current *Zeitgeist* are those that can contribute to science and technology. If intelligence and achievement tests don't discover the potential scientist, there is a good chance that the annual Science Talent Search will, though not until the high school years. Since

Westinghouse inaugurated in 1942 this annual search for the high school seniors most likely to become creative scientists, nearly 4,000 boys and girls have been picked for honors by Science Service out of the many thousands who have competed. As a result, "Science Clubs of America" now number 15,000 with a third of a million members—a twentyfold increase in a dozen years (2). As our need for more and better scientists is real and urgent, one can rejoice at what the talent search and the science clubs are accomplishing. One may regret, however, that the spirit of the times is not equally favorable to the discovery and encouragement of potential poets, prose writers, artists, statesmen, and social leaders.

But in addition to the over-all climates that reflect the *Zeitgeist,* there are localized climates that favor or hinder the encouragement of given talents in particular colleges and universities. I have in mind especially two recent investigations of the differences among colleges in the later achievement of their graduates. One by Knapp and Goodrich (4) dealt with the undergraduate origin of 18,000 scientists who got the bachelor's degree between 1924 and 1934 and were listed in the 1944 edition of *American Men of Science.* The list of 18,000 was composed chiefly of men who had taken a PhD degree, but included a few without a PhD who were starred scientists. The IBM cards for these men were then sorted according to the college from which they obtained the bachelor's degree, and an index of productivity was computed for each college in terms of the proportion of its male graduates who were in the list of 18,000. Some of the results were surprising, not to say sensational. The institutions that were most productive of future scientists between 1924 and 1934 were not the great universities, but the small liberal arts colleges. Reed College topped the list with an index of 132 per thousand male graduates. The California Institute of Technology was second with an index of 70. Kalamazoo College was third with 66, Earlham fourth with 57, and Oberlin fifth with 56. Only a half-dozen of the great universities were in the top fifty with a productivity index of 25 or more.

The second study referred to was by Knapp and Greenbaum (5), who rated educational institutions according to the proportion of their graduates who received certain awards at the graduate level in the six-year period from 1946 to 1951. Three kinds of awards were considered: a PhD degree, a graduate scholarship or fellowship paying at least $400 a year, or a prize at the graduate level won in open competition. The roster of awardees they compiled included 7,000 students who had graduated from 377 colleges and universities. This study differs from the former in three respects: (a) it deals with recent graduates, who had not had time to become distinguished but who could be regarded as good bets for the future; (b) these good bets were classified according to whether the major field was science, social science, or the humanities; and (c) data were obtained for both sexes, though what I shall report here relates only to men. In this study the great universities make a better showing than in the other, but still only a dozen of them are in the top fifty institutions in the production of men who are good bets. In the top ten, the University of Chicago is third, Princeton is eighth, and Harvard is tenth; the other seven in order of rank are Swarthmore 1, Reed 2, Oberlin 4, Haverford 5, California Institue of Technology 6, Carleton 7, and Antioch 9. When the schools were listed separately for production of men who were goods bets in science, social science, and the humanities, there were eight that rated in the top twenty of all three lists. These were Swarthmore, Reed, Chicago, Harvard, Oberlin, Antioch, Carleton, and Princeton.

The causes of these differences are not entirely clear. Scores on aptitude tests show that the intelligence of students in a given institution is by no means the sole factor, though it is an important one. Other important factors are the quality of the school's intellectual climate, the proportion of able and inspiring teachers on its faculty, and the amount of conscious effort that is made not only to discover but also to motivate the most highly gifted. The influence of motivation can hardly be exaggerated.

In this address I have twice alluded to the fact that achievement in school is influenced by many things other than the sum total of intellectual abilities. The same is true of success in life. In closing I will tell you briefly about an attempt we made a dozen years ago to identify some of the nonintellectual factors that have influenced life success among the men in my gifted group. Three judges, working independently, examined the records (to 1940) of the 730 men who were then 25 years old or older, and rated each on life success. The criterion of "success" was the extent to which a subject had made use of his superior intellectual ability, little weight being given to earned income. The 150 men rated highest for success and the 150 rated lowest were then compared on some 200 items of information obtained from childhood onward (14). How did the two groups differ?

During the elementary school years, the A's and C's (as we call them) were almost equally successful. The average grades were about the same, and average scores on achievement tests were only a trifle higher for the A's. Early in high school the groups began to draw apart in scholarship, and by the end of high school the slump of the C's was quite marked. The slump could not be blamed on extracurricular activities, for these were almost twice as common among the A's. Nor was much of it due to difference in intelligence. Although the A's tested on the average a little higher than the C's both in 1922 and 1940, the average score made by the C's in 1940 was high enough to permit brilliant college work, in fact was equaled by only 15 per cent of our highly selected Stanford students. Of the A's, 97 per cent entered college and 90 per cent graduated; of the C's, 68 per cent entered but only 37 per cent graduated. Of those who graduated, 52 per cent of the A's but only 14 per cent of the C's graduated with honors. The A's were also more accelerated in school; on the average they were six months younger on completing the eighth grade, 10 months younger at high school graduation, and 15 months younger at graduation from college.

The differences between the educational histories of the A's and C's reflect to some degree the differences in their family backgrounds. Half of the A fathers but only 15 per cent of the C fathers were college graduates, and twice as many of A siblings as of C siblings graduated. The estimated number of books in the A homes was nearly 50 per cent greater than in the C homes. As of 1928, when the average age of the subjects was about 16 years, more than twice as many of the C parents as of A parents had been divorced.

Interesting differences between the groups were found in the childhood data on emotional stability, social adjustments, and various traits of personality. Of the 25 traits on which each child was rated by parent and teacher in 1922 (18 years before the A and C groups were made up), the only trait on which the C's averaged as high as the A's was general health. The superiority of the A's was especially marked in four volitional traits: prudence, self-confidence, perseverance, and desire to excel. The A's also rated significantly higher in 1922 on leadership, popularity, and sensitiveness to approval or disapproval. By 1940 the difference between the groups in social adjustment and all-round mental stability had greatly increased and showed itself in many ways. By that time four-fifths of the A's had married, but only two-thirds of the C's and the divorce rate for those who had married was twice as high for the C's as for the A's. Moreover, the A's made better marriages; their wives on the average came from better homes, were better educated, and scored higher on intelligence tests.

But the most spectacular differences between the two groups came from three sets of ratings, made in 1940, on a dozen personality traits. Each man rated himself on all the traits, was rated on them by his wife if he had a wife, and by a parent if a parent was still living. Although the three sets of ratings were made independently, they agreed unanimously on the four traits in which the A and C groups differed most widely. These were "persistence in the accomplishment of ends," "integration toward goals, as contrasted with drifting," "self-confidence," and "freedom from inferiority feelings." For each trait three critical ratios were computed showing, respectively, the reliability of the A-C differences in average of self-ratings, ratings by wives, and ratings by parents. The average of the three critical ratios was 5.5 for perseverance, 5.6 for integration toward goals, 3.7 for self-confidence, and 3.1 for freedom from inferiority feelings. These closely parallel the traits that Cox found to be especially characteristic of the 100 leading geniuses in her group whom she rated on many aspects of personality; their three outstanding traits she defined as "persistence of motive and effort," "confidence in their abilities," and "strength or force of character."

There was one trait on which only the parents of our A and C men were asked to rate them; that trait was designated "common sense." As judged by parents, the A's are again reliably superior, the A-C difference in average rating having a critical ratio of 3.9. We are still wondering what self-ratings by the subjects and ratings of them by their wives on common sense would have shown if we had been impudent enough to ask for them!

Everything considered, there is nothing in which our A and C groups present a greater contrast than in drive to achieve and in all-round mental and social adjustment. Our data do not support the theory of Lange-Eichbaum (6) that great achievement usually stems from emotional tensions that border on the abnormal. In our gifted group, success is associated with stability rather than instability, with absence rather than with presence of disturbing conflicts—in short with well balanced temperament and with freedom from excessive frustrations. The Lange-Eichbaum theory may explain a Hitler, but hardly a Churchill; the junior senator from Wisconsin, possibly, but not a Jefferson or a Washington.

At any rate, we have seen that intellect and achievement are far from perfectly correlated. To identify the internal and external factors that help or hinder the fruition of exceptional talent, and to measure the extent of their influences, are surely among the major problems of our time. These problems are not new; their existence has been recognized by countless men from Plato to Francis Galton. What is new is the general awareness of them caused by the manpower shortage of scientists, engineers, moral leaders, statesmen, scholars, and teachers that the country must have if it is to survive in a threatened world. These problems are now being investigated on a scale never before approached, and by a new generation of workers in several related fields. Within a couple of decades vastly more should be known than we know today about our resources of potential genius, the environmental circumstances that favor its expression, the emotional compulsions that give it dynamic quality, and the personality distortions that can make it dangerous.

## References

1. Cox, Catharine C., *The Early Mental Traits of Three Hundred Geniuses.* Vol. II of *Genetic Studies of Genius,* Terman, L. M. (ed.). Stanford: Stanford Univer. Press, 1926.

2. Davis, W., Communicating Science. *J. Atomic Scientists,* 1953, 337-340.

3. Keys, N., The Underage Student in High School and College. *Univ. Calif. Publ. Educ.,* 1938, **7**, 145-272.

4. Knapp, R. H., & Goodrich, H. B., *Origins of American Scientists.* Chicago: Univer. of Chicago Press, 1952.

5. Knapp, R. H., & Greenbaum, J. J., *The Younger American Scholar: His Collegiate Origins.* Chicago: Univ. of Chicago Press, 1953.

6. Lange-Eichbaum, W., *The Problem of Genius.* New York: Macmillan, 1932.

7. Learned, W. S., & Wood, B. D., The Student and His Knowledge. *Carnegie Found. Adv. Teaching Bull.,* 1938, No. 29.

8. Lehman, H. C., *Age and Achievement.* Princeton: Princeton Univer. Press, 1953.

9. Pressey, S. L., *Educational Acceleration: Appraisals and Basic Problems.* Columbus: Ohio State Univer. Press, 1949.

10. Terman, L. M., A Preliminary Study in the Psychology and Pedagogy of Leadership. *Pedag. Sem.,* 1904, **11,** 413-451.

11. Terman, L. M., Genius and Stupidity: A Study of Some of the Intellectual Processes of Seven "Bright" and Seven "Dull" Boys. *Pedag. Sem.,* 1906, **13,** 307-373.

12. Terman, L. M., The Intelligence Quotient of Francis Galton in Childhood. *Amer. J. Psychol.,* 1917, **28,** 209-215.

13. Terman, L. M. (ed.), *et al. Mental and Physical Traits of a Thousand Gifted Children.* Vol. I of *Genetic Studies of Genius,* Terman, L. M. (ed.). Stanford: Stanford Univer. Press, 1925.

14. Terman, L. M., & Oden, M. H., *The Gifted Child Grows Up.* Vol. IV of *Genetic Studies of Genius,* Terman, L. M. (ed.).Stanford: Stanford Univer. Press, 1947.

15. Terman, L. M., Scientists and Nonscientists in a Group of 800 Gifted Men. *Psychol. Monogr.,* 1954, **68,** in press.

16. Witty, P. (ed)., *The Gifted Child.* Boston: Heath, 1951.

17. *Bridging the Gap Between School and College.* New York: The Fund for the Advancement of Education, 1953.

18. *The Intelligence of Scottish Children.* Scottish Council for Research in Education. London: Univer. of London Press, 1933.

*Abraham J. Tannenbaum*

# A Backward and Forward Glance
# at the Gifted

*A* social critic once compared America to a rocking chair, always in motion but going nowhere. As cruel and fanciful as this characterization may be, it suggests something of the constant to and fro movement with which we approach and retreat from our deepest concerns. We thrust forward and confront a national problem, stay with it for a while, and then move backwards as though we've lost interest before we've even found a solution, only to return once again another day. Such has been the case in our dealings with the education of the gifted. After nearly a decade of waning attention to the needs of able children and youth, today's educators seem prepared to revive the old enthusiasm for excellence that flashed for four or five years after Sputnik.

About three years before Sputnick, I joined the newly formed Talented Youth Project at Teachers College, Columbia University, and collaborated with its director, A. Harry Pascow, in a search for durable programs for the gifted. We wrote to about 100 schools that had been singled out, because of their special enrichment practices, in a national survey published in 1941. Our intention was to learn about developments in these programs, particularly the mistakes and refinements that had been made over the intervening thirteen years, and to pass on the benefits of such information to schools interested in initiating their own programs. Unfortunately, none of the respondents had anything to report. Every school had long since dropped its programs, usually because the key people responsible for inspiring and directing them had long since departed from the scene, as had the funds needed for the extra support.

This modest but abortive investigation taught us a lesson that has been reinforced over and over again ever since: namely, that special provisions for the gifted are primarily luxuries rather than necessities in the educational enterprise. Whenever schools can afford to introduce some kind of enrichment, it becomes icing on the curriculum cake, not part of the cake itself. As a result, despite repeated distinctions educators make between equality and

Tannenbaum, Abraham J. "A Forward and Backward Glance at the Gifted". *The National Elementary Principal.* Vol. LI, No. 5, February, 1972, pp. 14-23.

sameness of educational opportunity, the gifted get their fair share of stimulation at school only when there is enough money to pay the bill and their cause is supported by public figures whose opinions command attention. In fact, a school's failure to challenge able pupils to the limit of their abilities could hardly stir up the general indignation or legal action that would result if the victimized children had some kinds of learning handicaps.

With the launching of Sputnick into orbit in 1957, there was a sudden outpouring of widespread interest in the gifted. The Russian gambit damaged America's self-image as a world leader in technology, and the nation became conscience stricken over its failure to produce sufficient high-level manpower to meet the threat of its ideological and cold war adversary. Public education was singled out as the scapegoat, much as the Pearl Harbor military had been when America was caught napping at the time of another kind of surprise enemy attack. Educators turned down their attention to earlier warnings by academicians who were appaled at the plethora of so-called Mickey Mouse courses in the public schools, which made few demands on pupil intellect and allowed the gifted to coast through their studies understimulated and poorly equipped for leadership in a modern industrial society.[1]

Similar sentiments were expressed by Admiral Hyman G. Rickover, a special kind of military hero who achieved fame for fathering the first atomic submarine rather than for bravery in combat.[2] As a symbol of the link between national security and technology, Rickover added a strong note of alarm when he warned that the nation's position in the world would be endangered unless it raised its educational standards, particularly for the gifted. There was hardly room for counterargument: Manpower surveys showed that only half of the top 25 per cent of high school graduates went on to earn college diplomas and that only three per cent of those capable of earning Ph.D.'s actually did so.[3]

The perceived threat of Russian superiority in stockpiling sophisticated human resources, together with exposés of how America's gifted children were being all but neglected at school, produced a massive response to correct the inequity. Enormous public and private funds became available for crash programs in pursuit of excellence, primarily in the fields of science and technology. Academic coursework was telescoped and stiffened to test the brainpower of the gifted. Courses that had been offered only at the college level began to find their way into special enrichment programs in high schools and elementary schools.[4] There also appeared a rich outcropping of honors curricula, radically different from previous offerings and eventually affecting the educational diets of the non-gifted as well. Most important, it became virtually unthinkable for a gifted child to bypass the tougher courses in favor of the less challenging ones that easily yielded high grades but little of substance. It certainly was no time for youth to do their own thing or to enjoy the privilege of doing nothing. Instead, they were brought up in a period of total talent mobilization, requiring the most able minded to fulfill their potentials and submit their developed abilities for service to society.

Although the growing efforts on behalf of the gifted were generally scattered and uncoordinated, the new need for school programs comprehensive enough to accomodate human diversity without shortchanging the gifted was codified in a report by a renowned public servant, James B. Conant, a former president of Harvard University who had gone on to become U.S. High Commissioner of Germany and then ambassador to that country. The report, entitled *The American High School Today*,[5] recommended a rigorous program that was compatible with the popular sentiment of that era, and the author's personal reputation helped him gain a wide audience of opinion leaders in education. The high school was becoming the scene of a national talent hunt comparable in scope and vigor to the search for promising athletes. Once identified, the gifted student would undergo special counseling and exposure to an enriched curriculum in preparation for recruitment into a major college where he could continue on to advanced studies. Few efforts were spared in learning how to bring his talents to fruition. Universities and school systems researched the relative efficacy of special curricular and administrative procedures, the possible causes and cures of academic underachievement, the problems of measurement and prediction, and the effects of various social climates on school achievement. So rapid was the buildup of professional literature in the field that one writer claimed there were more articles published in the three-year period from 1956 to 1959 than in the previous 30 years.[6]

Despite the post-Sputnick flurry of activity, hindsight suggests that some unfinished business has remained to haunt us ever since. For one thing, the idea of special provisions for the gifted never really entered the bloodstream of American education. Instead, gifted children were considered ornaments to be detached and discarded when the cost of upkeep became prohibitive. Then too, the fervor with which guidance counselors ushered gifted youth into science programs backfired to some degree as large numbers of these students switched their academic majors by the time they reached the sophomore year in college, and many who did stay on to pursue the careers mapped out for them became victims of the shaky fortunes of the aerospace industry. On the other hand, little more than lip service was paid to the needs of the special breed of students not gifted academically but possessing exceptional talent in the arts, mechanics, and social leadership. Whatever work was done in defining and measuring creative productivity remained in the research laboratory. Few people attempted to develop ways of cultivating this kind of mental activity and translating it into curriculum sequences. Finally, the national talent hunt failed to penetrate the socially disadvantaged minorities whose school achievement records were well below the national norm and whose children with high potential were much harder to locate because their environments provided too little of the requisite encouragement and opportunity to fulfill whatever promise they might have shown under other circumstances. A notable exception to this general neglect of talent among the underprivileged was the much celebrated P.S. 43

project in New York City, which was later expanded into the even more widely heralded Higher Horizons Program.[7] But these efforts were shortlived, coming to an end when a subsequent evaluation revealed no special accomplishments in the program, perhaps due to an underestimate of costs, personnel, curriculum planning, and just plain hard work needed to duplicate on a much larger scale the earlier successes of P.S. 43.[8]

By the early 1960's, national attention was beginning to turn to the civil rights movement. Alleviating the plight of the inner-city ghettos became a cause celebre soon to be near the top of the list of America's priorities. Grave social injustice was seen in the way ghettoized masses suffered from racial inequality, and the only hope for rectifying the situation was an enormous public investment in upgrading their education, housing and employment opportunities. Schools could no longer afford the luxury of investing extra funds in provisions for the gifted. Moreover, the socially disadvantaged were poorly represented in special programs for the gifted, so conventional means of identifying highly able children were condemned as discriminatory. The IQ test, a major instrument for assessing academic potential ever since Terman initiated his monumental studies of genius in the early part of the century, came under heavy attack for being biased against some racial minorities and the socioeconomically depressed. Many schools discontinued the use of these tests, ignoring the arguments of some educators[9][10] that the instruments per se are not prejudiced but merely reflect the biases of the society by assessing potentials of children growing up in a system that fosters human inequality; therefore, eliminating the tests will accomplish nothing if the system is not corrected.

The decline of attention to the gifted in the 1960s is evident in the contrasting number of professional publications on that subject at the beginning and end of the decade. The number of entries under "Gifted Children" in the 1970 volume of The Education Index was less than half the number in the 1960 volume. It would seem, therefore, that the country was exchanging one fad for another much as it changes clothing styles and other habits. But the situation was not nearly so simple. What may have been operating instead is democracy's perennial dilemma over championing excellence and equality simultaneously.[11] By leaning too far in the direction of excellence, the country is in danger of creating a special kind of elitism out of meritocracy; by leaning heavily in the direction of equality, it easily loses sight of real human differences and ignores outstanding potential rather than offering special privileges for its cultivation. At this point in history, any neglect of the principle of equality can tear the nation apart from within; neglect of our need to build the largest possible reservoir of excellent human resources can make us vulnerable to attack from without. There is always the danger that the pursuit of excellence can only be accomplished by a retreat from equality, and vice versa. Thus, we rock back and forth between the two in order to show how reluctant we are to neglect either for too long. The most serious task facing us today is to place both goals in the same direction so that they can be pursued with equal vigor at the same time.

24

There are now unmistakable signs of a revival of interest in the gifted, but it remains to be seen whether it will be at the expense of commitments to the socially disadvantaged. Probably the biggest boost came from a 1970 Congressional mandate that added Section 806, "Provisions Related to Gifted and Talented Children," to the Elementary and Secondary Educational Amendments of 1969 (Public Law 91-230). This document expressed a legislative decision to include the gifted and talented students among those benefiting from Titles III and V of the Elementary and Secondary Education Act and the Teacher Fellowship Provisions of the Higher Education Act of 1956. It also directed the commissioner to:

1. determine the extent to which special education educational assistance programs are necessary or useful to meet the needs of gifted and talented children.

2. show which federal assistance programs are being used to meet the needs of gifted and talented children.

3. evaluate how existing federal education assistance programs can be more effectively used to meet these needs.

4. recommend new programs, if any, needed to meet these needs.

The target population has been defined as the upper three to five percent of school-age children who show outstanding promise in general intellectual ability, specific academic aptitude, creative or productive thinking, leadership ability, visual and performing arts, and psychomotor ability.

In response to the mandate, Commissioner Marland issued a report of his findings and recommendations that set the stage for doing something significant about the deteriorated condition of programs for the gifted.[12] He estimated that only a small percentage of the 1.5 to 2.5 million gifted and talented school children are benefiting from existing school services and that such services have a low priority at virtually all levels of government and school administration. Furthermore, even in those localities where there are legal or administrative directives for providing special services, little is accomplished due to other funding priorities, more threatening crises, and the absence of adequately trained personnel. Clearly, Marland saw the gifted as a deprived group whose talents are in danger of serious impairment unless appropriate intervention strategies are planned. He therefore declared his intention to initiate a series of major activities at the federal level with the hope of inspiring and pressing for more commitment on behalf of the gifted throughout the nation's schools.

The revival of interest in the gifted should not be interpreted simply as the restoration of post-Sputnick sentiments and programs for promoting excellence. Aside from the fact that it would be impossible for us to recapture the past even if we wanted to, the chances are that such an attempt would be foolish and wasteful. A great many changes have taken place in our social climate over the past fifteen years, and the kinds of excellence that we think are needed today appear quite different from those thought necessary at a time when our major fear was that the Russians would surpass us in aerospace exploits and modern military hardware. Judging from the little that we know about gifted high school graduates in the late 1950's, they were probably unlike their earlier counterparts in Terman's group, who were followed since their childhood in the early 1920's into middle age. Whereas the Terman adolescents were more often attracted to academic majors and careers in the social sciences than to any other studies,[13] the Sputnik generation of able teenagers gravitated primarily to the natural sciences and engineering.[14] It isn't easy to fathom what the present-day educational diet ought to be for gifted youth, but any assessment of our youth culture and the world in which it lives would indicate that the major emphasis of school enrichment cannot be simple carbon copies of those in the past.

It would be naive to force our so-called Now Generation into a characteristic mold as if it were homogeneous in any way. Young people are as diverse today in their values, habits, and aspirations as they have ever been in the past. Yet, they seem to be expressing certain distinctive moods that make it not only difficult but near presumptuous to define talent along traditional lines. For many years, consuming or producing knowledge was regarded as a human virtue, particularly if it helped conquer nature in order to make man's life more comfortable. There was hardly much doubt that gifted children would derive great personal satisfaction and a certain measure of power and freedom if they became highly knowledgeable. More recently, however some of the glamour has become tarnished. Significant segments of campus youth began to sour on knowledge factories, and Marcuse, one of their most influential, though not so young, spokesmen, warned about the mechanizing, denaturalizing and subjugating impact of knowledge.[15]

There may indeed have been something dehumanizing about the way we treated talent in the not so distant past. Our approach to the development of precious human resources was not much different from our handling of natural resources. Just as we mine and drill for vital raw materials below the earth's surface, we developed elaborate testing programs to locate promising young brains. We then proceeded to educate, counsel, and typecast our able students to fill needed roles in the brain pool in much the same way that we refine, package, and sell our natural resources to the highest bidder. One process is as impersonal as the other to students who resent being exploited by a society that takes a utilitarian view of individual skills. The situation is aggravated by the growing strain between the social system and many of its youth. Large numbers of gifted students resent being groomed to service the critical requirements of a state they consider guilty of aggression abroad and oppression at home. There is no doubt that the Vietnam war and racial strife have dampened allegiance to the flag at schools and campuses throughout the country. It has reached the point where students (and some faculty) are willing to retard certain kinds of scientific progess if they serve the interests of national defense. Witness the powerful protests against university-based research sponsored by the military.

To a great extent, the school world has mirrorec the strife of the larger society. In both school and society, young people are being led by some of their most gifted peers against entrenched establishments. There are the nonviolent malcontents groping for new meaning in their lives, and there are the militants who want a piece of the old action with themselves in the seat of power. The latter group can't wait to taste the privilege and independence usually reserved for adulthood and are willing to fight the older incumbents to make their presence felt. They are the ones who storm the offices of college deans and school principals to insist on a greater voice in the governance of their educational experience. Their struggle, in short, is to get in. The malcontent, on the other hand, want out. They, too, see themselves as victims of a world that threatens to suffocate rather than nurture the individual, but their response is a refusal to play the game by traditional rules, a willingness to withdraw from the rat race, sometimes with the help of drugs or some brand of bohemianism. The gifted among them are either school dropouts or charter members of free universities engaging in their own version of relevant education.

If there is a difference between disaffected youth today and their counterparts in the past, it is probably the extent to which they have carried their message. As one observer remarked, "The key difference between the Berkely riots of 1964 and the Columbia crisis of May 1969 is that in the pre-Columbian case the major impetus for unrest stemmed from the perceived abuse or misuse of authority ('Do not bend, fold, or mutilate'), whereas the later protest denied the legitimacy of authority."[16] One might add that when attention is called to the misuse of power, it is an expression of protest, but when there are doubts about the legitimacy of power, it is a sign of revolution. The revolt is not only against institutions (educational or otherwise) and their leaders, it is also against a tradition of rationalism that has sanctified ivory-tower scholarship. When Columbia rioters willfully destroyed a professor's research files, the act may have carried a message that goes beyond ordinary vandalism. It seemed to imply that all the work invested in accumulating those files was a waste of the professor's talent, which ought to have been dedicated to building a better society rather than dabbling in esoterica. And to make matters worse, the educational establishment expects its brighter students to follow in the footsteps of the professors like him.

Even the sciences have come under closer scrutiny than ever for their influence on the human condition. Sputnick-age gifted were bombarded with the message that a lifetime devotion to achievement in science was not only in the interests of the state but of mankind in general. Such pursuits had their own built-in ethic, that any efforts at solving the mysteries of the universe deserve the highest commendation because they attest to man's divine-like power of mastering his environment and creating his own brand of miracles in it. Now we are told that man's science is as fallible as he is himself. Among the most vocal critics are the environment-minded scientists who warn that, in our enthusiasm for conquering nature, we may be destroying ourselves in the process unless we impose restraints on such activity.[17] Perhaps the best-known writer to forecast doom if science continues on its present course is the biologist Barry Commoner whose Science and

Survival has had wide circulation and influence. Commoner takes the ecological point of view that the elements of nature are integrated but our knowledge of these elements so limited that we don't see their connectedness. Expressing deep concern about science's preoccupation with the elegance of its methods rather than the danger of its products, he directs much of his fire at the polluting effects of such symbols of technological giantism as nuclear testing and industrial waste. He acknowledges the brainpower needed to enrich scientific thinking, but he warns that "no scientific principle can tell us how to make the choice, which sometimes may be forced upon us by the insecticide problem, between the shade of the elm tree and the song of the robin."[18] With such caveats it may be difficult to convince gifted children that a life dedicated to science is the kind of high calling it once was unless closer links are made between the intellect and the conscience.

The recent upheavals in the academic community and the exposure of sacred cows in the scientific world raise serious questions among young people as to whether they ought to funnel their psychic energies into a life of the mind. Many are attracted to the sensitivity training movements, which tell them that "talking is usually good for intellectual understanding of personal experience, but it is often not as effective for helping a person to experience—to feel."[19] Accordingly, man should not be seen simply as a thought machine but rather as a complex biological, psychological, and social animal who can fulfill himself through all of these dimensions of his being. Every part of the body has to be exercised to its fullest potential, which means building up the strength and stamina of its muscles, its sensory awareness and aesthetic appreciation, its motor control, and the gamut of its emotional and social feelings. Inhibiting other aspects of self for the sake of the intellect amounts to robbing life of its multidimensionality, so the task of the individual is to make something of all his capacities, even if in so doing he cannot make the most of any one of them. What emerges is a brand of anti-intellectualism that places the mind in some kind of human perspective rather than discrediting it entirely. It may also signal a partial decline of the familiar controlled, achievement-oriented youth culture and the ascendance of an emancipated, awareness-oriented youth faction that has won the allegiance of many gifted individuals. To depict the change more clearly, it is useful to adapt Bennis's paradigm for trends in America's cultural values:

| Achievement-Oriented Youth | | Awareness-Oriented Youth |
|---|---|---|
| Self-advancement | v. | Self-actualization |
| Self-control | v. | Self-expression |
| Independence | v. | Interdependence |
| Endurance of stress | v. | Capacity for joy |
| Full employment | v. | Full lives |

Of course, the foregoing notes on changes in the youth culture are only speculations, but to the extent that they make sense, there is need to reassess the kinds of educational issues and research usually associated with the gifted. Questions about whether to accelerate, enrich, or group by ability, which aroused so much interest not so long ago, seem archaic and trivial in the 1970s. The same is true for the problems of underachievement, despite the enormous amount of scholarly time devoted to it over the years. More important, these concerns make sense only for a school world powerful enough to manipulate the young lives of its gifted in the interest of a national talent hunt. But you can't hunt by the old methods if the target is sensitive to being dismembered diagnostically and his parts coded in a language that data banks can understand. It is bad enough to be reduced to a code number that denotes the characteristics of a live commodity rather than qualities in a human being; it is even worse to make such a self-sacrifice at the behest of a social system that has lost most of its credibility among youth. Besides, the gifted young person who feels that the explosion of knowledge over the past quarter century has not brought us closer to utopia may resist the idea of devoting his life to learning on the ground that it isn't worth the sacrifice.

If faith in the advancement of knowledge is to be restored, it will have to be done with an understanding of what Commoner calls the "humane consequences" of knowledge. Therein lies the key to a new perspective on the educational needs of the gifted. It is no secret that superior young minds come to school uniquely sensitized to the problems of right and wrong. In her classic studies of children with IQ's above 180, Leta Hollingworth noted that the very gifted child often wonders about human destiny and problems of evil but feels powerless to resolve these problems.[20] In a similar vein, research on more moderately gifted children has shown that they possess an exceptional measure of social concern as evidenced by their idealization of humanitarian contributions.[21] Our problem is that we never really capitalized on these qualities in our enrichment programs. Instead, we have tried to stay as neutral and value-free as possible, much to the dismay of many thoughtful young people who don't want their school experience to be so antiseptic. They amy be trying to communicate some of this disappointment when they criticize education for being irrelevant.

It must be emphasized that the gifted are no better equipped to come to grips with the value dimensions of their studies than they are able to solve problems in non-Euclidean geometry without prior training. And it is unrealistic to think that the home, church or community can provide sufficient training for one subject of study any more than it can for the other. Social concern has to become the context in which all studies are couched, or else gifted youth will be saddled with the question, "Knowledge for what?" The recent push by young people to become a greater part of the nation's conscience suggests that they are indeed ready to explore the humane consequences of all aspects of their schooling. This readiness has to be fulfilled through careful planning and programming in a more serious way than ever

before. Otherwise, we will succeed at best in producing a breed of technocrats who possess only a pragmatic view of how their talents should be used. Any enrichment program that reflects such a short-sighted view of the nation's talent needs will probably never amount to more than another curriculum appendage to be discarded when our newly aroused interest in the gifted tapers off.

## References

1. Bestor, A. E. *Educational Wastelands.* Urbana: University of Illinois Press, 1953.

2. Rickover, H. G. *Education and Freedom.* New York: E. P. Dutton and Co., 1959.

3. Wolfle, D. *America's Resources of Specialized Talent.* New York: Harper & Row, Publishers, 1954.

4. Tannenbaum, A. J. "Recent Trends in the Education of the Gifted." *Educational Forum* 26: 333-43; March 1962.

5. Conant, J. B. *The American High School Today.* New York: McGraw Hill Book Co., 1959.

6. French, J. L. editor. *Educating the Gifted.* New York: Henry Holt and Co., 1959.

7. Landers, I. *Higher Horizons Progress Report.* New York: Board of Education of the City of New York, 1963.

8. Wrightstone, J. W., and others. *Evaluation of the Higher Horizons Program for Underprivileged Children.* New York: Board of Education of the City of New York, 1964.

9. Lorge, I. "Difference of Bias in Tests of Intelligence." *Proceedings: Invitational Conference on Testing Problems.* Princeton: Educational Testing Service, 1953.

10. Tannenbaum, A. J. "The IPAT Culture Fair Intelligence Test: A Critical Review." *Sixth Mental Measurements Yearbook,* O. Buros, editor. Highland Park, N. J.: The Gryphon Press, 1965.

11. Gardner, J. W. *Excellence: Can We Be Equal and Excellent Too?* New York: Harper & Row, Publishers, 1961.

12. Marland, S. P., Jr. *Education of the Gifted and Talented.* 2 vols. Washington, D.C.: U.S. Government Printing Office, 1971.

13. Terman, L. M., and others. *The Gifted Child Grows Up.* Stanford, Calif.: Stanford University Press, 1947.

14. Nichols, R. C., and Astin, A. W. *Progress of the Merit Scholar: An Eight-year Follow-up.* Evanston, Ill.: National Merit Scholarship Corp., 1965.

15. Marcuse, H. *One-Dimensional Man.* Boston: Beacon Press, 1964.

16. Bennis, W. G. "A Funny Thing Happened on the Way to the Future." *American Psychologist* 25: 595-608; July 1970.

17. Bereano, P. L. "The Scientific Community and the Crisis of Belief." *American Scientist* 57: 484-501; Winter 1969.

18. Commoner, B. *Science and Survival.* New York: The Viking Press, 1966. p. 104.

19. Schutz, W. C. *Joy.* New York: Grove Press, 1967. p. 11.

20. Hollingworth, Leta S. *Children Above 180 I.Q.* Yonkers-on-Hudson, N.Y.: World Book Co., 1942.

21. Martinson, Ruth A. *Educational Programs for Gifted Pupils.* Sacramento, Calif.: California State Department of Education, 1961.

*Lewis M. Terman*

# A New Approach to the Study of Genius

*T*hree stages may be noted in the study of genius during the last century. The first of these is typified by the work of Moreau de Tours, Lombroso, and Grasset. Its methods were impressionistic and anecdotal. Its characteristic procedure was the search for striking cases which would lend support to a preconceived theory.

The second stage is represented by the researchers of Galton, de Candolle, Odin, Ellis and Castle. Here the method is inductive, the selection of cases is based upon objective criteria, and the data are subjected to statistical treatment. Although the studies of this period marked a tremendous advance, they were limited by the nature of the biographical material upon which they were based. In the first place, the genius of biographical encyclopaedias represents a selected type, namely, the socially successful. Extraneous factors doubtless operate to influence the personnel of such encyclopaedias and the amount of space given to individual cases. In the second place, the biographical data are so incomplete and, what is worse, often so unreliable, that only an extremely limited number of facts can be assembled for as many as 75 per cent of any objectively selected group. Information regarding early life and training is likely to be especially scanty and untrustworthy.

A third and very significant advance is marked by Cattell's study of living American men in science. Here the selection of cases is accomplished by vastly improved methods, the desired data are obtainable from practically 100 per cent of his subjects, and the facts treated can be accepted as really facts. It is to be regretted, however, that it has not been possible in Cattell's study to secure the data which would be necessary to give a reliable picture of the juvenile traits and early mental development of his subjects. Those of us who have envied Professor Cattell his opportunity to witness the dramatic rise of his subjects from the mid-forenoon of their careers to their zenith, and their later subsidence or replacement by other luminaries,

Reprinted from *Psychological Review,* Vol. 29, No. 4 (July, 1922), pp. 310-318. By permission of the American Psychological Association.

naturally regret that the author has not been able to extend his observations back to the period of childhood.

The logical next step is the study of genius in the making, that is, the investigation of gifted children. This approach has the great advantage that the number of obtainable facts is limited only by the time, patience and resources of the investigator. It opens the way to a more thorough-going study of the genetic aspects of the problem, of the environmental factors which affect genius, and of the exact nature of its deviation from the average. Tests and measurements in unlimited number can be made, and norms can readily be secured for the interpretation of data so collected. Moreover, follow-up work with large numbers of gifted children will throw light upon genius which aborts or deteriorates, as well as open that which fulfills its promise. By this method we may even hope to learn something in time about the pedagogy of genius. We shall be able to test the theories of Witte, Berle, Wiener, Sidis, and others who believe that it is possible to make any child a prodigy. We shall find out to what extent, if at all, nature tends to even up the score of gifts by taking from him who has more than his fair share of one desirable quality some other advanatge. We shall find out what truth there is in the widespread view that gifted children are usually conceited, freakish, socially eccentric, and prone either to illness and early death or to nervousness and insanity.

Perhaps a brief personal note in this historical sketch will be pardoned. My own interest in gifted children dates back to a master's thesis on leadership in 1903, to a review in 1904 of the literature on precocity, and to an experimental study of bright and dull children for the doctorate in 1905. It is unnecessary to recount the scanty results of these juvenile studies. By the time it became possible for me to return to the problem, in 1910, the progress which has been made in mental testing had created a new situation. For certain ages, at least, it was now possible to determine with some degree of approximation the relative brightness of a given child as compared with unselected children of his age.

It was in 1911 that we began more or less systematically to collect data at Stanford on children who had made exceptionally good records in a mental test. In 1913 three schools in San Francisco were sifted for bright children, and the following year certain data were published on 35 cases testing above 120 I.Q. Ratings on several traits were secured and a brief information schedule was filled out by the teacher. The results of this explorative study were considerably out of line with my own expectations and in contradiction to earlier views which I had published on the dangers of precocity. In passing it might be noted that one of the bright children tested in 1911 is now a teaching assistant in Stanford University, that another was recently awarded a scholarship for meritorious record, and that a third had just received his Ph.D. degree and been awarded an $1,800 research fellowship by the National Research Council. Not one has yet to become insane or developed symptoms of post-adolescent stupidity!

In 1916 the methods were considerably revised. The teacher's information schedule was enlarged, a similar information schedule was prepared for the parents to fill out, and ratings on twenty traits were secured both from parents and teachers. Data were collected on 59 cases testing for the most part above 140 I.Q. The results have been summarized elsewhere and need not be reported here.

The establishment by the university of a special research fellowship in 1919 was the occasion for further revision of method and a stimulus to renewed search for cases. Unwisely, as it now appears, the number of traits to be rated was increased from 20 to 46. However, the information schedules were materially improved and an interest blank was arranged for the child. By the spring of 1921 approximately 180 cases testing for the most part above 140 I.Q. had been located, and for 121 of these fairly complete supplementary data had been secured. Some of the outstanding results for this "first group" are as follows:

1. The number of very high cases is larger than the standard deviation of the I.Q. distribution for unselected children would lead one to expect. It is doubtful therefore whether the incidence of superior intelligence follows the normal probability curve.

2. The sex for all the cases together is 60 to 40 in favor of boys. Above 160 I.Q. it is 65 to 35, and above 180 it is 70 to 30. These figures are not conclusive, however, owing to the fact that only a minority of the cases were discovered by a systematic canvass of the sexes.

3. As regards physical traits, it may be tentatively stated that these children, as a group, are above the average in height and weight, that they were precocious in learning to walk and talk, that they show no apparent excess of nervous symptoms, and that their general health conditions appear to be at least as good as the average for unselected children.

4. As regards school progress, the average acceleration is about two grades beyond the standard for their life ages; but as compared with the standard for their mental ages, there is an average retardation of more than two years. All but four have skipped one or more grades, and there are no genuine cases of grade repetition. According to the statements of their parents, about one sixth have been mildly encouraged to make rapid school progress, one sixth have been deliberately held back, and the remaining two thirds have been allowed to 'go their own pace.' Possibly three or four have been more or less systematically 'stuffed' but only one of these is near the top of the list.

5. Family data show strikingly superior heredity. On the Taussig fivefold classification of occupations about 50 per cent of the fathers belong to class 1 (the professional group), as compared with 4 or 5 per cent of the general population, while 37 per cent belong to class 2 and 13 per cent to class 3. Neither class 4 nor class 5 (the semi-skilled and unskilled occupations) is represented at all (in this 'first group'), unless we rate a barber as belonging to class 4. Fifteen of the 121 cases belong to seven families. More than a third of the parents are known to have one or more relatives who have attained a considerable degree of prominence. About 20 per cent

of the father's and mother's sibs belong to one or another of the learned professions.

6. The parents whose families are reckoned complete have an average of only 2.53 children. The average age of fathers at the birth of the gifted child was 36.2 years; that of the mothers, 31.4 years.

7. As regards racial differences, there are two outstanding facts: there is a noteworthy excess of Jewish cases and still a more striking deficiency among Italians, Portuguese, Mexicans and Spanish, all of whom are numerous in the vicinity of Stanford.

8. The trait ratings, owing to the usual halo effects, have yielded data of only limited value. The halo largely invalidates any comparison of our group with normal children on the traits in question, although it does permit a comparison of parents' and teachers' ratings with each other, also a comparison of average ratings on different types of traits. Classifying the traits under the five headings, intellectual, volitional, social, emotional, and psychophysical, we have the following average ratings by parents and teachers for the traits of each group, where the rating 1 is highest, 3 is the average and 5 is the lowest.

|  | Intellectual | Volitional | Social | Emotional | Psycho-physical |
|---|---|---|---|---|---|
| Parents | 1.67 | 1.98 | 2.13 | 2.18 | 2.28 |
| Teachers | 1.64 | 1.99 | 2.08 | 2.04 | 2.27 |

It is seen that both parents and teachers tend to rate these children high on all types of traits; but especially high on those which are classed as intellectual and volitional. Teachers tend to rate rather consistently higher than parents, but the rank order of the traits based upon the ratings accorded by parents and correlates .76 with a similar rank order based upon ratings by teachers.

9. The data on social adaptability and allied traits have been examined with special care, with the result that approximately two thirds of our cases have been classified as entirely normal or superior in this respect. A case study of the remaining one third shows that only three or four are seriously maladjusted. The difficulties of the large majority in social adjustment are readily accounted for by the natural tendency to jealousy and resentfulness on the part of their older classmates whom they almost invariably surpass, a form of reaction to which even teachers do not seem to be entirely immune.

The above conclusions are tentative only. The data on which they are based are faulty in more ways than we can here enumerate. What had been learned thus far, was, largely, what not to do; also, that what needed doing would be too costly for the little budget available. Fortunately at this time the directors of the Commonwealth Fund came to the rescue with a grant of $20,300. This subvention is being devoted to the search of 1,000 cases and to the immediate collection of psychological, educational, and social data concerning them. The expense of follow-up work will be borne for an indefinite period by Stanford University. Four full-time assistants began field work in September, 1921. The plan is to secure the following data from as many as possible of the 1,000 cases:

1. At least two intelligence tests;
2. Achievement tests in all the main school subjects; involving altogether three hours of testing;
3. A general information test oof about an hour's duration:
4. A two-hour test of certain moral and emotional traits (for at least a part of the subjects);
5. About 20 anthropometric measurements;
6. A record of all the books read during two months, together with the child's rating of each book;
7. A test of interest in and knowledge of 90 typical plays, games, and amusements permitting the computation of deviations from age and sex standards;
8. Ratings from parents and teachers on 25 traits, by a much better method than we had formerly used;
9. Data to be supplied by the parents in a 16-page School Information Blank, and by the child himself in a 4-page Interest blank;
10. Home and neighborhood ratings on the Whittier scale;
11. Of a small number of the highest cases more intensive studies will be made, especially with reference to heredity.

All of the tests and information schedules will be used with 500 or more unselected children from 8 to 16 years of age, in order to secure the necessary background of comparative norms.

A report of salient findings will be made in 1923 but the detailed treatment of data may occupy several years and the follow-up work an additional decade or two. Naturally the value of the data will be greater twenty or thirty years hence than at present.

A word about the selection of cases. For many reasons it did not seem feasible to attempt to locate *the* 1,000 brightest children in the state. The effort is simply being made to locate that number having a Binet I.Q. above 140 (also, by methods we cannot here describe, children of very exceptional special ability). The search is being confined in the main to the grades from 3 to 8 inclusive. Entire cities and counties are being taken in order to avoid, as far as possible, undesirable selection. A certain amount of arbitrary selection is, however unavoidable. This would be true even if it were possible to give a mental test to all the children in the territory covered, for the test itself is of course an arbitrary criterion. Since it is not possible to test all, additional selection is necessary. At present we are testing in each classroom (by the National Intelligence Tests) the three children who are rated by the teacher as the brightest, second brightest, and third brightest, respectively, and in addition the child who is youngest. Those who test in the top 5 per cent for their ages by the National are then given either an abbreviated or a complete Binet, according to the promise shown. Of our cases to date who test above 140, about one third were not nominated as brightest, second brightest, or third brightest, and were caught only by virtue of being youngest.

Notwithstanding the use of such an inclusive drag-net method we have found by sheer accident a number of high I.Q.'s which it had failed to catch. In one case, the youngest child was at home, because of broken glasses, and the teacher substituted the second youngest, not otherwise nominated. This was the only pupil in the room who tested above 140. Another pupil brought to the test by mistake, by a child messenger, tested 149. Another, who was the only child to qualify in a school of 500, was erroneously named by the teacher as youngest as a result of his name appearing alphabetically adjacent to that of the youngest and being confused with it. Of four cases above 170 I.Q. located by one assistant, not one was named as first choice by the teacher. Two of the four were not named as first, second, or third choice and would have been missed but for the fact that they were youngest. It is no wonder that in the old-time school with its narrow curriculum and untrained teachers, the genius often escaped notice as completely as if he had worn an invisible cap. A pupil nominated by one of our teachers as brightest, was a ten-year-old in the first grade with I.Q. considerably below 100. By testing all the children in certain of the smaller cities, after the nominations have been regularly made, we are now trying to get a line on the number who are missed by the usual method of selection.

No results have been worked up, but the following miscellaneous facts may be of interest.

1. The ratio of boys to girls is now only about 55 to 45, and, as before, is slightly higher in the upper I.Q. ranges.

2. The individual schools of a given city differ enormously in the proportion of children who are gifted to the required degree. The average number with I.Q. above 140 is, in the larger cities of California, about 1 pupil in 250.

3. The proportion of Jewish children is even larger than in our earlier data.

4. Several of our new cases are of very inferior social status and a few are living in extreme poverty. Several have grown up with a minimum of home supervision and training. C.M., for example (I.Q. 141), is the son of a common Mexican laborer. B.S., who tests at 154, has lived most of his life with his mother, who is feeble-minded by test. One of his sisters is insane, another is feeble-minded, and two others are decidedly subnormal.

Our present undertaking, laborous as it is, will at best only help to open the field. Minute studies will have to be made of a large variety of individual cases. More searching and detailed information will have to be collected on health and heredity. The non-intellectual traits will have to be explored by methods which do not yet exist. Special intellectual abilities will have to be investigated. The pedagogy of genius offers unknown worlds to explore. The science of biography, as a special branch of psychology, is still to be created.

Until our knowledge of the social significance of genius has been made more exact, our conception of democracy will remain an illogical patchwork. Until an appreciation of the extent and meaning of individual differences has become more general, the eugenics movement will remain a futile hobby of a handful of enthusiasts, the present unfavorable differential birth rate will continue, and for want of creative thinkers and doers, the struggle of civilization will be, not to advance, but to hold its own against a relatively increasing spawn of inferior mentality.

Paul A. Witty

# The Education of the Gifted and the Creative in the U.S.A.

*T*he advent of the intelligence test in America ushered in a period in which most schools recognized the problem of caring for individual differences. There was frequent adaptation of the curriculum to care more adequately for slow-learning and retarded pupils, and occasional attempts were made to enrich and extend the experiences of the rapid-learning and gifted pupil.

The gifted child was typically considered to be a pupil whose IQ was very high, a concept which has persisted over a very long period of time among educators. The practice is traceable, to a large extent, to the work of L. M. Terman and his associates who devised an individual intelligence test and administered it to large numbers of pupils who were assigned to categories according to their ratings. Pupils who earned IQ's of 130 and higher were designated as "gifted" and those of IQ 140 and higher were classified as "genius or near genius." Early studies of elementary school pupils revealed that about one per cent earned IQ's which placed them in the "gifted" group. More recent studies have yielded somewhat higher percentages.

Large scale genetic studies of the gifted were initiated about 1920 and were summarized by L. M. Terman and Melita H. Oden (16a). In a magazine article, Terman concluded that gifted children are:

> ...in general, appreciably superior to unselected children in physique, health, and social adjustment; markedly superior in moral attitudes as measured either by character tests or by trait ratings; and vastly superior in their mastery of school subjects as shown by a three-hour battery of achievement tests. In fact, the typical child of the group had mastered the school subjects to a point about two grades beyond the one in which he was enrolled, some of them three or four grades beyond(15).

In the foregoing investigation, the remarkable academic achievement of the gifted child was revealed. Subsequent study showed that this superiority was generally maintained. Terman wrote:

Witty, Paul A. "The Education of the Gifted and the Creative in the U. S. A." *The Gifted Child Quarterly,* Summer, 1971, Vol. XV, No. 2.

...close to 90 per cent entered college and 70 per cent graduated. Of those graduating, 30 per cent were awarded honors and about two-thirds remained for graduate work(15).

Continued investigation of the gifted as adults, as well as study of proven geniuses, convinced Terman that:

...the genius who achieves the highest eminence is one whom intelligence tests would have identified as gifted in childhood(15).

Although the findings of the writer's early studies of high IQ children corroborated Terman's reports, he differed markedly in his interpretation of the data. He doubted whether one is jusified in asserting that a high IQ may be used to predict attainment that may be regarded as the work of "genius," and stressed the importance of other factors such as unusual opportunity, drive, and interest. However, he recognized the value of intelligence test ratings in selecting pupils of high academic promise. Such ratings seem suitable, when supplemented by other data, for the identification of the verbally gifted pupil.

## *Administrative Procedures Recommended for the Gifted*

Perhaps the most conspicuous finding of the early studies was the demonstration of the rapid learning and educational promise of the gifted pupil. About half of the pupils in the writer's studies learned to read before entering school, almost forty per cent before they were five years of age, and some at ages three and four. Moreover, they mastered academic materials with such rapidity that by the time they had reached the fifth or sixth grade in school, they had, on the average, knowledge and skills of pupils classified two full grades above them. As they grew older, the attainment of many pupils grew less commensurate with their early promise. It became clear that the typical curriculum was unsuitable to offer these pupils sufficient challenge and motive for effective and continuous learning. Accordingly, it was recommended that moderate amounts of acceleration of school progress be employed and that enrichment be provided in special classes and in the regular classroom. In the twenties, special classes were formed in a few cities in various states such as California, Ohio, New York, and Pennsylvania. The practice was not widely employed because of inadequate numbers of gifted pupils in many communities and because of the prevailing attitude which led to a fear of the creation of an intellectually elite group through special attention to the gifted. Moreover, many administrators believed that the gifted pupil could take care of himself. As a result, relatively few efforts were made to enrich opportunities for the gifted during the period 1925-1950.

An increased interest in providing special opportunities for the gifted transpired following the publication of Terman and Oden's *The Gifted Child Grows Up* (16a), and *The Gifted Child* (25) edited by Paul A. Witty for the *American Association for Gifted Children,* an organization formed after World War II to foster interest in the education of the gifted. Impetus was given to efforts to identify and encourage gifted children by widespread dissemination of facts concerning the neglect of our greatest human resource at the time when the need for personnel of outstanding ability in science and related fields was crucial. During the following decade, a large number of books, articles and lengthy bibliographies reflected the expanding interest in the gifted. Special classes, partial segregation, and acceleration (or grade skipping) were used more frequently in the elementary school, and in the secondary school "honors classes" (especially in science) and "honors schools" were organized for the gifted. In some schools, provisions were made for superior high school students to enter college early or to obtain college credit for enriched courses taken in high school(13, 20).

Notable was the provision of scholarships and awards which served to offer further motivation and incentive for gifted high school students. For example, in 1956 the National Merit Scholarship Corporation granted 556 awards. By the end of its fourth year, more than 3,000 superior students had entered college with Merit Scholarships according to the Fourth Annual Report of the National Merit Scholarship Corporation. Magazines addressed to teachers and administrators also indicated steps that might be taken to provide more frequent identification of gifted pupils and ways to make more adequate provisions for them. One such article, addressed to school administrators by the present writer, was distributed widely by the editors of The Nation's Schools (February, 1956) and thousands of reprints were sent on request. Thus, a movement to offer the gifted child greater opportunities gained recognition in schools throughout the United States.

The foregoing educational practices were designed primarily to furnish increased opportunities for verbally gifted pupils in the elementary and the secondary school. These gains were heartening. There were, however, some conspicuous limitations in these commendable efforts. For example, the research studies, on which the selection of the gifted was based, were made when pupils were of school age. Very young children were not included.

During this period, opportunities for intellectual stimulation of young children were seldom found in the typical home, preschool center, and traditional kindergarten. One of the chief obstacles to the provision of such opportunities was the prevailing belief that the IQ was relatively constant, fixed, and unchangeable. It was believed that inborn factors accounted in large measure for the child's intelligence (or IQ) and that by the side of heredity, all other factors were "dwarfed in comparison."

## Failure to Recognize the Significance of Early Learning

In the years around 1960, a group of "cognitive" psychologists began to explore the nature and extent of learning in early childhood under varying conditions. The studies showed clearly the child's need for intellectually stimulating experiences during the early "crucial" years. In a recent book entitled *Revolution in Learning: The Years from Birth to Six,* Maya Pines states:

> Millions of children are being irreparably damaged by our failure to stimulate them intellectually during their crucial years ... from birth to six. Millions of others are being held back from their true potential(12).

Maya Pines pointed out further that "The child's intelligence grows as much during the first four years of life as it will grow during the next thirteen."(12). It was indicated, too, that failure to provide stimulation and nurture during the early years would have far-reaching adverse effects. Moreover, it was held that opportunities offered at this time have a marked positive influence in increasing learning ability and heightening intelligence, particularly in areas where "disadvantage" prevails. Thus J. McV. Hunt writes:

> ...it is not unreasonable to entertain the hypothesis that, with a sound scientific educational psychology of early experience, it might become feasible to raise the average level of intelligence — by a substantial degree ... this "substantial degree" might be of the order of 30 points of IQ(11).

The foregoing hypothesis will need to be examined and tested carefully. It is, however, clear that the IQ is no longer looked upon as a product chiefly of hereditary factors. The pendulum has swung to an emphasis on environmental influences. Accordingly, programs in early education have been proposed to improve intelligence(2, 5). Remarkable attainment in reading and language has already been reported for children who have been accorded early learning opportunities(4).

## Identification of the Creative Pupil

During the period of increased interest in the gifted pupil, it became evident that intelligence tests would not enable one to identify successfully pupils having a high potential for creative expression. This fact was long ago pointed out by the present writer who indicated that the intelligence test does not usually elicit imaginative, original, or unique response. Repeatedly, it has been found recently that if one were to limit selection of "gifted" pupils to those of IQ 130 and higher, he would fail to include the majority of creative pupils (17, 18). The present writer proposed, therefore, that the definition of the gifted be expanded to include "any child whose performance in a worthwhile type of human endeavor is consistently or repeatedly remarkable."

Efforts have been made in recent years to construct tests of "creativity" without marked success. Critics have emphasized the limitations in certain tests and the desirability of caution in using them. It has become clear that creativity is not a general trait, and that an individual who is creative in one area will not necessarily be creative in another (9).

## *Techniques for Identifying Creative Pupils*

Despite the limitations of tests of creativity, there are a number of practical approaches which are being increasingly used to find children whose creative promise is great. For example, in a study made by the present writer, the remarkable film of the Swedish photographer Arne Sucksdorff, *The Hunter and the Forest,* was shown in many schools in a large number of American cities. There is no commentary for the film, but a musical score and the sounds of animals and birds are employed as accompaniments.

After large numbers of pupils had seen the film, they were asked to write a commentary, a poem, or a story about it. The products of slightly more than ten per cent suggested unique creative ability. If a very high IQ had been used as the criterion for the gifted, a majority of these pupils would not have been included. Moreover, many of the outstanding compositions were written by pupils who had not previously been observed as having unusual aptitude in writing. If additional outstanding performance substantiated the first demonstration of exceptional ability by these pupils, they would be considered potentially gifted in this area.

Because of such findings, the present writer suggested that a search be made, not only for pupils of high verbal ability, but also for those of promise in mathematics and science, writing, art, music, drama, mechanical ability, and social leadership.

Motivated by the research of J. P. Guilford, scholars are increasingly recognizing the prevalence of undiscovered talent, and some are stressing multiple talents in children and youth (9, 10). For example, Calvin W. Taylor points out that there are many kinds of talent and indicates that if a search is limited to one type among seven talent groups, 50 per cent of the pupils would be included since they would be above average. If six types were included, the per cent would be about 90 for children above average in one or more items (14a). Such approaches for selecting talented pupils are promising, but will need to be studied further.

## Differences Between the Gifted and the Creative

The writer has already noted some of the characteristics of gifted children identified by intelligence tests. They were found to be well-adjusted socially and congenial with their peers. Creative pupils differ markedly from the verbally gifted in these respects. E. P. Torrance stresses the problem in adjustment displayed by the creative pupil:

> In no group thus far studied have we failed to find relatively clear evidence of the operation of pressures against the most creative members of the group, though they are far more severe in some classes than in others (18).

Support is given to the findings of Torrance by a remarkable study reported by Victor and Mildred G. Goertzel (8). These authors chose 400 persons, acknowledged as "eminent" by the large numbers of biographies recently written about them; in childhood:

> They showed their greatest superiority in reading ability; many read at the age of four. Almost all were early readers of good books. They were original thinkers and had scant patience with drill and routine. They were likely to be rejected by their playmates...(8).

The authors concluded that "Three out of five of the Four Hundred had serious school problems."

> Now as in the days of the Four Hundred, the child who is both intelligent and creative remains society's most valuable resource. When we learn to work with him instead of against him, his talents may reward us in ways beyond our ability to imagine (8).

It is at once clear that reading may be used advantageously in helping to meet the needs of gifted and creative pupils. Not only will wide reading enable a pupil to satisfy and extend his interests, but it may also help him to meet personal and social problems successfully and build an appropriate ideal of self (21, 23, 24).

## Promising Trends in the Education of the Gifted

We may note two encouraging trends in the education of the gifted. The first is the adoption of a broader concept of the gifted to include children demonstrating a capacity for high level creative response, and the extension and development in schools, generally, of programs for identifying and encouraging such pupils. The second is found in the notable efforts of parents and teachers to recognize the problem and to become involved in meeting it more adequately. Already there is evidence that increased involvement is being practiced by parents of young children who are employing helpful suggestions found in books such as Joan Beck's *How to Raise a Brighter Child* (2). They are being aided further by following recommendations included in books such as *Helping the Gifted Child* (22). Kits of materials such as the one developed in association with the television program *Sesame Street,* and the *Adventures in Discovery* program of the Western Publishing Company are also being used successfully.

Teachers, too, are becoming involved in programs for gifted and creative students as is suggested in a Reading Aids Booklet entitled *Reading for the Gifted and the Creative Student.* In Chapter III, Walter B. Barbe and Joseph Renzulli present the results of their recent survey of practices in the education of the gifted and the creative student in various states (1). The teachers participating in these programs are to be commended for their efforts to foster the development of gifted and creative pupils in their classrooms. Many of the programs are designed to encourage creative expression in the form of *divergent* and *evaluative* behavior as well as creative reading in the classroom (17, 18).

Despite the above gains, there continues to be a very great neglect of gifted and creative pupils. In a provocative article entitled "Characteristics of Gifted Children" published in 1967, Stanley Krippner indicates that "... society still allows many of its brightest young people to pass by unnoticed" and that "...most school systems have not reached a stage where creativity is properly cultivated or where giftedness is widely appreciated" (26).

Not only is the regrettable condition found in elementary and secondary schools, but it also persists in colleges where, as Krippner states, "The scope of student protest at colleges and universities demonstrates that professors and administrators — are sometimes inept caretakers of America's most valuable resource, its gifted individuals" (26).

It is to be hoped that the present meager opportunities will be greatly extended in the future, since as Arnold Toynbee has written:

> To give a fair chance to potential creativity is a matter of life and death for any society. This is all-important, because the outstanding creative ability of a fairly small percentage of the population is mankind's ultimate capital asset, and the only one with which only Man has been endowed (19).

## References

1. Barbe, Walter B., and Renzulli, Joseph. Chapter III in *Reading for the Gifted and the Creative Student,* Reading Aids Booklet. Newark, Delaware: International Reading Association, 1971.

2. Beck, Joan. *How to Raise a Brighter Child.* New York: Trident Press, 1967.

3. Chall, Jeanne S. *Learning to Read: The Great Debate.* New York: McGraw-Hill, 1967.

4. Durkin, Dolores. *Children Who Read Early.* New York: Teachers College Press, Columbia University, 1966.

5. Engelmann, Siegfried, and Engelmann, Therese. *Give Your Child a Superior Mind.* New York: Simon and Schuster, Inc., 1966.

6. Gallagher, James J. *Teaching the Gifted Child.* Boston: Allyn and Bacon, Inc., 1964.

7. Getzels, J. W., and Jackson, P. W. *Creativity and Intelligence.* New York: John Wiley and Sons, Inc., 1962.

8. Goertzel, Victor, and Goertzel, Mildred G. *Cradles of Eminence.* Boston: Little, Brown and Company, 1962.

9. Guilford, J. P. "Potentiality for Creativity," *Gifted Child Quarterly,* 6 (Autumn, 1962).

10. Guilford, J. P. *Intelligence, Creativity, and Their Educational Implications.* San Diego, California: Robert R. Knapp, Box 234, 1968.

11. Hunt, J. McV. *Intelligence and Experience.* New York: The Ronald Press Company, 1961.

12. Pines, Maya. *Revolution in Learning — The Years from Birth to Six.* New York: Harper and Row Publishers, Inc., 1967.

13. Pressey, S. L. "Educational Acceleration: Appraisals and Basic Problems," *Educational Research Monographs,* No. 31. Columbus, Ohio: The Ohio State University, 1949.

14a. Taylor, Calvin W. "Be Talent Developers," *Today's Educational,* (December, 1968).

14b. Taylor, Calvin W., and Barron, Frank (Editors). *Scientific Creativity: Its Recognition and Development.* New York: John Wiley and Sons, 1963.

15. Terman, Lewis M. "The Discovery and Encouragement of Exceptional Talent," *The American Psychologist,* 9 (June, 1954).

16a. Terman, Lewis M., and Oden, Melita H. *The Gifted Child Grows Up.* Vol. IV of *Genetic Studies of Genius,* edited by Lewis M. Terman. Stanford, California: Stanford University Press, 1947.

16b. Terman, Lewis M., and Oden, Melita H. "The Stanford Studies of the Gifted," Chapter Three in *The Gifted Child,* edited by Paul A. Witty. Boston: D. C. Heath and Company, 1951.

17. Torrance, E. Paul. "Explorations in Creative Thinking," *Education,* 81 (December, 1960).

18. Torrance, E. Paul. "Problems of Highly Creative Children," *Gifted Child Quarterly,* 5 (Summer, 1961).

19. Toynbee, Arnold. "Is America Neglecting Her Creative Minority?" *Accent on Talent,* 2 (January, 1968).

20. Witty, Paul A., and Wilkins, W. L. "The Status of Acceleration or Grade Skipping as an Administrative Device," *Educational Administration and Supervision,* 19 (May, 1933).

21. Witty, Paul A. "The Gifted Pupil and His Reading," *Highlights for Teachers,* No. 7 (February, 1967).

22. Witty, Paul A. *Helping the Gifted Child.* Chicago: Science Research

Associates, 1952. Revised in collaboration with Edith H. Grotberg, 1970.

23. Witty, Paul A. "Reading for the Gifted" (Featured Address) in *Reading and Realism,* Proceedings of the Thirteenth Annual Convention of the International Reading Association, edited by J. Allen Figurel. Newark, Delaware: International Reading Association, 1969.

24. Witty, Paul A., *et. al. Reading for the Gifted and the Creative Student,* Reading Aids Booklet. Newark, Delaware: International Reading Association (forthcoming).

25. Witty, Paul A. (Editor). *The Gifted Child.* Boston: D. C. Heath and Company, 1951.

26. Witty, Paul A. (Guest Editor). *Education* (September—October, 1957). See article by Stanley Krippner entitled "Characteristics of Gifted Children," pp. 15-20. In addition to Stanley Krippner's article, this issue of *Education* (September-October, 1967) contains an excellent annotated bibliography on the gifted and the creative by Edith H. Grotberg, pp. 52-56.

*E. Paul Torrance*

# Emerging Concepts of Giftedness

$M$any teachers, school administrators, counselors, school psychologists, and parents complain that there is no commonly accepted definition of giftedness, even among national and international authorities. When educational and civic leaders plead for support for programs for educating teachers of gifted children or for appropriate educational programs for gifted children, many legislators oppose such support, arguing that not even the experts know how to identify those who are gifted. They contend that if there is disagreement about identifying the gifted it is futile to attempt to educate teachers especially for the gifted and to provide special kinds of educational opportunities for them.

The problem, strangely, is not that the experts do not know how to identify gifted children, nor even that there is any genuine disagreement among the national and international authorities. The truth is that we have been expanding our concept of giftedness and that we have been learning an increasingly large number of ways of identifying a greater number of different kinds of gifted children.

Another problem is that many of those who have sought support for programs for gifted children have had fixed notions about giftedness. In many cases their ideas have been so patently erroneous that their proposals have not made sense to legislators and other would-be supporters. In some cases these fixed ideas have centered around one type of giftedness, usually the type identified by an intelligence test and represented by the index known as the "IQ." Until recently there has been little support for Paul Witty's (1951) definition of giftedness as "consistently superior performance in

---

Torrance, E. Paul *Gifted Child in the Classroom.* The MacMillan Company, New York, 1965.

any socially useful endeavor." Others have been overconcerned about the degree of giftedness and have argued that the gifted must have IQ's of 180, 150, 140, or some other figure. From arguments around this point there has arisen a great deal of confusing terminology, such as "genius," "highly gifted," "extremely gifted," "moderately gifted," "talented," and the like. Other arguments have centered around the fixity of the intelligence quotient.

Generally, however, serious students of the problem of educating gifted children agree that our expanding knowledge makes it clear that the problem is complex but not necessarily confusing. It is quite clear that there is a variety of kinds of giftedness that should be cultivated and are not ordinarily cultivated without special efforts. It is clear that if we establish a level on some single measure of giftedness, we eliminate many extremely gifted individuals on other measures of giftedness. It is also clear that intelligence may increase or decrease, at least in terms of available methods of assessing it, depending upon a variety of physical and psychological factors both within the individual child and within his environment.

The complexity engendered by our expanding knowledge of the human mind and its functioning should be exciting and challenging rather than confusing. The author hopes that the reader will find it so because this is the nature of things as teachers and parents experience them in trying to educate gifted children. Furthermore this complex view of the nature of giftedness permeates this book. The author hopes that it will help the reader feel more comfortable, yet excited and challenged, in his efforts to teach gifted children in elementary and high-school classrooms.

## Challenge of a Complex View of Giftedness

The acceptance of a realistically complex view of the human mind is itself a tremendous advance. In moving from an oversimplified (and patently erroneous) view of giftedness to a more complex one, we have reached a position where we can avoid many of the errors of the past. We should be able to develop a more humane kind of education for gifted children—one in which children will have a better chance to achieve their potentialities.

This more complex view of giftedness is causing us to reevaluate many of the classical experiments upon which we have built educational practices. From this reexamination it is becoming clear that children should be provided opportunities for mastering a variety of learning and thinking skills according to a variety of methods and that the outcomes of these efforts should be evaluated in a variety of ways. It will be one of the purposes of this book to illustrate some of this variety of learning and thinking skills, methods of learning, and evaluation procedures.

It is to be hoped that young teachers, as well as experienced educational leaders, will not be impatient with the complexity or the incompleteness of knowledge about giftedness. We do not yet know the end of the complexity of the functioning of the human mind and personality. This book, however, is inspired by the conviction that it is high time that we begin developing the strategies, methods, and materials that have built into them an acceptance of this complexity. In large part it is derived from the author and his associates' experimental work with gifted children.

In his own studies of creative giftedness the author has continued to be increasingly impressed by the wonderful complexity of this single aspect of man's intellectual functioning. Many fascinating insights concerning the functioning of children's minds occur even when we limit ourselves to the examination of such qualities of thinking as fluency of ideas, spontaneous flexibility, originality, and elaboration. Some children are exceptionally fluent in the production of ideas expressed in words but are unable to express ideas in figural or auditory symbols. Others may be tremendously fluent in expressing ideas in figural form but appear paralyzed mentally when asked to express them in words or sounds. Similar phenomena seem to occur when we consider creative movement or kinesthetic behavior.

A child may not be able to express his ideas verbally, visually, or any other way with a great deal of fluency and yet be quite gifted in other kinds of constructive, creative behavior. He may produce a small number of ideas, but each idea may be quite original or unusual and of high quality. He may be able to take a single idea and do an outstanding job of elaborating or expanding it, or he may produce ideas which show a great deal of flexibility of thinking.

The complexity of children's creative thinking does not end here. A child might respond quite creatively to one task and barely respond to another. For example, some children show tremendous originality and elaboration on the Incomplete Figures Test and respond very poorly to the Circles Test and vice versa (Torrance, 1962a). The Incomplete Figures Test confronts the child with incomplete structures, and this produces tension in most observers, making them want to complete the structures and integrate or synthesize their relatively unrelated elements. The pages of circles of the Circles Test, however, confront the subject with "perfect structures." In order to produce pictures and objects which have as a major part a circle, the child has to disrupt or destroy these "perfect structures," the circles. In the creative process there seems to be an essential tension between the two opposing tendencies symbolized by these two tasks: the tendency toward structuring and synthesizing and the tendency toward disruption and diffusion of energy and attention. Most children seem able to express both tendencies with equal skill, but others seem able to express only one of these tendencies to any great degree.

The author has mentioned here only a few of the ways he has devised for measuring the mental abilities involved in creative thinking, yet he realizes that he has only begun to represent psychometrically the different ways children can express their creative giftedness.

# Some of the Scientific Bases of Emerging Concepts

Many educators and psychologists have been struggling for years to tear themselves away from concepts of a single type of giftedness. Undoubtedly this struggle has been motivated by vague anxieties that such concepts lead to errors and inhumane treatment for many children. The difficulty has been in finding a way to conceptualize the various kinds of intellectual giftedness and to develop measures of the different kinds of mental abilities involved. There have been numerous brave but unsuccessful attempts. For example, on the basis of the report of the Norwood Committee in England (Burt, 1968), the Education Act of 1944 in that country gave recognition to the hypothesis that there are different kinds of intellectual giftedness. Burt, in fact, maintains that the Education Act of 1944 assumes that children differ more in quality of ability than in amount. This act recommended a tripartite classification of secondary school, based on the idea that there are three main types of giftedness: a literary or abstract type to be educated at grammar schools, a mechanical or technical type to be educated at technical schools, and a concrete or practical type to be educated at modern schools. Burt argues that this scheme has not worked out as well as had been hoped. This may well be due, however, to still another oversimplification of the problem. Many believe, nevertheless, that this tripartite system in England is much more successful than earlier systems based on a single type of giftedness.

Guilford's structure of intellect (1956, 1959) and research related to the creative thinking or divergent production abilities have been especially effective in directing educators and psychologists away from their dependence upon a single measure of giftedness. Guilford has given what amounts virtually to a periodic table of different kinds of intelligence. His theoretical model of the structure of intellect has three dimensions: operations, content, and products.

In this model the operators are the major kinds of intellectual activities or processes, the things that the organism does with the raw materials of information. The first, *cognition,* includes discovery, awareness, recognition, comprehension, or understanding. The second, *memory,* refers to retention or storage, with some degree of availability, of information. Then there are two types of *productive thinking* in which something is produced from what has been cognized or memorized: *divergent production,* or the generation of information, from given information, where emphasis is upon variety and quantity of output from the same source, and *convergent production,* or the generation of information where emphasis is upon achieving unique or conventionally accepted best outcomes (the given information fully determines

*51*

the response). The fifth operation is *evaluation*, reaching decisions or making judgments concerning the correctness, suitability, adequacy, desirability, and so forth of information in terms of criteria of identity, consistency, and goal satisfaction.

These five operations act upon each of the kinds of content (figural, symbolic, semantic, and behavioral) and products (units, classes, systems, transformations, and implications). In this book the term *productive thinking* will be used to refer to what Guilford has defined as *convergent production* and *divergent production*. The term *creative thinking* will be used to refer to such abilities as fluency (large number of ideas), flexibility (variety of different approaches or categories of ideas), originality (unusual, off-the-beaten track ideas), elaboration (well developed and detailed ideas), sensitivity to defects and problems, and redefinition (perceiving in a way different from the usual, established, or intended way or use). *Measured creative thinking ability* will be used to refer to test scores which have been devised to assess these abilities.

Guilford and his associates' monumental work remained almost totally neglected by educators until Getzels and Jackson (1962) showed that highly creative or divergent thinking adolescents achieved as well as their highly intelligent peers, in spite of the fact that their average IQ was 23 points lower. Since at least 1898, psychologists had been producing instruments for assessing the creative-thinking abilities, making pleas for using such measures to supplement intelligence tests and recommending educational changes needed to develop creative talent. In the main these earlier efforts to generate interest in creative development and other types of intellectual tests were ignored or soon forgotten. Many of these earlier efforts are receiving attention now.

In selecting materials for this book, a serious effort has been made to provide ideas that can be used in teaching gifted children in both regular and segregated classrooms. The ideas presented have almost infinite possibilities for use with a variety of types of gifted children. It is to be expected that in the hands of some groups of gifted children the line of development from these methods and materials will be quite different from what will ensue in other groups. These materials and methods rarely require that specific questions be answered in a given way. It is to be hoped that teachers will not give severe disapproval when children answer questions or offer solutions to problems in a different way or ask different, more penetrating questions. Such questions and solutions are essential in many kinds of gifted performance.

Single studies such as those of Getzels and Jackson (1962) always leave many questions unanswered. Since the Getzels-Jackson data were obtained from a single school, one with an unusually large number of gifted students, their study did not tell us under what conditions their results could be anticipated. This author and his associates have undertaken fifteen partial replications of the Getzels-Jackson study, hoping to obtain some clues to answer this question. In ten of these studies the results have been essentially the same as in the Getzels-Jackson study. In the other five the high IQ group scored significantly higher than the highly creative group on tests of achievement. In general it has been our impression that the children in these five schools were taught primarily by methods of authority and had very little chance to use their creative-thinking abilities in acquiring educational skills. In most the average IQ was lower than in the schools where the Getzels-Jackson results were confirmed. These observations suggested that the phenomena Getzels and Jackson report may occur only in schools where students are taught in such a way that they have a chance to use their creative thinking abilities in acquiring traditional educational skills or where the average IQ in the entire school is rather high.

It was observed that the highly creative pupils in at least two of the five divergent schools overachieved in the sense that their educational quotients were considerably higher than their intelligent quotients. Thus we thought that an ability gradient might be operating. According to the concept of the ability gradient suggested by J.E. Anderson (1960), ability level can be thought of in terms of thresholds, and questions can be asked about the amount of the ability necessary to accomplish a task. Then consideration can be given to the factors that determine function beyond this threshold. There are cutoff points of levels about which the demonstration of ability in relation to minimum demands is determined by other factors. In other words the creative-thinking abilities might show their differential effects only beyond certain minimal levels of intelligence.

To test this possibility, Yamamoto (1964) in one of the Minnesota studies of creative thinking, reanalyzed the data from six of the partial replications already mentioned. In each case students who scored in the top 20 per cent on the test of creative thinking were divided into three groups according to IQ (above 130, 120 to 129, and below 120). In general the achievement of the first two groups did not differ from each other but was significantly higher than that of the third group (IQ below 120). This finding supports suggestions made previously by several people, including this author (Torrance, 1962a), Roc (1960), and MacKinnon (1961).

Still almost unnoticed by educators is that part of the Getzels-Jackson study (1962) dealing with two kinds of psychosocial excellence or giftedness—that is, high social adjustment and high moral courage. It was found that just as the highly intelligent student is not always highly creative, the highly adjusted student is not always highly moral. Further it was found that although the highly moral students achieved at a higher level than the highly adjusted students, the teachers perceived the highly adjusted students as the leaders rather than the highly moral ones. This is especially significant in a peer-oriented culture such as we have in the United States. It is well to recognize the dangers of giving the greater rewards to those who accept the peer-value system and adjust almost automatically to the immediate group, almost without reference to moral values.

It is the contention of the author that we can do a better job of helping children achieve excellence in both social adjustment and moral courage.

From time to time investigators have assaulted the concept of fixed intelligence. Despite this the view that intelligence is a capacity fixed once and for all by genetic inheritance is still held quite widely. Indeed a great deal of empirical evidence seems at first glance to support the idea of fixed intelligence. Recently, however, Hunt (1961) proposed alternative explanations and summarized evidence which undermines this hypothesis.

It has been shown that performances (scores, not IQ) on the Binet-type intelligence tests improves with age. Age-discrimination, however, was one of the criteria Binet used in selecting items. Although Binet himself (1909) regarded intelligence as "plastic," the fact that performance on tests selected on age-discrimination criteria showed improvement with age has been used to conclude that development is predetermined by genetic inheritance. Another argument has been that individual children show considerable constancy from one intelligence test to another. Since all intelligence tests traditionally have been validated against the Binet-type test, this is to be expected. It has also been shown that there are high intercorrelations among the various Binet-type tests, and this has been presented as evidence in favor of a high "g" (general ability) factor. Another argument of the adherents of fixed intelligence has been based on evidence which shows that intelligence tests are fairly good predictors of school achievement. Since curricula and achievement tests have been based on the intelligence-test concept of the human mind, this too is to be expected.

Studies involving hereditary versus environmental determination also have been used to support the idea of fixed intelligence. The evidence here, however, frequently has not supported the idea of fixed intelligence. Both hereditary and environmental influences interact in determining mental growth and educational achievement.

Hunt (1961) has summarized evidence from studies of identical twins reared apart, from repeated testing of the same children in longitudinal studies, and from studies of the effects of training or guided, planned learning experiences. He believes that studies of the constancy of the IQ within individuals pose the most serious challenge to fixed intelligence. These include studies both of the stability with which individuals maintain their positions within a given group of individuals from one testing to another testing and of the variations of IQ within specific individuals.

Studies of the effects of schooling have been fairly convincing. Out of a group of people tested at some earlier age, those who complete the most schooling show the greatest increases and fewest decreases in IQ. Hunt cites studies by Lorge (1945), Vernon (1948), and deGroot (1948, 1951). In the areas of early environmental influences, Hunt mentions the sustained work of Wellman, Skeels, and their colleagues of the Iowa group. This group continued their studies over many years, demonstrating many of the effects of training at the kindergarten and nursery level. The studies of Spitz (1945, 1946) have been quite influential in convincing psychiatrists and social caseworkers that intelligence is crucial during the early years of life. Children deprived of social interaction or mothering fail to develop naturally either physically or mentally.

AWAY FROM BELIEFS IN PREDETERMINED DEVELOPMENT

Long-standing beliefs in predetermined development have been used frequently to support the concept of fixed intelligence. Much evidence, however, indicates that deprivations of experience make a difference in rates of various kinds of growth. The more severe the deprivations of experience have been, the greater has been the decrease in the rates of development.

Arguments concerning inherited patterns of mental growth have also been placed in doubt by the work of Hunt (1961), Ojemann (1948), Ojemann and Pritchett (1963), and others. The evidence seems to indicate that intellectual development is quite different when chidren are exposed to guided, planned learning experiences from that which occurs when they encounter only what the environment just happens to provide.

This has led to the suggestion that educational programs should be based upon guided, planned experiences which in turn are based upon an analysis of the requirements of the learning task and the condition of the child. Analysis of the task must include a consideration of the structure of the task, possible strategies or processes by which the task can be achieved (alternative ways of learning, kinds of discriminations to be made, and so forth), and the settings or conditions which facilitate or impede achievement of the task (cultural, social, physical, and the like). Analysis of the child's condition should consider the stage of development relevant to the concepts or skills to be learned, the level of relevant abilities, especially the most highly developed ones (memory, logical reasoning, originality, judgments of space, and so forth), and the individual child's preferred ways of learning. The concern is with potentiality rather than norms. Examples of such educational experiences will be outlined in the section on classroom procedures.

## Conclusion

In this chapter an effort has been made to show how recent breakthroughs in research concerning the human mind and personality and their functioning have resulted in the emergence of a new and challenging concept of giftedness. This concept stresses the importance of emphasis upon potentiality rather than upon norms and single measures of giftedness. It involves movement away from concepts of a single type of giftedness and fixed intelligence and beliefs in predetermined development. In the following chapters an effort will be made to outline educational goals, identification procedures, strategies of motivation, and methods and materials of instruction appropriate for the education of gifted children.

*J. W. Getzels*

*P. W. Jackson*

# The Meaning of 'Giftedness'— An Examination of an Expanding Concept

*W*hen a concept becomes the focus of critical concern it is almost inevitable that its original meaning will simultaneously be expanded and differentiated. The concept of "giftedness" is, of course, of critical concern at this time, and the purpose of this paper is to examine the transformations this concept is presently undergoing and to suggest some additional modifications in its application

"Giftedness" as related to children has most frequently been defined as a score on an intelligence test, and typically the study of the so-called gifted child has been equated with the study of the single I.Q. variable. Involved in this unidimensional definition of giftedness are several types of confusion, if not outright error. First, there is the limitation of the single metric itself, which not only restricts our perspective of the more general phenomenon, but places on the one concept a greater theoretical and predictive burden than it was intended to carry. For all practical school purposes, the term "gifted child" has become synonymous with the expression "child with a high I.Q.," thus blinding us to other forms of excellence. Second, within the universe of intellectual functions themselves, we have behaved as if the intelligence test represented an adequate sampling of *all* these functions. For example, despite the growing body of literature concerning intellectual processes which seem closely allied to the general concept of "creativity," we tend to treat the latter concept as applicable only to performance in one or more of the *arts*. In effect, the term "creative child" has become synonymous with the expression "child with artistic talents," thus limiting our attempts to identify and foster cognitive abilities related to creative functioning in areas other than the arts. Third, there has been a failure to attend sufficiently to the difference between the *definition* of giftedness as given by the I.Q. and the variations in the *value* placed upon giftedness as so defined. It is often taken for granted, for example, that the gifted child is equally valued by

Reprinted from *Phi Delta Kappan*, Vol. 40, No. 2 (November, 1958), pp. 75-77. By Permission of the senior author and publisher.

teachers and by parents, in the classroom and at home; that he is held an equally good prospect by teachers and by parents to succeed as an adult; and that children themselves *want* to be gifted. It can be demonstrated that none of these assumptions regarding the value of the gifted child can be held without question. Empirical data related to these assumptions indicate that the gifted child is *not* equally valued by teachers and by parents, in the classroom and at home: he is *not* held to be an equally good prospect by teachers and parents to succeed as an adult; and children themselves do *not* necessarily want to be gifted, at least not in the traditional sense of the word.

Despite its longevity, there is nothing inevitable about the use of the I.Q. in defining giftedness. Indeed, it may be argued that in many ways this definition is only an historical happenstance—a consequence of the fact that early inquiries in this field has as their context the classroom and its attendant concern with academic progress. If we moved the focus of our inquiry from the classroom setting, we might identify qualities defining giftedness for other situations just as the I.Q. did for the classroom. Indeed, *without* shifting our focus of inquiry, if we only changed the original criteria of learning, we might change the qualities defining giftedness even in the classroom. For example, if we recognize that learning involves the production of novelty as well as the remembrance of course content, then measures of creativity as well as the I.Q. might become appropriate in defining characteristics of giftedness.

A research project, under the direction of the authors, is now being conducted at the University of Chicago in order to provide empirical data related to the considerations outlined above. As subjects of our research we have used a group of approximately 500 adolescents attending a Midwestern private school. The grade range covered by our group extends from the end of the sixth grade to the end of the senior year in high school. Because of the broad purpose of the research, we have inaugurated an extensive testing program involving the assessment of traditional qualities, such as intelligence and psychological health, and including attempts to assess less conventional dimensions such as creativity, morality, and the like. The study to be discussed here is but one small aspect of the larger investigation and concerns specifically a description of two of our experimental groups: one which we shall label the "highly intelligent" group, and the other the "highly creative" group.

## Two Groups Mutually Exclusive

Our "highly intelligent" subjects were defined as those who were in the top 20 per cent of the sample population on conventional I.Q. measures, but who were *not* in the top 20 per cent on measures of creativity. Our "highly creative" subjects were defined as those who were in the top 20 per cent of our sample population on measures of creativity, but who were *not* in the top 20 per cent in I.Q. The groups comprised twenty-eight and twenty-four subjects respectively, with approximately an equal proportion of boys and girls in each.

Limitation of space does not permit a complete description of the instruments included in the creativity battery. However, an adequate understanding of the way in which the term "creative" is used in the material to follow requires at least passing comment concerning these tests. Most briefly, all of the tests in the creative battery involved facility in dealing with verbal and numerical symbol systems, and object-space relationships. Some instruments called for rapid verbal associations to stimulus words; others called for the ability to structure quickly an incomplete or distorted perceptual stimulus; still others required remote, or clever, or original responses to complex verbal situations (e.g., supplying last lines to a fable). In one test the subject was to respond to a complex paragraph involving numerical values by suggesting all of the mathematical problems which could be solved with the information in the paragraph.

It should be noted that we did not include in our experimental groups those children who were high in *both* creativity and intelligence, and there were many such individuals. Our attempt was to isolate the two qualities under study from each other as much as possible in order to examine the relative contribution of each to the functioning of the child. Those individuals who excelled in both areas are the objects of further investigation still in progress.

Having identified our two experimental groups, we compared them to each other and to the population from which they were drawn on a number of relevant variables, including: school performance as measured by standardized verbal and numerical achievement tests appropriate to each grade level; teacher preferences as measured by teacher ratings of the pupils on how much they "liked to have them in class"; the preferences of the children themselves for personal qualities they would like to possess; the children's perception of the personal qualities they believed would lead to success in adult life and those they felt teachers would most prefer in children. In addition, the children were asked to write four-minute stories in response to six pictures flashed on a screen for twenty seconds each. An examination was made of the differences in the writing "style" of the two groups.

## Experiment Subjects Equal In Achievement

The results of these comparisons may be summarized as follows:

First, with respect to school achievement, despite a difference of twenty-three points between the *mean* I.Q.'s of the two groups, they were *equally* superior in school achievement to the student population as a whole.

Second, when asked to rate the children on the degree to which they would like to have them in class, the teachers exhibited a clear-cut preference for the high I.Q. child. The ratings given the high I.Q. group were significantly higher than those of the total student body; the ratings given the high creativity group did not differ significantly from those of the total student body. This occurred despite the fact, as we have seen, that *both* the high I.Q. and the high creative groups were *equally superior* to the other students in school achievement.

Third, comparing the personal aspirations of the children as reflected in the personal qualities they would like to possess, we find that the creative child himself rates high marks, I.Q., pep and energy, character and goal-directedness *lower* than do members of the highly intelligent group, and that he rates wide range of interests, emotional stability, and sense of humor *higher* than do members of the highly intelligent group. The last item, sense of humor, is particularly noteworthy since the value which the creative child puts upon this quality so far exceeds the ranking it receives from high I.Q. children as to make it one of the outstanding differences between the two groups, and indeed sets the creativity group apart most sharply from *all* other groups.

Fourth, the groups show distinct differences in the degree to which they aspire for "success" in adult life. The high I.Q. child desires to possess those qualities *now* which he believes will lead to success in adult life; the creative child does not seem to use this remote goal as criterion in the selection of his present aspirations.

Fifth, the relationship between the child's own personal aspirations and those qualities which he believes teachers prefer is quite different for the two groups. The high I.Q. child holds to a self-ideal which is consonant with the one he believes teachers will most readily approve; the self-ideal of the creative child is not only *not* consonant with what he believes to be the teacher approved model but shows a slight *negative* correlation with such model.

Sixth and finally, in their written responses to our six stimulus pictures, the creative students exhibited a degree of imagination and originality (not by any means the same as correct grammatical construction) unmatched by the high I.Q. students. Compared to the latter group, the creative students produced stories which seemed to "spring from" the stimulus rather than appeared to be "tied down" by it. Their stories made abundant use of humor, novel situations, and unexpected endings. They seemed to "play with" the picture stimulus for the pleasure of invention rather than "labor" the stimulus in order to find the "correct" theme.

## Some Important Implications

There is, it seems to us a consistency and unity even in these preliminary findings which may have important implications for defining and identifying so-called gifted children in the educational setting. We believe the high academic performance of our creative children coupled with the related lack of recognition which they may receive from teachers points to the core of the problem expanding the present conception of "giftedness," and of breaking the bonds that the I.Q. has on this concept in the school situation. The personal qualities of such presently neglected groups as our creatives which tend to estrange teachers from them may very well derive from the very neglect which these children suffer in the educational setting. With respect to our creative students, for example, the quality of "disillusionment" which appears to be reflected in the discrepancies between their personal aspirations and the aspirations they believed to be valued by teachers and by society in general may be a function of just the neglect to which we have been pointing. Despite their exceptional talents, they may miss identification by the usual I.Q. instrument; and despite their superior achievement, they may fail to gain the same personal preference from teachers that the high I.Q. children seem to have. We venture to suggest that a consideration of these discrepancies may deepen our appreciation at once of the need for expanding the concept of giftedness in the school setting and of the very real difficulties involved in such expansion.

## A Challenge of Educators, Researchers

Once we set a precedent by allowing an exception to the practice of labeling only high I.Q. children as "gifted," the possibility of expanding the concept to include other potentially productive groups becomes a genuine challenge to both educators and research workers. The not inconsiderable dangers inherent in the possibility of expanding the concept to a point where it becomes meaningless seem to us to be compenstaed by the possibility of increasing the effectiveness of our education for *all* children.

Virgil S. Ward

# Basic Concepts

$T$he development of those phases of the total school program which comprise proper education for the gifted demands intelligent thought and skillful development. In this section of the *Manual,* some fundamental concepts which will be needed by all who engage in any part of these endeavors are introduced. The intention is not necessarily to provide definitions in the exact form to which every local school should subscribe, but rather to provide certain educational and psychological concepts from which as a point of departure, each responsible educational group can think through its own needs, problems, policies, and practices. Close consideration of these concepts should aid substantially in the understanding of the various discussions of curriculum and programmatic arrangements in the sections which follow.

Some basic considerations pertaining to the nature of human abilities are presented first; a limited number of generally applicable concepts which pertain both to psychological abilities and to educational provisions designed to bring them to fruition, next; and finally, some general features—"cardinal principles"—which the SRPEG participants observed to characterize the more excellent of the programs observed in the various sections of the nation, and hence to be essential to any serious or ambitious program.

## The Nature of Giftedness

The rationale of differential education for the gifted, as has been indicated, involves the belief that identifiable groups of children with high abilities exist for whom different kinds of educational provisions are necessary to equality of educational opportunity. Such groups of children, endowed with various kinds of superior abilities, have been diversely termed "superior and talented," "the able and ambitious," "the academically

Reprinted from *The Gifted Student: A Manual For Program Improvement.* A Report of the Southern Regional Project For Education of the Gifted, 1962, pp. 25-36. By permission of the author and publisher.

talented" and other familiar designations. For convenience, all these may be and are in this *Manual* referred to as "the gifted."

The behavioral sciences recognize certain definable qualities around which subgroups of individuals with superior potential may be categorized with varying degrees of reliability for the purpose of special education. Clearest among these qualities are giftedness in:

1. *General Intelligence,* usually manifest in high I.Q. scores and
2. *Specific Aptitudes* (or talents), as measured by valid tests appropriately designated, or as evidenced through remarkable insights and skills in particular areas of knowledge or human endeavor.

Aptitudes are regarded as specific behavioral efficiencies, usually accompanied by above average general intelligence. These special abilities may be inferred through superior performance in subject areas such as mathematics and foreign languages, in skilled interpersonal relations which make for social leadership, in various forms of artistic expression such as music, dance or painting and in still other particular kinds of behavior.

Within both of these categories of giftedness, general intelligence and specific aptitude, it is practicable to recognize that *degrees* of superiority exist, such that school provisions may be devised respectively to meet the needs of those small numbers singularly exceptional in ability (e.g. one per cent or less), and the broader numbers (e.g. two, five, or ten per cent as variously suggested) still sufficiently above average to justify substantially modified educational procedures. In 1950 the Educational Policies Commission recognized two such levels of intellectual giftedness and identified these in terms of given intelligence quotients. Other organizations and individuals have similarly recognized varying degrees of giftedness in terms of I.Q., specific cutoff points beginning sometimes essentially where the usual demarcation for the upper limit of the "normal" or "average" group occurs. This recognition of levels of variation, of course, applies in substance also to the various aptitudes and to other recognizable clusters of abilities.

What is important to recognize is that any cutoff point on any measured psychological trait is by its nature arbitrary, and that no given demarcation can be defended on grounds of biological or psychological science. The search is for that degree of deviation in behavioral characteristics, comprising a potential for productive learning and thinking, which is so far above average that the graded materials and normal procedures devised for the education of children in the majority are less suited than curricular arrangements that can be deliberately devised to develop the exceptional qualities.

At the present time behavioral scientists are making significant efforts to distinguish other behavioral attributes worthy of special educational attention. Creativity, productive thinking as distinct from reproductive, and divergent thinking as opposed to convergent, are concepts representing attempts to isolate, define, and measure additional significant qualities of mind which relate to giftedness. The development of creativity is now being seen increasingly as a worthy educational objective. As these important behavioral characteristics become sufficiently well established at the levels of behavioral science, educators can and should devote particular thought to their appropriate development.

Finally, it must be recognized that certain aspects of personality, such as motivation, value orientation and cultural background weigh heavily in identifying particular individuals whose present behavioral patterns seem to promise superior performance in the future. Constructive combinations of these aspects of personality in persons of lesser relative ability may lead to higher ultimate attainment. On the other hand, even among youth of high ability-potential, aspects of personality arising from unfortunate experience may combine to hamper present performance, leading to *underachievement* or *emotional instability*. In the case of these gifted children, remediation should be undertaken as an initial phase of differential education in order subsequently to allow fuller operation of the natural potential. What is patently inexcusable is to exclude such children from developed provisions which promise to remove the obstacles to their "self actualization."

Remarkable demonstrations on the part of children in contemporary schools have been noted during the present wave of interest in the problems of the gifted. Reading, self-taught, prior to the age permitting entry into school; successful learning of higher mathematics on the part of elementary school youngsters; brilliant examples of children's insights into social and philosophical issues, and other striking manifestations of remarkable ability have occurred too consistently and too frequently to ignore. Such behavior suggests a potential for learning and thought hitherto undreamed of and defiant of management within the standard patterns and processes of education which serve children of ordinary abilities. Reliable studies indicate further that the prodigious childhood accomplishments tend, on the whole, to be followed in adulthood by similarly constructive behavior through which creative inventions in the arts and sciences occur, and advances in human welfare are made by gifted statesmen and leaders in social thought. These facts and realizations suggest further the absolute urgency that persons in possession of such priceless human assets be identified early and treated with every resource available to the educator.

Specific expressive behaviors which characterize the gifted may be detailed in lists that number into the dozens. These particular behavioral traits, however, derive from a more manageable number of broader psychological variables which serve typically to distinguish the group. The following categories embrace most of the educationally significant behaviors of gifted individuals as they are presently recognized.

*Capacity for Learning:* Accurate perception of social and natural situations; independent, rapid, efficient learning of fact and principle; fast, meaningful reading, with superior retention and recall.

*Power and Sensitivity of Thought:* Ready grasp of principles underlying things as they are; sensitivity to inference in fact, consequence of proposition, application of idea; spontaneous elevation of immediate observations to higher planes of abstraction; imagination; meaningful association of ideas; forceful reasoning; original interpretations and conclusions; discriminatory power, quick detection of similarities and differences among things and ideas; able in analysis; synthesis, and organization of elements; critical of situations, self, and other people.

*Curiosity and Drive:* Mental endurance; tenacity of purpose; stubbornness, sometimes contrarily expressed as reluctance to do as directed; capacity for follow-through with extensive, but meaningful plans; curiosity about things and ideas; intrinsic interest in the challenging and difficult; versatile and vital interests; varied, numerous and penetrating inquiries; boredom with routine and sameness.

From these basic considerations as to the nature of giftedness, the local school may devise serviceable definitions for those groups of youngsters in whose interest they intend to develop specifically applicable school procedures. Starting efforts will perhaps wisely center upon the most clearly known deviant characteristics, i.e., general intellectual superiority, and those for which the clearest educational processes pertain. The identification of groups may be expanded as the program matures to include other kinds of abilities and larger numbers of children. A fair understanding of these concepts on the nature of giftedness will be essential to the establishment of adequate screening and identification procedures in the process of selecting and placing children, and to the broader and more nearly ultimate search for educational provisions exactingly geared to each group distinguishable through deviant characteristics.

## A Glossary of Functional Terminology

Terminology can both facilitate and deter progress. The following concepts have been selected for their functional value in thinking through the various problems arising in the accomplishment of a recognizable pattern of provisions for fortunately atypical youth. As with all the "basic concepts" in this section, it is not intended that given school personnel should accept verbatim the definitions offered. The fine arguments necessary for obtaining agreements at such a level of particularity would quite possibly tend rather to impede than to propel the changes integral to a good program. On the other hand, careful study of these deliberated descriptions and explanations on the part of every staff member to be involved in discussions about or responsibilities in the program, should assure some communality of sound understanding around which both thought and action may proceed. Reasoned departures from what is here suggested by way of definitions should be, and quite possibly can be, defensible in terms of more refined insights into educational or psychological processes, or in terms of practical contingencies governing a school's efforts to establish or to improve upon its differential provisions for youth of superior abilities. Such departures should not, however, reflect simple bias of person or of locality.

*Ability Grouping:*  Also sometimes called "segregation." The practice of assembling or deploying students for instructional purposes who are somewhat nearer together in general capacity for learning, or in given specific aptitudes, so that instruction and learning may proceed at a pace and in terms of qualities suited to this (these) capacities. Contrasts with those forms of grouping which utilize chronological age or alphabet as criteria for homogeneity and developmental readiness. May take the form of special classes, special schools, multiple track curricula, etc., and may be arranged for part or for all of the school curriculum. Specific capacities for differing areas of knowledge or skill, with interests related thereto, are recognized as superior criteria for grouping, as opposed to general indices (e.g. composite I.Q.) applied across the range of school activities.

*Acceleration:*  Any administrative practice designed to move the student through school more rapidly than usual. Includes such practices as early admission, grade-skipping, advanced placement, telescoping of grade levels, credit by examination, etc.

*Articulation:*  The sequential arrangement of studies through the total school program so as to avoid undesirable repetition or duplication at various grade levels. Problems of articulation often arise when programs for the gifted are planned to affect given school years but not to encompass the entire graded sequence.

*Differential Education (for the gifted):*  Educational experiences uniquely or predominantly suited to the distinguishing behavioral processes of intellectually superior people and to the adult roles that they typically assume as leaders and innovators. Then successfully arranged to involve the capacities and needs of the gifted, the experience (concepts, studies, activities, courses) by definition is beyond the reach of and not appropriate to the capacities and needs of persons *not* exceptionally endowed with potential for learning and productive or creative behavior.

*Enrichment (for the gifted):*  Practices which are intended to increase the depth or breadth of the gifted student's learning experiences. May include special assignments, independent study, individual projects, small group work, and other adaptations of routine school processes. This purported form of provision for the gifted often in fact merely camouflages do-nothingness.

*Identification:*  The process of finding those students who meet the criteria of giftedness adopted in a given school or system. Identification should begin as early as possible, should be systematic, i.e., follow a defensible plan, and should be continuous so as to improve the chances of discovering larger numbers of youth qualified for differential education. A variety of techniques exist for screening the pupil population, most of which have some virtue, and no one of which—particularly a single measure of intelligence—is sufficient alone.

*Mental Ability:*  An inclusive term, more properly referred to as "capacity," and including such conceptions as intelligence and aptitude (talent) and related processes such as creativity, productive thinking, divergent thinking, etc.

*Mental Tests:* Devices such as intelligence, aptitude, achievement, and personality tests, or rating scales for various skills, which are designed to provide relatively objective means of assessing or comparing certain of the capacities of characteristics of individuals.

*Motivation:* The basic psychological process involved in both under- and over-achievement in school. A subtle and complex literature on this aspect of personality exists in the behavioral sciences. As concerns the gifted, *underachievement* is recognized as a critical problem, and is thought of as a failure to perform as well as might be expected from scores on tests of aptitude or intelligence. No agreement exists as to how poorly a student must do, for how long, or in what activities, in order to be called an underachiever. Poor performance by gifted youngsters is not infrequently paralleled by singular out-of-school activities which possess intrinsic appeal to the child.

*Program (of special education):* A *pattern* of provisions within the total range of school activities which is designed to meet the distinguishable needs and abilities of intellectually superior and talented children. Single or scattered provisions such as advanced placement or early admission to first grade do not alone constitute a *program*.

## Ten Cardinal Principles

From a thoughtful review of all that was studied, attended, and observed, certain features which seem to characterize the more excellent programs of education for gifted youngsters appear to be mandatory in an ideal situation. These cardinal tenets, each excellently implemented, will be found altogether only in the rarest and most favored of school systems. On the other hand, unless the more modestly endowed school can show tangible evidence that it has realized as effectively as its circumstances permit each one of these ten disciplines to thought and practice, the chances are good that its claims toward differentiated education for the gifted are merely illusory.

Imaginative local school personnel in systems not yet really "off the ground" in this important respect may sense from a thoughtful perusal of these ten principles many of the particulars which will devolve upon them in developing educational services for supremely educable young people. For those school leaders already having substantially accomplished such special provisions in the total school program, the principles can serve as a broad check-list for systematic re-examination of its endeavors, and for improving those phases of the program revealed through the analysis to be less than what the school is capable of doing.

1. *Particularization of Objectives.* A philosophy of education which a given school might have adopted, and general objectives related thereto, provide a basis for the formulation of more specific realizations concerning

the nature and needs of those deviant groups identified by the school for differential provisions. These statements may take the form of particularized process goals, in order to distinguish them from general objectives of education for all youth. Such explicitly declared objectives should take account (1) of the exceptional abilities of the children intended to be reached—priceless abilities, sloughed off and neglected in the past—which point to potential for learning not yet dreamed of in the typical American school; (2) of the anticipated social roles which these youth characteristically assume as adults—leadership and reconstruction of the culture as distinct from simple participation therein; and (3) of the implications for these young people of the dramatic nature of the world in which they will spin out their lives as cultural frontiersmen—a material world rapidly being made all over by science and technology, and a social world characterized by close, but not necessarily friendly, interrelationships among interest groups of various kinds, and among nations, some of which are only presently emerging as powers on the world scene. Differential education for differentially endowed youth must take exacting account of all these demands in order to be adequate in more than name alone. Such particularized objectives for identifiable segments of the total pupil population are not only harmonious with democratic philosophies of education that are general in scope, but are essential to the fullness of these philosophies.

2. *Staff Training and Responsibility.* The typical school staff can scarcely hope to have within its ranks personnel already knowledgeable and skilled in the various phases of a program of education for the gifted. A wise selection of persons capable of the requisite learnings, and of skill in putting these understandings into practice, is a necessary early step, i.e. selection and then training. Training should be geared to the functions intended. These will cover a variety of needs, including excellence on the part of teachers in the challenging tasks of face-to-face instructional leadership and classroom management, imagination and reasoned thought in the development of curricular materials geared toward the specific task, and administrative ingenuity in leading staff and community through changes in habituated conceptions and established practices. Such staff training should be a bootstrap operation in the hands of committees of local personnel *only* when qualified consultative resources are *not* available. The costs are diverse and substantial when initial errors are made, though these are committed in good faith, and the efforts subsequently necessary for correcting concepts, materials, and actions mis-directed in the beginning are usually greater than what would have been involved in more adequately founded origins.

The time-honored administrative principle of clear designation of responsibility, with commensurate authority, in single persons pertains to this aspect of school practice. According to size and resources, single persons must be designated within the school system as responsible for leading in the hierarchy of functions essential to full-scale endeavor. A single head for system-wide collective efforts, one responsible to the building principal for the efforts of a given school, and further reasonable divisions of functions covering grade levels and subject matter will usually be indicated. Supervisory and guidance personnel must also be made clearly aware of their responsibilities in the special endeavor. In most schools of no greater than average size, it will likely be that these responsibilities are placed in the hands of persons who must continue to carry other duties as well. In any case, the assignment of responsibility is but an idle gesture unless corresponding time and provisions for implementing the required work are established in the process. The more thoroughly each person understands his function, has the requisite personal abilities to carry them out, and the time required for working in essentially uncharted territory, the more nearly adequate will the local program be.

3. *Community Interpretation.* Small and simple adjustments in the routine machinery of school operation will but mock the task at hand. Practices which will break with custom on numerous counts are much more likely to be sensed as necessary by the staff that takes this problem seriously. Ingenuity in interpreting these requisite changes to the community is needed. Forthrightness, perseverance, and patience pay good dividends in this respect, paving the way for active cooperation from resources outside the school setting, and for support by the majority of thoughtful citizens. Especially critical will be the school personnel's ability to obtain support on the part of those parents whose children are not destined to be involved in the highlighted efforts. If differentiated educational provisions for the gifted are shown to parallel provisions for the handicapped, and for groups with already recognized special abilities, as in athletics and music, and if the arguments are clearly made that the established educational program provides for the majority of youngsters according to their needs and capacities, this kind of community support can be developed.

4. *Systematic Pupil Identification.* A differentiated program of education cannot attain appropriate particularity without the tangible identification of persons to be involved in it. Explicit definitions, a knowledgeable utilization of existing psychological instruments, and a judicious involvement of the judgment of personnel closely acquainted with potential candidates for the program are essential to adequate processes of pupil identification. The identification process should begin in the primary grades, and extend continuously throughout the secondary school at least. Children mature and make manifest certain potentials at different times. And, of course, in schools beginning "small", with close and exacting definitions, each expansion in the adapted working conception of giftedness will call for additional screening of larger numbers of children than are expected ultimately to prove needful of the planned curricular processes.

5. *Distinguishable Curricular Experiences.* The demands which govern or delimit all studies and instruction intended to pertain with relative uniqueness to groups of gifted youth have been stated in the above discussion of particularized objectives. Units of the curriculum of the school, instructional patterns such as seminars or independent research projects, and materials devised for system-wide use—all these must involve those higher

powers of mind which bring bright and talented children to attention in the first place, and must be of such nature that they promote the child's natural capacities for judgment, critical analysis, and creative reconstruction of things as they now exist. Unless a school can point to such clearly identifiable provisions, and indicate how these provisions implement and validate the process goals or particularized objectives also on record, it is quite likely that nothing predominantly pertinent to the gifted exists, and that, rather, old merchandise has simply and unfairly been given new tags.

Curricular modifications which are adequate (and more hopefully excellent) for this task are perhaps among the most difficult matters the school staff has ever dealt with. Certain principles to guide these efforts are suggested in Section Five of this *Manual*. Equally mandatory are cautions that in the gradual development of increasingly pertinent processes, no *abusive* practices be allowed to creep in. Bright youngsters are being unwittingly subjected in today's heightened pressures to requirements and expectations some of which unquestionably serve to defeat their intended purpose, rather than to support it. And they are being allowed special courses and related experiences under conditions which connote *punishment* rather than *deserved privileges*. The direct and explicit purposefulness of all extraordinary requirements; the pursuit of unusual courses within the normal school day and week; and the evaluation of work by standards initially acknowledging the student's superior rank—all these must be designed and organically arranged so as to comprise in their totality a constructive and developmental array of experiences, as normal for these deviant youngsters as is the usual school regimen for his fellows in the main stream of organized education. Practices are likely to be inherently wrong if they lead to avoidance on the part of able youngsters and their parents, and if they require work in amount or kind which is not positively attractive in immediate nature and purposeful in ultimate objective.

6. *Flexible Pupil Deployment.* As with curriculum, where simple refinements and moderate rearrangements will not do, so it is with the inevitable placement of bright and talented pupils in instructional groups. Marked departures from traditional practices in administrative arrangements are necessary parallels to sound and forward-looking curricular adaptations. When conceived fundamentally, as the problem should be, a great variety of grouping patterns are feasible for youngsters as they pursue their course through the full range of knowledge provided, the activities conducing toward essential skills, and their progressive attainment of maturity in judgment and power of thought. Indeed, so diverse are the possibilities for variation in day-to-day shifting from group to group, short term reformulation of groups for the attainment of goals close at hand, separation of small numbers for fullest development of excellence in rare talents, and for flexible admission to the grades and movement through the graded structure, that *the only pattern clearly outmoded is the completely heterogeneous grouping of children, in relatively permanent and largely self-contained classes, which proceed by lock-step in a grade-a-year plan* as though this rusty pattern were

**69**

a condition of nature inflicted upon the school and its pupil clientele. So great is the distance between schools that lead and those that lag in respect to imaginative administrative practices that known instances exist in which bright children in communities an hour's drive apart endure or enjoy radically different kinds of developmental experience. And so frequent and widespread are schools who have made commendable departures, that the administrator or board member who "does not believe in newer methods" may see within this distance and with his own eyes real and effective differentiated patterns of pupil deployment such as he doesn't believe to exist.

7. *Comprehensiveness and Continuity.* Even in the face of the connotation which the term carries of a *variety* of provisions, numerous "programs" of education for the gifted are comprised of *single* features. Thus early admission to first grade may be practiced in one school system, and aptitude grouping in another, but not both in the same institution. Frequently, too, given provisions worthy of across the board application, are in fact utilized only at selective grade levels, or in selective schools within a system.

Instructional practices and administrative adaptations that are reasoned carefully in terms of reliable knowledge of human abilities and the educative process deserve to be brought to bear upon *every* differentially qualified child in a community, at *every* grade level in his entire school career, in *every* area of academic studies that involve those extremes in learning potential displayed by the identified gifted youngsters. Piecemeal and fragmentary allowances, selectively applied, while probably advantageous in and of themselves, fail in the in-between to provide what is equally necessary by way of properly gauged developmental learnings. Every phase of a total program of differential education for the gifted—identification, guidance, instruction, evaluation—should, therefore apply *comprehensively* across the pupil population and through the subject areas, and continuously (allowing variations on types of processes) through the maturing years of the selected children and the graded structure of the school from the kindergarten through general college.

8. *Progressive Program Development.* The various kinds of special provisions for bright and talented youngsters are not irresponsible devices in the nature of fads and passing fancy. Both careful reasoning and substantial experience lie behind successful practices. In the face of the intricate and highly significant task of developing within the local schools of any given community a full-scale pattern of differentiated educational provisions, it is likely that no school staff can rest satisfied with their present state of program development. A further earmark of excellence in a given program, therefore, is likely to be internal provisions for periodic re-examination of parts and of the whole structure erected to accomplish this function, and for refinement of effort where weaknesses are indicated.

9. *Financial Allocation.* No absolute sums can be indicated as essential to the attainment and maintenance of qualitative differential education for gifted youth. Nor is it necessary that every school system allocate similar amounts for each function within the program. On the other hand, it is

simply not realistic to expect that educational provisions which in their nature must be unusual ones, frequently involving extraordinary materials and facilities, can be accomplished within the same framework of allocations that pertained prior to the particular efforts. The usual school budget is characterized by all sorts of differing allocations. The nature of this selective spending reveals the values of the school system and its supporting community. Several activities which favor certain children over others are already heavily financed, and this practice is sanctioned by the community. The belated realization is that it is mandatory to provide differentially for youth of substantially deviant intellectual potential, and this at extraordinary cost proportionate to the economic strength of the system, in order to give these youngsters their fair share of educational opportunity.

In implementation, it is reasonable that any school system, no matter how well endowed, start with immediately clear and apparent outlets for increased funds, and progressively provide dissimilar allocations as the whole range of objectives of the program become more fully materialized. Schools with limited capital must judge where limited funds will do most good. What can no longer be excused is main failure to make selective allocations as demanded by the particular needs and capacities of these groups of deviant youngsters.

10. *Radiation of Excellence.* It is frequently remarked, and validly, that the studied attainment of a sound pattern of education commensurate with the heavily deviant abilities of brighter youth, will in the process lead to general improvements in the whole school program. What is equally true, but not so frequently remarked, is that one is not likely to find a good program for the gifted in other than generally good schools. Enlightened citizens or zealous professional members of the school staff are on sound grounds in pressing this cause to the point where tangible features of the total school program in their community can be identified which pertain with relative uniqueness to the higher degrees of human abilities represented in the concept of giftedness.

# Part II
## Characteristics of the Gifted and Creative

The concept of giftedness, as of intelligence itself, is today a much broader one than earlier in this century. Early research and especially the classic longitudinal studies of Terman tended to limit the concept of giftedness to high performance on tests of intelligence and academic achievement. Although few would deny that high intelligence and achievement are indeed very important types of superior ability, psychologists and educators in more recent years have asserted that man has a much broader repertoire of highly valuable behaviors. Each of these human behaviors, like intelligence and achievement, exist in the population and in the individual along a continuum, and thus, when we speak of a gifted or superior person, it is relevant to raise the questions, "Gifted in what ways?" or "Superior in what areas of performance?"

The broadened concept of giftedness grew out of a realization that an invaluable amount of human potential was being neglected because intelligence tests failed to measure such important characteristics as originality, leadership ability, foresight, and outstanding performance in non-academic areas. Furthermore, the use of intelligence tests as the sole criterion for determining giftedness often led to the conclusion that a person is either gifted or he is not! This limited conception of giftedness failed to take into account the indisputable fact that many people may have extremely superior potential in one or two areas, but that the same individuals may be mediocre or even below average in other areas of performance. Unless we view giftedness as a multidimensional set of traits that exist in varying degrees in the individual as well as the general population, it is quite likely that special educational efforts for the gifted will continue to focus on a relatively restricted number of abilities and a highly restricted portion of the population.

The articles that have been selected for Part II of this book reflect much of the thinking and research that has given rise to the broadened conception of giftedness. This section examines a number of cognitive processes that are not ordinarily measured in single factor tests of general intelligence. The articles by Guilford and Thurstone are considered by many to be classic studies of the nature and organization of mental abilities. They have particular relevance to the study of giftedness in that they call attention to the specific components of the intellectual processes. The article by Getzels and Jackson deals with the well-known but somewhat controversial distinction between creativity and intelligence.

This section also presents a series of articles dealing with the characteristics of persons who have been classified as gifted and creative. Factors such as family background, motivation to achieve, personality characteristics, and early childhood experiences are discussed in relation to highly creative production and outstanding school and occupational performance. Gallagher's comprehensive summary of research studies dealing with characteristics of the gifted is also included.

The final articles in Part II deal with some of the adjustment problems that are sometimes encountered by gifted and creative persons in our culture. Although the gifted do not experience a higher incidence of adjustment problems than the population at large, the articles in this section point out some of the relatively unique consequences that sometimes occur when outstanding abilities are thwarted. These selections have serious implications for educators who sometimes tend to ignore the importance of dealing with the affective as well as the cognitive development of highly able individuals.

*J. P. Guilford*

# Three Faces of Intellect

$M$y subject is in the area of human intelligence, in connection with which the names of Terman and Stanford have become known the world over. The Stanford Revision of the Binet intelligence scale has been the standard against which all other instruments for the measurement of intelligence have been compared. The term IQ or intelligence quotient has become a household word in this country. This is illustrated by two brief stories.

> A few years ago, one of my neighbors came home from a PTA meeting, remarking: "That Mrs. So-And-So, thinks she knows so much. She kept talking about the 'intelligence *quota*' of the children, 'intelligence *quota*'; imagine. Why, everybody knows that IQ stands for 'intelligence *quiz.*' "
>
> The other story comes from a little comic strip in a Los Angeles morning newspaper, called "Junior Grade." In the first picture a little boy meets a little girl, both apparently about the first-grade level. The little girl remarks, "I have a high IQ." The little boy, puzzled, said, "You have a what?" The little girl repeated, "I have a high IQ," then went on her way. The little boy, looking thoughtful, said, "And she looks like such a nice little girl, too."

It is my purpose to speak about the analysis of this thing called human intelligence into its components. I do not believe that either Binet or Terman, if they were still with us, would object to the idea of a searching and detailed study of intelligence, aimed toward a better understanding of its nature. Preceding the development of his intelligence scale, Binet had done much research on different kinds of thinking activities and apparently recognized that intelligence has a number of aspects. It is to the lasting

Reprinted from *American Psychologist,* Vol. 14, No. 8 (August, 1959), pp. 469-479. By permission of the American Psychological Association.

credit of both Binet and Terman that they introduced such a great variety of tasks into their intelligence scales.

Two related events of very recent history make it imperative that we learn all we can regarding the nature of intelligence. I am referring to the advent of the artificial satellites and planets and to the crisis in education that has arisen in part as a consequence. The preservation of our way of life and our future security depend upon our most important national resources: our intellectual abilities and, more particularly, our creative abilities. It is time, then, that we learn all we can about those resources.

Our knowledge of the components of human intelligence has come about mostly within the last 25 years. The major sources of this information in this country have been L. L. Thurstone and his associates, the wartime research of psychologists in the United States Air Forces, and more recently the Aptitudes Project at the University of Southern California, now in its tenth year of research on cognitive and thinking abilities. The results from the Aptitudes Project that have gained perhaps the most attention have pertained to creative-thinking abilities. These are mostly novel findings. But to me, the most significant outcome has been the development of a unified theory of human intellect, which organizes the known, unique or primary intellectual abilities into a single system called the "structure of intellect." It is to this system that I shall devote the major part of my remarks, with very brief mentions of some of the implications for the psychology of thinking and problem solving, for vocational testing, and for education.

The discovery of the components of intelligence has been by means of the experimental application of the method of factor analysis. It is not necessary for you to know anything about the theory or method of factor analysis in order to follow the discussion of the components. I should like to say, however, that factor analysis has no connection with or resemblance to psychoanalysis. A positive statement would be more helpful so I will say that each intellectual component or factor is a unique ability that is needed to do well in a certain class of tasks or tests. As a general principle we find that certain individuals do well in the tests of a certain class, but they may do poorly in the tests of another class. We conclude that a factor has certain properties from the features that the tests of a class have in common. I shall give you very soon a number of examples of tests, each representing a factor.

## The Structure of Intellect

Although each factor is sufficiently distinct to be detected by factor analysis, in very recent years it has become apparent that the factors themselves can be classified because they resemble one another in certain ways. One basis of classification is according to the basic kind of process or operation performed. This kind of classification gives us five major groups of intellectual abilities: factors of cognition, memory, convergent thinking, divergent thinking, and evaluation.

Cognition means discovery or rediscovery or recognition. Memory means retention of what is cognized. Two kinds of productive-thinking operations generate new information from known information and remembered information. In divergent-thinking operations we think in different directions, sometimes searching, sometimes seeking variety. In convergent thinking the information leads to one right answer or to a recognized best or conventional answer. In evaluation we reach decisions as to goodness, correctness, suitability, or adequacy of what we know, what we remember, and what we produce in productive thinking.

A second way of classifying the intellectual factors is according to the kind of material or content involved. The factors known thus far involve three kinds of material or content: the content may be figural, symbolic, or semantic. Figural content is concrete material such as is perceived through the senses. It does not represent anything except itself. Visual material has properties such as size, form, color, location, or texture. Things we hear or feel provide other examples of figural material. Symbolic content is composed of letters, digits, and other conventional signs, usually organized in general systems, such as the alphabet or the number system. Semantic content is in the form of verbal meanings or ideas, for which no examples are necessary.

When a certain operation is applied to a certain kind of content, as many as six general kinds of products may be involved. There is enough evidence available to suggest that, regardless of the combinations of operations and content, the same six kinds of products may be found associated. The six kinds of products are: units, classes, relations, systems, transformations, and implications. So far as we have determined from factor analysis, these are the only fundamental kinds of products that we can know. As such, they may serve as basic classes into which one might fit all kinds of information psychologically.

The three kinds of classifications of the factors of intellect can be represented by means of a single solid model, shown in Figure 1. In this model, which we call the "structure of intellect," each dimension represents one of the modes of variation of the factors (2). Along one dimension are found the various kinds of operations, along a second one are the various kinds of products, and along the third are various kinds of content. Along the dimension of content a fourth category has been added, its kind of content being designated as "behavioral." This category has been added on a purely theoretical basis to represent the general area sometimes called "social intelligence." More will be said about this section of the model later.

In order to provide a better basis for understanding the model and a better basis for accepting it as a picture of human intellect, I shall do some exploring of it with you systematically, giving some examples of tests. Each cell in the model calls for a certain kind of ability that can be described in terms of operation, content, and product, for each cell is at the intersection of a unique combination of kinds of operation, content, and product. A test for that ability would have the same three properties. In our exploration of the model, we shall take one vertical layer at a time, beginning with the front

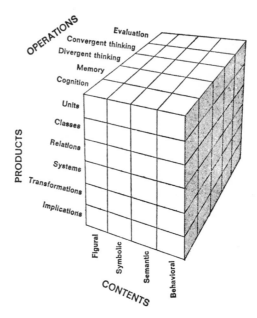

**FIG. 1. A Cubical Model Representing the Structure of Intellect**

face. The first layer provides us with a matrix of 18 cells (if we ignore the behavioral column for which there are as yet no known factors) each of which should contain a cognitive ability.

THE COGNITIVE ABILITIES.

We know at present the unique abilities that fit logically into 15 of the 18 cells for cognitive abilities. Each row presents a triad of similar abilities, having a single kind of product in common. The factors of the first row are concerned with the knowing of units. A good test of the ability to cognize figural units is the Street Gestalt Completion Test. In this test, the recognition of familiar pictured objects in silhouette form is made difficult for testing purposes by blocking out parts of those objects. There is another factor that is known to involve the perception of auditory figures—in the form of melodies, rhythms, and speech sounds—and still another factor involving kinesthetic forms. The presence of three factors in one cell (they are conceivably distinct abilities, although this has not been tested) suggests that more generally, in the figural column, at least, we should expect to find more than one ability. A fourth dimension pertaining to variations in sense modality may thus apply in connection with figural content. The model could be extended in this manner if the facts call for such an extension.

The ability to cognize symbolic units is measured by tests like the following:

78

Put vowels in the following blanks to make real words:

$$P\_\_W\_\_R$$
$$M\_\_RV\_\_L$$
$$C\_\_RT\_\_N$$

Rearrange the letters to make real words:

$$R \ A \ C \ I \ H$$
$$T \ V \ O \ E \ S$$
$$K \ L \ C \ C \ O$$

The first of these two tests is called Disemvoweled Words, and the second Scrambled Words.

The ability to cognize semantic units is the well-known factor of verbal comprehension, which is best measured by means of a vocabulary test, with items such as:

GRAVITY means _____
CIRCUS means _____
VIRTUE means _____

From the comparison of these two factors it is obvious that recognizing familiar words as letter structures and knowing what words mean depend upon quite different abilities.

For testing the abilities to know classes of units, we may present the following kinds of items, one with symbolic content and one with semantic content:

Which letter group does not belong?
XECM PVAA QXIN VTRO

Which object does not belong?
clam tree oven rose

A figural test is constructed in a completely parallel form, presenting in each item four figures, three of which have a property in common and the fourth lacking that property.

The three abilities to see relationships are also readily measured by a common kind of test, differing only in terms of content. The well-known analogies test is applicable, two items in symbolic and semantic form being:

JIRE : KIRE : : FORA : KORE KORA LIRE GORA GIRE
poetry : prose : : dance : music walk sing talk jump

Such tests usually involve more than the ability to cognize relations, but we are not concerned with this problem at this point.

The three factors for cognizing systems do not at present appear in tests so closely resembling one another as in the case of the examples just given.

There is nevertheless an underlying common core of logical similarity. Ordinary space tests, such as Thurstone's Flags, Figures, and Cards or Part V (Spatial Orientation) of the Guilford-Zimmerman Aptitude Survey (GZAS), serve in the figural column. The system involved is an order or arrangement of objects in space. A system that uses symbolic elements is illustrated by the Letter Triangle Test, a sample item of which is:

d    ——<br>
    —— <br>
b    e    —— <br>
a    c    f    ? <br>

What letter belongs at the place of the question mark?

The ability to understand a semantic system has been known for some time as the factor called general reasoning. One of its most faithful indicators is a test composed of arithmetic-reasoning items. That the phase of understanding only is important for measuring this ability is shown by the fact that such a test works even if the examinee is not asked to give a complete solution; he need only show that he structures the problem properly. For example, an item from the test Necessary Arithmetical Operations simply asks what operations are needed to solve the problem:

A city lot 48 feet wide and 149 feet deep costs $79,432. What is the cost per square foot?

A. add and multiply
B. multiply and divide
C. subtract and divide
D. add and subtract
E. divide and add

Placing the factor of general reasoning in this cell of the structure of intellect gives us some new conceptions of its nature. It should be a broad ability to grasp all kinds of systems that are conceived in terms of verbal concepts, not restricted to the understanding of problems of an arithmetical type.

Transformations are changes of various kinds, including modifications in arrangement, organization, or meaning. In the figural column for the transformations row, we find the factor known as visualization. Common measuring instruments for this factor are the surface-development tests, and an example of a different kind is Part VI (Spatial Visualization) of the GZAS. A test of the ability to make transformations of meaning, for the factor in the semantic column, is called Similarities. The examinee is asked to state several ways in which two objects, such as an apple and an orange, are alike. Only by shifting the meanings of both is the examinee able to give many responses to such an item.

In the set of abilities having to do with the cognition of implications, we find that the individual goes beyond the information given, but not to the extent of what might be called drawing conclusions. We may say that he extrapolates. From the given information he expects or foresees certain consequences, for example. The two factors found in this row of the cognition matrix were first called "foresight" factors. Foresight in connection with figural material can be tested by means of paper-and-pencil mazes. Foresight in connection with ideas, those pertaining to events, for example, is indicated by a test such as Pertinent Questions:

> In planning to open a new hamburger stand in a certain community, what four questions should be considered in deciding upon its location?

The more questions the examinee asks in response to a list of such problems, the more he evidently foresees contingencies.

THE MEMORY ABILITIES.

The area of memory abilities has been explored less than some of the other areas of operation, and only seven of the potential cells of the memory matrix have known factors in them. These cells are restricted to three rows: for units, relations, and systems. The first cell in the memory matrix is now occupied by two factors, parallel to two in the corresponding cognition matrix: visual memory and auditory memory. Memory for series of letters or numbers, as in memory span tests, conforms to the conception of memory for symbolic units. Memory for the ideas in a paragraph conforms to the conception of memory for semantic units.

The formation of associations between units, such as visual forms, syllables, and meaningful words, as in the method of paired associates, would seem to represent three abilities to remember relationships involving three kinds of content. We know of two such abilities, for the symbolic and semantic columns. The memory for known systems is represented by two abilities very recently discovered (1). Remembering the arrangement of objects in space is the nature of an ability in the figural column, and remembering a sequence of events is the nature of a corresponding ability in the semantic column. The differentiation between these two abilities implies that a person may be able to say where he saw an object on a page, but he might not be able to say on which of several pages he saw it after leafing through several pages that included the right one. Considering the blank rows in the memory matrix, we should expect to find abilities also to remember classes, transformations, and implications, as well as units, relations, and systems.

THE DIVERGENT-THINKING ABILITIES.

The unique feature of divergent production is that a *variety* of responses is produced. The product is not completely determined by the given information. This is not to say that divergent thinking does not come into play in the total process of reaching a unique conclusion, for it comes into play wherever there is trial-and-error thinking.

The well-known ability of word fluency is tested by asking the examinee to list words satisfying a specified letter requirement, such as words beginning with the letter "s" or words ending in "-tion." This ability is now regarded as a facility in divergent production of symbolic units. The parallel semantic ability has been known as ideational fluency. A typical test item calls for listing objects that are round and edible. Winston Churchill must have possessed this ability to a high degree. Clement Attlee is reported to have said about him recently that, no matter what problem came up, Churchill always seemed to have about ten ideas. The trouble was, Attlee continued, he did not know which was the good one. The last comment implies some weakness in one or more of the evaluative abilities.

The divergent production of class ideas is believed to be the unique feature of a factor called "spontaneous flexibility." A typical test instructs the examinee to list all the uses he can think of for a common brick, and he is given eight minutes. If his responses are: build a house, build a barn, build a garage, build a school, build a church, build a chimney, build a walk, and build a barbecue, he would earn a fairly high score for ideational fluency but a very low score for spontaneous flexibility, because all these uses fall into the same class. If another person said: make a door stop, make a paper weight, throw it at a dog, make a bookcase, drown a cat, drive a nail, make a red powder, and use for baseball bases, he would also receive a high score for flexibility. He has gone frequently from one class to another.

A current study of unknown but predicted divergent-production abilities includes testing whether there are also figural and symbolic abilities to produce multiple classes. An experimental figural test presents a number of figures that can be classified in groups of three in various ways, each figure being usable in more than one class. An experimental symbolic test presents a few numbers that are also to be classified in multiple ways.

A unique ability involving relations is called "associational fluency." It calls for the production of a variety of things related in a specified way to a given thing. For example, the examinee is asked to list words meaning about the same as "good" or to list words meaning about the opposite of "hard." In these instances the response produced is to complete a relationship, and semantic content is involved. Some of our present experimental tests call for the production of varieties of relations, as such, and involve figural and symbolic content also. For example, given four small digits, in how many ways can they be related in order to produce a sum of eight?

One factor pertaining to the production of systems is known as expressional fluency. The rapid formation of phrases or sentences is the essence of certain tests of this factor. For example, given the initial letters:

with different sentences to be produced, the examinee might write "We can eat nuts" or "Whence came Eve Newton?" In interpreting the factor, we regard the sentence as a symbolic system. By analogy, a figural system would be some kind of organization of lines and other elements, and a semantic system would be in the form of a verbally stated problem or perhaps something as complex as a theory.

In the row of the divergent-production matrix devoted to transformations, we find some very interesting factors. The one called "adaptive flexibility" is now recognized as belonging in the figural column. A faithful test of it has been Match Problems. This is based upon the common game that uses squares, the sides of which are formed by match sticks. The examinee is told to take away a given number of matches to leave a stated number of squares with nothing left over. Nothing is said about the sizes of the squares to be left. If the examinee imposes upon himself the restriction that the squares that he leaves must be of the same size, he will fail. Other odd kinds of solutions are introduced in other items, such as overlapping squares and squares within squares, and so on. In another variation of Match Problems the examinee is told to produce two or more solutions for each problem.

A factor that has been called "originality" is now recognized as adaptive flexibility with semantic material, where there must be a shifting of meanings. The examinee must produce the shifts or changes in meaning and so come up with novel, unusual, clever, or farfetched ideas. The Plot Titles Test presents a short story, the examinee being told to list as many appropriate titles as he can to head the story. One story is about a missionary who has been captured by cannibals in Africa. He is in the pot and about to be boiled when a princess of the tribe obtains a promise for his release if he will become her mate. He refuses and is boiled to death.

In scoring the test, we separate the responses into two categories, clever and nonclever. Examples of nonclever responses are: African Death, Defeat of a Princess, Eaten by Savages, The Princess, The African Missionary, In Darkest Africa, and Boiled by Savages. These titles are appropriate but commonplace. The number of such responses serves as a score for ideational fluency. Examples of clever responses are: Pot's Plot, Potluck Dinner, Stewed Parson, Goil or Boil, A Mate Worse Than Death, He Left a Dish for a Pot, Chaste in Haste, and A Hot Price for Freedom. The number of clever responses given by an examinee is his score for originality, or the divergent production of semantic transformations.

Another test of originality presents a very novel task so that any acceptable response is unusual for the individual. In the Symbol Production Test the examinee is to produce a simple symbol to stand for a noun or a verb in each short sentence, in other words to invent something like pictographic symbols. Still another test of originality asks for writing the "punch lines" for cartoons, a task that almost automatically challenges the examinee to be clever. Thus, quite a variety of tests offer approaches to the measurement of originality, including one or two others that I have not mentioned.

Abilities to produce a variety of implications are assessed by tests calling for elaboration of given information. A figural test of this type provides the examinee with a line or two, to which he is to add other lines to produce an object. The more lines he adds, the greater his score. A semantic test gives the examinee the outlines of a plan to which he is to respond by stating all the details he can think of to make the plan work. A new test we are trying out in the symbolic area presents two simple equations such as $B - C = D$ and $z = A + D$. The examinee is to make as many other equations as he can from this information.

THE CONVERGENT-PRODUCTION ABILITIES.

Of the 18 convergent-production abilities expected in the three content columns, 12 are now recognized. In the first row, pertaining to units, we have an ability to name figural properties (forms or colors) and an ability to name abstractions (classes, relations, and so on). It may be that the ability in common to the speed of naming forms and the speed of naming colors is not appropriately placed in the convergent-thinking matrix. One might expect that the thing to be produced in a test of the convergent production of figural units would be in the form of figures rather than words. A better test of such an ability might somehow specify the need for one particular object, the examinee to furnish the object.

A test for the convergent production of classes (Word Grouping) presents a list of 12 words that are to be classified in four, and only four, meaningful groups, no word to appear in more than one group. A parallel test (Figure Concepts Test) presents 20 pictured real objects that are to be grouped in meaningful classes of two or more each.

Convergent production having to do with relationships is represented by three known factors, all involving the "eduction of correlates," as Spearman called it. The given information includes one unit and a stated relation, the examinee to supply the other unit. Analogies tests that call for completion rather than a choice between alternative answers emphasize this kind of ability. With symbolic content such an item might read:

pots  stop      bard  drab      rats  ?

A semantic item that measures eduction of correlates is:

The absence of sound is_____ .

Incidentally, the latter item is from a vocabulary-completion test, and its relation to the factor of ability to produce correlates indicates how, by change of form, a vocabulary test may indicate an ability other than that for which vocabulary tests are usually intended, namely, the factor of verbal comprehension.

Only one factor for convergent production of systems is known, and it is in the semantic column. It is measured by a class of tests that may be called ordering tests. The examinee may be presented with a number of events that ordinarily have a best or most logical order, the events being presented in scrambled order. The presentation may be pictorial, as in the Picture Arrangement Test, or verbal. The pictures may be taken from a cartoon strip.

The verbally presented events may be in the form of the various steps needed to plant a new lawn. There are undoubtedly other kinds of systems than temporal order that could be utilized for testing abilities in this row of the convergent-production matrix.

In the way of producing transformations of a unique variety, we have three recognized factors, known as redefinition abilities. In each case, redefinition involves the changing of functions or uses of parts of one unit and giving them new functions or uses in some new unit. For testing the ability of figural redefinition, a task based upon the Gottschaldt figures is suitable. In recognizing the simpler figure within the structure of a more complex figure, certain lines must take on new roles.

In terms of symbolic material, the following sample items will illustrate how groups of letters in given words must be readapted to use in other words. In the test Camouflaged Words, each sentence contains the name of a sport or game:

> I did not know that he was ailing.
> To beat the Hun, tin goes a long way.

For the factor of semantic redefinition, the Gestalt Transformation Test may be used. A sample item reads:

From which object could you most likely make a needle?

> A. a cabbage
> B. a splice
> C. a steak
> D. a paper box
> E. a fish

The convergent production of implications means the drawing of fully determined conclusions from given information. The well-known factor of numerical facility belongs in the symbolic column. For the parallel ability in the figural column, we have a test known as Form Reasoning, in which rigorously defined operations with figures are used. For the parallel ability in the semantic column, the factor sometimes called "deduction" probably qualifies. Items of the following type are sometimes used.

> Charles is younger than Robert
> Charles is older than Frank
> Who is older: Robert or Frank?

EVALUATIVE ABILITIES.

The evaluative area has had the least investigation of all the operational categories. In fact, only one systematic analytical study has been devoted to this area. Only eight evaluative abilities are recognized as fitting into the evaluation matrix. But at least five rows have one or more factors each, and also three of the usual columns or content categories. In each case, evaluation involves reaching decisions as to the accuracy, goodness, suitability, or workability of information. In each row, for the particular kind of product of that row, some kind of criterion or standard of judgment is involved.

In the first row, for the evaluation of units, the important decision to be made pertains to the identity of a unit. Is this unit identical with that one? In the figural column we find the factor long known as "perceptual speed." Tests of this factor invariably call for decisions of identity, for example, Part IV (Perceptual Speed) of the GZAS or Thurstone's Identical Forms. I think it has been generally wrongly thought that the ability involved is that of cognition of visual forms. But we have seen that another factor is a more suitable candidate for this definition and for being in the very first cell of cognitive matrix. It is parallel to this evaluative ability but does not require the judgment of identity as one of its properties.

In the symbolic column is an ability to judge identity of symbolic units, in the form of series of letters or numbers or of names of individuals.

Are members of the following pairs identical or not:

825170493 _____ 825176493
dkeltvmpa _____ dkeltvmpa
C. S. Meyerson _____ C. E. Meyerson

Such items are common in tests of clerical aptitude.

There should be a parallel ability to decide whether two ideas are identical or different. Is the idea expressed in this sentence the same as the idea expressed in that one? Do these two proverbs express essentially the same idea? Such tests exist and will be used to test the hypothesis that such an ability can be demonstrated.

No evaluative abilities pertaining to classes have as yet been recognized. The abilities having to do with evaluation where relations are concerned must meet the criterion of logical consistency. Syllogistic-type tests involving letter symbols indicate a different ability than the same type of test involving verbal statements. In the figural column we might expect that tests incorporating geometric reasoning or proof would indicate a parallel ability to sense the soundness of conclusions regarding figural relationships.

The evaluation of systems seems to be concerned with the internal consistency of those systems, so far as we can tell from the knowledge of one such factor. The factor has been called "experiential evaluation," and its representative test presents items asking "What is wrong with this picture?" The things wrong are often internal inconsistencies.

A semantic ability for evaluating transformations is thought to be that known for some time as "judgment." In typical judgment tests, the examinee is asked to tell which of five solutions to a practical problem is most adequate or wise. The solutions frequently involve improvisations, in other words, adaptations of familiar objects to unusual uses. In this way the items present redefinitions to be evaluated.

A factor known first as "sensitivity to problems" has become recognized as an evaluative ability having to do with implications. One test of the factor, the Apparatus Test, asks for two needed improvements with respect to each of several common devices, such as the telephone or the toaster. The Social Institutions Test, a measure of the same factor, asks what things are wrong with each of several institutions, such as tipping or national elections. We may say that defects or deficiencies are implications of an evaluative kind. Another interpretation would be that seeing defects and deficiencies are evaluations of implications to the effect that the various aspects of something are all right (3).

## Some Implications of the Structure of Intellect

### FOR PSYCHOLOGICAL THEORY.

Although factor analysis as generally employed is best designed to investigate ways in which individuals differ from one another, in other words, to discover traits, the results also tell us much about how individuals are alike. Consequently, information regarding the factors and their interrelationships gives us understanding of functioning individuals. The five kinds of intellectual abilities in terms of operations may be said to represent five ways of functioning. The kinds of intellectual abilities distinguished according to varieties of test content and the kinds of abilities distinguished according to varieties of products suggest a classification of basic forms of information or knowledge. The kind of organism suggested by this way of looking at intellect is that of an agency for dealing with information of various kinds in various ways. The concepts provided by the distinctions among the intellectual abilities and by their classifications may be very useful in our future investigations of learning, memory, problem solving, invention, and decision making, by whatever method we choose to approach those problems.

### FOR VOCATIONAL TESTING.

With about 50 intellectual factors already known, we may say that there are at least 50 ways of being intelligent. It has been facetiously suggested that there seem to be a great many more ways of being stupid, unfortunately. The structure of intellect is a theoretical model that predicts as many as 120 distinct abilities, if every cell of the model contains a factor. Already we know that two cells contain two or more factors each, and there probably are actually other cells of this type. Since the model was first conceived, 12 factors predicted by it have found places in it. There is consequently hope of filling many of the other vacancies, and we may eventually end up with more than 120 abilities.

The major implication for the assessment of intelligence is that to know an individual's intellectual resources thoroughly we shall need a surprisingly large number of scores. It is expected that many of the factors are intercorrelated, so there is some possibility that by appropriate sampling we shall be able to cover the important abilities with a more limited number of tests. At any rate, a multiple-score approach to the assessment of intelligence is definitely indicated in connection with future vocational operations.

Considering the kinds of abilities classified as to content, we may speak roughly of four kinds of intelligence. The abilities involving the use of figural information may be regarded as "concrete" intelligence. The people who depend most upon these abilities deal with concrete things and their properties. Among these people are mechanics, operators of machines, engineers (in some aspects of their work), artists, and musicians.

In the abilities pertaining to symbolic and semantic content, we have two kinds of "abstract" intelligence. Symbolic abilities should be important in learning to recognize words, to spell, and to operate with numbers. Language and mathematics should depend very much upon them, except that in mathematics some aspects, such as geometry, have strong figural involvement. Semantic intelligence is important for understanding things in terms of verbal concepts and hence is important in all courses where the learning of facts and ideas is essential.

In the hypothesized behavioral column of the structure of intellect, which may be roughly described as "social" intelligence, we have some of the most interesting possibilities. Understanding the behavior of others and of ourselves is largely nonverbal in character. The theory suggests as many as 30 abilities in this area, some having to do with understanding, some with productive thinking about behavior, and some with the evaluation of behavior. The theory also suggests that information regarding behavior is also in the form of the six kinds of products that apply elsewhere in the structure of intellect, including units, relations, systems, and so on. The abilities in the area of social intelligence, whatever they prove to be, will possess considerable importance in connection with all those individuals who deal most with other people: teachers, law officials, social workers, therapists, politicians, statesmen, and leaders of other kinds.

FOR EDUCATION.

The implications for education are numerous, and I have time just to mention a very few. The most fundamental implication is that we might well undergo transformations with respect to our conception of the learner and of the process of learning. Under the prevailing conception, the learner is a kind of stimulus-response device, much on the order of a vending machine. You put in a coin, and something comes out. The machine learns what reaction to put out when a certain coin is put in. If, instead, we think of the learner as an agent for dealing with information, where information is defined very broadly, we have something more analogous to an electronic computor. We feed a computor information; it stores that information; it uses that information for generating new information, either by way of divergent or convergent thinking; and it evaluates its own results. Advantages that a human learner has over a computor include the step of seeking and discovering new information from sources outside itself and the step of programming itself. Perhaps even these steps will be added to computors, if this has not already been done in some cases.

At any rate, this conception of the learner leads us to the idea that learning is discovery of information, not merely the formation of associations, particularly associations in the form of stimulus-response connections. I am aware of the fact that my proposal is rank heresy. But if we are to make significant progress in our understanding of human learning and particularly our understanding of the so-called higher mental processes of thinking, problem solving, and creative thinking, some drastic modifications are due in our theory.

The idea that education is a matter of training the mind or of training the intellect has been rather unpopular, wherever the prevailing psychological doctrines have been followed. In theory, at least, the emphasis has been upon the learning of rather specific habits or skills. If we take our cue from factor theory, however, we recognize that most learning probably has both specific and general aspects or components. The general aspects may be along the lines of the factors of intellect. This is not to say that the individual's status in each factor is entirely determined by learning. We do not know to what extent each factor is determined by heredity and to what extent by learning. The best position for educators to take is that possibly every intellectual factor can be developed in individuals at least to some extent by learning.

If education has the general objective of developing the intellects of students, it can be suggested that each intellectual factor provides a particular goal at which to aim. Defined by a certain combination of content, operation, and product, each goal ability then calls for certain kinds of practice in order to achieve improvement in it. This implies choice of curriculum and the choice or invention of teaching methods that will most likely accomplish the desired results.

Considering the very great variety of abilities revealed by the factorial exploration of intellect, we are in a better position to ask whether any general intellectual skills are now being neglected in education and whether appropriate balances are being observed. It is often observed these days that we have fallen down in the way of producing resourceful, creative graduates. How true this is, in comparison with other times, I do not know. Perhaps the deficit is noticed because the demands for inventiveness are so much greater at this time. At any rate, realization that the more conspicuously creative abilities appear to be concentrated in the divergent-thinking category, and also to some extent in the transformation category, we now ask whether we have been giving these skills appropriate exercise. It is probable that we need a better balance of training in the divergent-thinking area as compared with training in convergent thinking and in critical thinking or evaluation.

The structure of intellect as I have presented it to you may or may not stand the test of time. Even if the general form persists, there are likely to be some modifications. Possibly some different kind of model will be invented. Be that as it may, the fact of a multiplicity of intellectual abilities seems well established.

There are many individuals who long for the good old days of simplicity, when we got along with one unanalyzed intelligence. Simplicity certainly has its appeal. But human nature is exceedingly complex, and we may as well face that fact. The rapidly moving events of the world in which we live have forced upon us the need for knowing human intelligence thoroughly. Humanity's peaceful pursuit of happiness depends upon our control of nature and of our own behavior; and this, in turn, depends upon understanding ourselves, including our intellectual resources.

## References

1. Christal, R. E., Factor Analytic Study of Visual Memory. *Psychol. Monogr.,* 1958, **72,** No. 13 (Whole No. 466).

2. Guilford, J. P., The Structure of Intellect. *Psychol. Bull.,* 1956, **53,** 267-293.

3. Guilford, J. P., *Personality.* New York: McGraw-Hill, 1959.

*Thelma G. Thurstone*

# *Primary Mental Abilities of Children*

*F*or many years psychologists have been accustomed to the problems of special abilities and disabilities. These are, in fact, the principal concern of the school psychologists who deal with children who cannot read, have a blind spot for numbers, or do one thing remarkably well and other things poorly. It seems strange with all this experience in differential psychology that we have clung so long to the practice of summarizing a child's mental endowment by a single index, such as the mental age, the intelligence quotient, the percentile rank in general intelligence, and other single average measures. An average index of mental endowment should be useful for many educational purposes, but it should not be regarded as more than the average of several tests. Two children with the same mental age can be entirely different persons, as is well known. There is nothing wrong about using a mental age or an intelligence quotient if it is understood as an average of several tests. The error that is frequently made is interpreting it as measuring some basic functional unity when it is known to be nothing more than a composite of many functional unities.

The researches on the primary mental abilities which have been in progress for several years have had as their first purposes the identification and definition of the independent factors of mind. As the nature of the abilities became more clearly indicated by successive studies, a second purpose of a more practical nature has been involved in some of the studies. This purpose has been to prepare a set of tests of psychological significance and practicable adaptability to the school testing and guidance program. The series of studies will be summarized in this paper, the battery of tests soon to be available will be described, and some of the problems now being investigated will be discussed briefly.

Reprinted from *Educational and Psychological Measurements,* Vol. 1, No. 12 (1941), pp. 105-116. By Permission of the author and publisher.

## Previous Studies

The first study in this series involved the use of 56 psychological examinations that were given to a group of about 250 college students. That study revealed a number of primary abilities, some of which were clearly defined by the configuration of test vectors while others were indicated by the configuration but less clearly defined. All of these factors have been studied in subsequent test batteries in which each primary factor has been represented by new tests specially designed to feature the primary factors in the purest possible form. The object has been to construct tests in which there is a heavy saturation of a primary factor and in which other factors are minimized. This is the purification of tests by reducing their complexity.

These latter studies of the separate abilities were in each case made in the Chicago high schools—one study emphasizing the perceptual factor at the Lane Technical High School, one study of the inductive factor at the Hyde Park High School, an intensive study of the memory factor or factors in four high schools, and a study of numerical ability by Coombs in six high schools. In each series of tests, one factor was represented by a large number of tests, but all factors were well represented. In all of these studies the same primary abilities were identified as had been found in the experiment with college students. These studies led to the publication by the American Council on Education of an experimental battery of tests for the primary mental abilities, adaptable for use with students of high school or college age.

The identification of the same primary mental abilities among high school students as we had previously found among college students encouraged us to look for differentiation among the abilities of younger children. In the Chicago Public Schools, group mental tests are made of all 1B, 4B, and 8B children in the elementary schools and of 10B students in the high schools. The demand for a series of tests to be used in the guidance program for high school entrants and the advisability of not making too broad a leap in age led us to select an eighth-grade population for the next study.

## The Eighth-Grade Experiment

In view of the purpose of investigating whether or not primary mental abilities could be isolated for children at the fourteen-year age level, the construction of the tests consisted essentially in the adaptation for the younger children of tests previously used with high school students. In some of the tests little or no alteration was necessary, while for other tests it was considered advisable to revise vocabulary and other aspects of the tests to suit the younger age level. A number of new tests were added to those selected from previous experimental batteries. Sixty tests constituted the final battery.

When the tests had been designed and printed, they were given in a trial form to children in grades 7A and 8A in several schools. Groups of from 50 to 100 children in these two grades were used for the purpose of standardizing procedures and, especially, for setting time limits.

Fifteen Chicago elementary schools were selected by Miss Minnie L. Fallon, Assistant Superintendent in charge of elementary education, and by Dr. Grace E. Munson, Director of the Bureau of Child Study, as experimental schools for this study. The tests in the main investigation were administered in the schools by the adjustment teachers. These adjustment teachers had had special training in testing procedures with the Bureau of Child Study and also had had considerable experience in giving psychological and educational tests. Special instructions in the procedures for these tests were given to the adjustment teachers, as well as written instructions for each day's testing program.

Eleven hundred and fifty-four children participated in this study. The complete battery of 60 tests was given in 11 one-hour sessions to the children in the 8B grades in each of the 15 schools. The children enjoyed the tests and, with very few exceptions, the sustained interest and effort were quite evident. One thing which a psychologist might fear in such a long series of tests would be fluctuating motivation on the part of the students. Although the adjustment teachers administered the tests, every session was observed by a member of our staff, and we were highly gratified by the sustained interest and effort of the pupils.

In addition to the 60 tests we used three more variables: chronological age, mental age, and sex. The latter test data were available in school records. They were determined by the Kuhlmann-Anderson tests which had been given previously to the same children. Therefore, the battery to be analyzed factorially contained 63 variables.

The total population in this study consisted of 1,154 eighth-grade children. When all the records had been assembled, it was found that 710 of these subjects had complete records for all of the 63 variables. We decided to base our correlations on this population of complete records rather than to use the large population with varying numbers of cases for the correlation coefficients. For convenience of handling with the tabulating-machine methods, the raw scores were transmuted into single digit scores from which the Pearson product-moment correlation coefficients were computed. With 63 variables there were 1,935 Pearson correlation coefficients.

This table of intercorrelations was factored to 10 factors by the centroid method on the tabulating machines by means of punched cards. Successive rotations made by the method of extended vectors yielded an oblique factorial matrix which is a simple structure.

Inspection of the rotated factorial matrix showed seven of the factors previously indicated: Memory, Induction, Verbal Comprehension, Word

Fluency, Number, Space, Perceptual Speed, and three less easily identifiable factors. One of these is another Verbal factor; one is involved in ability to solve pencil mazes; and one is present in the three dot-counting tests which were used.

We have computed the intercorrelations between the 10 primary factors. Our main interest centers on the seven primary factors that can be given interpretation and, especially, on the first six of these factors for which the interpretation is rather more definite. Among the high correlations we note that the Number factor is correlated with the two Verbal factors. The Word Fluency factor has high correlation with the Verbal Comprehension factor and with Induction. The Rote Memory factor seems to be independent of the other factors. These correlations are higher than the correlations between primary factors for adults.

Because of the psychological interest in the correlations of the primary mental abilities, we have made a separate analysis of the correlations for those factors which seem to have reasonably certain interpretation. If these six primary mental abilities are correlated because of some general intellective factor, then the rank of the correlation matrix should be one. Upon examination, this actually proves to be the case. A single factor accounts for most of the correlations between the primary factors.

The single factor loadings show that the inductive factor has the highest loading and the Rote Memory factor the lowest loading on the common general factor in the primary abilities. This general factor is what we have called a second-order general factor. It makes its appearance not as a separate factor, but as a factor inherent in the primaries and their correlations. If further studies of the primary mental abilities of children should reveal this general factor, it may sustain Spearman's contention that there exists a general intellective factor. Instead of depending on the averages or centroids of arbitrary test batteries for its determination, the present method should enable us to identify it uniquely.

We have not been able to find in these data a general factor that is distinct from the primary factors, but the second-order general factor should be of as much psychological interest as the more frequently postulated, independent general factor of Spearman. It would be our judgment that the second-order general factor found here is probably the general factor which Spearman has so long defended, but we cannot say whether he would accept the present findings as sustaining his contentions about the general factor. We have not found any occasion to debate the existence of a general intellective factor. The factorial methods we have been using are adequate for finding such a factor, either as a factor independent of the primaries or as a factor operating through correlated primaries. We have reported on primary mental abilities in adults, which seem to show only low positive correlations except for the two verbal factors. In the present study we have found higher correlations among the primary factors for eighth-grade children. It is now an interesting question to determine whether the correlations among primary abilities of still younger children will reveal, perhaps even more strongly, a second-order general factor.

## Interpretation of Factors

The analysis of this battery of 60 tests revealed essentially the same set of primary factors which had been found in previous factorial studies. Six of the factors seemed to have sufficient stability for the several age levels that have been investigated to justify an extension of the tests for these factors into practical test work in the schools. In making this extension we have been obliged to consider carefully the difference between research on the nature of the primary factors and the construction of tests for practical use. Several of the primary factors are not yet sufficiently clear as regards psychological interpretation to justify an attempt to appraise them generally among school children. The primary factors that do seem to be clear enough for such purposes are the following: Verbal Comprehension V, Word Fluency W, Number N, Space S, Rote Memory M, and Induction or Reasoning R. The factors which in several studies are not yet sufficiently clear for general application are the Perceptual factor P and the Deductive factor D.

The Verbal factor V is found in tests involving verbal comprehension, for example, tests of vocabulary, opposites and synonyms, completion tests, and various reading comprehension tests.

The Word Fluency factor W is involved whenever the subject is asked to think of isolated words at a rapid rate. It is for this reason that we have called the factor a Word Fluency factor. It can be expected in such tests as anagrams, rhyming, and producing words with a given initial letter, prefix, or suffix.

The Space factor S is involved in any task in which the subject manipulates an object imaginally in two or three dimensions. The ability is involved in many mechanical tasks and in the understanding of mechanical drawings. Such material cannot be used conveniently in testing situations, so we have used a large number of tasks which are psychologically similar, such as Flags, Cards, and Figures.

The Number factor N is involved in the ability to do numerical calculations rapidly and accurately. It is not dependent upon the reasoning factors in problem-solving, but seems to be restricted to the simpler processes, such as addition and multiplication.

A Memory factor M has been clearly present in all test batteries. The tests for memory which are now being used depend upon the ability to memorize quickly. It is quite possible that the Memory factor will be broken down into more specific factors.

The Reasoning factor R is involved in tasks that require the subject to discover a rule or principle covering the material of the test. The Letter Series and Letter Grouping tests are good examples of the task. In all these experimental studies two separate Reasoning factors have been indicated. They are perhaps Induction and Deduction, but we have not succeeded in constructing pure tests of either factor. The tests which we are now using are more heavily saturated with Inductive factor, but for the present we are simply calling the ability R, Reasoning.

In presenting for general use a differential psychological examination which appraises the mental endowment of children, it should not be assumed that there is anything final about six primary factors. No one knows how many primary mental abilities there may be. It is hoped that future factorial studies will reveal many other important primary abilities so that the mental profiles of students may eventually be adequate for appraising educational and vocational potentialities. In such a program the present studies are only a starting point in substituting for the description of mental endowment by a single intelligence index the description of mental endowment by a profile of fundamental traits.

## The Final Test Battery

In adapting the tests for practical use in the schools for the appraisal of six primary mental abilities, we must recognize that the new test program has for its object the production of a profile for each child, as distinguished from the description of a child's mental endowment in terms of a single intelligence index. For many educational purposes it is still of value to appraise a child's mental endowment roughly by a single measure, but the nature of such single indices must be recognized.

The factorial matrix of the battery of sixty tests was inspected to find the three best tests for each of seven primary factors. In making the selection of tests for each primary factor we consider not only the factorial saturations of the tests, which are, of course, the most important consideration, but also the availability of parallel forms which may be needed in case the tests should come into general use. Ease of administration and ease in understanding of the instructions are also important considerations.

The three tests for each primary factor were printed in a separate booklet and the material was so arranged that the three tests for any factor could be given easily within a 40-minute school period. The main purpose of the larger test battery was to determine whether or not the primary factors could be found for eighth-grade children, but the purpose of the present shorter battery was to produce a practical, useful test battery and to check its factorial composition. The selected tests were edited and revised so that they could be used for either hand-scoring or machine-scoring. The Word Fluency tests constitute an exception in that none of the tests now known to be saturated with this factor seems to be suitable for machine-scoring.

In order to check the factorial analysis at the present age level, we arranged to give the selected list of 21 tests to a second population of eighth-grade children. The resulting data were factored independently of the larger battery of tests. There were 437 subjects in this population who took all of the 21 tests. This population was used for a new factor analysis. The results of this analysis clearly confirmed the previous study. The simple structure in the present battery is sharp, with only one primary factor conspicuously present in each test, so that the structure could be determined by inspection for clusters.

A battery of 17 tests has been assembled into a series of test booklets for use in the Chicago schools. An experimental edition of 25,000 copies has been printed, and the plan for securing norms on these tests includes their administration to 1,000 children at each half-year grade level from grade 5B through the senior year in high school. These records have been obtained during the school year 1940 to 1941. The use of such a wide age range in standardizing the test is at first thought, perhaps, rather strange. The effort was made in order to secure age norms throughout the entire range of abilities found among eighth-grade children since the tests are to become a part of the testing procedure for all 8B children in the Chicago schools. Separate age norms will be derived for each of the six primary abilities. If a single index of a student's mental ability is desired, it is recommended that the average of his six ability scores be used.

As soon as the norms are established, the tests will be published by the American Council on Education under the title "Chicago Primary Mental Abilities Tests." It is expected that the tests will be ready for distribution during the summer of 1941. The norms provided with the tests will be of a wide enough range to make the tests useful at the high school and upper grade levels.

The complete test program consists of 17 tests, all of which have been reduced to machine-scoring form except the three tests for the Word Fluency factor W. In the nature of the case there seem to be difficulties in reducing this test to machine-scoring form, and hence it has been retained in hand-scoring form. It should be said, however, that the W tests can be scored almost as fast, if not as fast, as the tests which are machine-scored. Since all of the test can be hand-scored, their use is not limited to schools large enough to avail themselves of the scoring machine. The hand-scoring of all the tests is very easily accomplished by the use of perforated stencils to be provided with the tests. Hand-scoring is facilitated by the use of the scoring board distributed by the Stoelting Company.

The new battery represents six primary mental abilities, namely, Verbal Comprehension V, Space S, Number N, Memory M, Word Fluency W, and Reasoning R. They enable the skilled psychologist to tabulate a profile of six linearly independent scores instead of a single measure, such as the intelligence quotient.

Principals, teachers, adjustment teachers, and school psychologists have expressed their satisfaction with the profile of abilities plotted for each child. Probably the children themselves have found the profiles most interesting and have profited most from an examination of their own profiles. In the school year 1941-1942, these tests will be installed as a part of the educational guidance program in the Chicago schools by administering them regularly to 8B elementary school pupils and 10B high school pupils.

Some of the features of the tests should be mentioned. The tests are so arranged that machine-scoring and hand-scoring tests are directly comparable and will have the same norms. The child's task does not vary with the type of scoring; only the scorer's job is changed. Another feature is the use of fore-exercise booklets printed on yellow paper. The time limits for the practice exercises are approximate. When a test proper is started, the student places his white test booklet on top of his yellow practice booklet, and the examiners and proctors can check at a glance that every child is working in the right place. The tests proper are to be timed exactly. The three tests of each of the six abilities are arranged in a booklet for administration within a 40-minute school period. It is recommended that the successive booklets be given on successive school days.

## Further Problems

One of our principal research interests at the present time is to determine whether primary abilities can be identified in children of kindergarten or first-grade age. A series of about 50 tests is well under way, and some of them are now being tried with young children. If we succeed in isolating primary abilities among these young children, our next step will be to prepare a practical battery of tests for that age. A subsequent problem will be to make experimental studies of paper-and-pencil tests for appraising the primary abilities of children in the intermediate grades, approximately at the fourth-grade level. We are fairly confident that such tests can be prepared for use in the intermediate grades.

It is a long way in the future, but it is interesting to speculate on the possibility of using the tests of the primary mental abilities as the tool with which to study fundamental psychological problems of mental growth and mental inheritance. Absolute scaling of the tests at the different age levels will make possible studies on the rates of development of the separate abilities at various age levels. Modifiability of the abilities will be another problem to which we shall later turn attention.

*J. W. Getzels*

*P. W. Jackson*

# The Study of Giftedness:
# A Multidimensional Approach

$A$lthough few would argue that the terms "creative" and "intelligent" refer to independent classes of phenomena, still fewer would seriously propose that the two terms are synonymous. Despite this recognition of relative independence at the theoretical level, when turning to practical problems involving the assessment of the two qualities, one finds that the well-established intelligence test is most frequently used as *the* indicator of creativity. Individuals are grouped by IQ, and generally there is disappointment if the high-IQ person is not also creative. Sometimes he is not. There is also bewilderment when the creative individual has a relatively low IQ, as is often the case. Theoretical issues in the study of higher cognitive functioning and current practical problems in the search for talent make the importance of differentiating the two concepts in empirical terms self-evident.

## Problem

The central purpose of this research is to discover significant variables differentiating the creative from the intelligent person. Specifically, the present study examines the achievement motives, fantasy productions, school performance, and teacher preferences of two types of adolescents: those exceptionally high in creativity but not in IQ, and those exceptionally high in IQ, but not in creativity.

Getzels, J. W. and Jackson, P. W. "The Study of Giftedness: A Multidimensional Approach". *The Gifted Student,* OE-35016, Cooperative Research Monograph No. 2, pp. 6-18.

## Subjects, Instruments, and Procedures

The subjects were drawn from 449 adolescents comprising the total population of a midwestern private secondary school. The experimental groups were composed on the basis of performance on the following tests:

*Standard IQ tests.*—A Stanford-Binet, a WISC, or a Henmon-Nelson score was available for each adolescent. The scores obtained from the WISC and the Henmon-Nelson were converted by regression equation to comparable Stanford-Binet IQ's.

*Five creativity tests* taken or adapted from Guilford and Cattell or constructed especially for the study:

> 1. Word Association. The subject was asked to give as many definitions as possible to fairly common stimulus-words; e.g., "bolt," "bark," "sack." His score depended upon the absolute number of definitions and the number of different categories into which these definitions could be put.
> 2. Uses for Things. The subject was required to give as many uses as he could for objects that customarily have a stereotyped function attached to them; e.g., "brick," "paperclip." His score depended upon both the number and originality of the uses he mentioned.
> 3. Hidden Shapes. The subject was required to find a given geometric form that was hidden in more complex geometric forms or patterns.
> 4. Fables. The subject was presented with four fables in which the last lines were missing. He was required to compose three different endings for *each* fable: a "moralistic," a "humorous," and a "sad" ending. His score depended upon the number, appropriateness, and originality of the endings.
> 5. Make-Up Problems. The subject was presented with four complex paragraphs, each of which contained a number of numerical statements; e.g., "the costs involved in building a house." He was asked to make all the mathematical problems he could that might be solved with the information given. His score depended upon the number, appropriateness, and originality of the problems.

On the basis of the IQ measure and the mean of the five creativity measures, two experimental groups were formed:

> 1. *The high creativity group* (26 students: 15 boys, 11 girls)—students in the top 20 percent in creativity, compared to students of the same age and sex, but not in the top 20 percent in IQ.
> 2. *The high intelligence group* (28 students: 17 boys, 11 girls)—students in the top 20 percent in IQ, compared with students of the same age and sex, but not in the top 20 percent in creativity.

The two groups were then compared to each other and to the population from which they were drawn on the following variables: School performance as measured by standardized verbal and numerical achievement tests appropriate to each grade level; teacher preferences on having them in class; N-Achievement as measured by conventional scoring of responses to six of McClelland's stimulus-pictures. In addition to the conventional scoring, the N-Achievement protocols were also sorted "blind" for the creative and a matched noncreative group and finally analyzed systematically for the creative and intelligent groups by categories suggested in the blind sorting.

## Results

The results (see Tables 1 and 2) may be summarized as follows: (1) Despite the striking differences in mean IQ, the creative and the intelligent groups were *equally* superior to the total population in school performance as measured by standardized achievement tests. (2) Although it might be expected that creativity would contribute to status in a school setting, especially since the achievement of the highly creative subjects was at least as good as that of the highly intelligent subjects, it was actually the *intelligent* group rather than the *creative* group that was preferred by teachers when compared with the average student. (3) The two groups did *not* differ from the population in N-Achievement as scored conventionally. (4) Although failing to show differences when scored for N-Achievement, the fantasy productions of the creative group were clearly dissimilar from those of the popula-

**TABLE 1**

**Means and Standard Deviations of
Highly Creative and Highly Intelligent Groups
on Experimental Variables**

| Variables<br>1 | Total<br>population[1]<br>(N = 449)<br>2 | High-IQ<br>(N = 28)<br>3 | High<br>creative[2]<br>(N = 24)<br>4 |
|---|---|---|---|
| IQ | | | |
| Mean | 132.00 | 150.00** | 127.00 |
| Standard deviation | 15.07 | 6.64 | 10.58 |
| School achievement | | | |
| Mean | 49.91 | 55.00** | 56.27** |
| Standard deviation | 7.36 | 5.95 | 7.90 |
| Teacher preference ratings | | | |
| Mean | 10.23 | 11.20* | 10.54 |
| Standard deviation | 3.64 | 1.56 | 1.95 |
| Need for achievement<br>(T.-scores): | | | |
| Mean | 49.81 | 49.00 | 50.04 |
| Standard deviation | 9.49 | 7.97 | 8.39 |

[1]For purposes of comparison the scores of each experimental group were extracted from the total population before *t*-tests were computed.
[2]Two subjects were omitted from the sample of 26 high creatives because they failed to furnish data on the McClelland N-Achievement instrument.
*Significant at 0.01 level.
**Significant at 0.001 level.

tion as a whole, so much so that the "blind" sorting of 47 creative and non-creative protocols resulted in only 7 misplacements. (5) A more systematic differentiation of the protocols using content-analysis procedures showed that the two experimental groups differed significantly in their fantasy responses. The creative group made greater use of stimulus-free themes, unexpected endings, humor, incongruities, and playfulness.

**TABLE 2**
**Categories of Fantasy Production of Highly Creative and Highly Intelligent Groups**

| | Group | | | | |
|---|---|---|---|---|---|
| | High creativity[1] (N = 24) | | High IQ (N = 28) | | |
| Content-analysis categories 1 | Frequency[2] 2 | Percent 3 | Frequency[2] 4 | Percent 5 | $x^2$ 6 |
| Stimulus-free theme | 18 | 75 | 11 | 39 | 5.31[3]* |
| Unexpected ending | 22 | 92 | 17 | 61 | 5.05* |
| Presence of humor | 17 | 71 | 7 | 25 | 9.16** |
| Presence of incongruity | 17 | 71 | 10 | 36 | 5.06* |
| Presence of violence | 18 | 75 | 13 | 46 | 3.27 |
| Playful attitude towards theme | 21 | 89 | 9 | 32 | 14.04** |

[1]Two subjects were omitted from the sample of 26 High Creatives because they failed to furnish data on the McClelland N-Achievement instrument.

[2]Numbers in the frequency column represent the subjects whose fantasy productions fit the corresponding categories.

[3]Yates correction was applied in the computation of chi-squares.

*Significant at 0.05 level.

**Significant at 0.01 level.

Here, for example, are typical stories by highly intelligent and by highly creative subjects to two of the McClelland stimulus-pictures.

One picture-stimulus was perceived most often as a man in an airplane reclining seat returning from a business trip or conference. A high-IQ subject gave the following story: "Mr. Smith is on his way home from a successful business trip. He is very happy and he is thinking about his wonderful family and how glad he will be to see them again. He can picture it, about an hour from now, his plane landing at the airport and Mrs. Smith and their three children all there welcoming him home again." A high-creative subject wrote this story: "This man is flying back from Reno where he has just won a divorce from his wife. He couldn't stand to live with her anymore, he told the judge, because she wore so much cold cream on her face at night that her head would skid across the pillow and hit him in the head. He is now contemplating a new skid-proof face cream."

This story was in response to a stimulus-picture usually perceived as a man working late (or very early) in an office:

The High IQ Student: "There's ambitious Bob, down at the office at 6:30 in the morning. Every morning it's the same. He's trying to show his boss how energetic he is. Now, thinks Bob, maybe the boss will give me a raise for all my extra work. The trouble is that Bob has been doing this for the last three years, and the boss still hasn't given him a raise. He'll come in at 9:00, not even noticing that Bob had been there so long, and poor Bob won't get his raise."

The High-Creative Student: "This man has just broken into this office of a new cereal company. He is a private-eye employed by a competitor firm to find out the formula that makes the cereal bend, sag, and sway. After a thorough search of the office he comes upon what he thinks is the correct formula: He is now copying it. It turns out that it is the wrong formula and the competitor's factory blows up. Poetic justice!"

These stories were written in group sessions with often more than a hundred adolescents in the same room and a maximum writing time four minutes per story. "Skidproof face cream!" "Cereal that will bend, sag, and sway!" It seems that the ability to restructure stereotyped objects with ease and rapidity—almost "naturally"—is the characteristic mark of the high creative as against the high IQ subjects in this investigation.

## Discussion and Summary

The essence of creativity appears to lie in the ability to produce new forms, to conjoin elements that are customarily thought of as independent or dissimilar; not merely the propensity for seeing the bizarre but rather the aptitude for achieving new meanings having social value. Guilford has given the name "divergent" to intellectual activities expressing this ability, in contrast to activities which he calls "convergent." It is chiefly the latter type of performance that is tapped by conventional measures of intelligence. Whether or not one adopts the terminology of Guilford, there is little doubt that the ability required for what has been called "divergent" intellectual activity is not well sampled by the usual intelligence-test items, and accordingly this ability contributes but little to the IQ score. In these terms, the high IQ subjects of the experimental groups are superior in "convergent" intellectual performance and the high-creativity subjects in "divergent" intellectual performance.

The evidence of this report centers attention on the difference in the fantasy quality of the two groups. It is tentatively concluded that a *sine qua non* of creative functioning is a rich and available fantasy life.

The difference between the person with a convergent and the person with a divergent orientation toward problem solving appears to be that the former focuses on the stimulus, since he seeks objective precision of the sort others will recognize as "right" and therefore successful by conventional standards. In effect, he may be said to intellectualize the ambiguities presented by a problem in an effort to find the right answer. The latter detaches himself from the stimulus, since he prefers subjective playfulness that he himself will find "delightful." In effect, he may be said to personalize the ambiguities presented by a problem in an effort to attain an enjoyment which may or may not be shared with others. If the former "latches on" *to* a stimulus, the latter "takes off" *from* a stimulus.

The search for variables differentiating the "creative" from the "intelligent" person is the focus of much theoretical and practical concern. This study examined the achievement motives, fantasy productions, school performance, and teacher preferences of two types of adolescents, those exceptionally high in creativity but not in IQ and those exceptionally high in IQ but not in creativity. The results indicated that: (1) Despite striking differences in IQ, the two groups were equally superior in school achievement; (2) The intelligent subjects rather than the creative ones were preferred by teachers; (3) There were no differences in N-Achievement; (4) There were significant differences in fantasy productions, the creative group using more stimulus-free, humorous, and playful themes.

## Occupational Choice and Cognitive Functioning: A Study of the Career Aspirations of Highly Intelligent and of Highly Creative Adolescents

The relationship between an individual's cognitive style and his personal orientation to the world is of central importance to the understanding of both cognitive functioning and social behavior. This study investigates the relationship between cognition, as defined by performance on intellective tasks, and personal orientation, as defined by long-term occupational choice and career aspiration.

### Problem

The purpose of the investigation is two-fold: At the substantive level, to determine the occupational preferences of the two groups of adolescents described in the previous section; at the theoretical level, to ascertain the relationship between types of cognition and types of career aspiration. Two guiding empirical questions were posed: (1) What is the nature of the long-term occupational goals of the two groups? (2) To what extent do perceived "teacher standards" and the criterion "success in adult life" enter as motives in the aspirations of the two groups?

## Subjects, Instruments, and Procedures

The experimental groups were the 26 highly creative and the 28 highly intelligent adolescents previously described. Four instruments were used to obtain the data:

A DIRECT SENTENCE COMPLETION TEST. Among the 60 items comprising this test were such career-preference items as: "When I grow up I want to become a . . . .," "If the choice of a permanent occupation were left up to me, I would choose . . . ," "The work that has the greatest appeal to me is . . . ," "I always wanted to be a . . ." The student was required to respond directly to these items by completing each stub so as to reflect his own preferences. The responses of the two groups were analyzed for the number and kind of occupations mentioned.

AN INDIRECT SENTENCE COMPLETION TEST. This test was parallel to the direct test, except that the sentence stubs were written in the third person and used boys' names for the male subjects and girls' names for the female subjects: "When Stan [Jean] grows up he [she] wants to become a . . . , etc. The subject was required to respond "projectively" to the items by completing the stubs as a verbal speed test. The responses of the two groups were analysed for the number and kind of occupations mentioned.

A PARENT QUESTIONNAIRE. This instrument required the parents of the students to respond to two questions regarding their children's occupational goals as follows: "Has the pupil expressed interest in a particular career?" "If yes, specify. . . ." The responses from the parents of the two groups were analyzed for the number and kind of occupations mentioned.

AN OUTSTANDING TRAITS TEST. This was the same test described in detail in the first section. It contained descriptions of 13 children, each description exemplifying some desirable personal quality or trait. The subjects were required to rank the 13 hypothetical children in 3 ways: (1) On the degree to which they would like to be like them; (2) On the degree to which they believed teachers would like them; (3) On the degree to which they believed people with these qualities would succeed in adult life. The rankings given by the two groups within each category and the relationships among the rankings for the different categories were analyzed.

## Summary of Results

1. Differences between the two groups appeared in both the *quantity* and *quality* of occupational goals. The *quantity* of occupational possibilities mentioned is significantly greater for the high creatives than for the high IQ's, the latter group having mentioned an average of 1.82 different occupations on the Direct Sentence Completion Test and 3.57 on the Indirect Test, the former group an average of 2.61 and 5.00 on the respective tests. The *quality* of the different occupations mentioned as possibilities is also significantly different for the two groups. When the occupations mentioned were divided into conventional (lawyer, doctor, professor) and unconventional (adventurer, inventor, writer) categories, it was found that the high

creatives mentioned a significantly greater proportion of unconventional occupations than did the high IQ's. For example, on the Direct Sentence Completion Test, only 18 percent of the high IQ's mentioned any unconventional occupation, whereas 62 percent of the high creatives mentioned at least one such occupation as a possibility. (See Table 3.)

The findings of the reports of the adolescents are supported by the data from the Parent Questionnaire. Parents of 24 of the high-IQ children and 24 of the high-creativity children replied to the questionnaire. Parents of 16 high-IQ and 20 high-creativity children reported that their children had expressed an interest in some career. What is most noteworthy in these reports is that 12 (75 percent) of the parents of high-IQ children mentioned occupations in but five career categories: engineering and architecture, science, medicine, law, and teaching; only 7 (35 percent) of the parents of high-creativity children mentioned career choices exclusively in these five categories. Instead, the parents of high-creativity children tended to mention such rather unconventional occupations as "veterinary" or "entertainer," such unresolved combinations as "law or music," "teaching or art," and such expressive professions as "writing" or "dancing." None of the latter were mentioned as possibilities by the parents of the high-IQ children. A summary of the data is presented in Table 4.

With respect to the *quantity* of occupations considered, depending on one's point of view, one might say that the high-creativity adolescents are more "diffuse" in occupational goals than the high-IQ adolescents, or that they are more able and willing to deal with a greater range of career pos-

**TABLE 3**

**Number and Type of Occupations Mentioned by the Experimental Groups on Direct and Indirect Sentence-completion Tests**

| Type of sentence-completion test and group<br>1 | Number of occupations mentioned | | | Unusual occupations | |
|---|---|---|---|---|---|
| | Total<br>2 | Mean<br>3 | Standard deviation<br>4 | Number mentioned<br>5 | Number of students mentioning<br>6 |
| Direct: | | | | | |
| High-IQ | 51 | 1.82* | 1.09 | 6 | 5** |
| (N = 28) | | | | | |
| High-creative | 68 | 2.61* | 1.41 | 24 | 16** |
| (N = 26) | | | | | |
| Indirect: | | | | | |
| High-IQ | 100 | 3.57** | 1.81 | 12 | 10* |
| (N = 28) | | | | | |
| High-creative | 130 | 5.00** | 1.80 | 29 | 17* |
| (N = 26) | | | | | |

*t* used to test differences between mean in column 3.
$x^2$ used to test differences between frequencies in column 6.
*Significant at 0.05 level.
**Significant at 0.01 level.

**TABLE 4**

**Career Choices Mentioned by Parents**

**of High-IQ and High-creative Adolescents**

| | Parents of— | |
|---|---|---|
| Career choice mentioned | High-IQ's<br>(N = 16) | High-creatives<br>(N = 20) |
| A single major profession such as engineering or architecture, law, medicine, teaching | 12 | 7 |
| Other professions and occupations or several career choices | 4 | 13 |

$x^2 = 5.71$.
$p < 0.02$

sibilities. As for the *quality* of occupations considered, again depending on one's point of view, one might say that the high-creativity adolescents are either more "eccentric" in their occupational goals or more able and willing to deal with career risks; that is, to take liberties with accepted standards of adult success.

2. Data with respect to the second empirical question, the "success" orientation of the two groups, were obtained from the Outstanding Traits Test and provide further insight into the career aspirations of the high-IQ and high-creativity adolescents.

The high-IQ's ranked the qualities in which they would like to be outstanding in the following order: (1) character, (2) emotional stability, (3) goal-directedness, (4) creativity, (5) wide range of interests, (6) high marks, (7) IQ, and (8) sense of humor. The high creatives ranked the qualities in the following order: (1) emotional stability, (2) sense of humor, (3) character, (4.5) wide range of interest, (4.5) goal-directedness, (6) creativity, (7) high marks, and (8) IQ. Most noteworthy here was the extraordinarily high ranking given by the high-creativity group to "sense of humor," a ranking which not only distinguishes them from the high-IQ group (who ranked it last) but from all groups to which the test had been given.

The most relevant and striking differences, however, between the two groups in the context of the present inquiry are observed in the relationship of the qualities they want for themselves, the qualities they believe lead to adult success, and the qualities they believe teachers favor. For the high-IQ group, the rank-order correlation between the qualities they would like to have themselves and the qualities they believe make for success in adult life is 0.81; for the high-creativity group, it is 0.10. The rank-order correlation between the qualities the high-IQ group would like to have and the qualities they believe teachers favor is 0.67; for the high-creativity group, it is −0.25. (See Table 5.)

In effect, the high-IQ adolescent wants the qualities he believes make for adult success and qualities similar to those he believes teachers like; the high-creative adolescent favors personal qualities which have no relationship to those he believes make for adult success and are in some ways the reverse of those he believes his teachers favor. The high-creativity adolescents are thus more "rebellious" or more "autonomous" than the high-IQ adolescents with respect to adult standards of success, depending on one's point of view, and the high-IQ adolescents are more "compliant" or more "realistic." In any case, it seems clear that there is a systematic relationship between types of cognitive functioning and types of career aspiration. The high-IQ and the high-creativity groups are characterized by differences in their career aspirations: differences all the more basic since the school achievement of the two groups as measured by standardized verbal and numerical subject-matter tests was the same.

## Discussion

Several existing conceptual formulations may be cited to account for the present data. Guilford's factors of convergent and divergent thinking are highly relevant.

> In tests of convergent thinking there is almost always one conclusion or answer that is regarded as unique, and thinking is to be channeled or controlled in the direction of that answer. . . . In divergent thinking, on the other hand, there is much searching about or going off in various directions. . . . Divergent thinking . . . is characterized as being less goal-bound. There is freedom to go off in different directions. . . . Rejecting the old solutions and striking out in some new direction is necessary, and the resourceful organism will probably succeed.

In this sense, the high-IQ adolescents tend to favor "convergent" modes of problem-solving, and the high-creativity adolescents tend to favor "divergent" modes of problem-solving, whether in the cognitive function represented by performance on the intelligence and creativity measures, or in the personal-social function represented by occupational and career choice.

### TABLE 5
#### Rank Order Correlations among Subsections of the
#### Outstanding Traits Test, for High-IQ and High-creative Students

| | Students | |
| Components of correlation | High-IQ (N = 28) | High-creative (N = 26) |
| --- | --- | --- |
| Personal traits believed "predictive of success" and "favored by teachers | 0.62 | 0.59 |
| Personal traits "preferred for oneself" and "believed predictive of adult success" | .81 | .10 |
| Personal traits "preferred for oneself" and "believed favored by teachers" | .67 | −.25 |

In the context of motivational theory, Maslow's formulations of defense and growth are similarly relevent to the present issues. He writes:[1]

> Every human being has both sets of forces within him. One set clings to safety and defensiveness out of fear, tending to regress, hanging on to the past . . . afraid to take chances, afraid to jeopardize what he already has, afraid of independence, freedom, separation. The other set of forces impels him forward toward wholeness of self and uniqueness of self, toward full functioning of all his capacities, toward confidence in the face of the external world at the same time that he can accept his deepest, real, unconscious Self . . . This basic dilemma or conflict between the defensive forces and the growth trends I conceive to be existential, imbedded in the deepest nature of the human being, now and forever into the future . . .
>
> Therefore we can consider the process of healthy growth to be a never-ending series of free choice situations, confronting each individual at every point throughout his life, in which he must choose between the delights of safety and growth, dependence and independence . . . Safety has both anxieties and delights; growth has both anxieties and delights.

In this context, the high-IQ adolescent may be seen as preferring the anxieties and delights of safety, the high-creativity adolescent the anxieties and delights of growth.

It seems that the essence of the performance of the high-creativity adolescents lay in their ability to produce new forms, to risk conjoining elements that are customarily thought of as independent and dissimilar, to "go off in new directions." The creative adolescent seemed to possess the need to free himself from the usual, to diverge from the customary behavior; he seemed to enjoy the risk and uncertainty of the unknown. In contrast, the high-IQ adolescent seemed to possess to a high degree the ability and the need to focus on the usual and to be "channeled and controlled" in the direction of the right answers, the socially accepted solution. He appeared to shy away from the risk and uncertainty of the unknown and to seek the safety and security of the already known.

Moreover, the differences between the high-IQ's and the high-creatives are not restricted to their intellectual performance or to their occupational choice. The data concerning both cognitively-oriented and socially-oriented behavior are of a piece; the characteristics that describe one describe the other. The high-IQ's tended to converge upon stereotyped meanings, to perceive personal success by conventional standards, to move toward the model provided by teachers, to seek out careers that conform to what is expected of them. The high-creatives tended to diverge from stereotyped meanings, to move away from the model provided by teachers, to seek out careers that do not conform to what is expected of them. It seems that the outstanding feature of all the data is the consistency of the cognitive (as defined by performance on intellective tasks) and the personal-social (as defined by occupational choice and career aspiration) aspects of behavior.

[1]Maslow, A. H. Defense and Growth, *Merrill-Palmer Quarterly*, 3:37-38, No. 1, Fall 1956.

Turning to the educational implications of the research projects reported in these sections and, indeed, of the great bulk of research dealing with creativity, there seems to be little doubt as to which of these two personal orientations is more acceptable in the majority of our social institutions. Guilford, who clearly perceived this bias, says that education "has emphasized abilities in the areas of convergent thinking and evaluation, often at the expense of development in the area of divergent thinking. We have attempted to teach students how to arrive at 'correct' answers that our civilization has taught us are correct. This is convergent thinking. . . . Outside the arts we have generally discouraged the development of divergent thinking abilities unintentionally but effectively."

Failure to distinguish between convergent and divergent talent in our schools may have serious consequences for the future of our society. Both kinds of talent are sufficiently important to warrant attention in educational theory and practice, and it is unwise to think of divergent fantasy as simply rebellious, rather than germinal, or unconventional career choice as invariably unrealistic rather than courageous.

It is hoped that a multidimensional approach to the study of giftedness along the lines attempted in these studies will bring about an increased appreciation of the motivational and cognitive variability of children.

*Walter B. Barbe*

# A Study of the Family Background of the Gifted

$O$f what influence has heredity and environment been in the development of the gifted child? Specifically, how does the family background of the gifted child differ from that of the child who is average in intelligence? Unfortunately, it is not possible to determine from such a study as this whether heredity or environment played a larger part in the development of the superior intellect of the subject. But by means of such a study, factors in the development of the gifted may be revealed. In a follow-up study of a group of gifted Negro subjects, Jenkins concluded:

> . . . desirable as it would be to know which of these factors (heredity or environment) has been most potent in the development of our subjects, the writer is unable to present any crucial data on the question. The data relative to heredity are meager, and to some extent, superficial; and while the picture of the cultural background is more complete, even here there are intangible factors which elude objective evaluation (1).

The 456 subjects in this study received an I.Q. of 120 or above on the 1917 Form of the Stanford-Binet. These data were taken from the records of the Psychological Clinic of the Cleveland Board of Education. The range of I.Q. is from 120 to 164, with a mean I.Q. of 130.2. The largest number of subjects were in the 125-129 range (37.3 per cent), while almost sixty-two per cent were between 125 and 135. This placed all of the subjects in about the upper ten per cent (2) of the population of the United States at the time they were tested. A large percentage of the group (forty-four per cent) were in the upper one per cent of the population in intellectual ability as measured by this particular test.

Reprinted from *Journal of Educational Psychology*, Vol. 47, No. 5, (May, 1956), pp. 302-309. By permission of the publisher.

All of the subjects were graduates of the Major Work Program of special classes for public school children in Cleveland, Ohio. The data for this study were obtained from information reported on a five-page printed questionnaire which was distributed to the graduates of the program over the last fifteen years. Of those who received the questionnaire, a return of seventy-seven per cent was received.

## Racial and Religious Background

It is difficult to determine the racial background of a group of subjects. The question arises just how far back the subject should trace his ancestry. With regard to the ancestry of gifted subjects, Hollingworth states: "So few data have been gathered to show the proportion of gifted children in relation to race, that it is perhaps scarcely worth while to discuss the topic except to say that we are ignorant of the facts. We have, however, a few studies of the proportion of gifted in samplings of the various races found at present in the United States (3, pp. 68-69)."

In a study by Witty (4), the "racial stock included a preponderance of English, Scotch, German, and Jewish ancestors." Ninety-six per cent of the parents were American-born. These findings are similar to those of Terman and Oden: "The reports on racial origin indicate that, in comparison with the general populations of the cities concerned, there is about a one hundred per cent excess of native-born parentage, a probable excess of Scottish parentage and a deficiency of Italian, Portuguese, Mexican, and Negro ancestry (5)."

The racial stock of the subjects in the present study is predominantly German, nearly half (47.6 per cent) of the subjects reported having some degree of German ancestry. The next highest group mentioned, twenty-three per cent, was English. The next most frequent were: Hungarian, 14.7 per cent; Russian, 14.4 per cent; and Polish, 10.2 per cent. Hardly any European country was not at least mentioned.

The fact that the population of Cleveland consists of such a diverse foreign element would tend to make the racial background of the subjects different from the subjects in both Terman and Witty's studies. According to the 1940 Census (6) of the City of Cleveland, the largest foreign-born element, about thirteen per cent, was Polish. Czech, Hungarian and Italian each made up about twelve per cent of the foreign-born population. German, Yugoslavian, English and Russian each represented about seven per cent.

Slightly more than two and one-half per cent of the total sample are Negroes. The percentage of Negroes has risen from less than one per cent in 1938 to nearly five per cent in 1952. According to the census, the per cent of Negroes in Cleveland has risen from eight per cent in 1930 to 9.5 per cent in 1940 (6).

About 11.3 per cent of the group was Catholic, 46.3 Protestant, and 38.8 per cent Jewish. Other groups make up the remaining 3.8 per cent. As Hollingworth reports of New York City (3), children of Catholic parents, many of whom are gifted, are commonly being educated in parochial schools. This explains the rather low percentage of Catholic subjects in Major Work classes. The Jewish group appears to be represented in far greater numbers than its proportional share. This is also true of the gifted in the public schools of New York where Hollingworth reports there is "a marked excess of Jewish parentage (3, p. 70)."

## Economic Background

An important phase of a study of the gifted which has not received adequate attention is their socio-economic background. This is difficult to determine and, when done in retrospect, is subject to many errors. The procedure followed in this study was to locate the economic tenth of the census tract in which the subject had lived while he was in public school (7). This gave an indication of the rent and property value of the neighborhood in which the gifted subject had been reared. The results of this phase of the study are presented in Table 1.

The economic tenth from which the greatest number of subjects came was the seventh, while the sixth and seventh economic tenths included more than fifty-eight per cent of the subjects. This indicates that the background of the majority of the subjects in the study may accurately be described as "upper middle-class."

**TABLE 1**

**The Economic Status of 456 Gifted Subjects**

| Economic Tenths | Per Cent |
|---|---|
| Highest | 1.1 |
| Ninth | 7.9 |
| Eighth | 10.3 |
| Seventh | 37.1 |
| Sixth | 21.3 |
| Fifth | 11.0 |
| Fourth | 5.0 |
| Third | 3.5 |
| Second | 2.2 |
| Lowest | 0.7 |

## Order of Birth and Size of Family

It has long been a popular belief that the gifted child is an only child, or, perhaps, has one sibling. In a study of 253 subjects (8), Goddard reported half as being first-born and three-fourths as being either first- or second-born. Of the first-born, forty-five (about eighteen per cent) were only children.

Hollingworth reported that the gifted child had few siblings. In a study by Cobb and Hollingworth, fifty-seven gifted children averaged less than one sibling each (3). With respect to the order of birth, they found that more than one-half of their subjects were first-born.

In 1940, Terman reported that "the parents of the gifted subjects had produced . . . an average of 3.09 (children) per family." He states that this rate would more than maintain the stock, but "it appears likely that the subjects themselves will not equal the fertility rate of their parents" (5, p. 18).

In the present study two questions were asked to determine the size of the family and the order of birth of the gifted child. About 21.8 per cent of the subjects had no siblings, while 42.6 per cent had only one. Almost twenty per cent had two siblings, and seven per cent three.

About twenty-two per cent of the subjects in this study are only children. This is not as large a number as that found by Cobb and Hollingworth, although their finding that "more than half were first-born" (3, p. 180) is substantiated by the fact that 52.5 per cent of the subjects in this study were first-born. About twenty-nine per cent are second-born, and only 9.3 third-born. The data indicate that in this group the gifted child was the first-born in a family of two children.

## Parent or Guardian of Gifted Subjects

Eighty-seven and a half per cent of the gifted subjects were reared by their own parents. The next largest group, 7.2 per cent, were reared by only their mothers. Two per cent were reared by their own mother and a stepfather, and 1.5 per cent by their own father and a stepmother. The father or foster parents each reared 0.9 per cent of the total number of subjects.

Witty (9), in studying one hundred gifted children in Kansas, found that most of their parents were American-born. This was not true of the subjects in this study. Slightly less than fifty per cent of the subjects had one or both parents who were foreign-born. This is partially due to the large foreign element in the population of Cleveland.[1] It emphasizes the contribution of the immigrant to the mentally superior groups of the country. Table 2 presents these data.

---

1. About 20 per cent of the population of Cleveland were foreign-born.

TABLE 2

**Percentage of Parents of Gifted Subjects**
**Who Were Born Outside the United States**

| | |
|---|---|
| Both parents U.S.-born | 51.3 |
| One parent foreign-born | 21.1 |
| Both parents foreign-born | 27.5 |

Even though more rigid government controls have been placed on immigration, no trend is noted which would indicate that fewer of the subjects have parents who are foreign-born.

## Education of Parents

Hollingworth states (3) that the educational level of the parents of gifted subjects is far above the average for their generation. "In the majority of the cases where the gifted child has been born since 1915, both parents are graduates of high school, and in far more cases than in the population at large both parents are college graduates (3, p. 180)." Since all of the subjects in the present study were born after 1915, it is interesting to compare Hollingworth's statements with the data obtained for this group.

Of the fathers of the subjects, 38.4 per cent had a grammar school education or less; 33.6 per cent had a high school education; 8.8 per cent trade or business school; and 19.2 per cent had some college. Of the mothers of the subjects, 32.5 per cent had a grammar school education or less; 42.2 per cent had a high school education; 12.3 per cent trade or business school; and 13.0 per cent had some college. The mothers of the gifted subjects on the average appeared to be slightly better educated than the fathers through the high school and business school levels. However, there were more fathers than mothers who attended college.

## Marital Status of Parents

Terman reported (5) that until 1922, 5.2 per cent of the parents of his gifted group had been divorced and 1.9 per cent were separated. By 1940, the percentage of divorced and separated parents had risen to 13.9.

The data in the present study are not exactly comparable to the results of Terman's study. The information obtained in this study deals with the marital status of the parents while the subject was in public school. It is perhaps comparable to Terman's 1922 data but is definitely not comparable to his 1940 data.

Eighty-eight per cent of the parents of the subjects were living together while the subject was in public school. About 6.3 per cent were either divorced or separated. This is only slightly higher than the report for Terman's 1922 group and is certainly lower than that of the general population. The remaining five per cent consists of cases where one or both of the parents were deceased.

## Occupational Level of Parents of Gifted Subjects

The occupations of the parents were listed according to the U.S. census classification. The *Dictionary of Occupational Titles* (10) was used to classify the occupations into seven distinct groups: professional and managerial; clerical and sales; service; agriculture, fishery, forestry, etc.; skilled; semi-skilled; and unskilled. The subjects were asked the title and description of the father's occupation. It was possible to classify all but a few of the occupations listed. Where descriptions were not given and two classifications were possible, the data were omitted. Classifications of the parent's occupation were made for four hundred and thirty-seven subjects. Three of the remaining nineteen were on government pensions, while the rest gave no response to the question at all. The data are presented in Table 3.

**TABLE 3**

**Occupational Level of Parents of Gifted Subjects**

|  | Per Cent |
|---|---|
| Professional and managerial | 40.3 |
| Clerical and sales | 22.4 |
| Service | 3.7 |
| Agriculture, fishery, forestry, etc. | 0.2 |
| Skilled | 21.5 |
| Semi-skilled | 8.2 |
| Unskilled | 3.7 |

Hollingworth reports (3) that more than fifty per cent of the children testing above 140 I.Q. have fathers who are professional men or proprietors. The I.Q.'s of the subjects in the present study are not this high, which may partly explain why only about forty per cent of the parents fall into the professional and managerial group. Hollingworth also states (3) that half of the remaining fathers are in semi-professional and clerical occupations. This corresponds to the clerical and sales group of the U.S. Census Bureau, and the data for this group agree with the data in Hollingworth's study.

The fact that over thirty per cent of the parents are in the laboring class, and about forty per cent of these are semi-skilled or unskilled, is noteworthy. It indicates that while the majority of gifted children do come from parents of higher occupational status, the laboring class also contributes a sizeable number.

## Summary

In this study data were presented concerning the composition of the group being studied and their family background.

1. The range in I.Q. of the four hundred and fifty-six subjects was from 120 to 164 with a mean I.Q. of 130.2. Almost sixty-two per cent of the group were within the 125-135 range.

2. Slightly less than fifty-two per cent of the subjects are females; slightly more than forty-eight per cent are males.

3. Of the total samples, only 2.6 per cent are Negroes.

4. About thirty-nine per cent of the subjects are Jewish. The Jewish group is represented in far greater numbers than the size of this group in the total population would lead one to expect.

5. The economic tenth of the census tract in which the subjects lived while in public schools was most frequently the sixth and seventh. This would characterize the gifted child as being upper middle-class.

6. The gifted child appears to be either an only child or firstborn in a family of two.

7. Eighty-seven and one-half per cent of the gifted subjects were reared by their own parents.

8. Almost fifty per cent of the subjects had one or both parents who were foreign-born. These data indicate that the group studied is quite unlike other studies of gifted groups. Previously, the gifted child was found to have American parentage. The high percentage of foreign-born in Cleveland (approximately twenty per cent) partially explains these data.

9. The education of the mothers of gifted subjects is slightly higher than that of the fathers, even though more of the fathers went to college.

10. Forty per cent of the parents were in the professional and managerial group, 22.5 per cent in the clerical and sales, and thirty per cent in the laboring class.

The subjects in this study come from about average backgrounds with respect to occupational level, educational level and marital adjustment of their parents. Economically the majority of them come from an upper middle-class group.

## References

1. Martin David Jenkins, "A Socio-Psychological Study of Negro Children of Superior Intelligence." Unpublished Doctoral Dissertation. Graduate School, Northwestern University, Evanston, Illinois, p. 53, June, 1935.

2. Merle R. Sumption, *Three Hundred Gifted Children,* p. 6. Yonkers-on-Hudson, New York: World Book Co., 1941.

3. Leta A. Hollingworth, *Gifted Children.* New York: The Macmillan Co. 1926.

4. Paul A. Witty, "A Study of One Hundred Gifted Children." *Bulletin of Education,* University of Kansas, 2:8, February, 1930.

5. Lewis M. Terman and Melita H. Oden, *The Gifted Child Grows Up.* Stanford, California: Stanford University Press, 1947.

6. U. S. Department of Commerce, Bureau of the Census, Sixteenth Census of the United States, 1940, *Population,* 11:712, Part 5, Washington, D. C.: U. S. Government Printing Office, 1943.

7. Howard Whipple Green, *Census Tract Street Index for Cuyahoga County,* fifth edition. Cleveland Health Council, 1951.

8. Henry H. Goddard, *School Training of Gifted Children,* p. 129. Yonkers-on-Hudson, New York: World Book Co., 1928.

9. Paul A. Witty, "A Genetic Study of Fifty Gifted Children," In *Intelligence: Its Nature and Nurture.* Thirty-Ninth Yearbook, Part II, National Society for the Study of Education. Chicago: University of Chicago Press, 1940.

10. Job Analysis and Information Section, Division of Standards and Research, United States Department of Labor, *Dictionary of Occupational Titles, Part I,* second edition. Washington, D. C.: United States Government Printing Office, 1949.

*Anne Roe*

# A Psychologist Examines 64 Eminent Scientists

$W$hat elements enter into the making of a scientist? Are there special qualities of personality, mind, intelligence, background or upbringing that mark a person for this calling? Besides the natural interest in these questions, they have a practical importance, because the recruitment of qualified young people into science is a growing problem in our society. Where and how shall we find them?

During the past five years I have been making a study of the attributes of a group of scientists and the reasons why they chose this field of work. The most eminent scientists in the U.S. were selected as subjects, since they are most likely to exemplify the special qualities, if any, that are associated with success in research science. They were selected by panels of experts in each field of science. The study finally settled on a group of 64 eminent men who agreed to participate—20 biologists, 22 physicists and 22 social scientists (psychologists and anthropologists). A high percentage of them are members of the National Academy of Sciences or the American Philosophical Society or both, and among them they have received a staggering number of honorary degrees, prizes and other awards.

Each of the 64 individuals was then examined exhaustively by long personal interviews and tests: his life history, family background, professional and recreational interests, intelligence, achievements, personality, ways of thinking—any information that might have a bearing on the subject's choice of his vocation and his success in it. Each was given an intelligence test and was examined by two of the modern techniques for the study of personality: the Rorschach and the Thematic Apperception Test (TAT). The Rorschach, popularly known as the inkblot test, gives information about such things as the way the subject deals with problems, his manner of approach to them, the extent and efficiency of his use of rational controls, his inner preoccupations, his responsiveness to outside stimuli. The TAT gives information about attitudes toward family and society and self, about expectations and needs and desires, and something about the development of these.

From *Scientific American,* Vol. 187, No. 5 (November, 1952), pp. 21-25. Reprinted with permission. Copyright   1951, 1952 by Scientific American Inc. All rights reserved.

My study was financed during the first four years by grants from the National Institute of Mental Health and is being continued this year under a Guggenheim Fellowship. It has developed a great deal of material, much of which has been published in technical detail in special journals. In this brief article it is possible only to recapitulate the high points.

There is no such thing, of course, as a "typical" scientist. Eminent scientists differ greatly as individuals, and there are well-marked group differences between the biologists and the physicists, and between the natural scientists and the social scientists. Certain common patterns do appear, however, in the group as a whole, and the most convenient way to summarize these generalizations is to try to draw a picture of what might be called the "average" eminent scientist.

He was the first-born child of a middle-class family, the son of a professional man. He is likely to have been a sickly child or have lost a parent at an early age. He has a very high I.Q. and in boyhood began to do a great deal of reading. He tended to feel lonely and "different" and to be shy and aloof from his classmates. He had only a moderate interest in girls and did not begin dating them until college. He married late (at 27), has two children and finds security in family life; his marriage is more stable than the average. Not until his junior or senior year in college did he decide on his vocation as a scientist. What decided him (almost invariably) was a college project in which he had occasion to do some independent research—to find out things for himself. Once he discovered the pleasures of this kind of work, he never turned back. He is completely satisfied with his chosen vocation. (Only one of the 64 eminent scientists—a Nobel prize winner—says he would have preferred to do sometling else: he wanted to be a farmer, but could not make a living at it.) He works hard and devotedly in his laboratory, often seven days a week. He says his work is his life, and he has few recreations, those being restricted to fishing, sailing, walking or some other individualistic activity. The movies bore him. He avoids social affairs and political activity, and religion plays no part in his life or thinking. Better than any other interest or activity, scientific research seems to meet the inner need of his nature.

This generalized picture represents only majority traits; there are, of course, many exceptions to it, not only in individual cases but by groups; the social scientists, for instance, tend to be by no means shy but highly

| Field | Age at Time of Study | | Average Age at Time of Receiving College Degrees | |
|---|---|---|---|---|
| | Average | Range | B.A. | Ph.D., Sc.D., M.D. |
| Biologists | 51.2 | 38-58 | 21.8 | 26.0 |
| Physical scientists | 44.7 | 31-56 | 20.9 | 24.6 |
| Social scientists | 47.7 | 35-60 | 21.8 | 26.8 |

Average age of the subjects at the time of the study and at the time they received their degrees is given in this table. The upper age limit was set at 60; the lower limit was determined by the eminence of the subjects.

gregarious and social. Let us now consider the differences between groups. I have seperated the physicists into the theorists (12) and the experimentalists (10), because these two groups differ sharply. The biologists (physiologists, botanists, geneticists, biochemists and so on) are sufficiently alike to be grouped together, and so are the social scientists.

No standardized intelligence test was sufficiently difficult for these eminent scientists; hence a special test was constructed by the Educational Testing Service. To provide ratings on particular intellectual factors, the test was divided into three parts: verbal (79 items), spatial (24 items) and mathematical (39). (The mathematical test used was not difficult enough for the physicists, and several of them did not take it.)

While the group as a whole is characterized by very high average intelligence, as would be expected, the range is wide *(see table on page 123)*. Among the biologists, the geneticists and biochemists do relatively better on the nonverbal tests than on the verbal, and the other biologists tend to do relatively better on the verbal. Among the physicists there is some tendency for theorists to do relatively better on the verbal and for the experimentalists to do relatively better on the spatial test. Among the social scientists the experimental psychologists do relatively better on the spatial or mathematical than on the verbal test, and the reverse is true of the other psychologists and anthropologists.

On the TAT the social scientists tended to give much longer stories than the other groups did—verbal fluency is characteristic of them. The biologists were inclined to be much more factual, less interested in feelings and, in general, unwilling to commit themselves. This was true to a lesser extent of the physical scientists. The biologists and physical scientists manifested a quite remarkable independence of parental relations and were without guilt feelings about it, while the social scientists showed many

| Field | Visual | Verbal | Imageless | Totals |
|---|---|---|---|---|
| Biologists | 10 | 4 | 3 | 17 |
| Physicists | 10 | 4 | 4 | 18 |
| Psychologists and anthropologists | 2 | 11 | 6 | 19 |
| Totals | 22 | 19 | 13 | 54 |

Imagery of the scientists was correlated with specialty. The natural scientists were strong in visual imagery; the social scientists in verbal.

| Profession of Father | Visual | Verbal | Imageless | Totals |
|---|---|---|---|---|
| Verbal | 5 | 10 | 3 | 18 |
| Non-verbal | 8 | 2 | 2 | 12 |
| Totals | 13 | 12 | 5 | 30 |

Imagery of the father's Profession was strongly influential. The numbers on the right side of this table refer to the imagery of the sons.

dependent attitudes, much rebelliousness and considerable helplessness, along with intense concern over interpersonal relations generally. The biologists were the least aggressive (but rather stubborn) and the social scientists the most aggressive. The most striking thing about the TAT results for the total group, however, is the rarity of any indication of the drive for achievement that all of these subjects have actually shown in their lives.

On the Rorschach the social scientists show themselves to be enormously productive and intensely concerned with human beings; the biologists are deeply concerned with form, and rely strongly upon a non-emotional approach to problems; the physicists show a good deal of free anxiety and concern with space and inanimate motion. Again the social scientists, particularly the anthropologists, are the most freely aggressive.

Early in the course of the work it became apparent that there were some differences in habits of thinking, and a special inquiry was instituted along these lines. The data are unsatisfactory from many standpoints—there are no objective tests for such material, and I had to ask many leading questions in order to convey any idea of what I was after. Nevertheless rather definite and meaningful patterns did appear. The biologists and the experimental physicists tend strongly to dependence upon visual imagery in their thinking—images of concrete objects or elaborate diagrams or the like. The theoretical physicists and social scientists tend to verbalization in their thinking—a kind of talking to themselves. All groups report a considerable amount of imageless thinking, particularly at crucial points. Men whose fathers followed talkative occupations (law, ministry, teaching) are more likely to think in words.

The life histories of these 64 men show some general similarities, and there are patterns characterizing some of the subgroups. Geographical factors seem not to be particularly significant, except that only a few came from the South. The economic level was varied, ranging from very poor to well-to-do; among the anthropologists and the theoretical physicists a somewhat higher percentage came from well-to-do homes.

In several respects the scientists' backgrounds differ very much from the population at large. There are no Catholics among this group of eminent scientists; five come from Jewish homes and the rest had Protestant backgrounds. Only three of the 64 now have a serious interest in any church; only a few even maintain church memberships.

Another striking fact is that 53 percent of the scientists were the sons of professional men; not one was the son of an unskilled laborer and only two were sons of skilled workmen. Why do more than half of our leading scientists come from the families of professional men? It seems to me most probable, from more knowledge of the family situations of these men than I can summarize here, that the operative factor is the value placed by these families and their associates on learning—learning for its own sake. Most of the scientists developed intellectual interests at an early age.

Another remarkable finding is how many of them were their parents' first children. This proportion is higher than chance expectancy in all of the

| | | Verbal Test | | Spatial Test | | Mathematical Test | |
|---|---|---|---|---|---|---|---|
| | Number | Average | Range | Average | Range | Average | Range |
| Biologists | 19 | 56.6 | 28-73 | 9.4 | 3-20 | 6.8 | 6-27 |
| Experimental physicists | 7 | 46.6 | 8-71 | 11.7 | 3-22 | | |
| Theoretical physicists | 11 | 64.2 | 52-75 | 13.8 | 5-19 | | |
| Psychologists | 14 | 57.7 | 23-73 | 11.3 | 5-19 | 15.6 | 8-27 |
| Anthropologists | 8 | 61.1 | 43-72 | 8.2 | 3-15 | 9.2 | 4-13 |
| Total | 59 | 57.7 | 8-75 | 10.9 | 3-22 | 15.9 | 4-27 |
| Approximate IQ equivalents | | 163 | 121-177 | 140 | 123-164 | 160 | 128-194 |

Intelligence test results revealed minor variations among the specialties of the scientists. The theoretical physicists did better in the verbal test; the experimental physicists rated lowest. Both theoretical and experimental physicists did not take the mathematical test because it was not sufficiently difficult. Two anthropologists who took the verbal test did not take the other tests on the ground that they could not do them.

| Professions | Biologists 9 | Experimental physicists 5 | Theoretical physicists 10 | Psychologists 7 | Anthropologists 3 | Totals 34 |
|---|---|---|---|---|---|---|
| Research Science | 0 | 1 | 0 | 0 | 0 | 1 |
| Physician | 0 | 2 | 1 | 2 | 0 | 5 |
| Lawyer | 0 | 0 | 1 | 1 | 3 | 5 |
| Engineer | 0 | 0 | 3 | 2 | 0 | 5 |
| Clergyman | 2 | 0 | 1 | 0 | 0 | 3 |
| Editor | 2 | 0 | 0 | 0 | 0 | 2 |
| College teacher | 4 | 0 | 3 | 2 | 0 | 9 |
| School teacher | 0 | 2 | 0 | 0 | 0 | 2 |
| School superintendent | 1 | 0 | 0 | 0 | 0 | 1 |
| Pharmacist | 0 | 0 | 1 | 0 | 0 | 1 |
| | | | | | | |
| Business | 8 | 1 | 2 | 4 | 5 | 20 |
| Own business | 4 | 0 | 2 | 2 | 4 | 12 |
| Clerk, agent, salesman | 4 | 1 | 0 | 2 | 1 | 8 |
| | | | | | | |
| Farmer | 2 | 4 | 0 | 2 | 0 | 8 |
| Skilled Labor | 1 | 0 | 0 | 1 | 0 | 2 |
| Totals | 20 | 10 | 12 | 14 | 8 | 64 |
| Per cent professional | 45 | 50 | 84 | 50 | 38 | 53 |

Occupations of the fathers of the 64 eminent scientists showed a strong bias in favor of the professions. This was especially true of the 12 theoretical physicists, 10 of whose fathers had been professional. The anthropologists were an exception: five out of eight came from business backgrounds. Four of the 10 experimental physicists were the sons of farmers. None of the scientists were the sons of unskilled laborers.

subgroups. Thirty-nine were first born; of the rest five were eldest sons and two who were second born were effectively the eldest because of the early death of the first child. For most of the others there is a considerable difference in age between the subject and the next older brother (averaging five years). It seems probable that all this may point to the most important single factor in the making of a scientist—the need and ability to develop personal  independence to a high degree. The independence factor is emphasized by many other findings: the subject's preference for teachers who let them alone, their attitudes toward religion, their attitudes toward personal relations, their satisfaction in a career in which, for the most part, they follow their own interests without direction or interference. It is possible that oldest sons in our culture have a greater amount of independence or more indulgence in the pursuit of their own interests than other children have. On the other hand, there is some psychological evidence that first-born tend to be more dependent, on the average, than other children, and a good case could be made out for a hypothesis that reaction to this overdependence produced the scientists' strong drive to independence.

The early extracurricular interests of these men were varied, but here, too, there are some general patterns. More of the physicists than of the other groups showed early interests directly related to their later occupations, but this seems quite clearly to be due to the common small-boy preoccupation in  this country with physical gadgets—radio, Meccano sets and so on. The theoretical physicists were omnivorous readers, the experimentalists much less so. Among the social scientists many went through a stage of considering or even working toward a literary career. Half of the biologists showed some early interest in natural history, but for only five was it of an intense and serious sort, involving keeping field records of birds and flowers, and so on. Many of the biologists did not know during childhood of the possibility of a career in biology. This was even more true of the psychologists and anthropologists, since there are almost no boyhood activities related to professional social science.

It is of considerable interest that over half of these men did not decide upon their vocations until they were juniors or seniors in college. More important, perhaps, than when they decided, is why they decided. It certainly was not just a matter of always following an early bent. From fiddling with gadgets to becoming a physicist may be no great leap, but the attractions of theoretical physics are not so obvious or well known, nor are those of the social sciences or advanced biology. In the stories of the social scientists and of the biologists it becomes clear that the most important factor in the final decision to become a scientist is the discovery of the joys of research. In physics the discovery may come so gradually as not to be noticed as such, but in the other sciences it often came as a revelation of unique moment, and many of these men know just when and how they found it out. A couple of quotations will illustrate this:

"I had no course in biology until my senior year in college. It was a small college and the teacher was about the first on the faculty with a Ph.D. It was about my first contact with the idea that not everything was known, my first contact with research. In that course I think my final decision was really taken. It was mainly that I wanted to do something in the way of research though I didn't know just what, but working out something new."

"One of the professors took a group of us and thought if we wanted to learn about things, the way to do it was to do research. My senior year I carried through some research. That really sent me, that was the thing that trapped me. After that there was no getting out."

That research experience is so often decisive is a fact of very considerable importance for educational practice. The discovery of the possibility of finding things out for oneself usually came through experience in school with a teacher who put the students pretty much on their own.

There are other things in the general process of growing up that may have influenced the choice of career in subtle ways. One fourth of the biologists lost a parent by death or divorce at an early age. This may have tended to shove them to greater independence. Among the theoretical physicists there was a high incidence of serious illness or physical handicaps during childhood, which certainly contributed to the feelings of isolation characteristic of them. Among the social scientists there is an unusually intense concern with personal relationships, which often goes back to family conflicts during clildhood. A relatively large proportion of them seem to have come from homes in which the mother was dominant and the father inadequate in some way. The divorce rate among tle social scientists in this study was remarkably high—41 per cent.

Whereas the characteristic pattern among the biologists and physicists is that of the shy, lonely, over-intellectualized boy, among the social scientists the characteristic picture is very different. They got into social activity and intensive and extensive dating at an early age. They were often presidents of their classes, editors of yearbooks and literary magazines, frequently big shots in college. This contrast between the natural and social scientists was still evident after they grew up. It is true only in general, of course; even among the theoretical physicists there are some ardent party-goers.

The one thing that all of these 64 scientists have in common is their driving absorption in their work. They have worked long hours for many years, frequently with no vacations to speak of, because they would rather be doing their work than anything else.

*James J. Gallagher*

# Characteristics of Gifted Children: A Research Summary

*T*here is, naturally, an intimate connection between definition and characteristics; consequently, changes in the definition result in changes in the observed characteristics. In simpler days when a high IQ score was the sole criterion of high ability and was considered mainly a genetic property, then the characteristics of the gifted were based on how that sample appeared to compare with the average.

In line with the more complex views of human potential outlined in the previous chapter, this section will be divided into three identifiable subgroups—high IQ, high creative, and culturally disadvantaged talented. A further separate chapter on gifted underachievers follows as well.

## High IQ Students—
## The Terman Research

One of the most important sources of reliable information regarding the characteristics of gifted children, of the high IQ type, is the 40-year longitudinal study by Terman and his associates (1925, 1947, 1959).

Most of the investigations in child psychology, sociology, and education have been *cross-sectional,* that is a study of children at one given point in time. More useful and important information is often obtained from *longitudinal* studies in which the same individuals are studied over a long period of time. This longitudinal investigation of gifted children was undertaken by Lewis Terman and his associates in 1921. The goals of their research were to study the development of intellectually superior children from childhood into adulthood and to draw a composite picture of the characteristics of these children and chart their later achievements in life that could be related to childhood performance.

Gallagher, James J. *Research Summary on Gifted Child Education.* Department of Program Development for Gifted Children, Office of the Superintendent of Public Instruction, Illinois, 1966, pp. 25-44.

Approximately 1500 children whose Stanford-Binet IQ score was 140 and over (about the top 1 percent of the population) were studied. Many of these youngsters were studied in 1921 and re-examined in 1928, 1940, and in the middle 1950's. Thus, a large amount of information is available on these same individuals over a span of almost 40 years.

Let us consider first the adjustment these gifted children were making in school. Educational histories, teacher ratings, and achievement test scores were obtained for over 600 of these gifted children and for a comparison sample of more than 500 control children. These "control" children were selected on a basis of being those closest to the chronological age expected of that particular grade level, thus representing a sample of "typical" children.

## Teacher Ratings

Table VIII shows the five subject areas in which teachers rated the gifted children to have the greatest advantage over the control children and the five subject areas in which they had the least advantage over the control children. The teachers rated the gifted children markedly superior in the area of debating, U. S. history, composition, literature and ancient history. This suggests that the gifted children do their most superior work, relatively speaking, in subjects requiring *abstract thought.*

The areas which showed the least difference between gifted and control samples were penmanship, sports, and manual training, suggesting that the areas where the least differences existed were those in which motor ability or some special talent is a sizeable factor. Even in these areas the gifted children were still the equal of the control sample. This finding, of course, did not support the general notion that gifted children are somewhat inferior to other children in athletics or physical skills.

Among other things discovered on the basis of the Terman investigation were the following:

> 1. Only 1 percent of the gifted were reported by the parents as having positive dislike for school. Four percent reported only a mild attraction to school. The positive feeling for school was "very strong" for 54 percent of the boys and 70 percent of the girls.
> 2. Less than half as many gifted as control children displayed an undesirable attitude towards school.
> 3. Teachers' ratings of school work showed gifted children, as a rule, doing work of a superior quality in the grade where they were located.
> 4. Two and a half times as many gifted as control children were rated as very even or consistent in mental abilities, but twice as many of the gifted group were rated as very uneven, with the girls rated as less uneven than the boys.

TABLE VIII

**School Subjects Showing Greatest and Least
Differences Between Gifted and Control Children
by Teacher Rating**

**(after Terman et. al., 1925)**

| *School Subjects Showing Greatest Differences in Favor of Gifted* | *Subjects Showing Least Difference Between Gifted and Control* |
|---|---|
| 1. Debating or Speaking | 25. Penmanship |
| 2. U.S. History | 26. Games and Sports |
| 3. Composition | 27. Manual Training |
| 4. Literature | 28. Painting |
| 5. Ancient History | 29. Shop Work |

## Achievement tests

On the Stanford Achievement Tests administered to 565 of these gifted children, their performance was found to be consistently very superior to that of their age group. Terman and his associates developed what they called a Subject Quotient which was calculated by dividing a child's age score on a test of subject matter by his chronological age. Thus, if a child obtained an age score in reading of 10 years and his actual age was eight years, his Subject Quotient for reading was $10/8 \times 100 = 125$. The mean or average of all these quotients of gifted boys and girls for various subjects ranged from 135 to 148, none of them, however, exceeding the average IQ score for this group of 152. The children showed the greatest superiority in language usage with reading, spelling, and arithmetic following in that order. There is very little evidence in this study that these gifted children had any real difficulty in maintaining adequate performance for their classroom level in the type of subject matter being measured by these achievement tests.

From this result it will be seen that the problem of these gifted children does not rest in the academic area. It is rather a problem for the teacher to provide the necessary enrichment and challenge to keep up with their rapidly expanding abilities. The one reservation that might be placed on Terman's data was that the major method used in obtaining subjects (teacher ratings) was such that many youngsters with high ability who showed, however, poor motivation or inadequate cultural background might not have been identified or included in this group.

## Follow-up

What happened to these children when they grew up? Good school performance is not meaningful unless it predicts good life performance. Table

IX shows some individual examples of life success in the Terman group in 1941. These vignettes are only a few of the many possible examples that could be taken. The reader should also be aware of the fact that the majority of this group were in their early or middle thirties at the time of this study and not yet at their peak of professional achievement.

Although the women in the study did not achieve the same level of performance as that of the men, this may be due to the multiple responsibilities they have had in our society. Despite the dual responsibilities as wives and homemakers, a number of them have made important contributions. Two of them were nationally known writers, and another was both the author of a successful Broadway play and a noted actress. In the science fields, there was a bacteriologist in a leading medical school and a metallurgist in a responsible research position, plus a number of physicians, missionaries, concert pianists, etc.

Another follow-up study on the same Terman group over ten years later (Terman and Oden, 1959) indicated even further achievement beyond that indicated in the 1947 publication. The investigators commented that "there are men in nearly every field" who have won national prominence and 8 or 10 who have achieved international reputation. Among the tangible indications of achievement we find 70 of the men in the study listed in *American Men of Science* and 31 of the men listed in *Who's Who in America.*

Another tangible indication of intellectual productivity is the amount and quality of the writing done by this group. They have compiled a total of 2,000 scientific and technical papers and articles and over 60 books and monographs in scientific fields. Two hundred and thirty patents have been

**TABLE IX**

**Sample Life Achievement of Terman's Gifted Children**

**(after Terman and Oden, 1947)**

| Job Area | Accomplishment |
|---|---|
| Science | Physicist-Director of a great laboratory devoted to applications of atomic energy. |
| | Physiologist-Codirector on the most important investigation on the physiological and psychological effects of semi-starvation. |
| | Director of psychological research organization. Active in policy level of American Psychological Association. |
| Medicine | Chief of psychiatric therapy of large combat area—World War II; official psychiatrist at trial of Nazi war criminals. |
| | Widely known plastic surgeon. |
| | Director of public health department in leading medical school. |
| Government | State Department Chief of one of the critical areas in the Western Hemisphere. |
| | One of the youngest brigadier generals in the Army. |
| Arts | Noted motion picture director. |
| | Two fiction writers of national reputation. |
| | Noted lawyer who has mastered 15 languages as a hobby. |

awarded to the group, and there have been published 33 novels, 375 short stories and plays, and innumerable radio, television and movie scripts. This study has put an end in professional circles to the myths about gifted (high IQ) children not achieving in adulthood.

## Genetic influence

The great emphasis currently placed on the important role played by environment in the development of intellectual ability should not lead the reader to assume that heredity is no longer considered to have an important role in the development of those abilities. Nichols (1965) used as a basic sample 596,241 juniors who took the National Merit Scholarship Qualifying Tests. From this large sample, 1507 sets of twins were identified. These were divided into monozygotic and dizygotic twins on the basis of a questionnaire on physical similarity plus blood samples. Those sets of twins who could not be clearly classified by the index were omitted from the study.

The performances of these two groups were then compared on the National Merit Scholarship Tests consisting of five subtests: English, Mathematics, Social Studies, Natural Science and Word Usage. A composite score was obtained on the performance of these five tests. In all measures, for both male and female, the correlation between monozygotic twins was higher than dizygotic and this difference reached a statistical significance in all but one test—English Usage score for the males.

In order to account for a possible bias of the twins having differential experiences, the author determined by questionnaire which sets of twins had experienced periods of separation or specific illnesses. All sets of twins who reported such phenomena were then removed from the sample, and comparisons were made again. The correlations for both monozygotic and dizygotic twins increased with the elimination of these sets of twins, but the relative position remained the same, with the monozygotic twins always showing higher correlations.

Nichols feels that the correlations obtained are consistent with Burt's estimate (1958) that 77 percent of the observed variance in intelligence is attributable to heredity.

## Physical Abilities

Since Terman's longitudinal studies, it has been generally accepted that gifted students will show superiority to the average child in almost any measurable dimension, whether physical development or social or emotional adjustment. But is this superiority due to superior intellect or to the generally superior environment these gifted (high IQ) samples are drawn from?

Laycock and Caylor (1964) compared a sample of 81 gifted intermediate grade students (Binet IQ 120+ or CTMM 130+) with a less gifted sibling (at least 20 IQ points below gifted sibling) on a broad spectrum of physical and anthropometric measures. They found no differences on any of the physical measures between these matched pairs and concluded that when environmental differences are controlled, the gifted child does not reveal superiority in the physical dimension. The value of this study was somewhat diminished by an unaccountable failure to control for sex of sibling. There was also some overlap in IQ in the two groups because of the particular method of choosing the "non-gifted" siblings. Some of the "less gifted" (20 points below sibling) had IQ scores above some of the "gifted." Nevertheless, this study intimates that when various non-intellectual factors are controlled, the differences between gifted and average samples are not as impressive as previously held.

## Learning Ability

The very nature of their intellectual status makes it inevitable that gifted (high IQ) students learn more effectively than average students. The question raised in this section is whether their learning skills show a particular pattern of the use of specific strategies which would give some clues as to how they may enhance their superior status.

Klausmeier and his associates have done a series of studies comparing the learning characteristics of 40 gifted fifth grade boys and girls (WISC IQ 120+) with similar groups of average (WISC IQ 90-110) and slow students (WISC IQ 56-81) of the same life age. The slow group excluded glandular and neurological cases.

In one comparison, Feldhusen and Klausmeier (1962) found a negative relationship between IQ and scores on the children's manifest anxiety scale in both boys and girls; that is, the higher the IQ, the lower was the anxiety. The authors felt that superior mental ability may make it possible for a child to assess his environment and deal with it more effectively. The reader should remember that there were no controls for possible environmental factors that might influence these results. A substantial income, for instance, may dampen anxiety feelings also and would more likely be found in the gifted than the slow families.

The behavior of the same groups of children was studied during the process of solving arithmetic problems. A series of 29 problems, requesting the number of coins and bills needed to reach a particular sum, was selected by the experimenters (Klausmeier and Loughlin, 1961) and graded for difficulty. Each child received only one problem at their pretest level of performance. The time spent in solving the problems was not significantly different for any of the groups.

The gifted, average, and slow groups were compared on the degree to which they manipulated the figures and coins, withdrew from the situation, offered incorrect solutions, verified their results and showed a logical approach. The gifted group performed significantly better than the average group in persistence, in not offering incorrect solutions, in verifying their results and using a more logical approach. Thus, high ability students showed a performance style that was likely to enhance these already large differences between them and average or slow students.

However, a third study (Klausmeier and Check, 1962) in which retention and transfer was studied found little differences between the ability groups. Each of the youngsters was given an arithmetic problem at his level of difficulty. Solutions to the problems were reached in 15 minutes, with cues or help being given by the examiner as needed at regular intervals. After the solution was reached, five minutes of recorded stories and songs were introduced; then the original problem was presented to 60 of the subjects (retention). A transfer problem, based on the same principle, was given to the other 60. Seven weeks later, the original problem was given to the same retention group and a new transfer problem of the same level of difficulty was given to the transfer group. On these tasks, no differences between ability groups were obtained on either the retention or transfer tasks, although the retention group did significantly better than the transfer. The authors believed the lack of differences lay in the correct selection of level of difficulty for the problem.

Carrier, Malpass, and Borton (1961) compared the learning performance of 118 children from 11 to 14 years of age who were divided into three IQ categories—Bright (WISC IQ 120-150), Normal (WISC IQ 90-110), and Educable Mentally Handicapped (WISC IQ 50-80). These subjects were matched on age and sex and grouped into triads for assignment of tasks. A series of tasks that ranged from the conceptual to the manipulative were presented to the subjects in an air-conditioned mobile laboratory which also allowed for the collection of other data not usually collected in such experiments. Four measures of emotional tension: electrical skin resistance, vasodilation, respiration, and gross body movements were tallied.

The investigators expected to find a negative relation between intelligence and emotional tension. In other words, the more intelligence the less anxiety would be produced. They did find the cognitive tasks more tension arousing than the manipulative tasks but the relationships between emotional tension and learning performance were low.

In other words, the crucial variable in this situation was not that the student becomes anxious in a learning situation, but what he did about such anxiety. Some students will grasp the nettle, or the difficult problem, and through solution of the problem will reduce their anxiety. Other students will attempt to reduce their anxiety by avoiding or withdrawing from the problem. These different reactions to the same internal stimuli have vastly different implications for learning. These authors also commented on the need for a variety of measures for such characteristics of learning, emotion and motivation, since the relationship between measures attempting to get at these broad classes of concepts were not too high.

The learning ability of 13 gifted, 24 average and 36 retarded junior high students from a metropolitan area was tested by Jensen (1963). The groups were matched on CA but differed in ethnic origin and sex distribution, and had mean IQ's of 142, 103, and 66 respectively. The subjects were presented a series of colored geometric forms on a screen and asked to predict which would be the next form that would appear. They were given the reinforcement of a colored light when correct. Significant differences were obtained among all three groups with the gifted being most superior.

The ability to predict such answers rests in the mental capacity to hold a hypothesis regarding the system or pattern that is being followed by the experimenter while examining stimuli. This may be one type of specific description of what is functionally meant by superior intelligence.

Another approach to the problem is to look for qualitative patterns that result from performance on standard psychometric intruments. Gallagher and Lucito (1960) have pointed out that when the *relative* intellectual strengths and weaknesses of gifted, average, and mentally retarded children are compared on tests of intelligence, there are sizable differences in patterns of intellect among the three groups. They found that the gifted children had their strongest area of success on tasks relating to a factor of *Verbal Comprehension* which encompasses meaningful manipulation of verbal symbols. The mentally retarded groups were relatively strongest, on a factor of *Perceptual Organization* composed of nonverbal tasks. The average group did not show a characteristic pattern related to known factors of the tests.

A similar finding was obtained by Thompson and Finley (1962). Comparing the WISC profiles of 400 gifted and 309 mentally retarded children (CA 10), they found the gifted highest in tests of verbal comprehension while the retarded were relatively strongest in tests of perceptual organization. These results would emphasize a difference in mental development in a qualitative as well as quantitative sense.

Much of the available literature on learning skills is based upon simple rather than complex problem-solving ability. One of the most puzzling aspects of the intellectual development of gifted students is *how* they think and solve problems. Many times, the observer or teacher can only see the problem and the apt solution. What goes on in the mind of the student between these two points is often a dark, though impressive mystery.

Koeppe and Rothney (1963) compared the oral problem-solving performance of 200 gifted students (top 5 percent of their class) divided by sex and by grades nine through twelve. Each student's task was to solve twelve problems. After the student gave the answer to the problem, he told the examiner how he arrived at the solution. All answers were tape recorded. The problems were designed so as to require no specific field of knowledge and there was only one correct answer to each problem.

On only four of the twelve problems were there sex differences noted:

two problems on which boys were superior and two on which the girls excelled. The nature of the items themselves suggested that variations in interest were more responsible for the differences than basic problem solving abilities. No substantial differences were found by grade level either!

The analysis of the problem-solving process used by the students revealed that no single style or method was systematically applied. Instead, the students used different approaches to reach the answers in the various problems. But students who verbalized in "if-then" relationships gave more correct answers than those who did not. Although no significant differences were found between the sexes, the boys were more certain of the correctness of their answers than the girls.

Boehm (1962) compared four groups of students through the use of story telling methods on the development of conscience or moral values. The samples were divided according to upper and working class, sex and intellectual level (gifted vs. average). For each student in the sample, ages six to nine, four stories were presented in a projective-type environment, and students were asked how the story should come out. The results of the experiment were as generally expected. The academically gifted children showed earlier maturation and moral judgment particularly concerning a distinction between the intention and outcome of an action than did children of average intelligence. The upper-middle class students appeared superior on this dimension to the working-class children. Greater differences were found between the gifted and average students of the upper-middle class level than of the gifted and average ability students in the working class. To some extent the degree of morality shown depended on the situation.

Each of the stories were scored independently on tape recordings by three judges and classified according to Piaget's three levels of morality, cooperation, intermediary and constraint. The work of Piaget has been recently receiving deserved recognition in American psychology and education. One of the frequent criticisms of Piaget's discussion of stages of development has been his unwillingness to consider individual differences among youngsters and, instead, to make statements about what the seven-year-old or nine-year-old could do without particular consideration as to either the ability level or home background of the particular student. On the basis of this study, it would appear that these criticisms were valid and future discussions of developmental ages of moral development must take into account both ability level and social class.

## Achievement

Little has been added to the literature on the achievement of high IQ children since the Terman work. For the most part, they are redundant and confirm the Terman position that high ability children will do well in later schooling and in life performance.

For example, Gallagher and Crowder (1957) gave the Stanford Achieve ment test to a group of 38 highly gifted students (Binet IQ 150+) in a midwestern university city. In the *Paragraph Meaning* test the median (middle) score of the group was almost four grades above their chronological level while the *Word Meaning* median scores were about three-and-a-half grades in advance of their grade level. Clearly, it would require a very high-level curriculum program to challenge these fourth and fifth graders who have already surpassed average freshmen and sophomores in high school in their use and comprehension of language.

The case for arithmetic superiority was not quite so clear. In the *Arithmetic Reasoning* test, the median score was about two grade levels advanced and in *Arithmetic Computation* less than one grade level advanced. The difference between the reasoning and computation scores can probably be explained by the fact that the superior reading ability of these children could help them on the *Arithmetic Reasoning* subtest.

Their relatively low computation score can probably be accounted for by the fact that the test itself is developed on a vertical basis with a few problems in addition, another few in subtraction, and so on, to briefly cover each of the major arithmetic operations. Since these children were given, at the most, horizontal enrichment in arithmetic, they would not be expected to perform on those processes not covered at their grade level. Even the most gifted child would be hard pressed to learn how to do long division unless someone spent a little time explaining it to him.

This group's performance in social studies and science rather closely parallels their performance in the reading areas, as might be expected. All of these results should not be interpreted as meaning that there were no problems related to school work. The standard achievement tests, in most instances, usually test for knowledge of facts rather than the ability to apply those facts. Both teacher ratings and personality tests on the above group suggested that many of them were mediocre in their ability to do creative work. This fact should be received with some soberness since this group, above all others, should excel in this area.

Similar findings of superior academic performance have been reported for other groups of gifted children by Witty (1930), Hollingworth (1926), Miller (1957), Klemm (1953), and many others.


## Emotional Adjustment

While fairly adequate measures of achievement and intellectual status have been available on gifted children in the United States from the early 1920's, the same cannot be said concerning the measurement of motivational and personality characteristics. Although the early studies made valiant attempts to identify these characteristics, they were hindered by lack of adequate measuring instruments and the limited theoretical development of the field.

For example, some of the earlier Terman studies (1925) attempted to use measures of character development including tests which measured the tendency of students to falsify certain information. The children were asked to place a check on a list of books they had read. Some of the books on the list were fictitious, and the number of these books checked was a measure of falsification. However, these character traits seemed to be fairly specific to the task itself. Some children could be identified as fairly responsible regarding school assignments and very irresponsible concerning care of their younger brother or sister. Other children who would not dream of taking money, even if the theft could not be observed, might very well cheat on an exam where the danger of failure was so great as to put them under strong pressure.

Some indication of emotional adjustment was provided by the findings of the Terman and Oden (1947) follow-up study on their gifted children when they were young adults. As a group, they had a slightly lower rate of suicide and insanity and a better marital adjustment than expected of the general population. This finding was contradictory to some earlier views on genius.

## Genius and Insanity

For many years there has been a school of thought which has equated genius and insanity. Such a view, descending in large part from the works of Lombroso, *The Man of Genius,* has many supporters. A statement by Tsanoff (1949) is typical. "A home which nurses a genius may very likely also harbor a future criminal or a downright lunatic." (He concludes, however, that the relationship here is not a causal one.) The biographies of men of great talent such as Poe, Van Gogh, Beethoven, Napoleon, Oscar Wilde, etc., add substance to this point of view. What we would like to know is whether emotional instability must always accompany great work, whether great ability leads one to insanity, or whether the instability that has been coupled with high ability in individual cases is present through coincidence.

The danger of taking case histories as evidence is that it is easy to be selective and pick only those cases which illustrate your point of view and overlook such individuals as Verdi, Churchill, Shakespeare, etc. Also, if we judge persons of past ages on modern standards, we may conclude that every citizen of past eras was either immoral or insane. A more convincing argument for this point of view can be made if it could be demonstrated that there is a high degree of relationship between emotional difficulties and high intelligence in children today. There is considerable evidence available on this point.

## General Emotional Stability—Elementary Level

A series of research studies comparing gifted and other groups are available. Lightfoot (1951) compared, by means of tests and rating scales, 48 gifted elementary school children with 56 mentally retarded children in that same school. Comparison revealed the gifted to be slightly above average in adjustment while the retarded were below average. Characteristics particularly related to intellectual giftedness were creativity, dominance, affiliation, protectiveness, and achievement. Those characteristics particularly related to the mentally retarded were dependence, seclusion, rejection, and defensive behavior.

Gallagher and Crowder (1957) gave the Rorschach ink blot test to 35 highly gifted elementary school children (Binet IQ 150+), and found little or no evidence of serious emotional problems in all but two of the children. These results were confirmed by teacher ratings. The only characteristic in which the children showed less than "superior" was the area of creativity. In this respect, too, the Rorschach test and the teacher ratings showed agreement.

Mensh (1950) in a review of Rorschach studies used with gifted children found that they had a higher number of responses, a higher level of form quality, and qualitatively better records. This would suggest an overall better adjustment for this group. Gair (1944) found that seven-year-old gifted children showed better organization, wider range of interest, and much more adjustment than children of average or below average IQ. Hildreth (1938) found that in comparing a group of gifted children with a group of intellectually average children matched with the gifted on age, racial background, and socioeconomic background, the teachers had five times as many favorable ratings for the gifted as for the average.

## Emotional Stability—Secondary Level

The same general picture is revealed in studies of secondary level students. Ramaseshan (1957) compared a group of over 200 gifted (Binet IQ 120+) senior high school students in three Nebraska high schools with a group of average students on measures of personality and social adjustment. The two groups were rated by their teachers on personality, responsiblity, adjustment, initiative, and work habits, and the students were administered the Washburne Social Adjustment Inventory. On the teachers' ratings, the gifted group was significantly superior to the average on all variables and without regard to sex. On the Washburne scale the gifted were superior at a statistically significant level on all the variables with the exception of sympathy. On factors such as truthfulness, happiness, purposiveness, judgment, etc., the gifted group showed a clear superiority. The test results confirmed the teachers' ratings, although the differences between the groups were less on the tests than on the ratings.

Wrenn, Ferguson, and Kennedy (1962) compared to the top 5 percent on the ACE psychological examination with the lower 15 percent of a total student body of 9,990 junior college students. These groups were administered the Bernreuter Personality Inventory and comparisons were made between these two groups. The authors found no differences on the characteristic of emotional stability, but did find the highly intelligent junior college students were more self-sufficient and dominant than the junior college students of lower levels of ability or of the average of the college population.

Strang (1956) compared the viewpoints of gifted adolescents concerning the problems of growing up with those of their classmates. There were large areas of similarity in both groups. Both had typical attitudes of dissatisfaction with one's body and social status and were concerned with problems of their relationships with siblings and parents. Those characteristics which did seem to show differences from average children were that the gifted relied on peer acceptance and were less concerned with boy-girl relationships and with lack of rapport with parents.

The advent of the National Merit Scholarship program provided the basis for more information on superior secondary school students. Warren and Heist (1960) compared 659 men and 259 women who were National Merit Scholarship winners or semifinalists with an unselected sample of undergraduate students on personality characteristics. There was no great incidence of serious maladjustment as found on the MMPI test but there were considerable differences in favor of the Merit Scholars on variables of originality, imagination, inventiveness, and resourcefulness.

Nichols and Davis (1964) in a similar study compared 1184 National Merit scholarship semifinalists, who were college seniors at the time that they were studied, with a large sample representing the average college graduate. Again the differences found were in the attitudinal dimension. The investigators discovered the Merit Scholars to be less religious and conventional, more committed to political allegiance, and more concerned for freedom from supervision (a point which should not be lost on educators). Descriptive adjectives which they accepted as part of their self-concept included the following: intellectual, dominant, forceful, idealistic, rebellious moody, lazy, witty, and cultured. They identified themselves as less interested in the social and athletic dimension.

Kennedy (1962) compared the MMPI Profile of a sample of 100 gifted adolescents in a National Science Foundation Summer Institute for mathematics. These students had a mean chronological age of 17 and a mean Wechsler IQ of 135. The general profile on this personality test was well within normal limits and supported many other studies which suggested that high achieving, high IQ students do not have substantial personality adjustment difficulties. The difference between them and their less talented age mates apparently centers on attitudes and dimensions of cognitive style rather than dimensions of emotional maladjustment.

Lessinger and Martinson (1961) compared a group of gifted eighth graders on the California Psychological Inventory with gifted high school population and the general norms. They concluded that the gifted eighth graders were much more closely related in personality pattern to gifted high school boys and to the general adult population than to their own life age group. Similarly, the high school gifted boys differed greatly from the average high school population. In short, gifted students at the secondary school level seem to attain psychological maturity early and more closely resemble one another regardless of the wide range of chronological age. These results also have generally been either unnoticed or ignored in educational planning.

Several research studies have abandoned the search for gross emotional problems in the gifted and have searched instead for subtler indices of differences.

Lucito (1964) compared 55 bright (CTMM 120+) and 51 dull (CTMM 82−) sixth-grade children on an Asch-type task which attempted to measure their behavior along an independence-conformity continuum. The children were brought into a room in groups of six and asked to look at three lines and identify which line was the longest. The differences in line length were easily identifiable, but the problem was complicated by the administrator who provided each child with false information on the performance of the other five youngsters in the group. In some instances, the youngsters were given information that the other five members of his group had chosen the wrong lines before he had to register his own decision. His choice was either to follow the group members in a decision which was manifestly wrong or to reject the group and trust his own perceptions.

A comparison was then made to see if the bright or dull children tended to conform more to the false judgment of the group than to their own perceptions. Results indicated that the bright children, as a group, were significantly less conforming to their peers than were the dull children. None of the dull children fit into the most independent category of behavior as defined by Lucito, while 29 percent of the bright children fell into such category. These results would support the contention that increased intellectual ability does seem related to a more independent and less conforming behavior.


## Independence

Smith (1962) compared a group of 42 superior and 42 average adolescents matched on social class status, chronological age, religion, sex, and nationality background. Students scoring over the 95th percentile on intelligence tests represented the superior while the average was represented by students who fell between the 25th and 75th percentiles on the same tests.

The students were given the Thematic Apperception Test and interpersonal adjective check list that provided data on self and self-ideal concepts. In addition, teacher and classroom evaluations of the interpersonal behavior of the subjects were also collected. The most significant difference between the gifted and average groups was found in independence and dominance, with the gifted being significantly higher on these dimensions. No differences were found between the groups in responsibility or cooperativeness, self-acceptance, or accuracy of self-perception.

On the Thematic Apperception Test, the average group indicated more themes of a dependency-weakness-conformity basis than did the superior group but no differences were found on the other dimensions. As other investigators have found, when the socioeconomic variables are controlled, the differences between gifted and average are less dramatic than otherwise occur. The significant dimension of independence-dominance, however, fits in well with the previous work by Lucito and suggests that high intelligence may be a contributor to the degree of independence and dominance shown by the student.

Are the favorable personality characteristics associated with gifted individuals really caused by their intellectual giftedness or by some other factor? The crucial but often overlooked study by Bonsall and Stefflre (1955) throws some interesting light on this question. A sample of 1,359 high school senior boys were given the Primary Mental Abilities test and the Guilford-Zimmerman Temperament Survey. Enough information was obtained from the students to enable them to be classed on the Alba-Edwards scale on occupations. When the gifted youngsters were compared with youngsters of average intelligence, the usual results were found. The gifted boys were superior in thoughtfulness, general activity, restraint, ascendance, emotional stability, objectivity, and masculinity. *However, when these comparisons were controlled for socioeconomic level so that only the average youngsters from high socioeconomic level were compared with gifted youngsters in the same level, then little or no differences were found between the two groups.*

This result leads to the interesting speculation that the differences seen in comparisons of the personality of gifted and average children are really due more to socioeconomic status than they are to the factor of intellectual giftedness itself. Bonsall and Stefflre conclude, "It is possible that Terman in describing the multiple superiority of the gifted child is simply describing children from the upper socioeconomic levels?" If this is so, many of our assumptions about the "differences" of the gifted which call for special educational approaches and methods will need to be reconsidered.

## Summary

The evidence available regarding the superior emotional adjustment of the *intellectually gifted* child seems very strong. It is found consistently, whether the measuring instruments are teachers' ratings or personality tests, and whether the evaluation is on the present status of the child or follow-up studies of his later life. Whether similar results would be found in the *creatively gifted* is an interesting question dealt with in the next section.

*Independence* appears to be a particularly differentiating feature of gifted children and this fact has some obvious implication for educational planning.

There is a growing suspicion that the importance of intelligence in the development of personality characteristics may have been overestimated. We have demolished the point of view that high intellect is associated with instability. In its place, however, we have added the concept that high intellect has actually *aided* a person in making a good adjustment. Now studies that rule out other factors such as family stability or social status seem to find less significant relationships in either direction between intellect and stability.

## Social Adjustment

What of the social adjustment of the gifted child? Is he shunned by his intellectually average colleagues? Does he form a close-knit clique, associating only with others of his own ability level? What happens to his social adjustment under conditions where special programs for the gifted are initiated? All of these questions are of practical and theoretical importance to school teachers, psychologists, and administrators. While a number of research studies are now available on this subject, it is fair to say that none of these questions can now be answered with complete confidence.

Whenever investigations are made of the social adjustment of gifted children in a school setting, the studies almost invariably indicate a superior social adjustment for the gifted. Gronlund (1959), in summarizing these studies, stated, "Where the sociometric status of individuals has been correlated with their intelligence test scores, low positive correlations have been generally obtained."

## Elementary School

One illustration of the generally positive relationship between intelligence and social acceptance can be seen in Table X taken from Gallagher (1958b). This table relates intelligence to the number of friendship choices received in grades two through five in a midwest university community of superior socioeconomic status. The gifted children with IQ scores of 132 and above obtained an average of more than six friendship choices as opposed to an average of fewer than four for the children under IQ 100.

In another analysis, Gallagher (1958a) attempted to discover whether the bright students restricted their choices to other bright students or whether the average students picked average students. In grades two, three,

## TABLE X

### The Relationship of Intelligence to Social Popularity—Grades Two through Five

#### (after Gallagher, 1958b)

| Binet IQ Equivalent Groups | N | Number of Choices Received | Average Choices Received |
|---|---|---|---|
| 132+ | 18 | 114 | 6.33 |
| 116-131 | 95 | 463 | 4.87 |
| 100-115 | 147 | 617 | 4.20 |
| 84-99 | 61 | 220 | 3.61 |
| 68-83 | 11 | 31 | 2.82 |

and five, the intellectual ability of the child seemed unrelated to the intellectual ability of the chooser. In grades four, however, a definite relationship was discovered, with the bright children choosing other bright children and average children choosing other average children for their friends. This scatter of friendship choices agrees with Gronlund's conclusion that "there is little *direct* relationship between intelligence and the degree of acceptance by peers."

One of the other important factors that seem to be related to social popularity in children is propinquity or geographic nearness. A comparison of the friendship choices with distance from the child's home revealed highly significant relationships at each grade level and suggests that many of the social choices of the children in school are based on out-of-school contacts and neighborhood friendships.

When the extremes of intelligence are compared, the gifted show quite clearly their social superiority to mentally retarded children. Miller (1956), comparing superior, average, and retarded children, found the gifted children superior and able to predict the social status of other children more successfully than could children in the other groups. Gallagher (1958a) also found that gifted children were slightly superior to the others in their ability to guess who would pick them. Thus, the intellectually bright children seemed also to have somewhat superior social perception. Such social popularity does not square with the popular image of the bright youngster being a snob and acting superior to others.

Silverstein (1962) investigated this problem. He recorded the social choice behavior of five different IQ groups composed of 350 fifth grade pupils. The groups were divided by ten IQ point ranges. Group A, the top group had a 130 IQ or above on the Otis test; the bottom group consisted of students of 99 IQ and below. Each of these pupils were administered the Ohio Social Acceptance Scale which requires ratings of every child in the class by every other child on a five-point friendship scale. Silverstein believed that snobbishness would be represented by a person's expectation to be more favorably accepted than he is willing to be accepted by others. There were no differences between ability levels. In every IQ group, there was the expectation to receive favorable ratings that were greater than those that they were willing to hand out to others. It may be more blessed to give than receive, but our expectations generally run in the other direction.

## Secondary School

Martyn (1957) conducted a study of the social adjustment of gifted and highly gifted children in grades four through twelve in the Palo Alto, California, schools and was able to obtain information on the social acceptance of 354 gifted subjects as compared to the social adjustment of over 3,000 other students on the Cunningham Social Distance Scale. Martyn found, as many other investigators before him, that the social acceptance score for the total group of gifted children was significantly greater than that of their classmates. However, the mean acceptance score of 43 gifted students at the high school level and 91 gifted students at the junior high school *was not significantly higher than the averages of their almost 900 classmates.*

Thus, while the gifted children were more popular at the elementary school levels, they were not significantly more socially acceptable than their classmates at the secondary school level. This result seems to support the popular observation that intellectually superior children are at their lowest peer popularity level during the high school period where the peer values are the most important. The gifted youngster who is concerned about his social status may be tempted to deliberately mask his talents in order to gain the desired social popularity and prestige which appear to be especially important at this age.

## Why Are the Gifted Popular?

Although many investigators have indicated that gifted children tended to be more socially popular than children of average intellectual ability, there remains the question as to whether the children are being chosen because of their high intelligence or because of some of their many other favorable characteristics, personal and otherwise. Tannenbaum (1959) made an attempt to distinguish the characteristics of giftedness from the person himself by writing descriptions of stereotyped fictitious students. These students combined, in some way, three general characteristics; they were either *brilliant* or *average, studious* or *non-studious,* and *athletic* or *non-athletic,* These three characteristics were then listed in all possible eight combinations of these three characteristics, and 615 juniors in a large New York City high school were asked to respond to the particular combination of characteristics which most appealed to them.

On the basis of mean acceptability ratings, the characteristics were ranked as:

144

(1) brilliant—non-studious—athlete
(2) average—non-studious—athlete
(3) average—studious—athlete
(4) brilliant—studious—athlete
(5) brilliant—non-studious—non-athlete
(6) average—non-studious—non-athlete
(7) average—studious—non-athlete
(8) brilliant—studious—non-athlete

A comparison of the ratings of the *average* and *brilliant* characters revealed no significant difference, nor were there differences found between the brilliant athletes and non-brilliant athletes. However, these results did suggest that "academic brilliance *per se,* as compared to average ability, is not a stigma among adolescents, but when combined with other relatively unacceptable attributes it can penalize its possessor." The non-studious athlete may demonstrate outstanding brain power without fearing social derogation by peers. However, a display of brilliance by one who is studious and indifferent to sports constitutes a definite status risk.

But of what does this "popularity" consist? It is a "pal" relationship or is it the social bond between a leader and a follower? Pielstick (1959) suggests that the gifted child is a type of ego ideal to the average youngster. A natural next question is, Are there special leadership characteristics in the gifted?

Cassell and Haddox (1959) compared the scores of 60 gifted and 100 typical high school students on two leadership tests. The mean IQ of the gifted group was 125 and 103 for the average students. The LQT Test assessed the individual's philosophy of leadership with categories of personal integrity, consideration of others, mental health, technical information, decision making, and communication. On this test, no differences were found between the gifted and intellectually average students.

On the LAT Leadership Ability Test there are four parts which include tendencies toward autocratic aggressive, autocratic submissive, democratic, and laissez-faire strategies. On this test, there was a difference between the gifted and the average, with the gifted emphasizing the use of parliamentary procedure decision processes and minimizing the use of more autocratic or laissez-faire patterns.

## Summary

In summary, it is possible to say on the basis of available research that gifted children are, as a group, almost invariably more popular and more socially accepted than children of other levels of intellectual ability. It is not all clear that high intelligence *causes* better social popularity or whether the gifted are capitalizing on other aspects of their personalities or family situations to gain their favorable social position.

What we really don't know is how social acceptance affects the other areas of adjustment. Does high social adjustment sometimes come at the expense of limiting academic performance? Do the gifted deliberately avoid the appearance of braininess in order to stay popular? Many people believe so. Can the gross judgments of social acceptance be refined into meaningful components such as leadership, respect, warmth, etc.? And what can these tell us about the gifted? These are important areas for future research.

## Children of Remarkably Superior Intelligence

Special concern has been felt for those students who are found at the very top of the distribution in performance on intelligence tests. While the results of Terman and his co-workers removed many of the questions regarding the positive characteristics and adjustment of the youngster of superior intellectual ability, serious questions remain regarding the problems, within the educational program, of children whose performance classifies them as 1 in 100,000 or 1 in 1,000,000. The research conducted on these youngsters is very sparse, one reason no doubt being that they are hard to find in sufficient number.

Much of the investigations have been case studies. The classic example of this approach is provided by Hollingworth (1942), who did an intensive analysis of twelve children who scored above 180 IQ on the Stanford-Binet. On the basis of this small sample, Hollingworth suggested that this type of youngster was likely to have a difficult time adjusting to school. She concluded that they have special problems in finding hard and interesting work at school, in avoiding a negativistic attitude towards authority, and in tolerating others of lesser ability.

It is interesting to note that ten of the twelve children in this classification were first born, and five were only children. In all cases, their very high intelligence was noted quite early in life, and all of the parents came from a middle class or upper-middle class background. Even in such a selection the variation *within* the group should be noted. Hollingworth suggested that four of the subjects showed notable signs of creativity; however, another four gave no indication of marked constructive originality at all.

Other investigators have concentrated on the social adjustment problems of these youngsters. Terman and Oden (1947) in a small aspect of their larger research found 25 youngsters of extraordinary intellectual ability (IQ 180+). These tended to fall more into the bottom range of the social adjustment scale, although the range of adjustment within the group was wide.

Gallagher and Crowder (1957) compared the social adjustment of 15 youngsters of Binet IQ 165 and above with youngsters ranging in Binet IQ ranging from 150 to 165. In this comparison the higher IQ group tended to have slightly more social problems. Thus, there did seem to be some reason to suspect that the optimum social adjustment level (IQ ranges between 125 and 155) was as Hollingworth and Terman had suggested. There is some indication from the work of Gallagher and Crowder that the nature of the group influenced the social acceptance of the gifted youngster. That is, if a highly gifted child was in a group of average or below-average ability children, he was more likely to have social problems than if he was a member of a group of high ability children.

Kerstetter (1952) tended to substantiate this position. She studied 25 children with Binet IQ 160+ in special classes for gifted children in New York City. These highly gifted children were found to be, on the whole, socially well adjusted, and there seemed to be little relationship between very high intelligence and poor social adjustment. Thus, in a situation where the very high IQ child did not differ dramatically from the average ability of the group in which he was placed, he was able to form more harmonious relationships.

Anastasiow (1964) studied the self-concepts of a group of 23 very gifted students who had either a WISC IQ score of 145 or a Binet IQ score of 155 or above. Their performance on the STEP battery in reading and mathematics was compared with their performance on the Sears-Spaulding Self-Concept Test, which measured self-assessment in such fields as physical ability, social relations, mental abilities, human relation skills, etc.

In order to draw a comparison, the author divided the students into those performing on the 99th percentile on the reading and mathematics tests who were called the *high achievement* group, and all others who were called the *low achievement* groups. These two groups were then compared on their performance on the Self-Concept Scale. Anastasiow found the high achievers tended to have high self-concepts in physical abilities and social relationships with their peers. Even at this rarified level of intellectual performance, it is possible to see how self-concepts influence the achievement of the students. It is unlikely, however, that the difference in academic performance would be noted by the teacher since the "low achievers" were still mostly performing in the 90th percentile in the achievement tests and would hardly be considered academic problems from the standpoint of the teacher, who is probably giving them all A's for their academic performance. This is an interesting illustration, however, of how good performance could be even better given more favorable attitudes toward oneself.

These limited results again illustrate the complexity of variables that influence school performance and student adjustment. No single factor, such as an abnormally high IQ, by itself can determine social adjustment. The most it can do, in conjunction with other factors, is to predispose a youngster in certain directions. The predisposition in this case is to a lower social adjustment for children of extraordinary performance, but a good proportion of these students have excellent social relations, and any generalization made on this subject would have to recognize the many exceptions.

# References

Anastasiow, N. J. A report of self-concept of the very gifted. *Gifted Child Quarterly*, 1964, 8, 177-178.

Boehm, Leonore. The development of conscience: A comparison of American children of different mental and socio-economic levels. *Child Development*, 1962, 33 (3), 575-590.

Bonsall, Marcella, and Stefflre, V. J. "The Temprament of Gifted Children," *California Journal of Educational Research*, 1955, 6, 162-165.

Burt, C. The inheritance of mental ability. *American Psychologist*, 1958, 13, 1-15.

Carrier, Neil Alan, Malpass, Leslie F., and Borton, Kenneth D. *Responses of bright, normal and retarded children to learning tasks.* Carbondale, Illinois, Southern Illinois University, 1961.

Cassell, R. N. & Haddox, Genevieve. Comparative study of leadership test scores for gifted and typical high school students. *Psychological Reports*, 1959, 5, 713-717.

Feldhusen, J. F., & Klausmeier, H. J. Anxiety, intelligence and achievement in children of low, average and high intelligence. *Child Development*, 1962, 33, 403-409.

Gair, Mollie. Rorschach characteristics of a group of very superior seven year old children. *Rorschach Research Exchange*, 1944, 8, 31-37.

Gallagher, J. J. Peer acceptance of highly gifted children in elementary school. *Elementary School Journal*, 1958a, 58, 465-470.

Gallagher, J. J. Social status of children related to intelligence, propinquity and social perception. *Elementary School Journal*, 1958b, 58, 225-231.

Gallagher, J. J. & Crowder, Thora. The adjustment of gifted children in the regular classroom. *Exceptional Children*, 1957, 23, 306-312; 317-319.

Gallagher, J. J. & Lucito, L. J. Intellectual patterns of gifted compared with average and retarded. *Exceptional Children*, 1961, 27, 479-482. (of. *Peabody Journal of Education*, 1960, 38, 131-136)

Gronlund, N. E. *Sociometry in the classroom.* New York: Harper, 1959

Hildreth, Gertrude. The educational achievement of gifted children. *Child Development* 1938, 9, 365-371.

Hollingworth, Leta. Gifted children, their nature and nurture. New York: Macmillan, 1926.

Jensen, A. Learning ability in retarded, average and gifted children. *Marrill-Palmer Quarterly*, 1963, 9, 123-140.

Kennedy, W. A. MMPI profiles of gifted adolescents. *Journal of Clinical Psychology*, 1962, 18, 148-149.

Kerstetter, Leona. A sociometric study of the classroom roles of a group of highly gifted children. (Unpublished doctor's dissertation, New York University, 1952.)

Klausmeier, H. J. & Check, J. Retention and transfer in children of low, average and high intelligence. *Journal of Educational Research*, 1962, 55, 319-322.

Klausmeier, H. J. & Loughlin, L. T. Behavior during problem solving among children of low, average and high intelligence. *Journal of Educational Psychology,* 1961, 52, 148-152.

Klemm, E. W. Reading instruction for gifted children in the elementary grades. (Unpublished doctoral's dissertation, Northwestern University, 1953)

Koeppe, R. P. & Rothney, J. W. Evaluation of first steps in the counseling of superior students. *Personnel and Guidance Journal,* 1963, 42, 35-40.

Laycock, F. and Caylor, J. S. Physiques of gifted children and their less gifted siblings. Child Development, 1964, 35, 63-74.

Lessinger, L. M., and Martinson, R. The Use of the California Psychological Inventory with Gifted Pupils. Personnel and Guidance Journal 39, 572-75, March 1961.

Lightfoot, Georgia. *Personality characteristics of bright and dull children.* Contributions to Education No. 969. New York, Teachers College, Columbia University, 1951.

Lucito, L. J. Independence-conformity behavior as a function of intellect: bright and dull children. *Exceptional Children,* 1964, 31, 5-13.

Martyn, K. A. The social acceptance of gifted students. (Unpublished doctoral dissertation, Stanford University, 1957)

Mensh, I. Rorschach study of the gifted child. *Exceptional Children.* 1950, 17, 8-14.

Miller, R. V. Social status and socioempathetic differences among mentally superior, mentally typical and mentally retarded children. *Exceptional Children,* 1956, 23, 114-119.

Miller, Vera. The superior child enterprise. *American School Board Journal,* 1958, 134, 43-46.

Nichols, R. C. *The inheritance of general and specific ability.* Research Report No. 1. Evanston, Ill.: National Merit Scholarship Corporation, 1965.

Nichols, R. C. & Davis, J. A. Characteristics of students of high academic aptitude. *Personnel and Guidance Journal,* 1964, 42, 794-800.

Pielstick, N. L. Perception of mentally superior children by their classmates in fourth, fifth and sixth grades. (Unpublished doctoral dissertation, University of Illinois, 1959.)

Ramaseshan, P. H. The social and emotional adjustment of the gifted. (Unpublished doctoral dissertation, University of Nebraska, 1957)

Silverstein, S. How snobbish are the gifted in regular classes? *Exceptional Children* 28: 323-324 F1962.

Smith, D. C. *Personal and social adjustment of gifted adolescents.* Washington, D. C.: Council for Exceptional Children, Research Monograph No. 4, 1964.

Strang, Ruth. Gifted adolescents' views of growing up. *Exceptional Children,* 1956, 23, 10-15; 20.

Tannenbaum, A. *Adolescent attitudes toward academic brilliance.* New York: Bureau of Publications, Teachers College, Columbia University, 1962.

Terman, L. M. et al. *Mental and physical traits of a thousand gifted children.* Genetic Studies of Genius — Vol. I. Stanford, Calif.: Stanford University Press, 1925.

Terman, L. M. & Oden, Melita. *Genetic studies of genius. Vol. V: The gifted group at mid-life.* Stanford, Calif.: Stanford University Press, 1959.

Terman, L. M. & Oden, Melita. *Genetic studies of genius — IV. The Gifted Child Grows Up.* Stanford, Calif.: Stanford University Press, 1947.

Thompson. J. M. & Finley, Carmen J. A further comparison of the intellectual patterns of gifted and mentally retarded children. *Exceptional Children,* 1962, 29, 379-381.

Tsanoff, R. A. *The ways of genius.* New York: Harper, 1949.

Warren, J. R. and Heist, P. A. Personality attributies of gifted college students. *Science,* 1960, 132, 330-337.

Witty, P. A. *A study of one hundred gifted children.* Bulletin of University of Kansas, Vol. 2, 1930.

Wrenn, G. G., Ferguson, L. W. & Kennedy, J. L. Intelligence level and personality. *Journal of Social Psychology,* 1963, 7, 301-308.

Donald W. MacKinnon

# The Nature and Nurture
# of Creative Talent

$L$et me say first how deeply appreciative I am of the honor of having been chosen the Walter Van Dyke Bingham Lecturer for 1962. It has for me especial meaning to be provided this opportunity to honor the memory of a man I respected so much and whose work was such a pioneering contribution to that field of psychology to which I have given most of my energies as a psychologist. I am grateful, too, for this opportunity to express to Mrs. Bingham the gratitude of all psychologists for her generosity in establishing this series of annual lectures on the discovery and development of exceptional abilities and capacities. Our literature has been greatly enriched by the lectures which she has made possible.

I should like also to congratulate Yale University for having been chosen this year as the institution to be honored for its contributions to the study of talent, and to thank all those who have made such pleasant arrangements for this occasion.

There is a story, first told I believe by Mark Twain which, had Dr. Bingham known it, would have been, I am sure, one of his favorites. It is about a man who sought the greatest general who had ever lived. Upon inquiring as to where this individual might be found, he was told that the person he sought had died and gone to Heaven. At the Pearly Gates he informed St. Peter of the purpose of his quest, whereupon St. Peter pointed to a soul nearby. "But that," protested the inquirer, "isn't the greatest of all generals. I knew that person when he lived on earth, and he was only a cobbler." "I know that," replied St. Peter, "but if he had been a general he would have been the greatest of them all."

Dr. Bingham spent his life worrying about cobblers who might have been generals and indeed about all those who fail to become what they are

The Walter Van Dyke Bingham Lecture given at Yale University, New Haven, Connecticut, April 11, 1962.

MacKinnon, Donald W. "The Nature and Nurture of Creative Talent". *American Psychologist*, 17:484-495, 1962.

capable of becoming because neither they nor others recognize their potentialities and nourish their realization. Dr. Bingham was one of the first to insist that it is not enough to recognize creative talent after it has come to expression. He reminded us that it is our task as psychologists and as educators either through our insights or through the use of validated predictors to discover talent when it is still potential and to provide that kind of social climate and intellectual environment which will facilitate its development and expression.

Whatever light I shall be able to shed on the nature and nurture of creative talent comes in the main from findings of researches carried on during the last six years in the Institute of Personality Assessment and Research on the Berkeley campus of the University of California, and supported in large part by the Carnegie Corporation of New York.

In undertaking such a study one of our first tasks was to decide what we would consider creativity to be. This was necessary, first, because creativity has been so variously described and defined, and second, because only when we had come to agreement as to how we would conceive creativity would we be in a position to know what kinds of persons we would want to study. We came easily to agreement that true creativeness fulfills at least three conditions. It involves a response or an idea that is novel or at the very least statistically infrequent. But novelty or originality of thought or action, while a necessary aspect of creativity, is not sufficient. If a response is to lay claim to being a part of the creative process, it must to some extent be adaptive to, or of, reality. It must serve to solve a problem, fit a situation, or accomplish some recognizable goal. And, thirdly, true creativeness involves a sustaining of the original insight, an evaluation and elaboration of it, a developing of it to the full.

Creativity, from this point of view, is a process extended in time and characterized by originality, adaptiveness, and realization. It may be brief, as in a musical improvisation, or it may involve a considerable span of years as was required for Darwin's creation of the theory of evolution.

The acceptance of such a conception of creativity had two important consequences for our researches. It meant that we would not seek to study creativity while it was still potential but only after it had been realized and had found expression in clearly identifiable creative products—buildings designed by architects, mathematical proofs developed by mathematicians, and the published writings of poets and novelists. Our conception of creativity forced us further to reject as indicators or criteria of creativeness the performance of individuals on so-called tests of creativity. While tests of this sort, that require that the subject think, for example, of unusual uses for common objects and the consequences of unusual events, may indeed measure the infrequency or originality of a subject's ideas in response to specific test items, they fail to reveal the extent to which the subject faced with real life problems is likely to come up with solutions that are novel and adaptive and which he will be motivated to apply in all of their ramifications.

Having thus determined that we would limit our researches to the study of persons who had already demonstrated a high level of creative work, we were still confronted with the problem of deciding from which fields of creative endeavor we would seek to recruit our subjects.

The fields which we finally sampled were those of creative writing, architecture, mathematics, industrial research, physical science, and engineering.

If one considers these activities in relation to the distinction often made between artistic and scientific creativity, it may be noted that we have sampled both of these domains as well as overlapping domains of creative striving which require that the practitioner be at one and the same time both artist and scientist.

Artistic creativity, represented in our studies by the work of poets, novelists, and essayists, results in products that are clearly expressions of the creator's inner states, his needs, perceptions, motivations, and the like. In this type of creativity, the creator externalizes something of himself into the public field.

In scientific creativity, the creative product is unrelated to the creator as a person, who in his creative work acts largely as a mediator between externally defined needs and goals. In this kind of creativeness, the creator, represented in our studies by industrial researchers, physical scientists, and engineers, simply operates on some aspect of his environment in such a manner as to produce a novel and appropriate product, but he adds little of himself or of his style as a person to the resultant.

Domains of creative striving in which the practitioner must be both artist and scientist were represented in our researches by mathematicians and architects. Mathematicians contribute to science, yet in a very real sense their important creative efforts are as much as anything else personal cosmologies in which they express themselves as does the artist in his creations. So, too, in architecture, creative products are both an expression of the architect and thus a very personal product, and at the same time an impersonal meeting of the demands of an external problem.

If in reporting the findings of our researches I draw most heavily upon data obtained from our study of architects (MacKinnon, 1962), it is for two reasons. First, it is the study for which, in collaboration with Wallace B. Hall, I have assumed primary responsibility. Second, it is in architects, of all our samples, that we can expect to find what is most generally characteristic of creative persons. Architecture, as a field of creative endeavor, requires that the successful practitioner be both artist and scientist—artist in that his designs must fulfill the demands of "Delight," and scientist in that they must meet the demands of "Firmnesse" and "Commodity," to use the words of Sir Henry Wotton (1624). But surely, one can hardly think that the requirements of effective architecture are limited to these three demands. The successful and effective architect must, with the skill of a juggler, combine, reconcile, and exercise the diverse skills of businessman, lawyer, artist, engineer, and advertising man, as well as those of author and journalist, psychiatrist, educator, and psychologist. In what other profession can one expect better to observe the multifarious expressions of creativity?

It should be clear that any attempt to discover the distinguishing traits of creative persons can succeed only in so far as some group of qualified experts can agree upon who are the more and who are the less creative workers in a given field of endeavor. In our study of architects we began by asking a panel of experts—five professors of architecture, each working independently—to nominate the 40 most creative architects in the United States. All told they supplied us with 86 names instead of the 40 they would have mentioned had there been perfect agreement among them. While 13 of the 86 architects were nominated by all five panel members, and 9 nominated by four, 11 by three, and 13 by two, 40 were individual nominations each proposed by a single panel member.

The agreement among experts is not perfect, yet far greater than one might have expected. Later we asked 11 editors of the major American architectural journals, *Architectual Forum, Architectural Record,* the *Journal of the American Institute of Architects,* and *Progressive Architecture,* to rate the creativity of the 64 of the nominated architects whom we invited to participate in the study. Still later we asked the 40 nominated creative architects who actually accepted our invitation to be studied to rate the creativity of the invited 64 architects, themselves included. Since the editors' ratings of the creativity of the architects correlated +.88 with the architects' own ratings, it is clear that under certain conditions and for certain groups it is possible to obtain remarkable agreement about the relative creativeness of individual members of a profession and thus meet the first requirement for an effective study of creative persons.

A second requirement for the successful establishment of the traits of creative individuals is their willingness to make themselves available for study. Our hope was to win the cooperation of each person whom we invited to participate in the research, but as I have already indicated in the case of the architects, to obtain 40 acceptances, 64 invitations had to be sent out.

The invitation to this group, as to all the creative groups which we have studied, was to come to Berkeley for a weekend of intensive study in the Institute of Personality Assessment and Research. There, in groups of ten, they have been studied by the variety of means which constitute the assessment method—by problem solving experiments; by tests designed to discover what a person does not know or is unable or unwilling to reveal about himself; by tests and questionnaires that permit a person to manifest various aspects of his personality and to express his attitudes, interests, and values; by searching interviews that cover the life history and reveal the present structure of the person; and by specially contrived social situations of a stressful character which call for the subject's best behavior in a socially defined role.

The response of creative persons to the invitation to reveal themselves under such trying circumstances has varied considerably. At the one extreme there have been those who replied in anger at what they perceived to be the audacity of psychologists in presuming to study so ineffable and mysterious a thing as the creative process and so sensitive a being as a creative person. At the other extreme were those who replied courteously and warmheartedly, welcoming the invitation to be studied, and manifesting even an eagerness to contribute to a better understanding of the creative person and the creative process.

Here we were face to face with a problem that plagues us in all our researches: Are those who are willing to be assessed different in important ways from those who refuse? With respect to psychological traits and characteristics we can never know. But with respect to differences in creativeness, if any, between the 40 who accepted and the 24 who declined our invitation, we know that the two groups are indistinguishable. When the nominating panel's ratings of creativity were converted to standard scores and the means for the 24 versus the 40 were compared, they were found to be identical. When the editors' ratings were similarly converted to standard scores, the mean for the nonassessed group was slightly higher (51.9) than for the assessed sample (48.7), but the difference is not statistically significant.

Certainly we cannot claim to have assessed the 40 most creative architects in the country, or the most creative of any of the groups we have studied; but it is clear that we have studied a highly creative group of architects indistinguishable in their creativity from the group of 24 who declined to be studied, and so with the other groups too.

A third requirement for the successful determination of the traits of highly creative persons in any field of endeavor is that the profession be widely sampled beyond those nominated as most creative, for the distinguishing characteristics of the restricted sample might well have nothing to do with their creativeness. Instead they might be traits characterizing all members of the profession whether creative or not, distinguishing the professional group as a whole but in no sense limited or peculiar to its highly creative members. In the case of the architects, to use them once again as an example, two additional samples were recruited for study, both of which matched the highly creative sample (whom I shall now call Architects I) with respect to age and geographic location of practice. The first supplementary sample (Architects II) had had at least two years of work experience and association with one of the originally nominated creative architects. The second additional sample (Architects III) was composed of architects who had never worked with any of the nominated creatives.

By selecting three samples in this manner, we hoped to tap a range of talent sufficiently wide to be fairly representative of the profession as a whole; and we appear to have succeeded. The mean rating of creativity for each of the three groups—the ratings having been made on a nine-point scale by six groups of architects and experts on architecture—was for Architects I, 5.46; for Architects II, 4.25; and for Architects III, 3.54, the differences in mean ratings between each group being statistically highly significant.

So much for method and research design. I turn now to a discussion of the nature of creative talent as it has been revealed to us in our researches.

Persons who are highly creative are inclined to have a good opinion of themselves, as evidenced by the large number of favorable adjectives which they use in self-description and by the relatively high scores they earn on a scale which measures basic acceptance of the self. Indeed, there is here a paradox, for in addition to their favorable self-perceptions the very basic self-acceptance of the more creative persons often permits them to speak more frankly and thus more critically and in unusual ways about themselves. It is clear, too, that the self-images of the more creative differ from the self-images of the less creative. For example, Architects I, in contrast to Architects II and III, more often describe themselves as inventive, determined, independent, individualistic, enthusiastic, and industrious. In striking contrast Architects II and III more often than Architects I describe themselves as responsible, sincere, reliable, dependable, clear thinking, tolerant, and understanding. In short, where creative architects more often stress their inventiveness, independence, and individuality, their enthusiasm, determination, and industry, less creative members of the profession are impressed by their virtue and good character and by their rationality and sympathetic concern for others.

The discrepancies between their descriptions of themselves as they are and as they would ideally be are remarkably alike for all architects regardless of their level of creativeness. All three groups reveal themselves as desiring more personal attractiveness, self-confidence, maturity, and intellectual competence, a higher level of energy, and better social relations. As for differences, however, Architects I would ideally be more sensitive, while both Architects II and III wish for opposites if not incompatibles; they would ideally be more original but at the same time more self-controlled and disciplined.

As for the relation between intelligence and creativity, save for the mathematicians where there is a low positive correlation between intelligence and the level of creativeness, we have found within our creative samples essentially zero relationship between the two variables, and this is not due to a narrow restriction in range of intelligence. Among creative architects who have a mean score of 113 on the Terman Concept Mastery Test (1956), individual scores range widely from 39 to 179, yet scores on this measure of intelligence correlate $-.08$ with rated creativity. Over the whole range of intelligence and creativity there is, of course, a positive relationship between the two variables. No feeble-minded subjects have shown up in any of our creative groups. It is clear, however, that above a certain required minimum level of intelligence which varies from field to field and in some instances may be surprisingly low, being more intelligent does not guarantee a corresponding increase in creativeness. It just is not true that the more intelligent person is necessarily the more creative one.

In view of the often asserted close association of genius with insanity it is also of some interest to inquire into the psychological health of our creative subjects. To this end we can look at their profiles on the Minnesota Multiphasic Personality Inventory (MMPI) (Hathaway & McKinley, 1945), a test originally developed to measure tendencies toward the major psychiatric disturbances that man is heir to: depression, hysteria, paranoia, schizophrenia, and the like. On the eight scales which measure the strength

156

of these dispositions in the person, our creative subjects earn scores which, on the average, are some 5 to 10 points above the general population's average score of 50. It must be noted, however, that elevated scores of this degree on these scales do not have the same meaning for the personality functioning of persons who, like our subjects, are getting along well in their personal lives and professional careers, that they have for hospitalized patients. The manner in which creative subjects describe themselves on this test as well as in the life history psychiatric interview is less suggestive of psychopathology than it is of good intellect, complexity and richness of personality, general lack of defensiveness, and candor in self-description—in other words, an openness to experience and especially to experience of one's inner life. It must also be noted, however, that in the self-reports and in the MMPI profiles of many of our creative subjects, one can find rather clear evidence of psychopathology, but also evidence of adequate control mechanisms, as the success with which they live their productive and creative lives testifies.

However, the most striking aspect of the MMPI profiles of all our male creative groups is an extremely high peak on the *Mf* (femininity) scale. This tendency for creative males to score relatively high on femininity is also demonstrated on the Fe (femininity) scale of the California Psychological Inventory (CPI) (Gough, 1957) and on the masculinity-femininity scale of the Strong Vocational Interest Blank (Strong, 1959). Scores on the latter scale (where high score indicates more masculinity) correlate −.49 with rated creativity.

The evidence is clear: The more creative a person is the more he reveals an openness to his own feelings and emotions, a sensitive intellect and understanding self-awareness, and wide-ranging interests including many which in the American culture are thought of as feminine. In the realm of sexual identification and interests, our creative subjects appear to give more expression to the feminine side of their nature than do less creative persons. In the language of the Swiss psychologist, Carl G. Jung (1956), creative persons are not so completely identified with their masculine *persona* roles as to blind themselves to or to deny expression to the more feminine traits of the *anima*. For some, to be sure, the balance between masculine and feminine traits, interests, and identification, is a precarious one, and for several of our subjects it would appear that their presently achieved reconciliation of these opposites of their nature has been barely effected and only after considerable psychic stress and turmoil.

The perceptiveness of the creative and his openness to richness and complexity of experience is strikingly revealed on the Barron-Welsh Art Scale of the Welsh Figure Preference Test (Welsh, 1959), which presents to the subject a set of 62 abstract line drawings which range from simple and symmetrical figures to complex and asymmetrical ones. In the original study (Barron & Welsh, 1952) which standardized this scale, some 80 painters from New York, San Francisco, New Orleans, Chicago, and Minneapolis showed a marked preference for the complex and asymmetrical, or, as they often referred to them, the vital and dynamic figures. A contrasting sample of nonartists revealed a marked preference for the simple and symmetrical drawings.

All creative groups we have studied have shown a clear preference for the complex and asymmetrical, and in general the more creative a person is the stronger is this preference. Similarly, in our several samples, scores on an Institute scale which measures the preference for perceptual complexity are significantly correlated with creativity. In the sample of architects the correlation is +.48.

Presented with a large selection of one-inch squares of varicolored posterboard and asked to construct within a 30-minute period a pleasing, completely filled-in 8" × 10" mosaic (Hall, 1958), some subjects select the fewest colors possible (one used only one color, all white) while others seek to make order out of the largest possible number, using all of the 22 available colors. And, again citing results from the architects, there is a significant though low positive correlation of +.38 between the number of colors a subject chooses and his creativity as rated by the experts.

If one considers for a moment the meaning of these preferences on the art scale, on the mosaic test, and on the scale that measures preference for perceptual complexity, it is clear that creative persons are especially disposed to admit complexity and even disorder into their perceptions without being made anxious by the resulting chaos. It is not so much that they like disorder per se, but that they prefer the richness of the disordered to the stark barrenness of the simple. They appear to be challenged by disordered multiplicity which arouses in them a strong need which in them is serviced by a superior capacity to achieve the most difficult and far-reaching ordering of the richness they are willing to experience.

The creative person's openness to experience is further revealed on the Myers-Briggs Type Indicator (Myers, 1958), a test based largely upon Carl G. Jung's (1923) theory of psychological functions and types.

Employing the language of the test, though in doing so I oversimplify both it and the theory upon which it is based, one might say that whenever a person uses his mind for any purpose, he performs either an act of perception (he becomes aware of something) or an act of judgment (he comes to a conclusion about something). And most persons tend to show a rather consistent preference for and greater pleasure in one or the other of these, preferring either to perceive or to judge, though every one both perceives and judges.

An habitual preference for the judging attitude may lead to some pre-judging and at the very least to the living of a life that is orderly, controlled, and carefully planned. A preference for the perceptive attitude results in a life that is more open to experience both from within and from without, and characterized by flexibility and spontaneity. A judging type places more emphasis upon the control and regulation of experience, while a perceptive type is inclined to be more open and receptive to all experience.

The majority of our creative writers, mathematicians, and architects are perceptive types. Only among research scientists do we find the majority to be judging types, and even in this group it is interesting to note that there is a positive correlation (+.25) between a scientist's preference for perception and his rated creativity as a scientific researcher. For architects, preference for perception correlates +.41 with rated creativity.

The second preference measured by the Type Indicator is for one of two types of perception: sense perception or sensation, which is a direct becoming aware of things by way of the senses versus intuitive perception or intuition, which is an indirect perception of the deeper meanings and possibilities inherent in things and situations. Again, everyone senses and intuits, but preliminary norms for the test suggest that in the United States three out of four persons show a preference for sense perception, concentrating upon immediate sensory experience and centering their attention upon existing facts. The one out of every four who shows a preference for intuitive perception, on the other hand, looks expectantly for a bridge or link between that which is given and present and that which is not yet thought of, focusing habitually upon possibilities.

One would expect creative persons not to be bound to the stimulus and the object but to be ever alert to the as-yet-not-realized. And that is precisely the way they show themselves to be on the Type Indicator. In contrast to an estimated 25% of the general population who are intuitive, 90% of the creative writers, 92% of the mathematicians, 93% of the research scientists, and 100% of the architects are intuitive as measured by this test.

In judging or evaluating experience, according to the underlying Jungian theory of the test, one makes use of thought or of feeling; thinking being a logical process aimed at an impersonal fact-weighing analysis, while feeling is a process of appreciation and evaluation of things that gives them a personal and subjective value. A preference for thinking or for feeling appears to be less related to one's creativity as such than to the type of materials or concepts with which one deals. Of our creative groups, writers prefer feeling, mathematicians, research scientists, and engineers prefer thinking, while architects split fifty-fifty in their preference for one or the other of the two functions.

The final preference in Jungian typology and on the test is the well-known one between introversion and extraversion. Approximately two-thirds of all our creative groups score as introverts, though there is not evidence that introverts as such are more creative than extraverts.

Turning to preferences among interests and values, one would expect the highly creative to be rather different from less creative people, and there is clear evidence that they are.

On the Strong Vocational Interest Blank, which measures the similarity of a person's expressed interests with the known interests of individuals successful in a number of occupations and professions, all of our creative subjects have shown, with only slight variation from group to group, interests similar to those of the psychologist, author-journalist, lawyer, architect, artist, and musician, and interests unlike those of the purchasing agent, office man, banker, farmer, carpenter, veterinarian, and interestingly enough, too, policeman and mortician. Leaving aside any consideration of the specific interests thus revealed we may focus our attention on the inferences that

*159*

may be drawn from this pattern of scores which suggest that creative persons are relatively uninterested in small details, or in facts for their own sake, and more concerned with their meanings and implications, possessed of considerable cognitive flexibility, verbally skillful, interested in communicating with others and accurate in so doing, intellectually curious, and relatively disinterested in policing either their own impulses and images or those of others.

On the Allport-Vernon-Lindzey Study of Values (1951), a test designed to measure in the individual the relative strength of the six values of men as these values have been conceptualized and described by the German psychologist and educator, Eduard Spranger (1928), namely, the theoretical, economic, esthetic, social, political, and religious values, all of our creative groups have as their highest values the theoretical and the esthetic.

For creative research scientists the theoretical value is the highest, closely followed by the esthetic. For creative architects the highest value is the esthetic, with the theoretical value almost as high. For creative mathematicians, the two values are both high and approximately equally strong.

If, as the authors of the test believe, there is some incompatibility and conflict between the theoretical value with its cognitive and rational concern with truth and the esthetic value with its emotional concern with form and beauty, it would appear that the creative person has the capacity to tolerate the tension that strong opposing values create in him, and in his creative striving he effects some reconciliation of them. For the truly creative person it is not sufficient that problems be solved, there is the further demand that the solutions be elegant. He seeks both truth and beauty.

A summary description of the creative person—especially of the creative architect—as he reveals himself in his profile on the California Psychological Inventory (Gough, 1957) reads as follows:

> He is dominant (Do scale); possessed of those qualities and attributes which underlie and lead to the achievement of social status (Cs); poised, spontaneous, and self-confident in personal and social interaction (Sp); though not of an especially sociable or participative temperament (low Sy); intelligent, outspoken, sharp-witted, demanding, aggressive, and self-centered; persuasive and verbally fluent, self-confident and self-assured (Sa); and relatively uninhibited in expressing his worries and complaints (low Wb).
>
> He is relatively free from conventional restraints and inhibitions (low So and Sc), not preoccupied with the impression which he makes on others and thus perhaps capable of great independence and autonomy (low Gi), and relatively ready to recognize and admit self-views that are unusual and unconventional (low Cm).
>
> He is strongly motivated to achieve in situations in which independence in thought and action are called for (Ai). But, unlike his less creative colleagues, he is less inclined to strive for achievement in settings where conforming behavior is expected or required (Ac). In efficiency and steadiness of intellectual effort (Ie), however, he does not differ from his fellow workers.
>
> Finally, he is definitely more psychologically minded (Py), more flexible (Fx), and possessed of more femininity of interests (Fe) than architects in general.

There is one last finding that I wish to present, one that was foreshadowed by a discovery of Dr. Bingham in one of his attempts to study creativity. The subject of his study was Amy Lowell, a close friend of his and Mrs. Bingham's, with whom he discussed at length the birth and growth of her poems, seeking insight into the creative processes of her mind. He also administered to her a word association test and "found that she gave a higher proportion of unique responses than those of any one outside a mental institution" (Bingham, Milicent Todd, 1953, p. 11). We too, administered a word association test to our subjects and found the unusualness of mental associations one of the best predictors of creativity, and especially so when associations given by no more than 1% to 10% of the population, using the Minnesota norms (Russell & Jenkins, 1954), are weighted more heavily than those given by less than 1% of the population. Among architects, for example, this weighted score is for Architects I, 204; Architects II, 128; and Architects III, 114; while for the total sample this measure of unusualness of mental associations correlates $+.50$ with rated creativity.

And Dr. Bingham, like us, found that there are certain hazards in attempting to study a creative poet. His searchings were rewarded by a poem Amy Lowell later wrote which was first entitled "To the Impudent Psychologist" and published posthumously with the title "To a Gentleman who wanted to see the first drafts of my poems in the interest of psychological research into the workings of the creative mind." We, I must confess, were treated somewhat less kindly by one of our poets who, after assessment, published an article entitled "My Head Gets Tooken Apart" (Rexroth, 1959).

Having described the overall design of our studies, and having presented a selection of our findings which reveal at least some aspects of the nature of creative talent, I turn now, but with considerably less confidence, to the question as to how we can early identify and best encourage the development of creative potential. Our findings concerning the characteristics of highly creative persons are by now reasonably well established, but their implication for the nurture of creative talent are far from clear.

It is one thing to discover the distinguishing characteristics of mature, creative, productive individuals. It is quite another matter to conclude that the traits of creative persons observed several years after school and college characterized these same individuals when they were students. Nor can we be certain that finding these same traits in youngsters today will identify those with creative potential. Only empirical, longitudinal research, which we do not yet have, can settle such issues. Considering, however, the nature of the traits which discriminate creative adults from their non-creative peers, I would venture to guess that most students with creative potential have personality structures congruent with, though possibly less sharply delineated than, those of mature creatives.

Our problem is further complicated by the fact that though our creative subjects have told us about their experiences at home, in school, and in college, and about the forces and persons and situations which, as they see it, nurtured their creativeness, these are, after all, self-reports subject to the misperceptions and self-deceptions of all self-reports. Even if we were to assume that their testimony is essentially accurate we would still have no assurance that the conditions in the home, in school, and society, the qualities of interpersonal relations between instructor and student, and the aspects of the teaching-learning process which would appear to have contributed to creative development a generation ago would facilitate rather than inhibit creativity if these same factors were created in today's quite different world and far different educational climate.

In reporting upon events and situations in the life histories of our subjects which appear to have fostered their creative potential and independent spirit, I shall again restrict myself to architects. One finds in their histories a number of circumstances which, in the early years, could well have provided an opportunity as well as the necessity for developing the secure sense of personal autonomy and zestful commitment to their profession which so markedly characterize them.

What appears most often to have characterized the parents of these future creative architects was an extraordinary respect for the child and confidence in his ability to do what was appropriate. Thus they did not hesitate to grant him rather unusual freedom in exploring his universe and in making decisions for himself—and this early as well as late. The expectation of the parent that the child would act independently but reasonably and responsibly appears to have contributed immensely to the latter's sense of personal autonomy which was to develop to such a marked degree.

The obverse side of this was that there was often a lack of intense closeness with one or both of the parents. Most often this appeared in relation to the father rather than to the mother, but often it characterized the relationship with both parents. There were not strong emotional ties of either a positive or a negative sort between parent and child, but neither was there the type of relationship that fosters overdependency nor the type that results in severe rejection. Thus, if there was a certain distance in the relationship between child and parent, it had a liberating effect so far as the child was concerned. If he lacked something of the emotional closeness which some children experience with their parents, he was also spared that type of psychological exploitation that is so frequently seen in the life histories of clinical patients.

Closely related to this factor of some distance between parent and child were ambiguities in identification with the parents. In place of the more usual clear identification with one parent, there was a tendency for the architects to have identified either with both parents or with neither. It was not that the child's early milieu was a deprived one so far as models for identification and the promotion of ego ideals were concerned. It was rather that the larger familial sphere presented the child with a plentiful supply of diverse and effective models—in addition to the mother and father, grandfathers, uncles, and others who occupied prominent and responsible positions within their community—with whom important identifications could be made. Whatever the emotional interaction between father and son, whether distant, harmonious, or turbulent, the father presented a model of effective and resourceful behavior in an exceptionally demanding career. What is perhaps more significant, though, is the high incidence of distinctly autonomous mothers among families of the creative architects, who led active lives with interests and sometimes careers of their own apart from their husbands'.

Still other factors which would appear to have contributed to the development of the marked personal autonomy of our subjects were the types of discipline and religious training which they received, which suggest that within the family there existed clear standards of conduct and ideas as to what was right and wrong but at the same time an expectation if not requirement of active exploration and internalization of a framework of personal conduct. Discipline was almost always consistent and predictable. In most cases there were rules, family standards, and parental injunctions which were known explicitly by the children and seldom infringed. In nearly half the cases, corporal punishment was not employed and in only a few instances was the punishment harsh or cruel.

As for religious practices, the families of the creative architects showed considerable diversity, but what was most widely emphasized was the development of personal ethical codes rather than formal religious practices. For one-third of the families formal religion was important for one parent or for both, but in two-thirds of the families formal religion was either unimportant or practiced only perfunctorily. For the majority of the families, in which emphasis was placed upon the development of one's own ethical code, it is of interest to inquire into the values that were most stressed. They were most often values related to integrity (e.g., forthrightness, honesty, respect for others), quality (e.g., pride, diligence, joy in work, development of talent), intellectual and cultural endeavor, success and ambition, and being respectable and doing the right thing.

The families of the more creative architects tended to move more frequently, whether within a single community, or from community to community, or even from country to country. This, combined with the fact that the more creative architects as youngsters were given very much more freedom to roam and to explore widely, provided for them an enrichment of experience both cultural and personal which their less creative peers did not have.

But the frequent moving appears also to have resulted frequently in some estrangement of the family from its immediate neighborhood. And it is of interest that in almost every case in which the architect reported that his family differed in its behavior and values from those in the neighborhood, the family was different in showing greater cultural, artistic, and intellectual interests and pursuits.

To what extent this sort of cultural dislocation contributed to the frequently reported experiences of aloneness, shyness, isolation, and solitariness during childhood and adolescence, with little or no dating during adolescence, or to what extent these experiences stemmed from a natural introversion of interests and unusual sensitivity, we cannot say. They were doubtless mutually reinforcing factors in stimulating the young architect's awareness of his own inner life and his growing interest in his artistic skills and his ideational, imaginal, and symbolic processes.

Almost without exception, the creative architects manifested very early considerable interest and skill in drawing and painting. And also, with almost no exception, one or both of the parents were of artistic temperament and considerable skill. Often it was the mother who in the architect's early years fostered his artistic potentialities by her example as well as by her instruction. It is especially interesting to note, however, that while the visual and artistic abilities and interests of the child were encouraged and rewarded, these interests and abilities were, by and large, allowed to develop at their own speed, and this pace varied considerably among the architects. There was not an anxious concern on the part of the parents about the skills and abilities of the child. What is perhaps most significant was the widespread definite lack of strong pressures from the parents toward a particular career. And this was true both for pressures away from architecture as well as for pressures toward architecture by parents who were themselves architects.

The several aspects of the life history which I have described were first noted by Kenneth Craik in the protocols for the highly creative Architects I. Subsequently, in reading the protocols for Architects II and III as well as Architects I, a credit of one point for the presence of each of the factors was assigned and the total for each person taken as a score. The correlation of these life history scores with rated creativity of the architects is +.36, significant beyond the .005 level of confidence.

And now I turn finally to a consideration of the implications of the nature of creative talent for the nurturing of it in school and college through the processes of education.

Our findings concerning the relations of intelligence to creativity suggest that we may have overestimated in our educational system the role of intelligence in creative achievement. If our expectation is that a child of a given intelligence will not respond creatively to a task which confronts him, and especially if we make this expectation known to the child, the probability that he will respond creatively is very much reduced. And later on, such a child, now grown older, may find doors closed to him so that he is definitely excluded from certain domains of learning. There is increasing reason to believe that in selecting students for special training of their talent we may have overweighted the role of intelligence either by setting the cutting point for selection on the intellective dimension too high or by assuming that regardless of other factors the student with the higher IQ is the more promising one and should consequently be chosen. Our data suggest, rather, that if a person has the minimum of intelligence required for mastery of a field of knowledge, whether he performs creatively or banally in that field will be crucially determined by nonintellective factors. We would do well then to pay more attention in the future than we have in the past to the nurturing of those nonintellective traits which in our studies have been shown to be intimately associated with creative talent.

There is the openness of the creative person to experience both from within and from without which suggests that whether we be parent or teacher we should use caution in setting limits upon what those whom we are nurturing experience and express.

Discipline and self-control are necessary. They must be learned if one is ever to be truly creative, but it is important that they not be overlearned. Furthermore, there is a time and place for their learning, and having been learned they should be used flexibly, not rigidly or compulsively.

If we consider this specifically with reference to the attitudes of perceiving and judging, everyone must judge as well as perceive. It is not a matter of using one to the exclusion of the other, but a question of how each is used and which is preferred. The danger for one's creative potential is not the judging or evaluating of one's experience but that one prejudges, thus excluding from perception large areas of experience. The danger in all parental instruction, as in all academic instruction, is that new ideas and new possibilities of action are criticized too soon and too often. Training in criticism is obviously important and so widely recognized that I need not plead its case. Rather I would urge that, if we wish to nurture creative potential, an equal emphasis be placed on perceptiveness, discussing with our students as well as with our children, at least upon occasion, the most fantastic of ideas and possibilities. It is the duty of parents to communicate and of professors to profess what they judge to be true, but it is no less their duty by example to encourage in their children and in their students an openness to all ideas and especially to those which most challenge and threaten their own judgments.

The creative person, as we have seen, is not only open to experience, but intuitive about it. We can train students to be accurate in their perceptions, and this, too, is a characteristic of the creative. But can we train them to be intuitive, and if so how?

I would suggest that rote learning, learning of facts for their own sake, repeated drill of material, too much emphasis upon facts unrelated to other facts, and excessive concern with memorizing, can all strengthen and reinforce sense perception. On the other hand, emphasis upon the transfer of training from one subject to another, the searching for common principles in terms of which facts from quite different domains of knowledge can be related, the stressing of analogies, and similes, and metaphors, a seeking for symbolic equivalents of experience in the widest possible number of sensory and imaginal modalities, exercises in imaginative play, training in retreating from the facts in order to see them in larger perspective and in relation to more aspects of the larger context thus achieved—these and still other emphases in learning would, I believe, strengthen the disposition to intuitive perception as well as intuitive thinking.

If the widest possible relationships among facts are to be established, if the structure of knowledge (Bruner, 1960) is to be grasped, it is necessary that the student have a large body of facts which he has learned as well as a large array of reasoning skills which he has mastered. You will see, then, that what I am proposing is not that in teaching one disdain acute and accurate sense perception, but that one use it to build upon, leading the student always to an intuitive understanding of that which he experiences.

The independence of thought and action which our subjects reveal in the assessment setting appears to have long characterized them. It was already manifest in high school, though, according to their reports, tending to increase in college and thereafter.

In college our creative architects earned about a B average. In work and courses which caught their interest they could turn in an A performance, but in courses that failed to strike their imagination, they were quite willing to do no work at all. In general, their attitude in college appears to have been one of profound skepticism. They were unwilling to accept anything on the mere say-so of their instructors. Nothing was to be accepted on faith or because it had behind it the voice of authority. Such matters might be accepted, but only after the student on his own had demonstrated their validity to himself. In a sense, they were rebellious, but they did not run counter to the standards out of sheer rebelliousness. Rather, they were spirited in their disagreement and one gets the impression that they learned most from those who were not easy with them. But clearly many of them were not easy to take. One of the most rebellious, but, as it turned out, one of the most creative, was advised by the Dean of his School to quit because he had no talent; and another, having been failed in his design dissertation which attacked the stylism of the faculty, took his degree in the art department.

These and other data should remind all of us who teach that creative students will not always be to our liking. This will be due not only to their independence in situations in which nonconformity may be seriously disruptive of the work of others, but because, as we have seen, more than most they will be experiencing large quantities of tension produced in them by the richness of their experience and the strong opposites of their nature. In struggling to reconcile these opposites and in striving to achieve creative solutions to the difficult problems which they have set themselves they will often show that psychic turbulence which is so characteristic of the creative person. If, however, we can only recognize the sources of their disturbance, which often enough will result in behavior disturbing to us, we may be in a better position to support and encourage them in their creative striving.

## References

Allport, G. W., Vernon, P. E., & Lindzey, G. *Study of values: Manual of directions.* (Rev. ed.) Boston: Houghton Mifflin, 1951.

Barron, F., & Welsh, G. S. Artistic perception as a possible factor in personality style: Its measurement by a figure preference test. *J. Psychol.*, 1952, 33, 199-203.

Bingham, Millicent Todd. Beyond psychology. In, *Homo sapiens auduboniensis: A tribute to Walter Van Dyke Bingham.* New York: National Audubon Society, 1953. Pp. 5-29.

Bruner, J. S. *The process of education.* Cambridge, Mass.: Harvard Univer. Press, 1960.

Gough, H. G. *California Psychological Inventory manual.* Palo Alto, Calif.: Consulting Psychologists Press, 1957.

Hall, W. B. The development of a technique for assessing aesthetic predispositions and its application to a sample of professional research scientists. Paper read at Western Psychological Association, Monterey, California, April 1958.

Hathaway, S. R., & McKinley, J. C. *Minnesota Multiphasic Personality Inventory.* New York: Psychological Corporation, 1945.

Jung, C. G. *Psychological types.* New York: Harcourt, Brace, 1923.

Jung, C. G. *Two essays on analytical psychology.* New York: Meridian, 1956.

MacKinnon, D. W. The personality correlates of creativity: A study of American architects. In G. S. Nielsen (Ed.), *Proceedings of the XIV International Congress of Applied Psychology, Copenhagen 1961.* Vol. 2. Copenhagen: Munksgaard, 1962. Pp. 11-39.

Myers, Isabel B. *Some findings with regard to type and manual for Myers-Briggs Type Indicator, Form E.* Swarthmore, Pa.: Author, 1958.

Rexroth, K. My head gets tooken apart. In, *Bird in the bush: Obvious essays.* New York: New Directions Paperbook, 1959. Pp. 65-74.

Russell, W. A., & Jenkins, J. J. The complete Minnesota norms for responses to 100 words from the Kent-Rosanoff Word Association Test. Technical Report No. 11, 1954, University of Minnesota, Contract N8 onr-66216, Office of Naval Research.

Spranger, E. *Types of men.* (Trans. by Paul J. W. Pigors) Halle (Saale), Germany: Max Niemeyer, 1928.

Strong, E. K., Jr. *Manual for Strong Vocational Interest Blanks for Men and Women, Revised Blanks (Form M and W).* Palo Alto, Calif.: Consulting Psychologists Press, 1959.

Terman, L. M. *Concept Mastery Test, Form T manual.* New York: Psychological Corporation, 1956.

Welsh, G. S. *Welsh Figure Preference Test: Preliminary manual.* Palo Alto, Calif.: Consulting Psychologists Press, 1959.

Wotton, Henry. *The elements of architecture.* London: John Bill, 1624.

*Frank Barron*

# *Originality in Relation to Personality and Intellect*

$T$he purpose of this paper is two-fold: (*a*) to report relationships observed in a sample of normal men between a measure of originality and measures of certain other aspects of personal and intellectual functioning; and (*b*) more especially, to consider the statistically significant correlates of originality both when intelligence is partialled out and when it is systematically varied through special selection of *S*s.

The study employed a wide variety of psychological tests in a living-in assessment setting, using as *S*s a sample of military officers. Both because of the nature of the sample and because of the method employed for discovering significant relationships, several restrictions upon the generalizability of the results must be recognized. For one thing, correlation coefficients between the measure of originality and several hundred other variables were computed in a search for significant associations, and the observed correlations have not as yet been checked in any other sample. Moreover, the *S*s themselves were not selected with a view to discovering the traits of original persons; they had not engaged themselves in work which called for a high order of original thought, nor was originality an important value in their lives. In brief, the correlations to be reported may not reflect anything concerning the way in which highly creative people differ from the norm. The results therefore are germane to the question of how originality varies with other personal characteristics only if originality be considered as a variable which is distributed continuously throughout the general population.

In spite of these strictures inherent in the design of the study, there is some reason to believe that the results are generalizable to the problem of creative process in the highly original person. In an earlier report (4) on this

Barron, Frank "Originality in Relation to Personality and Intellect." *Journal of Personality,* 1957 25:730-742

This research was supported in part by the United States Air Force under Contract No. AF 18 (600) -8 monitored by Technical Director, Detachment #7 (Officer Education Research Laboratory), Air Force Personnel and Training Research Center, Maxwell Air Force Base, Alabama. Permission is granted for reproduction, translation, publication, use and disposal in whole and in part by or for the United States Government. Personal views or opinions expressed or implied in this publication are not to be construed as necessarily carrying the official sanction of the Department of the Air Force or of the Air Research and Development Command.

same group of *S*s, it was shown both that originality in free-response performance tests is sufficiently consistent across tests to be considered a dimension, and that in addition the test dimension itself is related to personality variables which had been hypothesized on theoretical grounds to be characteristics of highly original persons. Thus the testing of theory in that study suggests that generalizable relationships may be discovered in this sample.

## Test Measures of Originality

Eight tests which were presumed to measure originality or to provide a medium for its expression by the *S*s and its discernment by raters were used. Three of these tests were developed by Guilford and his associates in the Project on Aptitudes of High-Level Personnel at the University of Southern California, and have been shown by them to emerge with high loadings on a factor identifiable as originality (**12**). The three tests are: (*a*) Unusual Uses; (*b*) Consequences B; (*c*) Plot Titles B. Unusual Uses calls upon the *S* to list six uses to which each of several common objects can be put, and it is scored for infrequency, in the sample under study, of the uses proposed. In Consequences B the respondent is asked to write down what would happen if certain changes were suddenly to take place, and a score reflecting the cleverness or remoteness of the consequences suggested is obtained. In Plot Titles B the *S*'s score is the number of clever, as opposed to obvious or ordinary, titles he suggests for two story plots.

In addition to the three tests from the Guilford creativity battery, two standard projective tests, the Rorschach (**18**) and the Thematic Apperception Test (**17**), were used. The Rorschach O+ count was taken as one measure of originality, and the TAT stories were rated for originality by two raters working independently. A sixth test measure was provided by a Rorschach-like set of inkblots which had been developed by the present writer to measure threshold for the human movement response (**5**), but which in this context was scored simply for infrequency of the percepts reported by the *S* in protocols of the sample studied. A count of highly infrequent but correct anagram solutions to the test word "generation" provided a seventh measure, and a rating of the originality of a story composed by the *S* in which he was called upon to use all of the words in a standard list of fifty randomly selected common nouns, adjectives, and adverbs provided the eighth. These measures, their reliabilites, and their interrelations have been described in full elsewhere (**4**). In the present report the sum of the standard scores earned by each *S* on all eight tests is taken as a single measure of originality, and that variable will be referred to herein as the Originality Composite.

## The Ss and the Method of Study

The sample under study consisted of 100 officers in the United States Air Force; all were of the rank of captain, and they ranged in age from 27 to 50, with a mean of 33. As a group they were well above average in intelligence, in education, in physical health, and in personal stability. In preservice socioeconomic background they tended to be lower middle class. Most of them were combat veterans, and many had been decorated for valor either in World War II or in the Korean conflict. All but three were married, and most of them had at least two children. As a group they were less variable than men-in-general on a wide variety of psychological measures, and they were consistently above the average of the general population on variables favorable to personal effectiveness. A full description of the sample and of its standing relative to the generality on a variety of psychological tests is given elsewhere (16).

The Ss were studied in groups of ten for three full days at the Institute of Personality Assessment and Research. The method of study emphasized observation of the Ss in informal social interaction, situational tests, interviews, group discussions, charades, and the like. Thus there was ample opportunity for the social characteristics of the Ss to manifest themselves, and the raters were in a position to observe spontaneous and highly varied behavior. In addition, the subjects were administered an extensive battery of standard psychological tests.

Observations made by staff members during the assessment period were put in summary form and prepared for statistical analysis mainly through two techniques: a Q-sort deck of 76 statements descriptive of personal functioning,[2] and an adjective checklist consisting of 300 common, personally descriptive adjectives (16).[3] Both techniques were used by staff members at the conclusion of each assessment period to describe each assessee.

The Q-sort statements were sorted on a 9-point scale, while the adjectives were checked simply as characteristic or not characteristic of the given S. A composite Q-sort description of each S was obtained by averaging the placements of the items by four staff members. The composite adjective description consisted of all adjectives which had been checked as characteristic of the S by at least three of ten raters.[4]

These descriptions were given without knowledge of the objective test performances of the Ss. No rater knew any S's score on the Originality Composite at the time the descriptions were made.

Scores on the Originality Composite were correlated also with nearly 200 other assessment variables, most of which had proved upon inspection to be normally distributed. Space limitations prohibit the listing of all these variables here, but the nature of most of them may be indicated briefly. A full description of each variable, together with statistics descriptive of the variable's distribution in this sample, may be found in another report (16).

*Sources of variables:*

The Concept Mastery Test (20) : total score
The Wesman Personnel Classification Test (21) : Verbal and Numerical subtests and total score
The Minnesota Multiphasic Personality Inventory (13) : 14 scales
The Rorschach Psychodiagnostic (18) : 20 scores
The Personal Preference Survey (14) : 10 scales
The Strong Vocational Interest Blank (19) : 46 scales

[2]Developed by Drs. Jack Block and Robert E. Harris.
[3]Developed by Dr. Harrison G. Gough.
[4]The staff observers consisted of the following psychologists: Donald W.MacKinnon, Director of the Institute of Personality Assessment and Research; Richard S. Crutchfield, Associate Director; Jack Block, Harrison G. Gough, Robert E. Harris, and Frank Barron, senior staff members; Wallace Hall, Donal Jones, Betty L. Kalis, Paul Petersen, and Donald G. Woodworth, research assistants.

The Idea Classification Test (16) : total score
Charades (3) : four ratings and five scores
Staff ratings (16) : 30 traits
The Barron M-Threshold Inkblots (5) : threshold for human movement and volume of human movement
The Barron-Welsh Art Scale (2)
Improvisations (16) : 20 ratings
The Gottschaldt Figures Test (16) : total score
The Bennett Mechanical Comprehension Test (7)
The Minnesota Paper Form Board (15)
The Chapin Social Insight Test (8)
The Special IPAR Composite Personality Inventory (16) : 19 scales
The California Personality Inventory (10) : 20 scales
Form 60 of Berkeley Public Opinion Survey Scales (1) : 3 scales

# Differences in Staff Descriptions of High and Low Scorers

The 25 highest scorers on the Originality Composite were compared with the 25 lowest scorers on both the Q-sort descriptions and the composite adjective descriptions. The Q-sort items which showed statistically significant differences are given below.

*High Scorers*

At the .001 level:
1. verbally fluent, conversationally facile
2. high degree of intellect
3. communicates ideas clearly and effectively
4. highly cathects intellectual activity
5. is an effective leader
6. is persuasive; wins others over to his point of view

At the .01 level:
7. is concerned with philosophical problems and the meaning of life
8. takes an ascendant role in his relations with others.

*Low Scorers*

At the .001 level:
1. conforming; tends to do the things that are prescribed
2. is stereotyped and unoriginal in his approach to problems
3. has a narrow range of interests
4. tends not to become involved in things
5. lacks social poise and presence
6. is unaware of his own social stimulus value

At the .01 level:
7. slow personal tempo
8. with respect to authority, is submissive, compliant, and overly accepting
9. lacks confidence in self
10. is rigid, inflexible
11. lacks insight into own motives
12. is suggestible
13. is unable to make decisions without vacillation, hesitation, and delay

Adjectives which were applied differentially (at the .05 level or better) by the assessment staff to high and low scorers are given below, with the frequencies (i.e., number of cases out of 25 to which the adjective was applied) stated in parentheses after the adjective. Frequencies for high scorers are given first.

*High Scorers*
interests wide (12-1)
clever (9-1)
imaginative (9-1)
planful (9-1)
poised (11-2)
determined (10-2)
talkative (10-2)
logical (9-2)
rational (9-2)
shrewd (0-2)
civilized (8-2)
loyal (8-2)
mature (8-2)
versatile (7-0)
efficient (14-3)
initiative (13-3)
resourceful (12-3)
reflective (9-3)
quick (9-3)
enterprising (11-4)
energetic (10-4)
organized (10-4)
fairminded (13-6)

*Low Scorers*
dull (0-8)
commonplace (1-11)
simple (1-11)
slow (1-10)
apathetic (1-8)
rigid (1-7)
unassuming (5-12)
conventional (7-13)

From these Q-sort and adjective descriptions one is led to believe that considerable validity inheres in the originality measure. In brief, high scorers are seen as intelligent, widely informed, concerned with basic problems, clever and imaginative, socially effective and personally dominant, verbally fluent, and possessed of initiative. Low scorers are seen as conforming, rigid and stereotyped, uninsightful, commonplace, apathetic, and dull.

However, the marked relationship of originality to verbal fluency and to rated intellect raises a question concerning the extent to which this list of traits is determined by intelligence quite apart from originality. Perhaps these are in large part the traits of intelligent people, rather than of people who are not only intelligent but original as well. What we should like to know is the correlation between personality variables and that part of the variance in originality which is *not* associated with variance in general intellectual ability.

It is of course reasonable to expect that intelligence and originality will covary positively. If one defines originality as the ability to respond to stimulus situations in a manner which is both adaptive and unusual, and if one defines intelligence simply as the ability to solve problems, then at the upper levels of problem-solving ability the manifestation of intelligence will be also a manifestation of originality. That is to say, the very difficult problem which is rarely solved requires by definition a solution which is original.

It seems desirable, therefore, to partial out the effect of intelligence upon the correlations between the Originality Composite and other assessment measures. The Concept Mastery Test was here accepted as a good measure of general intelligence, though clearly with most emphasis upon the verbal comprehension factor in intelligence.

The product-moment correlation coefficient between the Concept Mastery Test and the Originality Composite in this sample is .33, a relationship significantly different from zero at the .01 level. When the Originality Composite is correlated with the other assessment measures and its relationship to the Concept Mastery Test is partialled out, the statistically significant partial $r$'s shown in Table 1 are discovered. (In Table 1 the variables are grouped, and the groups named, simply in a way which makes sense subjectively to the present writer; these are not clusters established statistically.)

With the effect of verbal intelligence thus removed, the forces determining original response emerge in an interesting pattern. One cluster of variables which are in fact uncorrelated with intelligence consists of responsiveness to color on the Rorschach, high scores on Block's scale purporting

### TABLE 1
#### Variables Significantly Associated with the Originality
#### Composite When Concept Mastery Test Scores
#### Are Partialled Out

| | Partial $r$'s |
|---|---|
| *Disposition towards integration of diverse stimuli:* | |
| 1. Rorschach: W | .52 |
| 2. Rorschach: number of different determinants used | .37 |
| 3. Idea Classification Test: number of classes discerned in sets of varied objects and property | .31 |
| *Energy, fluent output, involvement:* | |
| 4. Improvisations: degree of participation | .35 |
| 5. Word Fluency Test: total output | .41 |
| 6. Charades: motility | .39 |
| 7. Charades: fluency | .28 |
| 8. Staff rating: fluency of ideas | .49 |
| 9. Staff rating: drive | .42 |
| *Personal dominance and self-assertion:* | |
| 10. Improvisations: dominance | .37 |
| 11. Staff rating: dominance | .37 |
| 12. CPI: Dominance scale | .29 |
| 13 Personal Preference Scale: Active Phallic | .47 |
| *Responsiveness to impulse and emotion:* | |
| 14. CPI: Impulsive scale | .39 |
| 15. Block Ego-control Scale: undercontrol | .40 |
| 16. Rorschach: sum C | .38 |
| *Expressed femininity of interests:* | |
| 17. SVIB: Masculinity | —.31 |
| 18. MMPI: Femininity (Mf) | .33 |
| 19. PPS: Feminine Identification | .30 |
| *General effectiveness of performance:* | |
| 20. Charades: overall performance | .39 |
| 21. Improvisations: total effectiveness | .34 |
| 22. Staff rating: Overall effectiveness in staff function in the Air Force | .37 |

to measure undercontrol of impulse, and high scores on the CPI Impulsivity scale. Perhaps the rating of motility in Charades (defined as amount of motoric activity by the $S$ when attempting to convey a title to his teammates) is better grouped with this cluster too. What may be involved here is the tendency of the individual to discharge tension, through motor avenues of discharge, as immediately as possible, and hence to be relatively more under what in psychoanalytic terms would be called the domination of the pleasure principle rather than the reality principle.

Another cluster, that which is here labeled "energy, fluent output, involvement," would seem to indicate a higher level of drive, as well as ease of expression of the drive in work. This might well be a generic factor which shows itself interpersonally in the form of dominance and striving for power. The behavior apparently is effective as well, judging from the correlations with various ratings of effectiveness of performance.

The group of variables titled "disposition towards integration of diverse stimuli" suggests an openness in the more original $S$s to a variety of phenomena, combined with a strong need to organize those phenomena into some coherent pattern. This might best be described as a resistance to premature closure, combined with a persistent effort to achieve closure in an elegant fashion. In brief, everything that can be perceived must be taken cognizance of before a configuration is recognized as a possibly final one.

The relationships noted between originality and femininity of interest pattern may conceivably be explained in terms of some of the dynamics suggested above, although they lend themselves also to a quite different sort of speculation. In a sense, the recognition by men of impulses or interests which are considered more appropriate in women, or at least more characteristic of women than of men in this culture, may be seen as one aspect of the more basic disposition to allow more complexity and contradictions into consciousness; this assumes, of course, an initial biological bisexual disposition in both men and women. Thus the more original men would permit themselves to be more aware of tabooed interests and impulses, and would seek to integrate these superficially discordant phenomena into a more complex whole.

Another possible explanation is that some degree of cross-sex identification is important for creativity in men and perhaps women as well. The creative act is a kind of giving birth, and it is noteworthy that as an historical fact intellectual creativity has been conspicuously lacking in women, whose products are their children. At the risk of making too much of a linguistic parallel, it might be said that nature has literally arranged a division of labor. Men bring forth ideas, paintings, literary and musical compositions, organizations of states, inventions, new material structures, and the like, while women bring forth the new generation. Perhaps it is also true that women who do the kind of creative work usually done by men may themselves have some degree of reversal of the usual sexual identifications, being relatively more masculine in interests and impulses than the generality of women; at any rate, such an hypothesis seems worth investigating.

174

However, it may be that the present finding requires no very high-flown explanation, since this sample of military officers was on the average more masculine (in terms of scores on the tests mentioned) than men-in-general, and high scores on femininity in these subjects represented quite unremarkable deviations in the feminine direction.

## Correlates of Large Discrepancies Between Originality and Intelligence

Data gathered in a larger sample of officers, most of whom did not take part in living-in assessment, permit another approach to the question of what personality traits go along with originality in the absence (in this instance, the conspicuous absence) of the usually covarying verbal intelligence. In this study, 343 officers of the rank of captain, 100 of whom comprised the sample discussed previously, were scored on four of the eight measures used in the Originality Composite. The four measures were: Unusual Uses, Consequences B, Plot Titles B, and Word Synthesis Originality. The Concept Mastery test was also administered to these 343 officers. In addition, the officers themselves filled out the adjective checklist under instructions to give a candid and accurate picture of themselves.

Two groups were now selected for comparison with one another: all the $Ss$ (fifteen in number) who were one standard deviation above the mean on the abbreviated four-measure Originality Composite while being one standard deviation below the mean on the Concept Mastery test, and all the $Ss$ (23 in number) who were one standard deviation above the mean on the Concept Mastery test while being one standard deviation below the mean on the Originality Composite. The two groups will be referred to respectively as $O_1$-$I_1$ and $I_1$-$O_1$. The adjectives which each group applied to itself significantly more often (at the .05 level of confidence) are given below.

$O_1$-$I_1$: affected, aggressive, demanding, dependent, dominant, forceful, impatient, initiative, outspoken, sarcastic, strong, suggestible.
$I_1$-$O_1$: mild, optimistic, pleasant, quiet, unselfish.

When these extreme groups are compared, the impulse-control dimension emerges most clearly as a determinant of originality. Subjects who are relatively original in spite of being relatively unintelligent show a lack of ego-control. They describe themselves as persons whose needs demand immediate gratification and whose aggressive impulses are out in the open. They are willful, obstreperous, and extreme individuals. One would not be inclined to select them as companions for a long trip in a submarine. By contrast, their relatively unoriginal but more intelligent fellows seem very much on the pleasant side, although perhaps a bit *too* bland and unwarlike, all things considered.

When one compares these self-descriptions with the staff descriptions of $Ss$ who are *both* original and intelligent, it appears that intelligence represents the operation of the reality principle in behavior, and is responsible for such characteristics as the appropriate delay of impulse-expression and effective organization of instinctual energy for the attainment of goals in the world as it is. To use another of the distinctions proposed by Freud in his theory of the functioning of the mental apparatus (9), primary process thinking to the exclusion of the secondary process marks the original but unintelligent person, secondary process thinking which carries ego-control to the point where the ego is not so much strong as muscle-bound marks the intelligent but unoriginal person, and easy accessibility of both primary process and secondary process marks the person who is both original and intelligent.


## Some Speculations

If these conclusions from the observed results be permitted for the moment, a speculative formulation suggests itself. The effectively original person may be characterized above all by an ability to regress very far *for the moment* while being able quite rapidly to return to a high degree of rationality, bringing with him the fruits of his regression to primitive and fantastic modes of thought (a variant of the phenomenon termed "regression in the service of the ego" by Lowenstein and Kris). Perhaps when the cortex is most efficient, or intelligence greatest, the ego realizes that it *can afford to allow* regression—because it can correct itself. A basic confidence in one's ability to discern reality accurately would thus facilitate the use of the powers of imagination.

Another way of putting this is to say that when the distinction between subject (self) and object is most secure, the distinction can with most security be allowed to disappear temporarily. In such an individual there might therefore occur some transitory phenomena of the sort that in truly pathological form are characteristic of the very weak ego (such as hallucinations, sense of oneness with the universe, visions, mystical beliefs, superstitions, etc.). But in the highly creative individual the basis for these phenomena is precisely the opposite of their basis in mentally ill individuals. In paranoia, for instance, the fundamental ego-failure is the chronic *inability* to distinguish between subject and object, between inner and outer sources of experience, so that introjection and projection appear as characteristic mechanisms. In the creative person, this distinction may indeed have been attained with great difficulty and may have been won out of childhood circumstances which are ordinarily pathogenic, but once attained it is then maintained with unusual confidence. Thus the creative genius may be at once naive and knowledgeable, being at home equally to primitive symbolism and to rigorous logic. He is both more primitive and more cultured, more destructive and more constructive, occasionally crazier and yet adamantly saner, than the average person.

## Summary

Eight free-response performance tests which purport to yield measures of originality were administered to 100 captains in the United States Air Force. A composite score on the test variable Originality was derived from this test battery, and psychologists' descriptions of high-scoring Ss were compared with descriptions of low-scoring Ss. The contrasting pictures which thus emerged seemed to indicate considerable validity in the Originality Composite, but they also raised some question concerning the way in which verbal intelligence alone might have determined some of the observed differences. Verbal intelligence was therefore partialled out from the correlations between the Originality Composite and other test performances and ratings. The significant relationships which remained when the effect of intelligence had been thus removed were grouped under these headings: (a) disposition towards integration of diverse stimuli; (b) energy, fluent output, involvement; (c) personal dominance and self-assertion; (d) responsiveness to impulse and emotion; (e) expressed femininity of interests; (f) general effectiveness of performance. In a larger sample, consisting of 343 officers, the self-descriptions of Ss relatively high on Originality but relatively low on Intelligence were compared with self-descriptions of officers low on Originality but high on Intelligence. The former group characterized themselves by adjectives which suggested undercontrol of impulse, while the latter group described themselves as unusually well-controlled. An interpretation of these results in terms of the Freudian theory of the functioning of the mental apparatus was made, and some further speculations going beyond the present data were advanced.

## References

1. Adorno, T. W., Frenkel-Brunswick, E., Levinson, D., & Sanford, R. N. *The authoritarian personality.* New York: Harpers, 1950.

2. Barron, F., & Welsh, G. S. Artistic perception as a possible factor in personality style: Its measurement by a figure-preference test. *J. Psychol.,* 1952, **33,** 199-203.

3. Barron, F. Charades as an assessment device. Unpublished technical memorandum available from the Institute of Personality Assessment and Research, Berkeley, California.

4. Barron, F. The disposition toward originality. *J. abnorm. soc. Psychol.,* 1955, **51,** 478-485.

5. Barron, F. Threshold for the perception of human movement in ink-blots. *J. consult. Psychol.,* 1955, **19,** 33-38.

6. Barron, F. *The word rearrangement test.* Lackland Air Force Base, Texas: Air Force Personnel and Training Research Center.

7. Bennett, G. K., & Fry, D. E. *Test of mechanical comprehension.* New

York: Psychological Corp., 1947.

8. Chapin, F. S. Preliminary standardization of a social insight scale. *Amer. sociol. Rev.,* 1942, **7,** 214-225.

9. Freud, S. Formulations regarding the two principles in mental functioning. *Collected Papers,* Vol. IV. London: The Hogarth Press and the Institute of Psychoanalysis, 1950.

10. Gough, H. G. *Manual for the California Psychological Inventory.* Palo Alto: Consulting Psychologists Press, 1956.

11. Gough, H. G., & Krauss, I. *An assessment study of Air Force officers: Part II. Description of the assessed sample.* Lackland Air Force Base, Texas: Air Force Personnel and Training Research Center.

12. Guilford, J. P., Wilson, R. C., & Christensen, P. R. *A factor-analytic study of creative thinking: II. Administration of tests and analysis of results.* Los Angeles: Univer. of Southern California, 1952, Psychol. Lab., No. 8.

13. Hathaway, S. R., & McKinley, J. C. *Manual for the Minnesota multiphasic personality inventory.* Minneapolis: Univer. of Minnesota Press, 1943.

14. Krout, M. H., & Tabin, J. K. Measuring personality in developmental terms: the Personal Preference Scale. *Genetic Psychol. Monogr.,* 1954, **50,** 289-335.

15. Likert, R., & Quasha, W. H. *Revised Minnesota Paper Form Board Test.* New York: The Psychological Corporation, 1948.

16. MacKinnon, D. W., Crutchfield, R. S., Barron, F., Block, J., Gough, H. G., & Harris, R. E. *An assessment study of Air Force officers: Part I. Design of the study and description of variables.* Lackland Air Force Base, Texas: Air Force Personnel and Training Research Center.

17. Murray, H. *Thematic apperception test manual.* Cambridge: Harvard Univer. Press, 1943.

18. Rorschach, H. *Psychodiagnostics.* Bern: Huber (Grune & Stratton, New York, distributors), 1942.

19. Strong, E. K., Jr. *Vocational Interest Blank for Men.* Palto Alto: Stanford Univer. Press, 1938.

20. Terman, L. M., & Oden, M. H. *The gifted child grows up.* Palo Alto: Stanford Univer. Press, 1947.

21. Wesman, A. G. *Personnel classification test.* New York: Psychological Corp., 1947.

*Marie Dellas*
*and*
*Eugene L. Gaier*

# *Identification of Creativity:*
# *The Individual*

The present paper reviews creativity research within the cognitive and personological investigative orientations on five parameters of creativity as they
affect the individual: (*a*) intellectual factors and cognitive styles associated
with creativity, (*b*) creativity as related/unrelated to intelligence, (*c*) personality aspects of creativity, (*d*) the potential creative, and (*e*) motivational
characteristics associated with creativity. Despite differences in age, cultural
background, area of operation or eminence, a particular consistent constellation of psychological traits emerges. These persons also appear distinguished
more by interests, attitudes, and drives, rather than by intellectual abilities.
The assessment of creative potential should include not only singular intellectual characteristics but also cognitive styles and personality variables.
Creativity research pursued on the basis of compound criteria from disparate
psychological levels holds promise for more valid findings which may, in addition, contribute toward the resolution of conceptual dilemmas.

The thesis of the present paper is a conceptualization of the creative
person. The purpose of this critical review of the research and theory is to
probe the psychological makeup of the creative individual within the context of the question: Does an uncommon or unusual, but appropriate,
production occur fortuitously, or does it occur as a result of a particular
constellation of personal traits? That consistent, creative production is
manifested in a particular psychological condition is the position of the
authors.

Most economically, the literature on creativity can be classified into four
major orientations: (*a*) the nature and quality of the *product* created, (*b*) the
actual expression of creative acts and the continuing *process* during the
"creation," (*c*) the *nature* of the individual, and (*d*) environmental factors
and *press* that tend to initiate and foster creativity. Since the appearance of
Golann's summary statement on creativity in 1963, studies have focused on
two tangential but highly relevant topics dealing with the creative. First, is

Dellas, Marie and Gaier, Eugene L. "Identification of Creativity: The Individual."
*Psychological Bulletin*, 1970, Vol. 73, No. 1, pp. 55-73.

creativity independent of intelligence? Second, is personality, per se, a vital aspect of creativity?

In an effort to order the empirical evidence concerning the creative individual, the present paper is organized within two general trends. One may be designated the *cognitive* orientation in which analyses are made within the framework of intellectual dimensions—singular, intellectual traits and cognitive functioning and styles. The other position may be identified as the *personological* approach in which personality and motivational traits are the foci. Specifically, consideration is given to characteristics consistent with creative performance and issues involved in these domains. These include (*a*) intellectual factors and cognitive styles associated with creativity, (*b*) creativity as related/unrelated to intelligence, (*c*) personality aspects of creativity, (*d*) the potential creative, and (*e*) motivational characteristics associated with creativity.

## Cognitive Characteristics

Attempts to identify the creative individual by means of cognitive variables appear directed toward the investigation of either singular intellectual factors or cognitive styles.

### INTELLECTUAL ABILITIES

By means of multivariate methods of factor analysis, Guilford and his associates supported 16 of 24 hypothesized intellectual abilities postulated to be related to creative production. Among these are fluency of thinking, comprised of word, ideational, expressional and associational fluency; flexibility of thinking, composed of spontaneous and adaptive; originality; sensitivity to problems, redefinition; and figural and semantic elaboration. Beginning with the first major analysis of Wilson, Guilford, Christensen and Lewis (1954), in which air cadets and student officers were tested, a series of investigations (Guilford & Merrifield, 1960) isolated 15 of these separate factors in young adult populations. More recently, studies have recognized them at student levels. Guilford and Hoepfner (1966) identified all 16 at the ninth-grade level; Merrifield, Guilford, and Gershon (1963) found 7 at the sixth-grade level, and 6 were demonstrated by Lauritzen (1963) at the fifth-grade level.

Using students rated highly creative in the visual arts, Lowenfeld and Beittel (1959) also identified essentially the same factors. Five attributes—fluency, flexibility, redefinition, sensitivity to problems, and originality—were identical to those reported by Guilford.

Guilford (1967b) has collectively defined these factors as "divergent" thinking, a mode of productive thinking, typical of the creator, which tends toward the novel or unknown. It is this novel output which he considered the essence of creative performance. As compared to convergent thinking which is oriented toward the known or "right" solution, divergent thinking occurs where a problem has yet to be defined or discovered, and where no set way of solving it exists. Guilford has developed tests purported to measure these creative abilities and which have been used to discriminate between the creative and noncreative. Although these measuring devices have some face validity, the issue that arises with their use pertains in part to construct validity—whether or not these divergent production abilities are, in fact, responsible for creative potential. In order to demonstrate that these are, indeed, creative abilities, scores from instruments assessing divergent thinking have been related to other indices of creative performance. The results, thus far, have been contradictory and far from conclusive.

An analysis of the data in Drevdahl's (1956) study of arts and science students revealed that those rated as highly creative by independent judges on personal and objective creativity rating scales demonstrated superior performance on Guilford originality tests, the scores for originality correlating .33 with the ratings. When divergent production scores of high school students obtained on Guilford-like tests were correlated with teacher nominations for creativity (Merrifield, Gardner, & Cox, 1964; Piers, Daniels, & Quackenbush, 1960; Torrance, 1962), the correlations were generally low, on the order of .2. Yamamoto (1964a) noted similar low correlations between Torrance creativity measures and peer nominations as criteria.

Using instruments measuring three aspects of divergent thinking—redefinition, semantic spontaneous flexibility, associational fluency—Skager, Klein, and Schultz (1967) concluded that they yielded low and inconsistent relationships with artistic achievement at a school of design. This appears to substantiate Beittel's (1964) findings which indicated a lack of relationship between divergent thinking measures and performance in art.

When employed in the study of eminent creative adults, these divergent production tests have also correlated low or negligibly with criterion ratings of creativity. With respect to architects judged highly creative by experts in their own field, MacKinnon (1961) established that whether scored for quality or quantity of responses, the Guilford tests neither correlated highly nor predicted efficiently the degree of creativity demonstrated in their creative production. Gough (1961), substantiating this claim, presented evidence indicating that for research scientists, rated creativity correlated low or negligibly with various Guilford tests: Unusual Uses correlated $-.05$; Consequences, $-.27$, and Gestalt Transformations .27. With Air Force officers, Barron (1963a) found a positive multiple correlation of .55 between rated originality and a composite divergent production score including Guilford tests. Using semantic divergent production tests with public relations personnel nominated by their superiors as high or low creative, Elliott (1964) also noted that the groups were significantly discriminated on the basis of each of five of the eight Guilford-type tests.

The lack of success of these instruments in predictive efficiency and in correlating with demonstrated creativity and other indices of creative performance may be attributed to several factors. First, there is no consistency among the creativity ratings which appears inseparable from the major problem—the absence of an ultimate criterion for creativity. Gough (1961) rated his scientists on general science and research competence, mathematical-theoretical orientation, efficiency and productiveness, original potential, and general sophistication. MacKinnon (1964) used the indices of publicity and prominence, plus a 5-point scale including such items as originality of thinking, constructive ingenuity, and ability to set aside established conventions and procedures. The differences in these two examples are obvious, to say nothing of the ambiguity of such terms as "prominence" and "competence."

The ratings themselves are only as good as the criteria used for selection and are subject to bias, halo effects, and the judgment abilities of the raters. With respect to teacher ratings, the basis for making judgments is suspect since they typically see students only in the classroom situation. They may also lack an understanding of the dimensions to be rated. Sociometric peer nominations are subject to similar limitations. Thus, valid differential ratings may then be precluded.

Divergent production tests may also not be suited to the group investigated. Initially, it seems reasonable to assume that the particular content of divergent thinking measures—semantic, figural, and symbolic— would be significant in yielding differential results for persons in different fields. Appropriately, Elliott (1964) used semantic divergent production tests with advertising and public relations personnel, obtaining a significant positive relationship with the selected criteria. A significant relationship, however, did not obtain when Beittel (1964) correlated semantic test scores with criteria of creative performance of college art students.

The majority of Guilford's tests also leave unilluminated the personological context in which the creative process functions. As a great number of investigators now agree, personality factors are of great significance despite the fact that, for the most part, little is known regarding their contribution to creative production. Guilford (1966) appeared aware of this when he explained the low reliability of tests of divergent production. "This probably reflects the general instability of functioning of individuals in creative ways . . . and therefore, high levels of predictive validity should not be expected [p. 189]."

It is not surprising, therefore, in light of the above, that assessment instruments may not correlate with criterion ratings. Yet, despite the fact that the validity of Guilford-like creativity measures is still incomplete and unclear, the available evidence does suggest a relationship between creative performance and the divergent thinking attributed to the creative. Furthermore, the diversity of these intellectual aspects of creativity and the fact that they are relatively distinct components indicate that perhaps different types of creative talent exist, the scientific creative probably excelling in different abilities from the aesthetic creative. Consequently, the versatile, creative person may be the exception rather than the rule.

Since the recognition of the divergent production abilities, the many studies conducted to probe the relationship of creativity and intelligence concern the empirical distinction between them—whether or not they are separate domains.

Several prominent investigators in the field, Getzels and Jackson (1962), Guilford (1967b), and Torrance (1962), maintain that a valid distinction exists between the cognitive function designated "creativity" and the traditional concept of general intelligence. To buttress their position, they cite the relatively low correlations between IQ and creativity measures. Guilford and Hoepfner (1966) reported a mean correlation of .32 between 45 divergent production test scores of the ninth graders cited previously and the California Test of Mental Maturity. Studying highly gifted adolescents, Getzels and Jackson (1962) found the correlation between IQ and Guilford-derived creativity measures to be on the order of .3. Using his own tests in a replication of the Getzels and Jackson work at the elementary school level, Torrance (1962) obtained essentially similar results, his correlations with various intelligence tests ranging from .16 to .32.

Other investigators have reported consonant findings. A correlation of .3 was found by Yamamoto (1964b) between Torrance creativity test scores of creative adolescents and the Lorge-Thorndike measure. Investigating scientifically oriented, bright students, Herr, Moore, and Hansen (1965) did not find any relationship between the Guilford tests of creativity and scores on the Lorge-Thorndike, Watson-Glaser Critical Thinking Appraisal, and Terman Concept Mastery measures. Using seven creativity instruments and taking the Getzels and Jackson study as his starting point, Flescher (1963) reported the average correlation with California Test of Mental Maturity scores was .04 for his sample of 110 sixth graders, suggesting definite independence of creativity indices from intelligence.

Within the framework of the Campbell and Fiske (1959) concepts of convergent validity and discriminant validity, Wallach and Kogan (1965) reviewed many of the cited studies and a number of others which have attempted an operational distinction between creativity and intelligence. In a penetrating analysis, they concluded that few of these studies demonstrated both convergent validity, in which intercorrelation of many different measures of creativity were high, and discriminant validity, in which intercorrelations of the creativity measures with intelligence measures were low. These conclusions appear to be in essential agreement with the analyses by Thorndike (1966) and Marsh (1964) of the Getzels and Jackson (1962) investigation, with several Guilford studies, and with the more recent Wallach (1968) analysis of the Torrance tests.

Wallach and Kogan (1965) attributed his failure to obtain convergent and discriminant validation for creativity to the presence of either the time pressure, or evaluation pressure, or both. Therefore, the major innovation in their very comprehensive study of fifth-grade students involved a change in the assessment situation—the establishment of a relaxed, nonevaluative atmosphere with no time limit. An analysis of the data based on a Guilford-derived creativity battery, designed to test Mednick's (1962) associative theory of creativity, revealed that creative thinking was strikingly independent of the conventional realm of intelligence, and was a unitary and pervasive dimension in its own right. The correlation among the creativity factors was on the order of .5, among the intelligence measures on the order of .5, but the average correlation between the two sets of measures was .1. This distinction obtained, despite the fact that the measuring instruments required the use of verbal skills which are accepted as playing an important role in the measurement of intelligence. Cropley (1968), who also used this creativity battery in a group-test situation, came up with similar results. The Wallace and Kogan tests manifested a high degree of internal consistency and were relatively independent of the intelligence tests. However, he also found a substantial general factor loaded highly on both kinds of tests.

The assumption that pressures of time and evaluation may, indeed, be significant influences in the creativity-intelligence differentiation gains some support from Dentler and Mackler (1964). Although the rigid 5-minute limitation on the Torrance Tin Can Uses Test for originality was maintained, they found a greater mean originality produced by subjects in their "safe" group as compared to those in "routine," "indifferent," and "unsafe" groups.

Investigators at the Institute of Personality Assessment and Research (IPAR) provide additional support for the creativity-intelligence dichotomy where the creativity dimension was based on ratings. Among artists, correlations between creativity (rated quality of work) and measured intelligence (Terman Concept Mastery Test) were zero or slightly negative (Barron, 1963a). MacKinnon (1961) provided additional substantiating evidence gathered from creative architects. Within this group, the correlation of intelligence, measured by the Terman Concept Mastery Test, and creativity in architecture, as rated by experts, was −.08, which is not significantly different from zero. Even in fields such as mathematics and science where intelligence is prerequisite for the mastery of the subject matter, the correlation, although positive, was a low .07 (Gough, 1961).

Barron (1963a) has observed that commitment to creative endeavors is already selective for intelligence, so that the average IQ is already a superior one. Consequently, he has suggested that over the total range of intelligence and creativity, a low, positive correlation of about .4 exists. Beyond the IQ of 120, however, measured intelligence appears to be a negligible factor in creativity. McNemar (1964) appeared to be in agreement with this theory when he stated that "at high IQ levels there will be a very wide range of creativity whereas as we go down to average IQ, and on down to lower levels, the scatter for creativity will be less and less [p. 879]." It is hardly surprising that this "fan shaped" hypothesis, more recently reiterated by Guilford (1967b), was not confirmed by Mednick and Andrews (1967) and by Ginsberg and Whittemore (1968), who found a positive linear relationship throughout the range. The creativity measure was the Remote Associates Test which has been severely criticized as being a measure of convergent thinking rather than the divergent thinking attributed to creatives.

The IPAR data, along with findings previously cited, appear to provide some evidence for describing creativity as a concept at the same level of abstraction as intelligence. Even Thorndike (1966), who so severely criticized the Getzels and Jackson and Guilford studies, conceded that their data suggested that "there is some reality to a broad domain, distinct from the domain of the conventional intelligence test to which the designation of 'divergent thinking' or 'creative thinking' might be applied [p. 52]." He considered this distinguishable domain rather "nebulous and loosely formed," any different creativity measures being necessarily less interchangeable and equivalent than different intelligence measures.

In seeking, however, to identify the creative individual, immediate cognizance must be given to the fact that a test of creativity is not "creativity," just as a test of intelligence is not "intelligence." Furthermore, "tests of creativity" not concerned with affect or personality attributes may be an over-simplification and may, perhaps, be tapping a very low level of creativity—reception or differentiation—which may be far afield from the product or performance, and the life activities domain. The inconclusiveness of the data, therefore, seems to suggest that perhaps, until the personological context in which the cognitive variables are embedded is determined, real measures of the dimension of creativity remain elusive.


COGNITIVE FUNCTIONING

*Preference for cognitive complexity.* One of the stylistic variables emerging as particularly distinctive of the creative is a cognitive preference for complexity—the rich, dynamic, and asymmetrical—as opposed to simplicity. That this perceptual style or aesthetic preference is not limited simply to the creative artist, but is also typical of the creator in other fields, is revealed by the data of the IPAR investigations. Using the Revised Art (RA) Scale of the Welsh Figure Preference Test, that successfully discriminated between artists and nonartists in standardization and cross-validation samples (Barron, 1953; Barron & Welsh, 1952), Gough (1961) demonstrated this cognitive predisposition as characteristic of research scientists, MacKinnon (1961) of creative architects, and Barron (1963a) of creative writers.

Raychaudhuri (1966b), using this same instrument in India, furnished supporting cross-cultural evidence. Investigating musicians and painters, he reported that the mean RA scores of these artists were significantly higher than those of nonartists; these obtained differences were reinforced by the findings of another, comparable study (Raychaudhuri, 1966a).

Eisenman and Robinson (1967) used polygons of varying degrees of complexity to measure this variable. With high school students as subjects, they found that a preference for complexity in polygons was significantly related to a high score on a paper-and-pencil personality measure of creativity. The reported lack of significant correlation value (.14) between the Stanford-Binet and the polygon test or creativity test scores also suggested that this dimension was independent of the IQ domain. Evidence pointing toward the early development of this characteristic emerged in Rosen's (1955) investigation of art students. Scores on the Revised Art Scale did not increase as a funtion of training in art—the scores of the first-year art students not differing significantly from those of the advanced.

Thus, a cognitive predisposition for complexity appears to be a distinguishing feature of the creative person, regardless of the field of creative endeavor, at various developmental levels. Apparently, the creative individual has the capacity to integrate this richness of experience into a higher order synthesis that makes for the unusual in creative production or performance.

Empirical evidence also points to the Revised Art Scale as a promising, nonverbal measure of creative potential. It has had relatively consistent success in correlating with independent criterion measures of creativity—.41 with criterion ratings of creative scientists (Gough, 1961), and .48 with those of creative architects (MacKinnon, 1961). It also appears to be relatively independent of intelligence. Harris (1961) reported a correlation of −.07 between the Otis Quick-Scoring Mental Ability Tests and the RA for 390 ninth- and tenth-grade pupils. Welsh (1966), studying 368 gifted high school students in a residential summer school, found that though the correlation between the two intelligence measures—Terman Concept Mastery Test (CMT) and the nonverbal D-48—was significant, the correlation of both tests with the RA Scale was essentially zero, −.07 with the D-48 and −.03 with the CMT. In view of the controvertibility of other creativity tests, the use of this cognitive-perceptual instrument to identify the creative may result in more reliable and fruitful investigations into the domain of man's imagination.

*Cognitive flexibility.* Accumulating evidence suggests that cognitive flexibility is another stylistic feature distinguishing the creative. Investigations in this area have used an intrapsychic approach in which interactions and relationships among hypothetical mental structures have been examined. Hypothesizing that creative individuals, as compared with noncreative normals, have a greater availability of both the relatively mature and the relatively primitive processes (Hersch, 1962) studied the cognitive functioning of a group of recognized creators (artists), noncreative normals (firemen, salesmen, entrepreneurs), and schizophrenics. His findings, on the basis of responses to six categories of the Rorschach, confirmed this hypothesis and revealed that the primitive responses involving the association of affective attitudes with sensory stimulation were given most frequently by the creators, and best distinguished them from the other two groups. He attributed the creative individual's extensive use of primitive functioning to optimal, flexible controls which were readily accessible and facilitated quick return to secondary processes. By contrast, the noncreative normals, lacking the ability to function primitively, had rigid, self-limiting controls. An apparent weakness of this study lies in the fact that the control group, although matched for age and IQ, differed from the artists in education and social class.

An earlier study, however, by Myden (1959), in which he equated his controls on these variables, yielded essentially similar results. Using a battery of tests designed to offer clues to the whole pattern of mental functioning—Rorschach, Thematic Apperception Test (TAT), Vigotsky Concept Formation—he reported that the creative's significantly greater use of the primitive process was not an isolated phenomenon, but rather appeared to be a component of his thinking throughout the records, particularly the Rorschach, with the primary process well integrated with the secondary process, indicating its control by the ego.

Barron (1963a) also noted this biphasic regression-progression capacity in his study of 15 creative Air Force officers. Considering the correlates of originality when intelligence was covaried, he concluded that the impulse or ego-control dimensions emerged most clearly as a determinant of originality. The frequent regression to primary process thinking was attributed to the strong ego of the creator who allowed himself to regress momentarily far into primitive fantasies because he was secure in the control and flexibility of his ego. The importance of the ego-control variable in this process was demonstrated by Pine and Holt (1960). An assessment of expression and control of primary process by means of the Rorschach in 13 male and 14 female undergraduates revealed that these were statistically independent variables. The quality of a person's created production was unrelated to the amount of primary process expression, but was related to the effectiveness with which the expression was controlled.

Studying male undergraduate science majors, designated high creative on the basis of Guilford tests, Garwood (1964) discovered their responses to the Rorschach manifested a greater integration of nonconscious with conscious material than did the responses of the low creatives. The functioning of this style emerged at the adolescent level in the Getzels and Jackson (1962) study. The imaginative productions of the highly creative as manifested in TAT-type stories and drawings pointed to the movement of preconscious material into conscious expressions. That the preconscious was under ego control was evidenced in that their responses were both unique and adaptive to reality. The results of Clark, Veldman, and Thorpe (1965) were entirely consistent with these findings; the fanciful productions of their creative adolescents, as observed on the Holtzman Inkblot Technique, met the demands of adequate appropriateness.

The results of these last three studies, however, must be reviewed with reservation, inasmuch as no external or natural behavior criterion was designated. Creativity was restricted to a Guilford-type test battery whose validity was questionable. The findings of Wild (1965), who also presented evidence that creativity involved the ability to use psychological processes belonging to different developmental levels, must be considered in the same light since there was no interrater reliability on her creativity criterion for art students. Using the Rorschach to probe this dimension in third-grade children whose creativity was assessed by professional artists, Rogalsky (1968) emerged with inconclusive results. This suggests that the Rorschach may be an inappropriate instrument to use for this purpose at such an early age. Not having progressed much beyond operational thought (Baldwin, 1967), nor having developed full ego controls, the combinatory process required in the response may not, as yet, be mastered by children.

One general criticism of these investigations is their use of the Rorschach to measure this cognitive style. Despite a plethora of studies reporting the effectivness of this instrument in diagnosis, its validity, as well as its reliability, is still recognized as problematic. Furthermore, different scoring systems used in its interpretation (Hersch, 1962, employed the Rorschach Genetic Scoring System and Pine and Holt, 1960, applied a system devised by Holt and Havel, 1960) raise the question of comparability of results.

Although these studies point up certain limitations, the consistent findings, indicating that creative adults exhibit a strong degree of consensus regarding cognitive flexibility as manifested in adaptive regression, suggest that regression is an essential factor in the creator's makeup exploited toward productive, creative expression. Regression is not symptomatic of loss of ego control, but, rather, appears to be a part of the creative individual's thinking development, since primary process seems to be well integrated with secondary process. Barron (1963a) suggested that this seemingly necessary attribute is probably the reason the creator may appear simultaneously crazier yet saner, more naive and more knowledgeable, more destructive and more constructive. Though this stylistic cognitive feature appears at the lower developmental levels, the findings are less conclusive due possibly to the methodological and theoretical reasons discussed.

*Perceptual openness.* Perceptual openness, conceptualized as a greater awareness of and receptiveness to not only the outer world but also to the inner self, is another distinctive cognitive mode attributed to the creative. Some empirical evidence has accrued supporting its existence in his constitution, difficulties of operationalization notwithstanding.

Applying the Myers-Briggs Type Indicator, MacKinnon (1961) determined that a preference for this perceptual mode differentiated more creative from less creative architects. And Gough (1961) reported this same preference as discriminating between the high- and low-creative research scientists. Mendelsohn and Griswold (1964, 1966) also provided substantiating evidence. Dichotomizing psychology undergraduates as high or low creative on the basis of the Remote Associates Test, they observed that only the high creatives used peripheral cues effectively in solving anagram problems. The creatives, they suggested, deployed their attention more widely, were more aware and receptive, and retained more prior stimulus experiences in usable form, tending not to screen out the irrelevant. A serious limitation of these investigations, however, is their use of the Remote Association Test to identify the creatives. As Jackson and Messick (1965) pointed out, the items in this test have one recognized response and hence have limited value as indicants of originality. Furthermore, the theoretical basis on which this test has been constructed—the concept of the habit hierarchy and the interpretation of creativity in terms of traditional associative and mediation processes—was not supported in a recent study by Jacobson, Elenewski, Lordahl, and Lieroff (1968).

Within the psychoanalytic frame of reference, Barron (1963a) reported a study which may be construed as evidence of the existence of this cognitive style. Original persons, designated by a high composite score based on a variety of measures of originality, rejected suppression as a mechanism for the control of impulse. Since suppression would limit awareness and openness to both the internal and external stimuli, its rejection would make one more "open."

Propst (1962) attempted to demonstrate this mode of perception within the Rogerian framework employing an instrument developed to measure openness to internal experience through an introspection task. She found a positive relationship between this measure of openness and a combined score of originality for a sample of 60 male undergraduates. Some evidence is provided regarding the validity of the new instrument, yet it is apparent that, as any introspective method, it is subject to all the misperceptions and self-deceptions of self-report.

Although these data are far from conclusive, the cited research indicates that certain cognitive characteristics, idiosyncratic of the creative person's mental functioning, contribute to the originality or difference of the end products of his thinking, characterized by a certain intellectual freedom that is not goal-bound, controlled or channeled, but rather seeks the "unknown" and "confusion." It also points up a greater capacity and tolerance for flexibility, complexity, and openness.

## Personality Characteristics

Although the foregoing suggests that certain cognitive characteristics are essential to creativity, it is apparent, as Vinacke (1952) asserted, that they function not in isolation, but rather in relation to a total personality system of needs, attitudes, goals, and emotions. The importance of these personality factors is attested to even by those originally committed to a cognitive orientation, who have now modified their opinions. With respect to conditions affecting creative thinking, Guilford (1967a) proposed that consideration be given to "what motivates individuals . . . and needs, interests and attitudes that help the individuals to be productive creatively [p. 12]." Bloom (1963), while engaged in an extensive research of the cognitive dimensions associated with scientific creativity, concluded "rather reluctantly that personality and motivational factors are at least as important as aptitude in determining performance [p. 252]."

The most provocative concepts regarding personality characteristics of the creative individual have been derived from studies of the eminent and well established. Some of the most useful findings have emerged from the Institute for Personality Assessment and Research in California where recognized creative research scientists, writers, mathematicians, and architects were intensively studied. MacKinnon (1961) reported that on the California Psychological Inventory, highly creative architects emerged as self-confident, aggressive, flexible, self-accepting, little concerned with social restraints or other's opinions, and strongly motivated to achieve primarily in those situations where independent thought and action, rather than conformity, were required. They rated high on aesthetic and theoretical scales and their assertiveness and independence were again graphically displayed on IPAR scales measuring these variables. Other instruments revealed their perceptiveness, intuitiveness, and introversion, and though they indicated little desire to be included in group activities, which attested again to their introverted nature, they demonstrated marked social poise, dominance, and a desire to control others when they did interact. That architectural work requires both aesthetic and scientific creativity suggests that the notable personality traits of the highly creative architect would tend to be most generally characteristic of the creative person. Results from studies in other fields tend to support this hypothesis.

Except for the fact that creative research scientists were predominantly judgmental rather than perceptive, Gough's (1961) findings were in essential agreement with those of MacKinnon. The impulsivity, independence, introversion, intuitiveness, self-acceptance syndrome appeared again in the psychometric data of creative writers (Barron, 1963a), although this group differed in their significantly greater originality and emphasis on fantasy consistent with their profession. Creative male mathematicians (Helson, 1961) displayed comparable traits but differed from their female counterparts (Helson, 1967) in that they were more ambitious, sociable, professionally participative, self-accepting, and less eccentric. Raychaudhuri (1966c) established that on the basis of the Rorschach, TAT, and Szondi Test, professional musicians in India were more distinctly marked by emotional and temperamental, than by cognitive, characteristics. As compared to non-creatives, they appeared to be more egocentric, exhibitionistic, more stimulated by frustration, and preferred activities that permitted a greater range of individualism and self-expression.

While the above studies were conducted primarily within a psychoanalytic context, Cattell and his associates, using a factor-analytic approach with the Sixteen Personality Factor Test, which yields more easily quantifiable results, have come up with essentially similar data. Although more bohemian than creative scientists (Cattell & Drevdahl, 1955), creative artists and writers (Cross, Cattell & Butcher, 1967; Drevdahl & Cattell,

1958) demonstrated the same salient traits of ego strength, dominance, self-sufficiency, sensitivity, introversion, desurgence, and radicalism. Creative psychologists (Drevdahl, 1964) displayed the characteristic independence and nonconcern with social environment, but differed in lacking the dominance and aggressiveness manifested by other groups.

Findings by other earlier investigators were consonant with the above. On the basis of the Rorschach, TAT, and biographical data, Roe (1952), in her studies of the development of creative research scientists, described as salient among their characteristics strong curiosity, persistence, high energy level, and a strong need for independence. Stein (1956) found that various psychological tests revealed that more creative industrial research scientists, as compared with their less creative colleagues, were more autonomous and assertive, and had more integrative attitudes and their own value hierarchy. Comparing artists and nonartists on the Rorschach and TAT, Eiduson (1958) reported that the former had interests that were broader, theoretical, and abstract.

While there have been speculations on a possible relationship between creativity and neurosis, the empirical evidence demonstrates no basis for this assumption. Psychopathology in the creative's nature emerges in all the cited IPAR and factor-analytic studies, but the creative's distinctly superior scores on ego-strength scales (Barron, 1961, 1963a; Cross et al., 1967; Drevdahl & Cattell, 1958; MacKinnon, 1961) indicate that they presumably have adequate mechanisms to handle these deviations.

Exploring the relationship between job adaptation and creative performance, Heinze (1962) offered additional evidence of the creative's high ego strength. Highly creative scientists, compared to the less creative, exhibited qualities associated with ego strength in that they were relatively unimpeded by conflicting forces in the environment, demonstrating sufficiently flexible controls which enabled them to "transcend" these conflicts. Ego strength also appeared in the cited Wild (1965) and Hersch (1962) studies as the variable that differentiated the creatives from the schizophrenics. This appearance of pathology in the creative, therefore, which may be a necessary concomitant of openness, seems to be more suggestive of high intellect, greater sensitivity, richness, and complexity of personality rather than psychopathology, for the creative individual appears to have adequate resources and control measures to cope with these tendencies.

Sex ambivalence, designating a femininity of interests pattern in the male, and the evidence of a masculine pattern in the female, also emerges with some consistency to distinguish the creative. This high association between creativity and femininity appears on the scales of the MMPI and the California Psychological Inventory in all the IPAR investigations cited, regardless of profession, as well as in other studies using different instruments. Highly original military officers revealed this femininity of interests pattern on the Personal Preference Survey Scales (Barron, 1963a; Myden, 1959); and Hammer (1964) observed a higher incidence of feminine characteristics in artists on the basis of the Rorschach. Although these creative men did not deny expression of this more feminine aspect of their personality, which led them to recognize impulses and interests regarded, in our culture, as more characteristic of women, the data indicated that they were not characterized by an effeminate manner, nor were they homosexuals. Indeed a study by Ellis (1959), in which he confirmed his hypothesis that degree of homosexuality was directly related to loss of creative potential, attested to the contrary, as did MacKinnon (1961), Barron (1963a), and Hammer (1964), who stated that creative men demonstrated a high degree of masculine-associated traits such as assertiveness, confidence, determination, ambition, and power. One might conclude from these findings, that though feminine components appear to a greater degree in the creative male personality, it is the blending of the feminine and masculine, the integration of the necessary sensitivity and intuition with purposive action and determination, that is conducive to creativeness.

Probing this aspect of the female creative, Helson (1967) noted that creative women mathematicians differed from the less creative in that they retained their femininity despite admission of masculine characteristics. The less creative, afraid of their impulsivity, seemed to have donned masculine armor as protection. An earlier study (Helson, 1966), assessing female undergraduates, presented essentially similar conclusions. Although creative nominees were more intelligent and had stronger need for accomplishment, they were not significantly more assertive, skillful in analytical thinking, or generally more "masculine." Rees and Goldman (1961) also reported that though highly creative females displayed more masculine characteristics, they did not score as high on these masculine traits as the moderately creative. These data appear to buttress Barron's (1963a) suggestion that a certain amount of cross-sex identification is prerequisite to creativity in both men and women, with more creative women having salient masculine characteristics, just as creative men have salient feminine characteristics. Yet from these data, one might conclude that certain masculine traits in the female may inhibit rather than facilitate creativity; and may, in reality, be mere indicants of opposition to the feminine cultural role.

In comparing the cited evidence on personality, some limitations of the studies are immediately apparent. There were marked differences in criteria of creativity and nominees were only as good as the criteria upon which their selection was based and the judgment abilities of those making the selections. Sample sizes were often small; and, though males were studied predominantly (a further limitation on generalizability of results) when females were included, sex differences were not often examined (e.g., Barron, 1961). Some subjects were tested by mail (e.g., MacKinnon, 1961), the effects of which procedure are not known, and in this same study, a restriction of the range of indices existed within samples being contrasted. This lack of complete data for all subjects is a notable shortcoming.

Different approaches were used, the measuring instruments were heterogeneous, and the personality inventories utilized have been criticized for ambiguity, susceptibility to faking or malingering, lack of sufficient empirical validation, and liability to contamination of response sets and intelligence. MacKinnon (1964), however, has asserted that probably one of the most convincing checks in science is for different investigators, using a variety of approaches and tests, to come up with consonant findings—a situation that appears to exist with respect to this personality research. Despite the various approaches and heterogeneity of instruments, many similarities in the results can be seen across samples differing in cultural background, eminence, and profession. Independence manifested not only in attitudes but also in social behavior, consistently emerged as being relevant to creativity, as did dominance, introversion, openness to stimuli, and wide interests. Self-acceptance, intuitiveness, and flexibility also appeared to characterize the creatives, and though they had social presence and poise, they exhibited an asocial attitude and an unconcern for social norms. This may reflect antipathy toward anything encroaching on individuality or compelling conformance. Some of these characteristics appear more pronounced in aesthetic creativity—radicalism, rejection of external restraints—as opposed to scientific creativity; but the data reflect that the majority of these qualities appear to differentiate the creative from his noncreative counterparts. This evidence points up a common pattern of personality traits among creative persons and also that these personality factors may have some bearing on creativity in the abstract, regardless of field.

PERSONALITY TRAITS—YOUNG CREATIVES

One of the questions with which creativity research is concerned regards the similarity of personality traits of young creatives to those of recognized creative adults. Investigations of undergraduates (Drevdahl, 1956; Garwood, 1964; Rees & Goldman, 1961), high school adolescents (Cashdan & Welsh, 1966; Getzels & Jackson, 1962; Holland, 1961; Littlejohn, 1966; Parloff & Datta 1966) and elementary school children (Torrance, 1962; Weisberg & Springer, 1967) disclose that highly creative students have personality structures that are congruent to—but possibly less sharply delineated than—those of the mature recognized creatives.

Identifying the highly creative by means of self-report questionnaries (Holland, 1961; Rees & Goldman, 1961), ratings (Drevdahl, 1956; Parloff & Datta, 1965), and psychometrically, these investigators submitted essentially similar findings: high creatives, as compared to the low or noncreatives, manifested greater independence, dominance, autonomy, unconventionality, broad interests, and openness to feelings. Consistent with the evidence gathered from adults, emotional instability also appears controlled in the young creatives.

No significant differences on anxious insecurity versus self-confidence, will control, and instability or nervous tension were discovered by Drevdahl (1956) between creative and noncreative undergraduates. Rees and Goldman (1961) concluded that while the highly creative had high scores on the MMPI and Emotional Stability Scale of the Guilford-Zimmerman

Temperament Survey, no indication of maladjustment was demonstrated. They suggested that tendencies toward maladjustment may occur in connection with inhibition of creative production. In comparing high and moderate creatives, Parloff and Datta (1965) found that, though they were both below the norms on the sense of well-being and self-control scales of the CPI, it was the latter who displayed greater defensiveness, self-doubts, and irritability.

As measured by the McCandless Anxiety Scale, Reid, King, and Wickwire (1959) found creative children less anxious than the noncreative. Wallach and Kogan (1965), assessing manifest anxiety and test anxiety, reported anxiety at an intermediate level for their two groups high in creativity, regardless of intelligence level.

With respect to interpersonal relations, creative students also resemble eminent adults in that they display similar social poise and adequacy (Cashdan & Welsh, 1966; Garwood, 1964; Parloff & Datta, 1965). Conflicting evidence, however, regarding their sociability appears. Reporting on this dimension, Rivlin (1959) stated that high school students nominated as highly creative by teacher ratings, emerged as sociable, and more popular with their peers. Reid et al. (1959) lend support to this evidence with similar data derived from an investigation of creative seventh graders selected by peer nominations. Additional substantiation was produced by Cashdan and Welsh (1966). Their creative subjects, identified by the Revised Art Scale, appeared to welcome social contact and had more interest in social activities.

By contrast, Lindgren and Lindgren (1965) submitted evidence that creative undergraduates, selected by the Asymmetrical Preference Test, perceived themselves as asocial and "ornery." Holland (1961) described his creative adolescent subjects as asocial. For Getzels and Jackson (1962), the highly creative adolescent portrayed the outsider, the rejected and rejecting spectator, rather than the welcomed and committed participant. Torrance (1962, 1964) also observed that creative elementary school students were isolated from their peers in the classroom situation, and seemed less accessible psychologically. This contradictory evidence may be attributed to the different procedures used to define the creative individual. With respect to the studies of Rivlin (1959) and Reid et al. (1959), the ratings by teachers and peers may have been mere indices of sociability rather than creativity ratings.

Generally, the data indicate that the personality characteristics of young creatives bear similarities to those of creative adults, and, therefore, the conclusion seems tenable that these traits develop fairly early. Their manifestation at this level suggests that these characteristics may be determinants of creative performance rather than traits developed in response to recognition of creative behavior. It may be argued that any overall findings in these groups are ambiguous, since where the creative product is often intangible, idiosyncratically determined judgments of creativity may lack validity. However, since these investigations regarding young creatives appear to corroborate one another, the results and conclusions seem much more decisive. Ideally, of course, data regarding these groups should be obtained from longitudinal investigations. Except for Terman's (1954) pioneering study, these are customarily lacking.


## Motivational Characteristics

In identifying the creatives, there is also the "why" aspect which focuses on the nature and degree of motivations—conscious and unconscious—assumed to energize these individuals. That this would be a strong component of their nature is apparent, for with no propelling agent, actual production would be minimal or totally lacking. From one point of view, motivation for creativity is seen as a desire to maximize the experiencing of one's own expressive potentials. For Rogers (1959), the creative individual is attempting to realize and complete himself, to "become his potentialities." This view gains some empirical support from Golann's (1962) study of highly creative males, identified on the basis of the RA Scale, who indicated a preference for activities allowing for self-expression, independence, and the use of creative capacity, while low creatives tended to prefer activities essentially opposite.

Torrance and Dauw (1965) probing this motive in high school seniors through expressed aspirations, suggested that their subjects' greater striving and need for excellence, and greater attraction to unusual and unconventional types of achievement, indicated a strong desire to discover and use potentialities. These findings, consistent with Maddi's (1965) contention that the true creative is motivated by an intense need for quality and novelty, may be viewed as relatively concrete expressions of the general tendency toward self-actualization. He has presented empirical findings to buttress the posited relationship between creativity and need for novelty by citing significant correlations between novelty or imaginative productions and a tendency to prefer novel endings in a newly constructed Similes Preference Test.

Houston and Mednick's (1963) findings also appear germane, further supporting Maddi's speculation. Subjects were asked to choose between pairs of words—nouns that were followed by novel associations and non-nouns that were followed by common associations. The high creative group, identified by the Remote Associates Test, significantly increased, and the low creativity group significantly decreased, in the frequency of noun choices over the series of pairs. However, in the light of the questionable validity of the Remote Associates Test, and the lack of validation on the Similes Preference Test, these data must be interpreted with caution.

Risk-taking tendencies based on the need to achieve and to test limits have also been hypothesized as a form of motivation. McClelland (1963) and Kaplan (1963) suggested that creative research scientists have a greater interest in and are more willing to take long range, calculated risks where their own abilities make a difference in the odds. Although these speculations concern adults, similar contentions have been made concerning younger creatives. Getzels and Jackson (1962) and Torrance (1962) cited the asking of unusual questions, the joining together of dissimilar elements, and the choice of unconventional occupations as manifestations of risk taking in their subjects.

A systematic exploration of the relationship between risk taking and creativity is provided in a recent study by Pankove (1967). Defining creativity operationally in terms of two Wallach and Kogan (1965) tests, and risk taking in terms of scores obtained on three decision-making tasks, where subjects were free to choose the degree of risk under which they were willing to operate, she found a positive relationship between risk taking and creativity in fifth-grade boys. Low defensiveness enhanced the relationship while high defensiveness attenuated it.

Within this sphere Anderson and Cropley (1966) investigated the relationship of various nonintellective variables to originality. Identifying high and low creative seventh graders by means of Guilford-Torrance tests, they confirmed their hypothesis that originality was equated with the inability or unwillingness to internalize "stop rules." Rather than the posited impulsivity factor, it was risk taking that contributed most to the total variance of performance on originality. They suggested, therefore, that there was one super-ordinate "stop rule"—"Don't take risks" which differentiated the creative from the noncreative. The former apparently ignored or were unable to internalize this caveat.

Barron (1963b) stated that the creative individual's "exceptionally strong need to find order where none appears [p. 160]" may be considered a motivating factor. He proposed that the creative willingly admits into his perceptions the complex and disordered, and is challenged to make new order out of the apparent chaos through the use of his own abilities and experiences. The pleasure derived from the solution motivates him to search for situations defying rational construction and, therefore, to service the need to achieve order. Barron (1963a) also posited "the moral attitude" as a motivational characteristic of the creative. By this, he refers to the creative person's profound commitment to aesthetic and philosophical meanings expressed in work. He has maintained that the creator is constantly involved in the creation of his own private universe of meaning, and will "stake his life" on the meaning of his work. Barron believes that "without this cosmological commitment, no amount of mental ability will produce a genuinely creative act [p. 243]."

Various other motivational factors have been hypothesized as characteristic of the creative individual, yet here again, a paucity of empirical supporting data exists for this provocative aspect of creativity. This may be due to the lack of appropriate measuring instruments in this area (suggested by Taylor and Holland, 1964). Or, it may also be attributed to what Maddi (1965) referred to as the "child oriented" view of creativity. In focusing on the predisposing characteristics of the creative person, this viewpoint stresses the degree to which the creative style of functioning demonstrates playfulness, whimsical childishness, humor, relaxation, and uncritical freedom, rather than any sustained motivational qualities. It neglects to consider the long period of purposeful, relentless, organized thought, and motivated persistence generally preceding the creative insight. Creativity, after all, can only be recognized through some form of production or performance, and therefore, as Golann (1963) suggested, would be highly dependent on motivational characteristics. Though other attributes are relevant, they are not sufficient. The positive force of motivation which serves as an impelling and integrating factor would be one of the prime personality requisites for actual productivity.

## Summary Statement

With respect to the primary thesis of the present paper, the data suggest that the creative response, performance, or production is most likely to occur in a specific human condition. Despite differences in age, cultural background, area of operation or eminence, a particular constellation of psychological traits emerges consistently in the creative individual, and forms a recognizable schema of the creative personality. This schema indicates that creative persons are distinguished more by interests, attitudes, and drives, than by intellectual abilities. Whether these characteristics are consequents or determinants of creativity, or whether some are peripheral and of no value is moot. These questions remain insufficiently approached and elucidated.

The cognitive capacities that appear to be most frequently associated with the creative are an above-average intelligence and the effective use of this intelligence, the ability to produce unusual and appropriate ideas, an exceptional retention and more ready availability of life experiences, ideational fluency and the ability to synthesize remote or disparate ideas, discriminative observation, and a general cognitive flexibility.

In the realm of personality, a clearly differentiating factor that characterizes the creative is the relative absence of impulse and imagery control by means of repression. This relative lack of self-defensiveness seems to accord to the creative fuller access to his conscious and unconscious experiences, and therefore, a greater opportunity to combine dissociated items. An openness to internal and external stimuli is also indicated as a salient characteristic, and this is manifested in various forms. It appears in a predisposition to allow into the perceptual system complexity, disorder, and imbalance for the satisfaction and challenge of achieving an idiosyncratic order. It is also demonstrated in the creative male's lack of denial of the feminine side of his nature, which leads to wider interests, a greater openness to emotions and feelings, a greater aesthetic sensitivity, and self-awareness.

Although the creative appears to be subject to considerable psychic turbulence, empirical evidence has shown no basis for a significant and demonstrated relationship between psychopathology and creativity. Rather, it has demonstrated that the creative individual is possessed of superior ego strength and a positive constructive way of reacting to problems. Intuitiveness also comes through as a hallmark of the creative person. He appears to have an immediate apprehension of what is and what can be; and rather than accepting what is presented to his senses at face value, he searches for deeper meanings and eventualities.

Independence in attitudes and social behavior emerges with striking consistency as relevant to creativity. Possessed of an individualistic rather than a sociocentric orientation, the creative is not concerned with social activities, nor preoccupied with the opinion others have of him. Since he is little concerned with the impression he makes on others, he appears to be freer to be himself, to realize his own potentialities, and hence, may actually be a more fully functioning person than his noncreative counterparts. He appears to have a strong sense of identity and self-acceptance, knowing who he is, and what he wants to achieve. Strong aesthetic and theoretical interests also appear consonant with the creative personality, suggesting that the creative person has a high regard for the values of both truth and beauty.

Though the evidence can hardly be called overwhelming, it does seem to indicate that the creator is endowed with strong, intrinsic motivation, involving a degree of resoluteness and egotism that sustains him in his work. Indifferent to the fear of making mistakes, to social disapproval, and to the "anxiety of separateness," he seems endowed with a sense of destiny, an unshakable belief in the worth and validity of his efforts that could help him override frustrations and obstacles.

In brief, the roots of creativity do not seem to lie in convergent or divergent thinking, but rather, as Hudson (1966) suggested, in the personality and motivational aspects of character.

One of the great hopes of research on the creative person is the possibility that a finite number of personality characteristics is significant for creativity, as distinguished from those having significance for individual diagnosis, theory, or even academic performance. If some small number of parameters can be isolated, and defined in behavioral terms, great use of this might be mobilized for identifying creative potential.

## General Critique

Perhaps the most glaring deficit in the research on creativity has been the absence both of replicative studies, as well as follow-up investigations. The one-shot research study is typical. While little status or manifestation of originality may be accorded replication studies, they are a means of assessing reliability of results contributing both to their validity and generalizability. Follow-up investigations also serve this purpose and, certainly, could be of major import in providing support for the validity of psychometric instruments currently employed to "measure" creativity. Paradoxically, the paucity of replication studies simultaneously exists with the plethora of literature concerning one particular investigation that is merely rewritten with essentially the same information, but with a slightly different emphasis. This is at once disappointing, time-consuming, and exasperating.

Conceptual and semantic ambiguities continue to make communication a problem in reporting. The reader, seeking a clear picture of populations, or wishing to relate findings from one investigation with another, experiences particular difficulty when encountering such terms as "creative thinker," "divergent thinker," and "original thinker," insufficiently or inadequately defined. These same difficulties obtain in the use of such terms as "high," "medium," and "low" creativity. Unfortunately, the phrase "moderately creative," generally used, does not conjure in the mind of the reader the relatively clear picture projected by the words "100 IQ."

A host of studies deal with relatively small samples, thereby increasing the possibility of error and biased results. More important, however, in spite of relatively small, atypical samples and limitations in design, such as the arbitrary group classifications used by Getzels and Jackson (1962), Torrance (1962), and Yamamoto (1964b)—which result in a serious loss of information because of the exclusion of subgroups of considerable size and interest (deMille & Merrifield, 1962)—the inferences read as though applicable far beyond the studied groups. Age, sex, socioeconomic status, test setting, past experience, and other relevant variables have not always been controlled. Adequate rationale for the subjects selected is also often missing. It is not clear, for instance, whether children or adolescents are chosen in the interest of contributing toward a developmental theory of creativity or merely because of convenience and availability.

Precision is also sometimes lacking in reporting results. Some researchers have a tendency to be anecdotal (e.g., Torrance, 1962) which, while making for pleasant reading, tends to obscure the findings. This obscuration also obtains in those cases where results that do not support the hypothesis or may even contradict it are lost in the profusion of qualifications, interpretations, and explanations. Although data in these predominantly correlational studies merely indicate statistical prediction, use of the phrase "significant correlation" often carries the intentional or accidental implication of a causal condition, which, of course, is misleading.

A spate of researchers continue to rely on factor analysis (Vernon, 1964), multiple correlations, and other powerful statistical tools to isolate and identify the creative person, rather than on well-thought-out hypotheses grounded in adequate theoretical rationale. While broad group factors can be subdivided into smaller ones via factor-analytic techniques, this does not verify their validity, nor demonstrate that they are indeed parameters of creativity. With respect to multiple correlations, as Gough (1961) pointed out, some very dramatic relationships can be generated with sufficient data and sample numbers. When obtained with recognized creatives, however, the validity of these correlations cannot be easily ascertained especially in the absence of comparable sample groups.

One might also view a little critically the intentional or accidental overevaluation of creative abilities, or perhaps, more accurately, the devaluation of other abilities. The implication seems to be that creativity is the cardinal seed of existence and, if someone does not achieve creatively, he is of no particular value. In fact, the accusation of creative inferiority seems to have become a sharp form of criticism and everyone, therefore, wants to avoid this pejorative label. As data are released on creativity, and often couched in Olympian terms, one may find a counterpart to the "organization man"—a new pattern upon which everyone, having been "taught the tests" will model himself. Furthermore, the extolling of creativity to the detriment of mental discipline and the mastery of subject matter is inimical to creativity, and may defeat the ultimate purpose of this research (Kneller, 1965).

It is apparent that the criterion problem—fundamental to other aspects of research, yet far from solution—is of primary importance. The characteristics of such a criterion must come to terms with four dimensions: (a) the relevance or pertinence to the actual product or culture, (b) comprehensiveness, (c) the reliability and discrimination, and (d) freedom from bias. It is patent that the quality of research will depend upon the adequacy of the criteria utilized, since these are the standards by which other measures can be evaluated, or can serve to describe the performance of individuals on some success continuum. In spite of this importance, research directed specifically toward criteria is infrequent. Little time or attention has been devoted to the develpment of the criteria employed (Brogden & Sprecher, 1964).

Studies of creativity in adults have been primarily limited to men, and the manifestation of this dimension in women remains insufficiently elucidated. Helson's (1961, 1966, 1967, 1968) work, one of the few but major contributions in this area, indicates that different factors may be involved in its operation and emergence in women. Powell (1964) noted differences with respect to female creativity and the social desirability variable. Mendelsohn and Griswold (1964, 1966) concluded that the responses of women varied in creativity tests depending on differences in the experimenter. In the interests of a comprehensive portrait of the creative individual, research designed with a view to the deliberate and adequate investigation of male-female differences is warranted.

The necessity of longitudinal studies is obvious for determining qualities that contribute to creative performance, personality changes within the developing creator, and the interaction of personality, cognitive and environmental variables in the creative versus the noncreative. These longitudinal studies would also be basic to any developmental theory of creativity, and would be dependent for their initiation on the ability to identify early—perhaps preschool—those characteristics that may be related to creativity. Instruments that can be used for early identification are needed and these should be, as suggested by Starkweather (1964), not only of inherent interest to children but also, perhaps, independent of ability. Findings from the investigations concerning the beginnings of creativity in children thus far (Lieberman, 1965; Starkweather, 1964; Ward, 1966) remain inconclusive with little of definite substance reported.

The demonstrated lack of convergent validity, and discriminant validity with respect to intelligence, of various measures of creativity, and Yamamoto's (1966) factor-analytic studies of Minnesota test components, in which he found that scores with common semantic labels did not represent the same thing in each test, boldly underscore the need for more straightforward validation studies of measuring instuments to improve currently used predictors. It also appears that there is a necessity to develop creativity measures based on personality study rather than on task performance. The Preconscious Activity Scale of Holland and Baird (1968) is a step in this direction. That biographical items and past achievement have been rated as the most efficient predictors (Taylor & Holland, 1964) does not mean investigators have no further work in this direction. Rather, it does imply a necessity for a conceptualization and systematization of this evidence.

The implication of greatest significance regarding the psychological constitution of the creative individual is that a change in the dynamics of creativity research seems warranted. If the results of future investigations are to become more meaningful contributions to the cumulative literature on creativity, the data suggest that the assessment of creative potential cannot merely rely on singular intellectual traits, factor-analytically derived, but must also include cognitive styles and personality variables rooted in theoretical concepts. Creativity research, pursued within this framework of compound criteria from disparate psychological domains, holds promise for more valid findings which may, in addition, contribute toward the resolution of present dilemmas.

## References

Anderson, C. C., & Cropley, A. J. Some correlates of originality. *Australian Journal of Psychology,* 1966, **18,** 218-229.

Baldwin, A. L. *Theories of child development.* New York: Wiley, 1967.

Barron, F. Complexity-simplicity as a personality dimension. *Journal of Abnormal and Social Psychology,* 1953, **48,** 163-172.

Barron, F. Creative vision and expression in writing and painting. In, *Conference on the creative person.* Berkeley: University of California, Institute of Personality Assessment & Research, 1961.

Barron, F. *Creativity and psychological health: Origins of personality and creative freedom.* Princeton, N. J.: Van Nostrand, 1963. (a)

Barron, F. The needs for order and for disorder as motivation in creative activity. In C. W. Taylor and F. Barron (Eds.), *Scientific creativity: Its recoginition and develpment.* New York: Wiley, 1963. (b)

Barron, F., & Welsh, G. Artistic perception as a possible factor in personality style: Its measurement by a figure preference test. *Journal of Psychology,* 1952, **33,** 199-203.

Beittel, K. R. Creativity in the visual arts in higher education. In C. W. Taylor (Ed.), *Widening horizons in creativity.* New York: Wiley, 1964.

Bloom, B. S. Report on creativity research by the examiner's office of the University of Chicago. In C. W. Taylor & F. Barron (Eds.), *Scientific creativity: Its recognition and develpment.* New York: Wiley, 1963.

Brogden, H. E., & Sprecher, T. B. Criteria of creativity. In C. W. Taylor (Ed.), *Creativity: Progress and potential.* New York: McGraw-Hill, 1964.

Campbell, D. T., & Fiske, D. W. Convergent and discriminant validation by the multitrait-multimethod matrix. *Psychological Bulletin,* 1959, **56,** 81-105.

Cashdan, S., & Welsh, G. S. Personality correlates of creative potential in talented high school students. *Journal of Personality,* 1966, **34,** 445-455.

Cattell, R. B., & Drevdahl, J. E. A comparison of the personality profile (16 PF) of eminent researchers with that of eminent teachers and administrators, and of the general population. *British Journal of Psychology,* 1955, **46,** 248-261.

Clark, C. M., Veldman, D. J., & Thorpe, J. S. Convergent and divergent thinking abilities of talented adolescents. *Journal of Educational Psychology,* 1965, **56,** 157-163.

Cropley, A. J. A note on the Wallach-Kogan test of creativity. *British Journal of Educational Psychology,* 1965, **38,** 197-201.

Cross, P. G., Cattell, R. B., & Butcher, H. J. The personality patterns of creative artists. *British Journal of Educational Psychology,* 1967, **37,** 292-299.

deMille, R., & Merrifield, P. R. Review of J. W. Getzels & P. W. Jackson, *Creativity and intelligence: Explorations with gifted students. Educational and Psychological Measurement,* 1962, **22,** 803-808.

Dentler, R. A., & Mackler, B. Originality: Some social and personal determinants. *Behavioral Science,* 1964, **9,** 1-7.

Drevdahl, J. E. Factors of importance for creativity. *Journal of Clinical Psychology,* 1956, **12,** 21-26.

Drevdahl, J. E. Some developmental and environmental factors in creativity. In C. W. Taylor (Ed.), *Widening horizons in creativity.* New York: Wiley, 1964.

Drevdahl, J. E., & Cattell, R. B. Personality and creativity in artists and writers. *Journal of Clinical Psychology,* 1958, **14,** 107-111.

Eiduson, B. T. Artist and non-artist: A comparative study, *Journal of Personality,* 1958, **26,** 13-28.

Eisenman, R., & Robinson, N. Complexity-simplicity, creativity, intelligence and other correlates. *Journal of Psychology,* 1967, **67,** 331-334.

Elliott, J. M. Measuring creative abilities in public relations and in advertising work. In C. W. Taylor (Ed.), *Widening horizons in creativity.* New York: Wiley, 1964.

Ellis, A. Homosexuality and creativity. *Journal of Clinical Psychology,* 1959, **15,** 576-579.

Flescher, I. Anxiety and achievement of intellectually gifted and creatively gifted children. *Journal of Psychology,* 1963, **56,** 251-268.

Garwood, D. S. Personality factors related to creativity in young scientists. *Journal of Abnormal and Social Psychology,* 1964, **68,** 413-419.

Getzels, J. W., & Jackson, P. W. *Creativity and intelligence: Explorations with gifted students.* New York: Wiley, 1962.

Ginsberg, G. P., & Whittemore, R. G. Creativity and verbal ability: A direct examination of their relationship. *British Journal of Educational Psychology,* 1968, **38,** 133-139.

Golann, S. E. The creativity motive. *Journal of Personality,* 1962, **30,** 588-600.

Golann, S. E. Psychological study of creativity. *Psychological Bulletin,* 1963, **60,** 548-565.

Gough, H. G. Techniques for identifying the creative research scientist. In, *Conference on the creative person.* Berkeley: University of California, Institute of Personality Assessment and Research, 1961.

Guilford, J. P. Measurement and creativity. *Theory into Practice,* 1966, **5,** 186-189.

Guilford, J. P. Creativity: Yesterday, today, and tomorrow. *Journal of Creative Behavior,* 1967, **1,** 3-14. (a)

Guilford, J. P. *The nature of human intelligence.* New York: McGraw-Hill, 1967. (b)

Guilford, J. P., & Hoepfner, R. Sixteen divergent-production abilities at the ninth-grade level. *Multi-variate Behavioral Research,* 1966, **1,** 43-64.

Guilford, J. P., & Merrifield, P. R. The structure of intellect model: Its uses and implications. *Report of Psychological Laboratory,* No. 24. Los Angeles: University of Southern California, 1960.

Hammer, E. F. Creative and feminine ingredients in young male artists. *Perceptual and Motor Skills,* 1964, *19,* 414.

Harris, T. L., An analysis of the responses made by adolescents to the Welsh Figure Preference Test and its implications for guidance purposes. Unpublished doctoral dissertation, University of North Carolina, 1961.

Heinze, S. J. Job adaptation and creativity in industrial research scientists. Unpublished doctoral dissertation. University of Chicago, 1962.

Helson, R. Creativity, sex, and mathematics. In, *Conference on the creative person.* Berkeley: University of California, Institute of Personality and Assessment Research, 1961.

Helson, R. Personality of women with imaginative and artistic interests: The role of masculinity, originality and other characteristics in their creativity. *Journal of Personality,* 1966, **34,** 1-25.

Helson, R. Sex differences in creative style. *Journal of Personality,* 1967,

**35,** 214-233.

Helson, R. Generality of sex differences in creative style. *Journal of Personality,* 1968, **36,** 33-48.

Herr, E. L., Moore, G. D., & Hansen, J. C. Creativity, intelligence and values: A study of relationships. *Exceptional Children,* 1965, **32,** 114-115.

Hersch, C. The cognitive functioning of the creative person: A developmental analysis. *Journal of Projective Techniques,* 1962, **26,** 193-200.

Holland, J. L. Creative and academic performance among talented adolescents. *Journal of Educational Psychology,* 1961, **52,** 136-147.

Holland, J. L., & Baird, L. L. The preconscious activity scale: The development and validation of an originality measure. *The Journal of Creative Behavior,* 1968, **2,** 217-225.

Holt, R. R., & Havel, J. A method for assessing primary and secondary process in the Rorschach. In M. A. Rickers-Ovsiankina (Ed.), *Rorschach psychology.* New York: Wiley, 1960.

Houston, J. P., & Mednick, S. A. Creativity and the need for novelty. *Journal of Abnormal and Social Psychology,* 1963, **66,** 137-141.

Hudson, L. *Contrary imaginations: A psychological study of the young student.* New York: Schocken Books, 1966.

Jackson, P. W., & Messick, S. The person, the product and the response: Conceptual problems in the assessment of creativity. *Journal of Personality,* 1965, **33,** 309-329.

Jacobson, L. I., Elenewski, J. J., Lordahl, D. S., & Lieroff, J. H. Role of creativity and intelligence in conceptualization. *Journal of Personality and Social Psychology,* 1968, **10,** 431-436.

Kaplan, N. The relation of creativity to sociological variables in research organizations. In C. W. Taylor & F. Barron (Eds.), *Scientific creativity: Its recognition and develpment.* New York: Wiley, 1963.

Kneller, G. F. *The art and science of creativity.* New York: Holt, Rinehart & Winston, 1965.

Lauritzen, E. S. Semantic divergent thinking factors among elementary school children. *Dissertation Abstracts,* 1963, **24,** 629.

Lieberman, J. N. Playfulness and divergent thinking: An investigation of their relationship at the kindergarten level. *Journal of Genetic Psychology,* 1965, **107,** 219-224.

Lindgren, H. C., & Lindgren, F. Brainstorming and orneriness as facilitators of creativity. *Psychological Reports,* 1965, **16,** 577-583.

Littlejohn, M. A. A comparison of responses of ninth-graders to measures of creativity and masculinity-femininity. Unpublished doctoral dissertation, University of North Carolina, 1966.

Lowenfeld, V., & Beittel, K. Interdisciplinary criteria of creativity in the arts and sciences: A progress report. *Research Yearbook, National Art Education Association,* 1959, 35-44.

MacKinnon, D. W. The study of creativity and creativity in architects. In, *Conference on the creative person.* Berkeley: University of California, Institute of Personality Assessment and Research, 1961.

MacKinnon, D. W. The creativity of architects. In C. W. Taylor (Ed.), *Widening horizons in creativity.* New York: Wiley, 1964.

Maddi, S. R. Motivational aspects of creativity. *Journal of Personality,* 1965, **33**, 330-347.

Marsh, R. W. A statistical reanalysis of Getzels and Jackson's data. *British Journal of Educational Psychology,* 1964, **34**, 91-93.

McClelland, D. C. The calculated risk: An aspect of scientific performance. In C. W. Taylor & F. Barron (Eds.), *Scientific creativity: Its recognition and development.* New York: Wiley, 1963.

McNemar, W. Lost: Our intelligence. Why? *American Psychologist,* 1964, **19**, 871-882.

Mednick, M. T., & Andrews, F. M. Creative thinking and level of intelligence. *The Journal of Creative Behavior,* 1967, **1**, 428-431.

Mednick, S. A. The associative basis of the creative process. *Psychological Review,* 1962, **69**, 220-232.

Mendelsohn, G. A., & Griswold, B. B. Differential use of incidental stimuli in problem solving as a function of creativity. *Journal of Abnormal and Social Psychology,* 1964, **68**, 431-436.

Mendelsohn, G. A., & Griswold, B. B. Assessed creative potential, vocabulary level and sex as predictors of the use of incidental cues in verbal problem solving. *Journal of Personality and Social Psychology,* 1966, **4**, 423-433.

Merrifield, P. R., Gardner, S. F., & Cox, A. B. Aptitudes and personality measures related to creativity in seventh-grade children. *Report of the Psychological Laboratory,* University of Southern California, 1964, No. 28. (Los Angeles)

Merrifield, P. R., Guilford, J. P., & Gershon, A. The differentiation of divergent-production abilities at the sixth-grade level. *Report of the Psychological Laboratory,* University of Southern California, 1963, No. 27. (Los Angeles) Cited by S. W. Brown, Semantic memory and creative (divergent-production) abilities of senior high school students. Unpublished doctoral dissertation, University of Southern California, 1968.

Myden, W. Interpretation and evaluation of certain personality characteristics involved in creative production. *Perceptual and Motor Skills,* 1959, **9**, 139-158.

Pankove, E. The relationship between creativity and risk taking in fifth-grade children. Unpublished doctoral dissertation, Rutgers State University, 1967.

Parloff, M. D., & Datta, L. E. Personality characteristics of the potentially creative scientist. *Science and Psychoanalysis,* 1965, **8**, 91-106.

Piers, E. V., Daniels, J. M., & Quackenbush, J. F. The identification of creativity in adolescents. *Journal of Educational Psychology,* 1960, **51**, 346-351.

Pine, F., & Holt, R. R. Creativity and primary process: A study of adaptive regression. *Journal of Abnormal and Social Psychology,* 1960, **61**, 370-379.

Powell, M. B. The social desirability aspect of self concept in relation to achievement and creativity. Unpublished doctoral dissertation, New York University, 1964.

Propst, B. S. Openness to experience and originality of production. Unpublished master's thesis, University of Chicago, 1962.

Raychaudhuri, M. Creativity and personality: A review of psychological researches. *Indian Psychological Review,* 1966, **2,** 91-102. (a)

Raychaudhuri, M. Perceptual preference pattern and creativity. *Indian Journal of Applied Psychology,* 1966, **3,** 67-70. (b)

Raychaudhuri, M. *Studies in artistic creativity: Personality structure of the musician.* Calcutta: Express Printer Private, Ltd., 1966. (c)

Rees, M. E., & Goldman, M. Some relationships between creativity and personality. *Journal of General Psychology,* 1961, **65,** 145-161.

Reid, J. B., King, F. J., & Wickwire, P. Cognitive and other personality characteristics of creative children. *Psychological Reports,* 1959, **5,** 729-737.

Rivlin, L. Creativity and self-attitudes and sociability of high school students. *Journal of Educational Psychology,* 1959, **50,** 147-152.

Roe, A. *The making of a scientist.* New York: Dodd, Mead, 1952.

Rogalsky, M. M. Artistic creativity and adaptive regression in third-grade children. *Journal of Projective Techniques and Personality Assessment,* 1968, **32,** 53-62.

Rogers, C. R. Toward a theory of creativity. In H. H. Anderson (Ed.), *Creativity and its cultivation.* New York: Harper, 1959.

Rosen, J. C. The Barron-Welsh art scale as a predictor of originality and level of ability among artists. *Journal of Applied Psychology,* 1955, **39,** 366-367.

Skager, R. W., Klein, S. P., & Schultz, C. B. The prediction of academic and artistic achievement at a school of design. *Journal of Educational Measurements,* 1967, **4,** 105-117.

Starkweather, E. K. *Conformity and nonconformity as indicators of creativity in preschool children.* Tech. Rep. No. 1967; Stillwater: Oklahoma State University, 1964.

Stein, M. I. A transactional approach to creativity. In C. W. Taylor (Ed.), *The 1955 University of Utah research conference on the identification of creative scientific talent.* Salt Lake City: University of Utah Press, 1956.

Taylor, C. W., & Holland, J. Predictors of creative performance. In C. W. Taylor (Ed.), *Creativity: Progress and potential.* New York: McGraw-Hill, 1964.

Terman, L. M. The discovery and encouragement of exceptional talent. *American Psychologist,* 1954, **9,** 221-230.

Thorndike, R. L. Some methodological issues in the study of creativity. In A. Anastasi (Ed.), *Testing problems in perspective.* Washington, D. C.: American Council on Education, 1966.

Torrance, E. P. *Guiding creative talent.* Englewood Cliffs, N. J.: Prentice-Hall, 1962.

Torrance, E. P. *Role of evaluation in creative thinking.* Minneapolis: University of Minnesota, Bureau of Educational Research, 1964.

Torrance, E. P., & Dauw, D. C. Aspirations and dreams of three groups of creatively gifted high school seniors and comparable unselected group. *Gifted Child Quarterly,* 1965, **9,** 177-182.

Vernon, P. E. Creativity and intelligence. *Educational Research,* 1964, **6,** 163-169.

Vinacke, W. E. *The psychology of thinking.* New York: McGraw-Hill, 1952.

Wallach, M. A. Review of E. P. Torrance, *Torrance tests of creative thinking. American Educational Journal,* 1968, **5,** 272-281.

Wallach, M. A., & Kogan, N. *Modes of thinking in young children: A study of the creativity-intelligence distinction.* New York: Holt, Rinehart & Winston, 1985.

Ward, C. W. Creativity and impulsivity in kindergarten children. *Dissertation Abstracts,* 1966, **27,** 2127B.

Welsh, G. S. Comparison of D-48, Terman CMT, and Art Scale scores of gifted adolescents. *Journal of Consulting Psychology,* 1966, **30,** 88.

Wild, C. Creativity and adaptive regression. *Journal of Personality and Social Psychology,* 1965, **2,** 161-169.

Wilson, R. C., Guilford, J. P., Christensen, P. R., & Lewis, D. J. A factor-analytic study of creative-thinking abilities. *Psychometrika,* 1954, **19,** 297-311.

Yamamoto, K. Evaluation of some creativity measures in a high school with peer nominations as criteria. *Journal of Psychology,* 1964, **58,** 285-293. (a)

Yamamoto, K. Role of creative thinking and intelligence in high school achievement. *Psychological Reports,* 1964, **14,** 783-789. (b)

Yamamoto, K. An exploratory component analysis of the Minnesota tests of creative thinking. *California Journal of Educational Research,* 1966, **17,** 220-229.

Edith H. Grotberg

# Adjustment Problems of the Gifted

$S$cientific approaches to the study of the gifted, which followed the development and use of mental tests, yielded results inconsistent with beliefs held forty or fifty years earlier. The early works of Terman (10), Witty (12), and Hollingworth (4,5) dispelled the beliefs that the gifted are "the products of supernatural causes of human behavior," and that "intellectual precocity is pathological" (10). Indeed, Terman, Witty, and Hollingworth found the gifted to be physically superior, attractive, and generally well-adjusted.

Although these authors recognized that adjustment problems existed among the gifted, relatively little effort was made to investigate problem behavior until recently. It should be recalled, however, that Hollingworth (4) found that pupils of IQ's 180 plus had more adjustment problems than pupils whose IQ's fell between 130 and 180.

Recently a number of studies have appeared which tend to substantiate the findings of the early research endeavors as far as the generally superior adjustment of the gifted is concerned. But recent studies have attempted to determine the factors correlated with maladjustment.

Some of these studies have dealt with identifying the characteristics of underachievers, i.e., verbally gifted students who are not earning grades commensurate with IQ or test score expectancy. Haggard (3) found that by third grade high achievers responded to socialization pressures and accepted adult values readily. They co-operated, had good work habits, and maintained satisfactory relationships with parents, peers, and teachers. They were also highly competitive.

Gowan (2) reported that the underachiever experienced parental rejection and hostility frequently. Roesslein (8) found among high school male underachievers a pattern involving oversolicitous parents and resultant feelings of inadequacy. Armstrong (1), who studied the adjustment of underachievers in the ninth and eleventh grades, found that they were more in-

Reprinted from the April, 1962, issue of *Education.* Copyright 1962 by the Bobbs-Merrill Co., Inc. Indianapolis, Indiana.

fluenced by the desires of others rather than their own wishes and were regarded by their teachers as unco-operative, undependable, and poor in judgement.

Further, O'Leary (7) found the underachievers in the ninth grade to have poor work habits. Patterns of maladjustment found among underachievers at the college level by Wedemeyer (11) and Horrall (6) were similar to those noted in the elementary and high school pupils. And Shaw and Brown (9) found a high degree of hostility and hypercritical attitudes among underachieving college students.

## Institutionalized Gifted

Clearly the verbally gifted have adjustment problems, although their incidence is lower than that found in less intelligent individuals. A frequently used method for identifying the maladjusted gifted, as we have already indicated, has been in association with underachievement in elementary, high school, and college.

Another method of identifying the problems of the maladjusted gifted is to study gifted adults who have been institutionalized and whose conditions have been diagnosed. These individuals are to a large extent the underachievers or failures as adults. An examination of their records reveals a number of factors which should be of interest to educators. The remainder of this article is based on a study of institutionalized gifted in the Elgin, Illinois, State Hospital. This study was made by the writer in 1961.

## Test Groups and Tests

Forty gifted and forty non-gifted institutionalized patients comprised the experimental and control groups. Each group contained twenty male and twenty female patients. Psychological tests, consisting of a Wechsler-Bellevue or Adult Intelligence Scale, the Rorschach Test, a Thematic Apperception Test, and a Sentence Completion Examination, were given to ascertain the characteristics which differentiated the gifted population from the non-gifted population.

The gifted population was selected on the basis of high IQ. An IQ of 120 was set as the base, and the range was from 120 to 137. An IQ between 80 and 110 was used to designate the non-gifted population.

## A Summary of Characteristics

A summary of the findings concerning the characteristics of the gifted as compared to the non-gifted institutionalized population is organized around (1) age, (2) education, (3) occupation, (4) psychological controls, and (5) general diagnosis, frequency of paranoid tendencies, and incidence of obsessive-compulsive features.

1. *Age:* The institutionalized gifted and non-gifted had a median age of 33.5 to 34 years. The age differences are not significant. The gifted enter mental hospitals with the same relative frequency as the non-gifted. Another way of stating this fact is that the percentage of gifted in mental hospitals is the same as the percentage of gifted in the total population. Mental hospital populations represent the total population in terms of IQ distribution. The adjustment advantage of the gifted in childhood and youth apparently is lost in adulthood.

2. *Education:* The gifted have obtained on the average from three to five years more education than the non-gifted. The gifted male has continued his higher education more frequently and for more advanced degrees than the gifted female. Nine of the twenty gifted males were college graduates; two of these had master's degrees, three had doctor's degrees. Four gifted females, by contrast, were college graduates; two of these had master's degrees; none had a doctor's degree. Apparently the male is encouraged to pursue higher education more frequently and for more advanced degrees than the female.

3. *Occupation:* In spite of more education, the gifted female attained no higher occupational status than the non-gifted population. The gifted male holds the occupations associated with higher education, such as physician, teacher, publisher, pilot, and engineer.

4. *Psychological Controls:* The F score of the Rorschach was used to determine the degree of control that the patients indicated as they interact with their environment. No significant differences in control were found between the gifted and non-gifted populations. Further, the gifted demonstrated no greater control than that which would be expected by chance.

5. *Diagnosis:* The most frequently occurring diagnosis for the gifted male and the non-gifted population was schizophrenia or schizophrenic reaction. No significant differences existed. The gifted female was significantly more psychoneurotic than the non-gifted male (.01 level of significance) and the gifted male (.05 level of significance).

Statistically significant differences in incidence of paranoid tendencies did not appear between the gifted and the non-gifted. However, the gifted male showed the highest frequency of such characteristics. Over half of the gifted males could be so designated.

The gifted male also showed the highest incidence of obsessive-compulsive tendencies, although differences were not statistically significant.

## Feelings and Attitudes

Factors which may further contribute to an understanding of differences between the gifted and non-gifted institutionalized population are organized around (1) feelings of superiority, (2) perceptions of failure, (3) attitudes toward work, and (4) attitudes toward parental pressures in terms of parental expectations.

1. *Feelings of superiority:* At times, the gifted male tended to perceive himself as superior to others. The gifted female and the non-gifted populations

did not perceive themselves so often in this way. The feelings of superiority of the gifted male were significantly higher than the gifted female.

2. *Perceptions of failure:* Half of the gifted female population perceived themselves as failures while three-fourths of the gifted males so perceived themselves. The gifted female resembled more closely the non-gifted population. The gifted male felt significantly more of a failure than the non-gifted population. He felt more of a failure than the gifted female, but the difference was not significant.

3. *Attitudes toward work:* Negative attitudes toward work were held most frequently by both male and female gifted, while positive attitudes were held most frequently by the non-gifted. The gifted female had more negative attitudes toward work than the gifted male. She also had the least positive attitudes toward work. All of the relationships were significant at the .01 level.

4. *Attitudes toward parental pressures:* More male and female gifted resisted parental pressures than non-gifted, but the gifted submitted to parental pressure with about the same frequency as the non-gifted. The gifted showed a similar frequency of ambivalence toward parental pressures as the non-gifted. Both the male and female gifted showed a higher frequency of striving beyond parental standards than the non-gifted. All of the relationships were significant at the .01 or .05 levels.

## Discussion of Findings

The discussion is organized around two foci: (1) the characteristics and perceptions that distinguish the institutionalized gifted from the institutionalized non-gifted, and (2) educational implications of the findings.

The institutionalized gifted resembled the age groups of the institutionalized non-gifted and have developed no higher set of controls to ward off or postpone a psychotic or psychoneurotic disorder. The adjustment advantage found among gifted children and youth is apparently lost in adulthood.

The institutionalized gifted was better educated than the non-gifted. The gifted male continued higher education more frequently than the gifted female at a rate of more than 2 to 1. The gifted male also continued higher education for more advanced degrees than the gifted female. Gifted males held the better occupational positions and had the highest socio-economic status. Gifted females attained no higher socio-economic status than the non-gifted.

The institutionalized gifted male tended to become schizophrenic and to display paranoid or obsessive-compulsive features. He was more likely to project the blame for his failure onto others. He was not so likely to assume responsibility for his own failures. The gifted female more frequently developed psychoneurotic disorders.

The gifted male was more frequently aware of his superiority and also of his own sense of failure. Neither the gifted male nor female had marked positive attitudes toward work; indeed their attitudes were highly negative. Both the gifted male and female tended to reject pressure in terms of parental expectations. Yet as a group, they submitted to parental pressures about as frequently as did the non-gifted population. However, they more frequently attempted to surpass the expectations and achievements of their parents.


## Implications

Assuming that growth and development are continuous, and that adult adjustments are to a large extent contingent upon earlier experiences, a number of implications for education may be derived from the findings on institutionalized gifted. These findings may be suggested by the following questions:

1. What are the schools doing to determine and influence the gifted student's attitude toward work?
2. How does the school help gifted students deal with failure?
3. What are schools doing to help the gifted student develop a self-concept and ideal consonant with his promise?
4. How do the schools work with parents to foster achievement of a high order?
5. Are teachers and parents working together in efforts to stimulate more gifted girls to continue their education and make greater contribution in accord with their promise?

The institutionalized gifted have poor attitudes toward work. Is it possible that too many gifted meet school requirements without much effort? Perhaps these students acquire knowledge and information with a minimum of effort and therefore do not find it necessary to develop positive attitudes and desirable work habits.

The institutionalized gifted, especially the male, experience pervasive feelings of failure. Has academic work been so easy in the elementary school and high school that the gifted seldom experience failure and therefore do not learn to deal with it constructively? Does the gifted male's pattern of blaming others for his failures need to be examined and altered?

The institutionalized gifted male appears to feel superior to others. Have the schools contributed to the feelings of superiority on the part of the male? Similarly, have schools attempted to help girls develop a realistic appreciation of their abilities?

The institutionalized gifted report excessive conflict with their parents. Is the school helping parents to formulate realistic expectations for their gifted children? Are teachers helping the gifted relate effectively to those in authority?

The institutionalized gifted male is better educated and is higher in the occupational hierarchy than is the female. Do present programs for the gifted provide sufficient incentive for the full development of gifted girls?

Answers to these questions seem to be worthy of consideration by schools in their efforts to provide more adequately for gifted pupils.

## References

1. Armstrong, Marion E., *A Comparison of the Interests and Social Adjustments of Under Achievers and Normal Achievers at the Secondary School Level,* doctoral dissertation (Storrs, Connecticut: University of Connecticut, 1955). Abstract in *Dissertation Abstracts* 15, 1955, pp. 1349-1350.

2. Gowan, John C., "The Underachieving Gifted Child—A Problem for Everyone," *Exceptional Children,* Vol. 21 (April, 1955), pp. 247-249, 270-271.

3. Haggard, Ernest A., "Socialization, Personality, and Academic Achievement in Gifted Children," *School Review,* Vol. 65 (December, 1957), pp.388-414.

4. Hollingworth, L.S., *Children Above 180 IQ* (Yonkers-on-Hudson, N.Y.:World Book Company, 1942).

5. Hollingworth, L.S., *Gifted Children: Their Nature and Nurture* (New York: Macmillan, 1926).

6. Horrall, Bernice M., "Academic Performance and Personality Adjustments of Highly Intelliggent College Students," *Genetic Psychology Monographs,* Vol. 55 (February, 1957), pp. 3-83.

7. O'Leary, Maurice J., *The Measurement and Evaluation of the Work Habits of Overachievers and Underachievers to Determine the Relationship of These Habits to Achievement,* doctoral dissertation (Boston: Boston University, 1955). Abstract in *Dissertation Abstracts* 15, 1955, pp. 2104-2105.

8. Roesslein, Charles G., Differential Patterns of Intelligence Traits between High Achieving and Low Achieving High School Boys (Washington, D.C.: Catholic University of America Press, 1953).

9. Shaw, Merville, C., II, and Brown, Donald J., "Scholastic Underachievement of Bright College Students," *Personnel and Guidance Journal,* Vol. 36 (November, 1957), pp. 195-199.

10. Terman, L. M., and Oden, M., *Mental and Physical Traits of a Thousand Gifted Students,* Vol. I of *Genetic Studies of Genius* (Stanford, California: Stanford University Press, 1925).

11. Wedemeyer, Charles A., "Gifted Achievers and Non-Achievers," *Journal of Higher Education,* Vol.24 (January, 1953),pp. 25-30.

12. Witty, Paul, *A Study of One Hundred Gifted Children,* University of Kansas Bulletin in Education, Vol. II, No. 7 (Lawrence, Kansas: University of Kansas Press, 1930).

*E. Paul Torrance*

# Problems of Highly Creative Children

*I*nescapably, the individual who thinks of a new idea is in the very beginning a minority of one. Even when matters of demonstrable fact are involved, as in the Asch experiments, there are very few people who can tolerate being a minority of one. Since creativity involves independence of mind, nonconformity to group pressures, or breaking out of the mould, it is inevitable that highly creative children experience some unusual problems of adjustment. Thus, the highly creative child must either repress his creativity or learn to cope with the tensions which arise from being frequently a minority of one. Repression of creative needs may lead to actual personality breakdown. Their expression frequently leads to loneliness, conflicts, and other problems of adjustment. Educators of gifted children need to understand both types of problems.

## 1. Sanctions Against Divergency

In one of our studies, we have asked approximately 5,000 children in grades three through six to write imaginative stories concerning animals or persons with some divergent characteristic. These have given us many insights concerning the way children see the operation of their society's sanctions against being different. The following story by a sixth-grade girl illustrates many of these sanctions:

> Far into the jungle of Africa lived a flying monkey named Pepper. Pepper was a well-educated monkey and very cute . . . Pepper was unusual too. He was not like all of the other flying monkeys. You see, Pepper didn't eat bananas like everybody else. He wanted to be different. He ate peppers!
> No one ever went out of the jungle so Pepper, being different, decided to go to America! . . . When the people saw him, they began to laugh and then others began to scream. Then out of nowhere a man from a zoo came and took Pepper by surprise. . . .
> Now Pepper was sad. He didn't like the cage they put him in. He made a vow that if he ever got out he would never be different again and ten minutes later he saw some bent bars big enough to fly through. All of a sudden he flew

Reprinted from *Gifted Child Quarterly,* Vol. 5, No. 2 (Summer, 1961), pp. 31-34. By permission of the author and publisher.

out and in two days was back in the jungle. He kept his promise too. He was never different again. He was a good little flying monkey.

I suppose *he ate his bananas!*

About two-thirds of the stories about flying monkeys tell similar tales of conformity or of destruction. Some cultures, however, are more indulgent of divergency than others. Stories written by gifted children in special classes are far more hopeful in outlook than those of gifted children in regular classes. In about 70 per cent of the stories of pupils in classes for high achieving children, the flying monkey is in some way able to persist in his flying. The stories written by children in a small Oklahoma town composed of Indians, whites, and a few Negroes also reflect this tolerance of divergency. In 74 per cent of their stories, the flying monkey succeeds.

## 2. Creative Children May Not Be Well Rounded

The highly creative child is likely to have lagged in some phase of his development. Many investigators in a variety of fields have been disappointed to find that outstanding individuals in the field under study are not well-rounded, "all-American" boys. Verbal abilities frequently will be below some of their other abilities. Perhaps the most inventive and imaginative child we have tested is a boy who has had unusual difficulty in learning to read, yet his store of information and his ability to use it imaginatively in solving problems and developing ideas is fantastic.

This problem is particularly acute at the fourth-grade level. In a number of cases, fourth graders identified by our tests as highly creative have been reevaluated by teachers. Teachers then discover that these children are far more knowledgeable and thoughtful than they had imagined. One examiner after testing orally a certain fourth grade boy remarked: "This boy impresses me as the kind of individual who will become a top executive who can dictate to five secretaries at the same time without becoming confused." The boy's responses gave evidence of high inventive level, flexibility, and originality. This boy, however, has a serious reading disability and ranked near the bottom of his class on the written test of creative thinking.

Because verbal skills are highly valued in our society, tremendous pressures are placed on children to be "well-rounded" in this respect. The relentlessness of these pressures is symbolized in the following story by a sixth-grade girl:

"Quack! Quack! They were after him again—the Ladies Duck Aid Society, with their hair up in pin curls and their screaming, fat ducklings swimming and holding onto their skirts. They never failed. Alas! It was getting too much for little Glob-Blob. Every day there would be quacking and screaming of ducklings while poor Glob-Blob would run as fast as he could to get away from the vicious ducks.

"The reason for this was because poor Glob-Blob could not quack. So every day the Ladies Duck Aid Society would chase Glob-Blob, for they said it was for the good of the ducks, and it was not only right but they were doing a good turn.

"It was lucky for Glob-Blob that the ducks were fat and flabby, for if they were limber, I will not mention what would happen. But one day, these lazy ducks did reduce, and when chasing Glob-Blob dealt him a good many hard blows. And the next day, poor Glob-Blob was at last doomed. The vicious quackers had come and the chase was on. Glob-Blob was failing. It is a shame that so noble a duck should be doomed, but 'That's life,' said Glob-Blob to himself as, slowly but surely, failing, he dropped to the ground. The quackers, very pleased with themselves, sat down for a chat.

"But I shall always remember Glob-Blob and his death. So I shall let him finish his journey, where there will be no more quackers and chasers, and where at last, he may have passionless peace forever."

Many children must consider their counselors, teachers, and parents as "quackers and chasers" when we work so hard to make them become "better rounded personalities." They might contribute far more to society and be far happier and more successful by capitalizing upon their unique strengths rather than spending fruitless energy trying hopelessly to compensate for some divergent characteristic or behavior. I would not, of course, deny that it is necessary for some of our highly creative youngsters to achieve basic skills necessary for success in their chosen areas of specialization.

## 3. Creative Children
## Prefer to Learn on Their Own

Many creative children prefer to learn on their own and schools have been slow in providing such opportunities. Last year we conducted an exciting study in which we found that children would do a great deal of writing on their own, if properly motivated. In another it was found that gifted children in a split-shift school showed more growth in language development, science, and social studies than under a full-day schedule. Only in spelling was there significantly less growth among the split-shift children (seventh graders).

Since we have generally assumed that children do not learn on their own, we have seldom provided them with opportunities to do so. I have seen learning situations "accidentally" left "open" a sufficient number of times to have become quite excited about what would happen, if we should do so more frequently. The following story by an Oklahoma sixth grader, symbolizes this situation:

"Once there were some monkeys sitting in a group. They were all alike except three monkeys. They were very different because they could fly.

"One day some men from a park zoo were looking for some monkeys because theirs had died. They came upon the three that flew. So they took them in a cage. The cage didn't have a top to it. They were in the sun one day and the monkey said to the other, 'I wish we could get out of here.'

" 'Then, why don't we fly out of here?' said the other.

"They started to fly out. When they got about half a mile, some men came to feed them. When they couldn't find the three monkeys, they saw them flying away. One of them said, 'If we would have put them in a cage with a top, we would have had a real good thing here in the zoo.' "

One function of the school counselor might be to help highly creative children recognize or discover the "openings" in their cages to which they might be blinded.


## 4. Creative Children
## Like to Attempt Difficult Tasks

Frequently highly creative children strongly desire to move far ahead of their classmates in some areas. They always make us afraid that they are not "ready." Fortunately, however, educators of gifted children are rapidly revising many of their concepts about what can be taught at various levels of education. This terrifies many. The following recent headlines reflect such a fear:

"Caution Urged in Changing Primary into High Schools"

"Can We Rush Primary Education?"

"Don't Turn Grade Schools into High Schools, Educators Warn at Parley"

"Reading for Kindergarten, Language Too Soon Attacked."

Some of the panic may have been eased by a recent report of the Educational Policies Commission of the NEA and the American Association of School Administrators (*Contemporary Issues in Elementary Education, 1960*).

A very frequent theme in our imaginative stories is related to this problem. The young animal or fowl asks, "When can I roar? When can I crow? When can I quack? When can I fly?" Almost always, the answer is, "When you are a little older." We are always afraid that the young one might not be ready to learn and that he would be forever scarred by even the most temporary failure.

A common experience in the lives of many highly outstanding individuals has been their ability to cope with failure and frustration. Certainly, almost all highly creative scientists, inventors, artists, and writers attempt tasks which are too difficult for them. Had they not attempted such tasks it is quite unlikely that their great ideas would have been born.

217

## 5. Creative Children
## Are Searching for a Purpose

It has been said of most outstanding creative achievers that they seemed to be possessed by a purpose and to be "men of destiny." Creative children need some purpose which is worthy of enthusiastic devotion they seem capable of giving. Some of this need is symbolized in the following story by a sixth-grade boy:

> "There once was a South American monkey that didn't know what he was, who he was, or why he was even alive. He decided that he didn't know even the way to figure it out, so he thought he would make up a reason.
> "He had seen many airplanes fly overhead. He had seen many ferocious animals, many nice animals, and many machines. He had always thought that it would be nice to fly, so he pretended he was an airplane.
> "He had also heard that buzzing sound of the engines, so he called himself 'Buzz.' He also decided that he was a real fast flyer so that this was the reason he was alive.
> "Now, we all know that monkeys can't fly, but he didn't know this. Why he didn't even know that he was a monkey, so he kept trying and trying—and you know what? He flew!"

Perhaps this has some implications not only concerning the need for helping children discover their potentialities but for helping them achieve their self-concepts creatively rather than by authority.

## 6. Creative Children
## Search for Their Uniqueness

Counselors and teachers may become irritated with creative children who seem to create problems for themselves by trying consciously to be different—searching for their uniqueness. Barron maintains that creative individuals reject the demands of their society to surrender their individuality because "they want to own themselves totally and because they perceive a shortsightedness in the claim of society that all its members should adapt themselves to a norm for a given time and place."

One way in which the creative individual searches for his uniqueness is through his vocational choice. Getzels and Jackson, for example, found that their highly creative compared with their highly intelligent subjects gave a greater number of different occupations and more "unusual" or rare occupations. Their attitudes toward adult success were also different, the high creatives being less concerned with conventional standards.

## 7. The Psychological Estrangement
## of Creative Children

In no group thus far studied have we failed to find relatively clear evidence of the operation of pressures against the most creative members of the group, though they are far more severe in some classes than in others.

When we select the most creative members of each sex in each classroom and match them for sex and Intelligence Quotient with other children in the same classroom, three characteristics stand out as differentiating the highly creative children from the less creative ones. First, there is a tendency for them to gain a reputation for having wild or silly ideas. Their teachers and their peers agree on this. Second, their work is characterized by its productivity of ideas "off the beaten track." This explains one of the difficulties of teachers and peers in evaluating their ideas and perhaps why they show up no better than they do on traditional intelligence tests. Their ideas simply do not conform to the standardized dimensions, the behavioral norms, on which responses are judged. Third, they are characterized by humor and playfulness. All of these characteristics help explain both the estrangement and the creativity.

In the next issue, I shall discuss some of the problems which arise when highly creative children repress their creative needs and abilities.

*Harriet E. O'Shea*

# Friendship and the Intellectually Gifted Child

*F*ew areas in social psychology, in clinical psychology, and in developmental psychology are more confused semantically and more difficult ones in which to establish clear-cut measurement—than the area of friendship. Further difficulties attendant upon the original one lie in appraising the effect of friendship or of the lack of friendship upon the individual.

Close friendship involves in some fashion a personal, mutual awareness, a liking and confidence, and a secure satisfaction in interchange, which seem to be recognized introspectively by psychologists and sociologists. However, it is exactly here that measurement becomes so difficult. Presumably, there is a genuine difference between friendship, as such, and what has sometimes been called "popularity" in various sociometric and other studies. Presumably also, genuine close friendship has an effect upon the individuals involved which is different from the condition and experience of being "popular."

This paper reaffirms the assumption made by Lippitt (1) that "the power fields of friends strengthen each other." To the extent that this is true, it is manifestly important for developing human beings, for gifted children as well as others, to have friends. Maslow's (2) "self-actualizing people," in his observation, are those who seem to be especially at home in this life. One wonders whether the experience of constructive, close friendships may not be a contributing factor in reaching the condition of being self-actualizing.

If one looks for identities within the two experiences, it seems possible that the favorable relation of security with adults demonstrated by Spitz and Ribble and others to be so exceedingly important for infants, may, at its core, be something like the experience in the later preschool years, in the primary school years, and in the elementary school years of close friendships with peers. The possibility exists, in other words, that there is a central area of similarity, if not of identity, in the two experiences, with the attendant probability that the experience is comparably nourishing in both instances.

Reprinted from *Exceptional Children*, Vol. 26, No. 6 (February, 1960), pp. 327-335. By permission of the author and publisher.

## Friendship—A Potent Social Force

If the relationship of friendship is a potent force in the development of human beings, then this issue together with all other aspects of programs for gifted children should be taken into account as a major issue when educators and others are endeavoring to see how to meet the needs of gifted children. This issue becomes important if we are to insure their performing academically at top levels in order that they may, presumably, become especially productive for the benefit of society when they leave school and in order that they may have satisfying lives for themselves. All educational and clinical evidence shows that the individual must be complete and contented and "self-actualizing" within himself in order to be of maximum benefit to society. In other words, what is good for the individual gifted child will also be good for him as a social contributor. The question then becomes urgent: "Who are potential friends for gifted children? With whom can they establish relationships of friendship?"

Before we undertake a tentative answer to this question, it may be well to note further that there is a genuine need for the gifted child, as for all other human beings, to become a socialized person, both, again, for his own mental health and for his functioning in society. Undoubtedly relationships of friendship can be, and perhaps are, the most significant way to achieve socialization. The concept of making the intellectually gifted child "get along" with the child of the same chronological age in the center of the distribution of intelligence "because the world is full of such people and you have to get along with everyone" seems to the writer to be a thoroughly bankrupt concept. The contrary hypothesis is that it is only those persons who have experienced closeness and mutual trust and have thus achieved understanding of others throughout the years of childhood who can display sympathy and understanding and can achieve closeness to anyone as adults.


## Factors of Social Limitation

In the welter of studies of relationships between children, which frequently have probably been only "popularity studies," the choices in any case have almost always been strictly limited by geographical boundaries (friends are within a few blocks of each other) and by the child's most frequent contacts being within a narrow chronological age range imposed by the schools. Obviously, in such circumstances, the child with a higher mental age than his chronological age group has very little chance to find anyone of like mental age, even if he would take greater pleasure in such a relationship.

Even so, nothing correlates higher with mutual choices than mental age, and in various studies it stands considerably above any other factor. At the junior high school level, presidents of self-government groups typically are at about the 55th percentile of the group in mental age, and so on.

## Mental Age Factors

It is instructive to compare performances of different mental ages on various tasks and to think how completely communication must fail between children of two widely separated mental ages in the light of these radically different performances. Convenient examples of these phenomena for illustrative purposes can be seen in the Terman-Merrill Stanford-Binet Test Forms L and M. The tests for *comprehension* and for recognition of *similarities* show some clear mental age differences.

At the three-year mental age level, the simplest sort of answer to the following questions is acceptable:

a. What must you do when you are hungry?
b. What must you do when you are sleepy?

It is apparent that the questions at the five-year mental age level involve more coordination of different items, and more selection amongst material that should not be used for the answers, and more dealing with organized patterns:

a. What do we do with our eyes?
b. What do we do with our ears?

A child who has not yet reached the five-year mental age level would give answers that utilize simple associations to the objects mentioned without selection of what is appropriate and what is inappropriate. He does not see that the patterns imbedded in the questions make certain associations relevant and others totally irrelevant. A failing answer to "What do we do with our eyes?" would be *Sleep,* and to "What do we do with our ears?" would be *Wash them with soap,* or *Put hair over them.* It is apparent that the failing answers (below the five-year mental age level) have not been controlled by the abstract part of the questions, "What do we do with . . . ?" The main functions of eyes and ears have not been located by these respondents, and associations which are ruled out by the total pattern of the question have not been discarded.

At the eight-year mental age level, the requirement is to answer two of the following three questions satisfactorily:

a. What should a man do if he comes home and finds that a burglar has robbed his house?

b. Why is a train harder to stop than an automobile?

c. What should a man do if he finds that he is earning less money than it takes to live on?

It is apparent that much more material must be held together to answer any of these three questions than to answer the question, "What do we do with our eyes?" Not only must more material be brought together at once, but also many random, spontaneous reactions to each of the elements of the questions must be discarded under the control of the total pattern. Some satisfactory eight-year mental age reactions and some failing below-eight-year mental age reactions are the following:

1. (Burglar) "He would send down the police." This satisfactorily takes into account the problem, what the individual can do, and the facilities for dealing with it. Failing reactions are such as, "Find out who it was," or "Put it in the paper."

These two answers have not been controlled by the necessary steps for identifying the burglar or the possible results if one put an announcement in the paper, as contrasted with the series of actions necessary to meet the special conditions of a robbery in a house.

2. Similarly, in considering why a train is harder to stop than an automobile, a true eight-year mental age answer would be, "Trains are heavy and are hard to turn off" as contrasted with lower-mental age response such as: "Because a train has more things to stop—and in the automobile, you just have to push down the brakes."

It is apparent that this under-eight-year mental age answer has not seen the issue of weight and kinetic energy and has not been able to reject some immediate associations such as the one, "A train has more things," if that answer means more complicated machinery in the cab, as it appears to mean, in relation to the rest of the answer.

3. Finally, to the question of the man earning too little money, a satisfactory answer for an eight-year-old is: "He should go into another business." A below-eight-year mental age response could be, "Shouldn't spend so much money to live on" or "Borrow some." The response "Spend less money to live on" has not been ruled out by the specification in the question that, in effect, the man is already spending beyond his income for the minimum necessities of life. The less-than-eight-year-old answer which recommends borrowing has not been cancelled by the overall specification that the man is already on the way to being in debt.

As one considers the characteristics of these mental age levels, it becomes apparent that the five-year mental age cannot respond to or interact with the eight-year mental age. The first two groups are unable to keep track of all the items or perceive the abstract patterns that the eight-year mental age does automatically. The other way around, the three-year-old and five-year-old mental age levels would be exasperating and probably seemingly intentionally obstructive to the eight-year mental age level, because of omission of factual issues.

## Maturing Perceptual Contrasts

In the area of recognizing similarities, the contrast between the seven-year mental age level and the eleven-year mental age level shows up clearly how much more material is organized in one grasp of the situation at the eleven-year level, way beyond what the seven-year-old level can do. It is apparent also that more subtle abstract patterns are perceived by the eleven-year-old mind than by the seven-year-old mind.

*The seven-year-old mind can give two satisfactory similarities from the list below:*

*Seven year mental age*

(a) *Wood and coal*
(b) *Apple and peach*
(c) *Ship and automobile*
(d) *Brass and silver*

*The eleven-year-old mind can give three satisfactory similarities from the list below:*

*Eleven year mental age*

(a) *Snake, cow, sparrow*
(b) *Rose, potato, tree*
(c) *Wool, cotton, leather*
(d) *Book, teacher, newspaper*
(e) *Knife-blade, penny, piece of wire*

In the reactions of under-eleven-year mental ages to the above items, it is apparent that the lower mental age mind does not compare each entry with each other entry (snake, cow, sparrow) discarding in the similarities reported between two of them (taken two by two) all characteristics that would not include the third. In other words, the lower mental age uses without selections, or with very little selection, the first association that comes to mind for two of the stimuli, and it happily relaxes with no feeling of discrepancy even though the full pattern has not been met. For instance, for snake-cow-sparrow, some under-eleven-year answers are, "They can all hurt you" (ignoring the sparrow) and "All can walk" (ignoring the snake).

An under-eleven response for rose-potato-tree might be, "Rose grows like a tree, potato grows under ground." Here the under-eleven mind is not troubled by the fact that it has failed to unite the three ("Potato grows under ground") and is not troubled by differences between a rose bush and a tree, even in comparing those two. Perhaps there is a foggy feeling that there is some similarity between a rose bush and a tree but the under-eleven mind cannot cast out the inappropriate associations that come to mind and penetrate through to those characteristics that are identical for a rose and a tree.

In wool-cotton-leather, an under-eleven answer might be, "Comes from animals." Here the under-eleven mind is not troubled by cotton being non-animal. Again, first, early associations cannot be resisted to satisfy a controlling selector pattern.

A foggy perception of *something* similar in book-teacher-newspaper without the ability to penetrate through to the central characteristic shared by the three (giving information) is displayed by the under-eleven answer, "They belong to schools—newspaper has reading on it and we use it sometimes in school." Here, "belongs to school" may be moving in towards recognizing the information-giving characteristics of the three items but this reaction, among other things, fails to rule out many other aspects of a school such as having chairs, a furnace, and so on. This under-eleven reaction also fails to perceive the characteristic that both teacher and newspaper can give you information no matter where they may be, in school, on subways, in a living room, or wherever it may be.

Under-eleven reactions to knife-blade-penny-piece of wire are such as the following: "They are both strong." Among other things, this fails to utilize any scale of strength by which a usual piece of wire would be low in the scale and ignores the fact that a penny would be of very little use for leverage and so on. Another under-eleven reaction might be, "All made of the same metal" which is not controlled by the fact that a penny is never made of steel, which would be the almost invariable metal for a knife-blade, and does not take into account the fact that wire might be made of one of any number of different metals. The under-eleven mind cannot get to the more abstract, general category "All made of metal."

An eleven-year-old mind endeavoring to deal with a mind around seven would be bored or exasperated by the uninterestingness or the apparently obstructive action of the lower mental age. In the same way, the seven-year mental age which can only just manage to get two comparisons out of: wood and coal (fuel), apple and peach (fruit), ship and automobile (transportation), brass and silver (metal) would be completely bewildered in trying to deal with the ordinary, complicated, abstract thinking of the eleven-year-old mind illustrated by its ease of recognizing the similar element in three objects.

One can guess the discouragement of the higher mental age level child when he tries to talk and to play with the younger mental age level child who keeps missing the point and confusing issues and requiring endless explanations to get him into action at all, whereas it can be seen what a joy it is (all other things being equal) when one's companion sees instantly what one is talking about and says things that seem interesting, clear and important to one, even when he disagrees.

In the examples of reactions to similarities that have been quoted one might be seeing two seven-year-old children, one with an IQ of 100 and a mental age of seven, the other with an IQ of 157 and a mental age of eleven. In many school systems, or perhaps one has to say, in most school systems, these two seven-year-olds would be in the second grade together. The mental ages around seven would predominate in the class, perhaps 27 or 28 such children to only one or two with mental ages anywhere near our child of the IQ of 157. It then develops that day after day the eleven-year mental age confuses the majority, who usually protect themselves by cold shouldering him or even attacking him. He not only is starved for friendly interactions with equal minds but often, perhaps most of the time, the recipient of social exclusion or even hostility.

In Terman's (3) studies of "genius," although the gifted children were rated higher in personality traits than other children, there were no direct measures of friendship included in the data. However, in connection with these favorable personality ratings, it should be remembered that, typically, the gifted child in the study was the youngest in his classroom, which indicates that the gap between his mental age and that of the group was a little reduced. Also, it is interesting to note that, in the follow-up studies, the most successful group of these gifted children graduated from college younger than the least successful group, again suggesting less isolation from their classmates in mental age.

At the three-year-old level, there are data concerning who can be friends with whom. In a too-little-known study of spontaneous group formations in the nursery school, Hubbard (4) established what many would consider an extraordinary fact. In these little spontaneous groups, which averaged two or three children, which lasted perhaps six minutes, and which were engaged in twice in every 15 minutes, the question was: who played with whom? Hubbard investigated the occurrence of three factors in the choices made: chronological age, the general amount of social participation by the individual, and mental age. She measured her groups both in terms of the number of times that children joined each other and in terms of the length of time that they spent together in a group. The correlations between general amount of social participation or chronological age and the personnel of the little groups ran between $-.22$ and $+.19$. When, however, Hubbard calculated the relationships between mental age and spontaneous group participation, she found that those who played together most often showed a correlation of $+.41$ in mental age; in the case of those who played longest together in groups the correlation was $+.62$ for mental age. In other words, in these early years, an age when one is certain that the child is not standing around asking himself which is the appropriate child to play with, the most powerful factor pulling the membership of a group together appears to be similarity in mental age.

A direct comparison of the sociometric choices of gifted children within a gifted group and within their homeroom group assigned by chronological age has been reported by Mann (5). From a population of 1000 children, from kindergarten through sixth grade, he studied 67 intellectually gifted children who were taken for half of each day into a special workshop. The other half day, they were with their chronological age homeroom group. He utilized a sociometric technique in which each child chose those whom he would want to have with him at a school party, or whom he would want to have help him catch up with his work if he had been absent, or whom he would like to have on his side on a team. Mann also utilized the same factors in reverse, "Whom would you *least* like to have for . . ." Remembering that the gifted children spent an equal amount of time with the other gifted workshop children and with their chronological age homeroom children, the positive choices were found to be overwhelmingly for other workshop children. Also, the rejections were overwhelmingly for other workshop children. In other words, there seems to be revealed here a perfectly clear-cut difference in the lack of awareness of, and undoubtedly the lack of interest in, the lower mental-age children (of the same chronological age) and a greatly heightened awareness of and interest in the children of the same high mental ages.

In other words, the contention that keeping a gifted child with others of his own chronological age will help him have friendships with this group appears to be strongly refuted by Mann's findings. Insofar as a sociometric technique is measuring friendships (it is at least measuring "awareness of" and "interest in"), it is shown that friendships occur with those of like mental age, rather than with those of like chronological age.


## *"Like Attracts Like"*

Long ago, Hollingworth (6) reported many striking cases of the radical change in the life experience of highly gifted children, originally lonely, ineffectual, shunned non-participators who, when they were later moved into groups of comparable mental age, began to function richly in the new group, were well-liked, and frequently became some of the most valuable contributors to the life of the group, and, in each case, changed from a shy, lonely person into a happy, friendly, socialized individual.

The dynamics of the choice of like mental ages revealed by Hubbard amongst three-year-olds and of choices (and rejections) of like mental ages in the elementary school years as measured by Mann, and of the resuscitation of individuals placed among equals as reported by Hollingworth may be partly suggested by formulations of Lewin (7). He has stated that differences in mental age are closely related to the degree of differentiation of the person, and that increasing mental age means increasing flexibility, that is to say, increasing richness of behavior. It would seem highly likely that the three-year-old in the nursery school discovers those other children who provide him with appropriate richness of behavior, and who, in turn, are pleased by his richness of behavior. Less differentiation of the person presumably is unsatisfying and, in that sense, boring, and undoubtedly involves frustration of the higher mental age personality when some of his behavior and some of his advances are left hanging in mid-air or are rejected by the less rich and less flexible person who cannot deal with the higher mental age manifestations. Undoubtedly, the same dynamics exist in the elementary school years. It seems clearly apparent that those who are more differentiated as persons find the less differentiated, less rich personalities dull and uninteresting, and undoubtedly frustrating because there is no "comeback" to the gifted child's advances. On the other hand, the person of equal differentiation as a person, the one with greater flexibility and richness of behavior, provides interesting material to observe and to respond to and gives satisfying reactions to one's own behavior.

Assuming that close friendship, that genuine interaction with other persons does many favorable things—such as increasing the socialization of the individual, making his life more satisfying, widening and deepening his "power field," establishing and maintaining general mental health—then it is urgent that arrangements be made for intellectually gifted children (in school, on playgrounds, in community activities) which will offer them appropriate social contacts to enable them to build friendships. It seems highly probable that when the gifted child is externally bound to persons of lower mental age, who are less flexible and less rich in personality differentiation of the person, he is then, in effect, an isolated individual for whom activities tend to drop dead, and for whom there is malnutrition in the area of rich, constructive, developing, rewarding experience of close friendship.

## References

1. Lippitt, Ronald, "Studies In Topological and Vector Psychology: I. An experimental study of the effect of democratic and authoritarian group atmospheres," *University of Iowa Studies in Child Welfare,* 1940, 16, p. 45-195.

2. Maslow, A.H., "Cognition of Being in the Peak Experiences," *The Journal of Genetic Psychology,* 1959, 94, p. 43-66.

3. Terman, Lewis, *Genetic Studies of Genius.* Stanford University Press, California, 1925, 1926, 1930, 1947, 1959.

4. Hubbard, Ruth, "A Method of Studying Spontaneous Group Formation in: Thomas, Dorothy and associates," *Some New Techniques for Studying Social Behavior.*

5. Chapter IV, New York, 1929. Child Development Monograph, I, Bureau of Publications, Teachers College, Columbia University.

6. Mann, Horace, "How Real are Friendships of Gifted and Typical Children in a Program of Partial Segregation?" *Exceptional Children,* 1957, 23, p. 199-201.

7. Hollingworth, Leta, *Gifted Children: Their Nature and Nurture.* Macmillan, New York, 1926.

8. Lewin, K., *Dynamic Theory of Personality.* McGraw-Hill, New York, 1935.

# Part III
# Identification and Measurement
# of Giftedness

The primary purpose for identifying gifted and talented students is to determine if a particular individual possesses extraordinary ability in one or more areas to such an extent that his or her educational needs cannot adequately be met in the regular school program. A second purpose that can also be served by the identification process is to ascertain the types of program modifications which are necessary in order to accommodate the diversity of talent that may be present in a given school population. In other words, a comprehensive identification process should provide some direction for educational programming as well as determine which students will benefit the most from such programs. All too often, identification has been viewed as the process of fitting students to programs rather than developing programs that are based on the identified strengths of an individual or group. These strengths should include the interests and learning styles of the individual as well as the particular subject matter areas in which the student may excel.

Since giftedness appears in many different forms and can be found in all of the cultural groups in our society, a wide variety of identification procedures must be used to discover the great diversity of talents that can benefit from special educational programming. A comprehensive program for the identification of gifted and talented students should consist of both objective and subjective procedures that are designed to assess all of the types of abilities and interests that the gifted possess, and the degree to which these abilities and interests exist in the individual.

Perhaps more has been written about identification than any other topic within the field of the gifted. As the concept of giftedness began to expand beyond the earlier idea of one factor, the general intelligence factor, the problems of identification became increasingly more complex. Certainly both identification and special provisions for the gifted would be easier to provide if there were only a single factor. Recognition of a greater number of indicators of giftedness has, however, resulted in an increase in measurement problems associated with the identification process. Thus, we must continue to raise questions about such issues as the reliability of teacher rating scales and the predictive validity of tests that are administered to preschool youngsters or members of culturally different minority groups.

Although efforts are continually being made to improve the technology of identification procedures, many problems remain wholly or partially unresolved. One of our concerns in selecting material for Part III of this book was to choose articles that call attention to the major problems and issues that one must be aware of when he or she is involved in the identification process. The first two articles deal with measurement problems that are typically encountered in identifying intellectual giftedness and creativity. Problems such as the appropriateness of various measuring instruments at different age levels, the value of group as opposed to individual intelligence testing, and the criterion problem in creativity measurement are discussed. The articles point out a number of cautions and suggestions that are based on the extensive amount of research relating to intelligence and creativity assessment.

Pegnato and Birch report on seven different methods for identifying gifted children at the junior high school level. Since these authors used Stanford-Binet intelligence scores as a criterion measure for determining the efficiency and effectiveness of each method, the reader should keep in mind that the results of this study are restricted to the selection of intellectually gifted students. Another type of giftedness was investigated by Jerecky who studied the efficiency of seven different indicators of social giftedness. His results suggest that a combination of instruments can be used to predict the quality and effectiveness of social behavior among academically oriented, middle-class students. Again, the results of this study should be considered in view of the relatively restricted socioeconomic characteristics of the sample population.

In spite of the large number of psychometric problems involved in identification, research in the area of giftedness and creativity has led to the development of a number of specific instruments and procedures that can be used in the screening and selection process. Some of these instruments and procedures are discussed in this section.

Renzulli, Hartman, and Callahan have developed a four dimensional scale that is designed to guide teachers' judgment in the areas of learning, motivation, creativity, and leadership. The scale is based on a review of the literature dealing with characteristics of the gifted and was validated through a series of field studies. The "What Kind of Person are You?" instrument developed by Torrance and Khatena is a screening device for identifying creatively gifted adolescents and adults. A series of reliability and validity studies indicate that this instrument is a valuable tool for identifying a variety of creative behaviors.

The identification system developed by Gowan represents a practical method for gathering and processing information that is used in the identification process. Gowan's approach is based on a variety of selection criteria and is relatively economical in terms of time and expenses for testing. This method also makes provisions for the selection of students who might ordinarily be overlooked by traditional identification procedures.

For a number of years psychologists have wrestled with the problem of defining and measuring originality. In the final article in Part III, three different approaches to the measurement of this elusive trait are presented. Tests based on uncommoness of response, remoteness of associates, and cleverness of response were developed and evaluated through factor analytic procedures. The results of these studies are reported and the advantages and disadvantages of each approach are discussed.

*Ruth A. Martinson*
*Leon M. Lessinger*

# Problems in the Identification of Intellectually Gifted Pupils

*M*any problems beset the educator who recognizes the importance of providing for individual learning ability at the upper end of the ability scale. He is plagued by a number of questions and a considerable amount of confusion. Much of the confusion, though certainly not all, is related to the problem of identifying the intellectually gifted pupils.

Questions which arise concerning the identification of the intellectually gifted may be classified principally as follows:

1. Who are these persons? What should we call them?
2. What kinds of measures should be employed in the identification process? At what age should they be used?
3. Should criteria other than tests determine whether special provisions are needed?

In attempts to answer the questions satisfactorily, schools have developed a bewildering array of methods for selecting their gifted. The "New Deal" for the gifted has also produced a "New Deal" assortment of initials for designating the group. Witness the HAPs (high academic potential), HEPs (high educational potential), and HIPs (high intellectual potential), or the MRL (more rapid learner) and MCL (more capable learner).

The problem of proliferating percentages also confronts the educator. Should he include one or two percent of the total population, or would it be better to consider the upper 15 percent in this category? The larger percent is favored by some on the grounds that identification of the gifted will then be certain and comprehensive. In the extension of the group size the pupil with

Martinson, Ruth A. and Lessinger, Leon M. "Problems in the Identification of Intellectually Gifted Pupils". *Exceptional Children*, 26: 227-242, 1960.

special needs again may become lost in the press for providing for large numbers.

A third concern is that of complete identification. How can we be sure that we have identified all the intellectually gifted? Should the identification process begin at the third-grade level, or should it be confined to certain other selected grade levels?

Another important problem is that of adequate measurement. The question of whether group or individual tests should be used, in what ways they should be used, and the proper context for their use is perplexing. The problem of teacher judgment, and administrator judgment as part of the identification process also enters here.

The problems already mentioned are compounded when consideration is given to special provisions for the identified intellectually gifted pupil. Should provisions be made for the person with extremely high ability but with poor motivation and achievement? What of the child with personality problems? On what basis should we select from the selected?

The result of the dilemma, in some schools, may be obscure identification policies and procedures. A *range* of scores may include the exceptions within a given school district. IQ cutoff points may be given for group tests without specification of the test. Qualifications for admission may insure that only the high achieving well-behaved gifted child who needs the program least of the gifted will be admitted to it. Or partial and limited identification facilities may cause the gifted child to remain unidentified.

It is the conviction of the writers that much of the success of a program for the intellectually gifted is based upon sound identification procedures. So much of educational planning depends upon adequate knowledge of pupil potential that necessary time and expense should be invested to determine as accurately as possible what the potential is.

The problems outlined above are not simple. Some of them can be considered on the basis of evidence while others must be met through the application of common sense. That some will be dismissed more briefly than others does not make them less important within the present context.


## Questions: Who Are These Persons? What Should We Call Them?

The term *intellectually gifted* relates to the kind of abilities which are measured by individual intelligence tests. The term has the connotation of a small fraction of the total population who have exceptionally high learning ability. These children constitute the group of up to three percent of the population who, because they are exceptionally high in learning ability, have exceptional educational needs. On individual tests, they measure at two standard deviations or more beyond the mean. In measured general intelligence, they differ as much from the average as do the mentally retarded. In studies of intelligence levels within the general population, the mentally retarded and the intellectually gifted have been found to include approximately the same percent of the total population.[1]

It is important to think of the intellectually gifted, while a small percent, as including a *range* of potential. The following table shows the number of pupils within the total population who might be found at various IQ levels on the basis of expectancy. All of these pupils would be classified as intellectually gifted, yet the differences among the members of this group are exceedingly complex and diverse.[2]

**TABLE 1.**
**Number of Pupils From General Population**
**at Various IQ Levels**

| No. of Pupils | | IQ Level |
|---|---|---|
| 3 per | 100 | 130 |
| 1 per | 100 | 137 |
| 1 per | 1,000 | 150 |
| 1 per | 10,000 | 160 |
| 1 per | 100,000 | 168 |
| 1 per | 1,000,000 | 180 |

The fallacy of employing grade-level materials or of applying age-norms to the intellectually gifted is apparent when the mental age is considered. If educational provisions are made which are consonant with the potential of the child, the usual materials and experiences are inappropriate. The intellectually gifted child is capable of learning at an accelerated rate which should *widen* the differences between his attainment and that of the average child as he progresses in school. The hypothetical table which follows indicates the expanding differences as the child grows older, and as the IQ difference increases.

**TABLE 2.**
**Mental Age Equvalents of Various**
**Chronological Ages and IQ Levels**

| Actual Chronological age | Corresponding Grade | M.A. at 130 IQ Level | Corresponding Grade | M.A. at 150 IQ Level | Corresponding Grade | M.A. at 170 IQ Level | Corresponding Grade |
|---|---|---|---|---|---|---|---|
| 6 | 1 | 7.8 | 2 | 9.0 | 4 | 10.2 | 5 |
| 8 | 3 | 10.4 | 5 | 12.0 | 7 | 13.6 | 8 |
| 10 | 5 | 13.0 | 9 | 15.0 | 10 | 17.0 | 12 |
| 12 | 7 | 15.6 | 10 | 18.0 | 13 | 20.4 | ** |
| 14 | 9 | 18.2 | 13 | 21.0 | ** | * | ** |
| 16 | 11 | 20.8 | ** | * | ** | * | ** |

*Beyond test level
**Beyond normal school range

The higher the IQ, the wider the gap. The six-year-old with an IQ of 150 has the mental age equivalent of a beginning fourth-grader. At the age of 10 as a beginning fifth-grader, he has the mental age equivalent of a high school sophomore. It is clearly obvious that his needs cannot be met through the usual curriculum provisions.

## Questions: What Kinds of Measures Should be Used for Identification? At What Age?

Part of these questions relate to the age selected for identification of the gifted. Obviously, certain preliminary screening devices which are appropriate at one age level are not appropriate at another. And—those designated for certain age levels within the general population also may not be appropriate for this group. Another part of this question is whether identification is a single or multi-step process.

In deciding the age of identification and resultant special provisions for the gifted, it is well to recall that the educational needs of the intellectually gifted are not limited to certain grade levels, but that they exist throughout the grades. Hollingworth[3] and others have pointed out that the early grades are actually the time of greatest need for the gifted child.

Questions sometimes arise whether tests with primary-age pupils possess sufficient reliability to allow decisions. It may be worthwhile again to think of the intellectually gifted pupils in relation to his potential. He is mature far beyond his chronological age, when one considers his mental and intellectual development. It is more realistic, for example, to think of him as an upper-primary grade, or middle-elementary grade child than as a first-grader. In many schools, the age for first identification of mentally retarded children is set at third-grade level, because of the problem of test reliability. Yet the mentally retarded child with an IQ of 70 who is eight years of age is not as mature intellectually as the five-year-old child with an IQ of 130. It is reasonable, therefore, to continuously identify gifted children throughout the grades, including kindergarten.

Another question relating to early identification is whether the costs are prohibitive. This must be weighed against evidence, and against the value accruing to the child who through identification may be given the basis for a total school experience which is appropriate for him. The dollars invested then assume less importance.

To identify gifted kindergarten children for participation in a research study,[4] a multiple screening process was used. The screening included teacher judgment, a teacher identification form, the Pintner-Cunningham Intelligence Test, and the Goodenough Draw-A-Man Test. On the basis of the multiple screening criteria, 127 out of 1084 kindergarten children were referred for individual testing with the Revised Stanford-Binet Scale. Of the 127, 62 were identified as intellectually gifted on the criterion of a minimum IQ of 130.[5] Therefore, the group screening procedure was effective in nearly

50 percent of the cases. It seems legitimate, then, since we are responsible for educating gifted children from the time when they enter kindergarten, to identify them early.

The problem of identification changes from the lower primary grade level to upper grades with the increasing use of group tests. The problem becomes one of a differentiated process of identification in several steps. The first step is *screening*, which involves the use of carefully selected group tests and other devices. The second is *identification*, which is based upon preliminary screening, and which involves the establishment of the true potential of the pupil. This potential is determined by the use of individual tests in the hands of a specialist, given in such a way as to permit assessment of the level and quality of the pupil's ability to learn. The third step is *program planning,* an outgrowth of proper identification based upon thorough knowledge of pupils, their abilities, achievement levels, and personal attributes. All three of the steps listed precede any educational provisions.

The group test is suggested as a screening method rather than as an identification point for several reasons. One of these is the problem of group test ceiling. Group tests do not give the same kind of measure as the individual test when extremes at either end of the ability scale are considered. Evidence to this effect was found in the California Study[6] in which scores for the same group and individual tests were available for 332 gifted pupils. All of the pupils rated 130 or more on the Revised Stanford-Binet Scale.

If a criterion score of 125 or above on a group test (a score which is commonly designated for screening) had been used for selecting the gifted pupils, 82 of the 332 would have been eliminated. If the criterion score of 130 (the same as that for the individual test) had been applied, 51.5 percent of the gifted group would have been eliminated.

Essentially the same findings occurred within the context of a study of the entire population of a junior high school.[7] If a cut-off point of 125 on the group test had been employed, 49 out of 84 gifted pupils would have failed to qualify, including nine whose actual scores on the Binet ranged from 146 to 161.

The effect of test scores on curriculum planning requires sound planning of identification procedures. The sometimes vast discrepancy between group and individual scores causes educators to look upon the abilities of the gifted erroneously. In the Pegnato study, 45 pupils had Binet scores which were higher than the group test scores by 20 points or more, and 15 lost at least 30 points in the group test scores. The implications for educational planning are quite different when one considers the group test score of 134 and an individual test score of 178 for the same person, or a group test score of 115 and an individual score of 149, to cite two examples from this study.

Further evidence of the problem of differences between group and individual tests with the higher intelligence levels was subjected to study by a test publisher.[8] At the upper Binet levels, it was found that the group test scores were lower. Test scores within the average range, were comparable, and below the average range, the group test scores tended to be higher. The group test, therefore, gave the gifted pupils lower test scores, with algebraic differences of 33 points at the upper ranges. The discrepancy within the gifted group would actually make a difference in the kinds of curriculum experiences which were planned for these pupils.

The following partial table was adapted from the test publisher's report to show the algebraic differences between group and individual tests for pupils with IQ's above 130. The individual test score is consistently higher at each interval, with an increase at higher ability levels.

An analysis of group test manuals reveals the problem of applying a group test score criterion to a selected population. Three group tests, all widely used, were subjected to examination from the standpoint of adequacy for gifted pupils:[9]

The implications regarding the use of group tests in the identification process are clear. They should be used for screening purposes, and should be followed by measures which show the kinds of abilities and true potential of the gifted pupil. The group tests which are used for screening should be selected so that they possess adequate content of appropriate difficulty for the gifted pupil. On many occasions, group tests at an advanced grade level would be more useful for screening purposes than those of the child's actual grade level.

At the identification stage, the individual intelligence test is used to give trained examiners, under standardized conditions, a reliable assessment of the subject's responses to items which are important in school learning and

### TABLE 3.
### Differences in Test Scores Between Group and
### Individual Tests at Various Levels

| IQ Range | Number of Pupils | Algebraic Difference* |
|----------|------------------|-----------------------|
| 160-169 | 6 | 33.833 |
| 150-159 | 11 | 18.273 |
| 140-149 | 11 | 13.909 |
| 130-139 | 28 | 10.607 |

*In favor of the Binet

Test A required that the second-grader succeed on 77 percent of the items in order to attain an IQ of 125, and that the third-grader succeed on 84 percent for the same IQ. The third-grader would have to succeed on 138 out of 164 items. At the next level, the percent of success required is 63 percent for grade four; 72 percent for grade five; 81 percent for grade six; 89 percent for grade seven; and 94 percent for grade eight. Thus it is evident that the total number of items available for the measurement of pupil potential is low, and decreases at each succeeding grade level.

Test B is designed for grades 7-12. One form of this test does not yield an IQ of 125 or more beyond the ninth-grade level. The other form of the test requires success on 96 percent of the items in order to attain a score of 125. Therefore, although this test is used extensively in high schools, it does not measure the potential of the gifted pupil.

Test C is a primary level test. To attain a score of 125 on this test, the kindergarten child would have to succeed on 76 percent of the items, and the first-grader on 90 percent. The second-grader could not make a score of 125, although the test is designed to include this age level.

The advanced level of Test C shows the same pattern. This test, for ages 7-11, would not measure a sixth-grader with an IQ of 125 or over.

performance. The items evaluate such abilities as memory, verbal skill, comprehension, generalization, and synthesis, among others.

Individual administration of the test means that the ability of the gifted pupil is measured more directly and effectively than in a group situation. The group test is built upon items designed for the entire population, and therefore contains a number of items which serve no function in measuring the ability of the gifted pupil. In the individual test, on the other hand, the examiner is able to estimate the level at which he should begin testing, and thus save pupil energy, prevent frustration, and insure interest and motivation.

The individual test also must be evaluated from the standpoint of ceiling. One widely used individual test yields an IQ of 154 or less. Reference to Table 1 shows that certain individuals would be identified erroneously at less than true potential. *These are the individuals who most need special provisions.* Every effort should be made to utilize an individual test which will enable the gifted child to reveal his true ability. Curriculum planning otherwise would be unsoundly based.

## Question: Should Criteria Other Than Tests Determine Whether Special Provisions Are Made?

The purpose of multiple screening, followed by individual testing, is to locate and study those pupils whose learning abilities are exceptional. Any administrative planning and structuring of programs should *follow* the identification process, and should include whatever plans seem best for each individual.

Every intellectually gifted pupil, regardless of problems, ought to have an educational program planned to meet his needs. Identification does not assure achievement or motivation.[10] A "program" which includes only part of the identified gifted and excludes others is only a partial service. The intellectually gifted child who is excluded from special opportunities because he is poorly motivated, physically handicapped, or withdrawn may be the individual who could profit most from proper attention. Individuals with long histories of difficult behavior can make remarkable adjustments, and have, because they are given meaningful learning experience. The individuals with special problems will require special and skilled help, but this should be given, as it is with other types of exceptional children.

### Summary

The problem of identification is one of using the best available measures in order to arrive at an assessment of pupil potential which is as accurate as possible. Screening should be thought of as a preliminary step toward identification, in which multiple measures including group intelligence and achievement tests, teacher judgment, teacher check lists, and others are used. The final assessment of potential should be made with a measure which permits the pupil to perform at his true level and not with one which imposes ceiling limitations. This insures a proper basis for adequate curriculum planning.

Identification should begin at the kindergarten level, and should be a continuous process extending throughout the grades. The process should be aimed toward the identification of all intellectually gifted pupils, including those with special educational problems.

## Notes

1. Thompson, George C., *Child Psychology*. New York: Houghton Mifflin Company, 1952, p. 387.

2. Carter, Harold D., *Cut-off Points for Securing Groups of Pupils at Various Levels of Superiority as Indicated by 1937 Stanford-Binet IQ's,* (mimeographed).

3. Hollingworth, Leta, *Children Above 180 IQ*. New York: World Book Company, 1942, p. 282.

4. California Study Project on Programs for Gifted Pupils.

5. This study was done by Margery P. McIntosh, Director of Guidance, La Mesa-Spring Valley Schools.

6. California Study Project on Programs for Gifted Pupils.

7. Pegnato, Carl V., "Identifying Mentally Gifted in Junior High Schools." In James J. Gallagher (Ed.), *Teaching Gifted Students: A Book of Readings* (Boston: Allyn and Bacon, Inc., 1965), pp. 34-42.

8. Data through courtesy of California Test Bureau.

9. Data available in *Technical Supplement, California Study of Programs for Gifted Pupils.* Bureau of Education Research, California State Department of Education, Sacramento.

10. Jacobs, Norman, "Formal Recognition of Mentally Superior Children; Its Effect on Achievement and Achievement Motivation." Unpublished Doctor of Philosophy dissertation, Stanford University, January, 1959.

Donald J. Treffinger
Joseph S. Renzulli
John F. Feldhusen

# Problems in the Assessment of Creative Thinking

$A$ large number of studies dealing with various aspects of creative thinking have appeared in educational and psychological publications during the last two decades. Evidence of the extent of this interest appears in Razik's (1965) bibliography and this journal's attempts to update it in 1967 and 1968, as well as in recent volumes of *Psychological Abstracts* and *Dissertation Abstracts*. Yet there is a great deal of controversy regarding the nature of the creative process and the strategies that hold maximum promise for accelerating creative production. While such controversy is optimistically viewed as a healthy symptom in any relatively new line of scientific inquiry, our failure to master certain basic problems after nearly twenty years of intensified study has led to a decrease in interest among educational practitioners who at one time were eager to rally round the flag of creativity and to "do something" about this newly discovered (or rediscovered) human ability. Unless researchers can begin to find answers to many unsolved problems, the concept of creativity may be, at best, a catchall. At worst, there exists a very real danger that it could eventually be tossed upon the junk heap of discarded educational fads.

The purpose of this paper is to provide an overview of the major problems and issues that relate to the scientific study of creativity. By isolating the important dimensions of the problem, we hope that some direction may be provided for future research efforts.

There are two basic underlying assumptions upon which this paper is based. The first is that certain unique psychological processes, referred to as "creativity," do in fact exist in man's repertoire of behaviors, although in our investigation of those behaviors, we may have merely scratched the surface. The second assumption is that the creative process is complex, or multidimensional in nature.

This paper is based on the author's presentations in the symposium Assessing Creativity: Progress in Both Directions; at the Annual Meeting of the American Educational Research Association, Minneapolis, March, 1970, Richard E. Ripple, Chairman.

In this paper, we will consider two general and interrelated problems and several specific issues within each. The first set of problems involves the *theoretical description* of creative thinking; the second will be referred to as the *criterion problem.*

The first problem, then, is that there is no single, widely-accepted theory of creativity which can serve to unify and direct our efforts at specifying an adequate assessment procedure. The work of Mednick (1962) and his associates illustrates, perhaps as well as any, the formulation of a theory of creativity from which a particular method of assessment emerges. Yet, for a number of reasons, many researchers have not been attracted to this theory (cf. Jackson and Messick, 1965; Taft and Rossiter, 1963; Cropley, 1966), and it can hardly be described as widely accepted. Other theories, such as those of Rogers (1962) or Kubie (1958), have seldom resulted in the formulation of psychometrically adequate assessment procedures. Guilford's widely-known "structure of intellect" model (1967) does not constitute a theory of creativity *per se,* despite the fact that it has been heuristically or conceptually useful in describing some cognitive abilities which are related to creativity. It may be useful to describe it as a theory of human intelligence which subsumes some important cognitive aspects of creativity. Even though Guilford (1967) has argued in recent discussions that creative thinking is not merely a matter of divergent production, a comprehensive theory of creativity would necessarily consider in detail the nature and interrelationships of non-cognitive components of creative behavior, as well as the cognitive aspects.

Torrance's (1966) tests purport to be broadly eclectic, drawing from the "best" of theory available at the time of their development, but for that very reason—that they lack a unified, comprehensive, theoretical base—difficulties are inevitable. Of course, the variables assessed by the Torrance Tests (fluency, flexibility, originality and elaboration) are all classified in Guilford's "structure of intellect."

Given the existing array of ideas about creativity, and the absence of "theoretical unity," it is not in the least surprising that there exists a number of tests, all purporting to be measures of "creativity," but differing in a number of ways. Each instrument mirrors the particular set of beliefs and preconceptions of its developer concerning the nature of creativity. Sadly, the theoretical rationale for such tests is often not even sufficient to allow systematic tests of differential predictions.

An outgrowth of this problem, although a major concern in its own right, is that *we do not understand very completely the implications of differences in assessment procedures.* Variations in working time, test atmosphere, and directions given to the examinee, for example, seem to yield different kinds of results and different patterns of intercorrelations between creativity scores and other cognitive or achievement variables. It is quite clear that such changes occur (Wallach and Kogan, 1965; Van Mondfrans, Feldhusen, Treffinger, and Ferris, 1970). What is *not* clear is the reason for those changes, or under what conditions certain results might be predicted.

Van Mondfrans et al. (1970) argued that the matter is much more complex than merely removing the time limits and appearances of a test-like situation. Removing time limits, for example, had no significant effect on pupil performance on verbal tasks. The highest scores on these tasks were obtained under standard "test-like" conditions. On figural tasks, however, removing time limits did influence pupil performance; highest scores were obtained by pupils under "take home" conditions.

Continuing experimental work is needed to understand the problems of test procedures and their implications more completely. Such research would also be more profitable if predictions could be derived from a specific theoretical conception of creativity. In the meantime, a clear implication seems to be that researchers who use "creativity tests" should be extremely careful to report in detail the procedures for test administration, directions, and timing.

Another very controversial issue, which is related to theoretical problems and has probably prevented educators from achieving some closure in programming for the classroom, is a problem which we will refer to as *dimensionality*. (In measurement terms, the issue is more properly referred to as convergent and discriminant validation; see Campbell and Fiske, 1959.) Simply stated, the dimensionality issue involves the degree to which measures of creativity or divergent thinking are empirically distinguishable from other more traditional measures of cognitive processes such as intelligence and academic achievement. The development of defensible measures of creativity would seem to depend on constructing a series of tasks which share substantial variance with each other, but are at the same time generally independent of other traditional cognitive measures. The concern for this problem is reflected in the disproportionate amount of research that has been devoted to the creativity-intelligence distinction and our inability to arrive upon a generally acceptable operational definition. (Taylor, 1959, for example, has listed over one hundred definitions which have added to the semantic fog that envelops the study of creativity.) A great deal of the concern for the dimensionality issue, and the lack of resolution of this issue, stems from the problem of measurement and the adequacy of currently available tests of creativity and the divergent-thinking processes.

A number of research studies (Ripple and May, 1962; Thorndike, 1963a, 1963b; and Wallach and Kogan, 1965) have cautioned against the uncritical acceptance of the Getzels and Jackson (1962) hypothesis which suggested that creativity and intelligence were unrelated. In a historical perspective upon the measurement of cognitive processes, Ward (1963) called attention to aspects of Binet's and Wechsler's classic definitions of intelligence, parts of which sound surprisingly similar to many present-day definitions of creativity. Others (Guilford, 1967: Wallach, in press) have made a similar case for the relationship between creativity and the classic definitions of problem-solving.

As a result of the lack of a unified, widely-accepted theory of creativity, then, educators have been confronted with several difficulties: establishing a useful operational definition, understanding the implications of differences among tests and test administration procedures, and understanding the relationships of creativity to other human abilities.

The second general problem has been described as the *criterion problem*. What criteria exist against which the validity of creativity tests may be assessed? Although this problem has not generated as much concern as the creativity-intelligence controversy, its interrelatedness to all other aspects of the study of creativity demands that it be given high priority among areas in which research is needed.

Many researchers have tended, on the one hand, to view creativity entirely as a cognitive process, or, on the other hand, entirely as a complex set of personality traits. The former have tended to ignore the possibility that there may be an affective component to creativity, and the latter have tended to overlook the importance of underlying cognitive abilities in creative problem-solving. It is most likely, however, that a valid assessment procedure would, of necessity, consider both components. In the meantime, we must be very cautious about our willingness to make inferences about "creativity" from measures which are distinctly cognitive, particularly the divergent-thinking-type tests. This does not imply rejection of the usefulness of tests of divergent thinking. It may be true that some of the critics have been too severe (e.g. Covington, 1968; Wallach, 1968). While divergent-thinking measures certainly do not tell the entire story about creativity, it is quite likely that these measures do assess intellectual abilities which play an important role in creativity. If creativity is viewed as a complex kind of human problem-solving (in which case perhaps the term "creative problem-solving" would be preferable), divergent thinking may be a necessary, although not a sufficient, component.

There have been many difficulties in identifying acceptable external criteria for the validation of creativity tests. Foremost among them is the difficulty of any attempt to use teacher and peer judgements as a means of identifying creative youngsters. A number of studies which sought to use this approach (Holland, 1959; Wallen and Stevenson, 1960; Rivlin, 1959; Reid, King, and Wickwire, 1959; Torrance, 1966; and Yamamoto, 1964) have shown that when teachers and peers are asked to nominate very creative pupils or those with good imagination or many new ideas and ways of doing things, they usually produce a list of classmates who are the highest achievers or have the highest IQs. Further, there is considerable variability among teachers in the ability to rate pupils against a test criterion, even when specific definitions are provided. Research is needed on the effectiveness of procedures for training teachers or peers to be more effective raters, less influenced by other criteria.

Related attempts to establish external criteria for creativity have been the well-known series of studies that analyzed the characteristics of adults who have made significant contributions to their respective professions (e.g. MacKinnon, 1962; Barron, 1969). While these studies have provided us with excellent profiles and descriptions of the highly creative person, we must be careful not to confuse concurrent validity with predictive validity. MacKinnon (1962) cautioned that it is one thing to discover distinguishing characteristics, but quite another matter to conclude that traits observed several years after school or college truly characterized an individual when he was a student. Nor can we conclude that these same traits in youngsters today will identify individuals with the kind of creative potential that will be valued in tomorrow's world.

Another approach to the criterion problem would be to use products as indices of creative achievement. Thus great discoveries, inventions, works of art, or writings could be used as criteria. In the research by MacKinnon (1962) and Barron (1969), such indices were undoubtedly often used as the basis for judging an individual's significant contribution in a field. Miles (1968) has also attempted to develop tasks for concurrent assessment of an individual's ability to produce a creative object. While seemingly a hopeful approach to the development of criterion measures for validation of creativity tests, this approach through the use of products is beset by reliability problems.

There is also some reason to believe that some of the problems of assessing creative problem-solving relate to the heterogeneity and underdevelopment of the tasks that have been employed. As Davis (1966) and others have pointed out, the literature on problem-solving is very confusing. "Creative problem-solving" tasks have been used in one study and then never used again. Some people have attempted, as Davis did, to categorize or classify problem-solving, but this classification has tended to be rational rather than empirical. Some logical groupings or judgements about tasks may not hold up very well under closer examination; tasks which "on the face" seem to be attractive measures of creative problem-solving may reflect quite different appearances when studied empirically.

There is a great deal to be learned about the assessment of creative problem-solving. It is quite clear that simple measures of fluency, flexibility, and originality are not sufficient. Perhaps substantial effort must be given to finding new, more complex measures. Perhaps as a beginning we must at least look more carefully at the *interactions* among divergent-thinking scores (fluency-flexibility interactions, for example) and between divergent-thinking scores and other abilities; very little use of such combined sub-scores seems to have been made in the literature.

There are also a number of problems of a very practical nature to solve. How does the researcher know that what *he* considers creative tasks are creative and challenging for the examinee? It may be that the tasks he considers most unusual are boring, unexciting, even trivial, for the most imaginative of our examinees. Perhaps each task that purports to be an assessment of creative problem-solving should be accompanied by a simple rating scale: Have you ever worked on this problem before? Did you solve it? Were you given the solution? What did you think about the problems you have solved here? Were they interesting? Challenging? What did you think of your solutions?" Although many psychologists avoid using the term "introspection," it may be that quite a bit could be learned about measures of creativity by asking subjects to talk about their experiences. Perhaps the adequacy or creative strength of a response, or the extent to which a task captures the subject's attention and stimulates him to think creatively, are important matters, but only capable of being assessed by the subject himself.

Another dimension of the criterion problem concerns the appropriateness or inappropriateness of our current means for assessing originality. While a few have dissented, almost everyone who has grappled with creativity research appears to be satisfied with the statistical infrequency criterion for measures of originality. At least one researcher (Starkweather, 1964, 1968) has attempted to devise an alternate procedure, involving comparison of a child's response to all of his *own* responses, rather than to the responses of other children. Perhaps our easy acceptance of the statistical infrequency criterion has prevented us from identifying new methods which are useful for measuring this dimension of creative thinking. Ideally one would like a qualitative index with face validity.

An issue of critical importance in solving the problem of assessing creative thinking is concerned with the validity of our measures. Too often, in order to develop tests which are manageable from the psychometric point of view, we have relied on tasks which may have little or no logical relationship to creative behavior as it occurs in the "real world." While there exists a substantial difficulty (identifying adequate criteria against which the test tasks can be validated), the problem warrants our attention. The "creativity" assessed by our tests, after all, should be expected to bear a resemblance to creativity as it is actually manifested among people.

Finally, we should at least acknowledge the existence of a number of other important issues in research on creativity and its assessment: assessing the *relevance* of responses, distinguishing between sensible and bizarre responses, and establishing differential age and sex criteria. Most would agree that these are essentially unresolved problems, and thus appear to be topics that are worthy of the researcher's attention. Occasionally, the study of creativity has been described as a classic case of the blind leading the blind, but researchers in this area may prefer to look upon the situation as somewhat of a challenge, and to keep in mind that in the land of the blind, a one-eyed man can be king!

## References

Barron, F. *Creative person and the creative process.* New York: Holt, Rinehart, and Winston, 1969.

Campbell, D. T. & Fiske, D. W. Convergent and discriminant validation by the multitrait-multimethod matrix. *Psychological Bulletin,* 1959, 56, 81-105.

Covington, M. V. New directions in the appraisal of creative thinking. Berkeley, California: University of California, unpublished mimeograph, 1968.

Cropley, A. J. Creativity and intelligence. *British Journal of Educational Psychology,* 1966, *36,* 259-266.

Davis, G. A. Current status of research and theory in human problem-solving. *Psychological Bulletin,* 1966, *66,* 36-54.

Getzels, J. W. & Jackson, P. W. *Creativity and intelligence: explorations with gifted students.* New York: Wiley, 1962.

Guilford, J. P. *The nature of human intelligence.* New York: McGraw-Hill, 1967.

Holland, J. L. Some limitations of teacher ratings as predictors of creativity. *Journal of Educational Psychology, 1959, 50,* 219-223.

Jackson, P. W. & Messick, S. The person, the product, and the response: conceptual problems in the assessment of creativity. *Journal of Personality,* 1965, *33,* 310-329.

Kubie, L. S. Neurotic distortion of the creative process. Lawrence: University of Kansas Press, 1958.

MacKinnon, D. W. The nature and nurture of creative talent. *American Psychologist,* 1962, *17,* 484-495.

Mednick, S. A. The associative basis of the creative process. *Psychological Review,* 1962, *69,* 220-232.

Miles, D. T. Development of a test for an experimental research program. Final report, project no. 7-E-037, U.S. Office of Education. July 1968.

Razik, T. *Bibliography of creativity studies and related areas.* Buffalo, New York: Creative Education Foundation, 1965.

Reid, J. B., King, F. J., & Wickwire, P. Cognitive and other personality characteristics of creative children. *Psychological Reports,* 1959, *5,* 729-737.

Ripples, R. E., & May, R. B. Caution in comparing creativity and I.Q. *Psychological Reports,* 1962, *10,* 229-230.

Rivlin, L. G. Creativity and the self-attitudes and sociability of high school students. *Journal of Educational Psychology,* 1959, *50,* 147-152.

Rogers, C. R. Toward a theory of creativity. In Parnes, S. J. & Harding, H. F. (eds.) *A source book for creative thinking.* New York: Scribner's, 1962, 64-72.

Starkweather, E. K. Problems in the measurement of creativity in preschool children. *Journal of Educational Measurement,* 1964, *1,* 109-133.

Starkweather, E. K. Studies of the creative potential of young children. In F. E. Williams (ed.) *Creativity at home and in school,* Saint Paul: Macalester College, 1968, 75-122.

Taft, R. and Rossiter, J. The remote associates test: divergent or convergent thinking? *Psychological Reports,* 1966, *19,* 1313-1314.

Taylor, I. A. The nature of the creative process. In Smith, P. (ed.), *Creativity.* New York: Hastings House, 1959.

Thorndike, R. L. Some methodological issues in the study of creativity.

In *Proceedings of the 1962 invitational conference on testing problems.* Princeton, N.J.: Educational Testing Service, 1963b.

Torrance, E. P. Torrance Tests of Creative Thinking: Norms—technical manual. Princeton, N.J.: Personnel Press, 1966.

Van Mondfrans, A. P., Feldhusen, J. F., Treffinger, D. & Ferris, D. The effects of instructions and working time on divergent thinking scores. *Psychology in the Schools,* 1970, in press.

Wallach, M. Review of the Torrance Tests of Creative Thinking. *American Educational Research Journal,* 1968, *5,* 272-281.

Wallach, M. A. Creativity and the expression of possibilities. In Graubard, S. R. & Kagan, J. (eds.), *Creativity and Learning.* Boston: Houghton Mifflin, in press.

Wallach, M. A. & Kogan, N. *Modes of thinking in young children: A study of the creativity-intelligence distinction.* New York: Holt, Rinehart and Winston, 1965.

Wallen, N. E. & Stevenson, G. M. Stability and correlates of judged creativity in fifth grade writings. *Journal of Educational Psychology,* 1960, *51,* 273-276.

Ward, V. S. Developing productive thinking: Educational implications. Paper presented at the Second Conference on Productive Thinking, National Education Association, Washington, D.C.: May 2-4, 1963.

Yamamoto, K. Evaluation of some creativity measures in a high school with peer nominations as criteria. *Journal of Psychology,* 1964, *58,* 285-293.

Carl W. Pegnato
Jack W. Birch

# Locating Gifted Children in Junior High Schools: A Comparison of Methods

$T$his is a report on a study of the relative efficiency and effectiveness of seven different means of locating gifted children in junior high schools. The major purpose of the investigation was to discover which procedure or which combination of commonly used procedures would prove best.

The importance of finding gifted children has long been acknowledged (2). Only in the last quarter-century have the individual intelligence testing tools been shaped and sharpened sufficiently to allow psychologists to identify gifted children with a very high degree of certainty (4). The international events of recent years have heightened the urgency for the prompt and early discovery of all gifted children—those who show their capacity through exceptional achievements and those in whom great potentialities are latent—in order that they may be given the best possible guidance toward self-realization through education and training (1).

The gifted children in a junior high school could be discovered if every child in the school were individually examined by a psychologist (3). While some few schools in this nation have access to sufficient psychological service to provide for individual examination for all children, and while that amount of psychological service should ideally be available to all school districts, it is very rarely the case. In fact, it is the very shortage of psychological staff which makes it so necessary to find ways of choosing some small group of children from the total student body to refer for individual evaluation.

Several questions relating to locating children who might be gifted for referral to a psychologist seemed to need answers based on direct investigation.

---

Reprinted from *Exceptional Children,* Vol. 25, No. 7 (March, 1959), pp. 300-304. By permission of the senior author and publisher.

1. Do teachers recognize the mentally gifted children in their classes?
2. Are the children who win Honor status the gifted children of each class?
3. Are some gifted children to be found only through the interest and achievement they display in music or arts?
4. Are some gifted children identifiable primarily through the interest and ability they show in social, political, and other extra-curricular activities?
5. Does outstanding performance in mathematics call children to teachers' attention as gifted?
6. Can group intelligence tests be relied upon in the identification of gifted children?
7. Are group achievement test scores useful in selecting gifted children?
8. Are some gifted children overlooked even though all the criteria suggested above are employed in searching for them?
9. What screening method or combination of methods is most effective and efficient?
10. What is the magnitude of the problem of under-achievement among gifted children?

For the purposes of this inquiry, mental giftedness was defined in terms of a Stanford-Binet Intelligence Quotient of 136 or higher as determined from an examination by a school psychologist. This definition includes the most intelligent one percent of the general population, and, to that extent, is consistent with a number of current and widely used definitions.

As a setting in which to seek answers to these and other closely related questions, the junior division of a junior-senior high school in a large city (Pittsburgh, Pa.) was chosen. The school, in grades seven through 12, had 3600 students. The junior division enrolled 1400 students in grades seven through nine. In order to improve the prospect that a fairly large proportion of gifted children would be available for the study the school chosen was not only a large one, but it was situated in and drew upon a very favored group or neighborhood from a socio-economic standpoint.


## Methods of Screening for Referral

TEACHER JUDGEMENT.

The first step in the investigation was to find which pupils the teachers considered mentally gifted. This was accomplished by circulating a simple inquiry form which read as follows:

> We are in process of identifying mentally gifted children at the junior high school level. We feel that teachers have recognized most of these children in their classes. It would be helpful to have a basic and general list that we can share and use in program planning. Will you please, therefore, use the attached form to name the children you consider mentally gifted in your home room and in any of your classes. Make a statement for each child as to why you judge the child to be mentally gifted.

The form referred to in the directions simply provided blanks for the child's name, grade, and room, as well as space for any statement the teacher wished to make. No definition was given; each teacher was free to interpret the term "gifted" in his own way. No limitation was placed on the teachers' access to records on the children. Except that the teachers had been informed in a general faculty meeting that their help would be enlisted in finding all the gifted children in the schools, no further orientation was furnished. The forms returned by the teachers contained 154 different names.

HONOR ROLL LISTING.

A second step was to collect the names of children on the Honor Rolls for the different grades in the junior high school. An all-subject average of "B" or higher on an "A-B-C-D-E" scale of relative excellence of achievement was necessary for placement on the honor roll. The letter-grades used in arriving at the average were assigned by the teachers, and each teacher was free to use his own judgment in determining the child's letter-grade. At the close of the report period from which this list of names was taken, the 39 teachers involved had placed 371 children on the honor roll.

CREATIVE ABILITY IN ART OR MUSIC.

A third step in the investigation was aimed at locating mentally gifted children who might be displaying creative ability through art or music. The art and music teachers were asked to consider their students in terms of creativity and talent, and to submit the names of outstanding children. Teachers of vocal music, instrumental music, and arts contributed to a list of 137 children, 71 from music and 66 from art.

STUDENT COUNCIL MEMBERSHIP.

Social and political leadership might prove a special field of achievement for children who show mental giftedness in few or no other ways. It was felt that students selected in each home room to represent their peers in the Student Council would be classifiable as social and political leaders. A review of records on this point yielded 82 names.

SUPERIORITY IN MATHEMATICS.

Because mathematical skill is considered closely associated with mental giftedness, a fifth screening method was used. Arithmetic teachers were asked to name children who were outstanding. This was done about a month subsequent to the time all teachers were asked for the more general referrals. Again, there were no limitations placed on the teachers with respect to what information they might use in making their selections. The arithmetic teachers suggested 179 children's names.

GROUP INTELLIGENCE TEST RESULTS.

The investigation then turned to two somewhat more objective screening procedures which depended less upon professional judgment of teachers. These were group intelligence test scores and group achievement test scores.

The sixth step, then, was the review of cumulative records and the listing of children with group test intelligence quotients of 115 or higher. In the Pittsburgh school system the Otis Quick-Scoring Mental Ability Test, Beta Form, is administered at the end of the sixth grade and again at the end of the eighth grade. Scores were available on all the children at the school. The latest results were used. An IQ of 115 was chosen as the cut-off point for referrals for individual examination. This screening procedure produced 450 children with Otis IQ's 115 or higher.

GROUP ACHIEVEMENT TEST RESULTS.

The final screening procedure used the results of standardized achievement tests. Metropolitan Achievement Tests are administered at the close of each school year in Pittsburgh. The latest scores available were used. Subtest scores in two basic skill subjects, reading and arithmetic, were averaged. A list was compiled of the children with average scores at least three grade levels above grade placement. (Since the ceiling of the Metropolitan was 11th grade, the ninth graders who scored at the test ceiling were included.) This list contained 334 names.

## Procedure

When the lists from all of the seven screening methods were combined and analyzed, 781 different names appeared (394 boys and 387 girls). More than half of the total population of the junior high school grades (1400) had been recommended, by one or more screening method, for referral for individual examination to determine if they were actually mentally gifted.

At this point, the counselor and the vice-principal of the junior high school were asked to list the names of all children known to them to be emotionally or socially maladjusted and who might also be mentally gifted. When the names of those children were checked against the master list of 781, it was found that all had been included through some other screening procedure.

After the necessary individual psychological examinations were completed, the Stanford-Binet Intelligence Quotients of the 781 children were tabulated. The effectiveness and efficiency of the various screening procedures can be evaluated by reference to the material in Table 1, Effectiveness and Efficiency of Screening Procedures.

Effectiveness of a screening procedure is defined by the percentage of gifted children it locates. A screening procedure which includes all the gifted children among those it selects for referral to a psychologist is 100 percent effective. If it allows half of the gifted children to slip through its net and fails to refer them to the psychologist, it is 50 percent effective.

Efficiency of a screening procedure is defined by the ratio between the total number of children it refers for individual examination and the number of gifted children found among those referred. If the screening procedure refers 10 children and nine of them are found, upon individual examination, to be gifted, its efficiency is 90 percent.

The best screening method is one which combines high effectiveness and high efficiency, for that would result in most of the gifted being found with a minimum amount of wasted motion. Of course, if the main objective is to find as many of the mentally gifted children as possible, it may be necessary to use a highly effective screening method with less importance being placed on its efficiency.

## TABLE 1
### Effectiveness and Efficiency of Screening Procedures

| Screening Methods | No. Selected by Screening Method | No. Identified as Gifted by Stanford-Binet IQ | Effectiveness (Percent of Gifted Located; Total Gifted N = 91) | Efficiency (Ratio of No. Selected by Screening to No. Identified as Gifted, in Percent) |
|---|---|---|---|---|
| Teacher judgment | 154 | 41 | 45.1 | 26.6 |
| Honor roll | 371 | 67 | 73.6 | 18.0 |
| Creativity | 137 | 14 | 15.5 | 10.2 |
| Art ability | (66) | (6) | 6.6 | 9.1 |
| Music ability | (71) | (8) | 9.9 | 11.2 |
| Student council | 82 | 13 | 14.3 | 15.8 |
| Mathematics achievement | 179 | 50 | 56.0 | 27.9 |
| Group intelligence tests | | | | |
| Cut-off IQ 115 | 450 | 84 | 92.3 | 18.7 |
| Cut-off IQ 120 | (240) | (65) | 71.4 | 27.1 |
| Cut-off IQ 125 | (105) | (40) | 43.9 | 38.1 |
| Cut-off IQ 130 | (36) | (20) | 21.9 | 55.5 |
| Group achievement tests | 335 | 72 | 79.2 | 21.5 |
| Total | 781 | | | |

# Results

Of the 781 children selected by screening methods, 91 had Stanford-Binet IQ's of 136 or higher. To find 6.5 percent of the population of a junior high school with Stanford-Binet IQ's of 136 or above is quite unusual. However, the school was selected in part because other information had suggested that an extraordinarily large number of gifted children attended. While individual psychological examinations on the other 619 students might have uncovered more children who would rank among the most intelligent one percent of the population, it is doubtful if many were missed. Since the findings are to be interpreted largely in relative terms, it was not essential that every gifted child be located.

Some of the questions which prompted this investigation can now be answered in quantitative terms.

1. Teachers do not locate gifted children effectively or efficiently enough to place much reliance on them for screening. The category *Teacher Judgment* in Table 1 indicates that only 45.1 percent of the gifted children actually present were included in the teachers' lists. Not only were more than half of the gifted missing, but a breakdown of those children referred as gifted by the teachers revealed that almost a third (31.4 percent) of those chosen by the teachers were *not in the gifted or superior* range but in the *average* intelligence range on the Binet.

2. Almost three-fourths (73.6 percent) of the gifted children were on the Honor Roll. However 304 other children were rated Honor Roll status; therefore, the Honor Roll is among the less efficient screening methods.

3. Some gifted children do display unusual interest and achievement in music or art. However, these same children are noteworthy in other aspects of school work, too. All of the 14 gifted children among the 137 called outstanding in music or art were also screened for referral in at least two other ways.

4. The Student Council membership list contained no gifted children who were not among those already included by the group intelligence test screening. All of the gifted children on Student Council appeared on at least two other lists, also.

5. When mathematics achievement alone was the criterion used by teachers, the gifted children did not fare well. Almost half of them were overlooked, and for every mentally gifted child referred, more than two who were not mentally gifted were on the referral list.

6. Group intelligence tests like the one used in this study cannot be relied upon in the identification of gifted children in the junior high school grades. Reference to Table 1 indicates, when a cut-off point of IQ 130 is used that the group test located only 21.9 percent of the gifted children. Almost four out of five were missed. Even if the cut-off point of IQ 125 were used, more than half of the gifted children would be missed. The important point seems to be that the group test does not discriminate well between children who are a little above and those who are a great deal above average in learning capacity. The group intelligence test does seem to possess the best combination of efficiency and effectiveness as a screen. Using IQ 115 as the cut-off point a little better than nine out of 10 of the gifted will be found among the group so chosen when they are examined by a psychologist.

7. Group achievement test scores run a fairly close second to group intel-

ligence test scores in combined efficiency and effectiveness when used as they were in this situation.

8. Three gifted children were found who apparently did not make favorable showings in either group tests of intelligence or group achievement tests. One of these was located through the Honor Roll, and the other two were overlooked by all the screening procedures. The latter two were found because their cumulative records indicated that they had been examined by a school psychologist in the elementary grades and proved to be gifted.

9. By combining the group intelligence test list and the group achievement test list into one screening procedure, 88 of the 91 gifted children, or 96.7 percent of them, were found. Taken together the two group tests resulted in the most effective screening procedure.

10. This investigation did not set out to obtain detailed information on under-achievement among gifted children. However, analysis of the records of the 91 children with Binet IQ's 136 or higher showed six of them appearing on no list other than that of children with Otis IQ's 115 or higher. In addition, four others were on neither the Honor Roll or the list of children with achievement test scores three years above grade placement. There is good reason to think, therefore, that 10 of the 92 gifted children might be underachievers. The implication is strong that perhaps more than one out of 10 gifted children (10.8 percent in this study) is achieving markedly below an optimum level. Certainly the screening based on group intelligence test scores is helpful in locating gifted children who are not showing their potentialities either in letter-grades given by teachers or on group achievement tests.

## Summary

A major concern of our educational system is the identification and education of mentally gifted children. With reasonable certainty the identification of intellectually gifted students is now possible in the junior high school years through the use of individual intelligence tests administered by school psychologists. This identification procedure, though quite accurate, is both expensive and time consuming. Effective and efficient screening methods are necessary for choosing the children to be referred to the psychologist. Effective and efficient screening methods are those which make possible the identification of all the gifted children in a school while minimizing the total number of children who must be examined individually by the psychologist.

Seven kinds of screening procedures are considered. The use of group intelligence test results for screening is found to have advantages over other methods both in effectiveness and efficiency; they are of little value, however, for actual identification. The latter should be left to psychologists employing individual examination methods if measures of intelligence are to be the criteria used.

## References

1. Educational Policies Commission, *Education of the Gifted.* Washington,D.C.: National Education Association, 1950.

2. Hollingworth, Leta S., *Gifted Children, Their Nature and Nurture*. New York: The Macmillan Company, 1927.

3. Pegnato, Carl, *An Evaluation of Various Initial Methods of Selecting Intellectually Gifted Children at the Junior High School Level*. Doctoral Thesis, Pennsylvania State College, 1958.

4. Terman, Lewis M., and others, *Genetic Studies of Genius, Volumes I-II-III-IV*. Stanford, California: Stanford University Press, 1925 through 1947.

*Roy K. Jarecky*

# *Identification of the Socially Gifted*

*T*here has been slow but perceptible progress towards a liberalized interpretation of the concept of giftedness. A review of the literature suggested that probably it was not until after 1940 that serious attention was given to forms of gifted behavior other than intellectual. Westman's comment expressed what appears to be the currently accepted view of giftedness: ". . . the concept of giftedness has been broadened to include not only such areas as music and art, but areas such as mechanics and social maturity and personal relations as well. The child who displays unusual understanding of the physical forces in his world, and the child who exhibits unusual understanding and leadership of his peers, have been taking their place alongside the child who excels in performance on a test of mental ability (10, p. 4)."

Specifically, this paper summarizes a study with focus on the problem of identifying adolescent boys and girls possessed of an exceptional capacity for mature productive relationships with others—both peers and adults (5). This capacity was termed social giftedness.

## *Importance of the Socially Gifted*

The important contribution that the socially gifted adolescent can make, especially in the area of cooperative peer endeavor, cannot be overestimated. The young person who is highly skilled in relating to others and whose behavior is tempered by a mature social conscience acts as a sort of leavening agent among his fellows. For instance, he may help a group to integrate its efforts to achieve a common goal by forging new psychological channels of communication which in turn help group members to form more realistic and sympathetic perceptions of each other. Or he may, through a combination of warm good humor and gentle emphasis on ethical concerns, stimulate his peers to positive productive type behavior when the

Reprinted from *Exceptional Children,* Vol. 25, No. 8 (May, 1959), pp. 415-419. By permission of the author and publisher.

direction that the group behavior might take hangs in the balance. Socially gifted behavior is in fact a vital and hitherto neglected human resource.

The socially gifted person has an important function to perform in our society. His particular skills are as badly needed as those of the skilled technician and the scientist. The error that we are liable to make is to assume that somehow such skilled practitioners of human relations will always be available when needed. It should be abundantly clear that such is not the case. We can no more depend on a rich periodic harvest of socially gifted adults without special techniques of early identification and appropriate education than we can of biochemists. In all likelihood the socially gifted adolescent has benefited from a highly fortunate combination of heredity and environment. The socialization process of which he has been a part has instilled in him the psychological basis for effectiveness in interpersonal relationships. But, this potential must first be recognized and then nurtured to full maturity. Pritchard made this point with vigor and clarity:

> It should go without saying that the greatest need existing today is to find those who can lead in establishing the bases and means of wise living with our fellow men. It is of utmost importance to discover at an early age patterns of behavior which will predict unusual strength in the positive factors of emotional maturity, perseverance, social insight, and drive to accomplish. We need to discover those who excel in these attributes of "social intelligence" early in childhood in order that their unique gifts may be developed to the highest potential (7, p. 82).

## Characteristics of the Socially Gifted Adolescent

Prior to discussing the instruments that were used in the classroom to identify socially gifted adolescents the primary characteristics of socially gifted behavior as derived from the study will be presented. The social behavior of 76 fourteen-year-old boys and girls, members of two freshman classes of a large metropolitan high school, was observed and evaluated for a period of 15 weeks. Those young people finally designated as socially gifted appeared to have the following characteristics:

1. They were generally physically attractive and neat in appearance.
2. They were clearly accepted by an overwhelming majority of the people whom they knew, peers and adults alike.
3. They were generally involved in some sort of social enterprise to which they made positive, constructive contributions.
4. They were generally looked to as arbiters or as "policy makers" in their own group.
5. They related to peers and adults on an egalitarian basis, resisting insincere, artificial or patronizing relationships.
6. They maintained no facades. Their behavior was non-defensive in character.
7. They appeared free of emotional tension; that is, they were unafraid to

257

express themselves emotionally, but their demonstrations of emotion were always relevant.

8. They maintained enduring relationships with peers and adults. Socially gifted adolescents did not experience rapid turnovers in friendship.

9. They stimulated positive productive behavior in others.

10. They were gay young people who, in general, seemed to personify an unusual capacity for coping with any social situation. They managed to do so with a delightful mixture of intelligence, humor, and insight (5).

In short, these characteristics represent a life style peculiar to the socially gifted adolescent. These young people are to be recognized not by something specific that they can produce in the usual sense but by the extraordinary effectiveness of their social behavior.

## Design of the Study

In order to identify the socially gifted it was first necessary to devise a battery of differential tests of social behavior appropriate for use in a classroom situation. These instruments provided quantified assessments of the social behavior of the students and brought to light those patterns of overt behavior most closely associated with each individual by his peers, teacher, student teachers, and by himself. The behavior of these students with highest scores on the assessment instruments was then evaluated with reference to anecdotal records developed by the investigator over a three-month-observational period. Restated, the problem of evaluation was to determine whether certain students would consistently register high scores on the various tests and whether these scores would be supported by the evidence included in the anecdotal reports. High scores coupled with supportive anecdotal evidence then warranted careful comparison of the behavior patterns they represented with the characteristics of social giftedness derived from the literature and from questionnaire responses submitted by members of the American Association for Gifted Children.

Two freshman classes (referred to in the study as Class A and Class B) of a large metropolitan high school were selected as subjects for the research. These co-educational classes of 38 students each were part of an experimental program in which material in the social sciences, natural sciences, and communicative skills were integrated and presented in the form of projects to be mastered by individual study and small group discussion and review. Much time was spent at the beginning of each term teaching the students how to work together effectively in units of five or six. Emphasis was placed on the importance of individual responsibility for the total success of any group project. Thus, these two classes afforded a wealth of material relative to the social behavior of young adolescents in daily cooperative contact with each other.

The 76 students observed were all 13 to 15 years of age with the majority a few months past their 14th birthday. The group represented the middle-to-upper-middle socio-economic bracket in practically all cases. For the most part, fathers of the students were professional men, business men, merchants, or highly skilled workers. An administration of the American Council on Education Psychological Examination resulted in scores indicative of the high intellectual ability of the group. The mean score stood at the 80th percentile of ninth grade norms. Seventy-eight percent of the group had total scores at or above the 50th percentile. Only two students had total scores standing below the 25th percentile.

## Description of the Instruments

The students assessed each other by means of groupmate selection questionnaires and *Guess-Who?* questionnaires. The groupmate selection questionnaire is a type of sociometric device in which a group member is given the opportunity to indicate those members of his class with whom he particularly prefers to associate in dealing with some part of the term's work. The choosing of three fellow students as most desired groupmates represented a gross sort of evaluation of social acceptance and competence on the part of the class members for each other. The individual whose social ability was such that his influence was classwide tended to be chosen not only by the immediate members of his own subgroup but by members of other class subgroups as well. In general, the greater the number of choices cast for a particular individual the more certain that the class or group attitudes were uniformly positive toward that person. Groupmate choices were made on three separate occassions about one month apart when new project groups were to be formed. The scoring procedure was as follows. First, second, and third choices were weighted 5, 3, and 1 respectively. A student's score for a given selection period was the sum of the weighted choices cast for him. The mean of these selection period scores was considered the overall acceptance score for the total three month period.

The *Guess-Who?* type of questionnaire was first used in the Hartshorne and May studies of deceit and honesty among school children (3). It continues to be used as an effective technique in determining how young people in a relatively stable group perceive each other as well as themselves. The technique involved in constructing a *Guess-Who?* questionnaire centers on the development of short descriptive statements about social behavior. Generally the statements are developed in couplet form. One statement of the couplet is a positive or socially "good" type statement while its mate represents the negative side of the same social value. Thirty-one such statements were utilized in this study. Twenty-one were adopted from Tryon's monograph on the "Evaluation of Adolescent Personality by Adolescents" (9), while 10 others were devised by the investigator to reflect more specifically the characteristics of social giftedness as suggested by members

259

of the American Association for Gifted Children and articles in the professional literature dealing with the behavior patterns of socially successful adolescents. The directions presented at the administration of the *Guess-Who?* questionnaire were as follows:

> Below are some word pictures of members of your class. Read each statement and write down the names of the persons whom you think the descriptions fit. One description may fit several persons. You may write as many names as you think belong under each. The same person may be mentioned for more than one description. Write "myself" if you think the description fits you. If you cannot think of anyone to match a particular description, go on to the next one.

Scoring of the *Guess-Who?* questionnaire was accomplished by algebraically summing "plus" and "minus" votes for each student.

The second group of evaluative instruments were those used by appropriate adults to assess the social behavior of the students. These methods of assessment included a rating scale, a ranking procedure, and the Vineland Social Maturity Scale.

Two student teachers assigned to each class and the investigator rated the social behavior of the students using a modified version of the Integral Scale adapted from a study by Newman and Jones (6). As finally utilized, the scale incorporated eight items with ratings of 1-to-7 for each item. A rating of 1 represented complete concurrence with the positive aspect of the item whereas a rating of 7 represented complete concurrence with the negative aspect of the item. Scale items rated such aspects of behavior as sociability, social prestige, social self-confidence, attention seeking, stability in interpersonal relationships, and so forth. A total rating scale score was derived by averaging the eight subscores ascribed by each of the three raters and then summing the three averages. Thus 3 represented the most positive rating and 21 the most negative. If, for instance, each of the three raters assigned ratings of 1 for every item on the scale, the hypothetical student would receive three average ratings of 1. His total score would then be 3, the sum of the averages.

The ranking procedure represented an overall estimate of the social ability of each of the students by the classroom teacher. Each student was judged with reference to the proposed characteristics of social giftedness and then ranked accordingly. The individual considered to be the most socially gifted was ranked first, the next most socially gifted was ranked second, and so on.

The Vineland Social Maturity Scale was administered to each student by the investigator. The Scale was utilized since, in Doll's words, it "seeks to quantify the evaluation of social competence as a global aspect of individual maturation at successive age levels" (1, p. 81). The Scale measures social development in the areas of self-help, self-direction, locomotion, occupation, communication, and social relations. Doll believes that the value of the Scale lies in its synthesis of these six competencies into one total assessment which can be expressed in the form of a social quotient.

The student's perception of himself was obtained from a composition entitled "The Sort of Person I Am." This self-concept sketch was employed so that the adolescent could evaluate the adequacy of his relationships with others as he himself felt about it. A clinical psychologist, a social psychologist, and a college student personnel dean were asked to rate each of the 76 compositions on a 1 to 5 basis. A rating of 1 labeled a composition as devoid of any reference to criteria considered reflective of social giftedness whereas a rating of 5 represented a demonstration of much concern on the part of the writer for attitudes considered to play an important role in the complex of superior social behavior.

Besides keeping records of apparently socially gifted behavior, an attempt was also made to record examples of highly negative and/or ineffectual social behavior. This was done in order to accumulate evidence about students who otherwise appeared to be possible candidates for the characterization of socially gifted on the basis of the test scores they achieved. Anecdotal records were secured in as many different types of social situations as possible. The investigator spent time with the students outside of the classroom as well as in it. He visited with them in their homes, went to their parties, ate lunch with them, and accompanied them on various field trips.

## Intercorrelations Among Test Scores

The intercorrelations among test scores are presented in Table 1. The levels of significance of the correlation coefficients were derived from reference to Table 49 in Garrett (2, p. 299).

### TABLE 1
### Intercorrelations

1—Groupmate Choice
2—Guess Who? Questionnaire
3—Rating Scale

4—Teacher Rankings
5—Self-concept Composition
6—Vineland Social Maturity Scale

7—ACE Psychological Examination

| | 2 | | 3 | | 4 | | 5 | 6 | 7 |
|---|---|---|---|---|---|---|---|---|---|
| | A | B | A | B | A | B | | | |
| 1 | .69 | .71 | .66 | .61 | .71 | .67 | .40 | .24* | .38 |
| 2 | | | .74 | .78 | .67 | .74 | .42 | .45 | .41 |
| 3 | | | | | .72 | .71 | .30 | .37 | .52 |
| 4 | | | | | | | .31 | .45 | .45 |
| 5 | | | | | | | | .10** | .21** |
| 6 | | | | | | | | | .26* |

Note: Separate coefficients of correlation were calculated for class A and class B when both sets of scores being correlated were derived from intraclass assessments. Where one or both sets of scores represented a total assessment of both classes as one group, one coefficient and correlation was calculated. All correlations are positive and significant at the .01 level except as otherwise noted.

*Significant at the .05 level.

**Not significant.

Reference to the table of intercorrelations indicates that the most substantial relationships were found among those instruments whose scores reflected actual behavior in interpersonal relationships. Thus, there appeared to be general agreement among the students and adults regarding the quality and effectiveness of the social behavior of the students. Scores derived from the Vineland Social Maturity Scale, the self-concept compositions and the ACE Psychological Examination seemed to contribute less to an assessment of social ability than had been anticipated. For example, the investigator's experience with the Vineland Scale suggested that it may provide a better estimate of the young person's capacity for independent action than for finesse in interpersonal relationships. The self-concept compositions although affording important insights about their authors do not necessarily represent what the adolescents will do in a given social situation. Finally, the ACE Psychological Examination scores suggest that although social ability and intellectual ability are interrelated, the correspondence is certainly not a perfect one. As has often been noted, high intelligence does not guarantee social giftedness although obviously the socially gifted tend to be of above average intelligence.

## Selection of Adolescents as Socially Gifted

The selection of adolescents as most probably socially gifted was accomplished by utilizing the scores of the groupmate choice questionnaire, the *Guess-Who?* questionnaire, the rating scale, and the teacher ranking procedure to evolve a composite rank for each one of the students. The social behavior of the three highest ranked students in classes A and B as described in their anecdotal records was then reviewed. The pattern of social behavior delineated by these records agreed with the implications of the composite ranks. That is, the behavioral patterns of the highest ranked students were similar to what had been hypothesized as socially gifted behavior whereas the records of average and low scoring students contained practically no evidence of such behavior.

## Concluding Statement

The study indicates that social giftedness in adolescence can be ascertained and described. The groupmate choice questionnaire, the *Guess-Who?* questionnaire, the rating scale, and the teacher ranking procedure proved to be assessment techniques easy to administer and minimally disruptive of classroom routine. These instruments possess another advantage in that they are multifunctional. The data they provide can be used for purposes other than the identification of the socially gifted.

Finally, it is important to keep in mind that the testing procedures utilized in this study were administered to a group of middle-class, urban, academically oriented adolescents. Until the results of further research are available, the teacher interested in the socially gifted will have to experiment to determine how these instruments might best be modified if the students under consideration are considerably different in background from the subjects of this study.

## References

1. Doll, Edgar A. *The Measurement of Social Competence.* Minneapolis: Educational Publishers, Inc., 1953. 664 p.

2. Garrett, Henry E., *Statistics in Psychology and Education.* Third Edition. New York: Longmans, Green and Company, 1947. 487 p.

3. Hartshorne, M. and M. A. May, *Studies in Deceit.* New York: The Macmillan Company, 1928. 414 p.

4. Hollingworth, Leta S., *Gifted Children: Their Nature and Nurture.* New York: The Macmillan Company, 1926. 374 p.

5. Jarecky, Roy K., "The Identification of Socially Gifted Adolescents." Unpublished Doctor's Thesis. Teachers College, Columbia University, New York, 1958. 118 p.

6. Newman, Frances Burks, and Harold E. Jones, "The Adolescent in Social Groups; Studies in the Observation of Personality," *Psychology Monographs* No. 9. Berkeley: Stanford University Press, 1946. 94 p.

7. Pritchard, Miriam C., "The Contributions of Leta S. Hollingworth to the Study of Gifted Children," *The Gifted Child,* pp. 47-85. Edited by Paul Witty. Boston: D. C. Heath and Company, 1951. 388 p.

8. Terman, Lewis M. and Melita Oden, *The Gifted Child Grows Up; Twenty-Five Years' Follow-Up of a Superior Group.* Vol. IV of *Genetic Studies of Genius.* Edited by Lewis M. Terman. Stanford, California: Stanford University Press, 1947. 448 p.

9. Tryon, Carolyn, "Evaluation of Adolescent Personality by Adolescents," *Monographs of the Society for Research in Child Development.* Vol. IV, No. 4, 1939. 83 p.

10. Wesman, Alexander G. "Methods of Identifying Gifted Students," *Guidance News,* 9:4-5, October, 1956.

Joseph S. Renzulli
Robert K. Hartman
Carolyn M. Callahan

# Scale for Rating
# the Behavioral Characteristics
# of Superior Students

*I*n recent years a number of writers have called attention to a broadened conception of giftedness and the need for a wider range of criteria in the process of identifying gifted, talented, and creative youth (Getzels & Jackson, 1958; Jarecky, 1959; Witty, 1965). Although traditional tests of intelligence and achievement have been the major criteria for screening and selecting superior students, the role of teacher judgment is beginning to play an increasingly important part in efforts to place students in special educational programs that are designed to meet the needs of highly able youngsters (Cutts & Moseley, 1957; Pegnato & Birch, 1959).

In a comprehensive review of the literature dealing with the role of teacher judgment in the identification process, Gallagher (1966) pointed out some of the major weaknesses of teacher ratings. Because of the "frighteningly low level of effectiveness" of unstructured teacher judgment, Gallagher suggested a cautious approach to accepting teacher judgment as a basis for identification and concluded by saying that "most authorities would agree that teachers' opinions definitely need supplementing with more objective rating methods [p. 12]."

The development of the *Scale for Rating Behavioral Characteristics of Superior Students* (SRBCSS) represents an attempt to provide a more objective and systematic instrument that can be used as an aid in guiding teacher judgment in the identification process. It is not intended to replace existing identification procedures such as measures of intelligence, achievement, and creativity; rather it is offered as a supplementary means that can be used in conjunction with other criteria for identification.

## Procedures in the Development of the Scale

Initial "input" for the construction of the SRBCSS was derived from a comprehensive review of the literature dealing with characteristics or traits of superior students. Research studies relating to each of the four dimensions of the instrument were searched and categorized in an effort to isolate observable behavioral characteristics which were supported by common agreement among well known contributors to the literature. For a scale item to be included in the instrument, it was necessary that at least three separate studies had called attention to the importance of a given characteristic. These supportive studies are cited after each item in the scale.

The first experimental edition of the instrument was field tested in a number of school districts offering programs for gifted and talented students. Teachers and counselors completing the scale were asked to provide reactions about the effectiveness and usability of the instrument. Specifically, they were asked to make suggestions relating to clarity of expression, observability of traits, independence of items, and the ability of the instrument to make meaningful discriminations among students on each of the respective scales. This information led to the construction of the present edition, which includes several revisions based on the valuable feedback provided by classroom teachers, counselors, and special program personnel.

## Suggestions for Using the Scale

Teachers can use the SRBCSS most effectively by analyzing students' ratings on each of the four respective scales separately. The four dimensions of the instrument represent relatively different sets of behavioral characteristics, and therefore, no attempt should be made to add the subscores together to form a total score. Students can be rated any time during the school year; however, the earlier the observations are made, the more use can be made of the results in helping to identify and develop student abilities to the fullest. It is also valuable to obtain ratings from several teachers and counselors who are familiar with a youngster's performance.

Because of variations in student populations, methods of programing for superior students, and the availability of other data that can be used in the screening and identification process, it is impossible to provide the user with a predetermined set of cutoff scores for the scales. The instrument can be used most profitably by computing a mean score on each dimension for the total number of students who are being considered for enrollment in a special program. Those students who deviate markedly upward from the mean should be considered likely candidates for placement in a program or activity that is designed to enhance particular abilities; however, the reader is reminded that the instrument is offered as one means for guiding teacher judgment in the screening and identification process. Whenever possible, it should be used in conjunction with other instruments and techniques as part of a comprehensive system for the identification of superior students.

A guiding principle in using the SRBCSS emphasizes the relationship between a student's subscores and the types of curricular experiences that will be offered in a special program. Every effort should be made to capitalize on an individual's strengths by developing learning experiences that take account of the area or areas in which the student has received high ratings. For example, a student who earns high ratings on the Motivational Characteristics Scale will probably profit most from a program that emphasizes self initiated pursuits and an independent study approach to learning. A student with high scores on the Leadership Characteristics Scale should be given opportunities to organize activities and to assist the teacher and his classmates in developing plans of action for carrying out projects.

In addition to looking at a student's profile of subscores for identification purposes, teachers can derive several useful hints for programing by analyzing student ratings on individual scale items. These items call attention to differences in behavioral characteristics and in most cases suggest the kinds of educational experiences that are most likely to represent the youngster's preferred method or style of learning. Thus, a careful analysis of scale items can assist the teacher in her efforts to develop an individualized program of study for each student.

## Scale for Rating Behavioral Characteristics of Superior Students

### Joseph S. Renzulli/Robert K. Hartman

Name ———————————————— ———————————— Date ——— — ————

School ——————————————————————Grade ——— ——Age ———————————
                                                                                Years            Months
Teacher or person completing this form ——————————————————————————

How long have you known this child? ————————————————— Months.

**Directions.** These scales are designed to obtain teacher estimates of a student's characteristics in the areas of learning, motivation, creativity, and leadership. The items are derived from the research literature dealing with characteristics of gifted and creative persons. It should be pointed out that a considerable amount of individual differences can be found within this population; and therefore, the profiles are likely to vary a great deal. Each item in the scales should be considered separately and should reflect the degree to which you have observed the presence or absence of each characteristic. Since the four dimensions of the instrument represent relatively different sets of behaviors, the scores obtained from the separate scales should *not* be summed to yield a total score. Please read the statements carefully and place an X in the appropriate place according to the following scale of values:

1. If you have *seldom* or *never* observed this characteristic.
2. If you have observed this characteristic *occasionally*.
3. If you have observed this characteristic to a *considerable* degree.
4. If you have observed this characteristic *almost all* of the time.

Space has been provided following each item for your comments.

**Scoring.** Separate scores for each of the three dimensions may be obtained as follows:

- *Add* the total number of X's in each column to obtain the "Column Total."
- *Multiply* the Column Total by the "Weight" for each column to obtain the "Weighted Column Total."
- *Sum* the Weighted Column Totals across to obtain the "Score" for each dimension of the scale.
- *Enter* the Scores below.

Learning Characteristics ........................... —————————————

Motivational Characteristics ..................... —————————————

Creativity Characteristics ...................... —————————————

Leadership Characteristics ....................... —————————————

## Part I: Learning Characteristics

|   | 1* | 2 | 3 | 4 |
|---|---|---|---|---|
| 1. Has unusually advanced vocabulary for age or grade level; uses terms in a meaningful way; has verbal behavior characterized by "richness" of expression, elaboration, and fluency. (National Education Association, 1960; Terman & Oden, 1947; Witty, 1955) | ☐ | ☐ | ☐ | ☐ |
| 2. Possesses a large storehouse of information about a variety of topics (beyond the usual interests of youngsters his age). (Ward, 1961; Terman, 1925; Witty, 1958) | ☐ | ☐ | ☐ | ☐ |
| 3. Has quick mastery and recall of factual information. (Goodhart & Schmidt, 1940; Terman & Oden, 1947; National Education Association, 1960) | ☐ | ☐ | ☐ | ☐ |
| 4. Has rapid insight into cause-effect relationships; tries to discover the how and why of things; asks many provocative questions (as distinct from informational or factual questions); wants to know what makes things (or people) "tick." (Carroll, 1940; Witty, 1958; Goodhart & Schmidt, 1940) | ☐ | ☐ | ☐ | ☐ |
| 5. Has a ready grasp of underlying principles and can quickly make valid generalizations about events, people, or things; looks for similarities and differences in events, people, and things. (Bristow, 1951; Carroll, 1940; Ward, 1961) | ☐ | ☐ | ☐ | ☐ |
| 6. Is a keen and alert observer; usually "sees more" or "gets more" out of a story, film, etc. than others. (Witty, 1958; Carroll, 1940; National Education Association, 1960) | ☐ | ☐ | ☐ | ☐ |
| 7. Reads a great deal on his own; usually prefers adult level books; does not avoid difficult material; may show a preference for biography, autobiography, encyclopedias, and atlases. (Hollingworth, 1942; Witty, 1958; Terman & Oden, 1947) | ☐ | ☐ | ☐ | ☐ |
| 8. Tries to understand complicated material by separating it into its respective parts; reasons things out for himself; sees logical and common sense answers. (Freehill, 1961; Ward, 1962; Strang, 1958) | ☐ | ☐ | ☐ | ☐ |
| Column Total | ☐ | ☐ | ☐ | ☐ |
| Weight | 1 | 2 | 3 | 4 |
| Weighted Column Total | ☐ | ☐ | ☐ | ☐ |
| Total | | | ☐ |

*1—Seldom or never
2—Occasionally
3—Considerably
4—Almost always

**Part II: Motivational Characteristics**

| | 1 | 2 | 3 | 4 |
|---|---|---|---|---|
| 1. Becomes absorbed and truly involved in certain topics or problems; is persistent in seeking task completion. (It is sometimes difficult to get him to move on to another topic.) (Freehill, 1961; Brandwein, 1955; Strang, 1958) | ☐ | ☐ | ☐ | ☐ |
| 2. Is easily bored with routine tasks. (Ward, 1962; Terman & Oden, 1947; Ward, 1961) | ☐ | ☐ | ☐ | ☐ |
| 3. Needs little external motivation to follow through in work that initially excites him. (Carroll, 1940; Ward, 1961; Villars, 1957) | ☐ | ☐ | ☐ | ☐ |
| 4. Strives toward perfection; is self critical; is not easily satisfied with his own speed or products. (Strang, 1958; Freehill, 1961; Carroll, 1940) | ☐ | ☐ | ☐ | ☐ |
| 5. Prefers to work independently; requires little direction from teachers. (Torrance, 1965; Gowan & Demos, 1964; Mokovic, 1953) | ☐ | ☐ | ☐ | ☐ |
| 6. Is interested in many "adult" problems such as religion, politics, sex, race—more than usual for age level. (Witty, 1955; Ward, 1961; Chaffee, 1963) | ☐ | ☐ | ☐ | ☐ |
| 7. Often is self assertive (sometimes even aggressive); stubborn in his beliefs. (Buhler & Guirl, 1963; Gowan & Demos, 1964; Ward, 1961) | ☐ | ☐ | ☐ | ☐ |
| 8. Likes to organize and bring structure to things, people, and situations. (Ward, 1961; Gowan & Demos, 1964; Buhler & Guirl, 1963) | ☐ | ☐ | ☐ | ☐ |
| 9. Is quite concerned with right and wrong, good and bad; often evaluates and passes judgment on events, people, and things. (Getzels & Jackson, 1962; Buhler & Guirl, 1963; Carroll, 1940) | ☐ | ☐ | ☐ | ☐ |

| | 1 | 2 | 3 | 4 |
|---|---|---|---|---|
| Column Total | ☐ | ☐ | ☐ | ☐ |
| Weight | 1 | 2 | 3 | 4 |
| Weighted Column Total | ☐ | ☐ | ☐ | ☐ |
| Total | | | | ☐ |

**Part III: Creativity Characteristics**

| | 1 | 2 | 3 | 4 |
|---|---|---|---|---|
| 1. Displays a great deal of curiosity about many things; is constantly asking questions about anything and everything. (National Education Association, 1960; Goodhart & Schmidt, 1940; Torrance, 1962) | ☐ | ☐ | ☐ | ☐ |
| 2. Generates a large number of ideas or solutions to problems and questions; often offers unusual ("way out"), unique, clever responses. (Carroll, 1940; Hollingworth, 1942; National Education Association, 1960) | ☐ | ☐ | ☐ | ☐ |
| 3. Is uninhibited in expressions of opinion; is sometimes radical and spirited in disagreement; is tenacious. (Torrance, 1965; Gowan & Demos, 1964; Getzels & Jackson, 1962) | ☐ | ☐ | ☐ | ☐ |
| 4. Is a high risk taker; is adventurous and speculative. (Getzels & Jackson, 1962; Villars, 1957; Torrance, 1965) | ☐ | ☐ | ☐ | ☐ |

268

5. Displays a good deal of intellectual playfulness; fantasizes; imagines ("I wonder what would happen if. . . ."); manipulates ideas (i.e., changes, elaborates upon them), is often concerned with adapting, improving, and modifying institutions, objects, and systems. (Rogers, 1959; Gowan & Demos, 1964; Getzels & Jackson, 1962)  ☐ ☐ ☐ ☐

6. Displays a keen sense of humor and sees humor in situations that may not appear to be humorous to others. (Torrance, 1962; Gowan & Demos, 1964; Getzels & Jackson, 1962)  ☐ ☐ ☐ ☐

7. Is unusually aware of his impulses and more open to the irrational in himself (freer expression of feminine interest for boys, greater than usual amount of independence for girls); shows emotional sensitivity. (Torrance, 1962; Rothney & Coopman, 1958; Gowan & Demos, 1964)  ☐ ☐ ☐ ☐

8. Is sensitive to beauty; attends to aesthetic characteristics of things. (Wilson, 1965; Witty, 1958; Villars, 1957)  ☐ ☐ ☐ ☐

9. Is nonconforming; accepts disorder; is not interested in details; is individualistic; does not fear being different. (Carroll, 1940; Buhler & Guirl, 1963; Getzels & Jackson, 1962)  ☐ ☐ ☐ ☐

10. Criticizes constructively; is unwilling to accept authoritarian pronouncements without critical examination. (Ward, 1962; Martinson, 1963; Torrance, 1962)  ☐ ☐ ☐ ☐

Column Total ☐ ☐ ☐ ☐

Weight $\boxed{1}$ $\boxed{2}$ $\boxed{3}$ $\boxed{4}$

Weighted Column Total ☐ ☐ ☐ ☐

Total $\boxed{\phantom{xxxxx}}$

## Part IV: Leadership Characteristics

|  | 1 | 2 | 3 | 4 |
|---|---|---|---|---|

1. Carries responsibility well; can be counted on to do what he has promised and usually does it well. (Baldwin, 1932; Bellingrath, 1930; Burks, 1938)  ☐ ☐ ☐ ☐

2. Is self confident with children his own age as well as adults; seems comfortable when asked to show his work to the class. (Drake, 1944; Cowley, 1931; Bellingrath, 1930)  ☐ ☐ ☐ ☐

3. Seems to be well liked by his classmates. (Bellingrath, 1930; Garrison, 1935; Zeleny, 1939)  ☐ ☐ ☐ ☐

4. Is cooperative with teacher and classmates; tends to avoid bickering and is generally easy to get along with. (Dunkerly, 1940; Newcomb, 1943; Fauquier & Gilchrist, 1942)  ☐ ☐ ☐ ☐

5. Can express himself well; has good verbal facility and is usually well understood. (Simpson, 1938; Terman, 1904; Burks, 1938)  ☐ ☐ ☐ ☐

6. Adapts readily to new situations; is flexible in thought and action and does not seem disturbed when the normal routine is changed. (Eichler, 1934; Flemming, 1935; Caldwell, 1926)  ☐ ☐ ☐ ☐

7. Seems to enjoy being around other people; is sociable and prefers not to be alone. (Drake, 1944; Goodenough, 1930; Bonney, 1943)  ☐ ☐ ☐ ☐

| | | | | |
|---|---|---|---|---|
| 8. Tends to dominate others when they are around; generally directs the activity in which he is involved. (Richardson & Hanawalt, 1943; Hunter & Jordan, 1939; Bowden, 1926) | ☐ | ☐ | ☐ | ☐ |
| 9. Participates in most social activities connected with the school; can be counted on to be there if anyone is. (Zeleny, 1939; Link, 1944; Courtenay, 1938) | ☐ | ☐ | ☐ | ☐ |
| 10. Excels in athletic activities; is well coordinated and enjoys all sorts of athletic games. (Flemming, 1935; Partridge, 1934; Spaulding, 1934) | ☐ | ☐ | ☐ | ☐ |
| Column Total | ☐ | ☐ | ☐ | ☐ |
| Weight | [1] | [2] | [3] | [4] |
| Weighted Column Total | ☐ | ☐ | ☐ | ☐ |
| Total | | | | [_____] |

## References

Baldwin, L. E. A study of factors usually associated with high school male leadership. Unpublished Masters thesis, Ohio State University, 1932.

Bellingrath, G. C. Qualities associated with leadership in extra-curricular activities of the high school. *Teachers College Contributions to Education,* 193p, No. 399.

Bonney, M. E. The constancy of sociometric scores and their relationship to teacher judgements of social success and to personality self-ratings. *Sociometry,* 1943, **6,** 40o-424.

Bowden, A. O. A study of the personality of student leaders in colleges in the United States. *Journal of Abnormal and Social Psychology,* 1926, **21,** 149-160.

Brandwein, P. *The gifted student as future scientist.* New York: Harcourt Brace, 1955.

Bristow, W. Identifying gifted children. In P. A. Witty (Ed.), *The gifted child.* Boston: Heath, 1951. Pp. 10-19.

Buhler, E. O., & Guirl, E. N. The more able student: Described and rated. In L. D. Crow and A. Crow (Eds.), bEducating the academically able. New York: David McKayn 1963.

Burks, F. W. Some factors related to social success in college. *Journal of Social Psychology,* 1938, **9,** 125-140.

Caldwell, O. W., & Wellman, B. Characteristics of school leaders. *Journal of Educational Research,* 1926, **14,** 1-15.

Carroll, H. *Genius in the making.* New York: McGraw-Hill, 1940.

Chaffee, E. General policies concerning education of intellectually gifted pupils in Los Angeles. In L. D. Crow and A. Crow (Eds.), *Educating the academically able.* New York: David McKay, 1963.

Courtenay, M. E. Persistence of leadership. *School Review,* 1938, **46,** 97-107.

Cowley, W. H. Traits of face-to-face leaders. *Journal of Abnormal and Social Psychology,* 1931, **26,** 304-313.

Drake, R. M. A study of leadership. *Character and Personality,* 1944, **12,** 285-289.

Dunkerly, M. D. A statistical study of leadership among college women. *Studies in Psychology and Psychiatry,* 1940, **4,** 1-65.

Eichler, G. A. Studies in student leadership. *Penn State College Studies in Education,* 1934, No. 10.

Fauquier, W., & Gilchrist, T. Some aspects of leadership in an istitution. *Child Development,* 1942, **13,** 55-64.

Flemming, E. G. A factor analysis of the personality of high school leaders. *Journal of Applied Psychology,* 1935, **19,** 596-605.

Freehill, M. F. *Gifted children: Their psychology and education.* New York: Macmillan, 1961.

Garrison, K. C. A study of some factors related to leadership in high school. *Peabody Journal of Education,* 1935, **11,** 11-17.

Getzels, J. W., & Jackson, P. W. *Creativity and intelligence.* New York: Wiley, 1962.

Goodenough, F. L. Inter-relationships in the behavior of young children. *Child Development,* 1930, **1,** 29-48.

Goodhart, B. F., & Schmidt, S. D. Educational characteristics of superior children. *Baltimore Bulletin of Education,* 1940, **18,** 14-17.

Gowan, Jm C., & Demos, G. D. *The education and guidance of the ablest.* Springfield, Ill.: Charles C. Thomas, 1964.

Hollingworth, L. S. *Children above 180 IQ.* Yonkers, N.Y.: World Book, 1942.

Hunter, E. C., & Jordan, A. M. An analysis of qualities associated with leadership among college students. *Journal of Educational Psychology,* 1939, **30,** 497-509.

Link, H. C. The definition of social effectiveness and leadership through measurement. *Educational and Psychological Measurement,* 1944, **4,** 57-67.

Makovic, M. V. The gifted child. In W. F. Jenks (Ed.), *Special education of the exceptional child.* Washington, D.C.: Catholic University Press, 1953. Pp. 56-71.

Martinson, R. A. Guidance of the gifted. In L. D. Crow and A. Crow (Eds.), *Educating the academically able.* New York: David McKay, 1963. Pp. 176-182.

National Education Association. *NEA administration: Procedures and school practices for the academically talented student in the secondary school.* Washington, D.C.G NEA, 1960.

Newcomb, T. M. *Personality and social change.* New York: Dryden Press, 1943.

Partridge, E. D. Leadership among adolescent boys. *Teachers College Contribution to Education,* 1934, No. 608.

Richardson, H. M., & Hanawalt, N. G. Leadership as related to Bernreuter personality measures: I. College leadership in extra-curricular activities. *Journal of Social Psychology,* 1943, **17,** 237-249.

Rogers, C. R. Toward a theory of creativity. In H. H. Anderson (Ed.), *Creativity and its cultivation*. New York: Harper & Brothers, 1959. Pp. 75-76.

Rothney, J. W., U Koopman, N. E. Guidance of the gifted. In N. D. Henry (Ed.), Education for the gifted. *Yearbook of the National Society for the Study of Education,* 1958, **57,** (Part II), 346-361.

Simpson, R. H. A study of those who influence and of those who are influenced in discussion. *Teachers College Contributions to Education,* 1938, No. 748.

Cutts, N. E., & Moseley, N. *Teaching the bright and the gifted.* Englewood Cliffs, N.J.: Prentice-Hall, 1957.

Spaulding, C. B. Types of junior college leaders. *Sociology and Social Research,* 1934, **18,** 164-168.

Strang, R. The nature of giftedness. In N. D. Henry (Ed.), Education for the gifted. *Yearbook of the National Society for the Study of Education,* 1958, **57** (Part II), 64-86.

Terman, L. M. A preliminary study in the psychology and pedagogy of leadership. *Pedagogical Seminary,* 1904, **11,** 413-451.

Terman, L. M. (Ed.) *Genetic studies of genius.* Vol. 1. *Mental and physical traits of a thousand gifted children.* Stanford, Cal.: Stanford University Press, 1925.

Terman, L. M., & Oden, M. H. *The gifted child grows up.* Stanford, Cal.: Stanford University Press, 1947.

Torrance, E. P. *Guiding creative talent.* Englewood Cliffs, N.J.: Prentice-Hall, 1962.

Torrance, E. P. *Rewarding creative behavior.* Englewood Cliffs, N.J.: Prentice-Hall, 1965.

Villars, G. (Ed.), *Educating the gifted in Minnesota schools.* St. Paul, Minn.: Commissioner of Education, State of Minnesota, Department of Education, 1957.

Ward, V. S. *Educating the gifted.* Columbus, Ohio: Charles E. Merrill, 1961.

Ward, V. S. *The gifted student: A manual for regional improvement.* Atlanta: Southern Regional Education Board, 1962.

Wilson, F. T. Some special ability test scores of gifted children. In W. B. Barbe (Ed.), *Psychology and education of gifted.* New York: Appleton-Century-Crofts, 1965. Pp. 103-113.

Witty, P. Gifted children—Our greatest resource. *Nursing Education,* 1955, **47,** 498-500.

Witty, P. Who are the gifted? In N. D. Henry (Ed.), Education for the gifted. *Yearbook of the National Society for the Study of Education,* 1958, **57** (Part II), 41-63.

Zeleny, L. Characteristics of group leaders. *Sociology and Social Research,* 1939, **24,** 140-149.

Gallagher, J. J. *Research summary on gifted child education.* Springfield, Ill.: Superintendent of Public Instruction, State of Illinois, 1966.

Getzels, J. W., & Jackson, P. W. The meaning of "giftedness"—An examination of an expanding concept. *Phi Delta Kappan,* 1958, **40,** 75-77.

Hartman, R. K. Teachers' identification of student leaders. Unpublished paper, University of Connecticut, 1969. (Mimeo.)

Jarecky, R. K. Identification of the socially gifted. *Exceptional Children,* 1959, **25,** 415419.

Pegnato, C. W., & Birch, J. W. Locating gifted children in junior high schools: A comparison of methods. *Exceptional Children, 1959,* **25,** 300-304.

Witty, P. A decade of progress in the study of the gifted and creative pupil. In W. B. Barbe (Ed.), *Psychology and education for the gifted.* New York: Appleton-Century-Crofts, 1965, Pp. 35-39.

E. Paul Torrance
Joe Khatena

# "What Kind of Person Are You?" A Brief Screening Device for Identifying Creatively Gifted Adolescents and Adults

*B*oth teachers and researchers sometimes need a brief screening device for identifying creatively gifted adolescents and adults. Although high degrees of reliability and validity cannot be expected from a brief instrument designed to identify anything so complex as the creative person, for certain purposes moderate degrees of reliability and validity are acceptable. This is especially true when the purposes are didactic, exploratory, and/or preliminary screening. "What Kind of Person Are You?" should be viewed only in terms of these purposes.

The senior author had two major purposes in mind in devising this brief instrument. First, he was interested in creating materials for courses on creative ways of teaching that would at the same time obtain personal involvement and communicate course content (the results of research) to a large class of 200 or more students. The plan was to have students respond to the instrument, explain the procedure used in developing it, have students score their own responses, and explain the underlying rationale and research basis for each item. Second, he was interested in developing for research purposes a brief, easily administered and scored test that could be used in classifying adolescents and adults for experimental groupings to facilitate his search for better ways of teaching creatively-gifted or creatively-oriented people.

The data on which the instrument is based were derived from a survey made by the senior author several years ago of empirical studies of creative persons (Torrance, 1962, pp. 66-67). This survey resulted in a list of 84 characteristics that had been found in the over fifty studies surveyed to differentiate between creative individuals in some field of endeavor and similar but less creative people. Later, the list was reduced to 66 characteristics and

Torrance, E. Paul and Khatena, Joe "What Kind of Person Are You?" *Gifted Child Quarterly*, Summer, 1970, 14: 71-75.

used in a variety of studies of concepts of teachers and parents concerning what characteristics should be encouraged and discouraged in working with children and young people. A third previous step had been the collection of ratings by a panel of ten serious students of the creative personality (researchers who had been doing work in this area of investigation for at least two years) of these characteristics. Each of these 66 characteristics had then been ranked from 1 to 66 (Torrance, 1965).

Items for the "What Kind of Person Are You?" Test were constructed by pairing characteristics of differing ranks and arranging them in a forced choice format. In some cases, the item calls for a choice between two socially desirable characteristics and in others, between two socially undesirable characteristics. Similarly, there are items that call for choices between two characteristics that differentiate between creative and relatively non-creative people in a positive direction and some, in a negative direction. The rationale is that the creative person will choose the response that is more central or essential to creative functioning.

The following are sample items with the scored response indicated by an X.

__x__ A good guesser
_____ Receptive to ideas of others

__x__ Curious
_____ Self-confident

__x__ A self-starter
_____ Obedient

__x__ Intuitive
_____ Remembers well

__x__ Unwilling to accept things on mere say so
_____ Obedient

__x__ Altruistic
_____ Courteous

## Length and Timing

The present version of the test consists of 50 items and requires most subjects 5 to 10 minutes to complete. It is thus ideal for use in participation sessions with immediate feedback and application.

## Test-Retest Reliability

Four test-retest reliability studies have been conducted. Torrance had 18 subjects take the test twice, at intervals of one week and obtained a test-retest reliability coefficient of .91. Khatena had 26 subjects retake the test within the same day and obtained a reliability coefficient of .97. With 47 subjects and a one-week interval he obtained one of .71; with 27 subjects and a one-month interval, he obtained one of .73.

## Validity

Initial studies of validity have attempted to determine whether scores of "What Kind of Person Are You?" predict creative kinds of performances or identify persons who obtain high scores on other tests that purport to identify creative persons.

In one study, 41 St. Paul (Minnesota) teachers enrolled in a workshop on creative teaching, were administered both the "What Kind of a Person Are You Test" and the "Sounds and Images Test of Originality" (Cunnington and Torrance, 1965). The latter test requires the subject to produce imaginative and original images in response to recorded sound effects. Responses are scored on a scale ranging from 0 to 4 on originality, following a previously developed scoring guide. A product-moment coefficient of correlation of .75 was obtained between scores on these two measures, one a performance measure and the other a personality measure. In another study, 27 University of Georgia graduate students were administered these same two measures and a coefficient of correlation of .52 was obtained. In a third study, a coefficient of correlation of .26 was obtained for a group of 58 Eastern Carolina University music students. In each of these three cases, the validity coefficient is significant at better than the .05 level.

A class in Group Dynamics at the University of Minnesota was asked to write an imaginative and original story describing the interaction between three animate objects, such as Three Monkeys, Three Sailors, Three Giants, Three Fairies, and the like, as a part of a laboratory experience on the three person group. The stories were then scored for originality on a previously developed set of scales for evaluating the originality of imaginative stories (Torrance, 1964). These scales are concerned with picturesqueness, vividness, flavor, personal involvement, originality of solution, surprisingness of ending, original setting or plot, humor, invented words or names, and other unusual twists in style and content. A product-moment coefficient of correlation of .73 was obtained between the originality score obtained thereby and scores on the "What Kind of Person Are You? Test." Data were available for 47 subjects and the validity coefficient is a significant at better than the .01 level.

Two validity studies have been conducted with scores on

"Onomatopoeia and Images" (Khatena, 1969) as the criterion. This test requires the subject to produce images (word pictures) in response to onomatopoeic words in a repeated design such as employed in "Sounds and Images." Responses are scored for originality according to a guide. In the first, a validity coefficient of .48 was obtained with 58 Eastern Carolina University students in educational psychology; in the second, a validity coefficient of .37 was obtained with 67 Eastern Carolina University students. In both cases, the level of significance was better than .01.

In a group of 123 graduate students at the University of California at Berkeley, the senior author administered both the Provocative Questions Test (Torrance, 1966) and "What Kind of Person Are You?" A coefficient of correlation of .60 was obtained (significant at better than the .01 level).

For some time, the senior author has used the *Runner Studies of Attitude Patterns* (Runner and Runner, 1965) to group students for laboratory experience in terms of their creative motivations. The patterns used for this purpose include: high scores on Experimental Orientation, Intuitive Orientation, and Resistance to Social Pressure and low scores on Rules Orientation, Planfulness (Need for Structure), and Passive Conformity. In 48 students for whom results were available were divided into High, Moderate, and Low "Creative Orientations" on the basis of these criteria. Mean scores on the "What Kind of Person Are You? Test are: 33.12, 28.94, and 24.07. An analysis of variance yielded an F-ratio of 9.47, significant at less than the .01 level of confidence. The only scores below the overall mean on the "What Kind of a Person Are You? Test" were obtained by two subjects who were actually quite low on the Experimental Orientation scale, though otherwise high on the Creative Orientation scales. This experience suggests that the Experimental Orientation is quite critical in identifying people with Creative Orientations.

Data were available for a total of 101 students in two Group Dynamics classes on both the *Runner Studies of Attitude Patterns* and "What Kind of Person Are You? Test." This time, the subjects were divided into High,

**TABLE 1**

**Means, Standard Deviations, and F-Ratios of High, Moderate, and Low Creative Groups (What Kind of Person Are You?) on the Scales of the Runner Studies of Attitude Pattern**

| Scales | High | | Moderate | | Low | | |
|---|---|---|---|---|---|---|---|
| | Mean | S. D. | Mean | S. D. | Mean | S. D. | F-Ratio |
| Experimental | 7.61 | 1.74 | 7.70 | 1.81 | 5.74 | 1.92 | 12.49* |
| Rules, Tradition | 2.42 | 2.24 | 2.67 | 1.74 | 3.97 | 2.19 | 5.59* |
| Intuitive | 6.15 | 1.92 | 5.85 | 1.82 | 5.06 | 2.27 | 2.67* |
| Plan, Structure | 1.79 | 1.56 | 2.70 | 2.30 | 3.51 | 2.20 | 6.03* |
| Resistance to Social Pressure | 5.58 | 1.62 | 5.42 | 1.82 | 5.06 | 1.53 | 1.29 |

*F-ratio is significant at better than the .01 level

277

Moderate, and Low groups on the basis of scores on the "What Kind of Person Are You? Test " and compared on the basis of scores on each of the critical scales of the *Runner Studies of Attitude Pattern.* Differences in means were tested by the planned comparison method (Hays, 1963). The results are reported in Table 1. It would appear from these results that high Experimental and low Rules and Planfullness (need for structure) are most critical to the personality syndrome differentiated by "What Kind of Person Are You?"

Since 1958, the author has been developing a Personal-Social Motivation Inventory (Torrance, 1963) designed to study the motivations involved in creative behavior. The "Creative Motivation" scale of this inventory was administered to 27 students in education along with "What Kind of Person Are You?" A validity coefficient of .55 significant at better than the .01 level.

An indirect reflection of validity is found in the normative data obtained for various groups. The highest means have been obtained by students in creativity seminars conducted by the author. The highest mean obtained by such a group was one of 35.7 by 175 students in the senior author's class on "Creative Ways of Teaching" at the University of California at Berkeley. Means of 33.3 for 40 St. Paul (Minnesota) teachers and 33.1 for University of Georgia students in creativity seminars reflect this tendency. Graduate students in other classes conducted by the authors at the University of Minnesota, the University of Georgia, Eastern Carolina University, and Marshall University range from 23.35 to 29.4.

Further indirect reflections of validity are found in the means of entering freshmen enrolled in various majors in a midwestern university. The mean for the total group of 452 freshmen tested was 26.0 with a standard deviation of 5.00. In rank order, the means for majors having ten or more students are as follows:

| | |
|---|---|
| Speech and Drama | 29 |
| Art | 28 |
| Foreign Languages | 28 |
| English and Literature | 27 |
| Psychology | 27 |
| Elementary Education | 25 |
| Industrial Arts | 25 |
| Mathematics | 25 |
| Business | 24 |
| Home Economics | 24 |
| Social Science | 24 |

The mean for a sample of 170 University of Georgia elementary education majors was 26.5

It will be noted that students attracted to majors generally regarded as "creative" attain higher scores than those attracted to the majors generally assumed to require less creativity.

In summary, the validity evidence seems to be satisfactory to justify the use of "What Kind of Person Are You?" as a brief, coarse screening device for identifying creative adolescents and adults and for use in teaching and experimental grouping situations. Scores on this instrument are significantly related to ability to produce original images in response to both "Sounds and Images" and "Onomatopoeia and Images," to write original stories, to produce more provocative questions, to have freedom or creative orientations as measured by *Runner Studies of Attitude Patterns,* and to have creative motivations. Graduate students attracted to creativity seminars attain higher scores than graduate students in other classes in the same field and freshmen attracted to "creative" majors such as speech and dramatics, art and literature attain higher scores than those attracted to such majors as business, home economics, and social studies.

## References

Cunnington, B. F. and E. P. Torrance, *Sounds and Images.* Boston: Ginn and Company, 1965

Hays, W. L. *Statistics for Psychologists.* New York: Holt, Rinehart and Winston, 1963.

Khatena, J. "Onomatopoeia and Images: Preliminary Validity Study of a Test of Originality." *Perceptual and Motor Skills,* 1969, 28, 335-338.

Runner, K. R. and Runner. *Manual of Interpretation for the Interview From III of the Runner Studies of Attitude Pattern.* Golden, Colo. Runner Associates, 1965.

Torrance, E. P. *Guiding Creative Talent.* Englewood Cliffs, N. J.: Prentice-Hall, 1962.

Torrance, E. P. *Preliminary Manual for Personal-Social Motivation Inventory. Minneapolis: Bureau of Educational Research, University of Minnesota, 1963. (Mimeographed)*

*Torrance, E. P. Guide for Scoring Originality and Interest." In K. Yamamoto. Revised Guide for Scoring Minnesota Tests of Creative Thinking and Writing.* Kent Ohio: Kent State University, 1964.

Torrance, E. P. *Rewarding Creative Behavior.* Englewood Cliffs, N. J.: Prentice-Hall, Inc. 1965.

Torrance, E. P. *Torrance Tests of Creative Thinking: Directions Manual and Scoring Guide, Verbal Forms A and B.* Princeton, N. J.: Personnel Press, 1966.

*John C. Gowan*

# Identification — Responsibility of Both Principal and Teacher

$T$he following is suggested as a special identification program to be modified in specific particulars by local requirements.

1. Select beforehand an approximate percentage of the students for the program, depending upon local wishes and value judgements. It is suggested that this percentage should not be less than 1% and not more than 10%, except in exceedingly atypical schools. Let the percentage target be represented by P%.

2. Use a group test screen, and cut at a point which will give 5P%. Take the top tenth of this group and put them into the program without more ado. Put the rest of the group into the "reservoir".

3. Circulate to each classroom teacher a paper in which he or she is asked to nominate the:
   a. Best student.
   b. Child with the biggest vocabulary.
   c. Most creative and original.
   d. Child with the most leadership.
   e. Most scientifically oriented child.
   f. Child who does the best critical thinking.
   g. Able child who is the biggest nuisance.
   h. Best motivated child.
   i. Child the other children like best.
   j. Child who is most ahead on grade placement.
   k. Brightest minority group child in the class in case there are more than five, and one has not been named heretofore.
   l. Child whose parents are most concerned about increasing the enrichment of his educational progress.

4. Use an achievement battery and cut at a point which will yield 3P%. Make a list of all students who are in the top tenth in numerical skills; add both of these lists to the "reservoir".

5. Together with the principal, curriculum staff and guidance staff, plus

Gowan, John C. "Identification—Responsibility of Both Principal and Teacher." *Accent on Talent*, 2: 2, 1967.

a few teachers, go over and make a list of children who:

    a. Have held leadership positions.

    b. Achieved outstandingly in any special skill (such as arithmetic).

    c. Are the best representative of minority groups.

    d. Have influential parents.

    e. Are examples of reading difficulties but believed bright.

    f. Are believed bright but maybe emotionally disturbed.

    g. About whom any single individual feels he might be in the program. Put these in the "reservoir".

All pupils in the "reservoir" should now be ranked as to the number of times they have been mentioned.

All children having three or more mentions should be automatically included in the program.

All children having two citations should be sent to Binet Testing.

The Binet equivalent for the P% cut should be determined and any child above this cut placed in the program. If it is feasible, children with one mention should be Bineted with the same results. The remainder of the children are in the "hands of the committee". Each case should come up individually, and some of them should be placed in the program despite a Binet below the cut score. Special consideration should be given to (1) minority group children, (2) emotionally disturbed children, (3) children with reading difficulties and, (4) children with marked leadership or creative talents.

The committee should not be afraid to include children in the program because of social considerations, but each child who comes up before committee consideration should have an individual test.

It is believed that such an identification program:

1. Is reasonably effective in finding most of the able children.

2. Is reasonably efficient in cutting costs of individual testing to the bone and in conserving valuable committee time, which needs not be spent on consideration of children who obviously go into such a program.

3. Provides the multiple criteria which are so important in locating all of the able.

4. Is flexible enough to provide for special cases.

If such a program is adopted, it will be found that the size of P will tend to grow. This should not be a source of worry. The best answer of "where do we stop" is not to stop until at least one member of the screening committee thinks the committee has gone too far in letting students into the program. At any time in the program there ought to be children answering to the following descriptions that somebody thinks don't belong there: (1) a minority group child, (2) a slow-reader for his ability, (3) a "nuisance", (4) an emotionally disturbed child, (5) somebody's relative, (6) an original creative child, or (7) a school leader. If the program doesn't do anything for any one of these children, they can always be taken out with a minimum of educational damage. If it does do something for them, the guidance committee has the satisfaction of knowing either that (1) it has made a good guess, or (2) that it has acquired an important friend.

R. C. Wilson

J. P. Guilford

P. R. Christensen

# The Measurement of Individual Differences in Originality

$O$ne of the most important aspects of creative thinking is originality. This article discusses the problem of developing methods for measuring individual differences in originality. The problem arose in connection with a factor-analytic study of creative thinking conducted at the University of Southern California.

In that investigation various definitions of originality were considered in the light of their implications for measurement. Three definitions and corresponding methods of measuring originality were finally adopted and applied to specially constructed tests. The methods are based upon: (*a*) uncommonness of responses as measured by weighting the responses of an individual according to the statistical infrequency of those responses in the group as a whole; (*b*) the production of remote, unusual, or unconventional associations in specially prepared association tests; and (*c*) cleverness of responses, as evaluated by ratings of degrees of cleverness exhibited in titles suggested for short-story plots.

These three methods permit the operations of measurement of individual differences and, while recasting the definition of originality, they preserve much of the essential meaning usually assigned to the concept. In the following sections, some of the nonmeasurable aspects of originality are pointed out and each of the three proposed methods is discussed in conjunction with a description of tests developed to utilize the method. Since the tests were included in a factor analysis along with other tests of creative thinking, the three methods are evaluated in the light of the loadings of scores from these tests on a factor which has been called originality.

Reprinted from *Psychological Bulletin,* Vol. 50, No. 5 (September, 1953), pp. 362-370. By permission of the senior author and the American Psychological Association.

## Definition of Originality

In developing methods for measuring individual differences in originality, the meaning to be assigned to the term *originality* and the operations for measurement must be clearly specified. The term originality has several distinct meanings. We wish to use it as the name for a psychological property, the ability to produce original ideas. What we mean by an original idea will be further specified in relation to each of the proposed methods of measuring originality.

Many writers define an original idea as a "new" idea; that is, an idea that "did not exist before." They are frequently not in agreement, however, in their interpretation of "new," since they use it with different connotations. We shall point out the inadequacy of two of these connotations for the measurement of individual differences in originality.

In one connotation, a "new" idea is an idea that "has never previously been thought of by anyone who has ever lived." In practice, of course, it would be impossible to verify whether or not an idea meets these requirements of newness since one could never examine all the ideas of everyone who ever existed to determine whether the idea has been thought of before. This conception also presents a problem in the case of independent productions of the same idea. Two or more scientists may produce the same idea independently in different parts of the world. One of them may precede the others by a matter of months or weeks, or even hours or minutes. In trying to find creative scientists, we would probably not wish to regard the scientists who produced the idea later as unoriginal merely for having been preceded by someone unknown to them.

On the other hand, we find that "new," while meaning that which did not exist before, is sometimes interpreted, at least by implication, as including all human behavior that is not repetitive. That is, not only poetry, science, and inventions, but dreams, hallucinations, purposive behavior, and all perceptions are regarded as new. They are "new" in the sense that they are never duplicated exactly, even by the individual himself. Such a conception of "new" also fails to be fruitful, since it does not supply us with a basis for differentiating between more original and less original individuals.

For measurement purposes, we have found it useful to regard originality as a continuum. We have further assumed that everyone is original to some degree and that the amount of ability to produce original ideas characteristic of the individual may be inferred from his performance on tests. Rather than define original as "new" or "did not exist before" we have investigated three alternative definitions. We have regarded originality in turn as meaning "uncommon," "remote," and "clever." It was felt that these three definitions include significant aspects of what is commonly meant by the term original. Tests and scoring methods were developed for each of these approaches to originality.

# The Uncommonness-of-Response Method

Our first approach to the measurement of originality assumes a continuum of uncommonness of response. For this purpose originality is defined operationally as the ability to produce ideas that are statistically infrequent for the population of which the individual is a member. "Population" may here be regarded as any cultural group, professional group, or other aggregation of individuals having significant characteristics in common.

This definition of originality was utilized by constructing completion or open-end tests, which require the examinee to produce responses. The tests were administered to the group of individuals whose relative degrees of originality were to be determined. The responses of all the members of the group were tallied to determine their frequency of occurrence within the group. Weights were assigned to the various responses, the higher weights being given to the statistically more infrequent responses. A score was derived for each individual either by summing the weights assigned to his responses or by counting only the responses having high weights. On the basis of the score thus derived, those individuals with the highest scores were the individuals who had given the most infrequently mentioned responses.

This procedure may be clarified by an example. The items in the Unusual Uses test are six common objects. Each object has a common use, which is stated. The examinee is asked to list six other uses for which the object or parts of the object could serve. For example, given the item "A newspaper," and its common use, "for reading," one might think of the following other uses for a newspaper: (a) to start a fire, (b) to wrap garbage, (c) to swat flies, (d) stuffing to pack boxes, (e) to line drawers or shelves, (f) to make up a kidnap note. The test is given in two separately timed parts of five minutes each. Each part gives the names of three objects and their common use with spaces for listing six other uses per object.

All the responses given by a group of 410 Air Cadets and Student Officers to each object were classified, tallied, and weighted. A system of five weights was used. A weight of 5 was assigned for the (approximately) 1/5 most infrequently mentioned respones, a weight of 4 for the 1/5 next most infrequently mentioned responses, and so on down to a weight of 1 for the 1/5 most frequently mentioned responses. This gave a possible range of scores for each object (six responses) of 0 to 30 and a possible range of scores for the total test (six objects) of 0 to 180. The total scores actually obtained ranged from 5 to 129.

Let us consider the actual frequencies obtained for one of the objects. The 1,767 responses to the object given by the group of 410 Air Cadets and Student Officers were tabulated. One hundred and eighty-two different uses were mentioned. Eighty of these 182 uses were unique in that they were mentioned by only one member of the group. At the other extreme, one of the uses was mentioned by 173 individuals. The three most common uses mentioned, with frequencies of 173, 94, and 90, accounted for 357 responses and were assigned weights of one. The next six most common uses, with frequencies from 89 to 48, were assigned weights of two. Nine uses with frequencies from 45 to 29 received weights of three, 24 uses with frequencies from 23 to 9 received weights of four, and the 139 most uncommon uses, with frequencies from 8 to 1, received weights of five. It should be noted that there were not exactly 1/5 of the total number of responses in each weight category. Because of the way in which the responses distribute themselves it is usually not possible to designate an exactly equal number of responses for each weight. It is possible, however, to achieve a close approximation.

After the weight for each response had been determined for all six objects, each examinee's paper was scored by assigning the appropriate weights to his responses and summing them. By definition, those individuals who tended to produce the most infrequently given ideas were the ones with the highest total scores and were regarded as the most original members of the group. The mean score on the Unusual Uses test was 64.0, its standard deviation was 23.5, and its alternate-forms reliability was .74.

The same procedure was applied to the Quick Responses test and the Figure Concepts test (1). The Quick Responses test is similar to the conventional word-association test. It consists of a list of 50 stimulus words, derived principally from the Kent-Rosanoff list and a more recent list developed by D. P. Wilson (4). The 50 words were read to the examinees at the rate of one every five seconds, the examinee being instructed to respond with the first word that came to mind. Responses of 410 individuals were tabulated for each of the 50 stimulus words. Frequencies of occurrence for each response were determined, weights were assigned, and scores derived in a manner similar to that for the Unusual Uses test. The mean score on the Quick Responses test was 99.8 with the standard deviation of 18.7. The reliability estimate was .81 as computed for odd and even items and corrected for length.

The Figure Concepts test consists of 20 simple pen-and-ink drawings of objects and individuals. Each picture is identified by a letter. The examinee's task is to find qualities or features that are suggested by two or more drawings and to list the features and the letter designations of two drawings which possess them. For example, picture A might be a sketch of a child wearing a hat, picture B might be a sketch of a woman wearing a hat, picture C might be a sketch of young birds in a nest. The examinee might give such responses as "wearing a hat (a, b)"; "young (a, c)"; "family (a, b)"; etc.

All responses for all individuals were tabulated and classified according to frequency of mention. A further breakdown was made for each response mentioned in terms of the combinations of drawings used in identifying the feature. It was noted that while there were 190 possible pairs of drawings available, certain ones were rarely used, while others were used as a source of more than one feature. Weighting of responses was thus based on both the infrequency of the response itself and the infrequency of the drawing combination used as a source of that response.

How this dual classification affected an individual's score may be seen in the situation where two individuals gave the same response (feature name), but cited different combinations of drawings. If one individual's response was derived from a drawing combination that was frequently mentioned by others in connection with that feature, the weight assigned was low. The other individual's response, if derived from a drawing combination infrequently mentioned for that feature, was assigned a high weight.

As with the Unusual Uses test, weights were assigned so that an approximately equal number of all the responses given by the group received each weight. Each examinee's responses were then assigned their appropriate weights and the weights were summed to derive the individual's total score for the test. The mean score on this test was 29.9 with a standard deviation of 12.9. Since the format of this test did not permit the direct computation of a reliability estimate, the communality of the test (.41) found in the factor analysis is offered as an estimate of a lower bound of its reliability.

In the Number Associations test the examinee is given, in turn, four different numbers (digits) and for each is allowed two minutes in which to list as many synonyms, uses, and things associated with the number as he can. For example, for the number 4 he might list coach-and-four, for, fore, foursome, quartet, etc.

The associations listed by the group were tabulated and weights were assigned in a manner similar to that described for the Unusual Uses test. In order to try out a further variation of the uncommonness method, however, the individual's total score was derived in a slightly different manner from that previously described. Instead of summing the weights for all the responses given by the individual, his total score was derived by counting the number of responses with weights of 4 and 5. The mean score for this test was 12.5 with a standard deviation of 3.6 and an alternate-forms reliability of .57.

In the approach described in this section, we have chosen to define original as meaning "uncommon." An original idea or response is one that is uncommon or statistically infrequent, and an individual's degree of originality, as inferred from his scores on the tests described, is characterized by the degree of uncommonness of his responses.*

## The Remoteness-of-Association Method

The second approach is in terms of remoteness of association. Originality is here defined as the ability to make remote or indirect associations. To measure originality from this point of view, tests were constructed that required the examinee to make remote associations if he responded at

*The reader may recall that an uncommonness or idiosyncrasy score has previously used in connection with word-association tests in the assessment of abnormalities of behavior in clinical practice, particularly of the schizoid type. The fact that such a score measures an originality factor, as we shall show later, might be regarded as support for the popular idea expressed in the words of Seneca, "There is no great genius without some touch of madness."

all. Remoteness of association was imposed by the task. Three tests of this type were constructed. The degree of originality of an individual, according to this definition, would be manifested in terms of the number of remote associations he made.

The Associations I test presents 25 pairs of words. The associative connection between the two words is not immediately apparent. The examinee's task in each item is to call up a third word that serves as a link between them. For example:

Given:

Indian＿＿＿＿＿＿money

Write on the line between these words a word that associates the two.

There are several possible words that could be used such as penny, nickel, copper, and wampum, each of which is related to both Indian and money.

The examinee's score was the number of responses given to the 25 items in four minutes. The mean score for this test was 14.0 with a standard deviation of 4.9. The odd-even reliability estimate was .87, corrected for length.

The Associations II test is similar to the Associations I except that there is more emphasis on the correct response word having two different meanings in its relationship to the two stimulus words. It is also a multiple-choice test in which the examinee must indicate which one of five letters is the first letter of the correct association.

For example:

tree    *a  b  g  m  s*    dog

Which of the five letters is the first letter of a word that is associated with both tree and dog and has a different meaning in relation to each?

The word "bark" is the correct answer. It means the external covering of a tree and it also means the noise made by a dog. It also begins with *b* which is one of the choices, so the examinee circles the letter *b*.

The examinee's score was the number of correct responses given to 25 items in 12 minutes. The mean score was 14.0 with a standard deviation of 3.9. The odd-even reliability estimate was .62, corrected for length.

The Unusual Uses test, previously described, was also regarded as a test requiring the examinee to respond with remote associations. Since the six items composing the test were common objects, each with one well-known use, which was given, the examinee was compelled to utilize remote associations in seeking six additional uses for each object. Both a statistical-infrequency score and a simple-enumeration score were derived for this test. The correlation between these two scores was .94. There is, of course, much spurious overlap of the two scores. In view of the high correlation between the two scores and the similarity of their correlations with other tests in the creative-thinking battery, the simpler score was chosen for inclusion in the factor analysis. The mean for this score on this test was 22.1 with a standard deviation of 6.7 and an alternate-forms reliability of .80.

In the approach described in this section we have chosen to define original as meaning "remote." An original idea or response is "remote" to the extent that the individual is required to bridge an unusually wide gap in making associative responses. An individual's relative originality, as inferred from his scores on these tests, is characterized by the number of remote responses given in a limited time.

## Cleverness

According to the third approach, originality is defined as the ability to produce responses that are rated as clever by judges. This definition requires a test that calls forth responses showing variation on a continuum of cleverness. Weights are assigned to an individual's responses in proportion to their degrees of rated cleverness.

The Plot Titles test used to measure this type of originality presents two brief stories. For each story the examinee is allowed three minutes in which to write as many appropriate titles as he can. Although relevancy rather than cleverness is stressed in the instructions, an examination of the responses of the group revealed considerable variation in the ingenuity, cleverness, or striking quality of the titles suggested.

In an attempt to develop a reliable scoring procedure for evaluating cleverness, a sample of 50 individuals was selected from the total group of 410. These 50 individuals averaged approximately six responses for each plot. The approximately 300 titles for each plot were typed on separate slips of paper. Three judges, working independently, sorted the titles into six successive piles on the basis of their judgments of the relative cleverness of the titles. Weights from 0 through 5 were assigned to the titles in the successive piles, with the high weights being assigned to the more clever titles. Agreement among the judges is indicated by the interjudge correlations (of ratings) ranging from .53 to .76. Reliabilities of test scores derived from individual judges ranged from .69 to .77. These reliabilities were computed from the two cleverness scores, one from each story, for each of the 50 individuals. The reliability computed from the composite ratings of the three judges (.76) was not higher than that for the best individual judge. Since the most reliable judge was also the one who agreed best with the other two judges, it was decided to have this one judge do the scoring of the test for all examinees, with one of the other judges serving as a check scorer.

In an effort to simplify scoring, a study was made of total scores derived from the weights 0 through 5. That is, each test paper was scored by the number of responses at each of the cleverness levels of 0, 1, 2, 3, 4, and 5. Intercorrelations among the six scores were computed for the sample of 50 individuals. It was found that scores based on weights 0 and 1 intercorrelated well, and scores based on weights 2, 3, 4, and 5 intercorrelated well.

A combination of scores based on weights 0 and 1 had a low correlation with a combination of scores based on weights 2, 3, 4, and 5. It was decided to reduce the scale to two intervals, clever and nonclever. That is, responses receiving weights 0 and 1 would be called nonclever. This greatly reduced the fineness of discrimination required of the scorer. Utilizing the titles already rated as standard, the remainder of the tests were scored on this simple dichotomy. Two scores were recorded for each individual: the number of clever titles and the number of nonclever titles. It was decided to include both scores in the computation of the intercorrelation matrix and to determine, prior to the factor analysis, whether the cleverness and noncleverness scores were sufficiently independent to warrant including both of them in the factor analysis. The correlation between the two scores was −.031 and their patterns of intercorrelations with other tests in the battery were quite different; consequently, both scores were included in the factor analysis. The cleverness score (based on weights 2 to 5) emerged with a loading of .55 on the originality factor. The noncleverness scores (weights 0 to 1) had a loading of −.05 on this factor and had its highest loading (.59) on a factor identified as ideational fluency. The cleverness score had a loading of .07 on the ideational-fluency factor.

In the approach described in this section, we have chosen to define original as meaning "clever." An original idea or response is one that is rated as clever by judges. An individual's degree of originality, as inferred from this kind of test score, would be characterized by the number of clever responses given in limited time.

## Discussion

The seven test scores representing the three scoring methods described were included with 46 other test scores in a battery designed to explore the domain of creative thinking. The test battery was administered to 410 Air Cadets and Student Officers. The scores were intercorrelated and 16 factors were extracted. Orthogonal rotations resulted in 14 readily identifiable factors, a doublet, and a residual. Five of the seven originality test scores emerged with loadings regarded as significant (.30 and above) on one of the factors obtained. Following is a list of the tests, their scoring principles, and their loadings on the factor.

| | |
|---|---:|
| Plot Titles (cleverness) | .55 |
| Quick Responses (uncommonness) | .49 |
| Figure Concepts (uncommonness) | .32 |
| Unusual Uses (remoteness) | .31 |
| Associations I (remoteness) | .30 |
| Number Associations (uncommonness) | .25 |
| Associations II (remoteness) | .09 |

**289**

We have tentatively named this factor originality (3). Another test from the creative thinking battery which should be discussed in relation to this factor is the Consequences test. This test requires the examinee to list the consequences of certain unexpected events such as the sudden abolition of all national and local laws. Two scores were derived from this test on the basis of the degree of remoteness of ideas indicated by the individual's responses. The number of remote consequences was counted for one score and the number of immediate or direct consequences for the other. It was hypothesized that the remoteness of ideas represented by the remote-consequences score might refer to something different from the remoteness of ideas required by the originality tests already mentioned. A separate factor of penetration or the ability to see remote consequences in space, in time, or in a causal chain of circumstances was therefore hypothesized. No such factor emerged in the factor analysis. The remote-consequences score of the Consequences test came out with its highest loading (.42) on the originality factor. Evidently, the remoteness of ideas represented by this test score is not different from the remoteness of ideas required by the test scores hypothesized for originality. This finding lends additional support to the generality of the obtained originality factor.

Inasmuch as test scores representing all three methods of measuring originality have significant loadings on this factor, we may have some confidence in its generality. Had test scores of only one method emerged on the factor, we might wonder whether the factor were specific to the particular kind of scoring method.

It should be mentioned that this factor has some appearance of bipolarity since there were a few small negative loadings of other test scores in the battery on this factor. Those test scores with negative loadings are of the kind whose "right" responses are keyed on an arbitrary, conventional basis by the test constructor. The examinee who engages in an unusual line of thought is likely to be penalized for his originality in such tests. In this connection, the essentially zero loading for originality in Associations II (as contrasted with the significant loading in Associations I) is worth mentioning. In this test, too, one "correct" answer is given credit. It may be that the original examinees think of other appropriate responses whose initial letters appear among the alternatives, and for which they receive no credit.

The fact that five of our tests designed to measure originality have in common a single factor is regarded as evidence for the potential fruitfulness of the scoring methods described for the measurement of individual differences in originality. Further work is necessary in refining the tests and in validating them against objective criteria of originality. It is felt that considerable progress has been made toward the development of objectively scored tests of originality, with promise of satisfactory reliability.

As to the relative merits of the three approaches suggested, the uncommonness and cleverness methods have the greatest amount of the originality-factor variance but are the least economical in time and energy required to determine the scores.

In an exploratory study such as this one, expenditure of time and energy in scoring by the less economical methods may be justified in terms of the insights to be gained. In later studies, however, it is desirable to use more economical procedures. The remoteness principle is a more economical procedure, but does not yield factor loadings as high as the less economical cleverness and uncommonness procedures. The next steps will be to revise the remoteness tests in an attempt to increase their originality variance and to seek methods of simplifying further the cleverness and uncommonness scoring procedures without decreasing their originality variance.

## References

1. Guilford, J. P., Wilson, R. C., Christensen, P. R., & Lewis, D. J., A Factor-Analytic Study of Creative Thinking, I. Hypotheses and Description of Tests. *Reports from the Psychological Laboratory,* No. 4 Los Angeles: Univer. of Southern California, 1951.

2. Guilford, J. P., Wilson, R. C., & Christensen, P. R., A Factor-Analytic Study of Creative Thinking, II. Administration of Tests and Analysis of Results. *Reports from the Psychological Laboratory,* No. 8 Los Angeles: Univer. of Southern California, 1952.

3. Hargreaves, H. L., The "Faculty" of Imagination. *Brit. J. Psychol. Monogr. Suppl.,* 1927, 3, No. 10.

4. Wilson, D. P., An Extension and Evaluation of Association Word Lists. Unpublished doctor's dissertation. Univer. of Southern California, 1942.

# Part IV
## Developing and Encouraging Giftedness

While identification of the gifted and creative is a vital first step, any program that does not go beyond this is of little value. But the task of developing challenging educational experiences for highly able students is an extremely complicated one that does not lend itself to fixed formulas or mere rearrangements of the regular school program. Traditionally, special programs for the gifted were classified according to their administrative pattern or organization and the terms "ability grouping," "acceleration," and "enrichment in the regular classroom" were popular ways of describing a particular school's method for dealing with its gifted youngsters. In recent years, however, it has become increasingly apparent that various administrative patterns of organization do not in and of themselves constitute an adequate program. Unless there is some evidence that special efforts have been made to develop truly differentiated learning experiences regardless of how the program is organized, we must question whether or not any given practice is really capitalizing on the identified talents and abilities of its participants.

The first article in Part IV discusses administrative patterns of program organization and describes some of the unique advantages and disadvantages of each approach. A recurring theme in Ward's article is that organizational patterns *per se* do not constitute an adequate program unless they are accompanied by appropriate modifications in curriculum content and teaching strategies. Two administrative patterns, early school admission and homogeneous grouping, are dealt with in greater detail in the articles by Birch and Barbe. Both of these writers present research findings and case study material that help to point out the values and cautions of early admission and special group practices.

The article by Lanza and Vassar is a dialogue between a school principal and a consultant in the area of education for the gifted. Many of the questions that are ordinarily raised about program development are discussed and practical suggestions for program implementation are offered. The article by Renzulli deals with a study that was designed to determine the most important features in a program for the gifted. The research is based on the opinions of several of the leading researchers and writers in the field of gifted education.

During the past several years a variety of exciting new instructional approaches have emerged from the increased activity that has taken place in the areas of curriculum development and research on instruction. Although most of these approaches were not specifically designed for the superior learner, many of them have particular relevance for the gifted and talented. An attempt has been made to include in this section descriptions of some of the instructional approaches that encourage the learner to be a creative and productive thinker rather than a mere absorber of knowledge. Unfortunately, space limitation and the unavailability of concise descriptions prohibited us from including other promising approaches such as simulated learning games, the advance organizer method, and group encounter strategies.

Material dealing with creativity training would ordinarily be included in a section on instructional approaches, but because of the growing importance of this area in the education of the gifted and talented, we have included four articles that deal with various methods that can be used to stimulate the highly creative student. These selections provide a sampling of the numerous articles that have been written in recent years about methods for enhancing creative potential. An especially valuable resource article in this section is the selection by Treffinger and Gowan. These authors have gathered and classified into forty-three areas a representative listing of more than one hundred available methods, resources, and programs that can be used for studying the creative process and teaching creativity training skills to children and adults. Other articles in this section deal with both general strategies and specific methods for fostering creativity.

One of the most active areas of interest and investigation during the past few years has been the large number of gifted students who are typically overlooked in efforts to provide special programming. These students include low socioeconomic and minority group members, underachievers, and school dropouts. The last four articles in Part IV call attention to the many facets of what has been described as "the great talent loss." Factors such as test bias and the consequences of inferior schooling are discussed and several suggestions are made for improving identification and programming procedures.

*Virgil S. Ward*

# Program Organization and Implementation

## A. Introduction

Radical departure from the customary and conventional must characterize the organizational forms of programs for the gifted as well as their curricula. Procedures which govern the deployment of gifted students and their teachers, and which control the rate of movement of students through the graded sequence, must be related to the unusual abilities and needs of these students. Practices which can be shown by reason or research to be specifically appropriate for the gifted must replace those which have developed to meet the needs of average students.

This section of the report focuses on areas of administrative practice which have particular applicability to program organization and implementation for the gifted—especially ability grouping, acceleration, and independent study. Descriptions of the many forms of ability grouping and acceleration are available at large in the literature, as are discussions of the pros and cons of these practices. No comprehensive treatment of this easily obtainable normative material will be provided in this *Manual*. The present purpose, rather, is to discuss the process qualities inherent in these procedures, and to indicate a number of general observations regarding these and other administrative matters, which indications comprise guidelines to practice.

It should be recognized that ability grouping, acceleration, and independent study, alone or in combination, do not constitute an adequate program for the gifted. They are merely administrative procedures which allow and facilitate the development of known characteristics of gifted students and

Reprinted from *The Gifted Student: A Manual for Program Improvement*. A Report of the Southern Regional Project For Education of the Gifted, 1962, pp. 71-78. By permission of the author and publisher.

which support curriculum development of the kind outlined in the preceding section of this report.

The various methods of acceleration, for instance, constitute administrative recognition that gifted students accomplish standard learning tasks more rapidly than average students. Actually the school does not accelerate the student, who may enter the first grade already reading as well as the average third or fourth grader; rather, it accelerates instruction to keep pace with the student. The gifted student's learning ability does not lend itself to the neat sequential ordering of tasks according to grade levels. The school must acknowledge this and adjust itself to keep pace with him, sometimes making it possible for him to move ahead rapidly on one front while "marking time," or progressing slowly on another.

Grouping students according to selective ability patterns for all or part of their instruction is a practice which parallels the gifted student's ability to function in the classroom situation at intellectual levels not attainable by those of average ability. Only through ability grouping can the gifted student engage in stimulating discourse—discussion and debate—with his intellectual peers. This needed high level engagement of like minds cannot be carried on effectively or efficiently in the typically heterogeneous classroom.

Other characteristics of gifted children are recognized by the intellectual and behavioral involvements inherent in independent study. The value of independent study has already been noted in the preceding section where the concept of "reversed ratios" of teaching and learning was introduced. Independent study, as a recognized and formally adopted administrative procedure, makes possible learning of the nearly unlimited depth and breadth demanded by the wide range of interests and abilities of gifted students, and by the increasing amount and complexity of the body of man's knowledge.

Each administrative procedure employed in the program for the gifted thus embodies certain detailed mental processes of which this identified group of pupils are capable. These techniques are not merely grafted on to the educational program, but rather they grow naturally out of the needs and abilities of these students in the same manner that special curricular provisions are rooted in these needs and abilities.

The remainder of this section of the report will be devoted to further discussion of administrative procedures in the organization and implementation of programs for the gifted. The discussion will take the form of a limited number of generalizations which have been distilled from the total Project experience.

## B. Ability Grouping

### THE DESIRABILITY OF GROUPING.

Observers of special programs come quickly to the conviction that grouping of students according to ability for at least pertinent portions of their school experience is eminently desirable at every grade level. The mere grouping of pupils does not make a program, nor does absence of grouping necessarily mean that a program is absolutely ineffective. Nevertheless, ability grouping greatly increases the school's power to effect a marked improvement in the process of education for gifted students.

Ability grouping *makes possible* many teaching and learning experiences which cannot be accomplished in the typical classroom. This can be seen again and again in specially composed classes in all parts of the country. There is an electric quality, an aura of purposefulness, about such a class—whether it contains the remarkable five and six year olds of the Colfax School in Pittsburgh, lucid, earnest, and intensively engaged in making research reports or the 12th grade social studies students in Portland, Oregon, arguing political theory as though they were the Franklins, Paines, and Jeffersons of their generation. The kinds of intellectual activity that can be engaged in by a group of gifted children under the guidance of a carefully selected and specifically trained teacher simply cannot go on in the typical classroom, regardless of the kind of "enrichment" attempted.

ABILITY GROUPING AND THE TEACHER.

Perhaps the most important and yet the least controllable variable in the grouping situation is the teacher. Ability grouping is of no particular value when teachers do not or cannot capitalize on the fact that they are working with children who have special capabilities and needs. In many classrooms in schools renowned for their programs for the gifted, teachers can be observed using the same plodding, pedestrian techniques that are so often necessary in the typical classroom where students are slow to grasp even elementary facts and concepts—with frustration and boredom as the end products, instead of intellectual excitement and challenge. Whether or not the potential value inherent in ability grouping is realized is to a considerable extent the teacher's responsibility. If the teacher does not recognize these potentialities and fails to modify his or her approach to the teaching-learning situation, the potential value of ability grouping is lost. Too often, one suspects, this is why research data fail to show significant differences between the results of grouping and the results of "enrichment" in the regular classroom.

One common source of failure to translate well-conceived programs into good classroom practice is the administrative procedure of rotating the task of teaching gifted groups through the entire teaching staff of given grades. In many school systems staff members are required to take turns teaching the bright groups regardless of interest in or ability to work with such children. Teachers should be selected for work with gifted groups on the basis of ability and interest. There can be no doubt that some teachers are better teachers for gifted children than others, just as some teachers are better fitted through training, temperament, experience, and interest to teach retarded children. Teaching each type of student requires the development of skills and knowledge which can best be achieved by special training and by continuous experience of some duration. It is difficult to see what is to be gained by assigning a teacher whose real forte is teaching the gifted to a retarded group one year and an average group the next.

It is a matter of interest to note that in numbers of school systems with a successful pattern of experiences for the gifted, it is established practice to allow teachers of gifted classes additional time for preparation. Effective teaching of gifted children is a demanding task, more so than teaching average children whose range of interests is narrower and for whom drastic departures from standard curriculum and teaching methods already reasonably well developed need not be made.

Reducing the class loads of teachers of gifted classes need not be destructive of staff morale, provided the whole staff has been led to understand the purposes and the processes integral to this complicated task. *All* teachers should be involved in the planning and development of the gifted program, and the program itself should, of course, be thought of as a part of the total school program. The importance of this approach to program development has already been emphasized.

### THE FEASIBILITY OF ABILITY GROUPING.

Some form of ability grouping appears to be feasible (as well as desirable) for any school system regardless of size, wealth, or location. The kinds of grouping practices most suitable for any given system or school will, of course, depend on many factors such as the number of gifted children at various age levels, the number of schools in proximity to each other, and the availability of funds for compensating the factor of reduced teacher-pupil ratios. A sufficient number of "models" are described in the literature so that any school system—those in large, medium, or small cities, and those in suburban or in rural locations—should find help in planning and developing suitable ability grouping procedures. Practically every successful school in this particular has incorporated ability grouping of some kind into its program for the gifted, the forms varying from the massive complex of specialized high schools in New York City to the weekly seminars for general intellectual stimulation in rural Lewis County, New York. Everywhere the salutary effects of ability grouping upon motivation, achievement, and morale of able students is readily noticeable. There is little evidence in the experience of these school systems to substantiate the fears of those who believe that snobbishness and "elitism" are the inevitable by-products of ability grouping. Nor have they found grading of students in special groups to be an unmanageable problem. The collective experience of teachers and administrators who have worked in the midst of this kind of provision indicates that the common arguments against ability grouping are unfounded in fact.

# C. Acceleration

Despite the fact that research evidence supporting acceleration is unquestionably greater than that supporting ability grouping, systematic acceleration appears to be less often a formal feature of present programs for the gifted. Certain types of acceleration, especially advanced placement, are being increasingly practiced and seem to be gaining in acceptance. Others, such as early admission to first grade, early admission to college, and the "non-graded" primary are less frequently encountered. There seem to be several reasons for this widespread failure of the schools to adopt proven methods of acceleration. State laws prevent early admission to the first grade in some communities. Simple ignorance of existing research findings may account for some of the delay in adopting this and other practices where there are no laws to prevent such action.

Schools that deny, or fail to provide acceleration, frequently operate upon the now discredited belief that "social maladjustment" is the inevitable result of even moderate acceleration. It is not unlikely, however, that much of the reluctance to adopt certain techniques of acceleration may be correctly attributed to administrative inertia—unwillingness to sacrifice the convenience of the chronological age "lockstep" for flexible procedures which more adequately reflect known facts about individual differences in ability and total developmental readiness. Doubtless many gifted five year olds are refused admission to school not because they are not ready in every way but because a flexible admission policy would tend to create administrative "headaches" in the form of parental pressures to admit unqualified children. Such sacrifice of sound procedure to considerations of expediency is indefensible.

ACCELERATION A DESIRABLE PRACTICE.

Acceleration, like ability grouping, should be a part of every school program for the gifted. There is nothing startling about this observation, of course. Terman strongly suggested that many able students should be promoted sufficiently to allow them to enter college at age seventeen at the latest, and he claimed that many were ready at sixteen. *Any school system* can make such progress possible for its gifted students and the experience of those school systems which do practice moderate acceleration indicates that the benefits derived accrue not only to the gifted students but to the school as a whole. Teachers have found that a flexible promotion policy can help to reduce the range of variability within the classroom, and at the same time help to lessen the boredom and dissatisfaction of bright students. The anticipated administrative difficulties sometimes do not arise, and in any case they are outweighed by the positive gains derived from elimination of the "lockstep." Finally, and in addition to the benefits of acceleration for students and teachers, it should be pointed out again that society stands to benefit from the earlier entry into productive citizenship of its most able citizens. It seems unlikely that American schools can much longer ignore the compelling logic and impressive empirical evidence that can be marshalled in favor of moderately accelerated progress through the educational system for those who are capable of such progress.

### ACCELERATION ALONE NOT A PROGRAM.

It is perhaps unnecessary to point out again that acceleration alone, as with grouping, does not constitute an adequate program for the gifted. This fact is not universally comprehended, however. All too frequently administrators unblushingly talk of "programs" that consist solely of advanced placement classes at the twelfth grade level. While advanced placement is in many ways a useful concept, those who offer it as a "program" hold an impoverished concept of special education for the gifted. Acceleration is an administrative procedure which should be a part of every program for the gifted, but it does not obviate other modifications of the standard school routine, especially in the area of curriculum content and organization.

## D. Independent Study

### THE PROMISE OF INDEPENDENT STUDY.

It was suggested in the preceding section of this report that the unique characteristics of gifted children make possible a "reversed ratio" of teaching to learning; i.e., gifted students are capable of much learning with relatively little teaching. For this reason independent (individual) study is particularly suited to the needs of gifted students.

The Trump Commission prophesies that in the secondary school of the future even average students will spend perhaps forty per cent of their in-school time in individual study. How much American schools must change in order to make that prediction come true is apparent to observers who have like the SRPEG participants visited in school after school noting the frequency of given practices. Independent study as a formally recognized procedure, i.e., by inclusion into the administrative plan of the school of independent study courses for which credit is given, is quite rare. While it is true, of course, that teachers everywhere often make individual assignments which involve some degree of independent study, it is doubtful that the true potentialities of this method have been generally recognized. Understanding and acceptance of independent study as a salutary administrative procedure will greatly improve educational opportunity for gifted students. It will mark another step in the direction away from the rigid lock-step procedures still characteristic of American education and toward true individualization of education.

## E. Other Administrative Considerations

ARTICULATION.

The necessity of assuring continuity in the gifted student's school learning experiences was emphasized in the preceding discussion of curriculum development. Administrative innovations such as ability grouping and acceleration can disrupt established continuity and therefore the administrator must consider the probable consequences for all ensuing grade levels of any administrative decision affecting a level. Problems can arise, for instance, when junior high schools fail to take account of the high level of motivation, achievement, and expectancy of gifted students entering from valid differentiated elementary school programs. Administrative liaison between levels in the system can help to eliminate or reduce such potential problems. Establishing and maintaining continuity in the gifted student's school experience is extremely important. It can be accomplished only by administrators who can keep in focus the whole school program from kindergarten to college.

FINANCING SPECIAL EDUCATION FOR THE GIFTED.

It is impossible to say how much of a school budget should be allocated to the special education of gifted children. Obviously some provisions are far more expensive than others and may be beyond the reach of many school systems at the present time. On the other hand some provisions such as curriculum revision, most forms of acceleration, and many forms of ability grouping need add little or nothing to the budget.

There can be no question that expenditure of funds for special education of gifted students is fully justified. One of the tenets of the democratic philosophy of education is that each student should have an equal opportunity to develop his potentialities to the fullest. On this basis American schools provide special facilities and equipment for those who are athletically talented, musically promising, and for those who are blind, deaf, crippled, or mentally retarded. When the special intellectual capacities of children demand special educational provisions these should be provided whatever the cost.

## F. Conclusions

The unique abilities and needs of gifted students demand unusual administrative provisions. Traditional patterns of pupil and teacher deployment and of pupil progress through the graded sequence are inadequate. It has been suggested in this report that certain administrative procedures embody process qualities which parallel known characteristics of gifted learners. Acceleration implements the gifted learner's ability to accomplish school tasks more rapidly than average students. Ability grouping recognizes his need to engage in activities with his intellectual equals. Independent study capitalizes on his ability and motivation to learn without direct and constant teacher supervision. All of these administrative practices, plus others familiar and commonly reported to be feasible, should be part of every program for the gifted.

The overriding importance of the teacher in the implementation of programs for the gifted is an inescapable observation on the part of persons pointedly studying class upon class. In many cases programs which are outstanding from the standpoint of planning and organization are subverted in the classrooms by teachers who are unable to relate their teaching procedures to the needs and abilities of gifted students.

Ability grouping of some kind is a feature of practically every program for the gifted that has received any attention in the literature. Acceleration procedures, with the exception of advanced placement, are much less often included. The desirability of independent study as a formal administrative procedure has apparently been very largely overlooked by American schools. Thus even in schools noted for their attempts to provide differential education for the gifted there is evidence of inconsistency in philosophy and planning, poor articulation between schools, reluctance to begin special provisions in the early grades, and other evidences of inertia, lack of knowledge of research findings, and lack of imagination. The sum total of the experience of the Project participants suggests that despite the pioneering efforts of a few school systems there is still much room for improvement with respect to administrative aspects of program development for the gifted in American schools.

*Jack W. Birch*

---

# Early School Admission
# for Mentally Advanced Children

*T*his is a report on the adjustment and progress of 43 mentally advanced children who were accelerated one full year in school age-grade placement by early admission to first grade. The minimum age of entrance to first grade in Pennsylvania is five years and seven months as of the first day of September of the year of admission. A special case under regulation of the State Council of Education permits admission of children less than five years and seven months but over five years of age if recommended by a public school psychologist. In order to ascertain the effects of early entrance, periodic follow-up inquiries were made regarding children admitted early in September, 1951, September, 1952, and September, 1953. In 1951, in the Pittsburgh school system, six boys and eight girls were admitted early; in 1952, four boys and thirteen girls; in 1953, four boys and eight girls making the total of 43 children whose adjustment is studied here.

It is apparent that girls outnumber boys in this sample, although there is no obvious reason why this should be the case from the manner in which the sample was drawn. The newspapers gave wide publicity to the fact that parents could apply for examination for early admission consideration for their children. No applications for consideration were denied. Approximately nine times as many children were examined as were recommended for early admission. There seemed to be no considerable social or economic factor limiting the sample; the 43 early admissions recommended involved 27 different elementary schools representing all parts of the city. It may be that the important factors were that girls tend in general to develop verbal abilities earlier than boys and that bright girls tend to manifest their brightness to their parents earlier than do bright boys.

None of the children admitted early were very much younger than five years and seven months. Information on the children's ages as of the first day of September of the year of first grade admission follows:

The youngest child admitted early was five years, three months, and twenty-two days old, and the oldest child admitted early was just one day

---

Reprinted from *Exceptional Children*, Vol. 21, No. 3 (December, 1954), pp. 84-87. By permission of the author and publisher.

| Age at First Grade Admission (Below minimum general admission age of 5 years, 7 months) | No. of Children |
|---|---|
| 1 to 15 days | 8 |
| 16 to 30 days | 11 |
| 31 to 45 days | 4 |
| 46 to 60 days | 16 |
| 61 to 75 days | 4 |
| 76 to 90 days | 1 |
| 91 to 105 days | 1 |
| TOTAL | 43 |

short of being old enough to be admitted early without special examination.

The psychologists who made the examinations interviewed each child and at least one of the child's parents. In some cases the application forms which came to the psychologists contained comments by the principal of the school in the elementary district of the child's residence. These comments were particularly helpful in cases where the child had attended kindergarten for a period of time and the comments could include observations of the kindergarten teacher. However, not all children being considered for early admission had attended kindergarten, and there was not sufficient data to evaluate the possible effects of kindergarten attendance on later adjustment of children admitted early.

The information used by the psychologists in determining whether early admission should be recommended included the following:

1. Evidence from the interviews or other data of superior social maturity for the child's age.

2. Evidence from the interviews or other data of superior emotional maturity for the child's age.

3. Evidence from observation, interview, and other data of reasonably normal height and weight and robust physical health.

4. Evidence of superior reading aptitude from objective individual examinations of reading readiness.

5. Evidence of superior mental capacity from objective individual examinations of intelligence (mental age of seven years or higher and intelligence quotient of 130 or higher were considered advisable, although not required in every case).

6. Knowledge of the general characteristics of the first grade population and instuctional program of the school the child would attend.

Where it was feasible, two psychologists took part in examining the child, each doing a share of the examination separately, and then the psychologists pooled their judgments. When a decision either to admit or not to admit early had been reached, either by pooled judgments or where one psychologist did the complete evaluation, the decision was given to the parent at the time in an interpretive interview.

The interviews tended to follow one of three patterns. In about one out of 10 cases the psychologist recommended early admission, told the parent generally what to expect from the child, pointed out some considerations in preparing the child for first grade, and answered the parents' questions

304

about the child and the school. Second, in about one out of 40 cases the psychologist did not recommend early admission, but did not recommend against it. These were questionable cases, where a clear-cut decision was not easy to make. In such cases the psychologist explained the findings to the parent, presented both sides of the case, the factors which seemed to favor early admission and the factors which caused misgivings, and offered the choice to the parent. This usually occasioned discussion which resulted in a decision shared by the psychologist and the parent. The third pattern of interview, occurring in approximately nine out of 10 cases was that in which the psychologist recommended against early admission and explained why that decision had been reached. It seems appropriate to point out in this connection that the interviews in which early admission was refused did not present anything like the number of difficulties that might have been anticipated. No doubt there were a number of reasons for this, and certainly one of the most important was the skill of the psychologists involved. In addition, however, school principals and other school personnel had carefully informed many of the parents at the time they applied for consideration that the odds were heavily against a recommendation for early admission. Suggestions for dealing with this matter had been made to principals in an administrative letter. The local press, too, had proved a major aid by carrying accurate and informative articles about the early admission process. In the judgments of the psychologists involved, the examinations and interviews had positive values for most of the parents and children whether early admission was recommended or refused as well as positive values to the school from the data still useful when the children who were not recommended entered under the general age regulations a year later. At least one child each year was found whose mental development was retarded enough to justify the opposite of early admission—postponement of school admission even the following year. The early identification of both bright and dull children was an outcome of the process.

After the mentally advanced children were entered in school, a follow-up process began. Twice each year, winter and spring, a letter was addressed to the principal of each school. This letter listed the names of the children who had been admitted early to that school and asked the principal to offer such information about the adjustment of the children as might prove helpful in giving guidance to future policy and practice on early admission. For some of the children admitted in 1951 there are five follow-up comments, involving reaction from several teachers. These children are now in the second semester of the third grade. Some of the children were lost through moves out of the school system after one or more follow-ups. The total number of follow-up comments on all 43 cases is 116.

For the purpose of this report, the comments concerning the children have been classified into four kinds.

1. *Positive:* the report indicates that the child is making satisfactory or better school adjustment in all areas, academic, social, emotional, and physical.

2. *Positive—Questionable:* the report indicates that the child is making satisfactory or better school adjustment in all areas with the possible exception of one.

3. *Negative—Questionable:* the report indicates that the child, while not failing school, is definitely not making satisfactory or better school adjustment in one or two areas.

4. *Negative:* the report indicates that the child, while not failing in school, definitely shows evidence that early admission had contributed to current maladjustments.

Below are examples of statements.

*Positive:*

Marilyn has adjusted to first grade very satisfactorily. She is a superior child, mentally. Her social adjustment has been very good. Personality and attendance in kindergarten are contributing factors to this. I am not in favor of early entrance to first grade. It should be discouraged rather than encouraged. The majority of children under age will make better progress if they stay in kindergarten full time. Marilyn is the exceptional child, one in a hundred.

*Positive—Questionable:*

Carol is doing very well in reading and number work. She is alert and very intelligent. Socially she is shy and needs to be stimulated to associate with other children. She keeps busy at all times, but much to herself. Her attendance has been very irregular this first semester. She had chickenpox and has been out several times with colds. Altogether she was absent 33½ days. With an attendance of this sort, she has rated a B rating.

*Negative—Questionable:*

George is an easy-going child who lets nothing disturb him. He has shown no interest so far in achieving. His attention span is exceptionally short, even during development of a new lesson. George must be constantly reminded to finish the task to be done; without prompting he does nothing, but his work is correct when he does do it. His rating is high average, but he must be prompted to do each page. As a whole, George is still very immature in many ways, even to his size. Although he will learn to read I believe he would have profited more if he had remained in kindergarten another semester. He reads with the third (low) group.

*Negative:*

Wanda is a lovely child, but is so easily frustrated she cries often. Wanda's reading achievement is due largely to her learning to read with an older sister. She is not capable of reading independently or thinking for herself. At the first sign of difficulty she cries to go to her sister. It takes much reassurance to understand she must work alone. Although her mother wants her to be in first grade, she does not want her to do any work which presents any difficulty or upsets her. She reads with the second group, and seems to be able to tell about the coming lesson, although she cannot recognize the words. In my opinion Wanda definitely should have had more kindergarten.

It should be pointed out that Marilyn, Carol, George, and Wanda are all doing quite well in school now. George is still rather happy-go-lucky, and Wanda is still somewhat dependent; but their present teachers find these characteristics well within the normal range for all children.

The responses were classified so that a more objective evaluation could be made of the results of early admission. Table 1 shows the number of comments made on all the children in each category and the proportion of each classification of comments made regarding the children.

**TABLE 1**

**Proportions and Number of Comments**

| Number of Children | Number of Comments | Proportions |
|---|---|---|
| 30 | 64 | 100% Positive |
| 1 | 3 | 75% Positive |
| | 1 | 25% Positive—Questionable |
| 1 | 4 | 80% Positive |
| | 1 | 20% Negative |
| 1 | 3 | 75% Positive |
| | 1 | 25% Negative |
| 1 | 2 | 66% Positive |
| | 1 | 33% Positive—Questionable |
| 2 | 6 | 60% Positive |
| | 4 | 40% Positive—Questionable |
| 2 | 6 | 60% Positive |
| | 4 | 40% Negative |
| 1 | 1 | 50% Positive |
| | 1 | 50% Positive—Questionable |
| 1 | 1 | 33% Positive |
| | 2 | 66% Positive—Questionable |
| 1 | 1 | 20% Positive |
| | 2 | 40% Positive—Questionable |
| | 1 | 20% Negative—Questionable |
| | 1 | 20% Negative |
| 1 | 1 | 20% Positive |
| | 2 | 40% Positive—Questionable |
| | 2 | 40% Negative |
| 1 | 1 | 100% Positive—Questionable |
| 43 | 116 | |

The data in Table 1 indicate that an overwhelming majority of the children admitted early to first grade were making satisfactory school adjustments in all areas, academic, social, emotional and physical. The data also indicate that the preponderance of all ratings was on the combined Positive and Positive—Questionable side for all children, and no child had a majority of ratings on the Negative and Negative—Questionable side.

While the data in Table 1 do not illustrate this further finding, it was apparent by inspection that where some Negative and Negative—Questionable evaluations were given, these tended to be the ones given during the first year of school and that later evaluations of the same child, usually in second or third grade, swung toward the Positive side.

## Summary, Conclusions, and Implications

Forty-three children identified as mentally advanced were admitted early to first grade. The practice was evaluated by follow-up statements from their principals and teachers. The following conclusions can be drawn from the investigation:

1. Early admission of mentally advanced children to first grade is a very promising educational procedure in the general category of provisions for acceleration in age-grade placement, if it is practiced in accord with the procedures followed for the children in this investigation.

2. Further objective evaluation is advisable through follow-up of the same children and also of other children admitted at earlier ages to determine the practical limits on age of early admission.

Some of the implications of this report which appear of major importance are:

1. The early identification of mentally advanced children for optimum educational planning requires that all children have psychological examinations prior to first grade admission. Although only 1.1% of the five-year-olds would be eligible for early admission by State Council of Education early admission standards in Pennsylvania, examination of almost all children is necessary to locate that group.

2. It is crucial that the opportunity for early admission to first grade occurs only once in a child's lifetime. Individual psychological study of each apparently precocious child is essential in the pre-school years if this opportunity is not to be lost.

3. In formal school situations involving no kindergarten provisions, early admission to first grade is the earliest step, chronologically, that can be taken to adjust the prevailing public educational program to the gifted child's needs. Certainly it is not the only move, and it may not be the most important, but it is the first possible action of its kind in the child's school career.

4. Early admission to first grade seems to combine most of the favorable features associated with acceleration and to minimize the unfavorable features. It paves the way for such advantages as earlier entrance into post-college training and earlier marriage, while it does not require that a child start school with one group of children and then find himself forced to adjust socially with a new group after acceleration.

5. Six full years of education in the elementary school, rather than the five which usually result in cases of acceleration, are provided by early admissions to first grade. Not only need there be much less concern over gaps in skill sequences brought about by "skipping," but with a full six years of elementary education there is more time for the activities which are usually grouped under the much maligned, but valid, concept of enrichment.

6. If early admission and enrichment for bright children should become a prevailing practice in the early grades in public schools, success in the practice will depend in a large measure on the readiness of primary school professional personnel to provide the school learning program and the understanding needed by such children. Where there is reluctance to accept these younger children into first grade, and where there is the feeling that the children admitted early should begin immediately to behave like "geniuses," the implication regarding professional training, both pre-service and in-service, is evident.

7. Perhaps the most general implication of acceleration by early admission to first grade lies in the need which is pointed up for integration of educational practices regarding mentally advanced children at all levels in the school program. Acceleration at first grade entrance modifies the conditions under which attendance in special classes or later acceleration may operate. The same is true for any other special educational adjustment or combination of adjustments.

8. Finally, the systematic procedures presented in this paper for evaluating children referred for consideration for acceleration at the pre-first grade stage, with an attempt to objectify the evidence on how satisfactorily the procedures worked, should be thought of as indicative of the pressing need to develop and assess, by bona fide research techniques, the value of such procedures at all levels where acceleration or any other type of educational adjustment is to be attempted with mentally gifted children and youth.

*Walter B. Barbe*

---

# Homogeneous Grouping for
# Gifted Children

*T*he need for attention to the education
of gifted children has long been recognized. The development of provisions
for this, however, has not kept pace with the research findings on the nature
and needs of the gifted. To only a limited extent have special provisions been
made for them. Acceleration, enrichment and homogeneous grouping are
the major types of provisions. Few programs have been based solely upon
only one of these. Enrichment has come to be an essential part of any provision for the gifted, while homogeneous grouping is practiced to some extent
in every class.

But there are those who believe that formal provisions are necessary if
the gifted child is to be adequately provided for. There is much evidence to
prove that the gifted child frequently is neglected (1).

Recognizing this need for special attention to gifted children, in 1920
Cleveland, Ohio, began a program of special classes for gifted children.
This, known as the Major Work Program, was the beginning of a slow and
spasmodic increase in the belief that gifted children can best be provided for
in special classes (2).

The program of providing for gifted children in the schools of New York
City was started in 1922 by Leta Hollingworth. Even though Public Schools
No. 64 and 11 had reported grouping rapid learners shortly before this time,
"they did not carry with them the scientific research and evaluation begun
by Hollingworth in No. 165 (3)." These classes, known as Special Opportunity Classes, were given partial financial support by the Carnegie Corporation of New York.

In an article in *Ungraded* (4), Hollingworth, Cobb and others stated that
the purposes of the program were: "First, the particular children in it must
be educated—the class exists for them; but secondly, they must be studied—
our knowledge of such children must be increased, for we have, after all,
very little information to guide us in differentiating their schooling."

These early classes were entirely of an experimental nature and continued for a period of three years. Two groups of children were selected to

---

Reprinted from *Educational Leadership*, Vol. 13, No. 4 (January, 1956), pp. 225-229. By
permission of the copyright © owner, The Association for Supervision and Curriculum
Development.

be in the experiment. Group A was formed with children of 150 I.Q. and above, while Group B consisted of children with I.Q.'s between 135 and 154. All of the children were between the ages of 7 ½ and 9 ½ years and were accelerated in their school grade placement.

At the end of the three-year experiment, comparisons were made of achievement of the experimental groups and control groups of children who were of equal intellectual capacity but not in special classes. It was found that there was no great difference in the achievement scores of the segregated and non-segregated groups. In the evaluation, it was concluded that: "The advantages to be hoped for from the homogeneous grouping of gifted children lie not so much in the expectation of greater achievement in the tool subjects of reading, arithmetic and spelling as in an enrichment of scholastic experience (5)."

Hildreth recently reported on another attempt at special schools in New York. In 1940, Hunter College in New York City received authorization from the Board of Education to organize an elementary school for gifted pupils. Children from the ages of 3 to 11 who test above 130 I.Q. and "show other evidence of being mentally gifted and having other favorable traits (6)" are eligible for these classes.

Admission to the school is limited to those children living within a limited area of the Borough of Manhattan who meet the necessary mental and social qualifications. There is no tuition charge. An effort is made to keep the number of boys and girls as nearly equal as possible. Because of the enormous number of applicants, the staff believes that admission on the basis of objective tests is a fair method. An interesting point which Hildreth makes is that "the range [in I.Q.] . . . was around 60 points; the groups were seldom more homogeneous than in other schools except that the minimum rating was not below 130."

In telling of the children in the Hunter program, Hildreth describes them as having attractive personalities and possessing vitality and vivacity.

The parents of the Hunter group are a cross sampling of the population. Their occupations vary from day laborer to business executive. The majority of the parents have had some college, were born in New York, and would be ranked in the high-middle income bracket.

At the present time there are 22 classes for gifted elementary children. In addition to the one regular teacher for each class, there are five full-time special teachers. All of the teachers have the M.A. degree. The physical plant is, in itself, unique. All facilities for which a teacher could ask are available.

The goals of the educational program as outlined by Gertrude Hildreth are:

1. Mental health and adjustment.
2. Health and physical education.
3. Learning to become an economically efficient citizen, both as producer and as consumer.

4. Acquiring skill in social relationships.
5. Learning about one's role as an enlightened and active world citizen.
6. Education for initiative and originality (7).


Oliver (8) reports that an entire school is set aside in Baltimore for gifted junior high school students, while Allentown, Pennsylvania, brings superior students from all over the city to one school for "opportunity classes." A division within a school is described and the Cleveland Major Work Program is mentioned briefly as an example of this type. He mentions the differentiated high school programs in most cities where the college preparatory course, which is essentially for the gifted students, is offered to some, while a commercial curriculum is offered to others.

Colfax School in Pittsburgh, Pennsylvania, operates a partial segregation plan to "provide for better living conditions for its mentally superior children." The entire school, from the third grade on, is on the platoon plan. It is described by Pregler as a "workshop" plan: "The plan provides the maximum opportunity for group acceptance of the individual child, it encourages the pupil to work to capacity, and it makes it possible for superior children to work with and be challenged by their mental peers. Furthermore, it has enabled the school to develop special methods and materials well suited to the teaching of gifted children (9)."

The gifted children at Colfax School are segregated in the skill subjects and mix with their regular home room in the special subjects. Pregler points out that by use of the workshop plan, the gifted child still remains a part of the regular class. When he leaves the regular class, it is just as if a child in the typical school would go to orchestra practice. Actually, it amounts to segregation for half of the day. All of the skill subjects are taught either in the morning or afternoon, and the gifted child leaves his regular group for this period of time.

Baker (10) describes the program in Detroit for mentally superior children. Generally, he says, Detroit has a "mild amount of extra promotion." At the elementary school level, most schools follow the platoon plan of departmentalizing subjects. At the junior high level, the screening of gifted children is done by means of weighted formula. Five points are given for intelligence, four for school achievement, and two for chronological age. Children are then segregated according to the total points which they have. At the high school level, Baker says, the program consists of little more than the customary college preparatory courses.

Interest in provisions for the gifted has been outstanding throughout California. This is perhaps due to Terman's study (11) of gifted California youth.

A program described by Cora Lee Danielson, former supervisor of this work (12) was in operation for over twenty years. Los Angeles no longer has special classes but is attempting to meet the needs of the gifted through various other means.

In considering the merits of special classes, Goddard says that this is the best method by which the school can keep "the child happily employed with work that is educative, both because it is interesting to him and because it challenges his capabilities by calling for his best efforts continually (13)." The Educational Policies Commission says that in its broader sense, enrichment is a policy rather than a plan, and that special classes for the gifted have little justification if they do not provide enrichment. Activities especially appropriate for the gifted involve creative expression, ample opportunity for out-of-school contacts, and a chance for each child to learn more about his fields of special interest and to express his particular talents (14). Witty quotes Schwartz as saying:

> The real purpose of the special class seems to lie in the assignment of tasks which challenge the child's interest and capacity, the enrichment of the curriculum to include a wide variety of experiences which are not possible in a regular class, the opportunity to think and to discuss with other children of equal ability the problems of life within their grasp, the development of initiative and independence of thought, and last, but not least, the realization of responsibility to the community, looking toward the use of their powers for the benefit of mankind (15).

Carroll presents a strong argument for special education of the gifted: ". . . each child must receive the education best suited to his abilities and needs. To force upon all an education planned for average children, regardless of individual intellectual capacity, is to grant special privilege to the central group and to deny to the bright and the dull their rights (16)."

A large number and greater variety of learning experiences can be had by students in a homogeneously superior class, partly because less time is required for routine drill and remedial instruction (17). The enriched curriculum keeps the child's intellectual power active in an environment affording opportunities for association with children who are mentally and physically equal (18).

To the argument that the slower child is stimulated by the bright child, Goddard answered that the slower child is not stimulated but frightened (19). Instead of the special class making the gifted child feel superior, Carroll believes that it is the regular class where this happens and not the special class. He says that in an unselected group the gifted child is constantly made conscious of the fact that he is brighter than his classmates, so that different classes eliminate one of the causes of inflated self-esteem (20). Edith Carlson agrees with this view. She says that the "smugness, feelings of superiority, and other undesirable characteristics are alleviated when bright children are placed in special classes (21)."

Pregler recognizes (22) that there are advantages and disadvantages of each method of providing for the gifted child, but she believes, as do most educators, that it should be determined by what is best for the child. She believes that the partial segregation plan is the best yet devised for the particular situation in which she is located.

In a doctoral dissertation at Columbia University (23), Alice Keliher strongly opposes homogeneous grouping as a provision of caring for the gifted. Her major criticism is that segregation adversely affects society. Throughout her dissertation, however, she is careful to note that segregation, *as it exists today,* is not advisable. The dissertation, written in 1931, was aimed at the idea of complete segregation which was prevalent at that time. Today, in few programs is complete segregation followed. As is true about the Major Work Program, in Cleveland, Ohio, segregation, but not isolation, appears to be the more acceptable method.

Oliver summarizes present day thinking rather well in saying that mere segregation does not assure the gifted child of a better education. The ultimate need of the gifted child is an enriched program, whether it is in a homogeneous or heterogeneous classroom.

In discussing the criticisms of homogeneous grouping, Oliver says:

> There is considerable reason to believe that the alleged shortcomings [of special classes] are not inherent but are a matter of creating a proper environment and of establishing a proper attitude in the gifted, in the other pupils, in the teachers, and especially in the parents (24).

While no definite conclusions can be reached about the best method of providing for the gifted, it is important to recognize that the gifted child is being neglected and is in need of special attention.

## References

1. Walter B. Barbe, "Are Gifted Children Being Adequately Provided For?" *Educational Administration and Supervision,* Vol. 40, No. 7 (November 1954), pp. 405-413.

2. Walter B. Barbe and Dorothy Norris, "Special Classes for Gifted Children in Cleveland," *Exceptional Children,* Vol. 21, No.2 (November 1954), pp. 55-57.

3. Grace Loomis, "The Education of the Gifted Child," *Curriculum Bulletin,* No. 97 (December 12, 1951), Eugene, Oregon: School of Education, p.14.

4. Paul Witty, *The Gifted Child* (Boston: D. C. Heath, 1950), p. 55.

5. Howard A. Gray and Leta S. Hollingworth, "The Achievements of Gifted Children Enrolled and Not Enrolled in Special Opportunity Classes," *Journal of Educational Research,* Vol. XXIV (November 1931), p. 261.

6. Gertrude Hildreth, *Education of Gifted Children* (New York: Harper and Brothers, 1952), p. 40.

7. *Ibid.,* pp. 43-46.

8. Albert I. Oliver, "Administrative Problems in Educating the Gifted." *The Nations Schools,* Vol. 48, No. 5 (November 1951), pp. 44-46.

9. Hedwig O. Pregler, "Adjustment Through Partial Segregation," *National Elementary Principal,* Vol. 19 (September 1952), p. 243.

10. Harry J. Baker, "Characteristics of Superior Learners and the Relative Merits of Enrichment and Acceleration for Them." Supplementary Educational Monograph, No. 69. Edited by William S. Gray. Chicago: University of Chicago Press, October 1949, p. 157.

11. Lewis M. Terman and Melita H. Oden, *The Gifted Child Grows Up.* Stanford, California: Stanford University Press, 1947.

12. From personal correspondence with Miss Cora Lee Danielson.

13. Henry H. Goddard, *School Training of Gifted Children.* Yonkers-on-Hudson, New York: World Book Co., 1928, p. 1.

14. Educational Policies Commission, *Education of the Gifted.* National Educational Association of the United States and the American Association of School Administrators. Washington, D.C., 1950, pp. 56-58.

15. Witty, *op. cit.,* p. 189.

16. Herbert Carroll, *Genius in the Making.* New York: McGraw-Hill Book Co., Inc., 1940, p. 253.

17. Educational Policies Commn., *op. cit.,* p. 53.

18. W. J. Osburn and Ben J. Rohan, *Enriching the Curriculum for Gifted Children* (New York: The Macmillan Co., 1931), p.186.

19. Goddard, *op. cit.,* pp. 27-33.

20. Carroll, *op. cit.,* p. 213.

21. Witty, *op. cit.,* p. 188.

22. Pregler, *op. cit.,* p. 242.

23. Alice Keliher, "A Critical Study of Homogeneous Grouping." New York: Columbia University Press, 1931.

24. Oliver, *op. cit.,* p. 44.

*Leonard G. Lanza*
*William G. Vassar*

# Designing and Implementing a Program for the Gifted and Talented

*I*n this day of a thrust toward a more coordinated effort between general and special education, the principal's commitment to the needs of gifted and talented children is more important than ever before. Every school in the nation has some children with demonstrated or potential ability to reach extraordinary achievement levels. How a principal recognizes the needs of the gifted and talented and how he attempts to meet them will be determining factors in how successfully a given school meets the needs of its gifted.

Schools have always had some staff members who provide a stimulating cognitive and affective learning environment for such children. Today, with the wide-spread mobility of teachers in our schools, such fragmented opportunities do not assist a gifted child who is held to a rigid curriculum design geared to the middle of the continuum. The principal needs to be actively involved on a continuing basis if a school is going to provide a meaningful program for its gifted and talented children.

It is obvious that the plans a principal designs for the gifted and talented should be coordinated with any provisions already existing for such children in the school district. The principal should be well aware of the policies; the available instructional, pupil personnel, and special educational services; the local community's attitudes; and the various state and federal resources relating to all aspects of gifted and talented children. Limitations may be fostered by these conditions, and ways of reaching the goals may have to be varied depending on the local situation.

One basic thought must be kept in mind. Any special program or service for any exceptional child is basically one segment of meeting the needs of individual groups of children. It is not a design that gives special privileges to a select few for a narrow purpose.

To demonstrate some of the planning that might be involved in develop-

Lanza, Leonard G. and Vassar, William G. "Designing and Implementing a Program for the Gifted and Talented." *National Elementary Principal,* Vol. LI, No. 5, February, 1972.

ing a program for the gifted and talented, we have reconstructed the dialogue that took place between us prior to implementing a program for the gifted and talented in the elementary schools of Simsbury.

LANZA: *Several teachers and I have been talking recently about some of the youngsters in our school for whom we feel we are not doing enough. These are youngsters who have many superior traits. My staff has many questions that have resulted from a number of brainstorming sessions. We hoped that you could provide some assistance as we explore the possibilities for programs and services for the gifted.*

VASSAR: It might be a good starting point to discuss the education of the gifted and talented in the 70's. Who are they? Where are they? Are there more of them than we originally thought? We should probably discuss a broadened concept of giftedness. For many years, we discussed the kind of youngster we call the high IQ, highly motivated, highly interested child who, the American public figured, would make it anyway. This is one particular segment of giftedness that we have provided for to some extent. In the past 10 years, we have been able to broaden our definition of giftedness to include a number of other subgroups. The one we have already talked about is a legitimate subgroup. It's the kind that many school systems feel comfortable in starting with as a target group.

The second group is called highly creative, productive thinkers, youngsters who are very original, fluent, flexible, or divergent in their thinking. This is another identifiable target group with whom we can work in your school. A third group we might discuss is a group we call bright underachievers. Much has been written about bright underachievers, but many administrators are hesitant to recognize this group as a target group in the area of the gifted. These are children who score at a high level and should make it, if we just look at tests. However, because of some social or environmental inhibitors, they do not make it. There are certain kinds of stimulus programs we can provide for these children. Then we have the disadvantaged child in the urban and sparsely populated areas of the country. We have found from recent research that we are able to uncover potential giftedness in these areas, so again we find another category of giftedness in disadvantaged potential. These are children who are judged to possess potential superior ability but who have been inhibited by certain cultural, environmental, and economic limitations in their life style.

LANZA: *Are there other types of talented youngsters we should be thinking about, perhaps in some nonacademic areas?*

VASSAR: There is the whole area of the arts. You may want to consider a number of target groups of youngsters who may have outstanding talent, or the potential to gain talent, in the creative arts. The creative arts may be broken down into three subcategories: music, the visual arts (oils, sculpture, and so on), and the performing arts (theater, dance, media, and so on). For example, musical talent can be considered from both the composition and performance standpoint, and the performing arts from both visual and a performance point of view. As you can see, our concept of giftedness has really broadened in the last decade. We are talking about many more kinds of youngsters than we were following the launching of Sputnik, when we were searching for limited groups of academically oriented children.

LANZA: *You've mentioned all kinds of possibilities for working with a variety of students. It seems to me that we may have to limit ourselves in the beginning. Where do we begin? How can we identify these youngsters? How do we determine, pragmatically, what we should do with them?*

VASSAR: I don't really think we will ever reach the point where we have ultimate sophistication in an identification process for any child in our schools. Let's consider the Terman-type youngster, the high IQ or highly motivated youngster. You could come up with seven or eight different criteria based on both standardized testing and subjective criteria. If we talk about cuts, such as IQ cuts, on any kind of standardized testing, we're talking about roughly two standard deviations above the mean. We must also take into consideration the fact that there are many subjective factors we can utilize in terms of the academically bright or potentially bright. We can use teacher checklists, rating scales, observations, anecdotal records, physical well-being, and emotional stability. I think the key factor in the identification process is that we use a multiplicity of selection procedures for such children. In the area of the arts, which lends itself to an almost completely subjective analysis, we've had success in utilizing artists, musicians, and sculptors in the identification process. We should think in terms of conceptual attributes such as intense interest, involvement, and advanced skills in the specific talent area. In the creative-productive areas, we consider factors based on Guilford's Structure of Intellect, the hierarchy of intelligence, and things that evoke fluency, flexibility, and originality. In the area of disadvantaged potential, Torrance, for example, has given us much insight into the value systems of subcultures. When trying to identify the potential of the disadvantaged gifted, we should take into consideration the value system of the subdominant culture and utilize its various components in our identification process.

LANZA: *When looking at our specific needs, within our school or community, what other factors do we have to be concerned with?*

VASSAR: You should take a look at an administrative design. By this we mean the organizational design you use to provide time and space, staffing, and instruction to such children in your school setting. You should take a look at a number of different designs, such as special classes. This particular concept doesn't enjoy too much popularity today, since it completely separates special youngsters from their peer groups. You should also consider a semiseparation design in which the youngsters spend some of their time in a regular class and an appropriate span of time in a special setting with differentiated provisions for their academic ability or special talent area. This design seems to bridge the gap between the student's special education and general education needs. In some schools, a small group of children works with a special teacher in a special area of interest. Design may be considered a secondary component of programing, but much of it will be molded by the philosophy and objectives of your school and district, in addition to such things as availability of facilities, transportation, staff, and the feelings of the community.

LANZA: *How do we find out what the needs of our school are?*

VASSAR: The first thing you should do in your planning is to analyze the needs of these youngsters and the needs of the staff relative to providing services to such children. Perhaps you will want to set up a planning committee, including teachers, pupil personnel staff, administration, and parents. This team could determine which categories of gifted children they should start working with; that is, which group or groups of the gifted and talented demonstrate the top priority need in your school at this point in time. You should consider what kinds of staff you have to work with and whether you have the economic feasibility of hiring additional staff. The facility and transportation needs also have to be taken into consideration. After the analysis of needs has been completed, you should be ready to design your long-range and short-range objectives to meet the needs of your gifted and talented children.

LANZA: *Are there other program elements that are equally important or perhaps even more important that we should consider as we move ahead with our planning?*

VASSAR: It seems apparent that some program elements are more significant than others. Essentially, the key features put forth by Renzulli and Ward* are necessary elements for programs designed for education of gifted and talented children. These program characteristics are philosophy and objectives, identification and placement, the curriculum, the teacher, and program organization and operation. To be sure, each of these characteristics should be an essential ingredient in any school program. However, these aspects of differentiated education for the gifted are apt to be pushed aside in the mound of daily administrative trivia unless they receive specific, direct consideration. We shouldn't ignore a statement that is found constantly in the literature, "Time and qualified personnel must be made available if special education for the gifted is to be a meaningful reality."

LANZA: *You mentioned an area that we have not discussed yet. What are some of your feelings about teachers of the gifted? Are there certain characteristics we should take into consideration?*

VASSAR: It has been shown that teachers of the gifted and talented need to possess some degree of special preparation, characteristics, skills, and knowledge. However, specific credential requirements have not been designed for these teachers, and I see no immediate need for specific certification in this area of special education. Almost through necessity, it seems, educational programs for the gifted and talented are complex. Teachers of these students should be familiar with the literature and the research. They should also be able to translate research findings into

*Renzulli, Joseph, and Ward, Virgil. *Diagnostic and Evaluative Scales for Differential Education for the Gifted*, 1970.

workable, practical programs. These specific elements can be attended to by inservice programs and graduate courses in the education of the gifted and talented offered by various institutions of higher learning.

Far too often, the task of attempting to familiarize prospective teachers of these youngsters with modern advances in learning theory and their application to programs falls upon an already overburdened principal. Unless he is particularly inspired in that area, it is apt to be just another job, a reaction rather than a meaningful act. Differentiated curriculum designs stressing special qualities such as originality, fluency of ideas, intellectual curiosity, independence of thought, and conceptual elaboration require special preparation. Facing the prospect of having to provide assistance in this preparation adds to the staggering array of variables that often persuades administrators to postpone what they know should be done.

Just as with any "special" teacher, there are limitless possibilities for internal scheduling of teachers for the gifted. Variations will occur depending upon the number of students involved. Scheduling will vary depending on whether a teacher is full time in a given school or if he works in more than one school. Different administrative designs require different staffing considerations.

The teacher of a special class will certainly have different kinds of problems than an itinerant teacher or one who works in a semiseparation design. The full-time teacher of the gifted and talented, whether he works in a special class or semiseparation design, has the greatest opportunity for scheduling flexibility. His expertise with differentiated curriculum and teaching strategies can go far in benefiting other staff members. He should be able to function with his special students and also serve as liaison with the "feeder" teachers who send their gifted and talented to him for special instruction.

When scheduling a semiseparation program, for example, a number of factors should be considered. What subjects will the students miss? How often and for how long? Is the student responsible for any work that took place while he was out of his regular class? It is in these areas that the uninformed, nonsupportive feeder teacher can inhibit a special program. The attitude of other staff members in the school is an important factor that should be considered in designing a program. Many of these inhibiting attitudes come from myths and misinformation regarding the gifted and talented, and many can be eliminated through a comprehensive inservice orientation program for all staff members.

LANZA: *How much additional administrative detail will a special program necessitate?*

VASSAR: The amount of additional detail involved in a special program will depend on a number of factors, including the complexity of the program and the numbers and types of personnel involved. For example, a program that has the services of a guidance counselor at the elementary level will more than likely vary considerably from a program in which the school principal is primarily responsible for the administrative details.

Regardless of who does the work and what kinds of forms are used, some basic kinds of data should be compiled; at minimum, all available test data and teacher recommendations in some form. Beyond that, interest inventories, personality assessments, counseling anecdotes, case study reports, and evaluative data all add significantly to data banks. If one of the purposes of the program is to provide a differentiated curriculum for the gifted and talented, then it stands to reason that the more that is known about each youngster, the better the opportunity to meet his individual needs.

LANZA: *What has been your experience with the general public's reaction to special programs for gifted and talented children? What should we look for in terms of the various publics we will have to work with in the community?*

VASSAR: The best instructional programs can be doomed to failure if they are not based on sound public understanding and support. Today's communities feel a closeness to their schools, and they are increasingly sensitive to changes within them. Schools cannot move far from the ideas of the various publics without experiencing difficulties. Any school seeking to develop a sound program for gifted and talented children must be concerned with keeping the many interest groups of the community informed. Parents, for example, feel they have a right to be informed, and they are correct in that feeling. The first step toward effective community relations is an informed staff committed to the special program for the gifted and talented. A divided professional staff can quickly destroy the best efforts of a planned program. The principal should assume a major role in informing and working with the staff and the various publics. Those who help to develop a program are usually its best supporters. More so than with other groups, it seems, the parents of the gifted and talented are actively interested in their children's individual needs. As a group, they can be counted on to give active support to a program, if they are well informed.

LANZA: *Let's assume that we have decided which target group of children we are going to create a special program for and exactly what kind of program it is going to be. Am I correct in feeling that close contact with the parents of those youngsters will go a long way toward getting the program off to a smooth start?*

VASSAR: Opinions about counseling parents of gifted children range from one extreme to the other. There are those who do not want to rock the boat, so they sit back and say nothing until they are forced to react. On the other hand, there are those who advocate that school leadership is necessary in establishing parent groups. If a program is expected to operate successfully, parent counseling is necessary. The degree of involvement with parents will differ, depending on the complexity of the programs. The major task will, of course, occur during the first year of operation, when the identification process reveals that it will be necessary to communicate with a large number of parents. An effective informational group meeting or series of meetings, should be held to establish the groundwork for the special program. Everyone who is going to be involved with the program has to know what it is all about.

Parents should be informed about the nature of giftedness, its implications, how they can assist their child, and what the school intends to do. From that point on, counseling will be, more than likely, on an individual basis.

The individual who does the counseling must be familiar with the education of the gifted and talented, lest he do more harm than good when dealing with parents. Parents will be quick to notice uncertainty and a lack of commitment. They must have the feeling that the school is performing a worthwhile service for their children. With that feeling at the start, success can be predicted; without it, failure may result.

LANZA: *We certainly have a number of ideas with which to work. Believe it or not, we can really envision ourselves getting involved in some classroom activities with these gifted youngsters.*

VASSAR: It is certainly desirable for the principal to allow himself time to keep in touch with students involved in a special program for the gifted. He can evaluate student and program progress more accurately if he is directly involved.

Perhaps it is inevitable that the involvement will be at its peak during the first year of operation. It is during that year that the principal will be involved in the identification process and parent conferences. Of course, it is during that first year, also, that most of the "bugs" will occur, whether they be with other staff members, students, or one of the various publics. A working knowledge of what is being done with these youngsters will go a long way toward preventing some problems and solving others.

LANZA: *You've been extremely helpful. We now have a much clearer picture of the many factors that go into developing and designing a program for gifted and talented children. To summarize, let me enumerate the key items that we should be aware of:*

*1. The principal should be the key individual in designing and developing the program in his school.*

*2. Everyone involved must have a thorough understanding of the broadened concept of giftedness.*

*3. An analysis of existing student and staff needs must be made for the individual school.*

*4. The philosophy and objectives of the program must be established.*

*5. An identification process for the specific target group must be developed.*

*6. An organizational design for the placement of students must be developed.*

*7. The principal and staff must develop a differentiated curriculum for gifted and talented children.*

*8. Differentiated teaching strategies must be developed.*

*9. Appropriate instructional and supportive staff must be selected.*

*10. The role of various publics in the community must be considered for better public understanding.*

*11. Articulation and coordination with other programs in general and special education in the district has to be considered.*

*12. A definitive plan for evaluation must be developed.*

The foregoing reconstructed dialogue was designed to provide general direction for elementary school principals in the development of programs for the gifted and talented. By their very nature, such programs will vary greatly from school to school and even from classroom to classroom. If an elementary principal will consider the various factors mentioned in the dialogue, he can be reasonably certain that he will be operating on a solid foundation for meeting the needs of his gifted and talented children.

*Joseph S. Renzulli*

# Identifying Key Features
# in Programs for the Gifted

Abstract: A study was undertaken to determine which features and characteristics of programs for the gifted are considered by authorities in the field to be the most necessary and sufficient for comprehensive programing. The seven features that were considered to be relatively more essential than others have been designated as key features of differential programs for the gifted. Discussion includes a description of the important dimensions of these key features.

In recent years renewed attention and effort have been directed toward the development of special programs for gifted and talented students. Evidence of heightened interest in this area is found in the rapidly increasing number of states which have taken legislative action dealing with special provisions for the gifted. In addition to increased support at the state level, a number of communities have developed programs through the use of resources available locally and available under various titles of the Elementary and Secondary Education Act. In view of the renewed interest in this area, it may be useful to call attention to those aspects of differential education for the gifted which are considered to be the keystones of a quality program. Concentration upon a relatively limited number of indispensable program characteristics provides the complicated task of program development with structure and focus, and such an approach may be helpful in avoiding some of the hastily contrived adaptations that characterized the post Sputnik era—adaptations which, in many cases, suffered an equally hasty demise.

The study reported here was undertaken to identify characteristics considered to be the most necessary for a successful program of differential education for the gifted. The purpose of the study was to isolate through systematic procedures a basic core of key features that could be used for program development and evaluation. The concept of key features represents an essential part of the rationale upon which the study was based. Reflection upon the entire span of characteristics which any educational program might possibly include, from the quality of the classroom teacher to the adequacy of the supplies and materials that a teacher has at her disposal, leads to the conclusion that certain program features and characteristics are extremely more consequential than others. With respect to the whole array of practices and provisions that possess potential, although in varying degrees, to further the objectives of differential education for the gifted, the concept of key features holds that concentration on a minimal number of highly significant features will facilitate both program development and evaluation. This concept also holds that if the more essential features of a program are found to be present and operating excellently, then the probability of less critical features being similarly present is high.

## Procedure

The first step in carrying out the study consisted of searching the literature in order to identify the principal aspects of the problem and to locate relevant information and ideas that might prove useful in developing a comprehensive list of features and processes of programs for the gifted. This initial step included a nationwide survey aimed at locating lists of criteria used at state and local levels to evaluate special programs for the gifted.

The second step involved the selection of a panel of 21 expert judges. A larger group of persons who had made substantial contributions to the field of education for the gifted was identified according to a number of specified criteria; then this group was asked to nominate, from among themselves, those persons whom they considered to be the most qualified for judging the adequacy of educational experiences for superior and talented students.

The third procedure consisted of developing a relatively comprehensive list of general features and processes which represented various identifiable dimensions of programs for the gifted. This list was based upon those aspects of differential education which have received considerable and continued emphasis in both the general literature on the gifted and in the literature dealing more specifically with programs and program evaluation. The list was submitted to the panel of judges with the requests that (a) they rank in order of importance those features which they consider to be the most necessary for a worthy program, and (b) they stop ranking when that number of features which would assure a program of high quality had been reached. Thus, it can be seen that isolating the key features of programs for the gifted was based on the judgment of persons who were considered to represent the very best thinking in the field of education for the gifted.

The results of this inquiry were tabulated by means of a pooled frequency rating technique that was based on the popular method of assigning to the most frequently chosen response the rank of number one. In order that the rank numbers used in summing the data correspond to increasing magnitudes of importance, each rank was assigned a rank value. The rank values consisted of a series of numbers which were in the exact reverse order of the ranks. Since the maximum number of program features ranked by any one member of the panel of judges equalled 16, this rank value was assigned to rank one. Accordingly, rank two was assigned a rank value of 15 and so on, down to rank 16 which was assigned a rank value of one. These results are presented in Table 1. The pooled frequency rating of each program feature was expressed in terms of its total rank value. In addition to the 15 program features included in the original inquiry, Table 1 also contains 7 write ins submitted by various members of the panel and the total rank value of each. The program features are listed in hierarchical order according to total rank value.

**TABLE 1**

**Matrix of Frequencies with Which Each of 15 Program Features Were Ranked in Each of 16 Positions by 21 Selected Judges**

| Program features | 1 | 2 | 3 | 4 | 5 | 6 | 7 | 8 | 9 | 10 | 11 | 12 | 13 | 14 | 15 | 16 | Total rank value |
|---|---|---|---|---|---|---|---|---|---|---|---|---|---|---|---|---|---|
| *Rank value* | 16 | 15 | 14 | 13 | 12 | 11 | 10 | 9 | 8 | 7 | 6 | 5 | 4 | 3 | 2 | 1 | |
| The teacher: selection and training | 7 | 4 | 4 | 1 | 1 | 1 | 1 | | | | | | | | | | 274 |
| | (112) | (60) | (56) | (13) | (12) | (11) | (10) | | | | | | | | | | |
| The curriculum: purposefully distinctive | 3 | 4 | 6 | 1 | 2 | 1 | 1 | | | | | | | | | | 240 |
| | (48) | (60) | (74) | (13) | (24) | (11) | (10) | | | | | | | | | | |
| Student selection procedures | | 4 | 4 | 2 | 3 | 2 | 2 | | | | | | | | | | 220 |
| | | (60) | (56) | (26) | (36) | (22) | (20) | | | | | | | | | | |
| A statement of philosophy and objectives | 9 | 1 | 2 | 1 | | | | | 1 | | | | | | | | 208 |
| | (144) | (15) | (28) | (13) | | | | | (8) | | | | | | | | |
| Staff orientation | 1 | 6 | 2 | 1 | 1 | 3 | | | 1 | | | | | | | | 200 |
| | (16) | (90) | (28) | (13) | (12) | (33) | | | (8) | | | | | | | | |
| A plan of evaluation | | | | | 4 | 4 | 2 | 1 | 1 | | 1 | | 1 | | | | 139 |
| | | | | | (48) | (44) | (20) | (9) | (8) | | (6) | | (4) | | | | |
| Administrative responsibility | | 1 | 1 | 2 | 3 | 1 | 1 | | | 1 | | 1 | | | | | 125 |
| | | (15) | (14) | (26) | (36) | (11) | (10) | | | (7) | | (5) | | | | | |
| Guidance services | | | | 1 | 2 | 1 | 3 | 1 | 1 | | | | | | | | 95 |
| | | | | (13) | (24) | (11) | (30) | (9) | (8) | | | | | | | | |
| Ability grouping and/or acceleration | | | | 2 | 1 | 2 | 1 | 1 | 1 | | | 1 | | | | | 92 |
| | | | | (26) | (12) | (22) | (10) | (9) | (8) | | | (5) | | | | | |
| Special equipment and facilities | | | | 3 | 1 | 1 | | | | 1 | | | 1 | | | | 73 |
| | | | | (39) | (12) | (11) | | | | (7) | | | (4) | | | | |
| Use of community resources | | | 1 | | | | | 2 | 1 | 1 | | | | 1 | | | 50 |
| | | | (14) | | | | | (18) | (8) | (7) | | | | (3) | | | |
| Early admission | | | | 1 | | 1 | | 1 | 1 | | | | | | | | 41 |
| | | | | (13) | | (11) | | (9) | (8) | | | | | | | | |
| Community interpretation | | | | | | 1 | | 3 | | | | | | | 1 | | 40 |
| | | | | | | (11) | | (27) | | | | | | | (2) | | |
| Supplementary expenditures | | | | 1 | | 1 | | | | | 1 | 1 | | | | | 35 |
| | | | | (13) | | (11) | | | | | (6) | (5) | | | | | |
| A program of research | | | | 1 | | | | | 1 | | | | | 1 | | 1 | 25 |
| | | | | (13) | | | | | (8) | | | | | (3) | | (1) | |

Note:—The seven write ins, each receiving one vote, and their total rank values, are as follows: Community Support for Quality Education, 10; Morale and Esprit de Corps, 9; Student Assessment and Reassessment, 9; Student Performance, Evaluation, and Reporting, 10; Interpretation to Parents and Selected Students, 9; Small and Flexible Groups, 13; and Pupil Interpretation, 13.

Numbers in parentheses denote the weighted value of each frequency, i.e., the frequency multiplied by its rank value.

It is readily apparent from Table 1 that the uppermost 7 features of differential programs emerged as a relatively distinguishable group. It should be noted that the remaining features were both good and desirable elements of special programs; however, the ratings of the judges seemed to warrant the assignment of priorities to certain aspects of program development and evaluation. For this reason, the 7 features which achieved the highest collective ratings by the panel of judges were designated as key features. In the sections that follow, brief attention will be given to these important aspects of differential programs.

## Discussion

### KEY FEATURE A: THE TEACHER.

Although there is little question that all students should have well qualified teachers, the relatively greater demands made upon teachers by vigorous and imaginative young minds require that special attention be given to the selection and training of teachers for gifted and talented students. A number of statements in the literature in the form of principles (Ward, 1961; Williams, 1958) call attention to this important dimension of special programing and Newland (1962) has provided us with a breakdown of essential qualifications that can serve as guides in teacher selection.

### KEY FEATURE B: THE CURRICULUM.

Experiences comprising the curriculum for gifted and talented students should be recognizably different from the general educational program that is geared toward the ability level of average learners. These experiences should be purposefully designed to evoke and develop superior behavioral potentialities in both academic areas and in the fine and performing arts. A systematic and comprehensive program of studies should reach all children identified as gifted at every grade level and in all areas of the curriculum where giftedness is educationally significant. The careful development of distinctive syllabi, methods, and materials will help guard against a fragmentary or "more of the same" conception of differential education. A number of Ward's (1961) theoretical principles of education for the gifted are particularly relevant to curriculum development and can provide valuable guidance in constructing truly differential experiences.

### KEY FEATURE C: STUDENT SELECTION PROCEDURES.

The literature on giftedness is replete with information relating to the identification and placement of superior students. This key feature acknowledges the existence of all reliably identifiable types of giftedness and calls for the appropriate and discriminating use of several identifying instruments and processes. Periodic screening to obviate overlooking talent of any kind should be followed by increasingly refined, exacting, and fair appraisal of specific abilities. Identification and placement procedures should be carried out at least once annually, and provisions for succeeding search beyond the initial screening and for transfer into and out of the program should also exist.

KEY FEATURE D: A STATEMENT OF PHILOSOPHY AND OBJECTIVES.

The essential role played by statements of philosophy and objectives in guiding the developing of *all* educational enterprises is well known. Underlying statements of philosophy and objectives should take into account the arguments that support special programs, the broad and specific goals of the program, and the distinction between the objectives of general education and those that have particular relevance to differential education for the gifted. Although there is some possibility of well developed programs existing without written statement about the nature of philosophy and objectives, it seems highly improbable that school systems that have not taken the time to develop such documents will make serious inroads toward the implementation of comprehensive differential programing.

KEY FEATURE E: STAFF ORIENTATION.

In order to succeed, any educational venture needs the cooperation and support of those persons who are responsible for its implementation. A sympathetic attitude toward special provisions for the gifted and a basic understanding of the theory and operation of a special program on the part of all staff members are considered to be important elements in helping to realize a program's maximum effectiveness. In most instances, staff members not directly connected with the gifted student program usually participate indirectly by identifying and recommending students for placement. It is therefore necessary that they recognize the nature and needs of potential program participants, are knowledgeable about the available facilities, and are committed to the value of differential qualities of experience.

KEY FEATURE F: A PLAN OF EVALUATION.

Within the field of education for the gifted, the need for evidence of program effectiveness is well recognized. But the particularized objectives and relatively unique learning experiences that characterize truly differential programs require the use of objective evaluative schemes that take into account a variety of important program dimensions. One approach to program evaluation developed by Ward and Renzulli (1967) utilized each of the key features here reported as focal points around which a set of evaluative scales were developed. The instrument, entitled Diagnostic and Evaluative Scales for Differential Education for the Gifted, was designed to point out specific areas in which program improvement seems warranted.

A clear designation of administrative responsibility is an essential condition for the most efficient operation of all school programs. Although size and resources of a school system will determine the amount of administrative time that can be allotted to the gifted student program, it is necessary that the person in charge of even the smallest program be given sufficient time and resources to carry out his administrative duties in this area. Already overburdened administrators, supervisors, and teachers who are given the responsibility of a special program as an extra assignment without a corresponding reduction in other duties are likely to approach the task with less than optimal enthusiasm.

## Summary and Conclusions

The intent of this study was to isolate those features within programs for gifted that are considered by recognized authorities in the field to be the most essential for a worthy program. The effort was aimed at providing a sound rationale for decision making to persons who are involved in various aspects of programing for the exceptionally able. On the basis of the rankings by the panel of judges, there appears to be justification for designating certain program elements and characteristics as key features in programs for the gifted. Such a designation is considered to be useful in identifying areas in which concentration should be placed in the process of program development and evaluation. The key features isolated in the present study do not pertain to any given pattern or organization, but rather attempt to embrace excellent practices presently operating, either individually or in varying combinations, and practices that can and should be inaugurated in view of the behavioral potential of students who possess identifiably superior abilities.

## References

Newland, T.E. Some observations on essential qualifications of teachers of the mentally superior. *Exceptional Children,* 1962, 29, 111-114.

Ward, V.S. *Educating the gifted: An axiomatic approach.* Columbus, Ohio: Charles E. Merrill, 1961.

Ward, V.S., & Renzulli, J.S. Program evaluation in differential education for the gifted. In The Council for Exceptional Children, *CEC selected convention papers* 1967. Washington D. C.: CEC, 1967. Pp. 36-41.

Williams, C.W. Characteristics and objectives of a program for the gifted. In National Council for the Study of Education, *Education for the gifted,* 57th Yearbook. Chicago: University of Chicago Press, 1958. Pp. 147-165.

*William M. Griffin*

# Schedules, Bells, Groups, and Independent Study

$T$o produce students who are effective in independent study is what education should be all about. Independent study is not just a feature of organizational or curriculum change which can be added to or deleted from the school's program. It is the system of self-instruction in which each individual learner operates within the total system of the school's instruction. That these two systems are interdependent comes as no news to the astute practitioner bent on developing an independent study program. That there is need to explore the dimensions of these systems for factors which really make a difference also comes as no surprise.

What does it mean to be effective in independent study? How do you know? What are the conditions? How do they relate? One way of exploring the process of independent study is to set forth what effective students do in this kind of learning situation. It is possible to find many statements in the literature related to independent study which cite operational practices associated with the idea of independent study. These practices when edited for duplication of thought, overlapping of meaning, clarity of expression, and grouped into natural clusters, suggest a systems approach to the job of defining the process of independent study.

Approximately one hundred and fifty practices were collected, edited, and grouped into natural sub-trait clusters by the author. It was found that seven clusters would contain all of the practices. The definition contains five examples of practices to exemplify each sub-trait. These are the five ranked highest in importance by jury validation.

## Independent Study

The term independent study means a learning situation within the school

Griffin, William M. "Schedules, Bells, Groups, and Independant Study." from: Beggs, David W. III and Buffie, Edward G. (Eds.) *Independant Study,* Bloomington, Indiana: Indiana University Press, 1965, pp. 1-8.

day which allows a student to develop personal competencies through experiences as an individual but in interaction with others when needed. It is characterized by freedom from constant supervision. Students read, write, contemplate, listen to records and tapes, view, record, memorize, create, build, practice, exercise, experiment, examine, analyze, investigate, question, discover, and converse. Independent study emphasizes the individual's role in learning. It implies that all students possess potentialities for self-initiative, self-discipline, resourcefulness, productivity, and self-evaluation. In this respect, a student performing effectively in independent study is one who:

PERCEIVES WORTHWHILE THINGS TO DO: *for example,* pursues instructional leads for further study, compares various sources of information, asks relationship-type questions, integrates information from different subject-matter fields, summarizes findings and places them in correct frame of reference.

PERSONALIZES LEARNING: *for example,* casts about for a project of real interest and value, gives own unique reasons for doing what is done, prepares a plan to structure the study, distributes work schedule to allow for other commitments, expresses satisfaction in a task of own selection and implementation.

EXERCISES SELF-DISCIPLINE: *for example,* accepts limits of the school without denying self, displays sustained and conscientious industry, seeks procedural authority for own point of view and actions, works in harmony with others in groups of two or three, cooperates in maintaining a climate for individual work.

MAKES USE OF HUMAN RESOURCES: *for example,* initiates contacts with teachers, shares interpretations, interests, and ideas with a teacher in good exchange, comes prepared for conference discussions, uses contacts with teachers to clarify thinking with pertinent and relevant questioning, investigates suggestions which are offered.

MAKES USE OF MATERIAL RESOURCES: *for example,* broadens own knowledge through related readings, makes use of tapes, records, and projectuals to expand knowledge, displays deftness in locating library materials, recognizes and uses the tools of the trade, constructs special materials and devices for use in one's work.

PRODUCES RESULTS: *for example,* works at appropriate pace and follows through to completion, plans projects which are subject to accomplishment, states clear objectives, displays habit of getting down to work, finds application for a creative idea.

STRIVES FOR IMPROVEMENT: *for example,* seeks advice from competent people, corrects errors on own, studies authoritative sources for best practices, uses group sessions to test out ideas and clarify issues, evaluates material in light of personal experiences and firsthand knowledge.

These experiences under independent study may be either related or unrelated to course requirements.

The parts of this chapter that follow deal essentially with the conditions in the school's environment believed to foster independent study. Discussion will be directed to the relationship of independent study to the school's system of instruction (schedules, bells, and groups), and to various other components of the school's instructional system.

## The Student's Schedule and Independent Study

A student needs to have control of a substantial amount of his own time in school, and he should have this available to him in time modules appropriate for a variety of tasks. It takes time to read a book, to retrieve information from the library, to define a problem, to hold conferences, to exchange ideas, and to refine one's work.

Traditionally, the schedule maker has tried to avoid assigning a student to a study hall for more than a single period at a time. Now it is apparent that for many independent study purposes longer periods of time are not only desirable but also sometimes necessary. When the independent study portions of a student's week are developed in blocks of time and scheduled in spaces not used for classroom instruction, there is no necessity for the student in independent study to be interrupted by the classroom bell schedule. [Examples of schedules which facilitate the use of independent study as the method of learning are given in Chapter Seven.]

This ringing of bells has been the time-honored way to signal the beginning and end of classroom periods. Usually this has affected the entire student population in very much the same way. The rigidity with which students have been locked into this type of organization has, of course, become objectionable. The question as far as independent study is concerned is not whether bells ring or no bells ring. It is what the bell means to each individual in the school that counts. If it means something different from one individual to another, it would seem we are headed in the right direction.

For the most part, the things students do during their independent study time represent experiences which cannot be scheduled by the administration. Many students prefer to learn creatively—by questioning, experimenting, risking, testing, and modifying ideas. Educators must have faith enough in these young people to permit and encourage this to happen. Independent study opens improved ways of individualizing instruction.

## The Teachers's Schedule and Independent Study

A teacher needs to have control of a substantial amount of his own time in school in order to have the necessary flexibility to arrange individual conferences with students and to engage in professional preparation and planning. This is the interaction level between teacher and pupil and between teacher and teacher which lies beyond the mechanics of the master schedule. Here success depends to a large extent upon fresh diagnostic data. The teacher must see his role as that of motivating, encouraging, and helping the student to make effective use of the many resources around him. Independent study has been called education by appointment. The use of human resources in the process of independent study cannot be "scheduled" by the school in the usual sense of the word. Human resources can only be mobilized by those directly involved.

Independent study is not study carried out by a student entirely on his own. When a student is seeking procedural authority, defining a problem, developing ideas, testing points of view, taking certain risks, he needs to feel the undergirding influence of a teacher whom he respects. A skillful teacher can provide the right amount of help at a time when it is needed most and thus prevent a student engaging needlessly in large amounts of unproductive activity. In this role, the teacher counsels, advises, and plans. [This is discussed in some detail in Chapters Five and Eight.]

The availability of a teacher to a student engaged in independent study is increased when teachers work in teams. Under a team arrangement within a block of time or on a distributed schedule throughout the day, there is a great possibility that a student may find one of his teachers available. From a scheduling point of view, this is important. If independent study is to flourish in our schools, students should be given every opportunity possible to brush with exciting teachers. This is where the incentive for independent study rubs off.

## Group Instruction and Independent Study

Independent study probably thrives best when group instruction is of an "open system." When conducted for a period of several weeks an instructional unit can provide a host of leads for individual pursuit. If a teacher is to perceive his classroom group as individuals, in planning the study of a topic, an issue, a problem, or a theme he should first raise the question: What in this unit can students learn best by themselves? To resolve this question calls for acquaintance with individual students, cooperative planning, and some ideas for individual projects. The author has found that materials written for teacher use are sometimes helpful to students as they are casting about for a project of real interest and value. The concept that students are at times their own teachers is sometimes taken lightly. However, independent study is built on this premise.

Students vary in their ability to perceive worthwhile things to do. Guilford calls this trait "sensitivity to problems" and has developed scales for its measurement. Teachers who are sensitive to this kind of individual difference in students will make a special effort to help certain students get started.

Large group instruction with its multimedia impact serves to create ideas for independent study. In the area of the arts it is particularly effective to alert students to possibilities for developing their individual interests and talents. Independent study in the arts has particular significance for those students unable to elect courses in this area.

Independent study may be related to group instruction in other ways. This relationship can take one of several forms. Students in an "honors program" are sometimes excused from classes, but they continue to work with their teachers who act as consultants. In other instances, a formal tutorial arrangement between teacher and pupil is worked out; here the dialogue can strengthen the independent work. There are examples of contract plans and released time in which occasional checks with the group are a stimulant. Giving individual assignments to students within classes is an obvious approach to encouraging independent work. Another plan whereby pupils actually spend time each Saturday on a college campus in seminar work has been successful. This kind of experience gives incentive to pupils in small high schools. In any of these arrangements reports from schools indicate that students need access to a teacher or group activity in order to keep going.

## Spaces and Facilities and Independent Study

Secondary schools have been so completely scheduled with group instruction over the past half century that they have neglected to consider the potential of individual students to schedule themselves. They are expected to do this when they go to college, yet they have had little experience to sustain them.

If students are to take responsibility for their own learning throughout the school day, they must have access to appropriate spaces and facilities. In general, they should find the spaces and facilities for independent study to be open, staffed, and ready for use during all hours of the school day. Independent study facilities occupy a position in school life similar to that of service centers in community life. When we go to a store during business hours, we expect to find it open. When a student has need to use the language lab, for example, he should expect to find it open. Other facilities which fall into the same category of "open" utilization include: resource centers, libraries, programmed materials, study carrels, laboratory bench space, practice rooms, exercise rooms, testing services, audiovisual devices, conference spaces, guidance services, and specialized workshops and studios. Schools providing these facilities in their instructional environment should go further and make sure that they are available to students throughout the whole day.

## The Development of Competency and Independent Study

Webster defines the word "independent" as: "having or forming a competency, . . . hence, self-reliant, self-confident, self-respecting, . . . not subservient." These meanings are descriptive of the learner. In independent study it is not the study that is independent, it is the learner that is independent. Reasoning in this manner, an individual engaged in independent study is a person becoming competent in a particular choice of endeavor. Do we think of a high school pupil in the sense of becoming competent? Does he think of himself in this way?

In life, outside of school, when we meet a person who is an outstanding performer, we tend to take for granted certain things about him and how he got that way. We express ourselves like this: "I wonder who helped him get his start? He must have studied with a fine teacher. Think of the hours he must have practiced." Are not these dimensions of independent study? Competence as motivation is an intriguing theory to support the conduct so often observed in a person engaged in independent study.

## Evaluation and Independent Study

Independent study is a natural way to learn. It need not be restricted by subject-matter boundaries. There is nothing superficial about it. The learner owns what he does and what he has learned how to do. His experiences are as ungraded as life itself. The very nature of the work is a function of a personalized plan which calls for personalized evaluation and reporting.

The effective student in independent study is one who produces results and strives for improvement. The school should report both of these aspects to parents, college admissions officers, employers, and to interested members of the general public. Too, the student should be in a position to show what he has accomplished in his independent study endeavor. The art student who goes to be interviewed with portfolio in hand suggests a cue as to how to do this. Why should not a poem, a research paper, a painting, a project, a model, a write-up of an original experiment, a musical composition, a short story, a publication, a physically fit body, a piece of sculpture, a specimen of typing, a special device, or some other evidence of the quantity and quality of independent study be used as evidence of a productive high school experience? Placing a high value on student effectiveness in independent study and rewarding it when it occurs, the school will have little difficulty in establishing independent study as an integral part of each student's individual schedule. Teachers too will redefine their jobs to include the role of consultant to individual students and to accept the idea that young people are capable of vast amounts of learning apart from them. Parents and community people will also be encouraged to place as much value on a student's independent study time as they place on regular classroom instruction.

**335**

## J. Richard Suchman

# A Model for the
# Analysis of Inquiry

*I*nquiry has been variously described as an attitude, a state of mind, a way of learning, a process of investigation, an uncovering, and a search for the truth. Such descriptions serve to characterize phenomena only as they appear on the surface. To understand inquiry requires a look, however speculative, beneath the surface at the elements of the human condition and human functioning that play a role in the course of inquiry.

The purpose of this chapter is to present a model to provide a theoretical framework for the analysis of the behavior of inquirers. The model evolved through 7 years of research into the inquiry process as it is manifested by intermediate-grade children. This work was done at the University of Illinois with the outside support of the U.S. Office of Education. The initial purpose was to identify the necessary and sufficient conditions for stimulating and supporting inquiry in the elementary classroom and to develop methods and materials for creating these conditions. In time, the center of focus shifted toward the nature of the inquiry process itself, particularly the major psychological dimensions related to the processes of perception, motivation, storage and retrieval, overt action and the family of intervening functions loosely categorized as "thinking" or "information processing."

The process of inquiry can be made observable in the classroom setting by allowing children to formulate theories and gather data to test them in a group setting. Having seen discrepant physical events, they are challenged to formulate and test their own theories to account for the events. They have access to data through question-asking and can at any time verbalize their explanatory or theoretical formulations. Since no attempt is made by the teacher to either explain the events to the children or to render judgments about their theories, the children quickly learn that they have to judge the power of their own or each others theories and that this can be done through verbally mediated empirical tests or experiments.

Because of these specific conditions, the transactions between teacher

Suchman, Richard J. "A Model for the Analysis of Inquiry" in: Klausmeier, Herbert J. and Harris, Chester W. (Eds.) *Analysis of Concept Learning.* New York: Academic Press, 1966, pp. 177-187.

and pupil represent true and open inquiry where the responsibility for initiative and control in the learning situation rests squarely and consistently on the shoulders of the inquirers, the children. These transactions under these conditions are available for tape recording and analysis. It is thus possible to manipulate various personal and environmental independent variables to test relationships with a number of dependent inquiry process variables.

The model to be discussed in this paper grew out of and was to some extent verified through the observation and analysis of the inquiry process as it emerged in these studies. It should be understood that the population was restricted to fifth and sixth grade boys and girls and that the inquiries were verbal and focused largely on physical events presented on motion picture film.

We begin with a working definition: Inquiry is the *pursuit of meaning*. By this I mean that it is motivated by the desire to obtain a new level of relatedness between and among separate aspects of one's consciousness. Obviously, I am making the assumption that there is a consciousness, and that it plays a significant role in human behavior. I shall not argue the merits of that assumption at this time. It is also assumed that human beings do seek to make their encounters with reality more meaningful and that increments in meaning are satisfying. Inquiry, then, is a form of human behavior in which a person acts to increase the meaningfulness of his knowledge and experience. For example, a person who sees a strange object and examines it more closely is inquiring in that he is conducting his intensive examination in hopes of obtaining more data and thus finding a way to reduce the strangeness of the object. This may be achieved through increased familiarity and by finding ways to relate it to what he already knows or is familiar with. If the object turns out to be "like a rock," he then has available all that he knows about rocks to add to the meaningfulness of the object.

Consider for a moment the process by which we assign meaning to experience. Existence consists of an almost continuous series of *encounters* with the environment. Not all encounters, however, are equally meaningful. Indeed, a large proportion of daily encounters are totally ignored, let alone interpreted. In order to obtain meaning one must employ some form of *organizer* that serves to select out and pattern certain aspects of an encounter. We can reduce to symbolic form the statement that encounters, when processed through organizers, yield meaning (Fig. 1).

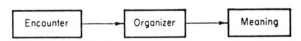

**Fig. 1. Encounters when processed through organizers yield meaning.**

But what exactly *is* an organizer? It is *any* idea, image, recollection, abstraction—any available pattern that can add to the meaningfulness of an encounter. A child's *second* encounter with a hot dog can be more meaningful to him in the light of his recollection of the first such encounter. Prior encounters as retrieved from storage can serve as organizers. A previously formed generalization or conclusion can also be an organizer. The belief that snakes can be harmful is in itself a meaningful notion and adds meaning to any encounter with a snake. Even a concept such as "balance" or "honesty" can enable a person to extract additional meaning from certain kinds of encounters. The former might have broad application to art, music, physics, mathematics, etc., whereas the latter is only appropriate in adding a new dimension of meaning to encounters with people.

The analysis of the generation of meaning in terms of encounters and organizers, has certain advantages. The examination of the teaching-learning process is considerably enhanced as we try to identify the kinds of encounters, organizers, and meanings available to the pupil. Does the teacher attempt to feed meanings to the children directly through verbal and other symbolic means or are meanings allowed to emerge as children apply organizers to analyze encounters? Where do the children obtain new organizers? Are they allowed to invent and test their own or are certain conceptual systems engineered into the children's thinking as the "proper" ways of interpreting encounters.

One can construct a simple taxonomy of teacher-pupil interaction from this model (Fig. 2). The vertical arrows feeding down into the boxes repre-

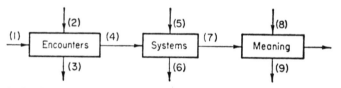

**Fig. 2.  A simple taxonomy of teacher-pupil interaction. See text for explanation.**

sent symbolic (verbal) teacher inputs. A teacher can generate a vicarious encounter (arrow 2) by description or by simply giving out raw data (e.g., "Bill had 10 marbles and lost 2"). He can didactically provide new *systems* (arrow 5), new ways of handling data (e.g., subtraction is a system). The teacher can also offer new meanings (arrow 8; conclusions, generalizations, or "truths") to the pupils (e.g., 10 minus 2 is 8).

By the same token, the teacher can elicit the same three kinds of knowledge from the pupil (arrows 3, 6, and 9). He can request a child to retrieve and report a previously stored encounter (arrow 3), a system (arrow 6), or a meaning (arrow 9). Much traditional teaching consists of feeding knowledge units in at one or more of these levels and later eliciting responses from the children *at the same level.*

The horizontal arrows represent transformations from one level of knowledge to the next. Encounters can lead to the generation of new systems by the learner himself (arrow 4), and systems can be applied to encounters to yield new meanings (arrow 7). Teachers can generate more pupil involvement by maximizing encounters (arrow 1) and allowing pupils to try out various systems or invent new ones. The value of a system is related to the amount of new meaning it can generate. Meanings can lead to action (arrow 10).

Described in terms of this model, inquiry is the active quest for increased meaning through (a) the generation of encounters, and (b) the selection and synthesis of systems for the purpose of analyzing, classifying, and interpreting encounters. Encounters, systems, and meanings can all serve as organizers. Since meanings result from an interaction of encounters and organizers, the inquirer avails himself of both elements and then tries to combine them in a way that is productive of new meaning. Strategies vary enormously, all the way from data gathering through a succession of almost random encounters to a series of experiments (highly controlled encounters) expressly designed to test a particular meaning (e.g., a generalization, theory, or conclusion).

To get on with the process of explicating the model, I shall start with a function called *storage*. Here we find the residue of experience, and the reservoir of organizers. These include encounters, systems, and meanings that have been given to the learner or synthesized by him. Any or all of these may be available to serve as organizers, to give meaning to new encounters. The storage function is represented in Fig. 3.

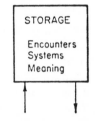

**Fig. 3. The storage function.**

The relationships among stored units greatly affect the retrievability and utilization of these units for inquiry or any other kind of cognitive operation. The Bloom taxonomy (1956) makes a careful distinction between knowledge and comprehension. The former consists in the retrievability of discrete informational units whereas the latter is the capacity to move meaningfully and deliberately among the parts of a lattice of related information with an understanding of the transformations that link the parts together. One can *know* that water boils at 212°F at sea level by simply applying two systems, temperature and altitude, to a few encounters with boiling water. The *comprehension* of the phenomenon of boiling requires the ability to relate temperature to vapor pressure through the concept of molecular motion and to relate altitude to atmospheric pressure through the concept of gravitation. Finally, boiling is accounted for in terms of the relationship between vapor pressure and atmospheric pressure.

Stored generalizations or conclusions have much greater power, flexibility and utility when they are well articulated with encounters and relevant systems. Such articulation is best achieved when generalizations are generated by the learner himself from encounters which he analyzes with systems he has selected or synthesized on his own. One comprehends best that which he has struggled to understand in his own terms.

Here we can see how the process of inquiry can affect the character of learning. If inquiry is the pursuit of meaning *through* the generation of encounters and the development of systems to interpret them, it would seem almost inevitable that an increase of comprehension would accompany an increase in inquiry. The intake function is represented in Fig. 4.

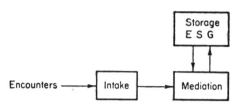

**Fig. 4.    The intake function.**

Encounters simply make new information available, but the meaning and significance derived from an encounter depends upon the organizers that are applied to it. A person encountering a tree may perceive a source of shade, a hiding place, an object of beauty, or perhaps all three. There will be differences from person to person and, within one person, differences from instance to instance. The model must, therefore, reflect the fact that there is no one-to-one relationship between a given encounter and the meaning derived from it. There is selection and control that regulates the retrieval of organizers from storage and the use of these gives form and meaning to intake. In Fig. 4 the regulatory function is represented by the box labeled "Mediation." The two arrows between mediation and storage represent the dual processes of storage and retrieval. The model does not show how the mediation function regulates the generation of meaning, it shows only that it *does* stand in a crucial pivotal position between storage and intake, the respective loci of stored organizers and new encounters.

The next function to be accounted for is overt action. The human can modify his environment and his relation to it. Actions take many forms and have at least two principal purposes: one is to produce new or altered environmental conditions; the other is to generate new data. A person may break a piece of chalk in two because he wants it broken—he prefers to have two pieces rather than one or because he wants to learn more about the properties of chalk, its strength or brittleness.

Figure 5 shows an arrow from mediation to action indicating that action is influenced by the same control system that regulates intake, storage, and retrieval. The action function has two efferent arrows, one directed back toward the external environment, representing action to change the environment and one directed toward the intake function, representing action for the purpose of generating new encounters.

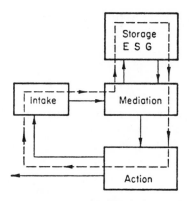

**Fig. 5. The action function completes the** *inquiry cycle* **(dotted lines).**

Notice now that the arrows connecting the four functions constitute a closed loop which I have designated as the *inquiry cycle* (dotted lines). It corresponds to the sequence of behaviors that can be observed in children as they pursue meaning through inquiry.

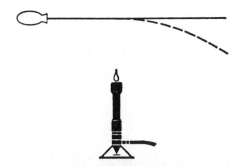

**Fig. 6. The bimetallic strip bends downward the first time it is heated; melting is generally thought to be the cause.**

Consider the example of a child who has witnessed a discrepant event, a demonstration of a blade that behaves in strange ways as it is held over a flame. First it bends downward as it is heated (Fig. 6). Then it straightens as it is cooled in a tank of water. The second time heat is applied it bends upward!

The first part of the event is assimilated by the child because he has two available organizers in storage, the concepts of melting and gravity. When combined they provide a satisfactory model to account for the behavior of the blade. As the demonstration continues, the blade is held in a tank of water whereupon it straightens out. It is then inverted and held over the flame again. This time it bends upward, *away from the flame* (Fig. 7)!

The child is surprised and puzzled. The event is clearly discrepant. He has no single stored encounter, no system, no meaning, in short, no organizer that will enable him to assimilate *in toto* this encounter.

His subsequent behavior can be translated in the terms of the model.

1. Encounter with blade bending upward.

2. Mediation function scans storage for organizer to match encounter.

3. No such organizer is available.

4. At this point the child usually wants to pick up the blade and examine it more carefully, flex it in his hands, perhaps hold it in the flame again, in short, learn more about the properties of the blade. In terms of the model, he is taking action to generate new encounters, taking in the data and scanning storage for organizers that will make the encounter more meaningful.

5. Without success he takes more action and generates more encounters.

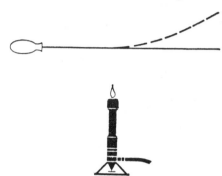

**Fig. 7.    The second time the bimetallic strip is heated, the blade bends upward—a discrepant event for most children.**

In time he will find some organizers that permit him to assimilate at least part of the encounter. He will surely associate heat (a system) with the bending and suspect that the expansion and contraction (two more systems) of the metal are relevant. He might test this theory through various measurements (controlled encounters). In time new data will bring new organizers into play and these will in turn suggest what new encounters are needed.

At all times, the decision as to what operation comes next is made through the mediating function. In other words, the process of inquiry is internally regulated and serves to bring encounters and theories together for matching so that each builds on the other. Whenever a match is made between a theory and an encounter, to a degree the theory is supported and the encounter assimilated.

Only an autonomous mediation function can operate in response to the shifting data-gathering and theory-modifying requirements of inquiry. Any attempt to intervene, such as programming data input or instructing the inquirer to utilize certain organizers tends to convert the process from pure inquiry into some form of externally manipulated learning. It is not my purpose here to argue the relative pedagogical merits of different proportions of inquiry as opposed to didactics. Suffice it to say that there are gains accrued from both and that an optimal educational program would probably vary widely between the two extremes.

In order to complete the inquiry model, one more function must be incorporated: *motivation*. It is necessary to account for the fact that the inquiry cycle does not swing into high gear with every phenomenon or problem posed to a person. People are selective and behave in accordance with a system of values which dictates the directions of inquiry and the degree of urgency with which it is undertaken. The urgency factor is particularly important since the behavior of the mediating function seems to change in relation to the amount of pressure it is under. High pressure reduces the tendency to accommodate, to modify, and regroup organizers. Urgency tends to prompt either total inaction or rigid action based on habital organizers. Low pressure allows the luxury of reflection and playfulness with ideas. Under these conditions the mediating function can retrieve a greater range of organizers from storage and generate more encounters, as well.

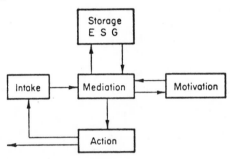

**Fig. 8. Model including the motivation function.**

Figure 8 presents the completed model with the motivation function linked to mediation by two arrows. The inward arrow represents the effects of motivation on the mediating process, effects that influence both direction *and* style of inquiry. The outward arrow represents the feedback, the fact that motivation is itself altered by the inquiry process and the intellectual products that it produces. For example, there is a marked effect on the motivation to inquire, once a sense of closure is gained. Furthermore, involvement in the process of inquiry accentuates another kind of motivation that seems to relate to the excitement of the act of inquiry, itself. When the mediation function is autonomous and in high gear the motivation to continue seems to become less and less related to the productiveness or closure generated by the activity and more and more by something even more intrinsic. There is a sense of power and competence that grows out of the manipulation of data and the constuction of workable theories. On the other hand, there is for some a sense of wonder and excitement in exploring unfamiliar domains. In any case, motivation is clearly interactive with inquiry and should be linked to mediation through a feedback loop.

One criterion for the value of a model is its validity, the degree to which it matches observable phenomena, and provides a basis for accurate prediction and/or control of behavior. For the present, my claim for validity is based mostly upon objective but unquantified evidence, the kinds of observational data that led to the construction of the model in the first place. Quantified data are more difficult to obtain but by no means impossible. For example, if the motivational and mediational characteristics of a learner could be controlled one might be able to predict inquiry productivity from the number and quality of encounters and organizers available.

A second criterion is generality. Is this simply a model for question-asking in physics or does it reflect the more general interrelation of functions that characterize the human intellective system regardless of the mode of activity? I believe I can make a case for the latter. This case is based upon the facility with which the model serves as an organizer for didactic teaching, the very antithesis of inquiry.

Suppose a teacher wants to provide his pupil with a new set of organizers that will enable him to comprehend the essential structure and functions vital to electronic tubes. He might begin by showing his pupil an actual tube or a cut-away model. This would be an encounter made available through direct sensory intake. He might then say, "A tube is something like a valve." In doing this he is instructing the pupil to retrieve from storage a particular organizer (in this case a system or concept) and bring it down into the arena of thought for further consideration. By bringing in the "valve" concept the teacher is also suggesting the model of a "flow being regulated," since that is what valves are for.

He continues, "But instead of a valve to regulate liquids, a tube regulates the flow of electrons, a kind of electric current." Some new organizers have been brought into the picture to modify the earlier one.

"Notice this object here," says the teacher pointing (and thus generating a new encounter). "Electrons flow from this anode to this plate." The encounter is extended verbally as more data is thrown in. "Between the anode and the plate is something which acts like a venetian blind, to admit varying amounts of current." Once again a model or system is retrieved from storage as an organizer. Past encounters plus a concept of a venetian blind make the grid of the tube immediately more meaningful.

Of course, the skillful teacher will check all along the way to be sure that he knows what organizers are actually being employed by the learner and what meanings for the learner they are generating when applied to the encounters.

The main distinction between this process and inquiry is in the role of the mediating function. It is, in this case, being carefully manipulated by the teacher. Each retrieval from storage, each new encounter taken in is the result of the teacher's decision, not the learner's. As a result the process and the resulting cognitive gains should match more closely the teacher's goals than the pupil's, providing the teacher is skillful. There is an enormous amount of conceptual growth that can be brought about by skillful teachers who can provide an optimal combination and sequencing of encounters and organizers. But he must have maximum feedback from the pupil in order to employ his skill as diagnostician and practitioner in deciding what next step is best for a given learner at a given time. Of course, anything less than a one-to-one teacher-pupil ratio reduces the effectiveness of the diagnostic didactic tutor.

What is missing here is the freedom of choice afforded the inquiring learner and hence the opportunity to develop learner autonomy, but education has many goals and must have an equal number of approaches to achieve them.

To summarize, this paper proposes, explicates, and illustrates a model for the inquiry process that is an attempt to relate the functions of storage, retrieval, perception, overt action, and motivation through a central, ego-like mediating function. Didactic teaching as well as inquiry were described in terms of the model.

## Reference

Bloom, B. S. (Ed.) *Taxonomy of educational objectives.* Handbook I. *Cognitive domain.* New York: McKay, 1956.

Hilda Taba

# Learning by Discovery: Psychological and Educational Rationale

$O$ne of the interesting phenomena in the development of ideas about learning and teaching today is the fact that the curriculum projects that were started to strengthen the role of content in the learning process have turned around and renewed the emphasis on cultivation of higher mental processes as the central outcome of learning (1).

Learning by discovery is one concept made popular by the new curriculums in mathematics and science. This concept is arousing the same kind of controversy that a few decades ago used to rage around the issue of content versus process.

## The History of the Idea

Learning by discovery is not the completely new invention that some of its proponents as well as its critics seem to assume. My own explorations take me back as far as 1904.

At that time Mary E. Boole published a little booklet called *Preparation of the Child for Science* (2). Influenced by the theories of thinking developed by her husband, George Boole, and Gratry, the French priest-logician, she developed ideas about learning and thinking that are amazingly similar to the characterization of discovery learning today.

She was concerned with the laws of the sequence of thought and was trying to evolve a way of guiding the child to the "working of the scientific mind which puts itself in relation to the 'As-Yet-Unknown-Truth' " (2: 15). She was especially concerned with the ways by which children can be led to "extract the truth from a series of impressions and statements, each of which is only partially true" (2: 20).

She spoke of the need for demarcation between "what the individual child has observed and what he has learned at second hand," of the impor-

Taba, Hilda "Learning by Discovery. Psychological and Educational Rationale." *Elementary School Journal*, 1963: 63, pp. 308-316.

tance for children to discover the laws of nature that govern what they explore. She stressed the importance of "unconscious cerebration" and advised parents and teachers to "keep silence even from good words" (2: 25) and to refrain from pushing children into premature awareness, because this "unconscious cerebration" takes place when children are occupied with explorations that they do not perceive as something for their own instruction.

She warned that there is no such thing as "*a* right method of performing any operation in elementary mathematics; because all rightness and all mathematicalness depends on getting each operation performed by *two methods:* the first, a roundabout one, which represents and registers the conscious action of the mind during the *process of discovery* [italics mine]; the second, a short method which condenses the roundabout one, assists in stowing its results away in the memory and facilitates the using of them subconsciously" (2: 101).

Something akin to learning set is suggested in her description of mathematical imagination, which, she wrote, "depends on the child being put into the right attitude towards mathematical conceptions in his earliest years" (2: 102).

These ideas could be matched almost point by point with current conceptions of the process of learning by discovery: helping learners get at the structure, or at the laws and principles of a subject, by allowing them to discover these laws and principles through intensive exploration of concrete instances; withholding verbalization of the basic principles until they are understood operationally and used intuitively; defining the process of learning as an active organization and reorganization of mental schemata with which to process information and to perceive relationships; strengthening the process of inference, that is, the process of going beyond that which was given (3, 4, 5).

Some elements of the current conception of discovery learning can also be found among the ideas of Maria Montessori (6), though in a more rigid form. She, too, was interested in the sequence of mental development. She maintained that abstractions were always a result of individual experience and required "pre-building" through a proper organization of these experiences.

Her mathematical games were organized to allow children to absorb impressions in their own way to promote a subconscious process of organizing, presumably independently of consciousness and will. She talked of the cultivation of the mathematical mind rather than of learning mathematics.

Inquiry as a method of learning was, of course, central to all Dewey's teaching and writing. In his *How We Think* he developed the theoretical concept of the nature of inquiry and of reflective thought. He identified learning with thinking, and thinking with active discovery of relationships and organizing principles. He considered the quality of searching to be the prime motive power of thinking and, therefore, maintained that the problem-solving processes are essential to active learning (7).

The advent of Gestalt psychology introduced a new stream of interest in learning by discovery. To describe active cognitive processes, Gestalt psychology introduced such concepts as insight, transposition, and meaning.

Insight was interpreted as the moment of discovering the organizing principle or the crucial relationship. Transposition was interpreted as an act of reorganizing one's conceptual scheme, something akin to what Wertheimer and Piaget call decentering (8, 9). These concepts are only now acquiring a firmer and a more operational definition (10: 33-36).

Several research studies have been conducted to examine the role of the discovery method and of insight in thinking. As early as 1934, T. R. McConnell conducted a study that compared discovery learning with authoritarian identification in the thinking of children (11). The volume that reports McConnell's study includes a report on a study by Lyle K. Henry (12), "The Role of Insight in the Analytic Thinking of Children."

The chief hypothesis of McConnell's experiment was that to learn is to discover. One learns through experience to discover "configurations" and to transpose them to carry out different tasks. One does not truly understand what one does not discover, and one cannot learn what one does not understand.

It was further assumed that achievement of insight involves differentiation and that habituation comes at the end rather than at the beginning of the sequence of learning acts. To test this assumption, the experimental group in McConnell's study manipulated the number relationships until they understood them before establishing or verbalizing the rules.

Henry found that insight was achieved when a correct transposition took place which enabled application. He further found that ability to apply principles meant that evidence was logically and psychologically related. Insight was characterized by suddenness of perception, a feeling of surety, and an inclination to ask heuristic questions (12). Later Swenson studied the role of organization and generalization in learning and in transfer (13).

## Two Dimensions of Learning

Learning by discovery, as pursued today, pertains largely to cognitive aspects of learning: the development and organization of concepts, ideas, and insights, and the use of inference and other logical processes to control a situation. The content of these explorations is, furthermore, limited to science and mathematics.

Naturally, there are other types of learning, such as mastering the skill of typing or memorizing a poem, in which the cognitive control of the situation is at a minimum. There are also other types of content in which cognition and valuing merge. To assume that the principles of learning by discovery apply to all varieties of learning or apply to all in a similar way leads to misapprehension.

Basic to the varied and partial definitions of discovery learning by different authors is the conception of learning as a transactional process that involves at least two different aspects: the assimilation of content of some sort and operations of cognitive processes required to organize and use this content.

In most past studies these two aspects of the learning process have been separated and unevenly stressed: either one or the other was represented as the chief focus, while the other was designated as an incidental by-product.

The so-called progressive practices tended to understress the role of content, largely because the early progressive education was a reaction against rote mastery of sterile subject matter. In contrast, those who have defended the primacy of content have often overlooked the importance of cultivating active mental processes, partly because they have assumed that assimilation of well-organized content automatically produces the necessary patterns of thinking.

The recent rationale of learning by discovery seems to bring process and content into a transactional relationship. The rationale stresses the need for a strategy for cultivating autonomous mental processes in relation to the requirements of the structure or the logic of the particular content.

The learner must construct his own conceptual schemata with which to process and organize whatever information he receives. Teaching is directed to enabling the learner to establish a relationship between his existing schemata and the new phenomena and to remake or extend the schemata to accomodate new facts and events. In doing this the learner has to decenter his current view of the situation or of the problem before him and reorganize his perception of it. He must also build a strategy of inquiry (5).

A different view of content is also involved. Content is seen not only as an array of facts to be absorbed, but as something that has structure, namely, a way of organizing detailed facts in the light of some concepts and principles.

A falling body can be viewed only as a discrete event or as an organization of gravitational forces. When one assimilates knowledge of the first sort, one has to learn each new fact anew. When one comprehends the principle of gravitation, one has hold of a more dynamic knowledge that enables one to explain and understand new phenomena and predict the consequences of events. One gets, as Bruner puts it, greater mileage from learning (3).

The act of discovery occurs at the point in the learner's efforts at which he grasps the organizing principle imbedded in a concrete instance or in a series of instances and can therefore transform this information: the learner can see the relationship of the facts before him, he can understand the causes of the phenomenon, and he can relate what he sees to his prior knowledge (4, 10). This point in the learner's efforts is also referred to as the moment of insight.

These acts of discovery are the product of the individual's intellectual effort; the nature of these acts, however, is dictated by the structure of the subject matter with which the learner deals. If the discovery is not related to the logic or the structure of the subject matter, we have what Wertheimer calls "dirty," "ugly," or "insensible" procedure (8: 24-33).

## An Inductive Sequence

Learning by discovery involves an inductive sequence. This sequence starts not with the exposition of the general principle, but with exposing the learner to some concrete instances of the principle that he can analyze, manipulate, and experiment with, either symbolically or actually.

Such an instance must be studied in considerable depth to discover the rule, the idea, the principle, or the generalization that underlies it, such as the generalization behind a particular mathematical operation or the anthropological meaning of the specific way of building houses in a specific culture (14: 356ff.). In such a sequence, an intuitive or operational grasp of the generalization precedes its verbalization.

Several proponents of this method argue that a premature verbalization of the generalization or the rule deprives the individual of the essential learning, namely, the reorganization of his own cognitive structure, and puts the student in the position of absorbing the generalization without necessarily understanding what it stands for or how to work it.

This differentiation between knowing the generalization and understanding what it stands for has led some proponents of discovery learning to insist that the subverbal or the intuitive process is the important and the essential characteristic of productive learning (4, 15).

This emphasis on intuitive learning as a prerequisite to conscious statement of the principle has often been interpreted as a negation of verbalization on any level. This interpretation does not do justice to what seem to be the actual operations in the classroom. It is only the premature verbalization of the central generalization to be learned that is delayed to allow the operational insight into its nature to take place and to permit the process of discovery to function.

The students must show operational evidence of their understanding before they are faced with formulating the rule or the principle for their operations, and the teacher must distinguish between the advent of the discovery and its verbalization. (Space does not permit me to deal with the problem of the relationship of language and verbalization to thinking.)

This distinction between the two levels of verbalization permits a clearer orientation toward the many claims made for discovery learning. The characteristics of discovery learning described here may also help to distinguish achieving meaningful learning from achieving intellectual potency. The two are often confused.

Ausubel, for example, argues that learning by the discovery method is not the necessary condition for meaningful learning, at least not for all kinds of learning or for all age levels. As the sophistication of the learner increases, the necessity for discovery learning decreases. He points out, further, that since learning by discovery is time-consuming, to use this method of learning exclusively would greatly reduce the scope of learning (16).

However, if one considers the intellectual potency or the productivity of cognitive activity as the chief outcome, one needs to redefine *meaningfulness* to include intellectual potency. Or else the effects of learning by discovery need to be considered in two different dimensions: the understanding of the meaning and the ability to use certain cognitive processes. Both need to be differentiated from mechanical or rote learning.

Hendrix, for example, differentiates knowing what a mathematical sentence stands for (meaning in the ordinary sense) from what she calls the "prerequisite for meaning" or understanding (15). For example, one can know the meaning of a geometric theorem and be able to reproduce it in a drawing, but not understand why it has to be, why certain proof can or should be employed, and how it was derived. She assumes this prerequisite to be an essentially non-verbal process that must precede verbal formulation. This "prerequisite" is very similar to what Mary Boole calls "subconscious" knowledge and to what Piaget calls "intuitive knowledge."

This intuitive or subverbal understanding is acquired by performing certain operations, such as comparing and contrasting prime and nonprime numbers until one gets the idea of what a prime number is and how it operates. This mastery can be demonstrated only by behavioral evidence. Only after the students have mastered operationally the meaning of a generalization, a principle, or a rule, are they ready for a verbal statement of it.

This distinction gives a definition of *meaningfulness* that avoids the black-and-white contrast with rote learning and admits other ways of gaining meaning: in other words, learning by discovery is not the only way of arriving at meaning.


## Cognitive Autonomy

Learning by discovery may, then, still be considered the chief mode for intellectual productivity and autonomy. When an individual has developed an organizing scheme for his own cognitive activity, he is presumably in a position to harvest a greater amount of knowledge as well as to become increasingly autonomous and independent of all forms of authority. He is better equipped to move into unknown areas, to gather data, and to abstract from these ideas and concepts. A person who can transform what Bruner (17) calls "episodic information" into systematic knowledge is in control of organizing ideas and thereby increases his intellectual power. Further, when the learner relies on his own cognitive processes, when he is aware of the relationship of the learning tasks to his own experience, and when he has developed an attitude of search and an expectation or a set to learn under his own steam, he is in a position to continue these processes on his own.

This type of learning is more permanent and more easily transferable (17), especially when it is addressed to the structure of subject matter. A student who understands the wave theory of sound is presumably in a position to explain the phenomena of light by the same theory. Having learned to look for patterns of prime numbers, the student can use the process on content that is dissimilar to that of prime numbers.

This idea of transfer has led some experimenters to search for the generic, highly transferable skills, such as universal skills of inquiry (5) or skills in problem-solving. How generic such intellectual skills are, and how independent they are of the particular context in which they are acquired, is as yet not too clear.

It is possible that the current models of inquiry and discovery, developed almost exclusively in the neat fields of science and mathematics, may not be applicable to the untidy and multivariant field of social and human problems. This is not to deny the transfer power of generalizations, inquiry skills, searching orientation, scientific attitude, or of the method of asking heuristic questions.

Too often extrinsic rewards only—such as grades—have been used to create motivation for learning. Those concerned with active and discovery learning rightly point out that children and young people are endowed with curiosity and with what White calls "competency motive" (18) and that some approaches to learning are more capable of cultivating this motive than others. Being an active process, learning by discovery is likely to mobilize the competency motive as a drive for learning behavior, to free the learning act from the immediate stimulus control, and to establish the cognitive control of the individual.

## Teaching Strategies

Learning by discovery requires a teaching-learning strategy that amounts to setting conditions to make discovery possible. All descriptions of discovery learning imply a specific teaching strategy, even though the existence of this strategy is not always so recognized.

Central in this strategy is the confrontation of learners with problem situations that create a feeling of bafflement and start the process of inquiry. Withholding certain kinds of information and certain kinds of crucial generalizations to challenge the search behavior and to preserve the opportunity for autonomous exploration and experimentation is also usually practiced. The teaching strategy is usually aimed at placing on the individual the responsibility of transforming information and reassembling it to get new insights.

So far, the experimental teaching strategies developed to foster learning by discovery are either imperceptibly imbedded in the programming of content, as in the curriculum in mathematics developed by the University of Illinois Committee on School Mathematics, or they are focused on specific tasks, as in the inquiry strategies developed by Suchman (5).

The first approach assumes that the thought processes are implicit in the sequence of the subject matter. The second approach assumes that a concentrated experience organized around selected instances suffices to produce a generic act of mental operations which, when acquired, are transferable to other settings.

Actually a bit more seems to be involved, namely, a cumulative curriculum and teaching strategy that spans time and various subjects.

When one faces the problem of providing for cumulative learning rather than training for discovery learning per se, one has to face several additional issues. Among these are the balance between assimilative or receptive learning and discovery learning, the balance between expository teaching and training in methods of inquiry, and the issue of depth study and scope. Not everything can be learned or even should be learned by the discovery method. It is time-consuming and, therefore, limits the scope of coverage. A good deal of learning must be accomplished by other means, such as deduction, logical inference, some form of exposition by the teacher, or by reading a book.

The task of organizing instruction, then, is to provide an appropriate balance between discovery learning, which requires depth study, and receptive learning to assure scope.

Depth study for discovery needs to be reserved for points at which new families of concepts or ideas are introduced, wherever or at whatever maturity level they occur. These experiences need to be alternated with intake experiences designed to extend information, generalizations, or their application to assure adequate scope.

Since the principles of depth and scope of curriculum organization are contradictory, the problem of curriculum organization is to replace the current concept of coverage with a concept of appropriate sampling of content that reduces the coverage of detail without reducing the essential idea content. This reorganization can probably be best provided by a curriculum design that focuses on fundamental ideas while judiciously sampling the detail with which to develop these ideas (14: 175-81; 352-59).

## References

1. This article is based on a talk given at the symposium of the convention of the American Educational Research Association, Atlantic City, New Jersey, February 20, 1962.

2. M. E. Boole. *Preparation of the Child for Science*. Oxford: Clarendon Press, 1904.

3. J. S. Bruner. *The Process of Education.* Cambridge, Massachusetts: Harvard University Press, 1960.

4. Gertrude Hendrix. "Learning by Discovery," *Mathematics Teacher,* LIV (May, 1961), 290-99.

5. J. Richard Suchman. "Inquiry Training: Building Skills for Autonomous Discovery," *Merrill Palmer Quarterly of Behavior and Development,* VII (July, 1961), 147-69.

6. Mario M. Montessori. "Maria Montessori's Contribution to the Cultivation of the Mathematical Mind," *International Review of Education,* XVII (1961), 134-41.

7. John Dewey. *How We Think.* Boston: D. C. Heath and Company, 1910.

8. Max Wertheimer. *Productive Thinking.* New York: Harper & Brothers, 1945.

9. Jean Piaget. *The Psychology of Intelligence.* London: Routledge and Kegan Paul, 1959.

10. Allen Newell, J. C. Shaw, and Herbert A. Simon. "Elements of a Theory of Human Problem-Solving." Santa Monica, California: RAND Corporation, March 7, 1957.

11. T. R. McConnell. "Discovery vs. Authoritarian Identification in the Thinking of Children," *Studies in Learning II.* Iowa Studies in Education, Vol. IX, No. 5, Iowa City University, 1934.

12. Lyle K. Henry. "The Role of Insight in the Analytic Thinking of Children," *Studies in Learning II.* Iowa Studies in Education, Vol. IX, No. 5, Iowa City University, 1934.

13. Esther J. Swenson. "Organization and Generalization as Factors in Learning, Transfer, and Retroactive Inhibition," in Esther J. Swenson, G. Lester Anderson, and Chalmers L. Stacey, *Learning Theory in School Situations.* Studies in Education, No. 2. Minneapolis, Minnesota: University of Minnesota Press, 1949.

14. Hilda Taba. *Curriculum Development: Theory and Practice.* New York: Harcourt, Brace and World, 1962.

15. Gertrude Hendrix. "Prerequisite to Meaning," *Mathematics Teacher,* XLIII (November, 1950), 334-39.

16. David P. Ausubel. "Indications and Contributions in an Approach to Learning by Discovery," *Educational Leadership,* XX (November, 1962), 113-17.

17. J. S. Bruner. "The Act of Discovery," *Harvard Educational Review,* XXXI (Winter, 1961), 21-32.

18. R. W. White. "Motivation Reconsidered: the Concept of Competence," *Psychological Review,* LXVI (September, 1959), 297-333.

*Mildred L. Krohn*

# Learning and the Learning Center

Objective: an eagerness for growth.

Is it pertinent to the topic to ask how we learn? By questioning, examining, exploring, experimenting, even sometimes when browsing without purpose. To help pupils learn more effectively, it is necessary to make available as many of the tools of learning as possible. To learn independently and at maximum potential for each pupil, instruction in work-study skills is basic. Such instruction can be enhanced and accelerated by the use of a wide range of materials and resources, in addition to books.

For the past two years work-study skills have been taught to elementary school children in Shaker Heights, Ohio, using large group instruction, and with the aid of an overhead projector. This approach grew out of an experimental plan that was tried for a year and then was presented to the Ford Foundation's Fund for the Advancement of Education for a possible grant. Purpose of the project was to help develop ideas for further experimental study. In May 1962, a matching grant was given in the amount of $45,000 to be used over a three year period to teach work-study skills and develop independent study habits. This involved pupils in grades 4, 5 and 6 in two schools: Lomond, with an enrollment of 625, and Ludlow, with 300 pupils.

Self-directed, independent study skills generally have been considered as suitable to the college and graduate study level. This experiment is attempting to prove that these skills can be acquired and used by pupils at an earlier age.

We must recognize that as the volume of knowledge becomes greater the teacher can no longer have all the answers. Consequently, there must be a shift in emphasis from the teaching to the learning aspect. We now see the self-motivated child bringing information to the classroom as a result of independent study which becomes a sharing, with teachers learning from as well as teaching pupils.

This requires a revolutionary shift in the teachers' thinking. Can Johnny actually learn without the teacher being present? We believe he can and does, as he has access to a wide range of materials, direction from teachers and librarians, and as he has motivation to interest him in finding answers, reports, truths, and in how to use these materials to his own best advantage.

Krohn, Mildred L. "Learning and the Learning Center." *Educational Leadership,* Vol. 21, pp. 217-222, Jan., 1974.

Many school libraries today are known as materials centers where all types of materials are provided to enrich and support the curriculum. However, "materials center" does not truly describe the activity taking place there, but rather suggests a place to store or house materials. For the schools in this project a more unique term was wanted that would indicate activity and the role of the library in the learning process. "Learning Center" was selected as the best descriptive term.

## The Learning Center

To implement this project, program changes in physical facilities were necessary. In the larger school a wall had to be removed to enlarge the room to about three and a half classrooms in size. Free-standing double-faced shelving is arranged in U-shaped areas down the middle of this large rectangular room to hold the 10,000 volumes. We find that books arranged this way absorb sound and allow several alcoves to accommodate children simultaneously doing different things without noise interference.

At one end of the room are five built-in study carrels, each with an electrical outlet and a filmstrip viewer, well lighted with cork board space on the walls which allows notes and papers to be tacked up for easy viewing. These carrels are extremely popular with the children and help to make their research and viewing a satisfactory and individual experience.

The listening area was developed by building a shelf in a small offset of the former main room and installing jacks so that earphones can be plugged in for student use. Tapes and records are also used here.

Another alcove has filmstrips and viewers on a built-in shelf. Here are also programed materials in the following areas: Organizing and Reporting; Reading Graphs, Charts and Tables; and Basic Library Skills. These are used independently by children, or assigned by the classroom teacher or librarian.

At the smaller school the center moved into the kindergarten room, the largest and one of the most attractive rooms in the school. Here perimeter shelving is used and is adequate for the 7,000 volumes. In this center six free-standing commercially built carrels are used instead of built-in carrels. These have a shelf where encyclopedia sets can be shelved and, with books in proximity, can create a reference area. The viewing area was formerly a closet, but by building a shelf on three sides, boys and girls can sit on stools and use the viewers which are placed on the shelf. The listening area is a table with earphones in one part of the Learning Center.

With this available space and a wide range of materials—books, filmstrips, pictures, recordings, tapes, transparencies—the tools of learning are readily available to the advantage of the learner. Learning becomes attractive in this kind of situation and achievement brings its own satisfactions.

A guide, outlining large group lessons, was used last year in grades four

356

through six. This was rewritten this summer and expanded to two booklets, one a guide, "Suggested Activities To Motivate and Follow Up Large Group Lessons" for the teacher and the other, a "Curriculum Guide for Large Group Instruction in Work-Study Skills," for the librarian.

## Teaching Needed Skills

Last year large group lessons were held every other week. This year the group lessons are being held every week, leaving the second semester for reviewing and reteaching skills where needed and for enrichment lessons. From the first year's experience it was learned that all the skills need to be taught as early as possible rather than spacing them throughout a school year. What was taught last May would have helped children use the skills more knowingly if they had been taught as needed.

The basic lessons outlined in the guide are as follows: Orientation to Learning Center; Listening; Card Catalogue; What Study Is; Outlining: Note Taking; Dewey Decimal Classification; Reference Books and Tools; Using the Audio-visual Section of the Learning Center; Techniques of Reporting; Oral Book Reports; Graphs, Charts, Tables and Diagrams; Using Many Sources in Preparing Reports; Map and Globe Studies; Bibliography; Parts of a Book.

These lessons are not listed in the order in which they are being taught, some are repeated in all three grades, but the scope and development varies for each lesson according to the grade level. These lessons are taught in the auditorium weekly by grade level. By teaching all classes of a grade at one time, the center is free from rigid scheduling and blocks of time are thus made available for practicing skills taught and for individual research.

For these lessons pupils are seated on folding chairs to which an arm has been attached to permit them to write. Each child is given a participation sheet which has blanks to be filled in as the librarian teaches the lesson. When completed, these sheets provide a good summary of what has been taught and are also helpful for absentees who miss the lesson.

Transparencies, shown on the overhead projector, have proven to be a most effective teaching aid, and the participation sheets have been the best method of getting total class participation which is not possible orally with a large group.

Last year lessons were taught by the three librarians, one being a former teacher who had recently completed her master's degree in library science. She taught the units that would ordinarily be considered classroom areas, e.g., maps and globes, outlining, graphs, charts, tables and diagrams. This year some lessons will be conducted by teachers and children as well as by the library personnel.

The total staff for this project includes, besides the three librarians, a library aide in each school, an audio-visual clerk and a half-time technician in the larger school. Having a technician to produce transparencies for use with the overhead projector is helpful to staff and students. They are used, not only for large group instruction, but also for class purposes, or for students giving special reports.

Overnight books and reserved book shelves have usually been associated with secondary and college levels. However, the project program has made it necessary to initiate these practices in our two program schools.

Teachers are asked to observe each lesson for their own information and for help in classroom follow-up. They are asked to write constructive criticism for whoever conducts the lesson to strengthen and improve wherever possible any future presentations.

Also this year the classroom teacher is to emphasize follow-up of lessons and utilize specific skills taught in large group lessons by applying them to use in current units in their daily teaching and thus make them more meaningful.

## Help for Individuals

Last year's emphasis was on the facilities and their use in the Learning Centers. This year the teacher is to play a more important role by utilizing skills in classroom follow-up and by checking and helping individual children improve their techniques.

In grades 4-6 there are no regularly scheduled library classes except for large group instruction. Instead, teachers are urged to permit pupils to come to the Learning Center as the needs arise logically in the classroom. In talking with teachers, they agree that this is the most difficult change to make in their teaching day. Their teaching methods have not changed, but their concepts of learning are being shifted. Children are not sent to the Center after work in the classroom has been completed, but rather as class discussion requires or provokes the need for immediate information.

One of the problems is what to do with the children in the classroom while six or ten of their classmates are sent to the Learning Center. With emphasis on independent study and individual learning according to ability, the individualized reading time is best to free children to do research without loss by being separated from the group, according to many teachers. Also available are times when children are working individually on projects in science, mathematics or social studies and no class presentation by the teacher is in progress.

Because good teachers are concerned about what and how much the children in their care learn they are naturally reluctant to allow them to leave the classroom and go off "on-their-own." However, after a year of trial, persuasion and observation, teachers are altering their thinking, revising their classroom schedules and witnessing children studying independently, using many kinds of materials on problems of real interest and value to them.

In summary, the "Activities" guide describes the goals of this experimental program in these words: "If we subscribe to the theory that children *want* to learn, that they are *eager* to grow in knowledge and their ability to apply this acquired knowledge to purposes which are meaningful to them, then we are ready to accept the basic goals of the experimental program in teaching work-study skills and in independent study. If the assignments we make to children in the intermediate grades have real meaning for them in that they help them to find answers to their immediate questions or to fill some present need (rather than as preparation for some nebulous career in the future), the children will not need to be *driven* to finding answers, nor will they need us, as teachers, to stand over them forcing them to study. These children will be ready for *independent study,* the ultimate goal of the experimental program."

After one year, the guide has been rewritten to become two, one for the teacher and one for the librarian; shifting teaching emphasis from factual to conceptual, emphasis has been shifted from the Learning Center to follow-up in the classroom; teaching large group lessons will now include teacher and student personnel. Additional changes will be made as experience warrants these.

Interest in this experiment has brought many visitors and inquiries for information and materials. To free the librarians and principals from conducting tours and answering correspondence, additional funds were granted this year by the Fund for the Advancement of Education. This money provided for an Information Officer to coordinate these duties; also to arrange visitors' schedules, and to publicize and promote the project. In the past month more than 150 sets of the "Curriculum Guide" and "Suggested Activities" books,[1] which were requested have been sent out.

How does one evaluate this project? The Iowa Work-Study Skills Test and the Educational Stimuli Library Skills Examination are being used but are inconclusive in their results to date. However, there is no test, to our knowledge, that truly measures how children have grown in independence in using the varied resources in the Learning Center. The use of the card catalogue and the location of materials improved considerably during the year, as did pupils' ability to work independently. Perhaps with more experience a test can be developed that can objectively evaluate this type of program.

While only two schools are involved in this experiment, all of our elementary schools have either moved libraries into larger existing quarters (kindergarten rooms or auditoriums), or have plans to enlarge by moving or enlarging existing libraries. It has also necessarily affected our secondary schools. If children are being taught work-study skills and have the opportunity to work independently in the Learning Center, this must continue in junior and senior high school.

[1]Available for $5.00 from Information Officer, F. A. E. Project, Shaker Heights City School District, 15600 Parkland Drive, Shaker Heights 20, Ohio.

The most important consequence of this experiment, hopefully, will come through the experiences children have in this program. If they can be developed into secondary and college students who pursue their academic interests in an independent, meaningful and increasingly successful manner, the true purpose of learning will have been served.

Harold K. Hughes

# *The Enhancement of Creativity**

$T$here are periods in history when one dominant idea characterizes many facets of intellectual life. In the seventeenth and eighteenth centuries, for example, mechanistic determinism flourished in physics and was reflected notably in philosophy, economics, and music. Possibly man is always in the midst of such periods, but he identifies them more clearly in perspective.

Taxonomists today describe the present scene variously as the second industrial revolution, the paper age, or the age of the anonymous man. Evolutionists speculate that man ceased to develop biologically a million years ago and chose, instead, the route of cultural evolution, a route that has led him through the paradox of his greatest intellectual triumph—the over-demonstration of his personal insignificance—and on to this ultimate tragedy, cosmology's imminent proof of the utter triviality of his species and his world.

At the risk of being declared myopic by taxonomists of the twenty-first century, I suggest that the common thread in these several classifications of the present scene is change, and that the dominant idea of our period in history is creativity.

As a research exercise, the serious study of creativity has long been the province of psychologists. In recent years, however, educators and business managers have culled the creativity literature and encouraged researchers in order, on the one hand, to accelerate discovery and, on the other, to increase profits through the more efficient use of personnel.

For nine years as an Associate of the Creative Science Program at New York University, I have studied scientific creativity in its many aspects and have lately begun to apply some tentative findings to my own teaching. The primary question to myself has been, Is it possible to stimulate the creativity

Hughes, Harold K. "The Enhancement of Creativity." *The Journal of Creative Behavior,* Vol. 3, No. 2, 1969, pp. 73-83.
*The material under this heading is abstracted from published research (see References) by Mooney, 1953; MacKinnon, 1962; Roe, 1953; Eiduson, 1962; Maslow, 1954; Pelz, 1958; Cattell, 1960; Dichter, 1959; Barron, 1958; Coler, 1959; and Drews, 1963.

of undergraduate and graduate students and, if so, will this enhanced creativity carry over into their later professional careers? Currently I have reason to think that the answer to that dual-faceted question is "yes," but I am not yet prepared to specify the boundary conditions between "yes" and "no." Tentatively, my hypothesis is, Scientific creativity in students can be enhanced in a climate and by techniques which can, in part, be created on the basis of a knowledge of those characteristics which distinguish creative from non-creative mature scientists (Terman, 1954). I present no data to support my hypothesis, nor are there any available that I know of. I merely present a series of reasoned and sometimes empirically based suggestions for the kind of ideal climate that may well produce more creative students, particularly scientists.

Naturally, not all future creative scientists have the characteristics which distinguish past or present scientists from their peers, nor would they necessarily benefit from this ideal climate that I propose. Higher education is, however, a group process. We must of necessity make decisions for the benefit of large numbers of students and hope that the flexibility that pervades the proposed climate can at least accommodate most of the exceptions without actually stifling them.

## Characteristics

Most creative scientists have good memories in both random and sequential access. A few display remarkable powers. Charles P. Steinmetz, for example, easily memorized the logarithms of the first 100 numbers. Herman P. Mark is reputed to remember the journal, volume, and page number of countless literature references. However, these creative scientists generally prefer to use their storage capacity selectively and decide for themselves what to store. Consequently, they have a low interest in enforced rote memory, seeing little reason to remember formulas which are easy to derive, facts that are readily available in books, or operations that are amenable to simple improvisation.

Creative scientists are particularly open to new experience. Possibly, this characteristic developed because the families of these children moved more often than most. Also, many of the scientists studied had, as children, been left alone for long periods of time during which they had to provide their own entertainment. They have wide interests and long interest spans and are not inclined to feel circumscribed by their environment. They work best when in frequent contact with colleagues having widely different orientations and experience.

The creative scientist works hard and persistently, is independent, antiauthoritarian, and attentive to detail. Apparently, his early home climate created strong drives which were self-controlled and channeled toward constructive and distant goals. Thus, early he experienced delayed satisfaction

362

of desires, as by working a year to get a longed-for bicycle. By attainment of a goal after much persistence, his resolve and creativity were stimulated.

Creative scientists on the average are emotionally cool, aloof, dominant and introspective. Often, as children, they chose to be alone although companionship was available. Nor were they very intimate with their families. Many observed some pathological disturbance at home and so learned to dislike interpersonal conflict. They are more socially concerned than sociable. Just as they enjoy a risk calculated on natural law but not on people, they prefer problems about things to problems that are people-related.

Albert Einstein (1950) illustrates the latter characteristic well when he writes, "My passionate interest in social justice and social responsibility has always stood in curious contrast to a marked lack of desire for direct association with men and women."

Of all the characteristics of a creative scientist, the one which is most related to his public image is his imaginative and unorthodox thinking. Nothing is spared his curiosity. He has neither veneration for the past nor respect for the present. With ideas, though not necessarily in behavior, he is future-oriented and is quite willing to make bold leaps into uncharted territory, guarded principally by intuition. This characteristic may well be a development of an overwhelming interest in reading and particularly in reading science fiction, which a creative scientist is likely to have at some stage in his life.

Likewise, he is not afraid of "way-out" daydreams, for he is confident that he can return to reality at will and appraise his dreams realistically. He is given to advocating changes for good logical but poor personal and political reasons. Being more interested in the goal than in the method of achieving it, he is likely to support his conclusions with vigor. This tendency makes him a disturber of the mental peace, and for the non-flexible teacher who wants to settle into a routine, the creative person creates havoc.

A creative scientist has a high tolerance for ambiguity and discomfort but little for boredom. Indeed, he actively seeks complex, discomforting situations and problems not only for the challenge they present but for aesthetic satisfaction in the elegant solution for which he hopes. Mental effort, then, is to the creative scientist what physical exercise is to an athlete— a chosen activity *and* a necessity. This strong drive almost automatically leads to the next characteristic.

Creative scientists find ways to reduce society's demands on them so that they have time to think. For example, many choose mates who, by competent management of home and children, relieve them of many common living chores. During these "think" periods, they may appear to be loafing. I remember when I was in industry a laboratory director would call me on the phone and say, "Bob has his feet on his desk again." Thus he would badger me about the most creative man in my section.

Creative scientists generally start slowly on a problem, look at many of its facets, and increase their pace as they proceed. Near the climax of success, they work furiously, and at this time observers become aware of the creative person's extraordinary capacity for involvement over extended periods of time. This, too, can be an explanation for the scientist's being so consistently described as an introvert.

The final characteristic of creative scientists that I wish to mention is their sensitivity to approval and disapproval. Although they have a good opinion of themselves, they need recognition and rewards in order to continue producing their best work. Similarly, they tend to learn most from those who are demanding yet fair. A typical creative scientist comes from a home where parental authority, although somewhat impersonal, was consistent, predictable, fair, and psychologically supportive. In general, rebellion was against ideas and seldom took the form of overt misbehavior.

## Toward a Total Creative Climate

Taking these eight characteristics into consideration and evaluating the needs inherent to their enhancement, and thus to creativity in general, a restructuring of the overall curriculum in most American colleges would appear to be desirable. Nor is the restructuring so major as to be improbable or even relatively time-consuming. For instance, American colleges commonly request that science students complete the liberal arts requirements in their first two years. This postpones the period of intensive concentration on their major interest and fails to utilize the enthusiasm for study that they bring to the campus. With a more flexible policy, general education courses could be distributed throughout the four years. We could maintain, then, a high level of interest in science for science majors while catering both to the creative person's adaptability and to his need for variety.

In a like vein, a science major should be required to take courses outside his major field—just as I am convinced that other majors should be required to take science courses. As T. S. Eliot has said, "It's a part of education to learn to interest ourselves in subjects for which we have no aptitude."

One, but by no means the only, value in required courses is that they train students in that quality of persistence without which there can be no creativity. Unfortunately, many advisors in the humanities do not share this view and they permit most of their majors to graduate illiterate in the facts and attitudes of science.

On the other hand, we must strike a balance, since, to be creative, an individual must have unprogramed time. Our pattern of required classes, convocations, homework and amusements must be liberalized in order that the student have the necessary opportunity for reflective and creative thinking. As an institution, the college, of course, should make sure that every student, and especially the creative one, is worked hard; yet, in many cases, the individual student can profitably be allowed to choose academically acceptable projects on his own. That is, schools must be rigid enough to force the lazy student to study and flexible enough to let the highly motivated one set his own pace. We need not, for example, be strict with all students about class attendance and deadlines; but we must demand adequate overall performance.

My own department offers credit for undergraduate courses called "Independent Study in Physics" and "Honors in Physics." Our experience with these courses is favorable and good students seem to like them, being able to direct their own theoretical and experimental activities in a wide variety of ways.

Thus, as I said, we have a paradox that needs equalizing: some students won't think unless they are forced to; others cannot exert their best efforts or develop to their full potential under excessive pressure to meet rigid requirements.

This paradox also seeps into the field of finances, in which scholarships and fellowships are needed (and should be provided) for those who are forced to devote a large fraction of each week to earning their support—and yet, a *moderate* level of financial pressure often increases the motivation for high achievement.

In order to resolve the paradoxes totally, of course, we would need a battery of individual-oriented educators supported by an extremely flexible, individual-oriented educational system. This is Educational Utopia. But, given the direction, the goal, we can come closer and closer in our lifetime to the ideal, with, as I see it, little lost and much gained.

In a final word about overall curriculum, the most creative students should be encouraged to change schools after receiving their bachelor's degree. Doctoral candidates thereby experience and benefit from a variety of equipment, emphases and teaching personalities, which is invaluable to their scientific and social maturing.

The college and its faculty should encourage nonclass activities such as attendance at professional meetings and lectures; publication; visits to other institutions, museums and libraries; and (for my particular group of students) a Student Section of the American Institute of Physics. The latter can also serve a social purpose. Whereas many future creative scientists are introverts, others like to be with people and benefit from close technical and social association with their classmates and professors. One graduate student wrote to me, "I find no greater stimulus to hard work and creative thinking than being in constant contact with intelligent, imaginative, critical and hardworking fellow graduate students."

Although we must teach students to expect a hostile or, at best, an indifferent climate from a society that frequently disapproves of creativity, we can easily provide them with lounges and library areas where they can converse with others who would otherwise lead similar lonely intellectual lives.

The teacher who fully understands the creative individual's tendency toward introversion will offer him a friendly, supportive relationship while respecting whatever psychological distance he prefers. In fact, a good instructor has a variety of relationships with his students. To one he is a friend, to another he is a taskmaster. In front of all he holds the carrot of achievement.

I remember one student calling me "a smiling executioner" for allowing him to devote an entire Christmas holiday to a high-gain amplifier which had no chance of working. He deserved the A he received for the course and he thanked me afterward for allowing him to learn so much electronics. Another student, however, complained that I gave him too many reasons why his inventions would not work. I do not pretend that it is easy to find the right way with the right student each time.

To encourage divergent thinking, a creative instructor will maintain an easy willingness to consider any question, any topic, any time. Thus, a good teacher is seen by his students as a "creative observer," according to Eric Barnes (1956), who describes one from a student's viewpoint: "He is perceptive, kind, appreciative, sometimes critical, but always detached. When he is on the sidelines, one's task immediately takes on new meaning and dignity. He finds the order latent in the apparent chaos of your life."

Obviously, to maximize student potential in the sciences or in any field, we must optimize the flexibility and *humaneness* of prospective teachers. They must be educated to be socially conscious, individual-concerned human beings first and educators second. An implication of the "adaptability" characteristic for the educational process is that there should be plenty of variety in course content and meeting formats. We should use audio and visual aids, reports, debates, outside speakers, instructors from other disciplines, visits to industry, and different seating arrangements and room assignments. Changes (particularly in the latter category) should appear logical and occur just often enough to be stimulating but not so often as to be disruptive or obviously capricious. It is perfectly natural, for instance, to have seating in the round for discussion meetings or seminars, since this arrangement is preferred by so many students.

In order to cater to the creative scientist's desire for resolvable disorder we should deal with complex concepts more often than we do now in lecture, laboratory, and homework. Too frequently in physics we simplify the assumptions in a problem in order to simplify the mathematics, but these two levels of difficulty need not be correlated. It is quite possible to devise complex problems without over-elaborating the mathematical tedium in their solution.

The essence of good engineering design is compromise, and problems requiring value-related compromise can be utilized more often. For maximum stimulation, these should cross the conventional boundaries of organized disciplines.

Another exercise in complexity is to devise problems as well as to solve them. Using my field of physics again as an example, one can ask for a pair of 3 by 3 matrices which commute and, therefore, have the same eigenvectors. We might also present a poorly defined situation, asking for a clarification of the problem and a tabulation of data which must be acquired before a solution can be found.

Is it not possible to raise a student's interest in complexity by admitting that much of what we teach him is incomplete and some of it even wrong? Few subjects in our freshmen and sophomore years are not simplified by assumptions: no friction, the absence of natural selection in the Hardy-Weinberg law of gene frequency stability, no chemical impurities present, circular Bohr orbits, etc. Having taught a topic under simplifying assumptions, the instructor might raise a student's creativity by revealing that the full story is really more complex. A good introduction to Heisenberg's uncertainty principle and to Godel's theorem (Nagel & Newman, 1958) is bound to help a science student realize that science is not always simple, or exact, or complete.

Conversely, intelligent simplification of complex situations should be taught as an important part of the creative treatment of scientific problems.

Certain techniques are known to promote divergent thinking. One can be called the "What would happen if. . ." question. John E. Arnold (1956), for example, populated a planet of Arcturus with unusual people for whom his students had to design a variety of products. Recently, I have had success by asking for the effects on the population of Terre Haute of a billion-fold increase in Planck's constant. In my experience, "What would happen if . . ." is a valid device for encouraging thinking and learning.

Puzzles, paradoxes and conundrums are also stimulants to divergent thinking. A story that I found useful concerns a panel truck I was following in my car. The driver stopped just short of a one-lane bridge and so I too had to stop. The driver alighted, seized a long pipe and proceeded to beat the sides of the truck vigorously. Wondering why, I too alighted and asked him what he was doing.

"Well," he said, "see that bridge? It will hold only 5 tons safely and I'm driving a 3-ton truck."

"Then you're all right," I said impatiently. "Go ahead and cross it."

"Oh, no," he replied. "You don't understand. The truck is also loaded with 3 tons of canaries and I'm trying to keep 1 ton of them in flight as I cross the bridge."

The class argued for two days about those canaries.

Another technique for stimulating science majors' creative thinking might well be the assignment of reading that is non-mathematical, reading the area of science fiction, and creative writing in all areas. All reading assignments should contain contradictory material.

At Indiana State University we are considering also a seminar in scientific methods and in the history and philosophy of science to broaden student perspectives after three years of emphasis on unintegrated facts and ideas. One of the reasons for studying the history of science is to allow students to derive emotional support from the past. To learn, for example, that Planck first obtained his equation for black-body radiation by curve-fitting data and only later realized it could have been derived from theoretical principles is to learn that even great men sometimes grope for answers.

Other techniques have proven valid in varying degrees. One of my colleagues is purposely vague about laboratory procedures in his advanced classes and claims that this stimulates the resourcefulness of students. In my thermodynamics class, I have found that I can break the pattern by which a student tends to answer questions in terms of the particular class he is attending: I simply ask a question in thermodynamic terms which really involves subject matter of a prerequisite course, such as mechanics or electricity.

An occasional dramatic stunt is stimulating, as I found out quite by accident. I once informed an elementary physical science class that we were to see a film on scientific methods. Not until the title flashed on the screen did I realize that the film was on superstitions. During the discussion afterward, I pretended to believe in the magic of rabbit's feet and water dowsing. Although most students know an instructor too well for him to deceive them totally, I feel that some of the students present learned as much about scientific method through dramatic use of contrast as they would have had the correct film been run.

Even the testing process can stimulate creativity. If we are to foster and take advantage of the creative person's tendency toward excellent but selective memory, we should give open as well as closed-book tests. The statement of problems in the latter type can include all data and complex formulas needed for their solution. To stimulate reflective thinking, throughout the year I sprinkle tests with problems that contain superfluous, contradictory or incomplete information along with more orthodox questions. A preliminary and admittedly subjective assessment of the value of these questions is that they do, in fact, stimulate students to more creative thinking.

Some tests should have essentially no time or resource limit. Three weeks before a term ends, for example, I distribute the first part of the final examination to some advanced classes. Students may consult any resource except another person. Limited time and extended time (take-home) tests rank students differently. It is not at all clear to me whether either ranking is the superior one. Life places a variety of demands on us and we should, I suspect, prepare students for leisurely problems as well as for urgent ones.


## Summary

Mature creative scientists are frequently distinguished from their less creative peers by their good but selective memory, openness to new experience, self-discipline, introversion, divergent thinking, attraction to resolvable disorder, insistence on free time, and need for a supportive climate. It is likely that these characteristics are but superficial manifestations of subconscious drives which produce extraordinary involvement in a problem for an extended period of time.

As a working hypothesis needing much more testing, I propose that these distinguishing characteristics imply that the ideal collegiate climate for the development of future creative scientists includes the following features: a moderate reliance on rote memory (open-book tests are, therefore, common); a variety of teaching methods, materials, topics and out-of-class experiences; formal course requirements in non-science areas; and self-directed education.

The ideal collegiate climate for creativity is supportive but only as personal as the student desires; it encourages divergent thinking about all problems, old and new; it stresses that all life is compromise and few subjects are completely knowable. Since one essence of creativity lies in the simplification of complexity, the ideal collegiate climate presents many complex problems, some of which are unsolvable. The climate is both leisurely and hurried.

The existence of this climate implies a staff capable of its creation, or, in other words, a staff of human beings sensitive to the needs of other human beings.


## References

Arnold, John E. The Creative Engineer. *Machine Design,* 3 May 1956, *28,* 119.

Barnes, E. W. *The man who lived twice: The biography of Edward Sheldon.* New York: Scribners, 1956.

Barron, F. The Needs for Order and for Disorder as Motives in Creative Activity. *Second (1957) University of Utah Research Conference on the Identification of Creative Scientific Talent,* Salt Lake City: Univ. of Utah Press, 1958, pp. 119-128.

Cattell, R. B. The Personality and Motivation of the Researcher from Measurements of Contemporaries and from Biography. *Third (1959) University of Utah Research Conference on the Identification of Creative Scientific Talent,* Salt Lake City: Univ. of Utah Press, 1960, pp. 119-131.

Coler, M. A. Creators of environment. *Teaching and learning.* New York: Ethical Culture Schools, 1959. Also, *Chem. & Eng. News,* 15 Aug. 1966, *44,* 72.

Dichter, E. Motivating the Technical Mind. *Industrial Research,* Spring 1959, *1,* 71.

Drews, E. M. Profile of creativity. *Nat. Educ. Assoc. J.,* Jan. 1963, *52,* 26.

Eiduson, B. T. *Scientists: Their psychological world.* New York: Basic Books, 1962.

Einstein, A. Quoted by Lin Yutang in *The wisdom of America,* New York: John Day, 1950, p.453.

MacKinnon, D. W. The Nature and Nurture of Creative Talent. *Amer. Psychol.,* 1962, *17,* 484.

Maslow, A. H. *Motivation and personality.* New York: Harper & Bros., 1954.

Mooney, R. L. *A preliminary listing of indices of creative behavior.* Columbus: Ohio State Univ. Bur. of Educ. Research, 1953.

Nagel, E., & Newman, J. R. *Godel's proof.* New York: New York Univ. Press, 1958.

Pelz, D. C. Social Factors in the Motivation of Engineers and Scientists. *School Sci. & Math.,* June 1958, *58,* 417.

Roe, A. *The making of a scientist.* New York: Dodd, Mead, 1953. Also, *Science,* 1961, *134,* 456.

Smith, R. F. W. The deliberate induction of new ideas. In M. A. Coler, *Essays on creativity in the sciences,* New York: New York Univ. Press, 1963.

Terman, L. M. Scientists and nonscientists in a group of 800 gifted men. *Psychol. Monog.,* 1954, *68 (7),* Whole No. 378.

Donald J. Treffinger
John Curtis Gowan

# An Updated Representative List of Methods and Educational Programs for Stimulating Creativity*

$T$his list of methods and programs has been developed for two major purposes: first, to serve as a source of references for further study of particular methods and programs; and second, as an indication of the relationship of a wide variety of methods and programs to the common goals of creative development and expression. Many of the items described first appeared in the *Creative Behavior Guidebook* by Sidney J. Parnes, published by Charles Scribner's Sons.

No attempt has been made to provide detailed explanations of any of the methods or programs. Nor is the list intended to be completely comprehensive or critical; certainly, we have not uncovered every possible resource which might have been included. Neither is every item which has been included of equal quality or importance. This compilation attempts to provide merely a representative listing of the great range of available methods, resources, and programs.

## 1. Affective Domain

Stimulation of the feelings and emotions of persons, to improve or enhance sensitivity to feelings, environments, and responses of others, as well as to develop values and release creative potential.

> Borton, T. *Reach, Touch, and Teach.* New York: McGraw-Hill, 1970.
> Brown, G. I. *Human Teaching for Human Learning.* New York: Viking, 1971.

Treffinger, Donald J. and Gowan, John Curtis "An Updated Representative List of Methods and Educational Programs for Stimulating Creativity." *The Journal of Creative Behavior,* Vol. 5, No. 2, Second Quarter, 1971, pp. 127-139.

*An updated version of an article which appeared in the "Creative Behavior Guidebook" by Sidney J. Parnes, published by Charles Scribner's Sons.

Casebeer, R. L. *Project Prometheus: Education for the Technetronic Age.* (1968). Jackson County Schools, 1133 South Riverside, Medford, Oregon, 97501.

Greenberg, H. M. *Teaching With Feeling.* New York: Macmillan, 1969.

Gunther, B. *Sense Relaxation.* New York: Collier, 1968.

Johnson, J. L. & Seagull, A. A. "Form and function in the affective training of teachers." *Phi Delta Kappan,* 1968, 50, 166.

Krathwohl, D. R., Bloom, B. S. & Masia, B. B. *Taxonomy of Educational Objectives, Handbook II: The Affective Domain.* New York: David McKay, 1964.

Mager, R. F. *Developing Attitude Toward Learning.* Palo Alto, California: Fearon, 1968.

Neill, A. S. *Summerhill: a Radical Approach to Child Rearing.* New York: Hart Publishing, 1960.

Rogers, C. R. *On Becoming a Person.* Boston: Houghton-Mifflin, 1961.

Rogers, C. R. *Freedom to Learn.* Columbus: Merrill, 1969.

Shaftel, F. *Role Playing for Social Values.* Englewood Cliffs: Prentice-Hall, 1967.

Spolin, V. *Improvisation for the Theater.* Evanston, Illinois: Northwestern University Press, 1967.

Weinstein, G. & Fantini, M. D. *Toward Humanistic Education: a Curriculum of Affect.* New York: Praeger, 1970.

## 2. Attribute Listing

Emphasizes the detailed observation of each particular characteristic or quality of an item or situation. Attempts are then made to profitably change the characteristic or to relate it to a different item. See: Crawford, R. P. *Direct Creativity* (with attribute listing). Wells, Vermont: Fraser, 1964.

## 3. Awareness Development

A program to increase the individual's sensitivity to what is going on within himself and how he relates to the here and now. See: Perls, F. S., Hefferline, R. F. & Goodman, P. *Gestalt Therapy.* New York: Julian Press, 1951.

## 4. Biographical Film Program

An educational program of ten documentary biographical films and a flexible textbook. It provides filmed contact with exemplary personalities and opportunity to draw from students' own inner resources in expressing themselves. Designed for college-bound students. See: Drews, E. M. & Knowlton, D. "The being and becoming series for college-bound students". *Audiovisual Instruction,* 1963 (January), 8, 29-32.

## 5. Bionics

A technique which seeks discovery in nature of ideas which are related to the solution of man's problems. For example, attributes of the eye of a beetle have suggested new types of groundspeed indicators for aircraft. See: "Bionics". *J. Creative Behavior,* 1968, 1, 52-57.

## 6. Brainstorming

Promotes rapid and unfettered associations in group discussions through deferment-of-judgment. See: Osborn, A. F. *Applied Imagination.* New York: Scribners, 1963.

## 7. Candid Camera Films

The Cornell Candid Camera Collection, which includes films originally made for and used by the television program, has many delightful short films which illustrate principles of creative problem solving and effective (as well as not-so-effective) thinking. Write for further information and catalog to: Du Art Film Laboratories, Du Art Film Building, 245 West 55th Street, New York, New York 10019.

## 8. Checklists

Focuses one's attention on a logical list of diverse categories to which the problem could conceivably relate. See: Osborn, A. F. *Applied Imagination.* New York: Scribners, 1963.
(See also Think Products).

## 9. Classroom Teaching and Creativity

Many articles and books have been addressed to the classroom teacher, providing ideas for encouraging creativity in the classroom. The following bibliography summarizes some useful resources:

Burton, W. H., Kimball, R. B. & Wing, R. I. *Education for effective thinking.* New York: Appleton-Century-Crofts, 1960. (pp. 323-6, 342-3 in partic.)
Carlson, R. K. "Emergence of creative personality." *Childhood Education,* 1960, 36, 402-404.

Cole, H. P. "Process curricula and creative development." *Journal of Creative Behavior,* 1969, 3, 243-259.

Givens, P. R. "Identifying and encouraging creative processes." *Journal of Higher Education,* 1962, 33, 295-301.

Hallman, R. J. "Techniques of creative teaching." *Journal of Creative Behavior,* 1967, 1, 325-330.

Hughes, H. K. "The enchancement of creativity." *Journal of Creative Behavior,* 1969, 3, 73-83.

Hutchinson, W. L. "Creative and productiive thinking in the classroom." *Journal of Creative Behavior,* 1967, 1, 419-427.

Kranyik, R. D. & Wagner, R. A. "Creativity and the elementary school teacher." *Elementary School Journal,* 1965, 66, 2-9.

Rusch, R. R., Denny, D. & Ives, S. "Fostering creativity in the sixth grade." *Elementary School Journal,* 1965, 65, 262-268.

Smith, J. A. *Setting conditions for creative teaching in the elementary school.* Boston: Allyn and Bacon, 1966. (Also: several companion paperbacks dealing with specific subject areas.)

Strang, R. "Creativity in the elementary school classroom." *NEA Journal,* 1961, 50, 20-22.

Taylor, C. W. & Harding, H. F. "Questioning and creating a model for curriculum reform." *Journal of Creative Behavior,* 1967, 1, 22-33.

Torrance, E. P. *Guiding creative talent.* Englewood Cliffs: Prentice Hall, 1962.

Torrance, E. P. *Rewarding Creative Behavior.* Englewood Cliffs: Prentice Hall, 1965.

Torrance, E. P. "Developing creativity through school experiences." In Parnes, S. J. and H. Harding (Eds.) *A Source Book For Creative Thinking.* New York: Scribners, 1962, pp. 31-47.

Torrance, E. P. *Encouraging Creativity in the Classroom.* Dubuque, Iowa: William C. Brown, 1970.

Torrance, E. P. & Myers, R. *Creative Learning and Teaching.* New York: Dutton, 1970.

Wodtke, K. & Wallen, N. "Teacher classroom control, pupil creativity, and pupil classroom behavior." *Journal of Experimental Education,* 1965, 34, 59-65.

## 10. Collective Notebook

Participants record their thoughts about a problem several times daily, then review the list, selecting the most promising ideas for further investigation. See: Haefele, J. W. *Creative Innovation.* New York: Reinhold, 1962.

## 11. Creative Analysis

A program of exercises designed to increase the college student's facility in discovering relationships within the knowledge he possesses, and thereby in creating new knowledge. Emphasizes words as tools of the mind and the thought process. See: Upton, A. & Samson, R., *Creative Analysis.* New York: Dutton, 1964.

## 12. Creative Instructions

Emphasizes how instructions are given (problem presented, etc.) as a key determinant in stimulating individual or group production of creative responses. See unpublished doctoral dissertation (67-15607), Colgrove, Melba, Annetta. "Stimulating Creative Problem Solving Performance Innovative Set". University of Michigan, 1967.

## 13. Creative Thinking Workbook

A program for adults and college-level students; many exercises suitable for high school students. The exercises are designed to remove internal governors and to provide practice in stretching the imagination problem-finding and problem-solving. Problems are included on product design and on presenting ideas. Can be self-instructional. Available from: W. O. Uraneck, 56 Turning Mill Road, Lexington, Massachusetts 02173 (1963).

## 14. Curriculum — General

Many recent developments in curriculum and instruction have been concerned with providing opportunities for creative growth. In this section, and the next five, several representative publications are listed in a variety of curriculum areas. (See also Affective Domain.)

Franco, J. M. *Project Beacon.* Public Schools, Rochester, New York 14608. (Concerned with the development of ego strength in primary grades.)

Gibson, J. S. *The Intergroup Relations Curriculum.* Medford, Massachusetts: Tufts University Press.

Jaynes, R. & Woodbridge, B. *Bowman Early Childhood Series.* Glendale, California: Bowman Publishing, 1969. (Designed to help develop positive self-awareness and identity, awareness of self as a person, ability to relate to others.)

Kreese, F. H. *Match Projects.* Boston: American Science and Engineering, Inc., 20 Overland Street. (Materials and activities across many areas, for grades 4-6+).

Massialas, B. G. & Zevin, J. *Creative Encounters in the Classroom.* New York: Wiley, 1967.

For anthologies dealing with educational and curricular implications of creativity studies:

Gowan, J. C., Demos, G. D. & Torrance, E. P. (Eds.) *Creativity: its Educational Implications.* New York: Wiley, 1967.

Davis, G. A. & Scott, J. A. (Eds.) *Training Creative Thinking.* New York: Holt, Rinehart, and Winston, 1971.

Treffinger, D. J. (Ed.) *Readings on Creativity in Education.* To be published by Prentice-Hall, Inc.

## 15. Curriculum—Mathematics

Davis, R. B. *The Madison Project*. Reading, Massachusetts: Addison Wesley. Five different curricula; grades 2-8.

Matthews, G. *Nuffield Mathematics Project*. New York: Wiley. A British program for ages 5-13.

Werntz, J. H. *MINNEMAST Project*. For grades K-6; write: 720 Washington Avenue SE, Minneapolis, Minnesota 55414.

## 16. Curriculum—Preprimary

Dunn, L. M. *Peabody Language Development Kit*. American Guidance Publishers, Circle Pines, Minnesota 55014.

Frostig, M. *Frostig Visual Perception Program*. Chicago: Follett.

Stendler, C. *Early Childhood Curriculum: a Piaget Approach*. Boston: American Science and Engineering.

For research on creativity among preprimary children, contact Professor Elizabeth Starkweather, Oklahoma State University, Stillwater, Oklahoma.

## 17. Curriculum—Reading, Literature, Language Arts

Clymer, T. et al. *Reading 360*. Boston: Ginn and Company, 1969. An innovative series, in which E. Paul Torrance served as creativity consultant.

Medeiros, V. *The Voices of Man Literature Series*. Reading, Massachusetts: Addison-Wesley. High school literature series for disadvantaged students.

Moffet, J. *A Student Centered Language Arts Curriculum*. (Volume 1: K-6; Volume 2: K-13). Boston: Houghton Mifflin, 1968.

## 18. Curriculum—Science

Brown, R. R. *Elementary Science Study*. (K-6). Manchester, Missouri: Webster Division, McGraw-Hill.

Karplus, R. & Thier, H. D. *Science Curriculum Improvement Study*. (K-6). Chicago: Rand-McNally.

LaSalle, D. Write for information concerning an independent science center. *Talcott Mountain Science Center*, Montevideo Road, Avon, Connecticut 06001.

Mayor, J. *Science: a Process Approach*. (K-6). New York: Xerox Corporation.

Washton, N. S. *Teaching Science Creatively*. Philadelphia: W. B. Saunders, 1967.

Anderson, R. D., DeVito, A., Dyrli, O. E., Kellogg, M., Kochendorfer, L. & Weigand, J. *Developing Childrens' Thinking Through Science*. Englewood Cliffs: Prentice-Hall, 1970.

# 19. Curriculum—Social Studies

Bruner, J. S. *Man: a Course of Study*. Curriculum Development Associates, 1211 Connecticut Ave., NW, Washington, D. C. 20036.

Edcom Systems. *Space, Time, and Life*. (Grades 4-6). EDCOM Systems, 145 Witherspoon Road, Princeton, N. J. 08540.

Educational Research Council of America. *Concepts and Inquiry*. (Gr. K-8). Boston: Allyn and Bacon.

Lippitt, R. *Social Science Laboratory Units*. (Gr. 4-6). Chicago: Science Research Associates.

Muessig, R. *Discussion Pictures for Beginning Social Studies*. New York: Harper and Row, 1967.

Taba, H. & Durkin, M. *Taba Social Studies Curriculum*. (Gr. 1-8). Reading, Mass.: Addison-Wesley Co.

# 20. Delphi Technique

Polling procedure resembling an absentee "brainstorming" effort used to generate alternative futures for a particular topic or series of topics. See: Helmer, Olaf. SOCIAL TECHNOLOGY Basic, 1966. For additional references, contact Book Service, World Future Society, P.O. Box 19285, Twentieth Street Station, Washington, D.C., 20036.

# 21. Developmental Stage Analysis of Creativity

See: Gowan, J. C. *The Development of the Creative Individual*. (1971). Robert Knapp Pub., Box 7234, San Diego, California, 92107.

# 22. Experimental Psychology Techniques

Caron, A. J. "A test of Maltzman's theory of originality training." *Journal of Verbal Learning and Verbal Behavior*, 1963, 1, 436-442.

Duncan, C. P. "Attempts to influence performance on an insight problem." *Psychological Reports*, 1961, 9, 35-42.

Gallup, H. F. "Originality in free and controlled association responses." *Psychological Reports*, 1963, 13, 923-929.

Maltzman, I. "On the training of originality." *Psychological Review*. 1960, 67, 229-242.

Maltzman, I., Belloni, Marigold, & Fishbein, M. "Experimental studies of associational variables in originality." *Psychological Monographs*, 1964, 78, 3. (Whole #580).

Maltzman, I., Brooks, L., Bogartz, W. & Summers, S. "The facilitation of problem-solving by prior exposure to uncommon responses." *Journal of Experimental Psychology,* 1958, 56, 339-406.

Maltzman, I., Bogartz, W. & Breger, L. "A procedure for increasing word association originality and its transfer effects." *Journal of Experimental Psychology,* 1958, 56, 392-398.

Maltzman, I. & Gallup, H. F. "Comments on 'originality' in free and controlled association responses." *Psychological Reports,* 1964, 14, 573-574.

Maltzman, I., Simon, S., Raskin, P. & Licht, L. "Experimental studies in the training of originality." *Psychological Monographs,* 1960, 74(6). Whole #493.

## 23. Forced Relationship Techniques

Specific types of exercises designed to derive new combinations of items and thoughts. See: Whiting, C. S. *Creative Thinking.* New York: Reinhold, 1958. (See also Management of Intelligence; Racking)

## 24. Futuristics

Predicting the future, with projections for five, ten, and fifty year periods. Write: Carl Gregory, California State College, School of Business, Long Beach, California 90801. Also contact: World Future Society, P.O. Box 19285, 20th St. Station, Washington D.C. 20036.

## 25. General Semantics

Approaches which help the individual to discover multiple meanings or relationships in words and expressions. See: Hayakawa, S. I. *Language in Thought and Action.* New York: Harcourt, Brace and World, Inc., 1964. For continuing current information, see ETC.: *a Review of General Semantics,* a quarterly journal with editorial offices at San Francisco State College, San Francisco, California 94132. (Business office: 540 Powell Street, San Francisco, California 94108.) See: True, S. R. "A Study of the Relation of General Semantics and Creativity." *Dissertation Abstracts,* 1964, 25 (4), 2390.

(Note: a conference on Creativity and General Semantics was held in conjunction with the 17th Annual Creative Problem-Solving Institute, in June 1971.)

## 26. Incident Process

A problem-solving approach (and/or training program) developed at the college and adult level. It stresses multiple viewpoints and a wide search for problem-elements; applies many methods similar to the older Job Relations Training program. See: Pigors, P. W. & Pigors, F. C. *Case Method in Human Relations: the Incident Process.* New York: McGraw-Hill, 1961.

## 27. Kepner-Tregoe Method

An approach (or training program) that emphasizes "what a man *does* with information," i.e., how he interrelates facts in analyzing problems and making decisions. Developed at adult level. See: Kepner, C. H. & Tregoe, B. B. *The Rational Manager.* New York: McGraw-Hill, 1965.

## 28. Management of Intelligence

A number of techniques for creative problem-solving, including negative ideation, 7 × 7 technique,, and others, are included in: Carl E. Gregory. *The Management of Intelligence: Scientific Problem Solving and Creativity.* New York: McGraw-Hill, 1967.

## 29. Morphology (or Morphological Analysis)

A system involving the methodical interrelating of all elements of a problem in order to discover new approaches to a solution. See: Allen, M. S. *Morphological Creativity.* Englewood Cliffs, N. J.: Prentice-Hall, 1962.

## 30. Problem-Solving Training

A program on problem-solving skills for high-IQ first graders. Consists of units called "games." Presented by the teacher as a programmed script for individual instruction (one child at a time). See: Anderson, R. C. "Can First Graders Learn an Advanced Problem-Solving Skill?". *Journal of Educational Psychology,* 1965, 56(6), 283-294.

## 31. Process Education Resources

A survey of materials and resources which can be utilized in process education: Seferian, A., & Cole, H. P. *Encounters In Thinking: a Compendium of*

*Curricula for Process Education.* Buffalo, New York: Creative Education Foundation, (Occasional Paper #6).

## 32. Productive Thinking Program

A self-instructional program for the upper elementary grades. It attempts to help children improve their creative problem-solving ability. To be published, in an expanded version, by Charles E. Merrill, Inc., of Columbus, Ohio. Considerable research has been conducted in which the original version of the *Productive Thinking Program* was used; much of this research is reviewed in: Treffinger, D. J. & Ripple, R. E. "Programmed instruction in creative problem-solving." *Educational Leadership,* 1971, 28, 667-675. Other published reports include:

Covington, M. V. "Some experimental evidence on teaching for creative understanding." *The Reading Teacher,* 1967 (Feb.), 390-396.

Covington, M. V. & Crutchfield, R. S. "Facilitation of creative problem-solving." *Programmed Instruction,* 1965, 4, 3-5, 10.

Crutchfield, R. S. "Creative thinking in children: its teaching and testing." In: H. Brim, R. Crutchfield and W. Holtzman (Eds.) *Intelligence: Perspectives 1965.* New York: Harcourt, Brace, and World, 1966 (pp. 33-64.)

Crutchfield, R. S. "Instructing the individual in creativity." In: Educational Testing Service's *Individualizing Instruction* (Princeton, 1965); also in Mooney and Razik's *Explorations in Creativity* (1967), pp. 196-206.

Crutchfield, R. S. & Covington, M. V. "Programmed instruction and creativity." *Programmed Instruction,* 1965, 4, 1-2, 8-10.

Evans, D., Ripple, R. E. & Treffinger, D. J. "Programmed instruction and productive thinking: a preliminary report of a cross-national comparison." In: Dunn, W. R. & Holyroyd, C., (Eds.) *Aspects of Educational Technology.* London: Methuen, 1968 (115-120).

Olton, R. M. "A self-instructional program for the development of productive thinking in fifth- and sixth-grade children." In: F. E. Williams (Ed.) *First Seminar on Productive Thinking in Education.* St. Paul, Minnesota: Macalester College, 1966, 53-60.

Olton, R. M. "A self-instructional program for developing productive thinking skills in fifth- and sixth-grade children." *Journal of Creative Behavior,* 1969, 3, 16-25.

Olton, R. M. & Crutchfield, R. S. "Developing the skills of productive thinking." In: Mussen, P., Langer, J. & Covington, M. (Eds.) *New directions in developmental psychology.* New York: Holt, Rinehart, and Winston, 1969.

Olton, R. M., Wardrop, J., Covington, M., Goodwin, W., Crutchfield, R., Klausmeier, H. & Ronda, T. "The development of productive thinking skills in fifth-grade children." Technical Report #34. Madison: University of Wisconsin Rand D Center for Cognitive Learning, 1967.

Ripple, R. E. & Dacey, J. S. "The facilitation of problem-solving and verbal creativity by exposure to programed instruction." *Psychology in the Schools,* 1967, 4, 240-245.

Treffinger, D. J. & Ripple, R. E. *The effects of programed instruction in productive thinking on verbal creativity and problem-solving among elementary school children.* Ithaca, New York: Cornell University, 1968. Final Report of USOE Research Project OEG-0-8-080002-0220-010.

Treffinger, D. J. & Ripple, R. E. "The effects of programed instruction in productive thinking on verbal creativity and problem-solving among pupils in grades four through seven." *Irish Journal of Education,* 1970, 4, 47-59.

Treffinger, D. J. & Ripple, R. E. "Developing creative problem-solving abilities and related attitudes through programed instruction." *Journal of Creative Behavior,* 1969, 3, 105-110.

Wardrop, J. L., Olton, R., Goodwin, W., Covington, M., Klausmeier, H., Crutchfield, R. & Ronda, T. "The development of productive thinking skills in fifth-grade children." *Journal of Experimental Education,* 1969, 37, 67-77.

## 33. Psychodramatic Approaches

These include a variety of techniques such as role playing and role reversal. In psychodrama the attempt is made to bring into focus all elements of an individual's problem; whereas in sociodrama the emphasis is on shared problems of group members. Elements of these techniques have been used in various types of educational settings and training programs. See: Moreno, J. L., *Who Shall Survive?,* New York: Beacon House, 1953. For current reading, see the quarterly journal *Group Psychotherapy* by the same publisher.

## 34. Purdue Creativity Training Program

The *Purdue Creativity Training Program* consists of 28 audio tapes and accompanying printed exercises, for the development of creative thinking and problem-solving abilities among elementary school pupils. For further information, write: John F. Feldhusen or Donald J. Treffinger, Educational Psychology Section, Purdue University, South Campus Courts G, Lafayette, Indiana 47907. Published descriptions and research reports include:

Bahlke, S. J. *A study of the enhancement of creative abilities in elementary school children.* Unpublished master's thesis, Purdue University, 1967.

Bahlke, S. J. *Componential evaluation of creativity instructional materials.* Unpublished doctoral thesis, Purdue University, 1969.

Feldhusen, J. F., Bahlke, S. J. & Treffinger, D. J. "Teaching creative thinking." *Elementary School Journal,* 1969, 70, 48-53.

Feldhusen, J. F., Treffinger, D. J. & Bahlke, S. J. "Developing creative thinking: the Purdue Creativity Program." *Journal of Creative Behavior,* 1970, 4, 85-90.

Robinson, W. L. T. *Taped-creativity-series versus conventional teaching and learning.* Unpublished master's thesis, Atlanta University, 1969.

WBAA. *Creative Thinking: the American Pioneers.* (A manual for teachers). West Lafayette, Indiana: Purdue University, 1966.

## 35. Racking Techniques

(also 7×7 technique and other forcing techniques)
See: Gregory, C. E. *Management of Intelligence: Scientific Problem-Solving & Creativity.* New York: McGraw-Hill, 1967.


## 36. Self-Enhancing Education

Emphasis on basic principles of creative problem-solving, including education for setting as well as solving one's own problems. See: Randolph, Norma & Howe, W. A. *Self-Enhancing Education, a Program to Motivate Learners.* Sanford Press, Sanford Office, 200 California Avenue, Palo Alto, California, 1967.


## 37. Self-Instructional Course in Applied Imagination

Programmed set of 28 self-instructional booklets. For complete curriculum No. 015677 or microfiche of report EDO-10382 write to ERIC Document Report Service, 4936 Fairmont Ave., Bethesda, Maryland 20014.


## 38. Sensitivity ("T Group")

A training program designed to help a person gain insight into himself and his functioning in a group. It attempts to increase the person's openness to ideas and viewpoints. See: Bradford, Leland P., Gibb, Jack R. & Benne, K. (eds.). *T Group Theory and Laboratory Method.* New York: Wiley, 1964. (See Affective Domain)


## 39. Structure of Intellect

A model devised by J. P. Guilford giving organization to the various factors of intellect, and arranging them into three grand dimensions: contents, operations, and products.
See: Guilford, J. P. *The Nature of Human Intelligence.* New York: McGraw-Hill Co., 1967.
Guilford, J. P. *Intelligence, Creativity, and Their Educational Implications.* San Diego: Knapp, 1968.

## 40. Synectics (or Operational Creativity)

A training program which stresses the practical use of analogy and metaphor in problem-solving. The Synectics mechanisms "force new ideas and associations up for conscious consideration rather than waiting for them to arise fortuitously." Developed at adult level. See: Gordon, W. J. *Synectics: the Development of Creative Capacity.* New York: Harper Bros. 1961.

## 41. Theoretical Issues

The question, "Can creativity be developed?" has interested many scholars, and the literature, both supportive and critical, contains many stimulating papers. Among them are:

Anderson, H. H. "Creativity and education." *College and University Bulletin,* 1961, 13.

Ausubel, D. P. "Fostering creativity in the school." *Proceedings of the Centennial Symposium, "How Children Learn."* Toronto, Ontario, Canada: Phi Delta Kappa and O.I.S.E., 1967, 37-49.

Ausubel, D. P. *Educational psychology: a cognitive view.* New York: Holt, Rinehart and Winston, 1968. ( Ch. 16, particularly pp. 549-555, 559-562.)

Ausubel, D. P. & Robinson, F. *School learning.* New York: Holt, Rinehart and Winston, 1969. (Ch. 17, partic. 523-540, 543-4).

Danziger, K. "Fostering creativity in the school: social psychological aspects." *Proceedings of the Centennial Symposium, "How Children Learn."* Toronto: Phi Delta Kappa and O.I.S.E., 1967, 50-59.

deMille, R. "The creativity boom." *Teachers College Record,* 1963, 54, 199+.

Gagne, R. M. *The conditions of learning.* New York: Holt, Rinehart, Winston, 1965. (partic. pp. 166-170.)

Getzels, J. W. "Creativity thinking, problem-solving, and instruction." In NSSE Yearbook, *Theories of learning and instruction.* 1964, 240-267.

Guilford, J. P. "Factors that aid and hinder creativity." *Teachers College Record,* 1962, 63, 391.

Hallman, R. J. "Can creativity be taught?" *Educational Theory,* 1964, 14, 15+.

Parnes, S. J. "Can creativity be increased?" In Parnes and Harding. *A source book for creative thinking.* New York: Charles Scribner's Sons, 1962, pp. 151-168.

Parnes, S. J. *Creative potential and the educational experience.* Buffalo: Creative Education Foundation, 1967. (Occasional Paper #2.)

Taylor, C. W. & Williams, F. E. (Eds.) *Instructional Media and Creativity.* New York: Wiley, 1966.

Taylor, C. W. & Williams, F. E. (Eds.) *Instructionnal Media and Creativity.* New York: Wiley, 1966.

White, W. F. *Psychosocial principles applied to classroom teaching.* New York: McGraw-Hill, 1969, (Ch. 7, particularly pp. 136ff.)

## 42. Think Products

A series of materials for teachers and industry to stimulate creative performance. Included is a series of TNT materials for teachers (techniques and tips) and a little magazine called "The Creative Thinker". Available from Think Products, 1209 Robin Hood Circle, Towson, Md. 21204.

## 43. Thinking Creatively

Gary A. Davis, Department of Educational Psychology, University of Wisconsin, Madison, Wisconsin, has been active in research on the development of creative thinking abilities, and in constructing instructional programs and materials as well. He has also published with Joseph A. Scott, an anthology entitled, "Training Creative Thinking". New York: Holt, Rinehart, and Winston, 1971. Related articles and materials include:

> Davis, G. A. "Training creativity in adolescents: a discussion of strategy." *Journal of Creative Behavior,* 1969, 3, 95-104.
> Davis, G. A. & Houtman, S. E. *Thinking creatively: a guide to training imagination.* Madison: University of Wisconsin Res. and Devel. Center for Cognitive Learning, 1968.
> Davis, G. A., Houtman, S., Warren, T. & Roweton, W. "A program for training creative thinking: I. Preliminary Field Test." Madison: University of Wisconsin, Res. and Devel. Center for Cognitive Learning, 1969.
> Davis, G. A. & Manske, M. "An instructional method of increasing originality." *Psychonomic Science,* 1966, 6, 73-74.
> Davis, G. A. & Roweton, W. "Using idea checklists with college students: overcoming resistance." *Journal of Psychology,* 1968, 70, 221-226.
> Manske, M. & Davis, G. "Effects of simple instructional biases upon performance on the Unusual Uses Tests." *Journal of General Psychology,* 1968, 79, 25-33.

## 44. Torrance's Materials

E. Paul Torrance, Professor of Educational Psychology at the University of Georgia, Athens, Georgia, has developed with colleagues several sets of instructional materials for fostering creative thinking among elementary school children. His *Ideabooks* series, with Robert Myers, includes "Can You Imagine?", "For Those Who Wonder," "Invitations To Thinking and Doing," "Invitations To Speaking and Writing Creatively," and "Plots, Puzzles, and Ploys." The *Imagicraft* series, with B. F. Cunnington, includes recorded exercises, based on biographical sketches of famous people and the "Sounds and Images" exercises. Most are intended for elementary school children, but contain imaginative exercises which might readily be used with adolescents and adults with minor modifications. For information, write

Ginn and Company, Waltham, Massachusetts 02154. The *Torrance Tests of Creative Thinking* are published by the Personnel Press, Princeton, New Jersey.

See also:

Britton, R. J. *A study of creativity in selected sixth-grade groups.* Unpublished doctoral thesis, University of Virginia, 1967.

Torrance, E. P. & Gupta, R. "Development and evaluation of recorded programed experiences in creative thinking in the fourth grade." Minneapolis: University of Minnesota, Bureau of Educational Research, 1964.

Torrance, E. P. "Priming creative thinking in the primary grades." *Elementary School Journal,* 1961, 62, 34-41.

.    (See also Classroom Teaching and Creativity above.)

## 45. Value Engineering (or Value Analysis, Value Innovation, Value Management, Etc.)

Training programs applying general principles of creative problem-solving to group efforts toward reducing costs or optimizing value. Adult level. See: Miles, L. D., *Techniques of Value Analysis and Engineering.* New York: McGraw-Hill, 1961; also Value Engineering Handbook, H111, U. S. Department of Defense, March 29, 1963 (U. S. Government Printing Office, Washington, D. C.). For current information, conference reports, bibliographies, etc., write Society of American Value Engineers, Windy Hill, Suite E-9, 1741 Rosewell Street, Smyrna, Georgia 30080.

## 46. Wff'n Proof

A symbolic logic game designed to increase one's ability to discover new relationships in a logical manner. Portions applicable at elementary level, proceeding through adult levels. Available from author, L. E. Allen (*WFF'N PROOF, The Game of Modern Logic*), P.O. Box 71, New Haven, Connecticut 06501.

## 47. Williams' Model

Frank E. Williams, Portland State College, Portland, Oregon, has developed an approach for helping teachers integrate the teaching of cognitive and affective skills with the presentation of subject matter. Recent published reports include:

Williams, F. E. "Fostering classroom creativity." *Cal. Teachers Assn. Journal,* March 1961.

Williams, F. E. "The search for the creative teacher." *Cal. Teachers Assn. Journal,* January 1964, 60, 14-16.

Williams, F. E. "Perspective of a model for developing productive-creative behaviors in the classroom." In: Williams, F. E. (Ed.) *First Seminar on Productive Thinking in Education.* St. Paul: Macalester College, 1966, 108-116.

Williams, F. E. "Training children to be creative may have little effect on original classroom performance, unless. . ." *Cal. Journal of Ed. Research,* 1966, 17.

Williams, F. E. "Models for encouraging creativity in the classroom by integrating cognitive-affective behaviors." *Educational Technology,* 1969, 9, 7-13.

Williams, F. E. *Classroom Ideas For Encouraging Thinking and Feeling.* Buffalo, New York: D. O. K. Publishers, 711 East Delevan Avenue, Buffalo, N.Y. 14215.

Williams, F. E. *Media For Developing Creative Thinking in Young Children.* Buffalo, New York: Creative Education Foundation, 1968 (Occasional Paper #3).

## 48. Work Simplification

An industrial training program that applies some of the general principles of creative problem-solving to the simplification of operations or procedures. Provides opportunity for personnel to use their mental resources in helping improve organizational operations, using simple industrial engineering principles. ("Job Methods Training," as well as other similarly named programs of World War II and thereafter, applied the basic concepts of this program.) See: Goodwin, H. F. "Work Simplification" (a documentary series of articles). *Factory Management and Maintenance,* July 1958. Briefer but more recent information may be obtained from Work Simplification Conferences, P.O. Box 30, Lake Placid, New York 12947 and from an article on Work Simplification by Auren Uris in the September 1965 issue of *Factory.*

## 49. Young Thinker (1964)

For children between 5-10 years of age. A series of more than 50 projects and exercises which can be used by the individual or by groups. These have been used in the home and in schools. Available from W. O. Uraneck, 56 Turning Mill Road, Lexington, Massachusetts 02173.

*Robert F. Eberle*

# Developing Imagination
# Through Scamper

## Overview

The past decade has witnessed a tremendous growth of interest in child-rearing. The perceptive, imaginative and creative abilities of youngsters have received their overdue share of attention from educators and psychologists.

All too frequently, adults who come in contact with children are obsessed with an urgency to prepare them for the 'real world' as quickly as possible. The pressures often generated by this feeling, perhaps more than anything else, tend to slow down if not entirely extinguish some children's imaginative and creative potential.

If we are to remedy the situation and effectively nurture creative behavior in children, then adults must: (1) be made aware of the conditions that tend to hamper creative-imaginative expression and (2) possess a working knowledge of the attitudes and behaviors that encourage this intellectual activity. Furthermore, we must expand our approach to education from (1) simply acquiring and retaining basic knowledge, to include (2) exploring the undetermined, revising the known and creating what might be.

Dr. Frank E. Williams, then Director for the National Schools Project, and his colleagues developed and tested techniques designed to encourage creative-imaginative expression in children. When exposed to these instructional strategies (which focused upon specific thinking-abilities) in a classroom environment which encouraged expression of particular kinds of feelings, the youngsters made statistically significant gains in their performance. These thinking processes—Fluent Thinking, Flexible Thinking, Originality, Elaborative Thinking—and the feeling processes—Willingness to take a calculated risk, Preference for complexity, Intuition—are the premises for newly devised *Scamper Games.*[1]

Scientific investigation has shown that individuals—whether children or adults—continually draw knowledge from their personal information-bank

Eberle, Robert F. "Developing Imagination Through Scamper." *The Journal of Creative Behavior,* Vol. 6, No. 3, Third Quarter, 1972, pp. 199-203.

[1]*Scamper, Games for Imagination Development* is published by the D.O.K. Publishers, Inc. 771 East Delavan Avenue, Buffalo, New York 14215. (Paper — 64 pages, $2.00)

and adapt, combine, rearrange or otherwise manipulate it to form creative ideas. Although the process does occur at the unconscious level (termed incubation by some), it is most frequently practiced at the conscious level.

Checklists—any form of questions or suggestions that stimulate ideation—have been found to be invaluable in the formation of creative ideas. Thus, the Scamper technique draws quite heavily on a list of Idea-Spurring questions developed by the late Alex F. Osborn founder of the Buffalo-based Creative Education Foundation.

## Scamper for Adults

During the development stage, Scamper games were tested on youngsters from three years of age to college students and teachers. Aside from its intended use at the lower age levels, the technique was found to be applicable to people of all ages and in different situations. As a form of 'intellectual calisthenics,' the technique is capable of (1) developing group spirit, (2) arousing curiosity, (3) stimulating involvement, and (4) providing strategies for creative listening and the development of imagination.

The directions are relatively simple. As few as two or as many as thirty-five can participate. Players are encouraged to meet the conditions of detachment, concentration, and reverie. A designated leader then reads a prepared script containing cues and directions followed by pauses. The pauses provide necessary time for the players to form eidetic images. During the pauses the leader observes the emotions, reactions and gestures of the participants as a means for determining when to continue with the next cue. By way of example, the following is the "Light Bulb"[2] game which can be used either with youngsters or adults.

## Light Bulb Example

We have so many wonderful things to help us live comfortably that we really don't give much thought about it. But if somebody hadn't given some thought to these things they would have never been invented. Have you ever thought what it would be like if light bulbs had never been invented? . . . I wouldn't like that, would you? . . . Light bulbs help us in many, many ways. But I think we could make them even better than they are now. I'm sure we could make them better . . . if we use our imagination.

Put a light bulb in your left hand. . . . Hold it out in front of you. . . . Very good. Now we are going to ask the light bulb to do whatever it is that we wish it to do. You may have to wish very hard for the light bulb to get

²The Light Bulb Game is reprinted with permission from D.O.K. Publishers, Inc., 771 East Delavan Avenue, Buffalo, New York 14215.

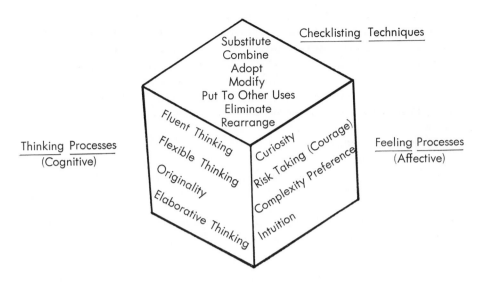

**FIGURE 1** Scamper model for creative imagination development.

your message, but let's try it and see if the light bulb will do what we desire it to do. . . . Wish for the light bulb to turn on. . . . Is it on. . . . Turn it off. . . . Now let's have the light bulb shine different colors. What color do you desire? Red? Green? Blue? Orange? Is there any other color that you desire? . . . Wish for the light bulb to shine whatever color you want it to shine. . . . Did it shine your color? . . . Would you rather the bulb shine warm or cold? . . . Take your choice and have the light bulb shine the way you want it to . . . . Do you feel the temperature changing in the room? . . . Put the light bulb aside. . . .

Get another light bulb and unscrew the bottom of it. . . . Take the bottom off and pour in some fly spray. . . . Screw the bottom back on. . . . Hold it out in front of you and wish for it to start shining. . . . As it shines have it kill all of the flies. . . . Now make the light bulb bigger and flat like a television tube. . . . Blink your eyes and have a program come on. . . . Blink your eyes and change the picture to another program. . . . Blink them again for another program. . . . Now blink your eyes and have the "Next Saturday Program" come on. . . . Are you going to be happy next Saturday? . . . Blink your eyes and turn off the T.V. . . .

Take another light bulb. . . . Make it about half as big as it is now. . . . Let's pretend that it is a magic flashlight. . . . Shine it at a cat and make the cat as small as a mouse. . . . Shine it on a mouse and make the mouse as big as a cat. . . . Have the mouse chase the cat. . . . Shine it on the dog and have the dog mee-ow like a cat. . . . Shine it on a bird and have the bird bark like a dog. . . . Shine it on a cow and have the cow grunt like a pig. . . . Shine it on a pig and have the pig sing like a bird. . . . Put your magic lightbulb on the shelf. . . .

Now put a light bulb in each hand. . . . Hold your arms out straight to the side. . . . Pretend that your light bulbs are jet engines and run down the street for a take-off. . . . Run faster. . . . Faster yet. . . . Zoom yourself up into the air. . . . Higher. . . . Higher. . . . Circle over your house. . . . Look down. . . . Do you see anyone you know? . . . Now zoom over town and look down. . . . Do you see any stores? . . . Zoom away from town and look down at the river. . . . Zoom away and look at the mountains. . . . Look at the ocean. . . . Zoom back toward home. . . . When you are over your house let loose of the light bulbs and have them zip away into space. . . . Open your parachute and float slowly to the ground. . . . As you float down, look all around you. . . . You are heading toward your back yard. . . . Touch your feet down, take off your parachute, and go tell people that you are home
. . . . I'll bet you never thought you could make a jet plane out of light bulbs. . . . Nothing is very hard to do. . . if you use your imagination.

## Summary

Scamper is a great leveling activity in which all players may become personally involved. Whether employed with children or adults, these creative-imagination games will lift individuals to new heights of learning and living enjoyment.

Robert A. Goodale

# Methods for Encouraging
# Creativity in the Classroom

"*T*eaching for creativity" has become a modern pedagogical fad, but, unfortunately, few educationists have taken the time to dig into the research literature to determine exactly what it means to "teach for creativity." The link between creativity and art, music, and dancing has made teaching for creativity synonymous in some instances with increased emphasis on art education and the banishment of "color books," and in other instances with encouraging students to simply "do whatever you'd like to do." Yet the research on creativity suggests that there is far more to the encouragement of creativity than the simple introduction of new books, audio-visual aids, or computer consoles. In an effort to relate this research to the process of encouraging creativity, I would like to spell out several specific ways in which teachers may encourage creativity in the classroom.

Such as it is, the research on creativity to date suggests that more important than the *types of materials* used to promote creativity is the *personality development of the learner.* All psychological studies conducted so far on creative people have concurred in their reporting of an admixture of certain "desirable" and "undesirable" traits in creative people as contrasted with noncreative people. Drevdahl and Cattell (1958) and Cattell (1963) found that writers, artists, and eminent researchers were significantly more intelligent, adventurous, sensitive, self-sufficient, and emotionally stable than the general population. At the same time these creative groups were also seen to be more socially withdrawn, dominant, aloof, nonconformist, bohemian and radical than the general population. Barron (1957) differentiated the 25 most original from the 25 least original of 100 Air Force captains and found the high scorers to be intelligent, widely informed, concerned with basic problems, clever and imaginative, socially effective, personally dominant, verbally fluent, and possessed of initiative. The low scorers were seen as conforming, rigid and stereotyped, uninsightful, commonplace, apathetic, and dull. Rees and Goldman (1961) separated 68 university students into high, middle, and low creative groups on the basis of honors and

Goodale, Robert A. "Methods for Encouraging Creativity in the Classroom." *Journal of Creative Behavior*, Vol. 4, No. 2, Spring, 1970, pp. 91-102.

prizes won in their fields. Personality traits were assessed by use of the Guilford-Zimmerman Temperament Survey and the Minnesota Multiphasic Personality Inventory. The initial division into three groups produced no significant differences, but when the high creativity group was further subdivided into high-high and low-high groups, the high-high group was seen as more impulsive, more aggressive, more domineering, and more ascendant than their "bridesmaid" counterparts. Personality adjustment or maladjustment was compared by Rees and Goldman for all three groups, and there was no indication that creativity was related to maladjustment.


## Personality Variables Among the Highly Intelligent

The work by Getzels and Jackson (1962), for all its methodological limitations, did serve to point out the wide differences in goals and behaviors between "Highly Intelligent" and "Highly Creative" students. The high creative group was less concerned with conventional vocational goals (teacher, doctor, engineer) and more interested in so-called off-beat vocations (inventor, artist, disc jockey). Neither were they overly concerned with whether or not they possessed the character traits admired by teachers or parents. These highly creative students were more self-reliant and independent, and despite the fact that they scored significantly lower (127) in mean IQ scores than their brighter classmates (150), they attained the same degree of academic achievement as the high intelligence group.

Since the Getzels and Jackson study it has become fashionable to point out that the highly intelligent person is not necessarily the most creative, and later investigations concerned with college grade-point averages have tended to bear this out (Harmon, 1963; Taylor, Smith & Ghiselin, 1963). However, in the haste for those on the short end of the standard intelligence scale to grab at this sign of redemption, they have frequently overlooked the fact that although measured intelligence is not a sufficient condition for high level creative output, it does show up again and again as being a necessary ingredient (Guilford, 1967). Terman's group of 800 men (Terman, 1954) with IQ's above 140 would certainly be tagged as creative by any criterion based on products or eminence. At the average age of 40 this group had published 67 books; 1400 scientific, technical, and professional articles; 200 short stories, novelettes, and plays; 236 miscellaneous articles; and more than 150 patents. Of 112 scientists in the group of 800, 42 were listed in the 1949 edition of *American Men of Science*. In addition, the group produced countless newspaper stories, radio and TV scripts, and secret documents not included in the above count. Surely this record far surpasses the productivity of any 800 men randomly selected from the general population.

What makes Terman's study more relevant for our discussion on the personality correlates of creative people is his further investigation into what he called his A group and his C group. Terman noticed that not all in his group of 800 men had contributed equally, and so he selected from this group the 150 rated highest for success and the 150 rated lowest for success. Success was defined as the extent to which an individual had made use of his superior intellectual ability. The A group was composed of the individuals achieving highest success, the C group those achieving the lowest amount of success. Neither group differed significantly in average IQ, and all were intelligent enough so that lack of intelligence was not a limiting factor in the attainment of success (all had IQ's of 140 or above). What Terman found was that personality and motivational factors prevented the C group from fulfilling their early promise. The C group was rated as non-persistent in striving toward goal achievement (quitters); they showed no "spark" or drive; they lacked self-confidence, and were immobilized by feelings of inferiority. Checking back through his earlier records, Terman found as early as 1922, 18 years before it even occurred to him to separate out the A and C groups from the 800 men, that the A group was then recognized by their raters as significantly superior to the C group in self-confidence, perseverance, and desire to excel. Thus the debilitating personality factors recognized as far back as their high school and college days apparently prevented members of the C group from contributing their expected share of creative products.

## Implications for the Teacher

The implications of these studies on the personality correlates of creative people suggests that a major step in encouraging creativity in the classroom is the support of activities which increase the student's self-confidence and persistence, and the toleration by teachers of student behaviors currently seen as "unpleasant." The quiet, well-behaved, bright student may be ideal from the teacher's point of view, since her crammed schedule requires smooth-running efficiency if all topics are to be adequately covered, and the creative child is more apt to want to ask questions or voice his own opinions, thus slowing down the machinery. Sometimes, too, the opinion the creative voices is a negative reaction to teacher-imposed tasks; a reaction which may quickly earn him the title of "troublemaker" from anxious, dogmatic, and authoritarian teachers. The curiosity of the creative child is such that he is more apt to "fool around" with lab materials and attempt things not outlined in the lab manual. Also, because he is less concerned with social conformity, he is more prone toward bohemian dress, and less motivated to gain the highest marks in the class.

The toleration of "unpleasant" (non-teacher-oriented) behaviors does not mean, of course, that teachers must give free license to all behaviors. A necessary amount of social responsibility is always associated with freedom. The young child allowed to get up from his seat and roam around the room when his seat work is completed is not at liberty to disrupt the reading group, nor is the college student who prefers to rephrase the exam question to be rewarded for shoddy work. The important point is that the child or student not be penalized for being different or for exhibiting his independence and curiosity. In most cases what is needed is a reshaping of the traditional classroom so that materials and facilities are arranged in ways that make it convenient for students to move from task to task, rather than in ways that make it easy and convenient for teachers to exercise complete and unyielding control.

Focusing on personality variables suggests that the teacher should be aware of her own personality. No teacher intends to squelch creativity, yet it is obvious that some do. The rigid and compulsive teacher is intolerant of deviations from the lesson plan and penalizes the student who passes his work in late. ("They need to learn to get their work done on time!") Thus, deadlines become more important than quality. The self-conscious teacher, unsure of her ability to control the class, dares not allow students to wander around the room or talk quietly among themselves for fear of precipitating chaos. The narcissistic teacher cannot bear the thought that students may sometimes think of better projects or solutions than she can, and the self-effacing teacher distrusts her own ability to experiment with new methods or materials because she doubts that she can implement them well and fears the ridicule which may accompany failure. Creative behavior is not apt to occur in an environment where creative activity is not encouraged. The teacher who demands that students abide by her wishes on matters that are not really important to social responsibility or intellectual skill can hardly be viewed as encouraging independent thinking.

As the purveyor of rewards and punishments for social and intellectual skills, the teacher stands in an advantageous position for encouraging creativity, curiosity, independence, and self-reliance. When the child shows some independent thinking the teacher can praise him, and when the child shows signs that his personal interests are not being satisfied by a proposed assignment, she can modify the assignment enough for that one child or any others, to include his interests. For example, if the child is interested in the sea and the assignment is on Colonial history, the teacher could suggest that the child write or report about the *Mayflower;* or if the assignment is about the first Thanksgiving, teacher might suggest that the child write about the wisdom of using fish as a fertilizer to grow corn.

The student can be made leader of a group project if he shows the requisite skills, or he can be made a one-man committee if he prefers to work alone. Reinforcement and feedback are powerful influences in shaping behavior, and if creative effort is to be encouraged then the teacher should be alert to see that every effort in the direction of creativity, curiosity, independence, and self-reliance is rewarded. Notes on the margins of college papers are every bit as good as the gold stars given in kindergarten. Papers should be graded as much for new ideas and generalization to other areas as for spelling, neatness, and factual content. Many graduate schools claim that their theses are graded on the former, when, as a matter of fact, they are graded mainly on the latter.

## Strategies for Creativity

If a response that is reinforced tends to be emitted again, then the first task for the teacher who wants to encourage creativity in the classroom is to get the student to emit a creative response so that it can be rewarded. This is not so difficult as it sounds, and it may not even require any new materials or texts, although such products are commercially available. What it does require is a change in how topics are taught or how questions about the topic are asked. Frank Williams has formulated an excellent approach to the problem in his enumeration of teaching strategies which encourage creative thinking (Williams, 1968). He lists 23 different strategies such as teaching by paradox (How can we explain poverty in the midst of plenty?), by analogy (Airplane cargo doors designed like the opening of a clam shell), by using examples of deficiencies (What are some things that man does not know?), by making allowances for thinking about possibles and making guesses; teaching the skill for change of things rather than adjustment to things; presenting unsolved social issues or scientific problems and asking the student to go off into his own areas of information to seek solutions; teaching about rigidities, fixations, and habit; showing how failures, mistakes, and accidents have led to the development of worthwhile things; studying creative individuals; etc. Massialas & Zevin (1967) also demonstrate how creative behaviors can be encouraged in the teaching of any subject through the use of open-ended discussions and problem solving. In one instance high school students were asked to interpret a textbook writer's prediction that the continued influx of non-Western immigrants into Israel would soon result in a shift of Israel's foreign policy. In another instance, students in a geography course were asked to select from a map a site for a large city and to defend their choice. A third example was that of students given ten haiku poems and asked to determine where the poems came from. Each task prompted a great deal of discussion in which opportunity arose again and again for students to be rewarded by both teachers and peers for opening up a new line of discussion.

For some years now, in a college course on the psychology of creativity, I have had great success with take-home examinations involving questions that as yet have no hard and fast answers. For example: What is a creative toy? How much conformity is necessary for society's safety? Has the concept of creativity been distorted or diminished by extending it to scientists, engineers, teachers, sales clerks, and plumbers? Are humor and creativity related? Why is J. P. Guilford seen as about to have a great impact on American education during the next 50 years?

Notice that with all of the preceding strategies no major change in curriculum content is required. Rather, what has changed is the opportunity for the student to offer his own ideas and evaluations, and to be rewarded for them. There is usually no single, correct answer, and the students accomplish all the usual goals of the curriculum as they are forced to give reasons for their choices or opinions. The nice part of this approach is that it fits in well with those intellectual factors believed to be part and parcel of the creative process as outlined by Guilford (1967); viz.: a variety of solutions (divergent production); changes or modifications of existing ideas (transformations); and sensitivity to the fact that things can often be made better than they are (sensitivity to problems).

## Establishing Confidence

A major move to increase creative production by increasing the learner's feelings of self-worth and self-esteem has recently been outlined by Randolph & Howe (1966) in *Self-Enhancing Education.* They describe an experimental elementary school program in California where children set their own behavior limits and expectations, establish the rules for their own self-management, increase their self-esteem by being seen by their teachers and peers as worthy, and also by valuing themselves as a unique resource. Of all the recent approaches to encouraging creativity in the classroom, this one seems to me to be far and away the best solution, since it calls for a change in the teacher from an authority figure to a "helping person," a change in the classroom environment from competition to mutual support, and a change in the learner's self-concept that leads him from fearing failure to contributing what he can.

John Holt (1964) has suggested that something like 40% of our children fail in school, and if we were to raise our academic standards as some would have us do, then the figure would increase substantially. While Holt confronts us dramatically with *how* children fail in school, he is not so sure *why* they do. The answer lies in Randolph & Howe's *Self-Enhancing Education.* While schools have been busily evaluating achievement and potential in the three R's, the large majority of less skilled learners have been quietly lowering their self-esteem, self-confidence, and perseverance. If schools are really interested in encouraging creativity, and salvaging the 40% who fail, then they are going to have to develop ways to give back these children's self-confidence and feelings of personal worth. Jonathan Kozol's (1967) *Death at an Early Age* describes too well what happens to young children at a time in their development when they do not have the emotional or intellectual defenses to cope with rigid teachers and a non-supportive environment. Somewhere along the line schools are going to have to move in the direction of educating students for full humanness if we sincerely value adventurous students.

## Some Teacher Aids

For those teachers who feel they must have tangible evidence that they are teaching for creativity, or a few props to help them get started, there are a number of workbooks available. Myers & Torrance (1964, 1965, 1966a,

1966b) have recently published a set of workbooks for elementary and secondary school children containing materials designed to encourage new ideas and to inhibit rigidity. These workbooks include open-ended questions such as: What kinds of fads might be beneficial to people? Would you rather be a frog, a deer, or on the moon? Why? What would happen if it was against the law to sing? When is the sky? What do the following have in common: a watch, a wagon, and an airplane? How many different ways can a ball be used? Other tasks include a few simple lines in which the child adds more lines to complete the drawing of a figure suggested by his own imagination, and invitations to write some silly stories. Myers & Torrance report that children are highly motivated to complete the exercises in the workbooks because they are "fun." No doubt one of the reasons children find such exercises interesting is because they deal more with experiences the child has been a part of and of which he can draw on from personal experience rather than what can be remembered from a study unit. More traditional curriculum content can also be approached the same way, as we saw with Massialas & Zevin, but it usually requires much more nose-grinding in order for the child to build up resources of knowledge to draw on.

Allyn & Bacon has brought out a whole series of instructive texts designed to stimulate creative teaching in a variety of subjects (Piltz & Sund, 1968; Smith, 1966, 1967a, 1967b, 1967c, 1967d; Westcott & Smith, 1967). The books describe a number of projects and ideas to stimulate creative thinking. The really nice part about the books is that the authors are fully aware of all the personality, environmental, and creative process variables brought to light so far by research on creativity, and they use the information to bring about the kinds of conditions that stimulate creative thinking in the classroom.

William Uraneck has published a couple of workbooks based largely on the factor of divergent thinking (1965, 1967). Most of the tasks revolve around giving ten or a dozen ideas: List 10 uses for a man's old belt; List 10 different birthday presents to give to a relative or a pet; What are some things you would do if you were small as a mouse? Again, the tasks draw a great deal on non-academic experiences.

My own feelings about the workbooks just described and other similar materials is that they are great for teachers who want to get started encouraging creativity and need some ideas. Presumably, such teachers will soon move on and develop their own ideas. As Smith himself says,

> . . . You will violate the very concept of creativity if you try to use [these books] as cookbooks. Copying in any form is a contradiction of the creative act. Creativeness follows no set pattern, but comes from the innermost being of each individual. This is not to say that you should not try the ideas from these books in your own classroom. Do so by all means! But every time you use an idea, ask yourself, 'What ideas do I as a creative person have that fit my particular group,' or 'What ideas do my children as creative people have that I could use to develop that creative ability?' [Smith, 1966. p.xiii]

The danger of such workbooks on creativity is that teachers who have no understanding of the creative person or the creative process will use them in rigid and authoritarian ways and thus continue to destroy the very thing they think they are encouraging. Fortunately, the Allyn & Bacon series includes a great deal of material on the creative person, the creative process and the creative environment in each book so that the teacher who uses them also learns a great deal about creativity in the process. The Myers & Torrance series also includes a teacher's manual with each type of workbook to help the unsophisticated teacher learn something about the entire concept of creativity and how the exercises in the workbooks are designed to stimulate it.

## Encouraging the Process

A less dramatic but no less important way of encouraging creativity is not to interfere with the creative process. All creative people report a period of incubation in which different alternatives are mulled over and over again prior to solution of a problem (Ghiselin, 1952). During such activity the person wishes to be left alone; not to be disturbed. It is not an uncommon experience for teachers to catch their pupils "daydreaming" now and then, and also not uncommonly the teacher asks the child if he has nothing to do. The implication is, of course, that children are not only supposed to be busy, they are supposed to look busy—which they do not show while thinking, although they may be very busy indeed. Teachers could be a little more tolerant of "daydreaming" and related behaviors when the child is obviously lost in his thinking. That is not to suggest that teacher is never to interrupt the process for, again, the child must meet his responsibilities, too. Neither is it to suggest encouragement of schizophrenic withdrawal. But there are occasions when teachers could respect the child's wish to stop and just "think" for a while, even if he may not be thinking about schoolwork.

Traditional exams disembowel the creative process completely, since they are usually strong on memory processes only and offer little opportunity for divergent production or evaluation. Little wonder that so many teachers complain that students do not think, when, as a matter of fact teachers do not ask the kinds of questions that require thinking, or give the student time to do so if he does have the opportunity. Many deadlines on term papers and other such projects are established for the teacher's convenience and not the student's.

Another method of encouraging creativity is to institute a program of breadth into the curriculum. One cannot help but get distressed at the fact that every year from grades 6-12, children are required to learn the parts of speech, but these same children are never given any instruction in anthropology, archeology, geology, philosophy, bird watching, or the history of Kenya. The same plays by Shakespeare are read by the same English classes year after year all over the U.S., but few students get a chance to read Chekhov, Gandhi, Darwin, or Marx. Mednick, in his paper on the associative basis of the creative process makes the following statement: "It would be predicted that the greater the concentration of associative strength in a small number of stereotyped associative responses the less probable it is that the individual will attain the creative solution" [1962, p. 223]. Breadth of experience has long been recognized as advantageous to creative insight (Bartlett, 1958; Birch, 1945; Hebb, 1949; Hymovitch, 1952; Osborn, 1953), yet every year teachers teach the exact same materials to a new group of students, and by graduation nearly all students have been exposed to nearly all the same things. It's a wonder that such a homogeneous group *ever* comes up with any new ideas. A little heterogeneity might generate more. Good school systems and colleges have recognized this principle for a long time and have looked for teachers and students from widely different backgrounds and geographic origins.

As a final way of encouraging creativity, educational systems might consider the administration of creativity tests, despite their present shortcomings. Although test interpreters and teachers still tend to abuse the purposes for which the tests are intended—guidelines only, tests are here to stay. They do offer objective measurement and predictive utility, and since it appears that some people will misinterpret test results despite all warnings to the contrary, one way of partially overcoming the problem would be to make creativity test scores available along with IQ and achievement scores. Such an additional measure may at least serve to suggest to the teacher that intellectual ability (as presently measured) is not *the* single most important quality that a student can possess, and that a child's imaginative processes need to be cultivated along with his reasoning and memory processes.

## References

Barron, F. Originality in relation to personality and intellect. *J. of Pers.*, 1957, *25*, 730-742.

Bartlett, F. *Thinking*. N.Y.: Basic Books, 1958.

Birch, H. G. The relation of previous experience to insightful problem-solving. *J. of Comp. & Physiol. Psychol.*, 1945, *38*, 367-383.

Cattell, R. B. The personality and motivation of the researcher from measurements of contemporaries and from biography. In C. W. Taylor & F. Barron (Eds.), *Scientific creativity: Its recognition and development*. N.Y.: Wiley, 1963. Pp. 119-131.

Drevdahl, J. E., & Cattell, R. B. Personality and creativity in artists and writers. *J. of Clin. Psychol.*, 1958, *14*, 107-111.

Getzels, J. W., & Jackson, P. W. *Creativity and intelligence*. N.Y.: Wiley, 1962.

Ghiselin, B. (Ed.) *The creative process*. N.Y.: Mentor Books, 1952.

Guilford, J. P. *The nature of human intelligence*. N.Y.: McGraw-Hill, 1967.

Harmon, L. R. The development of a criterion of scientific competence. In C. W. Taylor & F. Barron (Eds.), *Scientific creativity: Its recognition and development.* N.Y.: Wiley, 1963. Pp. 44-52.

Hebb, D. O. *The organization of behavior.* N.Y.: Wiley, 1949.

Holt, J. *How children fail.* N.Y.: Delta, 1964.

Hymovitch, B. The effects of experimental variations on problem solving in the rat. *J. of Comp. & Physiol. Psychol.,* 1952, *45,* 313-321.

Kozol, J. *Death at an early age.* Boston: Houghton Mifflin, 1967.

Massialas, B. G., & Zevin, J. *Creative encounters in the classroom.* N.Y.: Wiley, 1967.

Mednick, S. A. The associative basis of the creative process. *Psychol. Rev.,* 1962, *69,* 220-232.

Myers, R. E., & Torrance, E. P. *Invitations to thinking and doing.* Boston: Ginn, 1964.

Myers, R. E., & Torrance, E. P. *Can you imagine?* Boston: Ginn, 1965.

Myers, R. E., & Torrance, E. P. *For those who wonder.* Boston: Ginn, 1966a.

Myers, R. E., & Torrance, E. P. *Plots, puzzles, and ploys.* Boston: Ginn, 1966b.

Osborn, A. F. *Applied imagination.* N.Y.: Scribners, 1953.

Piltz, A., & Sund, R. *Creative teaching of science in the elementary school.* Boston: Allyn & Bacon, 1968.

Randolph, N., & Howe, W. *Self-enhancing education.* Palo Alto, Calif.: Stanford Press, 1966.

Rees, M., & Goldman, M. Some relationships between creativity and personality. *J. of Gen. Psychol.,* 1961, *65,* 145-161.

Smith, J. A. *Setting conditions for creative teaching in the elementary school.* Boston: Allyn & Bacon, 1966.

Smith, J. A. *Creative teaching of reading and literature in the elementary school.* Boston: Allyn & Bacon, 1967a.

Smith, J. A. *Creative teaching of the language arts in the elementary school.* Boston: Allyn & Bacon, 1967b.

Smith, J. A. *Creative teaching of the creative arts in the elementary school.* Boston: Allyn & Bacon, 1967c.

Smith, J. A. *Creative teaching of the social studies in the elementary school.* Boston: Allyn & Bacon, 1967d.

Taylor, C. W., Smith, W. R., & Ghiselin, B. The creative and other contributions of one sample of research scientists. In C. W. Taylor & F. Barron (Eds.), *Scientifiic creativity: Its recognition and development.* N.Y.: Wiley, 1963. Pp. 53-76.

Terman, L. M. The discovery and encouragement of exceptional talent. *Amer. Psychol.,* 1954, *9,* 221-230.

Uraneck, W. O. *The young thinker.* Lexington, Mass.: Author, 1965.

Uraneck, W. O. *Creative thinking workbook.* (Rev. ed.) Lexington, Mass.: Author, 1967.

Westcott, A. M., & Smith, J. A. *Creative teaching of mathematics in the elementary school.* Boston: Allyn & Bacon, 1967.

Williams, F. E. Perspective of a model for developing productive creative behaviors in the classroom. Unpublished manuscript, Macalester College, 1968.

*A. Harry Passow*

# *The Gifted*
# *and the Disadvantaged*

$M$ore than 15 years have elapsed since the inception of what has been called the "third wave of interest in the gifted." Fewer than a half dozen years have passed since such terms as *disadvantaged* and *deprived* were added to the educational lexicon. For some persons, the two populations—both lacking uniform, widely accepted definition—represent opposite ends of a continuum of talent potential. For others, both groups represent different aspects of the same problem of talent development. Certainly, one stimulus for the present concern for the education of the disadvantaged is the firm belief that children from low-income, ethnic, and racial minority groups represent the nation's largest unmined source of talent. Aside from the humanitarian aspects of overcoming poverty and discrimination, aside from the moral values in providing equal opportunity for all, the nation's welfare and survival depend on its success in identifying and nurturing talents of many kinds wherever they may be found.

Schemes for encouraging talent development among the disadvantaged tend to follow many of the patterns employed by planners of programs for the gifted a few years ago and, as might be expected, even commit some of the same errors. Many of the issues raised regarding programs for the gifted are now paraphrased to apply plans for the disadvantaged. Ironically, concern for the disadvantaged has triggered opposition to what had become established and accepted practices for the gifted. Most notably, special provisions for the gifted and particularly special groupings have become a prime target for attack on the basis of alleged "discrimination against the disadvantaged." Identification procedures, especially those involving standardized intelligence tests, have been condemned as being discriminatory against the poor and culturally different.

Stripped of polemics, the hard-nut question is basically one of how to

Passow, Harry A. "The Gifted and the Disadvantaged." *The National Elementary Principal,* Vol. LI, No. 5, Feb., 1972, pp. 24-31.

provide for the wide range of individual differences found in any school population. Having known for some time that identical experiences are not the same as equal opportunities, educational program planners continue to be concerned with the problems of individualization and differentiation of instruction. With respect to both the gifted and the disadvantaged, the perennial questions persist: What sorts of education will best educate? What constitutes adequate and appropriate education for all?

In a position paper prepared for the 1960 White House Conference on Children and Youth, seven problem areas in the education of the gifted and talented were identified as most pressing:

1. Improvements of means for measuring the multidimensions of high level ability, thus sharpening the identification of the talented.

2. Improvement of procedures for locating the potential underachiever at an early stage to prevent negative attitudes, learning patterns, and self-concepts from forming and choking his capabilities.

3. Recruitment, education, and retention of talented individuals in the teaching profession—in instruction, counseling, supervisory, and administrative positions.

4. Development of means for keeping abreast of new knowledge and revision of instruction to include these new insights and understandings.

5. Development and appraisal of instructional techniques, materials, and resources that will yield deeper learnings for the gifted.

6. Development of means for measuring deeper learnings that are untapped by the conventional achievement tests of today.

7. Increased understanding of the kinds of learning experiences that will nourish a love of learning; foster independence in thinking; feed the desire to experiment, to test, and to venture forth; and create a built-in standard of excellence in performance.

Miriam Goldberg's paper on the gifted, delivered at the 1965 White House Conference on Education, examined several issues that she felt needed clarification, since "the directions in which they are resolved may well determine the future of special provisions for the talented." The issues were listed under such headings as: The Climate for Talent Development, Current Oppositions to Special Programs, Expanded Conceptions of Talent, Increasing the Talent Pool—Womanpower and the Disadvantaged, and Administrative Arrangements for the Talented.

These five issues paralleled those identified five years earlier, even though programs for the gifted mushroomed throughout the country in the intervening years—spurred in part by Sputnik. To the 1960 conference, the major needs seemed to be for research and experimentation "to understand better the phenomenon of giftedness and its development, to assess the value of specific educational procedures and practices, to appraise proposals and plans, and to use available resources more effectively." These continue to be major needs in the area of the gifted, although there are now available research findings and operational experience that might be synthesized, interpreted, and applied to improved program planning. However, such issues

*403*

as racial isolation, student power, and community control were hardly considered at a time when most research on ability grouping, for instance, did not consider race or social class as significant variables.

Many innovations that were sharply debated a decade ago—even the need for special provisions for the gifted—have now become more or less institutionalized. A concern with nurturing creativity, productive thinking, and inquiry has become more focused as enthusiasm for novelty alone has been replaced with more tempered insights into the nature of these phenomena. True, there is still no adequate theory of talent development that might provide a framework for program planning, nor are we yet able to adequately define what constitutes "enrichment for the gifted." We have expanded our notions of giftedness and its multifaceted nature so that new assessment procedures have been developed to supplement or, in some instances, replace traditional techniques. Much of the so-called curriculum revolution, while not necessarily aimed at the intellectually gifted student, has since been found to be most appropriate for this population, since such programs deal with content and processes calling for the higher abstractions and conceptual abilities that are components of giftedness. Significant as such curricular changes have been, they tend not to contribute to integrated, articulated, sequential programs for the gifted, except in those few instances where some attempts have been made to attain such an end.

There have been curricular changes during the past decade that have opened alternatives for the gifted. Some of these can be described as *vertical,* moving courses or units down so that students have contact with material at an earlier age or in less time than is normal; some are *horizontal* changes, providing for greater depth and breadth than is usual; some are *reorganizational,* redesigning the curriculum content itself; and some may be called *augmentation,* introducing experiences that have not been part of the curriculum earlier. Seminars on standard and esoteric subjects have become part of school programs. Independent study has flourished. Extended school weeks and years have been provided for the gifted. Secondary schools and colleges have shared programs and resources, including staff. The Advanced Placement Program, featuring college-level work in high schools, has involved thousands of students in hundreds of schools.The National Merit Scholarship Program, with its related projects, has become part of an annual nationwide talent search. Early admissions to college have become standard across the nation.

Thus, in the area of the gifted and the talented, "new" and "promising" developments appear to be consolidations of what has been learned from the research and experience of the past dozen or so years. For example, there was a period during which the gifted underachiever was the target of much study, a great deal of research being supported by federal and state funds. The findings of such studies shed light on the relationships between motivational and personality variables, environmental conditions, and the instructional program as these factors affected the development of intellectual potential. However, our progress in moving from analysis and diagnosis to intervention and program has been painfully slow. We have, consequently, applied little of this research to the broader concerns with achievement, especially for the disadvantaged, probably because the populations studied have tended to be primarily the middle-class gifted.

Efforts to identify and nurture "creativity" provided considerable excitement and intense effort for a period, but the crest of that commitment passed quickly. We still do not understand the nature and causes of the so-called morning glories (individuals whose giftedness appears early but soon wanes or disappears) or the late bloomers (persons whose talents emerge somewhat late) or how these phenomena should influence identification or instructional and counseling procedures. We still profess concern for developing nonacademic talents (such as musical, artistic, mechanical, social, and dramatic), but we have given relatively scant attention to what kinds of provisions are appropriate and essential. The problems of adequate programs for highly gifted individuals—those with unusually rare genius—have been generally ignored on the tacit assumption that such talent will eventually come out anyway. Finally, we have hardly tackled, let alone resolved, the many issues regarding development of talent in its social context.

The problem of talent development continues to be one of devising educational opportunities that will unlock potential of all kinds to the fullest, programs that will be concerned with values, attitudes, self-concepts, and commitment to continued growth, not just the acquisition of knowledge and intellectual development. The research and development efforts of the late fifties and early sixties—many of them encouraged and supported by federal and state governments—helped broaden definitions of talent and helped us to understand that giftedness is multifaceted. Expanded notions of giftedness and its many-faceted nature suggest that, as David McClelland once observed, "talent potential may be fairly widespread, a characteristic which can be transformed into actually talented performance by various sorts of the right kinds of education." The drive for "quality education" and for "equal educational opportunity" represent, in some ways, a press to test the hypothesis. As students from impoverished backgrounds and from racial and ethnic minorities have "achieved" when provided with appropriate educational opportunities, they have demonstrated that "the right kinds of education" can indeed transform potential into "actually talented performance."*

The disappearance from the educational scene of some programs for the gifted, however, indicates our continued tendency to discard the baby with the bath-water. No program or provision for the gifted is so sacred that continuous assessment and evaluation is no longer needed. And, as education programs become inevitably intertwined with social and political processes within the school and the community at large, such educational processes must be continually examined in terms of overall effects.

*McClelland, David C., and others, editors. *Talent and Society*. New York: Van Nostrand Reinhold Co., 1958.

Ability grouping, for example, was viewed, along with acceleration and enrichment, as "a means of providing for the gifted." All three terms took on a variety of forms, of course, in different contexts and at different levels. When ability grouping in certain school situations led to a tracking system that segregated white, middle-class students from poor, nonwhite students, leading the former into college bound programs and the latter into dead-end terminal programs, clearly such provisions no longer contributed to full talent development. In abandoning grouping provisions, all too often schools failed to provide for curriculum differentiation, for appropriate teaching and learning strategies, for instructional resources—for all of the kinds of educational opportunities that grouping was originally intended to facilitate. Consequently, the gifted—white and nonwhite, middle and lower class—were deprived of appropriate educational opportunities.

The needs of gifted and talented chidren are, in a sense, the same as those of other children, differing in degree and quality. All children "need" opportunities to develop their individual talents, and the gifted and talented students are no exception. Such talented individuals come from all races, socioeconomic groups, geographic locales, and environments. To the extent that educational programs discriminate, sort out, and stifle talent development, they cannot be tolerated, no matter what political power is brought to maintain them.

The recently published report of the U.S. Office of Education survey of programs and provisions for the gifted (pursuant to Public Law 91-230, Section 806) uses language reminiscent of the 1950's, such as "the widespread neglect of gifted and talented children." In the sense of the school's inability or unwillingness to provide for the particular needs of the gifted, this neglect is even more intense and widespread among the disadvantaged and minority groups. These students are caught in a vortex of educational and environmental forces that mitigate against their being identified and having their talents nurtured.

In schools that are *de facto* segregated (as are many inner-city schools), where low achievement is widespread, teachers and administrators have low expectations, the curriculum is sterile and irrelevant, resources are limited, and individual diagnosis absent, the potentially gifted child may very likely be lost. Differing school milieus and predominant value systems affect general scholastic performance and individual attainment. Giftedness and talent always have a social referrent—those abilities that are identified and developed are those that are valued by the society—and the child in a depressed area who is potentially gifted may be doubly disadvantaged, for he lives in an environment that may be hostile or apathetic to his particular abilities. In some instances, outstanding scholastic achievement is perceived as "The Man's Game" and not to be pursued by the poor and the nonwhite lest they be coopted.

In schools where desegregation has taken place, integration may not have occurred, and the minority group students are often a minority. The schools from which they have come are frequently perceived as inferior, the levels of past performance lower, and potentials for outstanding performance limited. All too often the result has been a resegregation through grouping and tracking procedures that relegate the blacks, the poor, and the non-English speaking to the "slower" or "nonacademic" programs, where they are provided with an education that is basically inferior in quality. Since such procedures tend to be "class actions," in that all members of the minority group are treated as if homogeneity existed, the gifted and the talented among them are particularly vulnerable and suffer as a result of such discrimination. Furthermore, the social conditions in the classroom and the school, the nature of acceptance or rejection and the minority group student's perception of these interactions, the peer values—all affect the pupil's achievement motivation and the extent to which he will manifest and develop his giftedness. When students are black, red, or brown, are different culturally from the majority group, are non-English speaking or have "non-standard" dialects, those who are gifted or talented among them may be particularly disadvantaged because of discriminatory practices.

The gifted and talented among disadvantaged and minority groups pose a particular challenge and opportunity for educators. To begin to meet this challenge, educators must examine their own expectations regarding this untapped talent pool: To what extent have the biases of educators contributed to the limited development of gifted minority group youth? The fact that some unusually gifted black or Chicanos or Puerto Ricans have emerged and demonstrated outstanding ability does not change the urgent need for planners and researchers to attend to the special problems within this more general area of concern. More specifically, attention will have to be given to the following dimensions of the problem:

*Identification.* Procedures used to locate gifted and talented individuals, given all the problems that exist with the population in general, are even more problematic in identifying the gifted among the disadvantaged. Some educators have argued for discarding existing instruments and procedures and developing "culture fair" tests. Others, questioning the possibilities of such bias-free instruments and techniques, propose that the focus be on the interpretation of the data so as to take into account the disadvantaged background of the child. Still others urge that efforts emphasize the creation of settings that will encourage self-identification of the gifted through outstanding performance. Identification procedures that stress a search for talent rather than simply screen out and bar participation in programs for the gifted are crucial for minority group youth. As a start, such procedures should be more, rather than less, inclusive.

*Development of programs.* Experience of the past several decades has clearly indicated the need for differentiated opportunities for the gifted to develop their special abilities while, at the same time, they are given opportunities to develop certain general skills and abilities by interacting with students of less and greater potential. No single uniform program has emerged. However, educators need to turn their attention to the special problems of program development in educational and social settings where the disadvantaged are found. To recognize the nature of such problems would be a step forward at this point. The success of some mini- and prep schools in ghetto areas suggests one approach worth further exploration. By attending to the affective as well as cognitive development of students and by creating a climate for achievement, such schools seem to be providing another chance for able pupils who have been missed or turned off by the more traditional programs. Programs that provide opportunities for students to teach fellow pupils or for service in various community agencies can extend the possibilities for developing potentials. Education is not limited to the place we call school. Support is needed for encouragement of various opportunities for talent development in nonconventional settings, involving non-traditional personnel.

*Development of staff.* By creating the conditions for learning and by serving as the gatekeepers for programs and services, school staffs are critical in talent development. Staff development is needed in terms of altering expectations with respect to the identification and nurturing of talent among the disadvantaged. Coupled with attitudinal changes must come new teaching strategies and ways of using learning resources, in school and community.

*Enrichment of the learning environment.* For a variety of reasons, inner-city schools may be able to provide only limited resources for talent development. However, they are situated in urban centers, and the resources for learning are extremely rich. The entire community, not the classroom alone, must become the locus for learning. Not only will this extend opportunities for learning but it could, at the same time, alter the climate for learning—the attitudes toward unusual talents and their development.

*Development of strategies for bilingual and multicultural education.* The barriers to optimum development of the gifted among minority group students may include both the fact that the language of instruction differs from the child's mother tongue and the existence of discontinuities between the culture of the school and that of the home and neighborhood. If talent potential is to be realized, better strategies must be found for recognizing language needs and the potential richness of cultural differences.

*Development of appropriate guidance and other ancillary services.* In addition to the special guidance needs—personal and educational—of all gifted students, there are particular problems that may be encountered by the gifted minority group student. These may range from help with affective matters, such as peer and family attitudes toward the gifted child's "difference," to assistance in recognizing and selecting from the options available to him. Higher education opportunities, for example, have been expanded considerably in the last decade or so, and the gifted minority group student and his family may not be fully aware of the possibilities or the means for taking advantage of them.

*Development of financial resources.* Poor and minority group students need financial assistance to be able to develop their special abilities. While there has been increased support for minority group youth in the realm of higher education scholarships and stipends, it has not been sufficient. By

408

continuing to study, the poor child is unable to contribute to support of the family in any way, aside from answering his own intellectual needs. What is required are expanded opportunities to serve and to work as a means of earning some income, which will have a beneficial effect on both the talented individual and his family.

There is ample evidence that schools have failed to come to grips with the problems of identifying and developing giftedness and talent among various racial and ethnic minorities and children of the poor. When federal and state agencies, through appropriations for research and program development, encouraged and enlargement of opportunities for the gifted, there was a renaissance of interest and activity. The minority group gifted profited from that revived concern, but only to a limited extent.

In recent years, many school systems have misinterpreted the long over-due concern for the education of poor and minority group students as meaning that programs for the disadvantaged must take precedence over provisions for the gifted. What is needed now is a clear affirmation by educators and communities that they are concerned with the development of talent potential of all kinds, wherever such special abilities may be found. The issue is not one of providing for the gifted (meaning only white, middle-class, suburban children) or the disadvantaged (meaning only poor, nonwhite, ghetto dwellers). Gifted and talented individuals are found in all groups. There is no need or justification for depriving some students of opportunities at the expense of others. Nor is there any basis for not providing the disadvantaged gifted student with special opportunities that are essentially compensatory in nature.

What is needed is a real commitment to developing the total range of abilities and talents—including the unusually able and gifted. Such commitment would be manifested in the kinds of programs funded, the areas of research and development supported, the varieties of training programs underwritten, and so on. Unfortunately, too many educators and lay persons are unwilling to concede that there really are individual differences, that such differences should help determine the nature of appropriate education that must be provided, and that identical experiences do not make for equal opportunities. Certainly, in the last two decades we have acquired sufficient research data and program development experience to be able to provide the kinds of flexibility, openness, personnel, and material support to nurture individual talents more effectively than we are presently doing.

Talent is not the prerogative of any racial or ethnic group, any social class, or any residential area. It may lie untapped in some situations under some conditions, but no population has either a monopoly on or an absence of talents. Nor will depriving the gifted and talented pupil of opportunities to develop and use his gifts result in upgrading the attainments of his less able peers. Such misguided and meaningless egalitarianism contributes to the development of no one in particular. Obviously, with broadened insights into the natue of giftedness, some traditional identification procedures, college preparatory programs, and rewards systems are no longer valid. With the years of research and experience now behind us, we should view educational opportunities and engagement differently, based on modified values; and we should be more sensitive to the sociopolitical context in which learning takes place and programs function.

It was the civil rights movement and the war on poverty that underscored the failure of our schools to provide adequate educational opportunities for large numbers of our poor and disadvantaged groups. The U.S. Commissioner of Education has announced that he will become a "visible advocate for increased attention" to the gifted and talented. All educators must become advocates for increased, appropriate attention to the gifted, especially those among the disadvantaged and minorities, where discrimination and neglect have resulted in an even greater loss of talent development.

*Joseph S. Renzulli*

# Talent Potential
# in Minority Group Students

It seems probable that our society discovers and develops no more than perhaps half its potential intellectual talent.

*Robert J. Havighurst (1961)*

There can be little doubt that our nation's largest untapped source of human intelligence and creativity is to be found among the vast numbers of individuals in the lower socio-economic levels, particularly among the approximately 20 million black Americans. It would be a monumental task to explore all of the causes that have contributed to our failure to discover, stimulate, and make the most efficient use of this neglected source of talent. Intensified efforts to overcome this failure are based in part on the simple realization that an invaluable natural resource is being wasted daily by a system of education that has shut its eyes and turned its back on the children of the poor. The by-products of this waste are evident in unprecedented urban turmoil, in unemployment and underemployment, in rising crime and delinquency rates, and most importantly, in the human despair that accompanies thwarted expression and creativity.

Although massive efforts have been directed toward overcoming the inadequacies of educational programing for the culturally disadvantaged, relatively little attention has been focused on those youngsters within the total population of disadvantaged youth who have unusually high potentials for learning and creativity. The numerous compensatory programs that deal mainly with remediation in the basic skill areas and preparation for entrance into the labor market generally have overlooked the talent potential that exists in lower socio-economic and minority group youngsters. A number of persons have called attention to the dimensions of this untapped source of talent (Douglass, 1969; Torrance, 1968), and few would disagree that the time is long overdue for a systematic nationwide effort in talent retrieval. This article describes the dimensions of the talent potential among low socioeconomic and minority group members, and explores some of the is-

Renzulli, Joseph S. "Talent Potential in Minority Group Students." *Exceptional Children*, Vol. 39, No. 6, March, 1973, pp. 437-44.

sues and strategies involved in identifying talent potential and constructing educational programs which will maximize the development of this unidentified and under-stimulated segment of our school population.

## The Nature and Scope of Talent Loss

What exactly are the dimensions of the talent potential among minority groups, and what will be the costs of further delay in providing opportunities for the expression of such potential? A large body of accumulated research clearly indicates that gifted and talented children can be found in all racial groups and at all of society's economic levels. With respect to family background, Terman's (1925-1959) study of gifted children showed that, in actual numbers, the nonprofessional segment of the general population contains more than twice as many gifted children as the professional group. Regarding racial and ethnic origin, Miles (1954) reported that many high IQ black children can be found in black communities. Studies by Jenkins (1948) and Witty and Jenkins (1934) indicated that race per se is not a limiting factor in intellectual development, that black children with high IQ's come from a variety of backgrounds, and that educational achievement of highly able black children resembles that of other gifted youngsters. In more recent years, the works of Hunt (1961), Bloom (1964), and others have called attention to the significant role that environment plays in intellectual development. The massive number of research studies summarized in these works have crucial implications for the role that education can and should play in developing the high potential of youngsters from all races and social classes.

In addition to those studies concerned mainly with older or more traditional definitions of giftedness (i.e., giftedness in terms of IQ), a rapidly expanding body of literature dealing with a broader conception of talent development has recognized that children from depressed areas, low income groups, and racial minorities probably represent our largest unmined source of creative talent (Passow, 1966; Torrance, 1968). The importance of identifying and developing creative talent at all levels of society has caused leading philosophers and educators to focus their attention on this problem. In an article entitled, "Is America Neglecting Her Creative Minority?" Toynbee (1964) commented:

> To give a fair chance to potential creativity is a matter of life and death for any society. This is all-important, because the outstanding creative ability of a fairly small percentage of the population is mankind's ultimate asset, and the only one with which only man has been endowed [p. 4].

It cannot be denied that society stands to benefit from a systematic investment in the development of this vast source of untapped talent; yet, major inequalities of opportunity are still evident in our schools. The inferiority of existing schools for low income and minority group children has been indicated clearly by studies which show that the longer children stay in these schools, the further behind they become in achievement and the wider the gap grows between what they should know and their actual level of performance (Coleman, Campbell, Hobson, McPartland, Mood, Weinfeld, & York, 1966; Sexton, 1961). Average drops in measured intelligence of as much as 20 points have been recorded as black children progress (or perhaps it should be *re*gress) through grades (Passow, Goldberg, & Tannenbaum, 1967). Other studies dealing with delinquency, level of aspiration, self concept, aggressiveness, alienation, and a host of other variables reveal similarly ominous findings about the current state of the school situation for disadvantaged youngsters (Coleman et al., 1966; Mathis, 1969; Williams & Byars, 1968). Under circumstances such as these, even the most highly able and well motivated students from minority groups surely must lose faith in a system where the probability of nonsuccess is so high.

In spite of these grim statistics, there is a growing realization that a wealth of creative talent is lying unidentified and understimulated in schools that serve urban ghetto and rural poor youngsters. The decade of the 1960's may well be remembered as a period in our history when the education establishment began to pay serious attention to the detrimental effects which result from the inferior opportunities that exist for a large segment of our population. Books such as *How Children Fail* (Holt, 1966), *Death at an Early Age* (Kozol, 1967), *Pygmalion in the Classroom* (Rosenthal & Jacobson, 1968), and *Crisis in the Classroom* (Silberman, 1970) have literally shocked us into the reality of the situation. If we look upon the activities and pronouncements of the Sixties as the first step in a direct frontal attack upon the problem of educational equality, then the heightened interest of that decade certainly can be regarded with optimism. But our view should not be blurred by such optimism; for scattered attempts to "do something" for the culturally disadvantaged thus far represent little more than the proverbial "drop in the bucket" when compared to the great number of youngsters whose day to day school experience is nothing short of an educational and psychological disaster. If, on the other hand, the ground work laid during the Sixties has not been a false start, then action to correct this crucial problem in our schools remains the challenge and the task before us. The remainder of this article deals with some of the work that has been done in the area of identifying talent potential among low socioeconomic and minority group youngsters and developing educational programs to help this talent potential be realized.

## Identifying Talent Potential

A number of psychologists and educators who have wrestled with the problem of defining human abilities have advanced the thesis that a variety of talents contribute to the accomplishments of man. Early definitions of giftedness based solely on measures of intelligence have largely ignored the existence of a much broader spectrum of highly valuable human characteristics. In view of the heavy cultural loading of most standardized tests of intelligence and achievement, it is apparent that an identification process that depends mainly on traditional measures of performance will discriminate against youngsters who have not participated fully in the dominant culture. Attempts to circumvent this problem through the construction of culture free or culture fair intelligence tests have failed to yield measures that neutralize the influence of important factors in mental growth, such as perceptual and linguistic deprivation, the repression of constructive play activities, family insecurity and limited adult role models, and the effects of inferior school experiences. Thus, it seems safe to conclude that both traditional tests and so called culture free tests have had the effect of creating a limited conception of the abilities which our society values. Both reflect the emphasis which the dominant culture and formal education place on the ability to deal effectively with language, symbols, and abstraction.

A BROADENED CONCEPTION OF TALENT

In recent years a growing number of theorists and researchers have provided us with a much broadened conception of the nature of human abilities. Foremost among the newer models is the well known structure of the intellect cube developed by Guilford (1967) and his associates. This model consists of a three dimensional classification system designed to encompass and organize 120 possible talents according to (a) the type of mental operation employed, (b) the content involved in the thinking process, and (c) the type of product which results from the act of thinking. Williams and Eberle (1967) developed a similar model which identified 23 classroom teaching strategies that can be used to develop seven productive thinking operations in various subject matter areas, while Taylor's (1968) multiple talent model isolated an additional set of distinguishable abilities in areas such as creativity, decision making, planning, forecasting, and communications.

Taylor suggested a grouping of talents based on the world-of-work needs and pointed out that if we limit ourselves solely to academic talent, only the top 10 percent will fall into the highly gifted class and only 50 percent of our students will have a chance to be above average (i.e., above the median). On the other hand, if we measure students across several different talents, the percent of highly gifted students will increase tremendously:

> When we arrange a group of students on each of several talent ladders, those at the bottom of the old academic talent ladder—those heretofore labeled "educationally deprived"—will rise as a subgroup to be almost average as far as each of the other five types of talents are concerned. A third or more of them are likely to be above average on each new talent ladder. Since we have not been reaching these students, we should try eliciting as many different talents as possible. If we succeed, then those who had not been flourishing in

the old talent area will discover some areas where they are promising individuals and perhaps even star performers [Taylor, 1968, p. 68].

Thus, the application of a multiple talent approach in our schools will result in greater numbers of students achieving higher degrees of success both in and out of school. According to Taylor, a natural by-product of this approach will be an increase in the student's individuality. Each student will experience and display his own unique profile across talents and will thus become more self directed.

SUGGESTIONS FOR IDENTIFICATION OF MULTIPLE TALENTS

The taxonomies developed by Bloom (1956) and Krathwohl, Bloom, and Masia (1964) provide another classification system for isolating cognitive and affective processes that clearly identify dimensions of man's repertoire of behaviors. These behaviors often are not measured by traditional tests of intelligence or are "buried" in the general scores which many of these tests yield. A good example is the limited range of abilities sampled by the *Scholastic Aptitude Tests* (SAT). According to a recent report by the Commission on Tests (1970), the SAT has been found to be mainly a measure of developed verbal, mathematical, and reasoning abilities, and thus, it fails to take account of the educational potential of college applicants who for one reason or another have been educationally disadvantaged. The Commission has recognized the need for a broader conception of college admission criteria and has suggested that the SAT be expanded to include measures of the following abilities:

1. Adaptation in new learning situations.
2. Problem solving in situations that require varied cognitive styles and skills.
3. Analysis, search, and synthesis behaviors.
4. Information management, processing, and utilization skills.
5. Nonstandard information pools.
6. Comprehension through experiencing, listening, and looking, as well as reading.
7. Expression through artistic, oral, nonverbal, and graphic, as well as written symbolization.
8. Characteristics of temperament.
9. Sources and status of motivation.
10. Habits of work and task involvement under varying conditions of demand [Commission on Tests, 1970, vol. 2, p. 44].

The Commission further suggested that test procedures should be redesigned (a) to broaden the varieties of subject matter, competencies, and skills assessed; (b) to examine achievement in a variety of contexts; (c) to make greater use of opened and unstructured indicators of achievement; and (d) to assess nonacademic achievement such as social competence, coping skills, avocational skills, and artistic, athletic, political, and mechanical skills.

With these and other models to assist in defining and classifying a variety of human abilities, the next step should consist of the selection or development of appropriate instruments to identify a broad range of talent potential. Bruch (1971) suggested using Guilford's model to diagnose different patterns of abilities reflected in existing test items and to specify factors and clusters of factors that represent the strengths and weaknesses of particular individuals or cultural groups. Tests then could be designed to fit cultural strengths, and such tests could be used to measure both conventional abilities and those talents which are valued most by an individual's own culture. Bruch further suggested a case study battery for the identification of gifted disadvantaged youngsters that would include a profile of their strengths and developmental needs, ratios of time in school to developmental levels and achievement levels, and an analysis of positive and negative factors (both sociocultural and personal) which either enhance or inhibit further development of talents.

TORRANCE TESTS OF CREATIVE THINKING

Additional strategies for identifying hidden talent among the disadvantaged have been developed by Torrance (1969). Through the use of instruments such as the *Torrance Tests of Creative Thinking* (Torrance, 1966), youngsters are given an opportunity to respond in terms unique to their own culture. Such an approach avoids the problem of evaluating the child through experiences that are common to the dominant culture, and at the same time, helps to create a psychologically safe atmosphere which will motivate him to put forth his greatest effort. On the basis of research studies carried out with disadvantaged groups, Torrance (1964, 1967) has identified the following set of creative characteristics which he found to occur with relatively high frequency among disadvantaged children:

1. High nonverbal fluency and originality.
2. High creative productivity in small groups.
3. Adeptness in visual art activities.
4. High creativity in movement, dance, and other physical activities.
5. Ability to be highly motivated by games, music, sports, humor, and concrete objects.
6. Language rich in imagery.

Research conducted by Torrance and his associates over a period of 12 years has led to the conclusion that children of economically deprived and minority cultures seemed to perform as well as those from any other group. In a recent review of the literature dealing with the use of the *Torrance Tests of Creative Thinking,* Torrance (1971) summarized the results of 15 research studies which focused on the creative abilities of low socioeconomic and minority group children. Generally, these studies indicated that although whites surpassed blacks on verbal measures, there were no significant differences on scores of figural fluency, flexibility, and originality; and in some

416

cases, the so called disadvantaged groups surpassed the middle class groups. Although measures of intelligence have been found consistently to correlate positively with socioeconomic status, the research summarized by Torrance seems to indicate that creativity bears little relationship to factors such as race, social class, and level of parental education. Thus, a convincing argument is presented for a relatively culture free method of identifying a bountiful supply of creative talent. Torrance expressed the belief that in many ways the life experiences of low socioeconomic youngsters may actually be more supportive of creative achievement than the experiences of more advantaged children.

> Their lack of expensive toys and play materials contributes to their skill in improvising with common materials. The large families and life styles of disadvantaged families develop skills in group activities and problem-solving. Positive values placed by their families on music, rhythm, dance, body expressiveness, and humor keep alive abilities and sensibilities that tend to perish in more advantaged families [p. 79].

BIOGRAPHICAL INDICES

The recently developed *Alpha Biographical* (Institue for Behavioral Research in Creativity, 1968) provides another strategy for identifying creative talent among disadvantaged and minority group youngsters. This instrument, consisting of 300 items through which an individual is asked to describe himself and his background, is based on the belief that past behavior, experiences, and self descriptions can be used as indicators of future performance. A number of research studies carried out by the developers of the *Alpha* indicate that it can be used as an aid in identifying a number of different talents which are important for both academic performance and performance in a variety of work situations. The significance of this instrument lies in the fact that creativity scores and scores on a number of other factors bear little or no relationship to race. In other words, for certain abilities, the *Alpha* does not discriminate against persons from racial minorities.

The *Sub-Cultural Indices of Academic Potential* (SCIAP, Grant & Renzulli, 1971) is another instrument designed to take account of problems of test bias, the cultural distinctiveness of minority group members, and the growing concern on the part of high schools and colleges to identify high potential minority group students for supportive educational programs. The instrument consists of 145 items which ask students to indicate how they feel about themselves and how they would react in situations that are common to their every day experiences. There are no right or wrong answers to the SCIAP items, but rather, the instrument yields a profile that points out student preferences and learning styles in areas such as: the organization and management of information, commitment to social responsibility and leadership, flexibility in social situations, originality in cultural context, initiative and persistance, self concept, attitudes toward education, and support of family and school toward continuing education.

*417*

Two additional considerations should be pointed out in discussing the issue of identification. First, one of the major characteristics of the disadvantaged is their inability to master the linguistic and grammatical structures of the dominant culture. For this reason it is necessary to develop identification strategies which are not language dependent. Furthermore, because most youngsters have a greater facility with the spoken rather than the written word, it is especially important that the disadvantaged child not be required to "write down" all of his responses. Tape recorders or human recorders can serve in uncovering higher forms of thinking which might otherwise go undetected because of limited writing ability.

Finally, the identification of talent potential among the disadvantaged should be a continuous process that begins in the early years and that is carried out with unusual frequency. Until more and better predictive instruments are available, talent searches should take place in the classroom on a regular basis. Because of the dynamic nature of abilities such as creativity, efforts to make long range predictions should be replaced with frequent assessments of a variety of talents. These assessments should be followed by carefully designed classroom activities which are constructed specifically to enhance those talents which have been identified.

## Developing Talent Potential

Although strategies for identifying different types of human abilities are in varying stages of maturity, enough is known about developing talent potential to allow us to do some systematic programing in this area. Two major factors in the development of outstanding abilities are (a) the characteristics of the teacher and (b) the relevancy of the curriculum.

### TEACHER CHARACTERISTICS

One major generalization about teacher characteristics stands out from the vast amount of recent literature dealing with programing for the disadvantaged: "Experienced teachers who feel personal satisfaction in working with disadvantaged students are the key to successful compensatory education in poverty area schools [*Phi Delta Kappan*, 1970, p. 338]." This was the finding of a study which investigated 32 programs reporting substantial improvements in the achievement of low income students. Thus, careful teacher selection appears to be a major consideration in programing for the disadvantaged. Furthermore, in situations where talent development is a primary goal, it is especially important to select teachers who are committed to the task of working with disadvantaged youngsters in the development of a variety of talents. Teachers without such knowledge are likely to approach talent development in a piecemeal and haphazard fashion.

Space does not permit a detailed discussion of the several approaches to talent development which can be found in the literature (see for example, Gregory, 1967; Parnes & Harding, 1962; Williams & Eberle, 1967); however, two general suggestions are offered as necessary first steps for systematic programing in this area.First, the teacher should have a functional knowledge of one or more of the models described above. Using the model(s) as a guide enables the teacher to plan a wide variety of activities that are designed to nurture specific talents. If teachers are unaware of the behavioral characteristics and dimensions of various types of abilities, it seems unlikely that they will be able to plan purposeful activities to promote the development of these abilities.

A second suggestion relates to knowledge about specific strategies that have already proved their usefulness by promoting creative problem solving in business and industry. Techniques such as attribute listing, morphological analysis, brainstorming, and forced relationships are easy to learn and readily adaptable to a variety of classroom situations. However, it is the teacher's initiative in applying these techniques that will make the difference between an exciting, "mind expanding" experience and a routine classroom activity. The teacher who is coverage dominated, i.e., one who judges his effectiveness by the number of chapters or units that he covers during a given period, probably will never find time to develop abilities other than the so-called basic skills.

RELEVANCY OF THE CURRICULUM

While remediation in the basic skill areas must be an important goal of compensatory education, it should not, of course, be the only objective of the programs which serve the disadvantaged youth. Activities for talent development can be built into areas of the curriculum, and because of the inherent fun and excitement of activities such as the type described above, added dividends are likely to accrue in the form of increased motivation and improved performance in the basic skills of learning.

High potential disadvantaged youngsters are vitally interested in the social changes taking place around them in their neighborhoods and in the society at large. Thus, it is little wonder that they get "turned off" by a curriculum which deals with the exports of Brazil and the names of Columbus' ships when rallies against racism and demonstrations in Washington are the real issues with which they would like to deal. These issues provide excellent opportunities for constructing activities that promote decision making and social leadership skills. Exercises which encourage imaginative solutions to real life problems have a much greater likelihood of promoting creativity than the time worn chore of writing a story about "what I did last summer."

In their book, *Compensatory Education for the Culturally Disadvantaged,* Bloom, Davis, and Hess (1965) called attention to the importance of curricular relevancy by listing the following objectives as one of the four major goals of education for the disadvantaged:

Increasing stress must be placed on those aspects of interests, attitudes, and personality which will promote the further growth of the individual, enable him to find satisfaction in the things he does, and help him to find meaning and fulfillment in his life. The effects of automation, the shorter work week, urban living, and the fast pace of change on the national as well as international scene require individual character development which will enable each person to live with himself and with others under conditions very different from those which have prevailed [p. 3].

A somewhat simplified and yet operational definition of a relevant curriculum is: a set of experiences which deal with topics and issues that youngsters would talk about if given a free choice. If we are really serious about a process centered rather than content centered curriculum (and experiences that attempt to promote specific talents certainly must be considered process oriented), then the issues that youngsters prefer to talk about, those that they discuss before and after the school bell rings, provide fertile ground for the development of a wide range of talents.

## Basic Elements of a Total Program of Talent Development

Although highly qualified teachers and relevant curricular experiences are considered to be major factors in programing for high potential youngsters, a total approach to talent development also should include a number of other characteristics. Douglass (1969) pointed out four essential elements of an ideal system for maximizing the talent potential of low socioeconomic and minority group members.

The first element is greater flexibility in the ways in which schools are operated and performance is evaluated. The classroom unit must be broken down into small learning modules where individuals and small groups become the main focus of instructional efforts. Although the school may continue to serve as a "home base" for the learning process, Douglass suggested that early in the elementary school years students should be provided with extended periods of learning time in institutions that usually are not considered schools:

These would include places where knowledge is stored, such as art museums, science institutes, and libraries . . . places where knowledge is being put to work, such as farms, hospitals, airports, machine shops, sheet metal works, and construction . . . places in which some kind of education or learning or on-the-job training is under way . . . places where knowledge is being discovered such as research institutes and laboratories [Douglas, 1969, pp. 10-11].

The second element would consist of an early start in the education and socialization processes. Low socioeconomic group children often enter school with the accumulated deficits that result from poor nutrition and limited stimulation in infancy and early childhood. These deficits may lead to intellectual inhibition and an inability to take advantage of the educational opportunities that may be open to them in later life. Douglass advocated a program of nursing schools and day care centers where each child will be assured of services of professionals and paraprofessionals who are knowledgeable about early childhood experiences that are beneficial to later development. These centers might be located throughout the community in schools, hospitals, or factories, and they should provide continuing education programs for parents and substitute parents.

An early apprenticeship is the third element of a total program of talent development. Beginning at an early age, students should be given frequent exposure to different ways of making a living and of participating in leisure time activities. Too often, children from low socioeconomic group families have no real contact with a father figure or they see their parents employed only in lower level occupations. They have little opportunity to observe the variety of talents used in the broad spectrum of occupations, and thus, they have a limited conception of the many kinds of talents that are valuable to our society and available for their exploration. Early apprenticeship programs would help youngsters to see the real world's conception of talent rather than the school's traditionally limited concern for only academic ability.

A final element which is necessary in the development of talent potential is the creation of a more open system. The grade by grade progression has failed to meet the needs of students who do not "fit in" at the start or who are not willing to "play the game" by the existing rules. If we truly respect the individual differences and preferences of all people in our society, then we should not force them to follow a relatively prescribed system of learning. Students should be free to alternate school and work experiences with other experiences which they may wish to pursue. They should be free to drop out of school for a given period of time and allowed to reenter the system without fear of punitive action or relegation to programs which are essentially remedial in nature. Access to first rate educational programs should be readily available to every person at every stage of development regardless of his previous success or lack of success in the system. A more open system will allow adults as well as young people to have an opportunity to explore and develop talents that may have been thwarted earlier in life.

## References

Bloom, B.S. *Stability and change in human characteristics.* New York: John Wiley & Sons, 1964.

Bloom, B.S. (Ed.) *Taxonomy of educational objectives. Handbook I: Cognitive domain.* New York: David McKay, 1956.

Bloom, B.S., Davis, A., & Hess, R. *Compensatory education for cultural deprivation.* New York: Holt, Rinehart & Winston, 1965.

Bruch, C.R. Modification of procedures for identification of the disadvantaged gifted. *Gifted Child Quarterly,* 1971, 15, 267-272.

Coleman, J.S., Campbell, E.Q., Hobson, C.J., McPartland, J., Mood, A.M., Weinfeld, F.D., & York, R.L., *Equality of educational opportunity.* Washington, D.C.: USGPO, 1966.

Commission on Tests. *I: Righting the balance, II: Briefs.* New York: College Entrance Examination Board, 1970.

Douglass, J.H. Strategies for maximizing the development of talent among the urban disadvantaged. Paper presented at the annual meeting of The Council for Exceptional Children, Denver, Colorado, April, 1969.

Grant, T.E., & Renzulli, J.S. *Sub-cultural indices of academic potential.* University of Connecticut, 1971.

Gregory, C.E. *The management of intelligence.* New York: McGraw-Hill, 1967.

Guilford, J.P. *The nature of human intelligence.* New York: McGraw-Hill, 1967.

Havighurst, R.J. Conditions productive of superior children. *Teachers College Record,* 1961, 62, 524-531.

Holt, J. *How children fail.* New York: Dell, 1966.

Hunt, J. McV. *Intelligence and experience.* New York: Ronald Press, 1961.

Institute for Behavioral Research in Creativity. *Alpha Biographical Inventory.* Greensboro, N.C.: Prediction Press, 1968.

Jenkins, M.D. The upper limit of ability among American Negroes. *Scientific Monthly.* 1948, 66, 339-401.

Key to compensatory education. *Phi Delta Kappan,* 1970, 58, 338.

Kozol, J. *Death at an early age.* Boston: Houghton-Mifflin, 1967.

Krathwohl, D.R., Bloom, B.S. & Masia, B.B. *Taxonomy of educational objectives. Handbook II: Affective domain.* New York: David McKay, 1964.

Mathis, H.I. The disadvantaged and the aptitude barrier. *Personnel and Guidance Journal,* 1969, 47, 467-472.

Niles, C.C. Gifted children. In L. Carmichael (Ed.), *Manual of child psychology.* New York: John Wiley & Sons, 1954.

Parnes, S. J. & Harding, H. F. (Eds.) *A source book for creative thinking.* New York: Charles Scribner's Sons, 1962.

Passow, A.H. The talented among the disadvantaged. *Accent on Talent,* 1966, 1, 3-7.

Passow, A.H., Goldberg, M., & Tannenbaum, A.J. *Education of the disadvantaged.* New York: Holt, Rinehart, & Winston, 1967.

Rosenthal, R., & Jacobson, L.F. *Pygmalion in the classroom.* New York: Holt, Rinehart, & Winston, 1968.

Sexton, P.C. *Education and income.* New York: Viking Press, 1961.

Silberman, C.E. *Crisis in the classroom.* New York: Random House, 1970.

Taylor, C.W. Be talent developers . . . as well as knowledge dispensers. *Today's Education,* 1968, 57, 67-69.

Terman, S.M. *Genetic studies of genius.* Stanford: Stanford University Press, 1925-1959. 5 Vols.

Torrance, E.P. *Education and the creative potential.* Minneapolis: University of Minnesota Press, 1964.

Torrance, E.P. *Torrance Tests of Creative Thinking: Norms-technical manual.* Princeton, N.J.: Personnel Press, 1966.

Torrance, E.P. *Understanding the fourth grade slump in creativity.* Athens: Georgia Studies of Creative Behavior, 1967.

Torrance, E.P. Finding hidden talents among disadvantaged children. *Gifted Child Quarterly,* 1968, 12, 131-137.

Torrance, E.P. How creativity development can awaken unrecognized potential. Paper presented at the conference on "Developing Unawakened and Unrecognized Potential" sponsored by the Minnesota State Department of Education, Minneapolis, April, 1969.

Torrance, E.P. Are the Torrance Tests of Creative Thinking biased against or in favor of "disadvantaged" groups? *Gifted Child Quarterly.* 1971, 15, 75-80.

Toynbee, A. Is America neglecting her creative minorities? In C.W. Taylor (Ed.), *Widening horizons of creativity.* New York: John Wiley & Sons, 1964.

Williams, F.E. & Eberle, R.F. *Creative production in the classroom.* Edwardsville, Ill: American of Edwardsville, 1967.

Williams, R.L. & Byars, H. Negro self-esteem in a transitional society. *Personnel & Guidance Journal,* 1968, 47, 120-125.

Witty, P., & Jenkins, M.D. The educational achievement of a group of gifted Negro children. *Journal of Educational Psychology,* 1934, 45, 585-597.

Calvin W. Taylor

# Cultivating New Talents:
# A Way to Reach the
# Educationally Deprived

*I*n a mining region near Salt Lake City, large and efficient mills have been built in order to process raw materials from which valuable metals can be extracted. Rocks and boulders from the mountainside are ground in successive steps until, with the addition of water, they are turned into a stream of fine silt. Next, the stream is processed to yield copper, the metal initially sought.

At that point, the procedure used to end. But now, modern mining engineers are alert to any discoveries through basic research of the existence of new and sometimes rare and precious metals. The mining specialists immediately try to identify each newly discovered metal in the residual stream that was once poured off as a mere waste product. If a new metal is present, they try to find ways of adding other processes in order to develop this additional metal out of the total potential in the stream—continuing at the same time, of course, to extract copper.

As they look backward over the years, the Utah miners realize that they have dumped onto the valley floor waste products that may contain metals of a larger total value than the ones already extracted.

## Multiple Talents

Is our educational system "dumping" valuable human resources? Is it efficient as it could be in identifying and developing known talents? Is it alert to discover new talents, new resources?

The term "gifted" is one traditionally used to describe high scorers on an intelligence test (or the closely related academically talented). For the stu-

Taylor, Calvin W. "Cultivating New Talents: A Way to Reach the Educationally Deprived." *The Journal of Creative Behavior,* Vol. 2, No. 2, 1968, p. 83-90.

dents so identified, educators have set up special classes for which the curricula and the teaching methods have been designed specifically to nurture this general type of talent. And yet, the term "gifted" is in fact an adjective that can be used to cover eight to ten other broad or general high level talents, that may be equally important, such as creative talents, planning talents, wisdom or decision-making talents, forecasting talent, communication talents of several types, etc. Consequently, there are eight or ten types of giftedness that can be identified through testing (Taylor, 1966). Each of these general types is in turn composed of a particular sub-set of specific high-level talents. For example, Guilford has summarized and greatly augmented the work of Thurstone and his students who discovered about 20 specific talents initially called primary mental abilities. In Guilford's current version of his periodic table of the mind (called The Structure of Intellect), there are 120 possible specific high-level talents, with over 80 discovered to date (Guilford, 1964, 1967). Typical intelligence tests cover only a sub-set of about 8 specific talents or about 1/10th of those known—intelligence tests therefore do *not* cover the other 9/10ths known to date.

## Theory and Evidence

As a general rule, not all gifted persons excel in the same talents. If we conceive of each talent group as arranged on a ladder, we will find that those persons at the top of one ladder are essentially different ones than those at the top of another ladder. Furthermore, some of those at the top of one talent ladder may well be toward the bottom of another. If we begin to search for and develop a third talent, that ladder will show a composition of members quite different from the other two. Those at the bottom of a previous talent ladder may rise as a subgroup to be almost average as far as the new type of talent is concerned. A fraction of them (a third or more) are likely to be above average in the new talent area.

Let us turn to mathematics for a clearer picture of what happens on the talent ladders.

If there were merely one type of talent, only 50% of the students would be talented above the average (median). If there were two unrelated talents with 50% above average on each, 25% would be above average on both talents and 75% would be above average on at least one talent. For three uncorrelated talents, 87.5% would be above average on at least one talent.

| Number of Unrelated Talents | Percent Above Average in at Least One Talent |
|---|---|
| 1 | 50.0% |
| 2 | 75.0 |
| 3 | 87.5 |
| 4 | 93.8 |
| 5 | 96.9 |
| 6 | 98.4 |
| 7 | 99.2 |
| 8 | 99.6 |

Since high-level talents are not absolutely unrelated but tend to be lowly related in the positive direction, evidence indicates that the actual trends upward toward 100% do not climb as rapidly as in the theoretical picture above (based upon the extreme case of zero intercorrelations). In other words, there would be some slippage downward due to overlapping talents. In the case of two somewhat correlated talents, the expectation for the percentage above average would be in the high 60's (instead of 75%); for three talents it would be in the 70's (instead of 87.5%); for four talents in the 70's or possibly in the low 80's (instead of 93.8%), etc. The estimated downward slippage will depend upon the level of correlation found to be present—the more intercorrelation, the greater the slippage.

The same type of theoretical approach could be applied to the top end of the talent ladder. For example, considering the top 10% as highly gifted and looking across several types of talents or giftedness yields a similar important trend. If one type of talent is cultivated, only 10% will be "highly gifted." If talents are independent and two types are cultivated, 19% will be highly gifted. (One percent will be highly gifted in both types of talent and a total of 19% will be highly gifted in at least one.) This percent will likewise increase to 27 with three talents, to 35 with four talents, and will continue upward at a diminishing rate as each new type of talent is added, assuming that talents are completely unrelated.

However, in the usual case of talents being somewhat related, this percentage will not rise as rapidly. For example, if creativity is added as a second type of talent, the evidence suggests that a new 7% will be found to be in the top 10% of the highly talented in creativity along with 3% from the previous talent area who will have a high profile across both types of talent. Thus a total of 17% will be highly gifted in at least one of the two talent areas. By further taking into account the low interrelationships among different types of giftedness, approximately 22 to 23% will be found to be in the top 10% of at least one of three types of giftedness. This trend will continue so that if one cultivates at least six different types of giftedness in the classroom, about 30% of the students could be found to be highly gifted (in the top 10%) in at least one of the six high-level talent areas. Thus, the percent doubled with three talents and tripled with about six.

These calculations yield a beautiful phenomenon and a most promising picture for educators: Not only do new star performers emerge from almost all levels of the previous talent ladder, but those who had not been flourishing in the old talent areas will rise toward the middle of their class in each new talent area in turn. Moreover, nearly all students will have the rewarding experience of being above average in one or another talent area if we cultivate enough different talents in the classroom. In addition, about a third of the students will be found to be highly gifted in at least one major talent area.

This is a very heartening outlook in terms of motivation of students and the potential in our human resources. The sub-group heretofore classified as educationally deprived will almost approach an average group in a new gifted area, and individually they will spread widely up and down this new type of gifted ladder—certainly not highly concentrated at the bottom. A third or more of them will tend to be above average, and a somewhat different third of them will be above average in each new area of giftedness focused upon.

The implications of this phenomenon are exciting because, if a variety of talents are tested and trained for, a student can learn a great deal about himself and his abilities and consequently become self-directed. He can steer himself throughout his life into activities that call for his best talents—a course that can well lead to optimum self-actualization and productivity.

If we are to do well in preparing students for change, for keeping on the "right side of change," and even for bringing about needed changes in knowledge and practices, our talent searches should occur right in the classroom where we can, with no extra time required, develop the talents of students in the regular curriculum while they are simultaneously acquiring knowledge. Since the various talents tend to be unrelated or not highly related, a different classroom approach to each one will result in much greater variety in education. It will also provide the best hope of reaching each and every person in the classroom, because almost everyone will be above average in one or more of these high-level talents.[1] At one time or another, then, we would be reaching almost all of those children who, under less felicitous circumstances, would be considered educationally deprived, drawing them off the bottom more toward the average.

Using this new talent approach in the classroom presents no basic difficulties as far as course content is concerned. Students grow in subject matter knowledge at least as fast, if not faster, when they utilize and develop new talents while acquiring subject matter. Hutchinson (1963, 1967), for one, found this to be true. Using matched sets of classes of junior high students, he worked with two different teaching methods. First he had four teachers use their typical method, and then with a comparable set of students they used a productive thinking method in which the students were conceived to be "thinkers" and not merely "learners." He held the content dimension constant by having all students deal with the same two-week unit of social studies subject matter. He varied the teaching methods and observed the thinking and learning processes in the students.

The students in the productive thinking classrooms appeared to enjoy school more and learned at least as much or more subject matter. And a new group of students (independent of "IQ" type of talent) emerged as the star performers in this second type of classroom. To be specific, IQ scores correlated only $-.04$ with the amount of subject matter learned (post-test minus pre-test achievement scores). Thus, in the traditional classes, the IQ type of giftedness was being utilized while subject matter was being learned and in the second type of classes an almost entirely different (productive thinking) type of giftedness was being used while the same content was being learned.

[1] It is also realistic to recognize that, contrarily, almost everyone is below average in at least one talent.

**427**

And the poorest students in the first classroom were not the same type as those who were the poorest in the second classroom.

Recently Hutchinson decided to give a demonstration of his teaching methods to a set of teachers working in a poverty educational program. He again worked at the junior high level but he changed the subject matter to language arts. New groups of students continued to emerge as star performers when productive thinking processes were used in acquiring course content—and some of these star performers were below average students in the typical classroom.

## Program for Creative Talents

With the current emphasis on knowledge acquisition, a relatively narrow band of talents is probably being cultivated. In sharp contrast, if a multiple talent approach is used in the classroom, the band of talents would be deliberately widened, and, as an automatic by-product, the scope and type of knowledge acquired might also widen. In the cultivation of certain components of curiosity and creativity, for example, the student is required to expand his experience by working at and beyond the fringe of knowledge. To accomplish this particular expansion both of knowledge and of talents, an educator no longer needs to restrict himself solely to the academic talents but can break away initially to creative talents by experimenting with several approaches:

(1) Develop creative thinking and creative problem-solving characteristics.

(2) Develop creative personality and motivational characteristics.

(3) Overcome emotional hindrances and blocks to the creative processes.

(4) Develop an awareness of what is not yet known, encourage curiosity about it, and elicit ideas for launching creative ventures therein.

(5) Develop questioning abilities in teachers so that they learn to formulate thought-provoking questions about known subject matter and also about the unknowns, thereby giving students experience in dealing with contradictions and with knowledge of differing degrees of substantiation.

(6) Develop the ability of teachers to make direct statements that likewise provoke creative thought.

(7) Combine knowledge and creativity, or information and creativity, drawing upon cybernetics and information theory, including attempts to increase the creativeness of the input (receptional) processes and the output (expressional) processes.

(8) Elicit creative processes in classroom programs. (The creativeness of the internal central processes of students is a most challenging area.)

(9) Focus upon the creativeness of the students' products.

(10) Utilize related technology (such as inquiry training; discovery

methods used in the arts and mathematics; programs in art education, dance, and writing for fostering creativity; and various training programs in industry designed to develop creativity).

(11) Develop programmed instruction for creativity.

(12) Modify existing creativity testing materials to make them suitable for situational training and other classroom instructional uses.

(13) Develop other special instructional media for creativity.

(14) Identify those teachers who are most masterful in fostering creative processes and creative behaviors in students; analyze and then duplicate their approaches.

## Summary

Basic research has indicated that there are at least eighty specific talents that can be identified and tested. If one formulates meaningful subgroups of these many talents, a larger category called "giftedness" can be identified. There are at least eight or ten types of giftedness for which students can be tested and trained.

All evidence and demonstrations to date show strongly that a largely new group will be found to be most gifted as we either test or train in the classroom for each new type of giftedness. Classroom searches and development of talent also show that those who are seen as academically deprived will move upward as each type of giftedness becomes the focus of attention in classroom activities. In turn a different subgroup of people slip downward to the bottom of the talent ladder for that particular type of giftedness.

The challenge, then, is to devise and initiate various educational programs focused on developing creative and other new talents, for the sake of both the educationally deprived and the unrecognized, underdeveloped gifted persons.

This entire approach is a very healthy one indeed and should make our school systems much more efficient in identifying and developing the nation's important human resources for the overall benefit of the individuals, the communities, the nation, and the world. And, as we discover, identify, and process new human resources, we may, like the mining specialists, wonder how long we had previously been pouring such resources untouched through the mills and out on the world, unnoticed, undeveloped, unused.

## References

Guilford, J. P. Progress in the discovery of intellectual factors. In C. W. Taylor (Ed.), *Widening horizons in creativity*. New York: Wiley, 1964, pp. 282-297.

Guilford, J. P. *The nature of human intelligence.* New York: McGraw-Hill, 1967.

Hutchinson, W. L. Creative and productive thinking in the classroom. Unpub. Doctoral dissertation, University of Utah, June 1963.

Hutchinson, W. L. Creative and productive thinking in the classroom. *J. of Crea. Behav.,* 1967, *1* (4), 419-427.

Taylor, C. W. Questioning and creating: a model for curriculum reform. *J. of Crea. Behav.,* 1967, *1* (1), 22-23.

## Additional Readings

Taylor, C. W. Clues to creative teaching. A series of ten articles in *The Instructor* appearing from Sept. 1963-June 1964.

Taylor, C. W. (Ed.). *Creativity: progress and potential.* New York: McGraw-Hill, 1964.

Taylor, C. W. (Ed.). *Widening horizons in creativity.* New York: Wiley, 1964.

Taylor, C. W. (Ed.). *Creativity across education.* Selected papers from five annual creativity workshops held at the University of Utah. University of Utah Press, 1968.

Taylor, C. W., & Barron, F. (Eds.). *Scientific creativity: its recognition and development.* New York: Wiley, 1963.

Taylor, C. W., & Williams, F. (Eds.). *Instructional media and creativity.* New York: Wiley, 1966.

Taylor, C. W., Ghiselin, B., & Wolfer, J. A. Bridging the gap between basic research and educational practice. *NEA J.,* 1962, *51,* 23-25.

Taylor, C. W., Ghiselin, B., Wolfer, J. A., Loy, L., & Bourne, L. E., Jr. Development of a theory of education from psychological and other basic research findings. U.S. Office of Education Cooperative Research Project No. 621, August 1964. (Mimeo)

*Joseph L. French*

# The Highly Intelligent Dropout

*I*n recent years many people have assumed that all students of above average intellectual ability not only graduate from high school, but go on to college. Such an assumption is incorrect. Recent studies indicate that eight to 11 per cent of high school dropouts have IQ's of 110 or above. In a comprehensive study of Pennsylvania youth in 1964-65 we found more than 800 high ability dropouts. Nearly 500 had IQ's of 120 and above and 80 had IQ's of 130 or more. These figures are impressive when it is recognized that Pennsylvania has one of the lowest dropout rates in the country.

Some frequently mentioned correlates of school withdrawal were not substantiated in the findings of this study of dropouts with IQ's of 110 and above. Noticeably absent from the dropout data are indications of frequent school transfers, early part time employment, unemployment upon leaving school, generally low parental education, and lower parental employment status. What is noticed is that dropouts differ from "persisters" (students of the same age, IQ, neighborhood, and sex who were still in school) in such areas as personality, interests, educational skills, and family orientation toward school processes.

The male dropouts, when compared with the persisters, were found to be more frank, uninhibited, and happy-go-lucky. Although they tended to be easy going, their actions were marked with deliberateness. The male dropouts were more assertive, independent, unconventional, and rebellious than the persisters. Their overall response pattern, however, would suggest that they fell within normal limits with regard to their mental health.

The girls dropping out of school for reasons other than marriage were very similar to the boys. However, two-thirds of the female dropouts in this study were pregnant, married, and/or planning to marry when they withdrew.

The girls who withdrew because of pregnancy and/or marriage were far less socially oriented than the persisters; they were less prone to seek social recognition. These girls could be described as tending to be shy and retiring. Their personality pattern would indicate reason to suspect proneness to poor social adjustment in junior and senior high school.

Seldom did dropouts express attitudes which were opposite to those of

*431*

persisters. The differences found were generally a matter of degree. Both the male dropouts and persisters, for example, believed that their parents considered school to be important; the dropouts were not as implicit however. Male dropouts did not demonstrate a truly negative attitude toward the schools. They did point to a number of areas which they found to be difficult to accept. They often expressed concern that schools are not preparing students for the "real" world. There also appeared to be an emotional gap between the male dropouts and their teachers. The dropouts were not inclined to describe their teachers as being well prepared, knowledgeable with regard to subject matter, or concerned about the feelings and needs of the students. "Favoritism" was a problem listed by a number of dropouts. Dropouts tended to complain about the strong forces within the schools to conform. More than did the persisters, they expressed the importance of being able to be an individual.

The attitudes of the unmarried female dropouts were similar to those of the boys. They also expressed the notion that school training did not meet their needs as related to their vocational or professional goals. Although these girls also appeared to be estranged from their teachers, there was little reference made to unfair treatment or favoritism.

The married female dropouts were more similar to persisters than to unmarried female dropouts in their attitudes. They did not appear to feel as if teachers were partial in their treatment of students nor were they unhappy with their courses. They did, more so than the persisters or unmarried female dropouts, feel as if their parents weren't satisfied with the school setting.

# Part V
# Teaching the Gifted

The most appropriate education of gifted and talented students has for many years been a topic of great discussion and debate among educators. What kind of person should teach the gifted? What are the most effective teaching strategies for superior learners? Persons who have studied these and other questions relating to the gifted are the first to admit that there are no easy answers to these problems. Although some research has been done in the area of teaching and counseling the gifted, it is clearly the major area within the field that is in greatest need of continuing investigation.

The articles in Part V concern themselves with a variety of attempts to point out our present understanding about teaching the gifted and creative. The first article by Barbe and Frierson deals with the distinction between "product-oriented and process-oriented" teachers. The role of each type of teacher is described and practices that may limit the growth of gifted students are discussed. In a similar fashion, Nelson and Cleland have described the different teaching role that is necessary when the teacher attempts to respond to the unique capabilities and talents of each child. Although this article was written primarily for reading teachers, the teaching characteristics discussed are, in most cases, readily applicable to all areas of the curriculum. The authors do, however, deal with special teaching implications for the reading program and specific suggestions for instructing gifted children in reading are made.

The article by Bishop reports the results of a research study that was designed to identify characteristics of high school teachers who were judged to be successful by intellectually gifted students. Factors considered in the study were the intelligence and achievement levels of teachers, their interests and activities, their professional attitudes and viewpoints, and their classroom behavior. This study should be of special interest to those persons who are involved in teacher selection and training.

For a number of years E. Paul Torrance has been involved in a variety of studies dealing with the identification and development of creativity. In the final article in Part V, this renowned author and researcher discusses some of the ways that creative teaching can be used to reach the student who may not learn effectively through traditional teaching methods. Torrance reports some of the changes that took place in children and young adults as a result of creative teaching and several anecdotes describing specific changes in students' behavior are included. The article concludes with a list of teacher behaviors that Torrance considers to be important for creative teaching.

*Walter B. Barbe*
*Edward C. Frierson*

# Teaching the Gifted—
# A New Frame of Reference

$C$oncern for the gifted in the twentieth century may be traced through three distinct periods. Beginning with the work of Lewis Terman and Leta Hollingworth, emphasis was primarily upon the identification of individuals with superior mental abilities in an attempt to discover those characteristics which were unique to these individuals. Although Terman and Hollingworth considered the implications of their findings for education, their major contributions were to dispel false preconceived ideas and to arouse widespread interest in gifted children.

Terman and Oden's twenty-five-year follow-up study in 1947 clearly indicated that in addition to identification there was a need for specific educational programs for the gifted. The Educational Policies Commission and the American Association for Gifted Children followed Terman and Oden's report with publications that laid the groundwork for special educational planning. Interest in providing for gifted children became of national concern with the unexpected launching of man's first earth satellite.

Through these three stages educators have been primarily concerned with developing identification procedures and administrative provisions for the gifted. Extensive programming, which is the characteristic of the current stage, has brought with it the need for the development of teaching techniques designed specifically for the gifted.

There is a belated awareness today that teaching the gifted does not mean merely exposure to more work or the expectation of completing the same work in a shorter period of time. Administrative provisions have been successful in many situations, but except in the case of individual teachers there has been no consideration of the possibility that the learning pattern followed by the gifted child is different from that of the average child.

Reprinted from the April, 1962, issue of *Education* by permission of the Bobbs-Merrill Co., Inc., Indianapolis, Indiana.

If this is true, the teacher of the gifted must not be satisfied only to teach more, or more rapidly, but must teach differently.

## Product or Process?

Traditionally the teacher has been concerned with the product of learning rather than the process, the possession of knowledge rather than the projection of knowledge. Emphasis upon end-results fostered a teaching approach which called for the presentation of subject matter in a logical progression. Usually this meant simple to complex, concrete to abstract, cause to effect, singular to plural, and whenever possible in chronological order.

It is a credit to gifted students that they have been able to adjust themselves to this pattern of teaching. Underachievement might be only an indication of some gifted students' inability to fit themselves satisfactorily into this pattern of learning.

The process-oriented teacher, as opposed to the product-oriented teacher, is concerned with how gifted students learn, rather than how the material is learned by most students. Emphasis upon the learning pattern of the gifted fosters a teaching approach which calls for the introduction of material at the exploratory level.

The exploratory level is the point toward which the product-oriented teacher is working, but it is the beginning point of the process-oriented teacher. The exact point of the exploratory level can be defined by the process-oriented teacher no more clearly than the point at which the product-oriented teacher can say with assurance that the child "understands."

## Different Roles for Teachers

The role of the teacher in the product-oriented concept of teaching necessitates (1) mastery of the material to be taught in the course, (2) experience in teaching the subject in order that emphasis can be put on those areas which have proved to be difficult, (3) pre-planning to avoid confusion or interruption of the thought processes of the students, (4) sequential presentation of material and (5) quantitative measurement of how much was learned. Since the average student needs this structure in order to retain the vast amount of information to which he is being exposed, he learns best under the leadership of such a teacher.

The product-oriented classroom requires a teacher who is a leader-participant. This teacher must be able either to answer students' questions or direct them to the answer.

The product-oriented teacher is primarily concerned with how much and how rapidly each child has learned. Therefore her effectiveness is measured in terms of how much progress the students have made on an achievement test.

The role of the teacher in the process-oriented concept of teaching is different. It necessitates (1) mastery of a teaching approach that introduces students to material at the exploratory level, (2) experience which manifests itself in the continuing pursuit of knowledge, (3) pre-planning to insure presentation of materials at the exploratory level, (4) intentional interruption of the "lock-step"sequential development of ideas and (5) teacher involvement in the learning process to the extent that there is an awareness of individual students' involvement.

The process-oriented approach requires a teacher who is a learner-participant. She must involve herself skillfully in the learning process itself, teaching by example the pursuit of knowledge. The absence of predetermined goals allows her to use her experience of the learning process to involve the students in the process. The evaluation of the involvement of the student becomes not only the function of the teacher-participant, but also the function of the student himself.

## Direction of Learning

As has been pointed out, in the product-oriented pattern of teaching, the direction of learning is the same for all students. In process-oriented teaching for the gifted direction is determined by each student for himself.

The material is presented at the exploratory level, but the direction which the learning process takes is then determined by the student and not the teacher. Some students may work in the direction of established facts, while others may work toward the discovery of novel solutions or applications.

Creativity, about which there is so much concern today, can result from either product-oriented or process-oriented teaching. Since process-oriented teaching encourages individual direction, however, creative pursuits are more likely in this type of teaching. The very absence of rigidity in teaching will encourage creativity.

## Existence of "Content Bounds"

In both product-oriented and process-oriented teaching there are "content bounds." In product-oriented teaching these bounds evolve from resources the teacher has at her disposal. They may be bounds or limitations imposed by textbooks, library facilities, curriculum guides, school policies, the teacher's educational background, or any number of other things which might be called teachers' resources.

In process-oriented teaching the bounds are also present, but they evolve not from predetermined teachers' resources but instead from students' resources. The age of the students, their experiences both real and vicarious, their interests and a variety of other individual student characteristics establish these bounds. The important point is that the bounds are determined by characteristics of the students, not of the teacher or the school.

## Summary

It must be recognized that teaching gifted children effectively requires a different concept of teaching. This results in a different perspective and role as well as different teaching techniques and evaluative emphases.

The differences in emphasis of these two types of teaching, product-oriented teaching and process-oriented teaching, can best be demonstrated as follows.

| Product-Oriented Teaching for the Average | Process-Oriented Teaching for the Gifted |
|---|---|
| Emphasis on end-result (product) | Emphasis on learning pattern (process) |
| Leader-participant teacher | Learner-participant teacher |
| Predetermined learning direction | Learning direction is determined by each student for himself. |
| Content-bounds evolve from teachers' resources. | Content-bounds evolve from students' resources. |
| Teacher is evaluated and evaluates students on the basis of quantitative measurement of the end-result (product). | Teacher is evaluated and evaluates students on their involvement in the learning process. |

*Joan B. Nelson and Donald L. Cleland*

# The Role of the Teacher
# of Gifted and Creative Children

*I*n all educational programs, the teacher is the key to effective learning. This fact has been shown repeatedly in studies of the value of various methods of teaching reading to primary grade children (6). In Chapter 2 of this monograph, studies are discussed which make it clear that the way the teacher proceeds is more important than the materials or the specific methods utilized. It is the teacher who sets the environment which inspires or destroys self-confidence, encourages or suppresses interests, develops or neglects abilities, fosters or banishes creativity, stimulates or discourages critical thinking, and facilitates or frustrates achievement.

Implicit in the consideration of the role of the teacher of gifted and creative children is the assumption that this role differs in some substantive way from the role of the teacher in general. Are there specific traits which characterize the successful teacher of the gifted? Does the role require deviance in intellectual aptitude and creativity similar to gifted children themselves? Are there knowledges, understandings, methods, techniques, and materials which are unique to effective teaching of the gifted?

There has been little research indicating characteristics that identify successful teachers of the gifted. Indeed, there is little research to indicate those traits which differentiate between good and poor teachers in general. The attributes most frequently cited as appropriate for teachers of the gifted are the same attributes as those desirable for any good teacher. Lists of desirable traits usually include good health and stamina, knowledge of content field, broad background of information in related fields, a knowledge of the psychology of learning, familiarity with varied teaching methods, patience, creativity, flexibility, and a supportive attitude. Case studies have suggested rather clearly the importance of the teacher's ability to employ child-study techniques to determine the nature and needs of gifted children. Studies have revealed also the value of proficiency on the part of the teacher

Nelson, Joan B. and Cleland, Donald L. "The Role of the Teacher of Gifted and Creative Children." In: Witty, Paul A. (Ed.) *Reading for the Gifted and Creative Student.* Newark, Delaware: International Reading Association, 1971.

in using children's literature to satisfy interests and needs (8). Surely, the teacher of gifted children should possess the aforementioned characteristics and should be acquainted with the particular needs and interests of the gifted (7, 8).

The special problems associated with the teaching of the gifted are often basically the problems of dealing with individual differences in children (3, 4). The apparent differences in teaching roles may be based upon the unique characteristics that the gifted child brings to the learning situation and the way that the teacher reacts and responds to these characteristics. If one subscribes to the philosophy of education which recognizes individual differences and seeks to develop each child's unique capabilities and talents to that child's full potential, there can be no doubt that teacher's roles must vary according to the attributes of the students they teach.

What are the implications of this philosophy for the teacher of gifted children? What should be the components of a reading program for the gifted?

## Implications for the Teacher

*The teacher must possess an understanding of self.* The learning of children is influenced not only by what teachers do but also by what they are. It would be foolish to assume that a person can understand the needs, feelings, and behaviors of others if he does not understand himself. In dealing with students, the good teacher is constantly evaluating his own feelings, perceptions, motivations, and abilities.

Even the decision to work with gifted children must be based on the teacher's awareness of his own strengths and limitations. Gifted children progress most satisfactorily under teachers of superior intelligence who have a broad, general knowledge as well as a thorough mastery of subject area. To meet the demands put upon them, teachers must know subjects and their sources. It is very difficult to "fake it" with gifted students. Their superior reasoning ability and questioning attitude are apt to cause the faker some very uncomfortable moments. A simple, "I don't know; let's find out," creates greater respect and trust between student and teacher than any attempt to deceive. A persistent gap, however, between student need for information and guidance and teacher ability to present or direct students to significant data can be discouraging. Only the teacher who knows his limitations can make an intelligent assessment of his ability to work with the gifted.

Teachers must also examine their feelings about gifted children. The inquisitiveness and questioning attitude typical of gifted children can be a constant source of irritation for an authoritarian teacher. Explanations which are accepted by most children may be questioned or rejected by gifted children. If a teacher shows resentment at a challenging question, he may destroy incipient curiosity. The teacher who is open to new ideas and experiences expands the dimensions of student interests.

*The teacher must possess an understanding of giftedness.* Giftedness has been defined in various ways (*2, 3*). Some educators define it in terms of intellectual capacity; others, as consistently outstanding performance in one or more areas of endeavor. Some educators believe that the gifted child may be identified by a constellation of factors which includes intelligence, creativity, drive, perseverance, and performance.

It is extremely important that the verbally gifted child's ability be recognized early in his school career to insure a learning program that challenges him. Though we rarely hear of gifted children failing in school work, many do fail to develop more than a small measure of their potential for learning because of pressure to conformity in undifferentiated programs. Since it is the teacher who comes in personal contact with all the children, it is he who is most likely to identify the gifted children in his charge. For this reason it is vital that every teacher know the characteristics of gifted children.

Although there is no entirely adequate composite of traits for the gifted child, there are several compilations which provide a basis for the teacher in the identification of gifted children (*7, 8*). Included are the following items which apply primarily to the verbally gifted:

*Better health, social adjustment, and physical endowment
*Longer attention span
*Larger vocabulary
*Greater fluency of ideas
*Greater intellectual curiosity
*More rapid and efficient learning
*Greater ability to generalize and form concepts
*Greater insight into problems
*More curiosity and interest in intellectual tasks
*Earlier reading attainment (sometimes before school entrance)
*Wider range of interests

Teachers should be aware also of certain traits and behaviors which characterize highly creative children:

*Less concern with convention and authority
*More independence in judgment and thinking
*Keener sense of humor
*Less concern with order and organization
*A more temperamental nature

Once the gifted child is identified, the teacher must provide a learning environment appropriate to the development of the child's outstanding ability to conceptualize, generalize, create, initiate, relate, organize, and imagine.

The teacher should be a facilitator of learning rather than a director of learning. A function of education is to prepare the student for lifelong learning. Every child has an innate curiosity which expands and renews itself in the act of learning. Who has not marveled at the boundless energy and enthusiasm of the bright preschool child as he looks, listens, tastes, smells, and touches everything in sight to satisfy his curiosity? He is open to each new experience and learns from each that which is relevant to his needs. His learning is self-initiated, self-sustaining, and self-satisfying. The act of learning is, in itself, both the result and cause of his increasing curiosity. It is only when the child comes to school that his natural desire to learn is blunted by the imposition of an undifferentiated learning program and a rigid curriculum. Teachers who believe that they must control what a child does, learns, and feels, overlook the built-in drive for learning which resides in each child. If this natural drive is thwarted by the school, the curiosity dies and apathy takes its place. It is only then that external motivation and reward systems are necessary to arouse interest.

The bright child—with his heightened curiosity, wide range of interests, and insight into problems—is particularly thwarted by rigid curriculum requirements. The following suggestions, while appropriate for all children, are vital to the enhancement of lifelong learning habits for gifted children.

1. Build learning experiences around the child's natural curiosity by dealing with problems relevant to his own needs, purposes, and interests.

2. Allow the student to engage in the organization and planning of learning activities.

3. Provide real-life experiences that call for the active participation of the child, and then stress the skills necessary for that participation.

4. Act as a resource for learning rather than as a dispenser of information; resist temptation to impose knowledge upon a child before he is ready for it.

5. Keep programs flexible enough to encourage exploration and invention.

6. Encourage and reward initiative, inquisitiveness, originality, and a questioning attitude.

7. Allow a child to make his own mistakes and to accept the consequences (as long as the consequences are not dangerous).

One may wonder about the difference between direction and facilitation of learning. It is perhaps a difference in orientation as well as in behavior. Imagine the director standing in front of children and imposing his purposes, desires, and needs upon them; the facilitator stands behind the children and guides them in the realization of their own purposes, desires, and needs. The director imposes assignments, set requirements, and evaluates outcomes; the facilitator supports the students' self-initiated learning and self-determined goals and provides feedback for self-evaluation.

*The teacher must provide challenge rather than pressure.* The role of the facilitator of learning implies acceptance of the principle that children should be challenged rather than pressured. Because of his initiative and perseverance, the gifted child is particularly receptive to a challenging situation. He enjoys pitting his abilities and experiences against a task that has meaning for him. He doesn't want easy answers. He may even resent being told how to do something because it deprives him of the chance to figure it out for himself. The bright child is far more willing than his less-gifted peer to strike out on his own to explore the difficult and the unknown. He has experienced the exhilaration of accomplishment. This remark is not to suggest that less bright children cannot experience the same exhilaration. The fact is that persistent failure in school makes the less talented child afraid to try. The gifted child is not "turned off" quite so easily.

By the same token, a gifted and creative child is impatient with routine or repetitive assignments. Pressure will not suffice to inspire a child when the teacher views education as the coverage of a body of knowledge. Challenge, on the other hand, gives the child the opportunity to gain confidence in his own powers to think, analyze, organize, and act. The teacher's wise use of questions that ask not only *what* and *when* but *why, how, for what reason, with what intent,* and *to what purpose* aids in challenging a bright student to the kind of thinking that provides the building blocks for speculative theory and philosophy. Assuming that the challenge is appropriate to the child's maturity and experience, it gives him a chance to explore the extent of his powers and to know himself.

*The teacher must be as concerned with the process of learning as with the product.* In spite of recognition given to an educational philosophy that stresses *learning how to learn,* many teachers act as if education consists of the mastery of a body of knowledge. To make matters worse, educational progress is measured largely through the use of standardized achievement tests which emphasize the acquisition of skills and the memorization of facts. This narrow view of learning is highly undesirable since the abilities involved in recall and application of learned facts are low in the hierarchy of intellectual processes. Much more important to the individual in lifelong learning are the thought processes such as comprehending, analyzing, synthesizing, organizing, and evaluating.

The gifted child is often shortchanged in a system that sees the learner as the passive receiver of knowledge. The gifted child's superior learning ability allows him to score well on most standardized achievement tests, making it appear as though he is doing very well when, in fact, he is failing to develop more than a small fraction of his potential. Emphasis on the following kinds of activities will aid the teacher of gifted children in stressing the importance of the processes of learning rather than the product:

*Problem solving (emphasizing the process rather than the solution)
*Classifying and categorizing
*Comparing and contrasting
*Making judgments according to criteria
*Using resources (dictionaries, encyclopedias, libraries)
*Conducting research projects
*Discussing and debating
*Taking part in class meetings involving group process
*Planning future activities
*Evaluating experiences

In Chapter 3, there are descriptions of programs which have successfully emphasized these processes.

Knowledge of things as they are now becomes obsolete in this world of rapid and inevitable change. The only secure knowledge is the understanding of the processes involved in learning and the ability to apply these processes to new and constantly changing experiences.

*The teacher must provide feedback rather than judgment.* To become independent and self-reliant adults, children must learn early to evaluate their own learning experiences and achievements. Gifted students are ready for self-assessment and self-evaluation from the time they enter school. It is the job of the teacher to provide feedback information and a behavior model, but the seat of evaluation should be within the child. He should be encouraged to evaluate his own work not in terms of grades and norms but in terms of his own needs, purposes, and goals. Extrinsic evaluation of the child's efforts should be subordinate to intrinsic evaluation. This statement does not mean that the teacher may not evaluate the child's progress and achievement to learn his strengths and weaknesses as a basis for helping him to improve. It does mean, however, that the teacher should refrain from imposing his judgment on the child. Instead of red-penciling and grading a child's composition, the teacher might write a note and point out where the child failed to communicate because of spelling, mechanical, or organizational errors. This approach represents the difference between feedback and judgment.

*The teacher must provide alternate learning strategies.* One of the most important things a child can learn is that usually there is more than one way to accomplish an objective or attain a goal. There may be several solutions to a problem, several ways of categorizing objects, or several points of view in a discussion. All too often teachers insist that a learning goal be attained in a specified way. Creative children may be quick to point out different strategies which lead to the same outcome. The direct path to a goal may not be the most interesting. Children should be allowed to explore different pathways and even to pause along the way if their interest is captured by a more relevant goal.

For the gifted child who is less creative, alternative learning strategies should be pointed out and demonstrated by the teacher. Creativity is fostered in an atmosphere which provides freedom to experiment. Strategies that are being employed successfully in schools are indicated in Chapter 3.

*The teacher must provide a classroom climate which promotes self-esteem and offers safety for creative and cognitive risk-taking.* Every child has the right to feel safe to try out novel procedures and to explore new ideas in the classroom (5). The fearful child may consume so much energy in compensating for his repressions and anxieties that he has little energy left to apply to productive and joyful learning. Many creative children are blocked in freedom of expression through fear of criticism, of not pleasing the teacher, of failing, of not being liked, of making mistakes, of being wrong, of not meeting parents' expectations, or by other repressive influences and pressures. New ideas and other forms of divergent response must be welcomed in the classroom which fosters creativity.

Teachers can combat fear by creating a classroom atmosphere in which each child has a sense of belonging, a feeling of self-worth, and a sense of value in his own individuality. How is such an atmosphere created? Some suggestions follow:

*The teacher is supportive and accepting.
*Coercion is not used to manipulate children (i.e. threats about grades, loss of approval, loss of prestige, or banishment).
*The teacher recognizes, accepts, and values individual differences.
*The teacher provides differentiated learning experiences.
*Each child shares in planning his own work and the work of the group.
*The teacher provides enough structure for the child to feel secure but not enough to limit or stifle creative response.
*The teacher accepts and empathizes with strong feelings.
*The teacher recognizes his own limitations.
*The teacher values creativity and welcomes new ideas.

Gifted and creative children are willing to take risks in a warm supportive climate. They will risk the exploration of a new field; they will experiment with different learning techniques; they will share cherished ideas; they will define difficult problems; they will reveal their feelings; they will make mistakes and discover that they can learn from their mistakes; and finally, they will not fear to be themselves.

## Implications for the Reading Program

Reading programs for gifted children will deviate in methods, materials, and content utilized; but certain features, such as the following, will be recognized as necessary components of a program for the gifted.

*Early assessment of intellectual, perceptual, and reading abilities is vital.* Many gifted children learn to read before they come to school. This accomplishment is not necessarily the result of formal instruction but rather of a combination of high interest, extraordinary discrimination, and generalizing abilities. Gifted children often discover phonic elements on their own and use context and picture clues readily.

Children who learn to read early may be considered problems when they enter school. Placed with other children in a readiness program or the first preprimer, these gifted children may become bored, restless, and disruptive. Worse, they may withdraw into fantasy to escape the boredom, lose their eagerness to read, and become disillusioned with school in general.

A combination of intelligence and readiness tests, along with careful teacher observation and skill checklists, will give a fair indication of the child's level of competency. The ultimate test is, of course, whether the child can and does read and comprehend written materials.

Gifted children who have not learned to read before school entrance should also be observed carefully since they will be ready to move ahead to advanced work more rapidly than other children. Nothing is more discouraging to the bright, eager child than to be required to persist in drills or activities that are below his level of readiness (9).

*The reading program should be highly individualized.* With early and accurate assessment of children's abilities, the teacher can individualize the reading program for the gifted child (1). By analyzing his strengths and weaknesses in reading skills, the teacher may decide where the child will profit from instruction with the rest of the group and where he will profit from individual instruction. Each child should be permitted, indeed be encouraged to move ahead as rapidly as he desires and is able to proceed. The reward of accomplishment is a stronger inducement to further effort than we have yet realized.

Care should be taken to assure that the program includes the mastery of skills that provide the foundation for reading growth. Thus, basic word recognition skills should be stressed so that the child gains early independence in reading. It should be noted, however, that phonics, generalizations, and rules of structural analysis are merely tools to aid in word recognition. If it is obvious that the child has achieved independence in word attack and that he is skilled in using the generalizations successfully, then there is no point in continued emphasis and drill on memorizing the rules or practicing their application.

A child should not be discouraged from reading books at higher grade levels than his own. A truly individualized reading program will assess the child's ability at each level and not require him to reread any material that he has read before. It has been suggested that the gifted child's ability to decode sometimes outstrips his ability to comprehend the material he is able to read. It is likely that the child will discontinue efforts to read materials that are not relevant or meaningful to him at some level. Indeed, he may not be able to appreciate the more sophisticated nuances of a selection on first reading. Melville's *Moby Dick* is a prime example of a piece of literature that can be read at different ages with increasing levels of appreciation and understanding. Surely, no one would discourage a youngster from reading the novel because he could not fully grasp Melville's subtle use of symbolism.

*The reading program should emphasize development of higher mental processes.* Since gifted children attain independence in reading earlier than other students, they also are ready earlier for instruction in inferential, interpretive, and critical reading. Beginning in the primary grades, the gifted will profit from instruction in the following skills:

*Discovering clues from which to infer hidden meanings and probable outcomes
*Analyzing selections to detect author bias and subtle propaganda
*Locating materials on a given topic
*Organizing and synthesizing materials for purposes of reporting

*Evaluating materials in terms of worth and relevancy to purpose
*Understanding the use of connotation, figures of speech, plot, setting, and characterization in reading selections
*Appreciating the motives, intents, and feelings of the author and..or characters in a selection
*Selecting a reading technique and speed appropriate to the difficulty of the material and the purpose for reading it

*The reading program should extend interest in reading.* The importance of adequate reading skills instruction for the gifted cannot be overstated, but reading is much more than just knowing how to read. The ultimate goal of reading instruction is to establish permanent interest in reading.

An abundance of reading material is required. The voracious reading appetite of the gifted child makes it necessary to provide not only a wide range of materials in terms of variety of subject matter but also material in which in-depth study may be undertaken according to the interests of the student.

It is not enough, however, to provide interesting reading material. Even eager readers need help in choosing books to broaden and enrich their interests as well as to satisfy them. The teacher should become skilled in using child-study techniques, such as an interest inventory, in order to ascertain interests and employ them in the guidance of reading (*8*). Combining reading with social experience through the use of group projects, play writing and production, creative dramatics, discussion of favorite books, debate of a social issue, and sharing of creative writing broadens reading interests and enriches social relations.

We must be sure that our gifted youth are being provided with the best possible reading instruction not only to develop skill in reading but to nurture a love of learning that guarantees that their education will continue as long as there are good books to read.

## References

1. Barbe, Walter B. (Ed.). *Psychology and Education of the Gifted: Selected Readings.* New York: Appleton-Century-Crofts, 1965.

2. French, Joseph L. (Ed.). *Educating the Gifted.* New York: Holt, Rinehart and Winston, 1960. (Revised, 1964.)

3. Gallagher, James J. (Ed.). *Teaching Gifted Students: A Book of Readings.* Boston: Allyn and Bacon, 1965.

4. Smith, James A. *Creative Teaching of Reading and Literature in the Elementary School.* Boston: Allyn and Bacon, 1967.

5. Torrance, E. Paul. *Rewarding Creative Behavior.* Englewood Cliffs, New Jersey: Prentice-Hall, 1965.

6. Wittich, M. L. "Innovations in Reading Instruction: For Beginners," in Helen M. Robinson (Ed.), *Innovation and Change in Reading Instruction,*

Sixty-seventh Yearbook of the National Society for the Study of Education, Part II. Chicago: University of Chicago Press, 1968.

7. Witty, Paul A. "Who are the Gifted?" *Education for the Gifted,* Fifty-seventh Yearbook of the National Society for the Study of Education, Part II. Chicago: University of Chicago Press, 1958.

8. Witty, Paul A., Alma M. Freeland, and Edith H. Grotberg. *The Teaching of Reading.* Boston: D.C. Heath, 1966.

9. Witty, Paul A. *Helping the Gifted Child.* Chicago: Science Research Associates, 1952. (Revised with Edith H. Grotberg, 1970.)

William E. Bishop

# Characteristics of Teachers Judged Successful By Intellectually Gifted, High Achieving High School Students

$\mathcal{T}$he purpose of this study was to analyze selected characteristics of high school teachers who were identified as successful by intellectually gifted, high achieving students and to discover what differentiates these teachers from teachers not so identified. More specifically, the study was concerned with personal and social traits and behaviors, professional attitudes and educational viewpoints, and classroom behavior patterns of effective teachers of gifted high school students.

Data for this investigation were obtained from three groups of teachers from throughout the State of Georgia. One study group included 109 teachers who were selected by one or more gifted students as his "most successful" high school teacher. The students who selected the teachers were high school seniors who had participated in the First Governor's Honors Program in Georgia. Another study group included ninety-seven teachers who were selected at random from a list of teachers who had formerly taught students in the First Governor's Honors Program but who had not been selected by any of these students as his "most successful" teacher. The group of 109 identified teachers is called the Identified Group; the group of ninety-seven "non-selected" teachers is called the Validity Sample.

The third study group included thirty teachers in the Identified Group who were selected for intensive study, including a personal interview. This group was called the Interview Sample. The Interview Sample was a stratified random sample of the total number of identified teachers.

Every teacher in the study completed a copy of the Teacher Characteristics Schedule which provided estimates of the teacher's classroom behavior, attitudes, educational viewpoints, verbal ability and emotional adjustment. A response analysis of the T.C.S. items provided additional data relative to the personal and professional status of teachers in the different study groups.

Questionnaires were completed by the students who selected the teachers

Bishop, William E. "Characteristics of Teachers Judged Successful by Intellectually Gifted, High Achieving High School Students." Unpublished Doctoral dissertation, Indian Central College, Indiana (Last chapter of dissertation).

for this study. These questionnaires provided extensive data relative to the identified teachers.

In addition to information obtained from the T.C.S. and the student questionnaires, data on the Interview Sample were collected from the following sources:

1) Personal interview with each teacher
2) Wechsler Adult Intelligence Scale (verbal section)
3) Edwards Personal Preference Schedule
4) College transcripts.

The data obtained from these sources provide the bases for the major findings of this study. The major findings of the study are summarized in the following section.

## Summary of Major Study Findings

Major study findings are presented within the framework of the specific questions listed in the Statement of the Problem. The first question was stated as follows:

> What are the unique personal and social traits and behaviors which characterize high school teachers who are identified as successful by intellectually gifted, high achieving students?

It has been proposed that "teachers of the gifted should be deviant with respect to those qualities common to the gifted group."[1] Several findings of this study lend empirical support to the validity of this proposal. One of the areas where this is best demonstrated is the intellectual level and interests of the identified teachers.

### INTELLIGENCE LEVEL OF IDENTIFIED TEACHERS.

Several findings suggest the intellectual superiority of teachers identified as successful by gifted high school students. The most cogent is the mean score earned on the Wechsler Adult Intelligence Scale (W.A.I.S.) which was given to teachers in the Interview Sample. Their mean score of 128 on the W.A.I.S. places them 1.87 standard deviations above the mean or in the upper 3 percent relative to the general adult population. While giftedness is generally conceded to be a broader concept than can be represented by a single I.Q. it is recognized that those who score in the upper 3 percent on an individually administered test of intelligence evidence mental superiority.

Additional evidence of the superior mental ability of the identified teachers is revealed by their mean score on Characteristic I on the Teacher Characteristics Schedule. This score is purported to estimate the respondent's verbal ability (comprehension). The mean score of teachers in the

Identified Group was significantly higher than the mean score of teachers in the Validity Sample on this T.C.S. dimension.

TEACHER INTERESTS AND ACTIVITIES.

Several significant differences between the Identified Group and the Validity Sample are revealed in the intellectual nature of the personal interests and activities they pursue. These data suggest a total life pattern of the identified teachers which is dissimilar to other teachers. This is perhaps best demonstrated in their literary interests. A significantly higher percent of the Identified Group than the Validity Sample follow what they call a literary hobby. Their higher literary interest is evidenced in several ways. A significantly higher percent belong to a book purchasing club. A significantly larger number frequently read collections of poems, essays, stories and so forth. The same is true relative to the reading of biographies. A larger proportion of the Identified Group indicate that they frequently read fiction, read book reviews in newspapers or magazines and prefer *Harper's Magazine* to *Saturday Evening Post, Popular Mechanics* or *Redbook*.

Teachers in the Identified Group also indicate a higher level of cultural interest and involvement. A significantly higher proportion state that they attend concerts, exhibits and the like when the opportunities are available. A higher percent have visited an art gallery or museum within the past year and a significantly greater number have bought some painting or art work within the past year.

The desire for intellectual growth is cited as a reason for choosing teaching as a career by a significantly greater number of the identified teachers. Continued evidence of this desire may be reflected in the higher incidence of teachers in the Identified Group who have taken a college course within the past two years.

ACHIEVEMENT LEVEL OF TEACHERS.

It has been suggested that gifted students have much to gain from teachers who manifest high intelligence and characteristics positively correlated with superior intellect.[2] High achievement tends to be positively correlated with high intelligence. Several data obtained in this study indicate that the identified teachers are characterized by a high achievement level.

A strong need to achieve on the part of the successful teachers is reflected in their mean score on the Achievement scale of the Edwards Personal Preference Schedule. Edwards defines Achievement as "the need to do one's best, to be successful, to accomplish tasks requiring skill and effort . . . to do a difficult job well . . . to be able to do things better than others."[3] In six of seven comparisons with normative and parametric data, the Interview Sample shows a higher mean score on Achievement. In three comparisons the mean score on Achievement is significantly higher.

Evidence of high achievement is also reflected in the past scholastic performance of teachers in the Interview Sample. These teachers earned a mean grade-point average at the undergraduate level of 2.95 in professional education courses and 3.14 in courses in their major teaching area, based on a 4.00 system. At the graduate level, they earned a mean grade point average of 3.30 in professional education courses and 3.48 in the teaching area preparation. Over seventy percent of the teachers in the Identified Group indicate that they were "good" or "outstanding" students while in college.

Less direct data relative to the identified teachers' high achievement level are provided by other study findings. Ninety-three percent of the identified teachers indicate that they chose teaching as a career because they enjoyed past satisfactory experience in school work. A significantly greater number of teachers in the Identified Group were advised by former teachers that they would be good teachers. While the teacher-advisor may have had numerous and varied reasons for his advice, it seems unlikely that the suggestion would have been proposed to a low achiever.

Student descriptions of the selected teachers included repeated testimony to the achievement level of the teachers. A thorough command of their subject matter and a patent desire to increase their own knowledge and understanding were frequently noted by the students.

Several other personal traits and behaviors of teachers were considered in this study. On several variables there were no significant differences between teachers identified as successful by gifted students and teachers not so identified. These included such variables as sex, marital status, type of undergraduate institution attended, highest degrees held, course work preparation and extent of association with professional organizations.

Two personal variables on which teachers in the two groups did differ were age and length of teaching experience. These differences were not great, however, and could not be tested for statistical significance. The median age of teachers in the Identified Group is in the forty to forty-four age range. The median age of teachers in the Validity Sample is in the forty-five to forty-nine age range. The median length of teaching experience for the two groups is between ten to fourteen years and fifteen to nineteen years respectively.

The use of student evaluations as a research procedure in studies on teaching effectiveness has been criticized because students will choose a teacher who is "young, genial, and entertaining, while the serious, more experienced individual . . . is rarely popular."[4] This criticism of student evaluations for research purposes does not seem justified relative to the present study. Less than 2 percent of the selected teachers are in the twenty to twenty-four age range while more than 8 percent are in the sixty or over category. Fewer than 3 percent of these teachers have less than three years' teaching experience while nearly 30 percent have twenty or more years' experience. It is true, however, that the students preferred teachers who are slightly younger and less experienced than their teaching colleagues.

## Professional Attitudes
## and Educational Viewpoints

The second question posed in the Statement of the Problem was:

> What professional attitudes and educational viewpoints characterize these teachers (those identified as successful by gifted students)?

Data relative to this question were collected from several sources and are discussed in this section.

Two of the teacher characteristics estimated by the T.C.S. which relate to professional attitude and philosophy are Characteristic R (favorable versus unfavorable attitudes toward pupils) and Characteristic B (learning-centered "traditional" versus student-centered "permissive" educational viewpoints). The Identified Group scored significantly lower than the Validity Sample on Characteristic B. This suggests that teachers in the Identified Group have more student-centered educational viewpoints. This finding is also reflected in the difference in mean scores on Characteristic R. The Identified Group scored significantly higher than the Validity Sample on Characteristic R. This result indicates that teachers in the Identified Group have more favorable attitudes toward students.

The results of the E.P.P.S. administration lend additional support to the conclusion that identified teachers are characterized by sensitivity to others which is probably reflected in a student-centered approach to teaching. Mean scores on five E.P.P.S. variables are especially suggestive of this attitude.

The E.P.P.S. variable on which the Interview Sample scored most consistently and significantly higher than comparison groups was Intraception. Edwards defines Intraception as follows:

> To analyze one's motives and feelings, to observe others, to understand how others feel about problems, to put one's self in another's place, to judge people by why they do things rather than by what they do, to analyze the behavior of others, to analyze the motives of others, to predict how others will act.

An E.P.P.S. variable on which both male and female teachers in this study scored lower than all comparison groups was Autonomy. In five cases the difference was statistically significant. Autonomy has been defined as the need "to act without regard to the opinion of others."[6] An E.P.P.S. variable on which female teachers in the study scored significantly lower than the three groups with which they were compared was Exhibition, which has been defined as the need "to talk cleverly for the sake of impressing others, to be the center of attention."[7]

Male teachers in the Interview Sample scored significantly lower than three of the four groups with which they were compared on two E.P.P.S. variables, Succorance and Aggression. Succorance reflects a self-centered interest in the need "to gain encouragement and sympathy from others when one is depressed or hurt."[8] Aggression has been defined as "the need to show anger and criticize others openly."[9]

This profile of E.P.P.S. results suggests that the teachers in this study are not overly concerned with themselves. They seem to be sensitive to the feelings and needs of others; e.g., their students.

The teachers' favorable attitudes toward students also manifests itself specifically in relation to gifted students. All teachers in the study were asked to indicate what type of class they would prefer to teach. A significantly higher percent of the Identified Group than the Validity Sample stated that they would prefer to teach a class of exceptionally bright students rather than a class of average students, a class of slow and retarded students or a class of children of widely varying ability. Nearly three-fourths of the Identified Group stated this preference. Not one of them stated that he would prefer to teach a class of slow or retarded students.

Favorable attitudes toward gifted students were further evidenced in the teacher interviews with the Interview Sample. Every teacher in the sample expressed his support for special educational attention to the gifted, though the specific proposals for meeting the need varied widely.

## Teacher Classroom Behavior

The third specific question listed in the Statement of the Problem was stated as follows:

> What are the patterns of classroom behavior of teachers who are judged effective by gifted students? How do these teachers perceive their teaching role and responsibility and how do they assess their success in this regard?

This section presents conclusions based on study findings relative to this question.

Three of the dimensions estimated by the T.C.S. relate to teacher classroom behavior. On two of those three variables, the identified teachers differed significantly from the teachers not so identified. The Identified Group scored significantly higher on Characteristic Y, which provides an estimate of the respondent's responsible, businesslike, systematic versus evading, unplanned, slipshod classroom behavior. They also scored significantly higher than the Validity Sample on Characteristic Z which purports to measure the teacher's stimulating, imaginative versus dull, routine teacher classroom behavior.

It was noted in the previous section that teachers in the Identified Group also scored significantly higher on T.C.S. Characteristics B and R. These scores reflect favorable attitudes toward students and student-centered educational viewpoints.

The estimates of teacher classroom behaviors of the identified teachers indicated by T.C.S. results are supported by other study findings. Testimony of the identified teachers' stimulating and imaginative classroom behavior was provided by the student questionnaire responses. The most frequent reason the students mentioned for having selected the teachers for the study was the teacher's stimulating, motivational and inspirational qualities. The teacher's ability to present his subject in a meaningful and effective way and his success in increasing or instilling student interest in the subject were also frequently listed. The teacher's enthusiasm for this subject and for teaching were often cited by the students. One student described what he called his teacher's "contagious enthusiasm". Another noted that her teacher stimulates the willing and unwilling to accomplish on their own.

Additional evidence in this regard is provided by the teachers' self-descriptions. Teachers are asked to indicate characteristics which they feel are most descriptive of themselves. A significantly higher proportion of the Identified Group than the Validity Sample stated that enthusiasm is a strong trait in their own make-up.

Student comments also lend support to the findings that the identified teachers have a favorable attitude toward and interest in their students. The teacher's personal interest in his students was the fifth most frequently given reason stated by students for selecting a teacher.

Further evidence of identified teachers' permissive (student-centered) educational viewpoints was provided by their own expressions of opinion. A significantly *smaller* proportion of those in the Identified Group than in the Validity Sample stated that they believe that attentiveness of students is a more important indication of a good class than willingness of students to try and to volunteer, students who are well prepared or courtesy of students. A larger proportion of the identified teachers indicated that willingness of the students to try and to volunteer is a better indication of a good class than the other three factors mentioned above. The greater emphasis of the Identified Group on student activity and participation than on student attentiveness, which implies a passive student response, indicates a more student-centered philosophy. A larger proportion of the Identified Group indicated their belief that a severe and aloof manner is a more important failing in a teacher than inability to maintain a systematic or orderly approach or inadequate mastery of subject.

It should not be concluded from this finding and related findings reported above that the identified teachers de-emphasized the importance of subject matter. The majority of the identified teachers indicated their belief that inadequate mastery of subject matter is a more important teacher failing than inability to maintain a systematic and orderly approach or a severe and aloof manner. A larger proportion of the Identified Group than the Validity Sample also stated that they believe it is more important for a teacher to extend subject-matter knowledge rather than to keep up to date on educational theories or to take part in community activities.

Several other study findings indicate that teachers who are judged successful by gifted students emphasize the importance of subject matter. The students often cited the teacher's interest in and command of his particular discipline as their major reason for choosing him as their most effective teacher. The teacher's success in transmitting this interest in a particular subject to the students was also noted by many students.

ROLE PERCEPTION.

Interviews with the teachers in the Interview Sample provided data relative to the teachers' classroom behavior as they perceive it. These data provided additional support to the major conclusions suggested above.

The majority of teachers interviewed stated that they believe their major role is one of motivating students to want to study, learn and think independently. They frequently noted their responsibility to instill an interest in and appreciation for their particular subject as well as for learning in general. Very few, however, see their major role as imparting a specific body of knowledge. They emphasize the importance of demonstrating personal interest in each student.

Their descriptions of personal incidents which they feel represent effective and ineffective classroom behavior reflected this philosophical position. Effectiveness was usually defined in terms of methodological and/or motivational success experiences and ineffectiveness was represented by lack of success in these areas.

## Conclusions of Study

The conclusions which are suggested by the major study findings can be summarized as follows:

1. Teachers who are judged effective by intellectually gifted, high achieving students do not differ with respect to teachers not so identified relative to such variables as sex, marital status, type of undergraduate institution attended, highest degree held, course work preparation and extent of association with professional organizations.

2. Successful teachers of gifted students tend to be mature, experienced teachers.

3. Teachers who are successful with mentally superior students are mentally superior themselves. They stand in the upper 3 percent relative to the general adult population and significantly higher than their teaching colleagues.

4. The effective teachers tend to pursue avocational interests which are "intellectual" in nature. They have a significantly greater interest than their teaching colleagues in literature, in the arts and cultural life of their community.

5. The identified teachers are characterized by high achievement needs—they attempt to do their best and to succeed. This is reflected in past scholastic achievement as well as present teaching success.

6. A significantly greater number of the identified teachers decided to become teachers because of a desire for intellectual growth and because they were advised by a teacher that they would be a good teacher.

7. Effective teachers have more favorable attitudes toward students than other teachers. They take a personal interest in their students and are sensitive to the students' motives and behaviors; they attempt to see things from the students' point of view and to understand how they feel.

8. Effective teachers tend to be more student-centered in their teaching approach. They encourage students to participate in class activities and they take students' opinions into consideration.

9. Effective teachers are more systematic, orderly and businesslike in their classroom approach.

10. Teachers who are effective with gifted students are more stimulating and imaginative in the classroom than their teaching colleagues. They are well-grounded in and enthusiastic about their particular subject and about teaching. They define their success in terms of how well they motivate their student to want to study, to learn and to think independently. They are able to instill interest in and appreciation for their subject in their students.

11. Teachers identified as effective by gifted students support special educational provisions for gifted students. A significantly greater percent of them would prefer to teach a class of exceptionally bright students than would their fellow teachers.

In summary, these conclusions indicate that there are unique personal and social traits, professional attitudes and educational viewpoints and classroom behavior patterns which characterize successful high school teachers of intellectually gifted, high achieving students.

## *Implications*

The major findings of this study and the conclusions proposed above suggest several implications for educational planning and programming. It behooves those who have the responsibility for the pre-service education, placement and/or guidance of teachers to base their policies and decisions on the most reliable information available.

Assuming that the identified teachers in this study can serve as a prototype, the conclusions listed above are suggestive of factors which might guide the decision-making processes of those charged with the important responsibilities of educating, selecting and guiding teachers of gifted high school students. More specifically the following implications of this study are suggested.

1. School administrators should give careful consideration to the proper selection and placement of teachers for gifted students. Teachers placed with special classes of bright students should possess those qualities which are common to the gifted group. They should also have a special interest in

working with these students. The findings of this study indicate that a large percentage of teachers do not prefer to teach classes of gifted students while most of the teachers who are successful with these students state a definite preference for teaching students of exceptional ability.

A recent report of the National Commission on Teacher Education and Professional Standards notes that misassignment ranks fifth among the twelve most important factors which educators cite as limiting the quality of education. One of the violations mentioned in the report is the teachers' "lack of ability to understand particular groups of students."[10] The majority of misassignments is reported in grades ten through twelve.

Teachers are sometimes assigned to classes of gifted students on the basis of seniority. Another common practice is to assign high school teachers to several different types of classes (i.e., slow, average, gifted) on the pretext that such an assignment adds variety to a teacher's work schedule and effects a form of "distributive justice." Both of these practices undoubtedly result in misassignment of teachers for gifted students. While gifted students may continue to learn "in spite of" and not "because of" the teacher, the results of this study indicate that there are special qualities which characterize teachers who are successful with these students. Attempts should be made to identify those teachers who will provide the optimum educational experience for students of exceptional ability and teaching assignments made on this basis.

2. The special qualities and interests which characterize teachers who are successful with gifted students suggest the need for identifying preservice as well as in-service teachers to work with these students. The problem of attracting able young people into the teaching profession has received considerable attention in recent years. The report of the Commission on Teacher Education and Professional Standards calls this the number one problem limiting the quality of education today.[11]

If teacher education institutions were to develop special courses or programs at the undergraduate and graduate levels which would specifically prepare able young people to teach gifted high school students, more superior college students might be attracted to the teaching profession.

3. Special preparatory programs for teaching gifted students should result in special certification in this area. The unique nature and needs of gifted students call for the recognition of educational personnel who possess those personal qualities and professional competencies which will guarantee that gifted students receive the optimum educational experience which they deserve and the democratic ideal demands.

## References

1. Virgil Ward, *Educating the Gifted: An Axiomatic Approach* (Columbus, Ohio: Charles E. Merrill Books, 1961), p. 115.

2. *Ibid.,* p. 116.

3. Alan L. Edwards, *Edwards Personal Preference Schedule Manual* (New York: The Psychological Corporation, 1959), p. 11.

4. J. E. Morsh and E. W. Wilder, *Identifying the Effective Instructor: Review of Quantitative Studies* (San Antonio, Texas: U.S.A.F. Personnel Training Research Center, 1955), p. 61.

5. Alan L. Edwards, *E.P.P.S. Manual*, p. 11.

6. E. G. Guba, P. W. Jackson and C. E. Bidwell, "Occupational Choice and the Teaching Career," *Educational Research Bulletin*, XXXVIII (January 14, 1959), p. 3.

7. *Ibid.*, p. 3.

8. *Ibid.*, p. 3.

9. *Ibid.*, p. 4.

10. National Education Association, National Commission on Teacher Education and Professional Standards. *The Assignment and Misassignment of American Teachers: A Summary of the Complete Report.* (Washington, D.C.: The Commission, 1965).

11. *Ibid.*

*E. Paul Torrance*

# Creative Teaching
# Makes a Difference*

*A* few years ago, it was commonly thought that creativity, scientific discovery, the production of new ideas, inventions, and the like had to be left to chance. Indeed many people still think so. With today's accumulated knowledge, however, I do not see how any reasonable, well-informed person can still hold this view. The amazing record of inventions, scientific discoveries, and other creative achievements amassed through deliberate methods of creative problem-solving should convince even the most stubborn skeptic. Both laboratory and field experiments involving these deliberate methods of improving the level of creative behavior have also been rather convincing. In my own classes and seminars I have consistently found that these deliberate methods can be taught from the primary grades through the graduate school with the effect that students improve their ability to develop original and useful solutions to problems. The evidence is strong that creativity does not have to be left to chance.

I have similarly maintained that the development of the creative thinking abilities does not have to be left to chance. Here I find myself in a distinct minority. Indeed, some educators believe that it would be extremely dangerous to educate children to be creative while they are still children. They argue that the emphasis must be on obedience, conformity, discipline, and fundamentals like the three R's. One educator sought to clinch his argument by saying, "A child has to know the three R's in order to do anything! Isn't it enough that the schools teach him to read, write and figure? Let him dash off on his own errands later; let him specialize in college!" Such a statement, of course, reflects a gross misunderstanding of the nature of creative thinking. The development of the creative thinking abilities is at the very heart of the achievement of even the most fundamental educational objectives, even the acquisition of the three R's. It is certainly not a matter of specialization.

For years, students of creative development have observed that five-year olds lose much of their curiosity and excitement about learning, that nine-

Torrance E. Paul "Creative Teaching Makes a Difference." in Gowan, Demos and Torrance *Creativity: Its Educational Implications.* New York: John Wiley and Sons, 1967.

*The Florence S. Dunlop Memorial Lecture, Ontario Council for Exceptional Children, Point Credit, Ontario, Canada, October 30, 1964.

year olds become greatly concerned about conformity to peer pressures and give up many of their creative activities, that the beginning junior highs show a new kind of concern for conformity to behavioral norms with the consequences that their thinking becomes more obvious, commonplace, and safe. In 1930, Andrews published data to document the drops at about age five. Even earlier, the drops at about ages nine and thirteen had been documented and have been further supported in the Minnesota Studies of Creative Thinking (1962).

Those who have commented on the drops in creative thinking ability and creative behavior in general have almost always assumed that these were purely developmental phenomena. (For example, Wilt (1959) observed that creativity may all but take a holiday at about age nine or ten and returns only for a few after the crisis has passed. She concludes that about all that can be done is to keep open the gates for its return. Rarely, however, has anyone taken a contrary stand. One of these rare individuals, Susan Nichols Pulsifer (1960), has taken such a stand concerning the abandonment of creativity at about age five. She maintains that it is not a natural development change but is due to the sharp man-made change which confronts the five-year old and impels him by its rules and regulations.)

If our research at the University of Minnesota has contributed anything to thinking about this problem, it has come from my unwillingness to accept the assumption that the severe drops in measured creative thinking ability are purely developmental phenomena that must be accepted as unchangeable. As we entered into our longitudinal studies, it seemed obvious to me that many children needlessly sacrificed their creativity, especially in the fourth grade, and that many of them did not recover as they continued through school. It also seemed to me that many of our problems of school drop outs, delinquency, and mental illness have their roots in the same forces that cause these drops.

It will certainly take a great deal more research than we now have before very many people will be convinced about this matter. Personally, I consider the accumulated evidence rather convincing. One of the first positive bits of evidence came from my experiences in studying the creative development of two fourth-grade classes taught by teachers who are highly successful in establishing creative relationships with their pupils and who give them many opportunities to acquire information and skills in creative ways. There was no fourth-grade slump in these classes, either in measured creative thinking abilities or in participation in creative activities.

A somewhat more convincing line of evidence has come from our studies of the development of the creative thinking abilities in different cultures. As we have obtained results from the administration of our tests of creative thinking in diverse cultures, we have found that the developmental curve takes on a different shape in each culture and that the characteristics of the developmental curve can be explained in terms of the way the culture treats curiosity and creative needs.

For purposes of illustration, let us examine the developmental curve for non-verbal originality in the United States, Western Samoa, Australia, Germany, India, and in United States Negroes. There are no drops in the developmental curve for Samoan subjects. The level of originality begins in the first grade at the lowest level of any of the cultures studied but the growth is continuous from year to year. The second greatest continuity in development is shown by the U. S. Negro sample, although some of the specific cultural groups in India show curves almost identical to those of the Samoan subjects. Through the fourth grade, German and Australian children seem to show about the same level and pattern of development. Pressures towards standardization and conformity apparently occur quite early and continue for the Australian child but not for the German child. The overall pattern of growth among the children in India is much the same as in the United States, especially in the mission schools and public schools.

What are some of the things which make a difference? This is the search in which my staff and I have engaged for the past five years. We have studied the development of the creative thinking abilities in a variety of schools in the United States and in other countries. We have tried to discover what are the factors in nature and society which influence this development. We have conducted both laboratory-type experiments and field experiments in an attempt to see what effect certain changes in teaching procedures will have. We have tried to create various kinds of instructional materials which will have built into them many of the principles which have been discovered through this research.

These and other experiences have left me with the firm conviction that teaching can indeed make a difference insofar as creative development is concerned. Methods, materials, attitudes, relationships with pupils, and other aspects of teaching have been shown to make a difference. Yesterday I stated that I believe creative needs and abilities are universal enough to make creative ways of learning useful for all children, though not an exclusive way of learning for any children. Yet I am convinced that some children who do not learn in other ways will learn if permitted or encouraged to learn in creative ways. In other words, for these children learning in creative ways truly *makes the difference!*


## When Does Creative Learning Occur?

You may be asking, "How can I tell that creative learning is taking place?" I do not believe this is difficult. This summer I asked 200 students in my class in "Creative Ways of Teaching" to list within a five-minute period all of the signs they could think of to tell whether creative learning is taking place. When I analyzed their lists, I found that altogether they had listed 230 different signs I would accept as valid indicators that creative learning is occurring in a classroom or other learning situation. Since a person can be creative in an infinite number of ways, it is not surprising that a list of 230 signs was produced within a five-minute period. You might be interested in some of these signs. I have them arranged alphabetically, so let us examine the A, B, C's of creative learning, remembering that there are also D, E, F's and so on.

*Absorption*—there is absorbed listening, absorbed watching, absorbed thinking, or absorbed doing—sometimes irritating but searching for the truth

*Achievement*—there is a feeling of moving forward towards goals, getting things done

*Acceptance*—of individual differences in preferred ways of learning, differences in learning rates, faults, etc.

*Admission*—of errors, mistakes, and failures

*Alert*—listening and observation, intense awareness of the environment

*Aloneness respected*—there are times when the best learning can be done outside of the group but with purpose

*Animation*—there is movement, aliveness and spirit in whatever is done

*Analogizing*—there is play with various kinds of analogies as ways of stating and solving problems

*Arguments*—differences are permitted and used to correct mistaken ideas and find more creative productive solutions

*Art media* are used to develop and elaborate ideas and to give them concreteness

*Atmosphere* is tingling with excitement and communication of ideas

Behavior problems rare
Bells frequently unheard or unnoticed
Bodily involvement in writing, speaking, thinking, etc.
Boldness of ideas, drawings, stories, etc.
Brainstorming possible
Bulletin boards contain pupils' ideas
Bursting out to complete the teacher's sentence or to communicate some new idea or discovery
Busy hum of activity

Change of pace and approaches to learning or problem-solving
Challenging of ideas
Charged atmosphere
Changes in plans to permit one thing to lead to another
Checking many sources of information and ideas
Choice making
Close observations possible
Colorful, bold art work
Communication of ideas and feelings
Comparisons and contrasts are made
Community used
Combination activities cutting across the curriculum
Composing own songs
Consideration of apparently unrelated ideas and showing relationships
Concentration on work, not easily distracted
Conflicting ideas leading to new ideas
Continuation of activities after the bell
Continuity of activities, one thing leading to another
Control freedom
Curiosity evident in questions, experimenting, manipulating, and reading to find out.

## What Difference Does Creative Teaching Make?

Even from this partial list of signs of creative learning, logical reasoning would lead us to expect that changes will occur in the lives of the children who participate in such learning. In our experimental work we have usually been concerned about some effect of creative teaching on classes, schools, or school systems. From these studies, we know that creative teaching seems to result in increased creative growth as measured by changes in performance on tests of creative thinking ability, creative writing, and the like; increased participation in creative activities on one's own; increased liking for school; and changed career aspirations. These experiments do not tell us what differences creative teaching makes in individual lives over extended periods of time.

To obtain some exploratory data to develop some clues about this matter, I asked my California students to recall instances in which they had allowed or encouraged children, young people, or adults to express themselves creatively and then observed that the experience made a difference in achievement and behavior. These students included teachers, administrators, and school psychologists at all levels of education from nursery school to college and adult education. Of the 165 students present when this request was made, 135 or 82 per cent were able to recall such instances.

Only a few of these respondents denied that creative teaching can make a difference. In these rare instances the denial seems to stem from the mistaken notion that all changes in behavior and achievement are of a developmental nature and independent of teacher influence. For example, one teacher wrote as follows:

> "Right now, I can't really remember any particular child whom I've encouraged and where there has been a noticeable change. I have always felt that any change at the end of kindergarten year was due mainly to the natural development growth for the five-year old . . ."

This attitude is encountered frequently among teachers and developmental psychologists who have accepted the view that developmental processes are set, genetically determined, and unchangeable. I believe that this view results from a misinterpretation of developmental studies. These studies describe the developmental processes which occur when children experience only what the environment happens to provide. Recent studies are showing that the developmental processes can be quite different when children experience guided, planned experiences designed to lead to certain kinds of development.

Let us examine some of the changes mentioned most frequently by the 135 students who responded to my request to recall an incident in which creative teaching had made a difference:

From non-readers to average or superior readers
From vandalism, destructiveness and lack of school achievement to constructive behavior and improved achievement

From emotionally disturbed and unproductive behavior to productive behavior and even outstanding school achievement

From estrangement and lack of communication to good contact with reality and sensitive communication with others

From social isolation and rejection to social acceptance and productive group membership

From fighting and hostility to improved speech skills and lack of hostility

From bitter, hostile sarcasm to kindly, courteous, thoughtful behavior

From apathy and dislike of school to enthusiasm about learning

From lack of self-confidence and self-expression to adequate self-confidence and creative expression

From mediocrity of achievement among gifted pupils to outstanding performance

From diagnoses of mental retardation to diagnoses of normal or superior mental functioning

From a troublesome student to outstanding job performance

I was interested to note that some of these experienced teachers indicated that it was only a knowledge that teaching can make a difference that sustains them in their teaching roles.

Let us examine now a few examples which illustrate some of the different kinds of changes attributed to creative teaching.

### FROM NON-READER TO READER.

The most frequently mentioned type to change mentioned by the 135 respondents is from non-reader to reader, usually accompanied by improved behavior and achievement in general. Some of these changes occur in the primary grades, while others do not occur until the intermediate grades or the junior high school years. The following anecdote describes the occurrence of such a change during the second grade:

> In second grade we do lots of creative writing and I usually type the children's stories and let them illustrate them. John, a dreamy lad, artistic, sloppy, and a very slow reader, disturbed me by never getting more than a sentence or so written. Usually that was lost in the crumpled welter in his desk by the time the next chance to work on it came around. John was a "poor listener" and took offense over nothing. He often cried because he thought he was being slighted. (The sociogram showed him not so much rejected as ignored.)
>
> "One day I let him dictate to me and I typed his story as he talked. He wanted to tell the story of the *Spider*—from a TV horror story. I was tempted to censor this, but fortunately kept my mouth shut. John's story was long. It was a problem to take the time to do it all, but I did, while the class carried on. His choice of words, sentence structure, use of suspense, etc. were very vivid, imaginative, mature. When I read the story to the class, the reaction was one of wild enthusiasm. John was starry-eyed. He learned to read the story, did many more, and learned to read other things. His behavior improved and he made friends."

### FROM DESTRUCTIVE BEHAVIOR TO CONSTRUCTIVE BEHAVIOR.

Destructive behavior on the part of a child or adolescent is especially dis-

**465**

turbing to teachers, classmates, and administrative and custodial personnel. Students describing the consequences of creative teaching indicate that destructive behavior can be transformed into positive, creative energy and generally constructive behavior. The following is an account of one such instance:

"The principal, the janitor, the teachers all worked on the problem of John, the vandal. He was reported as being the culprit of many a weekend shambles at our school, but no one could prove anything. He couldn't stay still very long; his iron muscles seemed to need to move every minute; he was as strong, at 12 years, as most grown men. He was almost a permanent fixture in the office because of undesirable behavior. He was skilled, a *natural*, in things mechanical. He liked to boss and was often swaggering and bully-like in his playground behavior. The consensus as a result of brainstorming, was that John did not feel he belonged. The problem was how to make him feel he *did* belong.

"He was appointed by the Student Council (in which he could never be an officer, because of their strict code of grades and behavior) to be a chairman of the Lunchroom Committee. He organized a team of boys; they spent half their noon recess cleaning, moving tables, helping the janitor. He began to notice the litter which collected in certain windy corners of the schoolyard. His 'gang' cleaned it up. He helped park cars for Back-to-School-Night. One woman ran her car into a deep ditch, when she did not wait for John to show her the way. The way he directed her, telling her how to cramp the wheels and when was a marvel. She would have had to have a tow-away, except for his know-how. He had organized the entire parking area witout a hitch, where the drivers followed his directions, and all this done as well as an adult could have done it.

"Happily, as John became 'part' of the school, the vandalism became less and less. Reports came to us that he threatened (and coming from this boy that was no mean threat) othes who tried to destroy school property. Happily, he began to take an interest in school work. His father told us that John had at last said, 'I like school.' He said John had learned to read things around the house, in the neighborhood, at the store, and on trips for the first time in his life. His art work (racing cars, car engines and antique cars) was excellent. We all hope some of this progress will continue when he leaves us this fall to go to junior high school."

FROM TROUBLE MAKER TO STAR LEARNER AND TEACHER.

In the case of John, ability for verbal learning is perhaps limited although his capacity for art, mechanics, and leadership may be outstanding. Thus, the development of his potentialities might take a direction quite different from that reported for David, a younger learner:

"David had been a problem in kindergarten. He knew it and acted it out in the first and second grades. He had thoroughly convinced everyone he was a problem by the time he entered my third grade.

"A thatch of yellow hair, crystal clear blue eyes—as he walked along the path to school all he needed was a fishing pole over his shoulder to be the perfect Huckleberry Finn! He intrigued me and interested me beyond words— there must be a key to David, and I must try to find it.

"I set the stage in every possible way so he would do a few things at least that we could praise—this was a shock to him and he didn't know quite what to do with praise! . . . By Christmas time we had arrived at the point of mutual respect for one another.

"At Christmas in our room we take a trip around the world and explore the Christmas customs of the children in our countries. This year we had decided to go by plane. We had a representative from the airlines as a guest speaker—telling about tickets, traveling by plane, and showing some slides of various countries.

"The day came when each child was to make his ticket for the country he wished to visit. I was surprised as I watched David—usually he was one of the last ones to start, but this time he was well on his way immediately. As I 'toured' the room, I noticed David's ticket would be for Sweden. This surprised me as he had brought many things from Mexico in for Sharing Time, and I had rather thought his ticket would be for Mexico. The 'Captain' for the trip arranged his 'passenger' list by countries. David was the only one for Sweden. This seemed to please him, and as time passed we were all amazed at the responsibility he assumed in finding things to present about 'his country.'

"We found that he had chosen this country because his favorite grandmother had come from Sweden. . . . He found it necessary to write five or six letters to her for various items of information. I was surprised at the neatness and the care with which he did the job—would that he had done many of his other papers in like manner!

"He wrote some wonderful factual stories about Sweden. His Swedish fairy tales were really something! He often found expression at the easel—and such vivid colors.

"The day when the class were his 'guests' in Sweden he told of the customs and even taught us a game the Swedish children play. He also taught us to make little 'goodie' baskets they hang on their Christmas trees.

"Our children come to school by bus, but the two weeks before Christmas David walked nearly every morning because he wanted to get there early so he could get extra painting or writing done. As he was telling me goodbye on the last day of school before the holidays, he said, 'Gee, Miss T., this is the neatest Christmas I've ever had—I feel like I've almost been to Sweden.'

"I had found my 'key' to David. He needed to find out things and tell them—sometimes do a bit of embroidery on them—sometimes do a bit of dreaming and make-believe on them. He liked his real world much better too.

"This did change David—he no longer needed to be the 'bad boy'—he adjusted to the praise and found it 'fun' (as he said) to write stories, draw pictures, etc. of his 'secret world.' He was so busy doing this he didn't have time to revert to the 'old' David."

FROM ESTRANGEMENT AND RETARDATION
TO ADJUSTMENT AND ACHIEVEMENT.

A number of the anecdotes related by the respondents involved children who seemed to be estranged and out of contact with reality and regarded as mentally retarded. The following account of Jamie at the time he was in the fifth grade falls into this category:

"Jamie lived on another planet. He seemed to feel no need to relate to the world around him. As he entered the fifth grade, the children thought of him as a 'dumb kid.' In a flexible individual reading program I was able to let him skip around in the book as the spirit moved him and report in the way he was able through drawings. He completed one fourth grade and two fifth grade readers during the year and I feel he is ready to face my sixth grade reading material.

"At the same time in a 'slow' math class he was exposed to an imaginative teacher. By allowing him to use his interest in motors to develop a math project he was able to show a real flair for teaching others and his classmates discovered that Jamie had brains!"

## What Made the Difference?

The incidents I have just reported provide many provocative ideas about what makes a difference. In some ways, the teacher provided a responsive environment—one which involved a sensitive and alert kind of guidance and direction, the creation of an atmosphere of receptive listening, responding to children and young people as they are or might become rather than as they have been told that they are, fighting off ridicule and criticism, and making their efforts to learn worthwhile.

Now, I would like to give you a list of the factors mentioned most frequently by my students in "Creative Ways of Teaching."

Recognizing some heretofore unrecognized and unused potential
Respecting a child's need to work alone
Inhibiting the censorship role long enough for a creative response to occur
Allowing or encouraging a child to go ahead and achieve success in an area and in a way possible for him
Permitting the curriculum to be different for different pupils
Giving concrete embodiment to the creative ideas of children
Giving a chance to make a contribution to the welfare of the group
Encouraging or permitting self-initiated projects
Reducing pressure, providing a relatively non-punitive environment
Approval in one area to provide courage to try in others
Voicing the beauty of individual differences
Respecting the potential of low achievers
Enthusiasm of the teacher
Support of the teacher against peer pressures to conformity
Placing an unproductive child in contact with a productive, creative child
Using fantasy ability to establish contacts with reality
Capitalizing upon hobby and special interests and enthusiasms
Tolerance of complexity and disorder, at least for a period
Involvement
Not being afraid of bodily contact with children
Communicating that the teacher is "for" rather than "against" the child

## Permitting Children to Work Alone and in Their Own Way

In learning and in doing creative work, many people are unable to function very well in a group. They seem to need to "march to a different drumbeat" and to work at their own pace. Much in established ways of teaching creates a set which makes this difficult. Even beginning teachers find it possible, however, to permit such divergency. The following story of Mark's report on Latin America illustrates this point and suggests a number of other ideas as well:

"Last year was my first year of teaching. I had a student, Mark, whom I immediately recognized as an extremely creative student, and someone for whom I had an enormous respect.

"The study of Latin America is a required part of our social studies curriculum for the sixth grade. I followed every step of what I had been taught in 'Teaching Social Studies in the Elementary School' . . . letting the class decide what you need to learn about a people and a country to understand them and their needs, and then a secretary wrote the names of the various Latin American countries on the board, so that the children could select the country's committee they would like to be on to prepare written reports. We decided that the major countries would need more on a committee . . . Ecuador came up, and two people volunteered and were given that country to research and do a project on. After all of the countries had been spoken for, I noticed that Mark had not made a choice.

"Talking with him, I learned that he had wanted Ecuador, as he had been reading Darwin's journals and was fascinated by the Galapagos Islands, but he hadn't wanted to work with anyone, so hadn't held up his hand. Well, I said that was all right, and that he could make up a separate report on the Galapagos Islands, which he agreed to do.

"Three weeks later, Mark had not begun his report, in the sense that he had nothing on paper. He was just too busy reading books, interviewing anthropologists at the University of California, and thinking. I tried very hard to help him get something on paper, but when I saw that he just was too interested in Darwin's discoveries and their implications and the evidence of it that remains to this day on the Islands, I decided Mark's assignment would be changed to an oral report. He reacted very favorably to this, delivering a magnificent account of what kind of person Darwin was, an account of the voyage of the *Beagle*, and then delivered a very instructive lecture on the various forms of a single species as they appear on the different islands, drawing pictures of the variants on the chalkboard, complete with describing the different environment a different island would offer and asking the other students in the class to guess what variant they would imagine would result!

"Mark got such a good feeling out of this experience, I was able, when the next report came up, to talk with him in terms of being able to operate in more than one manner and thus be prepared to be flexible and able to choose—put it to him in terms of baseball; that a player might be a right-hander but it would be to his advantage to also learn to bat left-handed so that he could be a switch-hitter—that he decided he would prepare a written report, which he did—a very good one, and in on time and beautifully done, even as far as presentation—right down to the bibliography.

"The point is, I think, that in honoring his involvement at a particular time in research, he learned to respect me enough to consider the advantages when the next report came around of knowing how to prepare and get in on time a written report."

If we examine the teacher's report of this episode closely, we find several factors involved. It is likely that one of the more salient factors contributing to the success of the teacher in working with Mark was her willingness to change or bend her planned sequence of experiences to permit Mark to function in such a way to achieve his potentialities. He was able to function in terms of his abilities and interests, without actually upsetting the curriculum or the classroom organization. We find, however, that the teacher had already recognized Mark's creative potential and that she had an enormous respect for him. She recognized that she would be bucking a strong force to divert him at this time from his interest in the Galapagos Islands; furthermore, she saw how he might be able to contribute meaningfully to the curriculum for the entire class. She had not counted upon his absorption being so great that he could not find time to write his report. She remained open and flexible, however, and saw that he might contribute most by giving an oral report, a challenge which he met with unexpected skill. Having achieved success and having achieved respect for his teacher, he was then ready to learn some of the more conforming ways of behaving in the educational environment. In fact, he was even able to include a very proper bibliography documenting his report. He has learned adaptive and constructive ways of behaving which will doubtless stand him in good stead throughout his educational career.

## A Concluding Suggestion

My final suggestion is one created by J. H. Mohrman, one of my students, at the end of the course on "Creative Ways of Teaching." I shall present it to you just as he presented it to me—A Checklist for Creative Teaching:

"There is a story, common in the Navy and Merchant Marine, of the young third mate who had a great admiration for the Master of the ship in which he sailed. He was, however, puzzled about one of the Captain's habits. Quite occasionally while they were at sea, the Captain would take a dog-eared piece of paper from his pocket and study it intently for a few minutes. Following this ritual, the Captain was his usual picture of calm, self-assurance. Although he was never able to learn what was written on the paper, the Third Mate felt that it must contain the ultimate secret of the Captain's success as a seafarer. On one voyage the Captain died while they were at sea, and the Third Mate was given the task of inventorying and packing the Captain's belongings. He was in a high state of excitement as he went about this task knowing that, at last, he would discover the secret written on the slip of paper which the Captain had guarded so jealously. With trembling fingers, the Third Mate removed the paper from the Captain's jacket pocket and opened it to find this "secret" written inside: 'Starboard is Right—Port is Left.'

"We are all somewhat like the Sea Captain, and occasionally need some simple reminder of the elementary principles that we all 'know perfectly well.' For many reasons; partly because we all need a crutch for our courage from time to time, and a stiffner for our resolve, or perhaps more likely, simply a reminder of our good intentions, I have prepared a checklist to keep handy in my desk drawer to remind myself frequently of at least some aspects of the creative process. We all tend to be creatures of habit and to have our judgment beclouded by our ingrained prejudices and predelictions, particularly with regard to what the 'good' pupil or the 'good' classroom is like. Because of the many possibilities for conflict with our own personalities and the creative personality, or some aspect of the classroom where creative learning is taking place, I hope that this simple 'Starboard is Right—Port is Left' type of list will keep us closer to the creative course."

Don't be too "threatened" by the exceptional child—or the unexpected response.

Pay attention to the "atmosphere" of the room.

Don't be too concerned about a higher noise level—if it's a "busy hum."

Remember the creative need to communicate—maybe the whisper is all right.

Don't be blinded by "intelligence" test scores—they don't tell the *whole* story.

Don't be afraid to wander off your teaching schedule—stay flexible.

Encourage divergent ideas—too many of the "right" ideas are stifling.

Be accepting and forgiving of the "mistakes."

Remember, the "obnoxious" child may simply be escaping from the tedium of your class.

Don't let your pride get in the way of your teaching.

Different kinds of children learn in different ways.

Let them "test their limits."

Don't let the pressure for "evaluation" get the upper hand.

Give them a chance to "warm-up" to producing ideas.

Respect the privacy of their responses (especially the less successful ones).

Criticism is killing—use it carefully and in small doses.

How about those "Provocative Questions?"

Don't forget to define the problem.

Don't be afraid to try something different.

"This list could, of course, be added to indefinitely—and I intend to. Also these items won't 'translate' properly for everyone, but it's at least a start, and it will have served its purpose if it helps only me."

I would urge you to create your own list to fit yourself. Each teacher's way of teaching must ultimately be his own unique invention. I wish for you the very greatest success in perfecting you own invention—your way of teaching.

## References

Pulsifer, Susan Nichols. *Children Are Poets.* Cambridge, Mass.: Dresser, Chapman — Grimes, Inc., 1963.

Torrance, E. P. *Guiding Creative Talent.* Englewood Cliffs, N. J.: Prentice-Hall, Inc., 1962.

Wilt, Miriam E. *Creativity in the Elementary School.* New York: Appleton-Century-Crofts, 1959.

## Annotated Bibliography

Bedmar, R. L. and Parker, C. A. "The Creative Development and

Growth of Exceptional College Students." *Journal of Educational Research* 59: 133-136, Nov. 1965.

Guilford tests administered to 90 students in an honors program at Brigham Young University revealed no significant relationship or growth during three years.

Eberle, R. F. *Experimentation in the Teaching of the Creative Thinking Processes.* Edwardsville Junior High School, Edwardsville, Illinois, June 1965.

A research report which combines a search of the literature with a local study. Following a review of the literature the author reports that "aspects of creative thinking are learnable, and as such can be taught." Significant gains may take place in short periods and these are accompanied by personality changes. In the local study of 7 out of 16 cases significant differences on pre- and post-tests were obtained.

Lincoln, J. W. "Developing a Creativeness in People." (pp. 269-75) in Parnes, S. J., and Harding , H. F. *A Source Book for Creative Thinking.* New York: Charles Scribner's Sons, 1962.

The "Gordon technique" of synectics and its applications to operational creativity is discussed.

Maltzman, I. "On the Training of Originality." *Psychological Review* 67: 229-42; 1960.

Reviews his work on  training originality which he believes can be accomplished.

Mednick, Martha "Research Creativity in Psychology Graduate Students" *Journal of Consulting Psychology* 27:265-6, 1963.

The validity of the RAT (Remote Associates Test) was investigated by comparing ratings given individuals on a research creativity check list with the RAT. The correlation was .55 supporting the use of this test as a selection device for creativity.

Mednick, Martha, Sarnoff and Edward. "Incubation of Creative Performance and Specific Associate Priming." *Journal of Abnormal and Social Psychology* 69:84-88, July, 1964.

An ivestigation of the effect of associative priming on incubation of creative performance found that high scorers on the RAT (Remote Associates Test) performed better than low scorers and that the effect of specific priming was greater than no priming. Time relationship had no effect. Results support an associative interpretation of incubation.

Taylor, D. U., and others. "Does Group Participation When Using Brainstorming Facilitate or Inhibit Creative Thinking?" *Travail Humain* 24:1-20; 1961.

In attempting to test high pressure creation of new ideas, 96 Yale students were tested singly and in groups of 4. There were significantly more ideas produced in groups, although 4 persons produced slightly less than twice the number produced by persons working alone.

Torrance, E. P. "Factors Affecting Creative Thinking in Children: An Interim Report." *Merrill-Palmer Quarterly* 7:171-80; 1961.
Discusses psychological factors affecting the creative thinking of young children.

Yee, G. F. *The Influences of Problem-Solving Instruction and Personal-Social Adjustment upon Creativity Test Scores of Twelfth Grade Students.* Unp. Ed. D. thesis, Pennsylvania State University, 1964. (*Dissertation Abstracts* 26:916, 1965.)
High-ability students showed significant increase in creativity scores after problem-solving instruction as compared with matched controls. Low-ability students did not. Creative high-ability students have greater sense of personal worth, and fewer anti-social tendencies than counterparts; creative low-ability students also differ in the same way from their less creative counterparts. There was no significant difference, however, in adjustment among high-ability students varying in creativity or in low-ability students varying in creativity.

# Index

Abilities, mental use of 65
Ability gradient 53
Ability grouping 40, 65, 69, 295-298, 301-302, 310-314, 406
Acceleration 13-15, 17, 28, 34, 40-41, 65, 295-296, 298-309, 406
Achievement 4, 13-14, 17, 60, 195
  adult 130-131
  professional 10, 130-131
  school 9, 13-14, 40, 58-60, 101, 104, 129, 135-136, 147, 166, 251
Adjustment, (see also Social adjustment) 3-4, 18-19, 44, 62, 146-147, 214, 299, 467-468
  emotional 136-142, 156-157, 198, 208-221
Administration 40, 329
Adults 9-13, 40
Adventures in Discovery 45
Affective domain 371-372
Age 13-14
Allport-Vernon-Lindzey Study of Values 160
Alpha Biographical Inventory 417
American Association of Gifted Children 4, 258, 260
American Council on Education 92, 97
American Men of Science 130
American School of Mental Abilities 12
Analogies test 84
Anastasiow, N.J. 147
Anderson, C.C. 196
Anderson, J.E. 53
Andrews, F.M. 184
Antiintellectualism 28
Anxiety 133-194
Apparatus test 87
Aptitude 62
Architects 154
Armstrong, M.E. 208
Army General Classification Test 7
Arnold, J.E. 367
Articulation 65
Arts 10, 15, 43, 56, 62, 153, 181, 185, 250, 253, 317
Association for the Gifted 4
Associations test 286-287, 289
Attitudes of public 4, 15-16
Attlee, C. 82

Baird, L.L. 201
Baldwin, A.L. 188
Baker, H.J. 312
Barbe, W.B. 293, 433
Barnes, E.W. 366
Barron, F. 157, 181, 184-185, 187-192, 196, 218, 243-244, 391

Bartlett, F. 399
Beck, J. 45
Beittel, K.R. 180-182
Binet, A. 54, 230
  -type tests 54, 75-76, 100, 111, 128, 222-225, 235-237, 281
Bingham, W.V. 6-7, 151-152, 161
Biographical Data (See also Follow-up) 32, 44
Birch, H.G. 399
Birch, J.W. 230, 264, 293
Birth order 114, 122, 125, 146
Bishop, W.E. 433
Bloom, B. 189, 339, 412, 415, 419
Boehm, A. 135
Bonsall, M.R. 141
Boole, M.E. 246, 351
Borton, K.D. 133
Brainstorming 373
British school of mental abilities 12
Brogden, H.E. 200
Brown, D.J. 209
Bruch, C. 415
Bruner, J. 166, 349, 351
Burt, C. 51, 131
Butcher, H.J. 190

California Personality Inventory 160
Callahan, C. 230
Camouflaged Words test 85
Campbell, D.T. 183, 242
Campbell, J.Q. 413
Carlson, E. 313
Carrier, N.A. 133
Carroll, H. 313
Case studies of gifted (see also Follow-up) 8-13, 17-18
Cashdan, S. 193-194
Cassell, R.N. 145
Cattell, R.B. 32, 100, 190-191, 391
Caylor, J.S. 132
Characteristics of gifted (see Gifted child, characteristics of)
Check, J. 133
Christensen, P.R. 180
Churchill, W. 82
Circles test 50
Civil rights 24
Clark, C.M. 87
Cleland, D.L. 433
Cognition (see also Structure of Intellect) 51-52
Coleman, J.S. 413
College, gifted in (see also Gifted child, as college students) 9-10, 13-14, 16-17, 22, 26-27, 40, 45

Commoner, B. 27-29
Complexity, preference for 185-186
Conant, J. 23
Convergent production (*see also* Structure of Intellect) 51-52, 103, 108, 180-181
*Consequences* test 169, 181, 290
Council for Exceptional Children 4
Covington, M.V. 243
Cox, A.B. 181
Cox, C. 10-11, 18
Craik, K. 164
Creative
 press 179
 product 179, 436
 process 179, 436
 thinking 52
Creativity
 characteristics of 151-166, 171-172, 214-219, 274-275, 392, 441
 complexity of 153
 definition of 152-153
 and giftedness 43-44, 55
 identification 179-201, 264-270, 274-279
 relationship with intelligence 99-110, 156, 164-165, 180-185, 197, 208, 242
 tests (*see* Measurement)
Criterion problem (*see also* Measurement, problems in) 200, 240-241, 243-245
Cropley, A.J. 184, 196, 241
Cross, P.G. 190-191
Crowder, T. 138, 146-147
Culture (*see* Family)
Curiosity 63, 364
Curriculum (*see also* Education) 23, 25, 39, 55, 295-473
 planning 55, 238
Cutts, V.E. 264

Daniels, J.M. 181
Danielson, C.L. 312
Datta, L.E. 193-194
Dauw, D.C. 195
Davis, A. 419
Davis, J.A. 139, 244
deGroot, A.D. 54
Delinquency 9
deMille, R. 199
Dentler, R.A. 184
Development 55
Dewey, J. 347
Disadvantaged 42, 402-429
Discrimination against gifted children 4, 8
Discipline 163
Discovery (*see also* Problem solving) 346-353
*Disemvowled Words* test 79
Divergent thinking (*see also* Structure of Intellect) 45, 51-52, 103, 108, 180-182, 214-215, 243, 367, 396
Douglass, J.H. 411, 420-421

Drevdahl, J.E. 181, 190-191, 193, 391
Dropout 431-432

Early admission to school (*see* Acceleration)
Early development of gifted 5, 10-14, 17
Eberle, R.F. 414, 419
Education Act of 1944 51
Educational Policies Commission 4, 52, 312
Education
 for the gifted 13-15, 21-26, 28-30, 40-41, 61-67, 70, 229, 293-473
 enrichment of 15, 65, 297-473
Einstein, A. 363
Eisenmann, R. 185
Elaboration 50-52, 83
Elementary and Secondary Education Act 324
Elenewski, J.J. 189
Eliot, T.S. 364
Elliott, J.M. 181-182
Ellis, A. 192
Emotions (*see* Adjustment, emotional)
Environment 17-18, 54
 early childhood 54
Evaluation (*see also* Structure of Intellect) 52, 328, 335
Extracurricular activities 17

Factor analysis 76-77, 87, 93-97, 180, 199, 201, 282, 289, 291
Family 17-18, 34, 37, 111, 117
 parents in 114-117, 162-163, 211, 321-322
 size of 114
Fantasy 101-104
Feldhusen, J.F. 132, 141
Ferguson, L.W. 139
Ferris, D. 241
*Figure Concepts* test 84, 285, 289
Financing, educational 22, 25, 41, 70-71, 301, 408-409
Finley, C.J. 134
First born (*see* Birth order)
Fiske, D.J. 183, 242
Flescher, I. 183
Flexibility 50-52, 82-83, 180, 186, 189, 193
Fluency 50-52, 81-82, 180
Follow-up of gifted children 9-10, 12, 17-18, 25-26, 33-34, 36, 127, 129-130, 161, 200-201
Ford fund 13-14
*Form Reasoning* test 84
Franklin, B. 12
Frierson, S.C. 433
Freud, S. 176

"g" 10, 12, 54, 94
Gair, M. 138
Gallagher, J. 74, 134, 138, 142-143, 146-147, 264
Galton, F. 11

Gardner, S.F.  181
Garwood, D.S.  187, 193-194
Genetics (see also Heredity)  33, 37, 39, 41
Genius  32-40
Gershon, A.  180
*Gestalt Transformations* test  85
Getzels, J.  52-53, 74, 183, 185, 187, 193-194,
     196, 199, 218, 242, 264, 392
Ghiselin, B.  392, 398
Gifted child
  achievement of (*see also* Achievement)  4,
     9, 13-14, 17, 34-35, 39
  as college student (*see also* College, gifted
     in)  9-10, 13-14, 16-18, 27, 40, 45
  attitudes of  26, 210-212
  characteristics of  8, 33-36, 39, 59, 107-
     109, 111-117, 119-147, 441
  cultural effects on (*see also* Family)  22-
     26, 35, 37
  definition of  25, 39
  differences from 'average' child  4, 29, 33,
     37, 40
  early development of (*see also* Early
     development)  10-14, 17
  education of (*see* Education of gifted)
  ethnic background of  24, 35, 37, 112-113,
     117
  friendship patterns of (*see* Social accep-
     tance)
  health  9, 13, 17, 39
  identification of (*see also* Identifica-
     tion)  9, 11, 13-15, 34-36, 48, 65, 68,
     425-426
  insanity in  3, 33
  in school (*see also* School)  34-36, 40
     elementary  25, 40
     high school  25-26
     junior high school  25
  personality  63
  problems of  3-4, 13, 29, 44, 214-219
  sex differences in, (*see* Sex differences)
  social development of (*see also* Social
     development)  13-14, 44
  teaching of (*see* Education)
  traits of (see also Gifted child,
     characteristics of)  8-12, 17-18
*Gifted Child, The*  15
*Gifted Child Quarterly*  4
Giftedness
  characteristics of  57, 59, 63-64, 73-74,
     392-393
  complexity of  49-51
  definition of  25, 39, 44-45, 49, 56
  types of  51, 61-62
  value of  56-57, 71
Ginsberg, G.P.  185
Goddard, H.A.  312
Goertzel, M.  44
Goertzel, V.  44
Golann, S.E.  179, 195, 197

Goldberg, M.  403
Goldman, M.  192-193, 391-392
Goldsmith, O.  11
Gough, H.G.  157, 160, 181-182, 184-186,
     188, 190, 199
Gowan, J.C.  208, 230-231, 294
Grant, T.E.  417
Gregory, C.E.  419
Griswold, B.B.  188, 200
Guilford, J.P.  43, 51-52, 74, 100, 103, 108,
     110, 169, 180-185, 187, 189, 193, 241-242,
     333, 382, 392, 395-396, 414-415, 425

Haddox, G.  145
Haggard, E.A.  208
Hall, W.B.  153, 158
Hammer, E.F.  191-192
Hanson, J.C.  183
Harding, H.F.  419
Harmon, L.R.  392
Harris, T.L.  186
Hartman, R.  230
Hartshorne, M.  259
Hathaway, S.R.  156
Havell, J.A.  188
Hays, W.L.  278
Hebb, D.O.  399
Heinze, S.J.  191
Heist, P.A.  139
*Helping the Gifted Child*  45
Helson, R.  190, 192, 200
Henry, L.K.  348
Heredity  33-35, 37, 42, 54, 89, 131
Herr, E.L.  183
Hersch, C.  186, 188, 191
Hess, R.  419
Higher Horizons Program  24
Hildreth, G.  138, 311
Hobson, C.J.  413
Hoepfner, R.  180, 183
Holland, J.L.  193-194, 196, 201, 243
Hollingworth, L.A.  3, 29, 112-116, 136, 146-
     147, 208, 227, 235, 310, 435
Holt, J.  396, 413
Holt, R.R.  187-188
Honors programs  334
Horrall, B.M.  209
Houston, J.P.  195
Howe, W.  396
Hubbard, R.  226-227
Hudson, L.  198
Humor  59, 107, 256
Hunt, J.McV.  54-55, 412
Hutchinson, W.L.  427-428
Hymovitch, V.  399

Identification of gifted  34-36, 43, 229-270,
     280-281, 328, 407, 413-414, 425, 426
  early  9, 11, 13-14, 42-44
  instruments for (*see* Measurement; Tests)

purposes of 229, 248
*Incomplete Figures* test 50
Independence 140-141, 216-217
Independent study 300, 330-335, 468-470
Individual differences 39
Inductive study of genius 32
Inheritance (*see* Heredity)
Institute for Behavioral Research in Creativity 417
Institute for Personality Assessment and Research 152, 154, 170, 184-185, 190-191
Intelligence (*see also* Structure of Intellect) 3, 8, 10-11, 13-15, 17, 33-34, 39-43, 48-49, 52-60, 62, 64-66, 73-104, 127-128, 197, 233-239, 317, 392-393, 427, 450
  abstract 88
  and relationship with creativity 99-110, 156, 164-165, 180-185, 197, 208
  concrete 88
  relationship with originality 172, 175, 177
  social 77, 88
  tests of (*see also* Tests) 7-8, 10-11, 14-15, 24, 39, 54, 73-73, 100, 234-238, 414
Inquiry (*see* Problem solving)

Jackson, P. 52-53, 74, 183, 185, 187, 189, 193-194, 196, 199, 218, 241-242, 264, 392
Jacobson, L.F. 413
Jacobson, L.I. 189
Jenkins, J.J. 161
Jenkins, M.D. 111, 412
Jensen, A. 134
Jerecky, R.K. 230, 264
Jung, C.J. 157-159

Kaplan, N. 195
Keliher, A. 313
Kennedy, J.L. 139
Kennedy, W.A. 139
Kerstetter, L. 147
Khatena 230, 277
Klausmeier, H.J. 132-133
Klein, S.P. 181
Klemm, E.W. 136
King, F.J. 243
King, J.F. 194
Kneller, G.F. 200
Koeppe, R.P. 134
Kogan, N. 183-184, 194, 196, 241-242
Kozol, J. 396, 413
Krathwohl, D.R. 415
Krippner, S. 45

Lanza, L.G. 293
Laughlin, L.T. 132
Lauritzen, E.S. 180
Laycock, F. 132
Leadership 43, 145
Learning ability 40, 42, 132-135

Learning center 355-360
Lehmann, H. 13
Lessenger, L.M. 139
*Letter Triangle* test 80
Lewin, K. 227
Lewis, D.J. 180
Lieberman, J.N. 201
Lieroff, J.H. 189
Lightfoot, G. 138
Lindgren, F. 194
Lindgren, H.C. 194
Lippitt, R. 220
Littlejohn, M.A. 193
Longitudinal research (*see* Follow-up)
Lordahl, D.S. 189
Lorge, I. 54
Lowell, A. 161
Lowenfeld, V. 180
Lucito, L.J. 134, 140-141
Lumbroso, C. 3, 32, 137

Macaulay, D. 12
MacKinnon, D.W. 53, 153, 181-182, 184-186, 188, 190-193, 243-244
Mackler, B. 184
Maddi, S.R. 196
Malpass, L.F. 133
Mann, H. 226-227
Marcuse, H. 26
Mark, H.P. 362
Marland, S. 25
Marsh, R.W. 183
Martinson, R. 139
Martyn, K.A. 144
Masia, B.B. 415
Maslow, A.H. 109, 220
Massialas, B.G. 395, 397
*Matched Problems* test 83
Maturation 13-14
May, M.A. 259
May, R.B. 242
*McCandless Anxiety Scale* 194
McClelland, D. 100, 102, 195, 405
McConnell, T.R. 348
McKinley, J.C. 156
McNemar, Q. 184
Measurement (*see also* Tests) 230-291, 407, 415
  of creativity 43, 50, 62, 100, 156-158, 240-245, 274-291, 318, 399
  of giftedness 62, 230-270, 280-281, 318
  problems in (*see also* Criterion problem) 198-201
Mednick, S.A. 184, 195, 241, 398
Memory (*see also* Structure of Intellect) 51
Mendelsohn, G.A. 188, 200
Mensch, I. 138
Mental tests (*see also* Intelligence, tests of; Tests) 3, 7-8, 10-11, 14-15
Merrifield, P.R. 180-181, 199

Messick, S. 189, 241
Miles, C.C. 412
Miles, D.J. 244
Miller, R.V. 136, 143
*Minnesota Multiphasic Personality Inventory*
(MMPI) 156, 392
Mohrman, J.H. 470
Montessori, M. 347
Mood, A.M. 413
Moore, G.D. 183
Moral behavior 53, 135, 163, 196
and socioeconomic status 135
Mornay House test of intelligence 14-15
Moseley, N. 264
Motivation 40, 66, 195-197, 218, 343, 352,
359
Myden, W. 187, 191
Myers, I.B. 158, 396-398

Nagel, E. 367
National Association for Gifted Children 4
National Intelligence tests 36
National Merit Scholarship Corporation 41
Needs 26
for achievement 100-104, 160
*Necessary Arithmetical Operations* test 80
Nelson, J.B. 433
Newland, T.E. 326
Newman, J.R. 367
Nichols, R.C. 131, 139
Nisbet, J.F. 3
Norwood Committee 51
*Number Associations* test 286, 289

Objectives 66-67, 69, 89, 311, 328
Occupations (*see also* Vocational interests) 10, 104-110, 116-117, 123-126,
130, 159
Oden, M.H. 112, 130, 137, 146, 435
Office of the Gifted and Talented 5
Ojemann, R. 55
O'Leary, M.J. 209
Oliver, A.I. 312-313
Originality 50-52, 59, 83, 168-177, 180-181,
231, 282-291
characteristics of 171-172
definition of 283
relationship with intelligence 172, 175,
177
tests of 169, 282-291
Osborn, A. 387, 399

Pankove, E. 196
Parents (*see also* Family) 34-35, 114-117,
211, 321-322
Parloff, M.D. 193-194
Parnes, S.J. 371, 419
Pascal, B. 12
Passow, A.H. 412
Pegnato, C.W. 230, 236, 264

Personality 9, 18, 63, 226-227, 392-393
related to originality 168-177
*Pertinent Questions* test 81
Physical abilities 131-132
Piaget, J. 135, 348, 351
*Picture Arrangement* Test 85
Pielstick, N.L. 145
Piers, E.V. 181
Piltz, A. 397
Pine, F. 187-188
*Plot Titles* test 83, 169, 288-289
Powell, M.B. 200
Pregler, H.O. 312-313
Primary mental abilities 91-98
Pritchard, M.C. 256
Problem solving 336-353, 379
Productive thinking 51-52, 77
Productive Thinking Program 380-381
Programs for the Talented 21
Propst, B.S. 189
Pulsifer, S. 461
Purdue Creativity Training Program 381

Quackenbush, J.F. 181
*Quick Responses* test 285, 289

Ramasheshan, P.H. 138
Randolph, N. 396
Ratings 182
peer 181-182, 194, 243
teacher 58, 100, 128, 138, 181-182, 194,
209, 243, 249-250, 253, 262, 265-270, 280
Raychaud, M. 185
Razik, T. 240
Reading 445-447, 465
*Reading for the Gifted and Creative
Student* 45
Rees, M.E. 192-193, 391-392
Regression 187-188
Reid, J.B. 194, 243
Religion 112-113, 122, 163
*Remote Associates* test 195
Renzulli, J.S. 230, 294, 319, 328, 417
Rickover, H. 22
Ripple, R.E. 242
Risk taking 195-196, 217
Rivlin, L.G. 194, 243
Robinson, N. 185
Roe, A. 191
Roesslein, C.G. 208
Rogers, C.R. 195, 241
Rozalsky, M.M. 188
Rorschach (Inkblot test) 119, 138, 169, 186-
188, 191, 209-210
Rosen, J.C. 186
Rosenthal, R. 413
Rossiter, J. 241
Roth, K.R. 161
Rothney, J.W. 134

Runner, K.R. 277
Russell, W.A. 161

Scholastic Aptitude Test 415
Schultz, C.B. 181
Science 10-12, 15-16, 21-23, 27-28, 32, 40, 153, 181, 191, 362-364
Scientists 119-126, 181, 191
Science Talent Search 15-16
Scott, W. 11
Scrambled Words test 79
Screening of gifted (see Identification)
Segregation 406-407
Self concept 147, 156, 194, 198, 261, 313, 444-445
Sex differences 34, 37, 134-135, 174-175, 190-192, 198, 200, 210-213, 431-432
Sexton, P.C. 413
Shaw, M.C. 209
Silberman, C.E. 413
Silverstein, S. 143
Similarities test 143
Similes Preference test 195
Skager, R.W. 181
Skeels, H.M. 54
Smith, D.C. 140
Smith, J.A. 397
Smith, W.R. 392
Social acceptance 4, 13, 15-16, 23, 29, 44-45, 220, 228
Social adjustment 53, 142-144, 166, 194, 198, 214, 219
  in elementary school 142-144
  in secondary school 144, 194
Social interaction 35, 44
Social maturity 260
Socially gifted 256-263
  characteristics of 257-258
Socioeconomic conditions 37, 113, 117, 122, 141
Social Institutions test 87
Sociometry 226-227, 259-260
Spearman, C. (see also "g") 10, 12, 54, 94
Spitz, R. 54, 220
Spranger, E. 160
Sprecher, T.B. 200
Sputnik, effect on programs for the gifted 21-22, 25-27
SRPEG 61, 300
Starkweather, E.K. 201, 245
Steinmetz, C.P. 362
Stevenson, G.M. 243
Strang, R. 139
Street Gestalt Completion test 78
Strong, E.K. 157
Structure of Intellect 51-52, 75-90, 180, 241, 382, 416, 425
  content in 51-52, 76-78, 82
    behavioral 77-78
    figural 77-79, 81-83, 85-86

semantic 77, 79-85, 88
symbolic 77, 79, 81-82, 85-86, 88
implications for education 88
operations in 51-52, 76-78
  cognition 77
  convergent thinking 77, 84-85, 90
  divergent thinking 77, 81-83, 89
  evaluation 77, 85-88, 90
  memory 77-81
products in 51-52, 76-78, 88
  classes 77
  implications 77, 80-81
  relations 77, 79, 81, 84
  systems 77, 80-81, 86
  transformations 77, 80-81, 83, 85-86
  units 77, 79, 81, 86
tests of 78-87
Subcultural Indices of Academic Potential 417
Success 17
Suchman, J.R. 353
Sucksdorff, A. 43
Sund, R. 397
Swensen, E.J. 348
Symbol Production test 83

Taft, R. 241
Talent 22, 43
Talented Youth Project 21
Tannenbaum, A.J. 144
Taylor, C.W. 43, 196, 201, 242, 392, 414-415, 425
Teacher (see also Ratings, teacher) 33, 36-37, 41, 44-45, 439-447
  attitudes of 36-37, 393-394, 398, 440, 453-454
  characteristics of 449-458
  training 67-68
Thematic Apperception Test (TAT) 119, 140-141, 169, 187, 191, 209
Thorndike, R.L. 185, 242
Thorpe, J.S. 187
Terman, L. 3-4, 24, 39-41, 73, 75-76, 114-116, 127-131, 137, 141, 146-147, 195, 208, 226, 299, 312, 362, 392-393, 412, 435
Tests (see also Measurement) 14-15, 26, 33-37, 39, 58, 66, 105, 119, 169-171, 173, 183-188, 190-191, 193-195, 276-279, 282-289, 399, 407, 414-417
  ability 91-98, 445
  achievement 58
  spatial 80
Thompson, G. 14-15
Thompson, J.M. 134
Thorndike, E. 8
Thurstone, L.L. 74, 86, 425
Titles III and IV 25
Torrance, E.P. 50, 53, 181, 183, 194-196, 199, 230, 241, 243, 274, 276-278, 384-385, 396-398, 411-412, 416-417, 433-434

*Torrance Tests of Creative Thinking* 241, 416-417
Toynbee, A.  45, 412
Traits (*see also* Gifted child, characteristics of)  8-12, 17-18, 34-36
Treffinger, D.T.  241, 294
Tryon, C.  259
Tsanoff, R.A.  137
Twain, M.  151

Underachievement  28, 63, 66, 208, 215-216, 317
Underprivileged  23-24
University of California  152
University of Chicago  57
University of Southern California  76
*Unusual Uses* test  169, 181, 284, 286-287, 289
Uranack, W.O.  397

Validity  276-278
Van Mondfrans, A.P.  241-242
Vassar, W.G.  293
Veldman, D.  187
Vernon, P.E.  54, 199
Vinacke, W.E.  189
Vocational interests (*see also* Occupations)  159

Wallach, M.A.  183-184, 194, 196, 241-243

Wallen, N.E.  243
Ward, C.W.  201, 328
Ward, V.S.  242, 293, 319, 326
Warren, J.R.  139
Wedemeyer, C.A.  209
Weinfeld, F.D.  413
Wellman, B.L.  54
Welsh, G.S.  157, 185-186, 194
Wertheimer, M.  348, 350
Wesman, A.G.  256
Westcott, A.M.  397
White, R.W.  352
Whittemore, R.G.  185
*Who's Who in America*  130
Wickwire, P.  194, 243
Wild, C.  187, 191
Williams, C.W.  326
Williams, F.E.  387, 395, 414, 419
Wilson, R.C.  180, 193
Wilt, M.E.  461
Witty, P.A.  4, 48, 112, 136, 208, 264, 313, 412
*Word Grouping* test  84
Wotton, H.  153
Wrenn, G.G.  139

Yamamoto, K.  53, 181, 183, 199, 201, 243
York, R.L.  413

Zevin, J.  395, 397